01928

Group Dynamics

Second Edition

Donelson R. Forsyth
Virginia Commonwealth University

Brooks/Cole Publishing Company

Pacific Grove, California

Consulting Editor:
Lawrence S. Wrightsman, University of Kansas

Brooks/Cole Publishing Company, A Division of Wadsworth, Inc.

© 1990, 1983 by Wadsworth, Inc., Belmont, California 94002. All rights reserved. No part of this book may be reproduced, stored in a retrieval system, or transcribed, in any form or by any means—electronic, mechanical, photocopying, recording, or otherwise—without the prior written permission of the publisher, Brooks/Cole Publishing Company, Pacific Grove, California 93950, a division of Wadsworth, Inc.

Printed in the United States of America
10 9 8 7 6 5

Library of Congress Cataloging Publication Data

Forsyth, Donelson R., [date]
  Group dynamics/Donelson R. Forsyth.—2nd ed.
    p. cm.
  Rev. ed. of: An introduction to group dynamics. © 1983.
  Includes bibliographical references.
  ISBN 0-534-08010-3
  1. Social groups. I. Forsyth, Donelson R., [date] Introduction to group dynamics. II. Title.
HM131.F685 1990

                    89-25207
302.3′4—dc20   CIP

Subject Editor: *Claire Verduin*
Marketing Representative: *Bob Podstepny*
Senior Editorial Assistant: *Gay Bond*
Manuscript Editor: *William Waller*
Production Editor: *Ben Greensfelder*
Permissions Editor: *Mary Kay Hancharick*
Interior and Cover Design: *Lisa Berman*
Art Coordinators: *Sue C. Howard, Cloyce Wall*
Interior Illustrations: *Maggie Stevens-Huft*
Typesetting: *Omegatype Typography*
Cover Printing: *Phoenix Color Corporation*
Printing and Binding: *The Maple-Vail Book Mfg. Group*
(Credits continue on p. 594)

· Preface ·

Our scientific understanding of the physical and interpersonal world is growing at a remarkably rapid pace. Ten years ago physicists were certain that elements fuse only at very high temperatures, yet now laboratories across the country are studying the cold fusion process. A few decades ago physiological psychologists puzzled over the relationship between the brain and behavior, while now they use sophisticated imaging devices to observe the biochemical activities of various parts of the human brain directly. Each year researchers add to the list of subatomic particles that make up all physical matter and draw closer and closer to a comprehensive theory of the origin of the solar system.

Our knowledge of groups is also continually expanding as theorists craft new explanations for group behavior and researchers subject these notions to empirical test. Although social scientists in such fields as anthropology, sociology, and psychology have been studying groups for over half a century, their efforts continue to yield fresh insights and unexpected findings. Many of the ideas presented in the first edition of this book written seven years ago remain unchallenged, but others have been refined, augmented, or even expurgated in the intervening years. This edition keeps pace with these developments by taking an updated look at the scientific study of groups and their dynamics.

Orientation

Because this book is intended to serve as an introduction to group processes, I tried to maintain a balanced, integrative stance when presenting ideas, evidence, and viewpoints. Although a certain amount of personal bias is perhaps inevitable, from the first page to the last I worked to integrate areas of inquiry that too often remain independent of one another, including:

Theory and research. Conceptual analyses of groups are reviewed in depth, but empirical studies that highlight important principles derived from relevant theory are cited to show how theoretical systems are revised through research. The emphasis on theory-grounded knowledge sometimes means that less central, though nonetheless interesting, topics are sometimes slighted, but whenever possible I refer the curious reader to other sources for additional information.

Theory, research, and application.   Group dynamics appeals to theoretically minded basic research scientists and applications-oriented individuals who work with groups in industrial, organizational, educational, judiciary, and therapeutic contexts. As I noted above, the approach taken here stresses theory and research, but applications are introduced throughout the book in the text and in boxed sections, and entire chapters are devoted to questions of group productivity, decision making, and therapeutic applications.

Traditional and contemporary topics.   Our current understanding of groups was shaped by the work of Gustave Le Bon, Emile Durkheim, Kurt Lewin and many other early scholars. Although I focus on issues and topics that lie at the heart of contemporary group dynamics, classic analyses of groups are integrated with current topics to achieve an historically grounded overview.

Psychology, sociology, and other social sciences.   Researchers in a variety of fields are currently conducting studies of groups and their processes. Group dynamics is not a discipline that stands in isolation, but instead it draws on work carried out in the fields of psychology, sociology, social psychology, anthropology, speech and communication, political science, business, education, and psychiatry. Therefore, whenever possible the text integrates various perspectives to achieve a comprehensive analysis of group behavior.

Features
Every attempt has been made to create a textbook that teaches group dynamics rather than one that simply exposes the student to basic principles and research findings. Recognizing that the study of group dynamics can be a trying task with many stumbling blocks, several pedagogical features were used to make the material more accessible to the reader.

Organization.   The 15 chapters are sequenced to progress from basic issues and processes to the analysis of more specialized topics. First, two chapters examine the general nature of groups as well as research methods. Second, several chapters examine processes that occur early in the life of any group, including group formation, development, and the growth of structure. Third, several chapters focus on interpersonal processes that often operate within most groups, such as conformity, influence, and leadership. Fourth, we turn to consider both productivity and decision making in groups. Fifth, the book ends by considering a number of issues and implications of life in groups, including conflict, the behavior of large groups, and therapeutic groups. This order, however, is somewhat arbitrary and many may prefer to read the chapters in a different order.

The organization of each chapter can be grasped by reviewing the outline and overview presented on the first few pages of the chapter. Even though each chapter was written to stand as a single unit, overlap among the various topics means that the reader will be referred to information contained in other chapters from time to time. Also, each chapter consists of a number of independent subsections that examine specific aspects of the topic but form an integral component of the overall chapter. These subsections are short enough that they can be read from start to finish in a single sitting.

Boldface terms, glossary, and names.   As you read the book you will frequently encounter terms that are presented in boldface type. These key terms or concepts are defined in the text and in the glossary at the back of the book. The text also refers to the work of a number of theorists and researchers. In most cases the citation is presented in parentheses, and it states the investigator or investigators' last names and the date of the publication of the research report or book. When the individual is mentioned in the text proper, his or her first name is also included. Over 2000 works are cited, and all are listed in a reference section at the end of the book.

Outlines and summaries.   Before launching into your reading, you may find it useful to review the outline at the beginning of the chapter so that you can get a general idea of the topics you are about to encounter. Readers may even wish to add outlining indices, such as roman numerals by section headings (for example, "I. The Nature of groups") and letters next to subheadings (for example, "A. Some examples of groups") to further clarify the chapter's organization. Each chapter also ends with a comprehensive summary. All of the terms that appear in boldface in the text are italicized in these summaries.

Focuses.   Each chapter contains a number of boxed inserts, or "focuses," that present detailed information about a particular topic. These focuses examine specific topics in more detail, present applications of group dynamics to particular problems, or offer useful suggestions for improving groups. Even though this material is set apart from text, you should not assume that it is less important than other topics examined in the chapter.

Cases.   All of the chapters (except chapters 1 and 2) describe one group in considerable detail. The chapter on group formation, for example, focuses on the Beatles, and the chapter dealing with conformity highlights a jury in a murder trial. All the cases are or were real groups rather than hypothetical ones, and the incidents described are documented events that occurred within the group. The cases help clarify the concepts being examined, but the reader is reminded that the processes discussed in reference to the chapter's case group apply to other groups as well.

Revisions and Additions

If you are familiar with the first edition, then you will undoubtedly notice several changes that go beyond a general updating of the text material. These changes include: (1) the addition of a chapter on development and socialization; (2) moving the chapter dealing with conflict in groups so that it now precedes the chapter on intergroup conflict; (3) undertaking an analysis of norms in the conformity chapter (Chapter 6) rather than the chapter dealing with group structure; (4) examining coalitions in the chapter dealing with conflict (Chapter 12); and (5) integrating the material dealing with particular types of groups, such as juries and classroom groups, throughout the book. Also, coverage of certain topics, such as status differentiation, influence tactics, individual versus group performance, decision making, environmental stressors, conflict resolution, in-group/out-group biases, and crowds has been expanded considerably.

Acknowledgments

Most things in this world are accomplished by groups rather than by single individuals working alone. This book is no exception. Although I am personally responsible for the ideas presented in this book, many individuals provided me with assistance during the course of the project. Professor Lawrence Wrightsman of the University of Kansas, the consulting editor on the project, gracefully shared his expertise, enthusiasm, and knowledge with me. Thanks also go to students in my classes who gleefully provided me with feedback about ambiguities and weaknesses, as well as my colleagues who provided me with their comments and suggestions. They include Karl Kelley, of North Central College; Judy Nye, of Monmouth College; Betsy Singh, of The College of William and Mary; Stanley Strong, of Virginia Commonwealth University; Glenn Littlepage, of Middle Tennessee University; Wendy J. Harrod, of Iowa State University; Jamie McCreary, of California State University, Stanislaus; Richard Moreland, of the University of Pittsburgh; Carl W. Backman, of the University of Nevada, Reno; Duncan A. Ferguson, Sir Wilfred Grenfell College; Joan Rollins, Rhode Island College; and Robert Mauro, of the University of Oregon.

The Brooks/Cole staff, and Claire Verduin in particular, also deserve special thanks for their capable efforts.

I would also like to thank a number of people who provided me with intellectual and socioemotional support. Barry Schlenker, my mentor in social psychology, made many contributions to my training and development, as did Marv Shaw and Russ Clark. Elske Smith and Steve Danish are to be acknowledged for creating and sustaining an intellectual climate where scholarship can thrive, and Mark Leary earned my thanks many times over by helping me separate my good ideas from my dumb ones. I also owe my family and friends a debt of gratitude for the support they have provided me over the years. Bob Lesniak, Chuck and Laurie Savage, Paul Ware, Martha and Dale Travis, Bill Clegg, and Pete and Susan Riebsame deserve special mention, as do Bethia Caffery and Doug Tuthill. Lastly, I could not have completed this revision without the love, encouragement, and friendship of Suzanne Sonnergren. I remain forever in her debt.

Donelson R. Forsyth

· Contents ·

8
Leadership   211

9
Performance   249

10
Decision Making   283

15

Groups and
Change   459

·1·

The Science of
Group Dynamics

I am cast upon a horrible, desolate island; void of all hope of recovery. I am singled out and separated, as it were, from all the world, to be miserable. I am divided from mankind, a solitary; one banished from human society. I have no soul to speak to or to relieve me.

Daniel Defoe, *Robinson Crusoe*

With these words Robinson Crusoe, the hero in Defoe's classic novel, laments his fate. The climate of his island is comfortable, the food plentiful, and the animals peaceful. He has seed for crops, tools for working, weapons to protect himself, and clothes to cover himself. But despite these comforts, he feels that fate has done him a great wrong, for he is no longer a member of any human group.

Unlike the unfortunate Crusoe most of us live out our lives in the midst of groups. Of the billions of people populating the world, all but an occasional hermit, outcast, or recluse belong to a group. In fact, since most of us belong to several groups, the number of groups in the world probably reaches well beyond 5 billion. Everywhere we turn, we encounter groups: airplane crews, audiences, choirs, clubs, committees, communes, dance troupes, families, fraternities, gangs, juries, orchestras, sororitites, support groups, teams, and on and on. The world is literally teeming with groups.

Groups are a fundamental component in our social lives, but in some respects their pervasiveness prevents us from fully understanding them. In living most of our lives surrounded by groups, trying to get into groups, and trying to get out of groups, we can become so accustomed to them that their influence on our behavior goes unnoticed. We take our groups for granted, so much so that we must learn to look at them anew, from a different, more scientific perspective.

This book, in surveying what we know (and don't know) about groups, takes such a perspective. But before we plunge into our study, we must deal with some basic questions about groups and the methods used to study them. First, what, precisely, is a group? If we are to undertake a serious study of groups, then surely we must be able to identify one when we come across it. Second, what assumptions will serve as our guidelines as we describe, analyze, and compare the various groups that populate the planet? What approach will we take, as scientists, to the study of groups?

THE NATURE OF GROUPS

What would you include if you were asked to name all the groups in which you are a member? Would you list your family? your neighborhood association? a student club or organization? your political party? a handful of fellow students who often take the same classes you do? a bunch of co-workers who go out for drinks after work once in a while? Are all these collections of people groups? What kinds of social collectives qualify as *groups*?

Some Examples of Groups

The impressionists.   Art in 19th-century France was dominated by the classicists, who favored paintings depicting mythological, religious, or historical scenes. But not all artists accepted the standards established by the classical school. In 1860 Claude Monet met Camille Pissarro, and the two spent long hours airing their radical views. Two years later Edouard Manet and Edgar Degas, both sons of wealthy families, joined Monet and Pissarro in their search for alternative forms of artistic expression. Later that year Monet met three other disillusioned young artists (Pierre-Auguste Renoir, Alfred Sisley, and Frédéric Bazille) and persuaded them to join the informal gathering.

Over the next few years these young artists worked together in developing a new approach to painting, often journeying out into the countryside to paint landscapes. They sometimes painted side by side and patiently critiqued one another's work. They also met regularly, each Thursday and Sunday, in a café in Paris to discuss technique, subject matter, and artistic philosophies. For years their art was rejected by critics, and they scarcely earned enough money to survive, but by relying on one another for social support they were able to continue to develop their ideas. In time their approach was recognized by the art community as a new school of painting and was labeled impressionism (Farrell, 1982).

The survivors.   Piers Paul Read (1974) recounts the grim fate of the members of a rugby team who survived the crash of their chartered plane only to find themselves stranded in subzero temperatures high in the Andes Mountains. A lone individual would have certainly perished in the harsh climate, but by pooling their scant resources and skills, the group managed to survive. Each individual was responsible for performing certain tasks, including cleaning their sleeping quarters, tending to the injured, and melting drinking water. These activities were coordinated by the captain of the rugby team, but when he was killed in an avalanche, much of the business of running the group's activities fell on the shoulders of a coalition of three cousins.

The group lived for weeks by eating the bodies of those who had died in the crash and avalanche, but when starvation seemed imminent they sent two men down the mountain to seek help. After walking 14 days and sleeping in the open at night, the two "explorers" managed to reach a small farm on the edge of the great mountain range. Their sudden appearance after 70 days was followed by an air-rescue operation that lifted the remaining 14 from the crash-site. Those who had managed to stay alive later pointed out that "it was their combined efforts which saved their lives" (Read, 1974, p. 310).

The jury. On January 11, 1973, the jury in the case of *California v. Juan Corona* began its deliberations. For months, the 12 members had listened to the prosecution argue that Corona was guilty of having murdered the 25 men whose bodies had been found in shallow graves on a farm near Yuba City, California. They also listened as Richard E. Hawk, Corona's attorney, challenged the prosecution's witnesses and belittled the police. The case was built on circumstantial evidence, and many observers felt that the Anglo community had charged Corona because he was Hispanic.

Initially, the jurors spent considerable time discussing the evidence in general and clarifying among themselves the judge's instructions. The amount of evidence to be considered was almost overwhelming, and the jury was torn between reviewing each murder separately and considering the evidence as a whole. Concerned by the consequences of a guilty verdict, the group moved painstakingly, reviewing each bit of evidence and insisting that all members state their views openly. Each day, too, as they left the courthouse for dinner and their hotel rooms, they passed by a crowd of placard-waving Corona supporters. The waiting group included Corona's four young children, who were strategically placed where each juror would see them.

Gradually, those who believed that Corona was guilty began to dominate the group's discussion. The jury spent hours examining evidence found at one particular grave, and it concluded that Corona must have been the one who had dug it. Receipts bearing Corona's name had been found in the grave, and one juror persuasively argued that since Corona never threw away receipts and the receipts had been still folded together when found, they must have fallen from his pocket when he was digging the hole. She concluded with conviction: "I believe these receipts do place Corona at that grave while the dirt was being shoveled over that poor man's body" (Villaseñor, 1977, p. 73).

The group needed eight days to reach its conclusion, but on January 18, 1973, the jury emerged from its deliberations. The group concluded that Corona was guilty of all charges.

The People's Temple. Jim Jones was a dynamic speaker who could hold an audience in rapt attention. In 1963 he formed his own church, the People's Temple Full Gospel Church. His persuasiveness influenced many, and his message reached out to the rich and poor, young and old, and educated and uneducated. The membership soon swelled to 8000, united in their acceptance of Jones's political, religious, and social teachings. Rumors of improprieties began circulating, however. Former members reported that at some meetings those who had displeased Jones were severely beaten before the whole congregation, with microphones used to amplify their screams. Jones, some said, insisted on being called Father, and he demanded absolute dedication and obedience from his followers. Many members donated all their property to the church, and one couple even turned over their 6-year-old son on demand.

Jones eventually moved the group to Guyana, in South America, where he established Jonestown. Press releases described the settlement as a utopian community, but rumors still circulated; was Jonestown more like a prison than a utopia? Relatives in the United States became concerned, and they convinced a member of Congress, Representative Leo Ryan, to visit Jonestown. Jones's followers attacked the group, and five people were killed, including Ryan. When the assassins returned to tell Jones of their attack, he ordered his followers to take their own lives. Armed guards prevented all but a few from escaping, and Jones repeatedly told the members to accept their deaths with dignity. When authorities reached the settlement the next day, they were met by a scene of unbelievable ghastliness. On Jones's orders more than 900 men, women, and children had killed themselves. Jones's body was found near the "throne" from which he had directed the mass suicide. Over the chair remained the motto "Those who do not remember the past are condemned to repeat it" (Krause, 1978).

The presidential advisory committee.   The year was 1961, relations between Cuba and the United States had reached a new low, and the Central Intelligence Agency felt that the United States should help a force of 1400 exiles invade Cuba. President John F. Kennedy formed an ad hoc advisory committee of leading political figures to make the decision. The members boasted years of experience in making monumentally important governmental decisions, and various warfare specialists from the CIA and the military attended all the meetings. The group met for many hours, and a strong feeling of mutual respect soon welded the group into a cohesive unit. The CIA and military representatives were slightly removed from the inner circle, but the members of the committee were impressed by one another's competence.

The group decided to sponsor a small invasion. The committee members themselves chose the site for the landing: an inlet on the southern side of Cuba called Bahía de Cochinos, the Bay of Pigs. But on the day of the invasion little went according to plan. The committee had assumed that the Cuban army would be disorganized, ill-equipped, and small, but in less than 24 hours 200 men in the landing force had been killed, and the remaining 1200 were captured quickly. The attack that had been so carefully planned by the committee ended in complete disaster, and the members spent the following months wondering at their shortsightedness and cataloging all the blunders they had made (Janis, 1972, 1982, 1983).

The Rattlers and the Eagles. The 22 11-year-olds, all white and all boys, were camping near Robbers Cave State Park in Oklahoma. The boys were separated into two groups—the Rattlers and the Eagles—before spending several days hiking, swimming, and playing sports. During that time friendship bonds, rules, and rituals blossomed within each group, along with an undercurrent of animosity toward the other group. When the two groups met in a series of competitive games, in almost no time tempers flared and full-fledged hostility broke out. The Eagles stole and burned the Rattlers' makeshift team pennant. The Rattlers counterattacked that night by breaking into the Eagles' cabin, and the following day fistfights and small brawls broke out between members of the two groups.

Unbeknownst to the boys, the camp was part of a field study of relationships between groups, and the boys' behaviors were recorded continually by the camp counselors. When hostilities reached a physical level, the observers intervened and separated the two groups. They then staged a series of problems that could be solved only if the groups cooperated with each other. One problem required locating a leak in the camp's water supply. Another required them to move a truck that apparently had broken down. During and after the pursuit of these goals, animosity between the two groups diminshed. When camp was over, the boys went back home on the same bus (Sherif, Harvey, White, Hood, & Sherif, 1961).

The therapy group. The seven members of the group were outpatients at a university clinic. All seven reported problems in relating to other people, to the extent that they could not establish meaningful interpersonal relationships. Dr. R. and Dr. M., two experienced group psychotherapists, met with the group weekly. During these meetings the group members shared problems from their daily lives and received support from one another. More importantly, they learned to disclose information about themselves to others and received feedback that helped them acquire useful social skills.

Despite the fact that the group was composed entirely of people who had never been able to maintain friendships or intimate relationships, it became remarkably unified. The members rarely missed a session, and they grew more confident whenever they disclosed some previously unmentioned aspect of themselves. The therapists felt that the group seemed to plod at times, but the clients themselves were excited by their ability to interact successfully. The group lasted for 30 months, after which clinical testing indicated that the members "did extraordinarily well and underwent substantial characterologic changes as well as complete symptomatic remission" (Yalom, 1985, p. 267).

What Is a Group?

The groups in these examples differed from one another in many ways. Some were small, consisting of fewer than ten members (the therapy group), but others were large (the People's Temple). Nearly all the groups had leaders, but the power and duties of the leaders varied greatly. The artists, for example, seemed to take turns at leading, the presidential committee was run by an extremely powerful political authority, and the unofficial leader of the jury established his power through indirect means. Similarly, some of the groups formed spontaneously, whereas others were established deliberately for the purpose of achieving certain goals. Given these differences, can we accurately call all these collections of people groups?

Kurt Lewin, an eminent theorist who made many contributions to the scientific study of groups, offered an answer. He felt that despite their difference in size, structure, and activities, virtually all groups were based on interdependence among their members (Lewin, 1948). We understand intuitively that three persons seated in separate rooms working on unrelated tasks can hardly be considered a social group, for they cannot influence one another in any way. If, however, we create the potential for interdependence by letting at least one person influence or be influenced by the others, these three individuals can be considered a rudimentary group. The impressionists, for example, lived and worked together, influencing one another's ideas and techniques. Stranded in the Andes, the group of survivors helped one another overcome the many hardships they faced. The members of the therapy group provided one another with encouragement and support. Each Rattler's contribution brought the group closer to triumph over the Eagles. In all these examples, and in most other groups, members "have relationships to one another that make them interdependent to some significant degree" (Cartwright & Zander, 1968, p. 46).

By emphasizing the importance of mutual influence among members, we can define a **group** as *two or more interdependent individuals who influence one another through social interaction*. This definition, however, is fairly arbitrary. It implies that collections of people can be easily classified into two categories—group and nongroup—when in actuality such classifications are rarely so clear-cut. Indeed, the sampling of definitions in Focus 1-1 reveals that no single view has been accepted by all theorists and researchers. Moreover, even if we decide that a collection of people meets the definition of a group, our analysis is far from complete. When we study a group, whether a collection of struggling artists, a president's task force, or believers in an unorthodox religion, we must go beyond interdependence by considering the group's other important characteristics. Some of the most critical attributes to consider are examined in the next section. (Borgatta, Cottrell, & Meyer, 1956; DeLamater, 1974; Hare, 1976; Mullen, 1987; and Turner, 1985, discuss additional common features of groups.)

· ·

FOCUS 1-1: DEFINING A GROUP

A group exists when two or more people define themselves as members of it and when its existence is recognized by at least one other.

Brown, 1988, pp. 2–3

A group is a collection of individuals who have relations to one another that make them interdependent to some significant degree.

Cartwright & Zander, 1968, p. 46

For a collection of individuals to be considered a group there must be some *interaction*.

Hare, 1976, p. 4

We mean by a group a number of persons who communicate with one another, often over a span of time, and who are few enough so that each person is able to communicate with all the others, not at second hand, through other people, but face-to-face.

Homans, 1950, p. 1

A group is an aggregation of two or more people who are to some degree in dynamic interrelation with one another.

McGrath, 1984, p. 8

Two or more persons who are interacting with one another in such a manner that each person influences and is influenced by each other person.

Shaw, 1981, p. 454

A group is a social unit which consists of a number of individuals who stand in (more or less) definite status and role relationships to one another and which possesses a set of values or norms of its own regulating the behavior of individual members, at least in matters of consequence to the group.

Sherif & Sherif, 1956, p. 144

Descriptively speaking, a psychological group is defined as one that is psychologically significant for the members, to which they relate themselves subjectively for social comparison and the acquisition of norms and values, . . . that they privately accept membership in, and which influences their attitudes and behavior.

Turner, 1987, pp. 1–2

. . . .

The Characteristics of Groups

The dictionary defines a *cow* as "the mature female of domestic cattle, genus *Bos*," but dairy farmers are likely to be more interested in a cow's characteristics (four legs, tail, udder) rather than this definition (Webster, 1976, p. 421). Similarly, if you wanted to understand one of the groups we discussed earlier, you would need to be able to say more than "Yes, this aggregate is a group." You would need, for example, to describe how much members interact with one another and how each person is related to other members. You might also need to estimate the size of the group, catalog the goals that the group members pursued, index the group's unity, and chart the way the group changed over time. Interdependence among members is the hallmark of a group, but we should not overlook other crucial characteristics of groups: interaction, structure, size, goals, unity, and temporal change.

Interaction.   If you were to observe a group of people, you would probably notice first the many ways in which the members influenced one another's behavior. If you watched the French artists, you would see them offering one another advice, exchanging stories about their own hardships, and asking for reactions to their work. Observing the final day of the Jonestown group would reveal a very different form of interaction, with Jones demanding and winning obedience from all the church members. But regardless of the group setting, such influence usually requires interaction among the group members. Indeed, many theorists have underscored the importance of interaction to conclude that in groups the behavior of every member can potentially affect all the other members (for example, Bonner, 1959; Homans, 1950; Stogdill, 1959). Although interaction with other members may be discontinuous and short-lived, the interaction that does occur—physical, verbal, nonverbal, emotional, and so on—is a key feature of group life.

Structure.   All but the most ephemeral groups develop a stable pattern of relationships among the members. Although a wide variety of terms can be used to describe **group structure,** three of the most useful are **role, status,** and **attraction relation.** Consider, as an example, Kennedy's advisory group. From the outset of their deliberations the committee members adopted particular roles: some individuals became supporters, some defenders, some abstainers, and very few critics. These roles defined the behaviors expected of people who occupied given positions in the group. Stable patterns of authority and attraction also paralleled these roles, for some members of the group commanded much more respect than others, and some were better liked. If the group structure had developed differently, the group might have made a very different decision.

Size.   Groups vary considerably in size. Georg Simmel, noting these variations, developed a taxonomy of groups based primarily on size (Simmel, 1902). Shifting from smallest to largest, he identified the *dyad* (2 members), *triad* (3 members), the *small group* (4 to 20 members), the *society* (20 to 30), and the *large group* (more than 40 members). On average, however, most groups tend to be relatively small in size, ranging from 2 to 7 members. One researcher, after counting the number of people in 7405 informal, spontaneously formed groups found in public settings, reported an average group size of only 2.4 (James, 1953). He also found that deliberately formed groups, such as those created in government or work settings, included on the average 2.3 members (James, 1951). Although groups come in all shapes and sizes, they tend to "gravitate to the smallest size, two" (Hare, 1976, p. 215).

Size, per se, is not a critical quality of a group, but its indirect influence on other aspects of the group is considerable. Dyads, for example, possess many unique characteristics simply because they include only two members. The dyad is, by definition, the only group that dissolves when one member leaves and the only group that can never be broken down into subgroups (or coalitions). The same point can be made about very large aggregates, such as mobs, crowds, or congregations like that of the People's Temple. Such groups may be so large that individual members can never influence every other member, and as a result interdependence is minimal. And as groups increase in size, they tend to become more complex and formally structured (Hare, 1976). Thus, if we do not consider the group's size, we may fail to understand its other properties and characteristics.

Goals. Groups usually exist for a reason. For example, the artists wanted recognition for their work. The Andes team wanted to live. The jury was convened to make a decision about guilt or innocence. The members of the People's Temple were seeking religious and spiritual enlightenment. In each case the members of the group united in their pursuit of *common goals*.

Alvin Zander, in tracing the history of groups in society, points out that people have been using groups to accomplish goals since ancient times (Zander, 1985). By gathering in tribes, people protected themselves from dangerous animals, human enemies, and natural disasters. In ancient Egypt workers combined their efforts to build dams, irrigation systems, and colossal monuments. By 300 B.C. Chinese workers and merchants had formed organized guilds to monitor business practices. The Roman Empire made extensive use of groups, for its society was organized into various tribunes, legislative bodies, and associations. And, of course, people have traditionally conducted religious services in groups rather than in isolation.

Today's groups are no less goal-oriented, for much of the world's work is done by groups rather than by individuals. In groups we solve problems, create products, create standards, communicate knowledge, have fun, perform arts, create institutions, and even ensure our safety from attacks by other groups. Put simply, groups make it easier to attain our goals.

Cohesiveness. To understand any group we must consider its **cohesiveness** or the strength of the relationships linking the members to one another and to the group itself. As early as 1897 Emile Durkheim discussed how groups vary in terms of cohesiveness; he proposed that groups with greater solidarity had more influence over their members. A more formal analysis of cohesion was supplied by Lewin and his colleagues at the Research Center for Group Dynamics, which was founded at the Massachusetts Institute of Technology (MIT) but is now part of the Institute for

Social Research at the University of Michigan. Lewin and his associates believed that cohesion involved both individual-level and group-level processes. At the individual level cohesiveness derives from each member's attraction to other group members, whether this attraction is based on liking, respect, or trust. And at the group level cohesiveness reflects that "we-feeling" that joins people together to form a single unit (Cartwright, 1968; Festinger, 1950).

Enjoyment and satisfaction are usually much more pronounced in highly cohesive groups than in less cohesive groups. In closely knit groups members tend to participate more fully and communicate more frequently, and absences are much less likely. People in cohesive groups experience heightened self-esteem and lowered anxiety, apparently because the group provides a source of security and protection. Increases in cohesiveness also generally go hand in hand with increases in the group's capacity to retain its members (Mobley, Griffeth, Hand, & Meglino, 1979). Dorwin Cartwright, for example, actually defines cohesiveness as "the degree to which the members of the group desire to remain in their group" (1968, p. 91) and Leon Festinger calls it the "resultant of all the forces acting on the member to remain in the group" (1950, p. 274). Thus, cohesiveness "contributes to a group's potency and vitality; it increases the significance of membership for those who belong to the group" (Cartwright, 1968, p. 91). Extreme cohesiveness can be detrimental, as was the case with Kennedy's advisory committee, but without some minimal level of cohesiveness the group members would simply drift apart.

Temporal change. Some groups are so stable that their basic processes and structures remain unchanged for days, weeks, or even years, but such groups are rare. As complex systems of interdependent human beings, groups more typically *change*. In the weeks between crashing on the mountainside and the final rescue, for example, the Andes group changed dramatically. Throughout the ordeal conflicts surfaced and became submerged again, questions of authority were raised before being settled through change, and aspects of group structure took one form after another. The group was never static but, instead, developed continually.

Most group dynamicists currently believe that developmental changes in groups tend to follow one of two patterns (Hill & Gruner, 1973; Shambaugh, 1978). The *cyclical models* suggest that certain issues tend to dominate group interaction during the various phases of group development but that these issues can recur later in the life of the group. One model, for example, argues that group members strive to maintain a balance between task-oriented actions and emotionally expressive behaviors (Bales, 1965). The group tends to oscillate between these two concerns, sometimes achieving high solidarity but then shifting toward a more work-centered focus.

Successive-stage theories, in contrast, specify the usual order of the phases of group development. Bruce W. Tuckman's approach, for example, assumes that most groups move through five stages (Tuckman, 1965; Tuckman & Jensen, 1977). In the first phase the group forms, and members become oriented toward one another. In the second phase the group members often find themselves in conflict, and some solution is sought to improve the stormy group environment. In the next phase norms and roles develop that regulate behavior. In the fourth phase the group has reached a point at which it can perform as a unit to achieve desired goals, and the final stage ends the sequence of development with the group's adjournment. These theories of group change will be examined in more detail in Chapter 4.

Groups Are Dynamic

If you were limited to a single word, how would you describe the processes that take place in groups? What word illuminates the interdependence of people in groups? And what word adequately summarizes (1) the group's capacity to serve as an arena for social interaction, (2) the powerful impact of group structures on members' actions, (3) the diversity of groups in terms of size, (4) their usefulness as vehicles for accomplishing goals, (5) the way in which groups become cohesive, and (6) their ability to change over time?

Lewin chose the word *dynamic*. Groups tend to be powerful rather than weak, active rather than passive, fluid rather than static, and catalyzing rather than reifying. Lewin used the term *group dynamics* to stress the powerful impact of these complex social processes on group members.

Group dynamics, however, has a second meaning; it refers not only to the powerful processes that occur within groups but also to the scientific study of these processes. We turn to this topic in the next section.

THE NATURE OF GROUP DYNAMICS

How can we develop a deeper understanding of the people who inhabit the world? Each social science offers a different answer. Anthropology suggests that much knowledge can be gained by studying human cultures and civilizations, both past and present. Sociologists propose a different strategy: examine human societies, how they function and how they influence their members. And psychology offers yet another view: study the behavioral and mental processes of individuals.

Group dynamicists working in these disciplines also study human behavior, but they choose to focus on groups of people. Human behavior is often group behavior, for we typically work, play, worship, learn, eat, travel, and even sleep (sometimes) in groups (Battistich & Thompson, 1980). These groups not only have a pervasive impact on our social lives, but they are also fundamental components of society. In a sense each one of us belongs not to society at large but to groups that are, in turn, embedded in society. Thus, if we wish to understand ourselves, or our society, we must understand groups.

Lewin (1943, 1948, 1951) is generally given the credit for coining and popularizing the term *group dynamics* (see Focus 1-2). To Lewin group dynamics is both the powerful processes that influence individuals when in group situations and the study of these processes. Two of the most prolific researchers in the field, Dorwin Cartwright and Alvin Zander, later supplied a much more formal definition, calling it a "field of inquiry dedicated to advancing knowledge about the nature of groups, the laws of their development, and their interrelations with individuals, other groups, and larger institutions" (1968, p. 7).

FOCUS 1-2: THE LEGACY OF KURT LEWIN

Kurt Lewin is widely recognized as the "parent" of group dynamics. Born in Prussia in 1890, Lewin studied and taught in Freiberg, Munich, and Berlin before moving to the United States in 1933. For the next decade he taught at the Child Welfare Research Station at the University of Iowa and refined *field theory*, his psychological model of human behavior. **Interactionism**, one of the key assuptions of this theory, holds that behavior is a function of both the personal characteristics of the individual and the characteristics of the environment. The formula $B = f(P, E)$ summarizes this assumption. In a group context this formula implies that the behavior of group members (B) is a function (f) of the interaction of their personal characteristics (P) with environmental factors (E), which include features of the group, the group members, and the situation. These factors combine to form what Lewin called the *lifespace*.

In 1945 Lewin established the Research Center for Group Dynamics at MIT. At this center he continued to study the consequences of interdependence among group members. During his scientific career he and his colleagues examined leadership climates, industrial productivity, ways to reduce prejudice, and the influence of groups on attitudes, all within the general field-theory framework. Although he died unexpectedly of a heart attack just as group dynamics was beginning to develop more fully, his students and colleagues continue to carry on the Lewinian tradition in their theory, research, and applications (Lippitt, 1947; Marrow, 1969; Schellenberg, 1978).

Cartwright and Zander also pointed out what group dynamics was not. It is not, for example, a therapeutic perspective holding that psychological well-being can be ensured through participation in small groups guided by a skilled therapist. Nor is it the communication of certain rules or guidelines that enable individuals to develop the skills needed for smooth and satisfying social interactions. Finally, group dynamics does not refer to a loose collection of maxims concerning how groups should be organized—emphasizing, for example, such niceties as equal participation by

all group members, democratic leadership, and high levels of member satisfaction. Rather, group dynamics is an attempt to subject the many aspects of groups to scientific analysis through the construction of theories
and the rigorous testing of these theories through empirical research.

Group dynamics is not even a century old. Although ancient scholars
pondered the nature of groups, the first scientific studies of groups were
not carried out until the 1900s. Cartwright and Zander (1968), in their review of the origins of group dynamics, suggest that its slow development
stemmed in part from several unfounded assumptions about groups. For
example, many people felt that the dynamics of groups was a private affair, not something that scientists should lay open to public scrutiny. Others felt that human behavior was too complex to be studied scientifically
and that this complexity was magnified enormously when groups of interacting individuals became the objects of interest. Still others believed
that the causes of group behavior were so obvious that they were unworthy of scientific attention.

The field also developed slowly because group dynamicists disagreed
among themselves on many basic issues. It was not established by a single
theorist or researcher who laid down a set of clear-cut assumptions and
principles. Rather, group dynamics developed gradually as theorists debated basic issues and researchers developed new methods for studying
groups. Because these early efforts form the foundation of contemporary
group dynamics, the remainder of the chapter briefly examines the history of the field. (Allport, 1985; Jones, 1985; McGrath, 1978; Newcomb,
1978; Pepitone, 1981; and Steiner, 1986, also detail the development of
group dynamics.)

What Is the Group Dynamics Perspective?

Group dynamics seems to have two sides. To some the field is sociological,
for it focuses on groups of people and how these groups influence and are
influenced by societal forces. Others, however, maintain that group dynamics is a profoundly psychological science; the focus is on individuals'
thoughts, actions, and emotions, and these individuals just happen to be
in groups rather than alone. Is group dynamics a subfield of sociology or
psychology?

Ivan Steiner (1974), in an insightful analysis of the historical roots of
group dynamics, points out that sociologists and psychologists "discovered" groups almost simultaneously. Group dynamics owes much to the
work of early sociologists who proposed in the late 1800s that society was
based on a fundamental solidarity among people (Cooley, 1909; Durkheim, 1897/1966; Simmel, 1955). Durkheim, for example, asserts that social life is based on interpersonal relations within **primary groups**—small
groups characterized by face-to-face interaction, interdependency, and
strong group identification. Families, children's play groups, sets of emotionally close peers, and groups of business colleagues can be primary
groups. Because these small groups are the building blocks of society,

Durkheim argues sociologists must understand groups if they are to understand the processes that sustain society and culture (1964, 1897/1966).

At the same time, however, psychologists began studying how individuals react in group settings. In 1895 the French psychologist Gustave Le Bon published his book *Psychologie des foules (The Crowd),* which describes how individuals can temporarily lose their rationality when submerged in a mob. In 1897 Norman Triplett conducted one of the first laboratory studies of the effect of a group on an individual by asking children to perform a simple task while alone or with another child. These studies and those that followed suggested that if psychologists are to understand individuals, they must be able to explain how these individuals are influenced by groups.

In the intervening years group dynamics has become thoroughly embedded within many other branches of the social sciences. Although most group dynamicists would probably identify themselves as social psychologists, the relevance of groups to topics studied in many academic and applied disciplines gives group dynamics an interdisciplinary character. For example, researchers who prefer to study individuals may find themselves wondering what impact group participation will have on the individual's cognitions, attitudes, and behavior. Those who study organizations may find that these larger social entities actually depend on the dynamics of small subgroups within the organization and may therefore be forced to look more closely at small-group processes. Indeed, social scientists examining such global issues as the development and maintenance of culture may find themselves turning their attention toward small groups as the unit of cultural transmission.

To convey a sense of this interdisciplinary breadth, consider the fields listed in Table 1-1. Beginning first with the more academic disciplines, we see that theory and research dealing with groups are relevant to nearly all the social sciences. To oversimplify the complexities of these various fields: Psychologists tend to focus on the behavior of individuals in groups. Sociologists, in contrast, focus more on the group and its relation to society. Anthropologists find that group processes are relevant to understanding many of the common features of various societies; political scientists examine the principles of group relations and leadership; and communication researchers focus more specifically on the communication relations in groups. Although the overall aims of these disciplines may be quite different, all must consider groups.

Groups are also relevant to many applied areas, as Table 1-1 shows. The study of groups in the work setting has long occupied business-oriented researchers concerned with the effective organization of people. Although early discussions of business administration and personnel management tended to overlook the importance of groups, the 1930s witnessed a tremendous growth in management-oriented group research (for example, Barnard, 1938; Mayo, 1933). People in organizations ranging from businesses to hospitals to the armed forces began to take notice of

TABLE 1-1. Group dynamics: An interdisciplinary field.

Discipline	*Some Relevant Topics*
Psychology	Social facilitation, problem solving, attitude change, perceptions of others, social comparison
Sociology	Self and society, influence of norms on behavior, role relations, deviance
Anthropology	Groups in cross-cultural contexts, societal change, groups based on sex, age, and race
Political Science	Leadership, intergroup relations, political influence, power
Speech and Communication	Information transmission in groups, problems in communication, networks
Business and Industry	Motivation, productivity, improving organizational effectiveness, goal setting
Social Work	Improving adjustment through group participation, family counseling
Education	Classroom groups, team teaching, class composition and educational outcomes
Clinical/Counseling Psychology	Therapeutic change through group counseling, sensitivity training, encounter
Criminal Justice	Organization of law enforcement agencies, gangs, jury deliberations
Sports and Recreation	Team performance, effects of victory and failure, cohesion and performance

the critical role that interpersonal relations played in their own organizations, and soon principles of group behavior became an integral part of most philosophies of effective administrative practices. Other professions have both influenced and have been influenced by group work. Social workers frequently found themselves dealing with such groups as social clubs, gangs, neighborhoods, and family clusters, and an awareness of group processes helped crystalize their understanding of group life. Educators were also influenced by group research, as were many of the medical fields that dealt with patients on a group basis. Although this listing of disciplines is far from inclusive, it does convey the idea that the study of groups is not limited to any one field. As A. Paul Hare, the compiler of a useful handbook of group research (Hare, 1976) and his colleagues once noted, "This field of research does not 'belong' to any one of the recognized social sciences alone. It is the common property of all" (Hare, Borgatta, & Bales, 1955, p. vi).

Are Groups Real?

The roots of group dynamics in both psychology and sociology produced two different orientations to the study of groups. The first orientation, which Steiner labels the *individualistic approach,* focused on the individual in the group. Researchers who took this approach sought to explain the behavior of each group member, and they ultimately wanted to know if such psychological processes as attitudes, motivations, or personality were the true determinants of social behavior. Steiner contrasts this perspective to the *group-oriented approach*: "The individual is presumed to be an element in a larger system, a group, organization, or society. And what he does is presumed to reflect the state of the larger system and the events occurring in it" (1974, p. 96). Sociological researchers tended to adopt the group-oriented perspective, and psychological researchers favored the individualistic orientation (Steiner, 1974, 1983, 1986).

The disparity between these two views was most apparent in discussions of the concept of the groupmind. Extending the work of Le Bon and other crowd psychologists, Durkheim suggested that large groups of people sometimes acted with a single mind. He felt that such groups, rather than being merely collections of individuals in a fixed pattern of relationships with one another, were linked by some unifying force that went beyond any single individual. This force was so strong in some groups that the will of the individual could be completely dominated by the will of the group, which Durkheim called the **groupmind** or collective consciousness.

Psychologists interested in group phenomena tended to reject the reality of such concepts as groupmind or collective conscious. Floyd A. Allport, the foremost representative of this perspective, argued that such terms as groupmind were unscientific, since they referred to phenomena that simply did not exist. In his 1924 text *Social Psychology* he baldly wrote that "nervous systems are possessed by individuals; but there is no nervous system of the crowd" (p. 5). He added: "Only through social psychology as a science of the individual can we avoid the superficialities of the crowdmind and collective mind theories" (p. 8). Taking the individualistic perspective to the extreme, Allport also concluded that groups should never be studied by psychologists, since they did not exist as scientifically valid phenomena. Because Allport believed that "the actions of all are nothing more than the sum of the actions of each taken separately" (p. 5), he felt that a full understanding of the behavior of individuals in groups could be achieved simply through studying the psychology of the group members. Groups, in a scientific sense, are not real entities.

Allport's reluctance to accept such dubious concepts as groupmind into social psychology helped ensure the field's scientific status. His belief that groups could be completely understood from the individualistic perspective meant, however, that group processes and such concepts as role, leadership, and interpersonal communication were unscientific and therefore unimportant. Until the reality-of-groups question could be answered, many psychologists refused to study groups.

In time the rift between the two factions closed (Warriner, 1956). In the first place, psychologists came to realize that group was as scientific a concept as such individualistic notions as mind, attitude, and value. Lewin, for example, convincingly argued that groups possessed properties that could not be fully understood by piecemeal examination. Adopting the dictum of Gestalt psychology, "The whole is greater than the sum of the parts," he pointed out that when individuals merged into a group something new was created and that the new product itself had to be the object of study (Lewin, 1951). Second, researchers were able to demonstrate that the group phenomena that Allport considered to be unscientific reifications could be experimentally created, varied, and studied in laboratory settings. Muzafer Sherif, for example, conducted a landmark study of norms in 1936. **Norms,** although often unspoken, structure individuals' behaviors and judgments in group settings. Sherif created norms by asking groups of men to state aloud their estimates of the distance a dot of light had moved. He found that, over time, the men accepted a standard estimate in place of their own idiosyncratic judgments. This norm continued to influence individuals' perceptions even when they later responded alone. In view of Sherif's findings most theorists were forced to admit that the behavior of individuals in groups might be significantly influenced by unobservable, but potent, social forces such as norms.

Third, Donald T. Campbell (1958a) persuasively argued that groups become real when they possess the characteristics of entities. He pointed out that most people perceive common objects to be unified wholes, or entities. A building, for example, isn't perceived as a hodgepodge of walls and windows with a roof but as a single, unified structure. Collections of human beings, however, sometimes are but sometimes aren't perceived to be unified entities. For example, some of the gatherings of individuals you encounter on any given day may appear to you to be groups. If you observed the therapy group or the Rattlers attacking the Eagles, you would probably decide that you were observing groups in action. But if you chanced upon a gathering of strangers waiting for a bus, you might feel that these individuals did not look like a unified group. Campbell thus rejected the argument that groups must be labeled as either real or unreal; he suggested that groups vary in realness, depending on the observer's perspective. (Campbell used the term *entitativity* to describe the extent to which something is perceived to be a single unified whole. His work is described in more detail in Focus 1-3.)

. . . .

FOCUS 1-3: PERCEIVING GROUPS

Imagine that you must locate a group and record its characteristics as part of a class assignment. You go to the library and relax in a chair with a good view of four students seated at the same table. You watch these people read silently to themselves for a while, but as the minutes go by a question begins to disturb you: are these people really a group? Perhaps they are actually just four individuals seated at the same table, an aggregate of strangers who don't really fit the definition of group.

According to Donald T. Campbell (1958a), your misgivings stem from the absence of certain perceptual cues that can be taken as evidence of unity. Campbell based his analysis on the work of early psychologists who had wondered how the human mind decides whether something perceived is a Gestalt—a unified system of interrelated parts—or a random collection of unrelated elements (Kohler, 1947; Wertheimer, 1938). Applying this work to the perception of groups, Campbell coined the term *entitativity* to describe the extent to which something seems to be a unified entity. From one perspective, for example, the spectators at a football game may seem to be a disorganized mass of individuals who happen to be in the same place at the same time and not really a group at all. But at another level the tendency for the spectators to shout the same cheer, to express similar emotions, and to move together to create the "wave" gives the fans the appearance of entitativity.

What cues do we rely on to make our judgments about entitativity? Campbell emphasizes three:

1. common fate: the extent to which individuals in the aggregate seem to experience the same, or interrelated, outcomes
2. similarity: the extent to which the individuals display the same behaviors or resemble one another
3. proximity: the distance among individuals in the aggregate

Applied to the four individuals seated at the same table, the principle of common fate predicts that the degree of "groupness" you attribute to the cluster would increase if, for example, all the members got up and left the room together or began laughing together. Your confidence that this cluster was a real group would also be bolstered if you noticed that all four were reading from the same textbook or were wearing the same Greek organization shirt. Finally, if the members moved closer to one another, you would become even more certain that you were watching a group.

Perceived unity influences many other aspects of the group, including attraction among members, stability, and productivity. In one study, for example, researchers compared the responses of women who thought they were members of a group with those of women who thought they were behaving in an individualistic situation (Zander, Stotland, & Wolfe, 1960). The women were required to work on an experimental task in separate testing cubicles, so the researchers assumed that their perceptions of entitativity would be low—that is, that they wouldn't feel like members of a group. Half the women, however, were repeatedly told that the researchers believed that they were a group rather than just an aggregate of individuals. As predicted, these women attributed groupness to their aggregate, and in consequence they rated themselves more negatively after group failure rather than success. The self-evaluations of members of low-entitativity aggregates were uninfluenced by the group's outcome. Thus, even though a group may exist only in the eyes (and minds) of its members, this feeling of unity may still have profound consequences (Tajfel, 1982; Wilder, 1986).

· ·

Even though Allport himself amended his initial position on the issue by acknowledging the reality of groups (1961, 1962), vestiges of the rift remain (Archibald, 1976; House, 1977; Stryker, 1977, 1986). Group dynamicists in psychology or sociology tend to overlook theory and research that originates in the other discipline (Backman, 1983, 1986). Sociologists are content to study the group as a whole, psychologists concentrate on individuals in groups, but few try to integrate these two levels of analysis in a single overall perspective (Doise, 1986; Smith & White, 1983). To deal with these limitations, many advocate a unified treatment of groups and social processes (Stephan & Stephan, 1985, 1986). Toward this end, throughout my discussions of groups I will try to strike a fair balance between group-oriented analyses and individualistic analyses. Although in some cases I may fall short of full integration, drawing from both perspectives will increase the likelihood of achieving the primary goal: an understanding of groups.

Group Dynamics: A Basic or Applied Science?

In most sciences a line is drawn between basic and applied research. **Basic research** (sometimes called pure research) examines theoretical questions in an attempt to acquire more knowledge about a particular subject. **Applied research,** in contrast, assumes that usefulness is the supremely important quality of research and that accruing data about esoteric, inapplicable theories is misplaced effort. To exaggerate the differences between these two perspectives: The basic scientist assumes that the best way to proceed is through attention to theory-related research and seeks knowledge for its own sake. The applied scientist focuses on a specific problem and performs research that provides a solution; knowledge is a means to an end.

Group dynamics does not easily fit either of these classifications. Basic researchers testing theoretically interesting ideas often achieve results that have many useful applications. Moreover, practitioners who work with groups but have no interest in theoretically elegant conceptualizations nevertheless provide basic researchers with much raw material for theories. Overall, research in group dynamics can usually be called **action research,** Lewin's term for the use of the scientific method in solving questions that have significant social value. Lewin argued in favor of the intertwining of basic and applied research, for he firmly believed that there "is no hope of creating a better world without a deeper scientific insight into the function of leadership and culture, and of other essentials of group life" (1943, p. 113). To achieve this goal, he assured practitioners that in many instances "there is nothing so practical as a good theory" (1951, p.

169) while charging basic researchers with the task of developing theories that can be applied to important social problems (Cartwright, 1978; Forsyth & Strong, 1986).

What Aspects of Groups Should Be Studied? An Overview

Throughout the history of group dynamics some approaches that initially seemed promising have been abandoned after they contributed relatively little or failed to stimulate consistent lines of research. The idea of group-mind, for example, was discarded when researchers identified more likely causes of crowd behavior. Similarly, such concepts as syntality, groupality, and the lifespace initially attracted considerable interest but stimulated little research (see Cattell, 1948, Bogardus, 1954, and Lewin, 1951, respectively). In contrast, researchers have studied such topics as group development, leadership, and group performance continuously since these issues were first broached by some enterprising explorer.

Although the vast number of articles and books published about groups makes the task of reviewing past work on groups seem nearly insurmountable, to set limits on our task we will examine only those topics that have dominated group dynamicists' interests over the years. Table 1-2 presents a sampling of some these topics, organized in five broad, overlapping categories.

Orientation and methods.   This chapter and the next provide an introduction to the study of groups. This chapter has defined and described the characteristics of groups while also highlighting some of the important features of the field of group dynamics. Chapter 2 concludes this brief introduction to the field by examining measurement methods and research designs.

TABLE 1-2. Topics in group dynamics.

Category	Topic	Chapter
Orientation and Methods	The science of group dynamics	1
	Studying groups	2
Group Formation and Development	Group formation	3
	Development and socialization	4
	Group structure	5
Influence and Interaction	Conformity and influence	6
	Power	7
	Leadership	8
Group Performance	Group performance	9
	Decision making in groups	10
Issues and Application	Environmental process	11
	Conflict	12
	Conflict between groups	13
	Crowds and collective behavior	14
	Groups and change	15

Group formation and development.   Which topic should serve as the first step in our study of groups? The choices are limitless, but this text "begins at the beginning" by considering why groups form (Chapter 3) and how they develop (Chapter 4). This section also includes a chapter that focuses on the nature and development of group structure, including role, status, and attraction differentiation (Chapter 5).

Influence and interaction in groups.   A group is a complex social system, a microcosm of powerful interpersonal forces that significantly shape members' actions. Chapters 6, 7, and 8 consider how individuals react to interpersonal influence in groups and how they influence their group in return. Chapter 6 begins by considering how we sometimes conform to group pressure but how we can also influence the group by remaining independent. Chapter 7 extends this topic by considering how we make use of social power to influence others, and how people respond to such influence. We will then turn in Chapter 8 to leadership as an influence process.

Group performance.   Groups are performance machines. Much of the world's work is done by people working together rather than individuals working in isolation. In Chapter 9 we will consider factors that influence individual productivity in groups and Chapter 10 we will review some of the advantages and disadvantages of making decisions in groups.

Issues and applications.   Groups are neither all good nor all bad. Although they are so "beneficial, if not essential, to humans" that "it seems nonsensical to search for alternatives to human groups," evidence indicates that groups sometimes have a negative affect on humans (Buys, 1978, p. 568). Thus, although group membership leads to many positive consequences, we cannot ignore some of its more problematic aspects. Chapter 11 considers the impact of environmental factors, such as overcrowding and territoriality, on group processes. The next two chapters examine conflict, with Chapter 12 focusing on conflict in groups and 13 examining conflict between groups. Chapter 14 extends our analysis of groups by considering factors that can cause members of large groups, mobs, and crowds to engage in extreme, atypical behavior. Last, Chapter 15 concludes our study of groups by considering ways to harness group processes to help members change for the better.

SUMMARY

Consider several examples of people who have joined to form a social unit, such as a band of renegade artists, airline passengers stranded on a mountainside, a religious movement changing over time, or a governmental committee making an important decision. These social groupings possess many unique characteristics, but they are all *groups*: they include two or more interdependent individuals who influence one another through social interaction. Were we to observe these groups, we would soon notice a number of common features: (1) interaction among group members; (2) *group structure*, including *roles*, *status*, and *attraction relations*; (3) variations in size; (4) shared common goals; (5) *cohesiveness*; and (6) the tendency for these characteristics to change gradually over over time.

The term *group dynamics* refers to both the subject and the field. Lewin first used the phrase to describe the powerful processes that take place in groups, but group dynamics also names the "field of inquiry dedicated to advancing knowledge about the nature of groups" (Cartwright & Zander, 1968, p. 7). Despite variations among group dynamicists, virtually all agree with Lewin's basic concept of *interactionism*: behavior is a function of the person and the environment, or $B = f(P, E)$. This relatively young science has roots in many academic and applied disciplines. Sociologists, for example, have long recognized that *primary groups* are the bridges that link individuals to society, and psychologists have studied how people act when they are in groups rather than alone. This interdisciplinary heritage gives group dynamics a broad conceptual foundation, but it also leads to differences in opinion concerning how groups should best be studied. For example, although most researchers now agree that groups are real entities, there are two approaches to studying them. Psychologically oriented researchers still tend to take an individualistic approach by focusing on the individual and not the group. Others, in contrast, adopt a group-oriented approach that draws on early studies of mob behavior, the *group-mind*, and *norms*. Similarly, theoretically minded investigators emphasize *basic research*, problem-oriented researchers conduct *applied research*, and some combine these two perspectives by conducting *action research*.

·2·

Studying Groups

S uppose you find yourself elected leader of a small club or a committee. You tackle your duties enthusiastically, but never having been a leader you tend to have more failures than successes. Disheartened but not willing to admit defeat, you resolve to improve your understanding of the basic principles of leadership by careful study. But which sources should you consider? Should you turn to philosophy for answers? Great thinkers through the ages have discussed the courses and strategies of leadership. Should you heed the advice of expert authorities—presidents of nations, military heroes, or corporate executives—who have offered guidelines for effective leadership? Or should you try to diagnose the source of your problems by relying on intuition and common sense?

Scientific research offers an alternative. The great Roman orator Cicero argued that leaders must maintain firm control, since groups have "no judgment, no discretion, no discrimination, no consistency," but this recommendation may not apply to your group. The able industrialist Lee Iacocca (1984, p. 60) thinks that a good leader must "know how to delegate and how to motivate," but exactly how can you apply this advice in your group? Common sense may tell you that you need to make friends with the people in your group, but friendship could be the wrong solution to your problems. The writings of ancient scholars, the prescriptions of experts, and your own common sense offer suggestions about leadership, but the group dynamicist wants to know if these ideas can stand up when tested scientifically.

What makes a discipline a science? The sociologist George Caspar Homans offers one possible answer: "When the test of the truth of a relationship lies finally in the data themselves, and the data are not wholly manufactured—when nature, however stretched out on the rack, still has a chance to say 'No!'—then the subject is a science" (1967, p. 4). This definition is but one of many, but it aptly highlights two key aspects of science. First, researchers must find a way to "stretch nature out on the rack"; they must be able to measure the processes and phenomena they are interested in explaining. If, for example, you want to know if treating group members in a friendly way will prompt them to work harder, you must develop ways to measure the leader's friendliness and the members' motivational levels.

Measurement is so crucial a component of scientific research that the first half of this chapter is devoted to reviewing several measurement methods used by researchers. Measurement, however, is only part of the picture. As Homans notes, researchers must also test "the truth of the relationship" in some way. You may want to know if friendliness and motivation are related to each other, but what techniques can you use to gauge the strength of such a relationship? The second section of the chapter answers this question by describing several research methods that can be used to study groups.

MEASUREMENT IN GROUP DYNAMICS

Progress in science often depends on the development of tools for conducting research. The compound microscope, for example, provided biologists with the means of studying organic processes that had once been completely unknowable, just as the telescope enabled astronomers to observe distant celestial phenomena. Similarly, before the scientific study of groups could flourish, researchers had to develop the tools for doing group research. Recognizing the complexity of groups, these early investigators struggled to develop ways to assess group members' actions and reactions. The following sections trace the growth and impact of two important measurement tools—observational strategies and self-report measures—that gave group dynamics a foothold in the scientific tradition.

Observational Techniques

Early researchers relied heavily on **observational measures** in their initial studies of groups. After all, the approach had been used for centuries by historians, philosophers, and literary figures, and the idea of answering questions about groups by watching them seemed both reasonable and efficient (Cartwright & Zander, 1968). Over the years, however, researchers have developed various approaches to observation, so that the term *observational research* is now quite broad in meaning. Yet, despite these differences the goal of any observational measure is always the same: to watch and record events that transpire in groups in order to test the adequacy of some hypothesis concerning their dynamics (Kidder, 1981; Weick, 1985).

Consider William Foote Whyte's 1943 observational study of street corner gangs. Whyte wished to understand as completely as possible the groups and social structure of an Italian-American slum in the heart of Boston. He moved to the district, which he gives the fictitious name Cornerville, lived for a time with an Italian family, and joined the Nortons, a group of young men who gathered at a particular corner on Norton Street. He also participated in a more upwardly mobile social club known as the Italian Community Club. For 3½ years Whyte observed and recorded these groups, and his integrated notes yielded a detailed portrait of this community and its groups. In particular, Whyte's study underscored a strong link between the individual member and the group. For example, if a young man belonged to a corner gang such as the Nortons, his life was dramatically influenced by this group; he became a "corner boy" first, an individual second. Doc, the leader of the Nortons, pointed out that a corner boy would be lost without his gang.

> They come home from work, hang on the corner, go up to eat, back on the corner, up to a show, and they come back to hang on the corner. If they're not on the corner, it's likely the boys there will know where you can find them. Most of them stick to one corner. It's only rarely that a fellow will change his corner [Whyte, 1943, p. 256].

Whyte used observation measures in his study, but before he could carry out his observations, he had to answer a number of important questions. First, should he participate in the group or remain outside it? Second, should he reveal his identity to the group or keep his research purposes to himself? Third, he had to decide whether to structure the observations he would be making. As you will see, his answers to these three questions had a great impact on his final product.

Participant observation.   Whyte decided to study the Boston slum groups from within; he actually joined these groups. This technique of group observation is called **participant observation,** which can be defined as "a process in which the observer's presence in a social situation is maintained for the purpose of scientific investigation. The observer is in a face-to-face relationship with the observed, and, by participating with them in their natural life setting, he gathers data" (Schwartz & Schwartz, 1955, p. 344; see also Schwartz & Jacobs, 1979).

Participant observation offers both strengths and weaknesses. As a member of the group, Whyte gained access to information that would have been hidden from an external observer. His techniques also gave him a very detailed understanding of the gang. Rather than portraying the group as a static entity, he described groups as they are: dynamic interpersonal systems that evolve over time. He was also able to clarify formerly vague concepts such as leadership and power by tying these terms to directly observable, unambiguously described group events. Unfortunately, his presence in the group may also have changed the group itself. He went bowling with the Nortons, gambled with them, and even lent money to some of the members. His presence in the group undoubtedly modified its structure, and therefore the group he describes is not a typical corner gang, but, rather, a corner gang with a researcher in it.

Overt and covert observation.   Whyte was an overt observer of the group; the Nortons knew that he was a social scientist and that he was recording their behavior. Such openness meant that he did not have to mislead the group in any way, but by revealing his purpose he may have indirectly influenced the gang's behavior. As one corner boy once remarked, "You've slowed me down plenty since you've been down here. Now, when I do something, I have to think what Bill Whyte would want to know about it and how I can explain it. Before I used to do things by instinct" (p. 301). As Focus 2-1 explains, the tendency for individuals to modify their behavior when they know they are being observed is known as the **Hawthorne effect**.

FOCUS 2-1: THE DISCOVERY OF THE HAWTHORNE EFFECT

In the 1920s Elton Mayo and his associates at the Hawthorne Plant of the Western Electric Company carried out landmark studies of industrial behavior (Landsberger, 1958; Mayo, 1945; Roethlisberger & Dickson, 1939). To identify the physical features of the work setting that improved or impeded job performance, Mayo and his colleagues systematically varied a number of features while measuring the workers' output. For example, he moved one group of women to a separate room, where their performance could be carefully monitored. Next, he introduced factors into the situation that were expected to hurt performance, such as reduced lighting and fewer rest periods, and factors that he thought would help performance, such as brighter lighting and more rest periods. Surprisingly, all innovations led to improved worker output (although recent analyses suggest that Mayo may have overestimated the impact of these situational manipulations [Franke & Kaul, 1978]). To Mayo's credit he recognized that the physical features he had manipulated were not as important as the social factors present in the work group. Apparently, the group members felt that the company was taking a special interest in them, and so they responded by working particularly hard. (Varying views on these studies are presented by Bramel & Friend, 1981, and Franke, 1979.)

Mayo's work underscored the importance of considering interpersonal factors in the work setting, but at the same time it warned investigators of a serious research problem: group members act differently when they believe they are being observed by social scientists interested in their behavior (Barnard, 1938; McGregor, 1960). This change in behavior as a result of observation, or Hawthorne effect, continues to limit the generalizability of research findings based on field and laboratory situations in which group members know they are being studied.

Some researchers, worried that groups may react oddly if they know they are being observed, use **covert observation;** the observer records the group's activities without the subject's knowledge. Although such methods are commendable methodologically, their invasion of privacy is questionable (Cook, 1981; Douglas, 1976; Reynolds, 1979). The use of open, nondeceptive methods is generally considered to be less controversial.

Structuring observations.   Whyte decided to observe the Nortons each day, but he did not immediately try to structure his observations in any way. He simply took extensive notes and eventually integrated them to form an overall picture of the group. To some, such an open approach to observation is needed so that final conclusions are not biased by the researchers' preconceptions about the groups (Barton & Lazarfeld, 1969; Glaser & Strauss, 1967; Schwartz & Jacobs, 1979).

Others, however, argue that such openness should be avoided, because it puts too much trust in the observational powers of the researchers: they may let initial, though implicit, expectations shape their records (Mitroff & Kilmann, 1978; Weick, 1985). Consider, for example, a study conducted by Albert H. Hastorf and Hadley Cantril (1954). They asked college students to watch a film of two groups—two teams playing a football game. The game selected had been played between Dartmouth and Princeton and had been characterized by extremely rough play and many penalties. The Princeton quarterback, an all-American, left the game in the second quarter with a broken nose and a mild concussion. In the third quarter the Dartmouth quarterback's leg was broken when he was tackled in the backfield. Hastorf and Cantril asked Dartmouth and Princeton students to record the number and severity of the infractions that had been committed by the two teams.

As Hastorf and Cantril had expected, they found that some of their student observers weren't very objective (see Figure 2-1). Dartmouth students saw the Princeton Tigers commit about the same number of infractions as the Dartmouth players. Princeton students, however, disagreed with the Dartmouth observers; they saw the Dartmouth team commit more than twice as many infractions as the Princeton team. Apparently, the Princeton observers' preference for their own team distorted their perceptions of the group interaction.

Structured observational measures offer one possible solution to the problem of objectivity in observations by helping observers categorize group behavior. Like biologists who classify living organisms under such

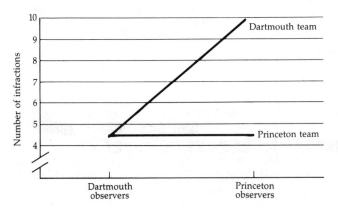

FIGURE 2-1. The number of infractions recorded by Dartmouth and Princeton students while watching the film of a Dartmouth/Princeton game.
Source: Hastorf & Cantril, 1954

categories as phylum, subphylum, class, and order or psychologists who classify people into various personality groupings or types, group researchers want to be able to classify each group behavior into an objectively definable category. To achieve this goal, they first decide which behaviors in the group are of interest and which are not. Next, they set up the categories to be used in the coding system. The researchers then note the occurrence and frequency of these targeted behaviors.

Researchers can now choose from a wide assortment of structured observational systems; indeed, one researcher has actually developed a structured coding system for classifying types of coding systems (Trujillo, 1986). Robert Freed Bales's method, however, has proven particularly useful (Bales, 1950, 1970, 1980). As shown in Table 2-1, an early form of Bales's **Interaction Process Analysis** (IPA) classified each bit of behavior performed by a group member into 1 of 12 categories. Six of these categories (1–3 and 10–12) pertain to *socioemotional activity*, or actions that are based on the interpersonal relationships within the group. Complimenting another person would be an example of a positive socioemotional behavior, whereas insulting a group member would reflect negative socioemotional behavior. The other six categories pertain to *task activity*, or behavior that focuses on the problem the group is trying to solve. Giving and asking for information, opinions, and suggestions related to the problem the group faces are all examples of task-oriented activity.

To use the IPA, observers must learn to identify the 12 types of behavior defined by Bales (see Table 2-1). They must practice listening to a group discussion, breaking the verbal content down into the smallest meaningful units that can be identified, and then classifying these units as to category (Bales, 1950, p. 7). Thus, considerable training is involved in this

TABLE 2-1. The categories of the original and the revised Interaction Process Analysis system.

General Categories	1950 IPA Categories	1970 IPA Categories
A. Positive (and mixed) actions	1. Shows solidarity 2. Shows tension release 3. Agrees	1. Seems friendly 2. Dramatizes 3. Agrees
B. Attempted answers	4. Gives suggestion 5. Gives opinion 6. Gives orientation	4. Gives suggestion 5. Gives opinion 6. Gives information
C. Questions	7. Asks for orientation 8. Asks for opinion 9. Asks for suggestion	7. Asks for information 8. Asks for opinion 9. Asks for suggestion
D. Negative (and mixed) actions	10. Disagrees 11. Shows tension 12. Shows antagonism	10. Disagrees 11. Shows tension 12. Seems unfriendly

(Source: Bales, 1970)

form of observation. As the group members interact, observers record on a profile form containing the categories listed in Table 2-1 who spoke to whom (for example, Person 1 to Person 2) and the type of statement made (say, a statement that shows solidarity or seems friendly). If Person 1, for example, begins the group discussion by asking "Should we introduce ourselves?" and Person 2 answers "Yes," the observers write 1-2 beside Category 8 (Person 1 asks for opinion) and 2-1 beside Category 5 (Person 2 gives opinion to Person 1). If later in the interaction Person 3 angrily tells the entire group "This group is a boring waste of time," the coders write 3-0 beside Category 12 (Person 3 seems unfriendly to entire group).

When used by well-trained observers, the IPA yields a reliable and valid record of group interaction. In addition, because it records the number of times a particular type of behavior has occurred, it allows comparison across categories, group members, and even different groups. Furthermore, in working with process analysis for more than 40 years, Bales has continually improved the IPA on the basis of available data. As Table 2-1 indicates, Bales revised several of the categories in 1970 to increase their usefulness during observation, and even more recently he proposed a further elaboration of the entire system. This newest version is called SYM-LOG, which stands for System of Multiple Level Observation of Groups. We will examine this advanced coding system in detail in Chapter 5 (Bales, 1980; Bales, Cohen, & Williamson, 1979).

Given the greater objectivity of structured observations, why did Whyte take an unstructured approach? At the time he conducted his study, very little research had been done on community groups. He therefore chose to observe as much as he could each day, make extensive notes when possible, and wait for some overall guiding theme to make itself evident. He was rewarded when it became clear after many hours and pages of observation that "an analysis of leadership would provide a means of integrating the study" (p. vii). Thus, if the research is more exploratory, designed to develop theory first and validate hypotheses second, then an unstructured observational approach is appropriate. If the researcher has a hypothesis in mind and can make use of more structured observational methods, the rigor and objectivity of a structured approach seems preferable.

Self-Report Measures

Imagine that you are a researcher and that you want to know how group members feel about something or why they performed a particular behavior. How can you find out? One simple solution is to ask them questions and record their responses. How you go about asking can vary; you can administer carefully constructed personality *tests*, distribute attitude *questionnaires*, or conduct face-to-face *interviews*. But these **self-report mea-**

sures are all alike in that they involve asking a question and recording the answer (Dawes & Smith, 1985).

Sociometry is an example of a self-report measure. This procedure was developed by Jacob L. Moreno in an early study of adolescent women living in 14 adjacent cottages of an institution. Although neighbors, the women were not very neighborly. Discipline problems were rampant, and disputes continually arose among the groups and among members of the same group who were sharing a cottage. Moreno's solution was to regroup the women into more compatible units and put the greatest physical distances between hostile groups. He achieved this goal by giving the women a confidential questionnaire that asked them to to indicate those in the community they liked the most. On the basis of these responses he was able to reduce the overall level of antagonism in the community (Moreno, 1953).

Thus, Moreno had developed sociometry, a technique for measuring the social relationships linking group members. A sociometric study begins by asking the group members one or more questions about their fellow members. Typically, the central question concerns which person in the group they like the most, but other questions have been used, such as "Whom in the group would you like to work with the most?" or "Whom do you like the least?" The number of choices permitted is limited by the researcher.

In the second phase the researcher summarizes these choices by drawing a **sociogram,** or a diagram of the relationships among group members. To start, the researcher graphs, in the shape of an oval, a number of circles representing all the group members. Next, he or she draws in the feelings of each group member about the others, using arrows to indicate the direction of relationships. Next, as depicted in Figure 2-2, the researcher draws the diagram again to organize it into a more meaningful pattern. For example, those individuals who are frequently chosen as most liked by others could be put in the center of the diagram, and the least frequently chosen people could be placed about the periphery.

In the final stage the researcher identifies the configurations of the group and the positions of each member. This step often includes the identification of (1) *stars,* the highly popular group members; (2) *isolates,* the infrequently chosen individuals; (3) *pairs,* two people who, by listing each other as their first choices, have reciprocal bonds; and (4) *chains,* clusters of individuals within the group who make up a subgroup, or clique. The researcher may also wish to calculate several indexes that summarize sociometric choice. Some of the more popular measures that can be computed from a sociogram include (1) the number of times a person is chosen by the other group members (choice status); (2) the number of times a person is rejected by others (rejection status); (3) the relative number of mutual pairs in a group (group cohesion); and (4) the relative number of

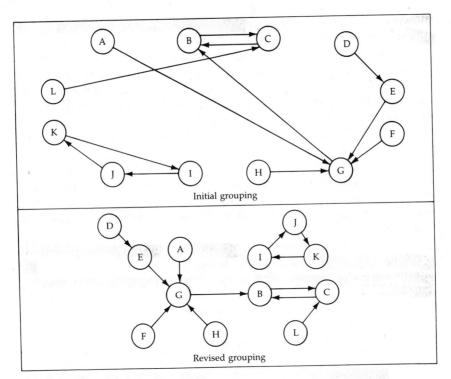

FIGURE 2-2. Sociogram of a 12-person group. *A* to *L* are all group members, but *G* is a star; *L* and *D* are isolates; *B* and *C* are a pair; and *I, J,* and *K* form a chain.

isolates (group integration). Lastly, if respondents have provided several nominations reflecting both liking and disliking, more elaborate statistical methods can be used to organize the choice and rejection data (see Lindzey & Borgatta, 1954; Moreno, 1960; Northway, 1967). (See Focus 2-2.)

. . . .

FOCUS 2-2: FAMILIES AS SMALL GROUPS

Of all the groups we belong to, one often influences us more than all others: our family. We become members of this group at birth, and during our childhood this group cares for and socializes us. As we grow older, our roles within the group may change, but even as adults many of our actions are constrained by our family's dynamics. Our family is usually the first group we join and the last one we leave.

Some group dynamicists, when initiating a study of a particular family or trying to help a family overcome a problem, use a form of sociometry to measure the general structure of the group. Because members of a family are linked both genetically and socially, such a diagram is sometimes termed a **genogram** (Guerin & Pendagast, 1976). The analysis begins with some basic questions about the immediate family: What are the names

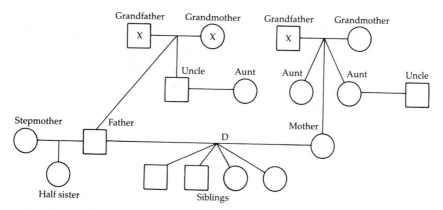

FIGURE 2-3. In this genogram circles depict females, boxes depict males, an X indicates the individual is deceased, and D signifies divorce.

and ages of the parents? When did they marry? Do they have any children? Are they boys or girls, and how old are they? Next, researchers can ask about close relatives, including grandparents, uncles, and aunts, and also inquire into the possibility of previous marriages that ended in divorce or death. Once the basic structure of the family is charted (see Figure 2-3), other aspects of family life can be considered. Who communicates with whom? In some families certain individuals often know most about what is happening within the group and frequently write and telephone the other group members. Where are the group members? If any have moved to distant locations, they may feel cut off from the rest of the group. Have any major events changed the group recently? Such events could include the death of grandparent, a serious illness in a child, an affair by one of the parents, or loss of employment.

Like a sociogram, a genogram only scratches the surface of a family's complex dynamics. If supplemented with observational data and other information about the group, however, it becomes a useful tool for both researcher and practitioner. Family therapists, in particular, have found that the genogram is very useful in helping families isolate the cause of their troubles and identify possible solutions (Guerin & Pendagast, 1976). In addition, it highlights how methods and concepts developed in studying groups can apply to the study of families. A family is a complex system of relationships, but at core it is just one type of group among many (Argyle, 1969; Okiishi, 1987; Steinhauer, 1987).

• •

Like observational methods, self-report methods such as sociometry possess both weaknesses and strengths. They depend very much on knowing what questions to ask the group members. The observer may be able to incorporate previously unnoticed variables into the research scheme once the project is launched. The self-report researcher, in contrast, is likely either to fail to notice unexpected variables or to experience great difficulty in adapting the survey to include them. A maze of technical questions also confronts the researcher designing questionnaires. Unless the questions are worded properly, the responses will be difficult to interpret. The link between the quality of the results and the quality of the survey itself is captured in the inelegant phrase "garbage in, garbage out." Questionnaires composed of poorly selected or ambiguously worded questions are always exceedingly difficult to interpret. Also, if subjects are unwilling to disclose their personal attitudes, feelings, and perceptions or are unaware of these internal processes, self-report measures will provide little in the way of useful data (Dawes & Smith, 1985).

Despite these limitations, self-report methods are indispensable research tools for many problems in group dynamics. For example, researchers may be interested in the hypothesis that the best-liked people in groups will also be the people who have the most favorable attitudes toward the group itself. Thus, two variables—liking and attitude toward the group—must be measured. Whereas the observer of a group may have difficulty determining whether a group member is well liked just by watching, survey researchers can easily test for liking by administering a sociometric self-report questionnaire. In addition, by asking the right questions of the right people, they can zero in on the specific problem of interest. They can ask questions that directly measure reports of feelings about others and the group, and the responses to such questions are relatively easy to interpret. Because questionnaire responses can be objectively coded, very specific conclusions can be drawn from questionnaire and interview responses. Thus, self-report methods are of value for two basic reasons: they can be used to tap variables directly that may be difficult to assess otherwise, and they can yield very specific conclusions about the relationships among variables.

Selecting a Measure

Unlike the earliest group dynamicists, modern-day researchers use a variety of tools when they embark on a study of group processes. But whether they select observation, self-report methods, or some other approach, they must remember that no measurement method is perfect. Observational techniques yield much information about group behavior, but researchers must guard against biases, such as the Hawthorne effect and subjectivity. Self-report methods, too, tell us much about group phenomena, but from the perspective of the participant rather than the observer. When the researchers are most interested in intrapersonal phenomena such as group members' perceptions, feelings, or beliefs, self-report methods may be the only means of assessing these private processes. But if participants are biased, their self-reports may not be as accurate as we could hope. Hence, some researchers ensure that the disadvantages of one approach are offset by the advantages of another by using multiple measures, including observations, self-reports, or other techniques (see Focus 2-3).

· ·
FOCUS 2-3: MEASURING GROUP COHESION

Cohesiveness, as noted in Chapter 1, is a key concept in many theories of group processes (Cartwright, 1968; Drescher, Burlingame, & Fuhriman, 1985; Mudrack, 1989; Stokes, 1983). A group's unity is a complex concept, however, and hence it can be assessed using a variety of methods.

Many researchers prefer to assess cohesion directly through observation. Homans (1950), for example, evaluated cohesion in work groups by watching the teams at work, and Bales (1980) uses his SYMLOG system to calculate unity. Cohesion can also be measured using nonreactive observational techniques that have little or no impact on the participants in the research (Webb, Campbell, Schwartz, Sechrest, & Grove, 1981). Such methods include measuring how frequently people wear apparel that connects them with their group or noting the pronouns that members use. People who say "We won that game" or "We got the job done" are assumed to be more closely linked to their group than people who say "They lost that game" or "I got the job done" (Cialdini et al., 1976, Experiment 1; Snyder, Lassegard, & Ford, 1986).

Sociometry provides yet another means of measuring cohesion. Leon Festinger and his colleagues used this method in a study of groups of people living in the same court of a housing project (Festinger, Schachter, & Back, 1950). After the residents supplied the names of all their good friends, the investigators calculated the ratio of in-court choices and outside-court choices. The greater the ratio, the greater was the cohesiveness of the court (Lott & Lott, 1965).

A second self-report approach assumes that group members are accurate observers of their group's cohesiveness and, if asked, are willing to communicate their perceptions to the researcher. Self-reports include such questions as these (Schachter, 1951; Schachter, Ellertson, McBride, & Gregory, 1951; Indik, 1965; and Terborg, Castore, & DeNinno, 1976; respectively):

- Do you want to remain a member of this group?
- How did you like your team?
- How strong a sense of belonging do you feel you have to the people you work with?
- How would you describe the way you and the other members of your survey party 'got along' together on this task?

Researchers, too, sometimes use multi-item scales that include many questions that can be combined to yield a single index of cohesiveness. For example:

1. The *Group Environment Scale* measures cohesiveness by asking for yes/no answers to items such as "There is a feeling of unity and cohesion in this group" and "Members put a lot of energy into this group" (Moos & Humphrey, 1974; Moos, Insel, & Humphrey, 1974).
2. The *Group Attitude Scale* assesses members' "desire to identify with and be an accepted member of the group" (Evans & Jarvis, 1986, p. 204) by asking them to indicate how much they want to remain a member of the group, like it, and feel included in it.
3. The *Sports Cohesiveness Questionnaire* focuses on three aspects of group cohesiveness, including the strength of member-to-member bonds, the strength of member-to-group bonds, and perceptions of group unity (Carron, 1980; Carron & Chelladurai, 1981; Martens, Landers, & Loy, 1972).

No matter what the method selected, researchers must make certain that their methods match their research goals. If they want to know about overt interpersonal processes, observational methods are most appropriate. Self-report methods, in contrast, should be used when researchers focus on group members' personal perspectives on group unity. Given the complementary advantages of the two approaches, many researchers use both methods in their studies of cohesion.

RESEARCH DESIGNS IN GROUP DYNAMICS

As barriers to the scientific study of groups were overcome through the development of measurement techniques, social scientists began studying groups in earnest. Interest in group phenomena seemed to explode upon the scientific community in the 1940s, and through the years researchers have refined and expanded their methods of testing the validity of hypotheses about groups. Despite the wide variety of techniques, however, most researchers still rely on one of the three basic approaches: (1) in-depth case studies of single groups, (2) correlational analyses of the relationship between various aspects of groups, and (3) experimental studies that require manipulating aspects of the group situation. These three approaches are examined in this section, along with three research projects that serve as examples. Thus, as you learn something about methods, you can also learn a bit more about group dynamics (Cook, 1985; Cook & Campbell, 1979).

Case Studies

When medical researchers encounter a patient who is suffering from a little-known illness, they often initiate a case study by gathering as much information about the patient's medical background and symptoms as possible. Similarly, group dynamicists sometimes carry out **case studies** by delving deeply into the nature of a single group. If the group has not yet disbanded, the researcher may decide to observe it as it carries out its functions. Alternatively, facts about the group may also be culled from interviews with members, descriptions of the group written by journalists, or members' biographical writings. On the basis of this information, researchers can construct an overall picture of the group and estimate the extent to which the examined case supports their hypothesis.

Researchers have used the case study to examine a variety of groups, including a doomsday group that prophesied the end of the world, naval personnel living in an underwater habitat called Sealab, government leaders meeting at a international summit, religious communes, warfare between nations, and rock-and-roll bands (see Festinger, Riecken, & Schachter, 1956; Radloff & Helmreich, 1968; Hare & Naveh, 1986; Stones, 1982; White, 1977; and Bennett, 1980, respectively). Irving Janis, for example, used this method to study the poor decision-making strategies used by groups responsible for such fiascoes as the Bay of Pigs invasion, the defense of Pearl Harbor before its attack in World War II, and the escalation of the Vietnam War. Relying on *archival methods*, Janis sought out available information about several such bumbling groups and then looked for their similarities. After making a thorough examination of historical documents, minutes of the meetings, diaries, letters, published memoirs of the group members, and public statements made to the press, he concluded that these groups had been the victims of **groupthink,** "a deterioration of mental efficiency, reality testing, and moral judgment that results from in-group pressures" (1972, p. 9). He specified the major determinants and symptoms of groupthink and suggested steps to take to avoid it. (We will return to the topic in far more detail in Chapter 10.)

Like all other research designs case studies offer both advantages and disadvantages. They allow in-depth understanding of the group or groups under study, and they yield descriptions of group events often unsurpassed by any other research procedure. Second, case studies carried out using archival methods are nonreactive; they do not disrupt or alter naturally occurring group processes. Janis, for example, studied groups that had already disbanded, so he did not need to worry about altering the phenomenon under study. Finally, and at a more pragmatic level, case studies can be relatively easy to carry out, and they make for fascinating reading.

Case studies, however, yield only limited information about groups in general. Researchers who use the method must constantly remind themselves that the group studied may be unique and therefore nonrepresentative of other groups. Also, because researchers can't always use objective measures of group processes when conducting case studies, their interpretations can be influenced by their own assumptions and biases. Even worse, the materials themselves may be inaccurate or unavailable to the researcher. Janis, for example, was forced to "rely mainly on the contemporary and retrospective accounts by the group members themselves, . . . many of which are likely to have been written with an eye to the author's own place in history" (1972, p. v). Finally, case studies can rarely yield statements concerning the causal relationships among important variables in the group under study. Janis felt that groupthink was causing the poor decisions in the groups he studied, but some other unnoticed factor could actually have been the prime causal agent.

Correlational Designs

Theodore Newcomb conducted his classic "Bennington study" in the mid-1930s. As a new member of the faculty at Bennington College, Newcomb was intrigued by the divergence in attitudes among the first-year students, the more advanced students, and the students' families. Most Bennington students came from well-to-do New England families whose strong conservatism was indicated by their presidential preferences. As Figure 2-4 indicates, in the 1936 presidential elections the majority of the families of the students favored Alfred M. Landon, the Republican candidate, rather than Franklin D. Roosevelt, the Democratic, and eventually victorious, candidate. First-year students shared the attitudes of their families, but the match between student and family attitude was much poorer where upper-class students were concerned (Newcomb, 1943).

Newcomb believed that the students' attitudes changed as their reference groups changed. **Reference groups** provide us with guidelines or standards for evaluating ourselves, our attitudes, and our beliefs (Hyman, 1942). Any group that plays a significant role in our life, such as our family, a friendship clique, colleagues at work, or even a group in which we would like to claim membership can become a reference group for us. The reference group for new students at Bennington, for example, was still their family—hence the close match between family attitudes and fresh-

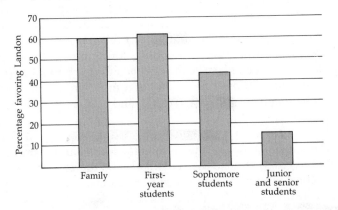

FIGURE 2-4. Attitude change at Bennington College.
Source: Newcomb, 1943

man attitudes. The longer students remained at Bennington, however, the more their attitudes changed to match the attitudes of their new reference group, the rest of the college population. Whereas most family groups had conservative attitudes, the college community supported mainly liberal attitudes, and Newcomb hypothesized that many Bennington women shifted their attitudes in response to this reference-group pressure.

To investigate his reference-group hypothesis, Newcomb used questionnaires, sociometry, and interviews to assess the attitudes, popularity, and family backgrounds of an entire class of Bennington students over a four-year period, from their entrance in 1935 to their graduation in 1939. He found a consistent trend toward liberalism in many of the students, and reasoned that this change resulted from peer-group pressure because it was more pronounced among the popular students. Those who endorsed nonconservative attitudes were (1) "both capable and desirous of cordial relations with the fellow community members" (1943, p. 149), (2) more frequently chosen by others as friendly, and (3) a more cohesive subgroup than the conservative students. Individuals who did not become more liberal tended to be isolated from the college's social life or to be very family-oriented. The impact of this group experience was deemed to be considerable, for the more liberal attitudes remained a part of the beliefs of many of the Bennington graduates 25 years later (Newcomb, Koenig, Flacks, & Warwick, 1967). (See Focus 2-4.)

• •
FOCUS 2-4: REFERENCE GROUPS AND PERSONAL CHANGE

Newcomb's study illustrates the way in which reference groups influence their members. We tend to think that we personally pick and choose our beliefs, attitudes, and values through thoughtful reflection. Yet the groups that we belong to are, in many cases, the true source of even our most private and cherished beliefs. If we join a country club, we may find that our attitudes gradually change until we adopt the same political views, enjoy the same recreations, and aspire to reach the same goals as our fellow members (Wright & Hyman, 1958). If we fall in with a group of juvenile delinquents, our beliefs about crime, violence, and justice may change to match those of our new peer group (Thrasher, 1927). If our classmates in school seem to be particularly gifted or limited academically, we tend to view ourselves as similarly bright or dull (Felson & Reed, 1986). Some theorists even suggest that our *self-concept*—our basic sense of who we are—is deeply rooted in the groups to which we belong (Tajfel, 1982; Turner, 1985). The influence of a reference group on its members is subtle but powerful.

Newcomb also documented the stresses that occur when people change reference groups. Since groups are the source of many attitudes and values, changing reference groups can cause distressingly significant changes in our self-concept. One Bennington student poignantly described these changes:

> An increasing crescendo of scattered remarks of my friends mounts up in my mind and culminates in a dissonant, minor-chord. What is the matter with these dissatisfied, bewildered, cynical girls? It's a simple answer, yet dishearteningly complex. Bennington is their trouble. I can't speak for all of us, but a hell of a lot of us are in this fix. We come from fine old Tory families who believe firmly in Higher-Education—Good God knows why. So they sent us to a well-spoken-of college with an interesting-sounding scheme of education. . . . We came home, some of us, talking a new language, some cobwebs swept out, a new direction opening up ahead we were dying to travel. Liberal, we thought we were. "What the hell's happened to you? Become a parlor Pink? . . . " The more education, the broader-minded—and narrower the circle of kindred souls. It's closing in on us now. Soon we'll graduate, and what then? Back to the old "set" which we've outgrown? To people we can never be completely satisfied with again as friends, and who distrust us now, if we've been brave enough to show our colors [Newcomb, 1943, pp. 11–12].

• •

Characteristics of correlational studies.   Newcomb's Bennington study was a **correlational study;** he examined the naturally occurring relationships among several variables without manipulating any of them. Newcomb felt, for example, that as students came to identify more closely with fellow students, their attitudes and values changed to match those of their peers. Therefore, he assessed students' popularity, their dependence on their families, and changes in their political attitudes. Then he examined the relationships among these variables by carrying out several statistical tests. At no point did he try to manipulate the group situation.

Correlational studies take their name from a statistic known as a **correlation coefficient** (which in mathematical notation is written as r). This statistic summarizes the strength and direction of the relationship between two variables, and it can range from $+1$ to -1. Distance from zero, (0), the neutral point, indicates the strength of the relationship. If Newcomb had found that the correlation between students' popularity and liberal attitudes was close to 0, for example, his study would have shown that the two variables were unrelated to each other. If, however, the correlation was significantly different from 0—in either a positive or negative direction— his study would have shown that these two variables were related to each other. The sign of the correlation ($+$ or $-$) indicates the direction of the relationship. If, for example, the correlation between popularity and attitudes was $+.68$, this positive correlation would indicate that both variables increased and decreased together; the more popular the student, the more liberal her attitude. If a negative correlation such as $-.52$ was found, the variables would be inversely related; more popular students tend to have less liberal atitudes. Thus, a correlation is a handy way of summarizing a great deal of information about the relationship between two variables.

Advantages and disadvantages.   The power of the correlational study is evident in the Bennington project. In many cases group dynamicists wish to know more about the relationship between variables. "Are group leaders usually older than their followers?" "Do groups become more centralized as they become larger?" and "Do people who are more committed to their group tend to express attitudes that match their group's position?" are all questions that researchers might ask about the relationship between variables. When coupled with accurate measurement techniques, correlational studies offer the means of clearly describing these relationships without disrupting or manipulating any aspect of the group.

Correlational studies, however, possess a significant weakness: they yield only limited information about the causal relationship between variables. Newcomb's data, for example, indicated that the attitude changes he measured were related to reference-group pressures, but he could not conclusively rule out other possible causes. Perhaps, unknown to Newcomb, the most popular women on campus all read the same books, which contained arguments that persuaded them to give up their conservative attitudes. This explanation seems implausible, yet it cannot be eliminated given the methods used by Newcomb. To draw conclusions about causality, researchers generally turn to experimental techniques.

Experimentation

Between 1937 and 1940 Kurt Lewin, Ronald Lippitt, and Ralph White investigated what effects, if any, a leader's style might have on group members (Lewin, Lippitt, and White, 1939; White & Lippitt, 1968). Lewin and his colleagues arranged for 10- and 11-year-old boys to meet after school in five-member groups to work on hobbies such as woodworking and painting. The adult who led the group assumed one of three particular styles of leadership: autocratic, democratic, and laissez-faire. The *autocratic* leader made all the decisions for the group, never asking for input from the boys. The boys rarely knew what the group would be doing next, were not permitted to decide for themselves how to approach the task at hand, and were even assigned a partner. The autocratic leader tended to give many orders, to criticize the boys unreasonably, and to remain aloof from the group. The *democratic* leader set no policies for the group; the group members themselves made all decisions while guided by the leader. The leader frequently explained long-term goals and steps to be taken to reach the goals, and members were free to choose their work partners. Democratic leaders rarely gave orders and commands, and the criticism they did give group members was always considered to be deserved. Lastly, the democratic leader did not remain apart from the group but attempted to foster a spirit of cooperation and egalitarianism. The final type of leader was labeled *laissez-faire*, a French expression meaning "let (people) do (what they choose)." The laissez-faire leader was, in a sense, not even a leader. He never participated in the group interactions, allowing the boys to work in whichever way they wished. He made it clear that he would provide information if asked, but he rarely offered information, criticism, or guidance spontaneously (Lewin, et al., 1939; White & Lippitt, 1968).

Once these three types of leaders were established in the groups, the researchers set about recording the many types of behavior they felt would be influenced by leadership style. Two of the most important variables they measured were group productivity and aggressiveness. The autocratic groups tended to spend more time working (74%) than the democratic group (50%), which in turn spent more time working than the laissez-faire groups (33%). Although these results would seem to argue in favor of the efficiency of an autocratic leadership style, the observers also noted that when the leader left the room for any lengthy period the democractically led groups kept right on working, whereas the boys in the autocratic groups stopped working. The second variable, aggressiveness, also revealed interesting differences among the groups. In general, most of these differences appeared when the laissez-faire and democratically led groups were compared with the autocratic groups. In the latter groups observers noted high rates of hostility among members, more demands for attention, more destructiveness, and a greater tendency to single out one group member to serve as the target of almost continual verbal abuse. Lewin suggested that this target for criticism and hostility, or scapegoat, provided an outlet for pent-up hostilities that could not be acted out against the powerful group leader.

The characteristics of experiments.   Lewin, Lippitt, and White's study of leadership styles possesses the three key features of an **experimental study.** First, the researchers selected a variable that they believed caused changes in group processes. This variable, which is called the **independent variable,** was manipulated by the researchers. In the leadership study this manipulation was achieved by giving groups different types of leaders, either autocratic, democratic, or laissez-faire. Second, the researchers assessed the effects of the independent variable by measuring such factors as productivity and aggressiveness. The variables measured by the researcher are called **dependent variables,** because their magnitude depends on the strength and nature of the independent variable. Thus, the leadership researchers hypothesized that group leadership style would influence productivity and aggressiveness, and they tested this hypothesis by manipulating the independent variable (style) and measuring the dependent variables (productivity and aggressiveness).

Third, the experimenters tried to maintain control over other variables that might have hampered interpretation of the results. The researchers never assumed that the only determinant of productivity and aggressiveness was leadership style; they knew other variables, such as the personality characteristics and abilities of the group members, could influence the dependent variables. In the experiment, however, the researchers were not interested in these other variables. Their hypotheses were specifically focused on the relationship among leadership style, productivity, and aggressiveness. Therefore, they made certain that these other variables were controlled in the experimental situation. For example, they took pains to ensure that the groups they created were "roughly equated on patterns of interpersonal relationships, intellectual, physical, and socioeconomic status, and personality characteristics" (White & Lippitt, 1968, p. 318). The groups were also assigned at random to the experimental conditions. Since no two groups were identical, these variations could have resulted in some groups working harder than others. The random assignment of groups to the three conditions helped ensure the evening out of these initial inequalities, thus making it clear that any differences found on the dependent measure were due to the independent variable, not to uncontrolled differences among the participating groups.

The key characteristics of an experiment, then, are the manipulation of the independent variable(s), the systematic assessment of the dependent variable(s), and the control of other possible contaminating factors. When the experiment is properly designed and conducted, researchers can assume that any differences among the conditions on the dependent variables are produced by the variable that is manipulated and not by some other variable they forgot to control.

Advantages and disadvantages. Why do group dynamicists so frequently rely on experimentation to test their hypotheses about groups? This preference derives, in part, from the inferential power of experimentation. Because of the way in which experiments are designed, they allow the researcher to make inferences about the causal relationships linking variables. As logic would suggest, if a change is recorded in some dependent variable, that change must have been caused by something. If every variable except one—the independent variable—has been held constant or controlled, the change must have been caused by the independent variable. Experiments, if properly conducted, can be used to detect causal relationships among variables.

Maintaining control is one of the keys to successful experimentation, but it can also undermine the value of such research design. The major problem is that in seeking rigorous control, experimenters may end up studying closely monitored but artificial group situations. Experiments are often performed in laboratories and use volunteers who work in the groups under study for relatively short periods. Although an experimenter can heighten the impact of the situation by withholding information about the study, such deception can be challenged on ethical grounds. In addition, although experiments can be conducted in the field using already existing groups, they will almost necessarily involve the sacrifice of some degree of control and will reduce the strength of the researchers' conclusions. Hence, the major advantage of experimentation, the ability to draw causal inferences, can be offset by the major disadvantage of experimentation, basing conclusions on contrived groups that have no parallels among naturally occurring groups.

Choosing a Research Design

Researchers use a variety of empirical procedures in their studies of groups. Some observe group processes and then perform a qualitative analysis of their observations, whereas others insist on quantitative measurement methods and elaborate controlled experiments. Some researchers conduct their studies in field situations using naturally occurring groups, but others bring groups into the laboratory or even create ad hoc groups for the research. Some exploratory studies of groups are undertaken by researchers who have no clear idea of what results to expect, whereas other research is designed to test hypotheses carefully derived from a specific theory. Some researchers study group phenomena by asking volunteers to role-play group members, and others simulate group interaction with computers.

The diversity of research methods doesn't reflect group dynamicists' uncertainty about which technique is best. Rather, the diversity stems from the unique advantages and disadvantages offered by each method. Case studies limit the researcher's ability to draw conclusions, to quantify results, and to make objective interpretations. But certainly some topics, such as groupthink, are difficult to study by any other method. As Janis himself points out, it would be difficult to examine groups that make decisions about national policies, including war and civil defense, through correlational studies or experimentation. But the real forte of the case-study approach is its power to provide grist for the theoretician's mill, enabling the investigator to formulate hypotheses that set the stage for other research methods.

Such stimulation of theory is also frequently a consequence of correlational research. These studies are limited in causal power, but they yield precise estimates of the strength of the relationships among variables. And when compared with experimentation, they are usually more ethical. Lastly, experimentation provides the firmest test of causal hypotheses predicting that variable X will cause such and such a change in variable Y. In the properly designed and conducted experiment, the researcher can test several hypotheses about groups, making the method both rigorous and efficient. But where an artificial setting would yield meaningless results, where the independent variable cannot be manipulated, or where too little is known about the topic even to suggest what variables are causal, some other approach would be preferable. The solution, then, is to use multiple methods for studying groups. As Joseph E. McGrath explains, "all methods have inherent flaws—though each has certain advantages. These flaws cannot be avoided. But what the researcher can do is to bring more than one approach, more than one method, to bear on each aspect of a problem" (1984, p. 30).

SUMMARY

Before group dynamicists could study groups scientifically, they first faced the task of developing methods for measuring group processes. As a result of these pioneering efforts, today's researchers can now turn to a range of *observational measures* when they wish to observe and record events transpiring in groups. Some researchers, such as William F. Whyte, prefer *participant observation;* Whyte actually joined a corner-gang to observe the group. Others, in contrast, remain outside the group under study, and guard against the biasing influences of the *Hawthorne effect* by keeping their research agenda a secret from the group members they are watching *(covert observation).* Researchers also use various *structured observational measures* in their studies, for such systems yield a more objective record of group members' actions. Bales's *Interaction Process Analysis* is an example of one such measurement system.

These observational methods are complemented by an array of *self-report measures.* Moreno's *sociometry,* for example, involves asking members to report whom they like the most. The researcher can then use this information to generate a *sociogram,* a visual image of the interpersonal relations in the group. A visual summary of a family's structure, in contrast, is termed a *genogram.*

Investigators can also choose from a variety of research designs when deciding how to test their hypothesis. Janis, for example, utilized a *case-study* approach in searching for the symptoms and causes of *groupthink* in governmental decision-making groups. At Bennington College, Newcomb investigated how *reference groups* can influence their members' attitudes and political beliefs by carrying out a *correlational study.* Rather than manipulating aspects of the situation, he gauged the strength of the naturally occurring relationships between such variables as political preferences and popularity. Often such information is summarized in the form of a *correlation coefficient.* Last, Lewin, Lippitt, and White studied the impact of autocratic, democratic, and laissez-faire leaders on groups by conducting an *experimental study.* They manipulated the *independent variable* (leadership style), assessed several *dependent variables* (aggressiveness, productivity, and so on), and limited the influence of other possible causal factors by controlling the situation and assigning groups to experimental conditions at random.

These three methods possess both strengths and weaknesses. The conclusions drawn from case studies can be highly subjective, but they stimulate theory and provide detailed information about particular groups. Correlational studies provide only limited information about causality, but they yield precise estimates of the strength of the relationship between two variables and raise fewer moral questions for researchers. Last, groups studied in experimental settings may not reflect the dynamics of naturally occurring groups, but experimentation provides the clearest test of cause/effect hypotheses.

·3·

Group Formation

Monet's *Le pont*. Pissarro's *Les toits rouges*. Renoir's *L'enfant à l'arrosoir.* Degas's *Les Danseuses*. When we see such paintings, we easily imagine the artist's long, solitary struggle to set down his personal vision of beauty on canvas. Yet these works of art were more the product of a group than of an individual. During the 1800s the Academy of Fine Arts in Paris dominated the art world. It sponsored an annual art exhibit but would allow only artists who used accepted techniques to display their work. Most artists, to make a living, followed the academy's guidelines. But in 1860 several disgruntled artists began meeting regularly to discuss new approaches to painting. These men were united in their belief that the academy was stifling their creativity, and they tried to develop alternative techniques in their own paintings. The group disbanded after several years, but not before its approach to art—*impressionism*—had been accepted by the academy and the rest of the world (Farrell, 1982).

This circle of artists was not unique; countless groups have sprung up, grown, and finally died out over the centuries. This group's case history, however, highlights the fundamental question that this chapter explores: why did this particular group come into being at that particular time? In 1858 the men who would eventually join the group—such notables as Manet, Monet, Degas, Cézanne, and Pissarro—were busy pursuing their careers independently. But by the mid-1860s they had joined to form one of the most influential artists' circles of all time. What were the circumstances that led these individuals to form a group?

Researchers have not developed a comprehensive theory that explains why groups form, but a number of views have been offered. Two of these perspectives, in particular, shed considerable light on the orgins of many groups. First, a *functional perspective* emphasizes the usefulness of groups for individual members (Mackie & Goethals, 1987). The artists, for example, needed reassurance and support each time they were rejected by the academy. They needed to discuss their ideas about painting and refine their techniques. Some of the impoverished members needed shelter, food, and paints. As Richard Moreland (1987, p. 104) notes in his theory of social integration, groups have formed throughout history "whenever people become dependent on one another for the satisfaction of their needs."

A second approach traces the origin of groups to the process of *interpersonal attraction*. This perspective suggests that groups form when several people find that they like one another and want to spend time together. Many of the artists joined the impressionists' group, for example, because they liked Pissarro. He was knowledgeable about art, was supportive of the younger members, and often stepped in to prevent conflicts in the group. As you will see in the second section of this chapter, groups are a medium for the exchange of interpersonal rewards among members.

THE VALUE OF GROUPS

If you were a modern-day Robinson Crusoe stranded on a deserted island, what one thing would you need the most? A rifle for protection? A supply of food? A tent for shelter? Another human being would prove far more useful than all these things. Another person would help you survive the hardships posed by your harsh environment. Moreover, because you are a social animal, you depend on other people for the satisfaction of many of your most basic psychological and informational needs. Other people are also a valuable source of social support during difficult times, and by joining with others you can solve problems that would overwhelm you by yourself. As you will see below, group life is very adaptive, for it satisfies many of our most basic survival, psychological, informational, interpersonal, and collective needs (Mackie & Goethals, 1987).

Survival Needs

In earlier epochs humans needed groups to survive the challenges of a harsh environment. As Table 3-1 indicates, living in groups offers far more advantages than disadvantages. If you had a partner on your deserted island, for example, the two of you could combine your efforts to find food and defend yourselves from predation. By dividing up the work, you

TABLE 3-1. Living in groups: Some advantages and disadvantages.

Function	Benefits	Costs
Feeding	Cooperative hunting More searchers to find food Cooperative cultivation Sharing of excess food Facilitation of feeding	The need to divide and share food
Defense	Greater alertness Stronger defense in larger numbers Confusion of predators by larger numbers	Greater conspicuousness
Nurturance	Care of sick, injured, young Reciprocal altruism	Spread of contagious diseases
Reproduction	Access to opposite sex Enhanced variety	Competition for mates

(Sources: Bertram, 1978; Harvey & Greene, 1981; Scott, 1981)

could complete essential tasks with greater efficiency. During times of sickness you could care for each other. Also, depending on the composition of your group, you could increase the population of your island home. For humans, and nearly all other species subject to predation, there is safety in numbers.

Some theorists, impressed by the adaptive advantages of living in groups, have suggested that the need to affiliate is not learned through experience but is a manifestation of an instinctive drive that is common in many species. Although the idea of a "herd instinct" in humans is not new (Edman, 1919; McDougall, 1908), a branch of biology known as **sociobiology** offers a provocative explanation for the origin of instinctive gregariousness. Sociobiology is based on Charles Darwin's theory of evolution. According to Darwin, living organisms evolve over time through a process of **natural selection:** species members with characteristics that increase their fitness tend to survive longer and be more successful in passing their genes along to future generations. Much of Darwin's work dealt with biological and anatomical fitness, but sociobiology strives to explain the behavior of animals in social situations. Sociobiologists believe that recurring patterns of behaviors among animals ultimately stem from evolutionary processes that increase the likelihood of adaptive social actions while extinguishing nonadaptive practices (Wilson, 1975).

In the modern world the advantages of group life over solitude become less important; people who buy their food in grocery stores and live in houses with deadbolts on the doors don't need to worry much about effective food-gathering strategies or protection from predation. Because affiliation offered so many advantages to our biological ancestors, however, the desire to affiliate became part of our genetic heritage, some sociologists believe. According to this theory, when our genetic ancestors left the protection of the trees of the rain forests to become ground dwellers, people who were predisposed to join groups were much more likely to survive and breed than people who avoided social contacts. Because affiliation increased our ancestors' fitness, over countless generations genes that promoted solitude-seeking were weeded out of the gene pool, whereas genes that encouraged affiliation prospered. The result: affiliation became a part of the biological makeup of humans (Barash, 1982; Crook, 1981).

Are humans driven by a herd instinct? Perhaps. In most situations and societies humans tend toward sociality rather than isolation (Mann, 1980). Studies indicate that infants seem to be predisposed to form strong attachments to others and that babies who are deprived of close human contact have higher mortality rates (Ainsworth, 1979; Bowlby, 1980). Even in adults protracted periods of social isolation can be extremely disabling (Zubek, 1973), and we prefer the company of others when we feel threatened or distressed (Rofé, 1984). Sociobiologists have also offered evidence suggesting that cooperative group life is a more stable strategy in evolutionary terms than competition and individualism (Axelrod & Hamilton, 1981).

Many theorists, however, believe that our tendency to join others is not instinctive but is, instead, learned during infancy and early childhood. Studies of infant monkeys, for example, indicate that early experiences can change affiliative tendencies (Harlow & Harlow, 1966). Although a genetic approach to affiliation would argue that monkeys raised in isolation should still display affiliative tendencies (since experience alone cannot alter instinctual drives), monkeys raised in isolation are antisocial when they reach adulthood. This dramatic impact of early experience on affiliative behavior also occurs in humans and attests to the learned, rather than genetic, determinants of group formation (Ainsworth, Blehar, Waters, & Wall, 1978). Additionally, sociobiology has yet to offer a convincing explanation for certain sex differences in group behavior, which are discussed in Focus 3-1. Thus, although most would agree that affiliation helps humans survive, the jury is still out on the instinct question (see Quadagno, 1979, for a critique).

. . . .

FOCUS 3-1: WOMEN AND MEN IN GROUPS

In many modern societies women have rarely joined certain kinds of groups: military units, governmental and judicial bodies, some social clubs, athletic teams, and businesses are still primarily male domains. To explain this sex difference, the anthropologist Lionel Tiger and his colleagues suggest that the "bonding instinct" is stronger in men than in women. Tiger notes that historically the division of labor in most human societies has been based on gender. Women tended to gather food and care for the young; these activities do not require close cooperation in groups. Men, in contrast, performed activities that required cooperative effort, such as hunting and defense. Thus, natural selection favored men who were predisposed to join groups and women who showed a flair for mothering. In time, Tiger argues, male bonding became more powerful than female bonding (Tiger, 1969; Tiger & Fox, 1971; Tiger & Shepher, 1975; Shepher & Tiger, 1983).

The available evidence, however, lends only minimal support to Tiger's contention that men form groups more readily than women (Booth, 1972; Latané & Bidwell, 1977). One survey of 800 adults found that men did, indeed, join more groups than females. Women, however, were more likely to participate in same-sex groups, and they spent more time in their groups than did men (Booth, 1972). Studies of community action groups find no consistent gender differences (Parkum & Parkum, 1980), and women are just as likely as men to join atypical groups, such as cults, satanic covens, and communes (Pittard-Payne, 1980). Women's groups also tend to be more unified than men's groups (Booth, 1972; Hill & Stull, 1981, Winstead, 1986), despite Tiger's assertion that "women seem to have special problems sustaining all-female work groups" (Shepher & Tiger, 1983, p. 283).

Researchers also argue that even when groups contain more men than women, sexist attitudes rather than genes are the probable cause of this imbalance. Women are minorities in some types of groups. Fewer women participate in conventional political groups such as meetings, rallies, and political parties; unconventional political groups such as demonstrations, riots, and terrorist groups (Lal Goel, 1980); and other types of groups (Smith, 1980). However, as attitudes toward the role of women have changed in contemporary society, these differences in rates of social participation have also begun to diminish (Lal Goel, 1980; Smith, 1980). These tendencies suggest that social and cultural forces rather than instincts are responsible the predominance of men in certain types of groups.

. . . .

Psychological Needs

In *Group Psychology and the Analysis of the Ego*, Sigmund Freud (1922) suggests that being a member of a group satisfies basic psychological needs and desires. For most individuals childhood experiences in the family group create these needs, for it is in this group that the child finds satisfaction through a sense of belonging, protection from harm, and acceptance. Freud maintains that, as adults, we unknowingly use groups as a means of *replacing* the original family group. The group's leader, for example, satisfies our need for a parental *authority figure*. The other group members represent siblings, and disputes among members are an adult form of *sibling rivalry* (Billig, 1976; Janis, 1963).

Need for affiliation.   Freud's replacement hypothesis, although highly speculative, stimulated subsequent studies of the basic psychological needs that can be satisfied by joining groups. Much of this work focused on the need for affiliation, which is abbreviated *n* **Affiliation.** When compared to "loners," individuals high in *n* Affiliation tend to join groups more frequently, communicate more with other group members, seek more social approval from others, and accept other group members more readily (see McClelland, 1985, for a review). In one illustrative study researchers measured *n* Affiliation with the Thematic Apperception Test (TAT). This measurement technique assumes that even when we aren't aware of our needs, we project these needs outward in making up stories about ambiguous pictures. The researchers then gave the subjects electronic pagers ("beepers") for one week and asked them to write down a description of what they were doing each time they were beeped. As expected, the subjects who were high in the need for affiliation were the ones who spent more time in groups (McAdams & Constantian, 1983).

Need for power.   Because group interactions provide many opportunities to influence people, those who feel a need to control others also tend to seek out groups (Winter, 1973). This need for power over other people, or *n* **Power**, was examined in one recent study of college students' friendship groups. The researchers, after measuring *n* Power with the TAT, asked the subjects to recall ten recent interactions that had (1) involved one or more of their friends, (2) occurred within the previous two weeks, and (3) lasted for at least 15 minutes. The subjects then described what had happened in each episode, what had been discussed, and their role in the group. Correlational analyses indicated that people with a high *n* Power motive took part in relatively fewer dyadic interactions but more large-group interactions (more than four members). They also reported exercising more control in these groups by organizing and initiating activities, assuming responsibility, and attempting to persuade others. These relationships between *n* Power and participating in groups were strongest for men (McAdams, Healy, & Krause, 1984).

FIRO.   William C. Schutz's Fundamental Interpersonal Relations Orientation, or **FIRO** (pronounced to rhyme with *Cairo*), also stresses the relationship between psychological needs and group formation (Schutz, 1958). Like Freud, Schutz believes that our behavior in groups often parallels either our own childhood behavior or our parents' behavior. Schutz, however, extends Freud's notions by identifying three basic needs that can be satisfied by joining a group. The first, *inclusion*, is the desire to be part of a group and to be accepted by a group. This need is similar to *n* Affiliation. The second, *control*, corresponds to *n* Power, for it is the need to guide the group by organizing and maintaining the group's processes. The third need, *affection* or openness, is the desire to establish and maintain open, positive relations with others.

Schutz believes that these needs influence group behavior at two levels: they determine how we treat other people and how we want others to treat us. Inclusion involves our desire to join with other people and our need to be accepted by them. Control refers to our need to dominate others but also our willingness to let others dominate us. Affection includes a desire to like others as well as a desire to be liked by them. (Schutz, 1973, 1983, also uses the term *openness* to describe the need for affection.) The FIRO-B, which Schutz developed, measures both the need to express and the need to receive inclusion, control, and affection (see Table 3-2).

Schutz argues that groups offer members a way to satisfy these basic needs. If, for example, Becky has a strong need to receive and express inclusion, she will probably prefer to do things in a group rather than to perform tasks individually (Leary, Wheeler, & Jenkins, 1986). If, in contrast, she needs to express control, she may seek membership in a group that she can control. Or if she wishes to receive affection from others, she may seek out other people who seem warm and friendly. In general, then, the greater the intensity of these needs in any given individual, the more likely that person is to take steps to create, or seek out membership in, a group (Schutz, 1958).

TABLE 3-2. Example items from FIRO-B.

Dimension	Need to Express the Behavior	Need to Receive the Behavior from Others
Inclusion	I try to be with other people. I join social groups.	I like people to invite me to things. I like people to include me in their activities.
Control	I try to take charge of things when I am with people. I try to have other people do things I want done.	I let other people decide what to do. I let other people take charge of things.
Affection (openness)	I try to be friendly to people. I try to have close relationships with people.	I like people to act friendly toward me. I like people to act close toward me.

(Source: Schutz, 1958)

Informational Needs

Leon Festinger (1950, 1954) suggests a third reason for joining a group: information. Festinger contends that physical reality rarely provides us with objective standards for the validation of personal opinions, beliefs, or attitudes. Therefore, we often compare our personal viewpoint to the views expressed by others to determine if they are "correct," "valid," or "proper." Festinger calls this information-seeking process **social comparison**. Stanley Schachter's classic studies of affiliation provide convincing support for Festinger's theory. Schachter (1959) assumed that individuals seek out other people whenever they feel uncertain of the validity of their attitudes or beliefs. To test this notion, he created an experimental setting that was both ambiguous and anxiety-provoking. The college women who served as subjects in the study were greeted by a researcher who claimed to be from the Medical School's Departments of Neurology and Psychiatry. In serious tones he told the women that he was studying the effects of electric shock on human beings. In one condition (low-anxiety) the room contained no electrical instrumentation; the experimenter explained that the shocks would be so mild that they would "resemble more a tickle or a tingle than anything unpleasant" (p. 14). The subjects who were assigned to the high-anxiety condition, however, faced a vast collection of electronic equipment and were informed, "These shocks will hurt, they will be painful . . . but, of course, they will do no permanent damage" (p. 13). The experimenter then told the subjects to wait their turn and asked if they wanted to wait alone, with others, or didn't really care one way or the other. Many more of the women in the high-anxiety condition (63%) than in the low-anxiety condition (33%) chose to wait with others, so Schachter concluded that "misery loves company."

But did the subjects join the group so that they could acquire information through social comparison? Maybe they just felt so frightened that they didn't want to be alone. To explore this possibility Schachter replicated the high-anxiety condition of his original experiment, complete with the shock equipment and the measure of desire to affiliate. In this second study anxiety was held constant at a high level, but the amount of information that could be gained by affiliating was manipulated. Half of the women were told that they could wait with other women who were about to receive shocks. The remaining subjects were told that they could join women "waiting to talk to their professors and advisors" (p. 22). Schachter felt that if the women believed that the others could not provide them with any social-comparison information, there would be no reason to join them. Supporting his prediction, 60% of the women in the same-state condition asked to wait with others, but no one in the different-state condition expressed affiliative desires. Writes Schachter: "Misery doesn't love just any kind of company, it loves only miserable company" (p. 24).

Schachter's studies, however, do not tell us if the women actually engaged in social comparison once they joined a group. He was interested only in their choice to wait with others or alone, so he terminated the studies as soon as the subjects had made their choices; the groups never formed. Fortunately, a subsequent team of researchers examined this question by asking four to six strangers to meet at a room labeled with the sign "Sexual Attitudes—Please Wait Inside." No experimenter greeted the subjects as they arrived, but the contents of the room were varied to create three experimental conditions. In the fear condition the otherwise empty room contained several electronic devices and information sheets suggesting that the study involved electric shock and sexual stimulation. In the anxiety condition the equipment was replaced by a number of contraceptive devices, books on venereal disease, and some color pictures of nude men and women. In the ambiguity condition the subjects found only two cardboard boxes filled with computer cards. Observers behind a one-way mirror watched the group for 20 minutes, recording interaction, action, withdrawal, controlled nonreaction (such as deliberate talking about something other than the experiment), and escape behaviors (Morris et al., 1976).

Analysis of the group's interactions indicated that affiliating individuals did indeed engage in social comparison. Groups in the fear condition interacted more, both verbally and nonverbally, and also displayed withdrawal reactions and controlled nonreactions. In the anxiety condition, where the subjects were presumably embarrassed about the situation they had gotten themselves into, interaction was low and withdrawal was high. Lastly, the completely ambiguous condition tended to fall between these two conditions (see Focus 3-2). These findings, when combined with the results of other research, indicate that in many ambiguous situations people join with others as a means of better understanding social reality. (Goethals, 1986, Goethals & Darley, 1987, and Suls & Miller, 1977, review a number of recent developments in this area.)

· ·

FOCUS 3-2: SOCIAL-COMPARISON BIASES

Researchers, by building on the theoretical foundations provided by Festinger's and Schachter's empirical studies, have generated a wealth of information concerning social comparison processes in groups. Many questions remain to be answered, but we now know considerably more about when people engage in social comparison, the kinds of people they select for comparison, and the consequences of this comparative process (Goethals, 1986; Goethals & Darley, 1987).

Group dynamicists have also used social comparison to better understand many naturally occurring groups, including classrooms, teams, support groups, families, and adolescent friendship groups (Levine, 1983; Nosanchuk & Erickson, 1985; Taylor, 1983; Tesser & Campbell, 1983; Tesser, Campbell, & Smith, 1984). These investigations confirm Festinger's basic assumption, but they also suggest that we aren't unbiased seekers of information. When given a choice, we prefer to make comparisons that will provide us with reassuring information rather than accurate information. Groups, for example, generally recruit new members who express attitudes that match the group's viewpoint. A person with a deviant opinion brings more information to the group, but the similar individual validates the group's position (Earle, 1986). Also, when selecting a target for our social comparisons, we often prefer a person who displays inferior skills and abilities. This tendency, which is called **downward social comparison,** is most likely when we are uncertain of our abilities and lack confidence in our beliefs (Wills, 1981).

In like fashion, in an ambiguous setting such as that created by Schachter we don't seek out individuals who seem nervous and upset. Instead, we prefer to wait with people who are experiencing very little fear. Rather than confirming our worst fears, we would prefer to discover that we have gotten worked up over nothing (Darley & Aronson, 1966; Friedman, 1981; Rofé, 1984). Thus, two motives seem to underlie social comparison: the desire for cognitive clarity and the desire for reassurance that nothing is wrong with ourselves or our situation. And when these motives clash, we generally sacrifice accuracy for reassurance.

· ·

Interpersonal Needs

Paul Simon's song *Bridge over Troubled Water* describes a fourth function of groups. Like a bridge that helps travelers by spanning obstacles, other people provide us with valuable **social support.** Different groups provide different forms of support, but we often turn to our network of friends, relatives, and acquaintances for emotional sustenance, advice, favors, and reassuring feedback about our worth (Barrera, 1986; Cutrona, 1986; Sarason, Sherarin, Pierce, & Sarason, 1987; Stokes & Wilson, 1984). (See Table 3-3.)

Why is social support such an important function of groups? First, the available evidence indicates that our social groups and networks protect us from stress and its aftereffects. One review of 17 studies concluded that people who receive support from others tend to experience less stress in their lives (Barrera, 1986). Evidence also supports the *buffering hypothesis:* during times of stress individuals who belong to a supportive group will experience fewer psychological and physical problems than individuals who receive no social support from their groups (Cohen & Wills, 1985). Admittedly, some groups fail as stress buffers, for during times of conflict over goals and disputes among members, groups can be the source of stress (Cooper, 1981; Hays & Oxley, 1986; Seeman, Seeman, & Sayles, 1985). If, however, group members display some of the supportive qualities listed in Table 3-3, then membership should help rather than hurt.

Second, social support protects us from the painful emotions associated with loneliness: sadness, uneasiness, self-doubt, and boredom. Unlike recluses who enjoy their privacy and solitude, lonely people feel that their personal relationships are too few or too unsatisfying. In the case of **emotional loneliness** we are dissatisfied because we lack a meaningful, intimate relationship with another person. **Social loneliness,** in contrast, occurs when we feel cut off from friends and acquaintances (Weiss, 1973; Wheeler, Reis, & Nezlek, 1983).

Some theorists believe that membership in a group offers a respite from one or both of these forms of loneliness. A tight-knit group of friends or a family, for example, may be so emotionally involving that members never feel the lack of a dyadic love relationship. In contrast, playing on an amateur athletic team, working each day with the same group of associates, or frequenting a neighborhood bar is often sufficient to prevent social loneliness. Indeed, some groups, such as communes, cults, or therapy

TABLE 3-3. Some forms of social support.

Type of Support	Example
Emotional support	Expressing concern for well-being Listening to self-disclosures of private feelings
Advice and guidance	Suggesting solutions to a problem Demonstrating a way to perform a task
Tangible assistance	Doing small favors Lending money
Positive feedback	Expressing admiration for some personal attribute Showing respect for abilities or skills

groups, may fulfill members' social and emotional needs (Rook, 1984; Shaver & Buhrmester, 1983). A poll taken in two U.S. cities indicated that people who belonged to more groups and organizations reported relatively less loneliness (Rubenstein & Shaver, 1980). College students who eat dinner and spend weekend evenings with others tend to describe themselves as less lonely (Russell, Peplau, & Cutrona, 1980). When the subjects in another study rated the quality of their family interactions, friendships, romantic relationships, and group activities, people who were satisfied with their groups and their friendships reported the least loneliness (Schmidt & Sermat, 1983). Membership in groups with extensive interconnections among all the members has also been linked to reduced loneliness (Stokes, 1985). Thus, group membership appears to be an antidote for loneliness.

Collective Needs and Group Goals

Groups sometimes form when individuals pool their individual efforts in the pursuit of a collective goal (Mackie & Goethals, 1987; Zander, 1985). In some cases groups form spontaneously when several people recognize that they can accomplish a desired goal more successfully, more efficiently, or with more enjoyment if they work together; examples shown in Table 3-4 include a buyers' cooperative, a citizens' action group such as Mothers Against Drunk Driving (MADD), or a mob of vigilantes. Many others—an army platoon, a business, a jury—are deliberately created by an organizer or core of organizers who want to achieve a particular purpose (Fine & Stoecker, 1985). In all these cases, however, the group forms when "the task to be done is too big for one worker and can be completed or can be done more cheaply, quickly, or better if taken up by several colleagues" (Zander, 1985, p. 37).

When are individuals likely to seek goals through collective action? Zander argues that one of the most important factors is degree of dissatisfaction with one's current outcomes; if a substantial number of individuals "realize that a situation is not what it might be and that something ought to be done" (p. 52), collective action becomes increasingly likely. A community group seeking lower taxes, the civil rights movement, and MADD exemplify such groups (Miller, 1983). Culture, too, plays a determining role. In most English-speaking countries cutural norms emphasize **individualism:** concern for one's own personal needs, interests, and goals. Other countries, in contrast, stress **collectivism:** a concern for group needs, interests, and goals (Hofstede, 1983; Leung & Lind, 1986; Wheeler, Reis, & Bond, 1989). These cultural differences are reflected in an increased tendency in collectivist countries to use groups to achieve goals. In Japan, for example, groups are used routinely for achieving a variety of goals. Men and women gather before work to perform calisthenics and travel to their jobs. In the workplace most activities involve groups rather than individuals. Zander writes that "a group—not a person—is the prime unit, and each group is assigned a definite set of duties to divide

TABLE 3-4. Collective goals sought by groups.

Purpose of the Group	Typical Groups
Protect members from physical harm	Neighborhood "watch" association, emergency squad, platoon in army
Solve a problem for members or for those who created the group	Committee, commission, task force, research staff
Reduce costs for members	Buyers' cooperative, trade association
Make resources available	Bank, rental agency
Accomplish heavy, arduous tasks	Construction crew, assembly line
Make routine individual tasks more tolerable	Picking apples, sewing quilts
Set rules or standards for others to follow	Legislative body
Change the opinions of persons outside the group	Citizens' action group, political party
Worship a deity	Religious body
Pay homage to ideas or objects	Patriotic society, veterans' group
Heal members and nomembers	Psychotherapy group, staff of surgery
Teach persons information or skills	Schools, tutoring agency
Improve a system of ideas or a theory	Academic department, professional society
Make things for consumers	Factory, production line
Enrich leisure time of members	Hobby club, discussion group
Give advice to those who seek it	Consultation firm, support group
Render decisions on guilt	Jury, supreme court
Engage in the performing arts	Orchestra, dance company, drama troupe
Capture those who break the law	Police, posse, vigilantes
Administer an organization	Executive committee, trustees, regents

(Source: Zander, 1985)

among participants as is best" (1983, p. 5). After work people frequently dine and relax in small groups. Zander puts it simply: "The people of Japan like to do things in groups" (p. 3).

The Functions of Groups: A Summary

We now have a partial answer to the question "Why did Degas, Manet, Pissarro, Renoir, and the other artists join to form a group?" The various perspectives examined in this section differ sharply in scope and emphasis, but all note the critical importance of groups in meeting human needs. These needs may be instinctive, or they may be learned. They may be the end product of early childhood experiences or a reaction to temporary, but stressful, situations. They may reflect our uncertainty about our social world or a desire to achieve important goals. But no matter what their origin or nature, groups offer a means of satisfying these needs.

By stressing the useful functions that groups serve, we can explain our preference for group life over isolation. The functional perspective, however, also helps us predict when groups will form. Sociobiology, for example, by stressing the adaptive advantages of groups, predicts that people will join groups when their survival is threatened. FIRO theory proposes that groups form when people with particular needs meet. Social-comparison theory assumes that groups form whenever people are uncertain about the validity of their beliefs and perceptions. Studies of the social support we gain through social interaction suggest that groups form whenever people experience stress and loneliness. And Zander's analysis of the practical uses of groups argues that groups form whenever individuals wish to achieve a goal that one person acting alone cannot attain. Thus, the functional approach explains both the "why" and the "when" of group formation.

INTERPERSONAL ATTRACTION

In 1860 Monet met Pissarro in a small studio in Paris. Pissarro was Monet's elder by ten years, but despite this age difference the two soon became good friends. During the next few years as we have seen, Pissarro and Monet met such artists as Cézanne, Manet, Degas, and Renoir in various studios in Paris. Some of these young artists were attracted to Monet and his ideas about art. Others were attracted to the friendly, supportive Pissarro. Drawn to one another by these feelings of interpersonal attraction, the artists began to associate, and in time the artists' circle took on a life of its own.

In many cases groups form when two or more individuals discover that they like one another. As was the case with the impressionists, feelings of attraction prompted people to join initially and thereby set the stage for the development of stronger, more involving interpersonal bonds. Thus, if we wish to understand why groups form, we must identify the factors that prompt us to like some people and dislike others.

The Rewards and Costs of Groups

Many theorists believe that attraction depends, at its core, on **social exchange:** "the exchange of rewards and punishments that takes place when people interact" (Berscheid, 1985, p. 429). This perspective assumes that social interaction is analogous to economic activity. Just as business executives base their decisions on projections about the profits they expect to gain by some new venture, individuals make decisions concerning the desirability of interaction with others by identifying the rewards and costs that the relationship will create for them. Rewards include any possible gratifications and satisfactions offered by the relationship, whereas any frustrations and dissatisfactions that result from membership are considered costs. In general, social exchange theory assumes that individuals' preferences for interaction are based on a "minimax" principle: people will join groups that provide them with the maximum number of valued rewards while incurring the fewest number of possible costs (Among the theorists who embrace these basic assumptions are Adams, 1965; Altman & Taylor, 1973; Berg & Clark, 1986; Blau, 1964; Foa & Foa, 1971; Hays, 1985; Homans, 1974; Huesmann & Levinger, 1976; Huston & Burgess, 1979; Kelley et al., 1983; La Gaipa, 1977; Lerner, 1974; Rusbult, 1983; and Thibaut & Kelley, 1959.)

Social-exchange theory is one of many alternative perspectives dealing with attraction (Berscheid, 1985; Perlman & Fehr, 1986). Its broad orientation, however, can account for a number of tendencies that have been documented by researchers.

The similarity/attraction effect. Newcomb once studied group formation by inviting 17 young men who were entering college to live, rent-free, in a dormitory near the campus. The young men began the semester as strangers, but soon after moving into the dormitory, they began clustering into several smaller units. When Newcomb examined these groupings, he was struck by the subgroup members' similarity in terms of values, beliefs, and interests. One clique, for example, contained men who endorsed liberal political and religious attitudes, were all registered in the arts college, came from the same part of the country, and shared similar aesthetic, social, theoretical, economic, political, and religious values. Members of the second subgroup were all veterans, were majors in engineering, and shared similar religious, economic, and political values. A third subgroup differed from the first two cliques in that its members were all from small Midwestern towns and were all Protestants. Lastly, the four men who did not belong to any subgroup displayed unique values and interests (Newcomb, 1960, 1961, 1962).

Newcomb had found strong evidence for the **similarity/attraction effect:** we like people who are similar to us in some way. This effect has been obtained in studies of several other groups, and it appears to be caused by a number of interrelated processes (Byrne, Ervin, & Lamberth, 1970; Curry & Emerson, 1970; Griffitt & Veitch, 1974; Hill & Stull, 1981; Kandel, 1978; Wright & Crawford, 1971, Study 4). First, people who adopt the same values and attitudes that we do reassure us that our beliefs are accurate (Festinger, 1954). We therefore find association with such people very rewarding (Byrne, 1971; Clore & Byrne, 1974). Second, similarity serves as a signal to suggest that future interactions will be free of conflict (Insko & Schopler, 1972). Third, once we discover that we are similar to another person, we tend to immediately feel a sense of unity with that person (Arkin & Burger, 1980). Two strangers chatting casually on an airplane, for example, feel united if they find that they share even the smallest similarity, such as the same middle name or a favorite TV program. Last, disliking a person who seems similar may prove to be psychologically distressing. After all, if a person is similar to us, it follows logically that he or she must be attractive (Festinger, 1957; Heider, 1958).

Complementarity of needs. The similarity/attraction effect exerts a powerful influence on groups, but in some cases we prefer the company of people who are dissimilar to us. If, for example, Robin enjoys leading groups, she will not be attracted to other individuals who enjoy leadership. Instead, she will seek out a group of people who wish to be led. According to the **complementarity-of-needs hypothesis,** we are attracted to people who possess characteristics that fulfill, or gratify, our own personal needs (Kerckhoff & Davis, 1962; Levinger, Senn, & Jorgensen, 1970; Meyer & Pepper, 1977).

Which tendency is stronger, the similarity/attraction effect or complementarity of needs? Some investigators, working primarily with dyads, have found that that similarity is much more common than complementarity (Levinger, Seen, & Jorgensen, 1970; Magaro & Ashbrook, 1985; Meyer & Pepper, 1977). Other researchers don't agree, however, for they find that the members of close-knit groups tend to possess compatible, and somewhat dissimilar, needs (Kerckhoff & Davis, 1962; Schutz, 1958). (See Focus 3-3.) Given the available evidence, it would be premature to draw any firm conclusions concerning the impact of complementarity on attraction.

· ·
FOCUS 3-3: SIMILARITY, COMPLEMENTARITY, AND GROUP FORMATION

William C. Schutz is one of the few researchers who has succeeded in finding any evidence that supports the complementarity-of-needs principle (1958). According to Schutz's FIRO theory, described earlier, we prefer to join groups that satisfy our need to express and receive inclusion, control, and, affection. In discussing similarity of needs, Schutz maintains that "interchange compatibility" is critically important. This type of compatibility occurs when individuals in groups agree about how much inclusion, control, and affection should exist in the group. For example, if one group member believes that members should exchange only a small amount of affection but a second member believes in exchanging a great deal of affection, these two individuals' needs will be incompatible.

Schutz argues that complementarity also influences attraction in groups. Consider, for example, four executives who all need to control the group's processes. Because the behavior of each person interferes with the needs of the others, Schutz predicts that the group will be unstable. What is needed for group formation, according to Schutz, is a form of complementarity called *originator compatibility.* People who wish to originate inclusion, control, and affection should be complemented by others who wish to receive inclusion, control, and affection (Schutz, 1958).

Schutz describes several other types of compatibility, but evidence indicates that interchange and originator compatibility are the most basic determinants of group formation. In one project Schutz constructed groups of varying compatibility by taking into account the members' FIRO-B scores. For compatible groups he created originator compatibility by placing in each group one member with a high need for control, one member with a high need for inclusion, and three members with lower needs for control and inclusion. In addition, interchange compatibility was established by grouping people with similar needs for affection. All the groups in this set were compatible, but levels of affection were high in half of the groups and low in the other half. A set of incompatible groups was also created by including group members who varied significantly in their need for affection, ranging from high to low. As Schutz predicted, (1) cohesiveness was higher in the compatible groups than in the incompatible groups, and (2) the compatible groups worked on problems far more efficiently than the incompatible groups. He found similar results in studies of groups that form spontaneously—such as street gangs and friendship circles in fraternities (Schutz, 1958).

. . . .

The proximity/attraction effect. Similarity was an important determinant of attraction among Newcomb's subjects, but so was sheer physical closeness: people who lived near one another tended to become friends. This **proximity/attraction effect** also occurred in two apartment complexes studied by Festinger and his colleagues. When they measured residents' sociometric choices, they were surprised to find that the physical distance between people was one of the most important determinants of friendship: people liked people who lived in apartments that they passed by daily (Festinger, Schachter, & Back, 1950; see also Arkin & Burger, 1980; Brockner & Swap, 1976; Ebbesen, Kjos, & Konečni, 1976; Hays, 1985; Newcomb, 1981).

Why do people tend to form groups with people who just happen to be nearby? First, small distances may create a sense of groupness, or unity (Arkin & Burger, 1980). As noted in Chapter 1, distance is a cue that we use when identifying groups. As a result we generally assume that people who are near us are part of our group. Others may add to this sense of unity by treating people who are near one another as if they were a group (Moreland, 1987).

Second, proximity may not be rewarding in and of itself, but it may make interaction among individuals more likely. Provided this interaction is enjoyable, proximity will encourage group formation (Gewirtz, 1969; Gewirtz & Baer, 1958a, 1958b).

Third, the effect may stem from a process known as **mere exposure:** we tend to like stimuli that we are exposed to repeatedly (Zajonc, 1968; for reviews see Grush, 1979, and Harrison, 1977). Although mere exposure to another person may seem to be insufficient to produce liking, the impact of exposure on group formation has been demonstrated in a number of studies that have varied the number of encounters between strangers (Brockner & Swap, 1976; Insko & Wilson, 1977; Saegert, Swap, & Zajonc, 1973; Tyler & Sears, 1977). In one study women tasted several pleasant-tasting or foul-tasting liquids. Between each tasting some of the subjects were moved from one tasting booth to another, and their rotations were carefully controlled so that each woman spent 10, 5, 2, 1, or 0 tasting trials with another subject. As predicted, the greater the exposure to another woman, the more this stimulus person was liked—the taste of the liquid was irrelevant (Saegert et al., 1973, Experiment 1).

Reciprocity.   Groucho Marx joked that "I wouldn't join a club that would want me as a member," but most of us respond very positively when we find out that others accept and approve of us. To test for the effect of approval on attraction, researchers often arrange for subjects to receive positive feedback (compliments, friendly advice, admiration of qualities) or negative feedback (criticisms, rebukes, insults) from a stranger or a group of strangers. In most cases subjects like the positive strangers and dislike the negative strangers (Jones, 1973; Shrauger, 1975). Also, because liking tends to be met with liking in return, attraction bonds are often mutual. This tendency, which is known as **reciprocity,** is pervasive in most groups. Newcomb (1979) found strong evidence of reciprocity, as have other investigators (Kandel, 1978; Segal, 1979, Wright, Ingraham, & Blackmer, 1984). Some group members, like Groucho, may not like to be liked, but these exceptions to the reciprocity principle are relatively rare (see Chapter 5).

Group members' characteristics.   If a group dynamicist approached you on the street and asked you to explain why you had joined a particular group, you probably wouldn't say "We all share the same opinions" or "All the group members seem to like me." Instead, you would probably point to the socially attractive qualities that the people in your group possess. Indeed, people generally report that they prefer to associate with people who are generous, enthusiastic, punctual, dependable, helpful, strong, truthful, and intelligent (Bonney, 1947; La Gaipa, 1977; Thibaut & Kelley, 1959; Lott, Lott, Reed, & Crow, 1970). In contrast, we tend to dislike individuals who possess qualities that we think are undesirable, such as tediousness, rudeness, and incompetence (Gilchrist, 1952; Iverson, 1964; Leary, Rogers, Canfield, & Coe, 1986) (See Focus 3-4.)

Part of the appeal of socially attractive people stems from our belief that interactions with them will be rewarding. Competent individuals increase our chances of achieving success, helpful people assist us with our problems, and sociable people make interaction more enjoyable. Also, as the adage "You are known by the company you keep" suggests, acceptance by attractive individuals is an indication of our social worth. High school students, for example, often seek out membership in one of the school's "in-crowds." Those who are members of the most prestigious groups generally report feeling very satisfied with themselves and their group.

· ·
FOCUS 3-4: BOREDOM IN GROUPS

Our fellow group members can do many things to undercut the rewarding aspects of our groups and increase our costs. They can, for example, make noise when we are trying to get work done (Chapanis, Garner, & Morgan, 1949). They can get in our way when the room in which we must work is limited in size (Heller, Groff, & Solomon, 1977). They can perform poorly at the task at hand and cause the group to fail (Zander, 1968). They can refuse to agree with us when we are certain we are correct (Brehm & Mann, 1975). They can ignore us (Zander & Cohen, 1955), reject us (Pepitone & Wilpinski, 1960), and fill the room with second-hand cigarette smoke (Bleda & Sandman, 1977).

One of the most unpleasant punishments meted out by group members, however, is also the most commonplace: boredom. It seems that too frequently our groups include at least one member who displays one or more of the boring behaviors listed in Table 3-5. These inducers of boredom, which were identified recently by Mark R. Leary and his colleagues, suggest that boring people tend to be passive in groups but that when they do take part in the interaction, they speak slowly, pause before making a point, and drag out the meeting. Bores also sidetrack the group unnecessarily, show little enthusiasm, and seem too serious and preoccupied with themselves. Worst of all, boring group members complain about their own problems (negative egocentrism) and talk incessantly about trivial topics (banality).

Leary and his associates found that if given the choice, we much prefer the company of interesting people to boring people. In one study they asked observers to listen to a tape recording of a conversation that included a boring group member (someone who displayed many of the behaviors listed in Table 3-5) or an interesting group member (someone who avoided these behaviors). When the observers later rated the discussers, they felt that the interesting targets were more likable, friendly, enthusiastic, popular, emotional, intelligent, personal, strong, and secure than the boring targets. The implications of these findings are clear: if you want people to leave you out of their groups, do all you can to be as boring as possible (Leary, Rogers, Canfield, & Coe, 1986).

TABLE 3-5. The components of boring behavior.

Dimension	Definition	Example Behaviors
Passivity	Participating at a low rate	Adds nothing to conversation Doesn't express opinions Doesn't hold up end of conversation
Tediousness	Communicating in a boring manner	Talks slowly Rambles Includes too much detail
Distraction	Interfering with the group's interaction	Talks about past too much Is excited by trivial things Is easily sidetracked
Low affectivity	Lacking emotion or expressiveness	Lacks enthusiasm Has monotonous voice Avoids eye contact
Boring ingratiation	Awkwardly trying to impress others	Tries hard to be funny Tries hard to be nice Tries to impress you
Seriousness	Maintaining a serious demeanor	Doesn't smile Is very serious
Negative egocentrism	Complaining about one's own problems	Is constantly complaining Acts bored
Self-preoccupation	Lacking interest in others	Talks about self Always talks about problems
Banality	Talking about trite and trivial topics	Talks about trivial, superficial things Repeats stories and jokes

(Source: Leary, Rogers, Canfield, & Coe, 1986.)

• •

Those students who want to be a part of an in-crowd but aren't accepted by this clique, in contrast, are the most dissatisfied (Brown & Lohr, 1986; Newman & Newman, 1976).

Because our sense of self-worth prospers when we are members of prestigious groups, people often draw attention to their membership in such groups. Robert Cialdini and his associates call this tendency basking in reflected glory (or **BIRGing**) and suggest that it enhances our social identity. In one study they found that college students subtly emphasized their allegiance to their university depending on the school's most recent football performance. For example, more students wore clothes bearing their university's name or mascot on days after the team had won. Also, when interviewed about their school, students used the word *we* more after a victory ("We're a good school") and the word *they* more after a loss ("They lost that game") (Cialdini et al., 1976; see also Cialdini & Richardson, 1980; Snyder, Lassegard, & Ford, 1986).

Associating with attractive, successful people can pose a problem, however. Although we can revel in the knowledge that we are accepted by such individuals, our sense of self-worth may suffer if we think that our own attributes and abilities are inferior to theirs. As noted earlier in the chapter, we often prefer the company of less competent individuals because they provide us with a target for downward social comparison. If we associate with people who have abilities that are superior to ours, our own talents pale by comparison.

Abraham Tesser, Jennifer Campbell, and their associates have developed an intriguing model that explains how people deal with the desire to associate with attractive people (BIRGing) and the need for downward social comparison. They argue that the relevance of the attribute or skill to our self-definition determines when we seek our inferiors or our superiors. Imagine, for example, that you are a mediocre football player who wants to be a great player. In this case you will probably avoid joining a group of all-conference football players. If, however, you play football for fun but take pride in your academic performance, you may feel very comfortable associating with better players. Indeed, Tesser and Campbell's **self-evaluation maintenance model** (SEM) assumes that the ideal co-member or friend is someone who performs worse than you do on tasks that you think are important but very well on tasks that you don't think are important. Such associates provide you with targets for downward social comparison, and you can also bask in the glory of their accomplishments in areas that don't interest you (Tesser & Campbell, 1983; Tesser, Campbell, & Smith, 1984).

Tesser and Campbell tested the model in one recent study by giving elementary school students a list of activities (sports, art, music, math) and asking them to pick out ones that they considered to be important or unimportant. The students also identified their most and least preferred classmate. One week later the students rated their ability, their close classmate's ability, and their distant classmate's ability in an area they felt was important and one they felt was unimportant. As Figure 3-1 indicates, if the students thought that the task was important, they judged their performance as superior to their close friend's. If the task was not important to them personally, they felt that they had performed relatively worse. The performances of disliked classmates were derogated for both important and unimportant tasks (Tesser et al., 1984).

Physical attractiveness. One characteristic of potential group members deserves special mention: physical attractiveness. Although most of us would deny that we pick our business associates, friends, or club members on the basis of their physical attractiveness, most people are drawn to physically attractive people.

Naturally, attractiveness is a particularly strong determinant of romantic relationships, but it also exerts an influence on group formation as well. In one investigation the researchers used sociometry to identify the

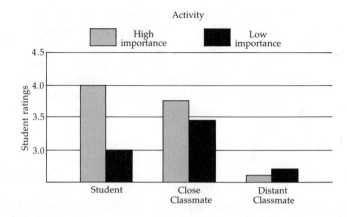

FIGURE 3-1 Students' ratings of their own performance, a close friend's performance, and a disliked classmate's performance on activities that the students designated as being important to their self-definition or unimportant to their self-definition.

Source: Tesser, Campbell, & Smith, 1984

four types of students shown in Figure 3-2. Students who received the most positive sociometric nominations were placed in the accepted group, those who received an average number of nominations were placed in the control group, students who were rejected were placed in the rejected group, and any students who went unnominated (in either positive terms or negative terms) were classified as isolated. Next, trained judges rated the physical attractiveness of the subjects using high school graduation photographs, and the average attractiveness scores of the students in the four groups were compared. As Figure 3-2 indicates, physical attractiveness was positively related to acceptance, with one important exception: extremely attractive individuals tended to be rejected by their classmates. Other evidence suggested that the highly attractive students in this study

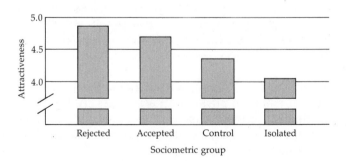

FIGURE 3-2. Physical attractiveness ratings of college students in four sociometric groups.

Source: Krebs and Adinolfi, 1975

tended to be individualistic, ambitious, and achievement oriented, so they may have been rejected for failing "to demonstrate a concern for their less attractive peers" (Krebs & Adinolfi, 1975, p. 251).

Social Exchange and Group Formation

Interpersonal attraction was once thought to be a mysterious process that pulled some people together while pushing others apart. As we have seen, however, social exchange theory demystifies this process by suggesting that we like similar people, people with complementary needs, people who are nearby, people who like us, and people who possess attractive qualities, because they offer us many rewards and pose few costs (Thibaut & Kelley, 1959).

Do we, then, join any group that promises us a favorable reward/cost ratio? Harold Kelley and John Thibaut, in their seminal theory of social exchange, argue that although we may be attracted to such groups, our decision to actually join is based on two additional factors: our comparison level and our comparison level for alternatives. **Comparison level** (CL) is the standard by which individuals evaluate the desirability of group membership. The CL derives from the average of all outcomes known to the individual and is usually strongly influenced by previous relationships. If, for example, Juan has previously been in groups that yielded very positive rewards with very few costs, his CL should be higher than someone who has experienced fewer rewards and more costs through group membership. According to Thibaut and Kelley (1959, p. 21), groups that "fall above CL would be relatively 'satisfying' and attractive to the member; those entailing outcomes that fall below CL would be relatively 'unsatisfying' and unattractive" (see also Kelley & Thibaut, 1978).

We cannot predict group formation on the basis of comparison level alone. Juan, for example, may be offered a choice of membership in several groups, all of which are around his CL. In this case the group with the best reward/cost balance will determine Juan's **comparison level for alternatives,** or CLalt. Thibaut and Kelley write that "CLalt can be defined informally as the lowest level of outcomes a member will accept in the light of available alternative opportunities" (1959, p. 21).

Thibaut and Kelley's predictions concerning CL and CLalt are summarized in Table 3-6. Consider, as an example, a student named Julie who is considering joining a study group that has been formed by her classmates. According to Thibaut and Kelley, she will first attempt to predict what positive and negative outcomes will result from membership in the group. Looking at rewards, she may believe that joining the group will make learning easier, will lead to increased interaction with several attractive individuals, and will also yield an improved course grade. On the negative side, however, she thinks that the group might be boring and she doesn't think she has much in common with most of the members.

Joining a group, then, is largely determined by CLalt, whereas satisfaction with membership is determined by CL. If Julie decides that the out-

TABLE 3-6. The impact of comparison level and comparison level for alternatives on satisfaction with group membership and decision to join a group.

		Membership in the Group Is	
		Above Her CL	Below Her CL
	Above her CLalt	Membership is satisfying , and she will join.	Membership is dissatisfying, but she will join.
Membership in the Group Is	Below her CLalt	Membership is satisfying, but she will not join.	Membership is dissatisfying, and she will not join.

(Source: Thibaut & Kelley, 1959)

comes that would result from group membership surpass her CL, she will be satisfied with membership. Before she joins, however, the value of alternative group membership must also be considered; the study group must exceed her CLalt. In fact, Julie may decide that remaining outside the study group will yield a more favorable reward/cost ratio; in this instance remaining alone will establish the lower limit of her CLalt.

SUMMARY

When and why do groups form? One answer to this question highlights the survival, psychological, informational, interpersonal, and practical advantages of membership in a group. First, in eons past groups offered protection against environmental dangers that threatened the survival of the human species. *Sociobiology,* a biological approach to understanding social behavior, argues that the process of *natural selection* thus favored individuals who preferred group living to isolation. Indeed, some evolutionary theorists, such as Tiger, suggest that humans are instinctively drawn to other humans.

Second, membership in groups satisfies many basic psychological needs. Freud, for example, suggests that adults' reactions in groups parallel their childhood family experiences. Other theorists, too, maintain that groups offer individuals the means of satisfying the need for affilitation (*n* Affiliation) and the need for power (*n* Power). Schutz's Fundamental Interpersonal Relations Orientation (FIRO), in particular, stresses the relationship between individuals' behavior in groups and their need to receive and express inclusion, control, and affection.

Third, Festinger suggests that in many cases we seek out other people so that we can evaluate the accuracy of our personal beliefs and attitudes. This process, which is known as *social comparison,* was investigated extensively by Schachter; he found that people who face an ambiguous situation will seek information through affiliation. Additionally, individuals engage in social comparison to acquire reassuring information. For example, we often protect our sense of self-worth by comparing ourselves with those who are performing less effectively (*downward social comparison*).

Fourth, our groups satisfy many of our interpersonal needs. Groups are an important source of *social support*, so they work as a protective buffer that shields us from the harmful effects of stress. Groups also provide a respite from *social loneliness* and *emotional loneliness*.

Fifth, groups are useful on a practical level. In many cases people face goals that they cannot attain working alone, so they join in a collaborative effort. Zander notes that people pursue goals in groups when they become dissatisfied with current outcomes, but he adds that cultures that are based on *collectivism* rather than *individualism* are more likely to stress group goals over individual goals.

A second approach to the question "When and why do groups form?" suggests that we join groups when interpersonal attraction creates feelings of liking for others. Although various theories have been developed to account for attraction, many emphasize the process of *social exchange*: the giving and accepting of rewards and punishments among individuals. This perspective explains a number of general tendencies identified by Newcomb in his studies of the acquaintance process, including:

1. the *similarity/attraction effect:* we like people who are similar to us in some way
2. the *complementarity-of-needs hypothesis:* we like people who possess qualities that fulfill our own needs
3. the *proximity/attraction effect:* we like people who are close by
4. *mere exposure:* we like people whom we have been exposed to repeatedly
5. *reciprocity:* we like people who like us
6. *basking in reflected glory (BIRGing):* we seek to associate with successful, prestigious groups

We also tend to avoid individuals who possess objectionable characteristics, people who are boring, and those who are physically unattractive. Last, as the *self-evaluation maintenance model* predicts, we prefer to associate with people who do not outperform us in areas that are very relevant to our self-esteem.

We do not, however, simply join any group that promises many rewards and few costs. As Thibaut and Kelley note, our reaction to any group depends on two standards: our *comparison level (CL)*, the standard value that the group must surpass before we consider it to be satisfying, and our *comparison level for alternatives (CLalt)*, the value of the least acceptable group available to us. They predict that our satisfaction with group membership is primarily determined by our comparison level, whereas our comparison level for alternatives determines whether we join, stay in, or leave a group.

·4·

Development and Socialization

I n 1970 the rumors about the breakup of the Beatles were finally confirmed. When Paul McCartney officially announced that he was leaving the group, the world's most successful rock-and-roll band was no more.

Only six years earlier the Beatles had jumped from small clubs and beer joints in Liverpool, England, to the international concert circuit. With a sound honed by years of practice, McCartney, John Lennon, George Harrison, and Ringo Starr rapidly became celebrities. Their strategically planned tours were overwhelming successes, their wit disarmed their critics, and their songs dominated the airwaves in England and the United States.

But the Beatles who sang *Let It Be* in 1970 were not the same Beatles who had sung *I Wanna Hold Your Hand* in 1964. From their earliest days the band was innovative and daring, and during the 1960s this restlessness led them to experiment with new music, drugs, and life-styles. Each Beatle undertook a solo project, and with each year the group members related to one another in new ways. All the members also changed personally during this time, and these changes reverberated through the group. These natural shifts and changes in the fabric of the group eventually culminated, predictably, in the group's demise.

All groups, whether the Beatles, a construction crew, a high school clique, or the choir in a Baptist church, share an important feature: they change. Initial uncertainties give way to stable patterns of interaction, tensions between members wax and wane, old members are replaced by new ones, and levels of productivity fluctuate. Moreover, just as the group undergoes change over time, so the individuals within it change their relationship to it. Harrison, once barred from the Beatles, became a key member. Lennon turned from the group to Yoko Ono for support and inspiration. As time passes, members of any group abandon old roles to take on new ones, and personal commitment to the group rises and falls.

This chapter explores time-dependent processes that operate at both the group level and at the individual level. First, we consider **group development:** patterns of growth and change that occur in groups throughout their life cycle, from formation to dissolution. Next, we turn to group socialization: patterns of change in the relationship between the individual members of the group and the group itself. The final section considers how these processes can be controlled to achieve organizational development.

GROUP DEVELOPMENT

The noted group dynamicist William Fawcett Hill was at one time so intrigued by developmental processes in groups that he maintained a collection of all the theories that pertained to the subject. Over the years his collection grew and grew, until finally the number of theories reached 100. At that moment, Hill notes, the "collecting bug was exterminated, as the object of the quest had lost its rarity" (Hill & Gruner, 1973, p. 353; see also Hare, 1982; Lacoursiere, 1980).

The morass of theoretical models dealing with development, though daunting, is not altogether irremediable. Theoreticians are at variance on many points, but most assume that groups pass through several phases, or *stages*, as they develop. Just as humans mature from infancy to childhood, adolescence, adulthood, and old-age, stage models of group development theorize that groups move from one stage to the next in a predictable, sequential fashion. The Beatles, for example, became a successful musical group, but this productivity was prefaced by earlier stages marked by confusion, conflict, and growing group cohesion.

What stages typify the developmental progression of groups? The number and names of the stages vary among theorists. Many models, however, highlight certain interpersonal outcomes that must be achieved in any group that exists for a prolonged period. Members of most groups must, for example, discover who the other members are, achieve a degree of interdependence, and deal with conflict (Hare, 1982; Lacoursiere, 1980). Therefore, most models include the basic stages shown in Table 4-1. Initially, the group members must become oriented toward one another.

TABLE 4-1. Five stages of group development.

Stage	Major Processes	Characteristics
1. Orientation (forming)	Exchange of information; increased interdependency; task exploration; identification of commonalities	Tentative interactions; polite discourse; concern over ambiguity; self-discourse
2. Conflict (storming)	Disagreement over procedures; expression of dissatisfaction; emotional responding; resistance	Criticism of ideas; poor attendance; hostility; polarization and coalition formation
3. Cohesion (norming)	Growth of cohesiveness and unity; establishment of roles, standards, and relationships	Agreement on procedures; reduction in role ambiguity; increased "we-feeling"
4. Performance (performing)	Goal achievement; high task orientation; emphasis on performance and production	Decision making; problem solving; mutual cooperation
5. Dissolution (adjourning)	Termination of roles; completion of tasks; reduction of dependency	Disintegration and withdrawal; increased independence and emotionality; regret

Next, they often find themselves in conflict, and some solution is sought to improve the group environment. In the third phase norms and roles develop that regulate behavior, and the group achieves greater unity. In the fourth phase the group reaches a point at which it can perform as a unit to achieve desired goals, and the final stage ends the sequence of development with the group's adjournment. These five stages, which Bruce W. Tuckman labeled *forming* (orientation), *storming* (conflict), *norming* (cohesion), *performing*, (performance) and *adjourning* (dissolution), are examined next (Tuckman, 1965; Tuckman & Jensen, 1977).

Forming: The Orientation Stage

When the group is forming, members often suffer through an *orientation* period marked by mild tension and guarded interchanges. McCartney and Lennon, for example, greeted each other with caution. Lennon knew nothing of this boyish, self-confident guitarist, and he questioned McCartney's guitar-playing skills. McCartney himself wasn't sure he wanted to become a band member, particularly in a group led by the older Lennon. Both men were unwilling to commit themselves to any future relationship.

This initial period of orientation is very typical in groups. When groups form, the members must deal with people they hardly know, and this initial unfamiliarity leaves them feeling uncomfortable and constrained. Often all the members of a new group are on their guard, carefully monitoring their behavior to make certain that they avoid any embarrassing lapses of social poise. Feeling as if they have been thrown together with a bunch of strangers, they may be reluctant to discuss their personal views and values with people they know so little about. This ambiguous situation is further complicated by the absence of any specific norms regarding the regulation of interaction and goal attainment as well as uncertainty about their role in the group. This tension is so intensely punishing that people who believe that they lack the social skills necessary to cope with the situation actively avoid group membership (Cook, 1977; Leary, 1983).

With time, tension is dispelled as the ice is broken and group members become better acquainted (Thibaut and Kelley, 1959). After the initial inhibitions that arise from interaction with strangers subside, group members typically begin exchanging information about themselves and their goals. As the individuals begin to function like a group, categorization processes may prompt them to redefine themselves as group members rather than individuals (Turner, 1987). Feelings of interdependence also increase during this period, and members reach a rudimentary level of trust.

Storming: The Conflict Stage

Most groups reach a minimal level of interdependence relatively rapidly; once Lennon and McCartney recognized each other's talents, they began to practice together regularly. This polite orientation stage, however, often ends when the actions of one or more members of the group are incompatible with, and resisted by, one or more of the other group members. This stormy outbreak marks the group's passage into the second stage of development: **conflict.**

Conflict in a group can take many forms. Disagreements that arise when one person misinterpets another's position or actions are termed *false conflicts* (Deutsch, 1973) or *autistic conflicts* (Holmes & Miller, 1976; Kriesberg, 1973). Other conflicts, sometimes called *contingent conflicts*, are easily solved by changing some minor situational factor. The group member who arouses the ire of others by consistently arriving for meetings ten minutes late can be told to show up on time or be dropped from the group; the discord over who sits where at the rectangular table may be alleviated by moving to a round table. Such disagreements, although of some importance to the group, are easily resolvable without any undue increase in group tension (Deutsch, 1973).

Escalating conflict, in contrast, can seriously disrupt the group's internal dynamics. Even when the conflict stems from a minor point of disagreement, such as how to control the flow of communication or when to break for lunch, it can lead to other, more basic points of contentiousness. More issues are brought out into the open, and soon the minor differences extend to many other areas. Furthermore, members who were reluctant to break the smooth preconflict interaction now realize that the damage is already done, and they join in the fray by expressing the dislikes and disagreements that they had previously suppressed.

Despite the negative connotations of conflict, disagreeing is a natural consequence of joining a group. Observers of all types of groups have documented clashes among members and have invariably concluded that group conflict is as common as group harmony (Bales, Cohen, & Williamson, 1979; Bennis & Shepard, 1956; Fisher, 1980; Tuckman, 1965). As a sociological perspective based on conflict theory suggests, the dynamic nature of the group ensures continual change, but along with change come stresses and strains that surface in the form of conflict. In rare instances group members may avoid all conflict because their actions are perfectly coordinated, but in most groups the push and pull of interpersonal forces inevitably exerts its influence (for example, Dahrendorf, 1958, 1959).

Lewis Coser goes so far as to suggest that although conflict can destroy a group, it can also promote group unity. The idea that conflict creates unification may seem paradoxical, but according to Coser,

> conflict may serve to remove dissociating elements in a relationship and to re-establish unity. Insofar as conflict is the resolution of tension between antagonists it has stabilizing functions and becomes an integrating component of the relationship. . . . Conflicts, which serve to "sew the social system together" by cancelling each other out, thus prevent disintegration along one primary line of cleavage. [1956, p. 80].

Others have noted that interdependency among members and the stability of a group cannot deepen until hostility has surfaced, been confronted, and been resolved (Bennis & Shepard, 1956; Deutsch, 1969). Low levels of conflict in a group could be an indication of remarkably positive interpersonal relations, but it is more likely that the group members are simply uninvolved, unmotivated, and bored. Coser notes that the absence of conflict tells us little about the stability of the group, since the more cohesive the group, the more intense is the conflict. Conflict also provides a means of venting personal hostilities, but members can reduce this stress by confronting the problem and communicating dissatisfactions honestly and openly. If hostilities are never expressed in the group, they may build up to a point at which the group can no longer continue as a unit (see Focus 4-1 and Chapter 12).

. . . .

FOCUS 4-1: THE THRESHOLD THEORY OF CONFLICT

Ernest Bormann emphasizes the positive value of conflict in his **threshold theory** of group tension (1975). According to Bormann, groups experience two types of social tension, primary and secondary. **Primary tension** occurs during the orientation phase when group members feel too restrained by the novelty of the group setting. **Secondary tension,** in contrast, usually occurs when the group's routine patterns of interaction are disrupted by intense disagreement. Although Bormann admits that uncontrolled secondary conflict can destroy the group, he argues that every group has a threshold for tension that represents its optimal level of conflict among members (see Figure 4-1). Conflict too far below this level

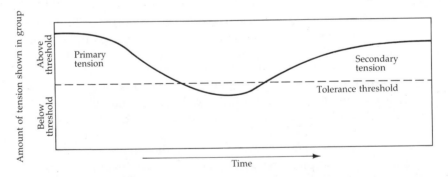

FIGURE 4-1. Primary and secondary tension areas in groups. As the curve illustrates, most groups experience considerable tension when they first convene. This primary tension, however, dissipates over time and the amount of tension in the group drops to a more comfortable level. So long as the tension among members remains below the tolerance threshold, secondary tension will not develop.

Source: Bormann, 1975

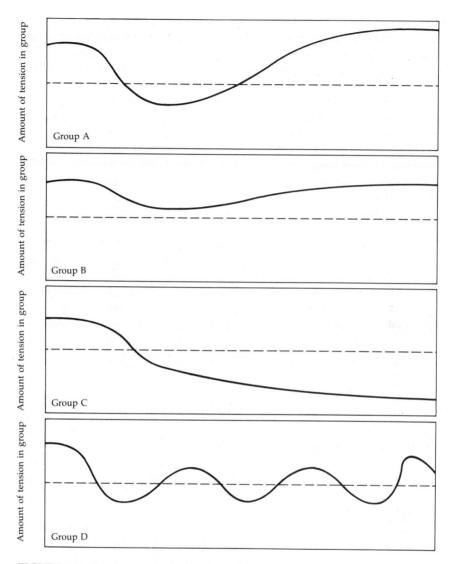

FIGURE 4-2. Tension curves in four hypothetical groups.
Sources: Bormann, 1975; Fisher, 1980

results in group apathy, boredom, and lack of involvement. Prolonged conflict above this level, on the other hand, causes shared disagreement, heightened hostility, and a loss of group effectiveness. What is needed, then, is a balance between too little tension and too much tension.

An application of the threshold theory of group tension to four hypothetical groups is shown in Figure 4-2. Group A, after initially reducing primary tension, experiences a large amount of uncontrolled secondary tension. The amount of tension is far above the tolerance threshold, and it remains at high levels for a prolonged period. Such a group will, in all likelihood, fail to exist for long unless steps are taken quickly to reduce the conflict. Group B, on the other hand, never gets past the primary-tension phase. Although such groups are not very common, they sometimes occur, as when group members are perhaps forced to join the group, remain uninvolved in the group interactions, or owe commitments to other groups or activities. Membership in such a group is often very unpleasant for group members, and again a short life-span is predicted. Group C may seem to be an ideal group because of its low level of secondary tension, but looks can be deceiving. The low level of tension may be the result of excellent internal group dynamics, but more notably it stems from boredom and apathy. The group members may be too uninvolved to argue about the issues at hand, or they may be unwilling to confront the problems that have arisen in the past.

   Ideal groups, according to the threshold notion of conflict, are similar to Group D. Although D clearly experiences frequent episodes of conflict, these episodes have mostly positive consequences: the clarification of goals, an increased understanding of differences and points of contention, successful discussion, stimulation of interests, and the release of hostility. The group has apparently managed to develop techniques that limit escalation and, thereby, to control the magnitude and longevity of the conflict. At a minimum the group interaction will probably be lively.

. . . .

   The Beatles, as a group, certainly supported Coser's arguments. When they were refining their sound and culling poor musicians from their midst, conflicts regularly shattered the group's harmony. Pete Best, their drummer at one time, was the target of regular criticism. McCartney picked arguments with various guitarists until he drove each one from the group. The group even argued about how they should style their hair; Harrison refused for sometime to go along with the others when they began wearing their hair long and brushed forward. These conflicts, however, were only the precursors to their developing unity.

Norming: The Cohesion Stage

The Beatles struggled through a long period of low popularity paired with high internal strife. Drummers, managers, and guitarists quit one after another when McCartney and Lennon criticized their musical talents and personal attributes. But something happened when the group played an extended engagement in Hamburg, Germany. Playing nightly in a foreign city, isolated from their family and friends, the Beatles tried new techniques and songs. They bonded tightly, to the point that they spent virtually all their time together. In McCartney's account, during this period the group functioned as a single entity: "We're all really the same person. We're just four parts of the one" (quoted in Stokes, 1980, p. 53).

During the third developmental stage intermember conflict is replaced by cohesiveness: a feeling of group unity, camaraderie, and esprit de corps. In part this increased cohesiveness reflects the growth of group norms that regulate and stabilize the group's internal dynamics. Beyond this "norming" process, however, we also find changes in other aspects of the group, including increased group unity, membership retention, and satisfaction (see Table 4-2).

Unity. A heightened sense of unity is one of the most basic changes that takes place when a group becomes cohesive. Not only do relationships among the group members become more positive, but members also develop a sense of belonging to the group as a whole. During this stage they often proudly identify themselves as group members and defend the group against criticism or attack by outsiders. As "we-ness" emerges, members begin to feel that they share important commonalities, such as similar personal qualities, goals, or outcomes, with the other members. For the Beatles this stage was marked by an increased inner confidence in themselves and an outward uniformity of appearance.

Stability. Perhaps because of this feeling of unity, cohesive groups tend to retain their members. Indeed, Cartwright (1968, p. 91) defines cohesion as "the degree to which the members of the group desire to remain in their group." This relationship between cohesiveness and member retention is strongest, moreover, when cohesion is based on the members' commitment to the group-as-a-unit rather than their attraction toward other individual members. In studies of cohesion and turnover in industrial settings, strong liking for one's co-workers is not a strong predictor of decreased turnover. A strong, group-level positive link between the member and the group, however, is associated with lower turnover (Mobley, Griffeth, Hand, & Meglino, 1979).

TABLE 4-2. Changes associated with increases in group cohesion.

Attribute	Type of Change
Unity	Increased sense of "we-ness," or "groupness"; high level of camaraderie and esprit de corps; development of group identity
Membership stability	Low turnover; low absence rates; high involvement by members; greater participation in activities
Member satisfaction	More enjoyment by members; increases in self-esteem and sense of security; lower levels of anxiety
Internal dynamics	Stronger influence of group; greater acceptance by members of group's goals, decisions, and norms; low tolerance for disagreement; increased pressures to conform

Satisfaction.   Group cohesion and satisfaction with membership generally covary. Across a range of groups in industrial, athletic, and educational settings, people who are members of highly compatible, cohesive subgroups report more satisfaction and enjoyment than members of noncohesive groups (Darley, Gross, & Martin, 1951; Hare, 1976; Stokes, 1983a; Wheeless, Wheeless, & Dickson-Markman, 1982). Members of cohesive groups also tend to report more positive self-esteem, a heightened sense of security, and lower levels of anxiety (for example, Myers, 1962; Pepitone and Reichling, 1955). Studies conducted in industrial work groups, for example, indicate that employees reported less anxiety and nervousness when they worked in cohesive groups (Seashore, 1954). Typically, the atmosphere in cohesive groups is cooperative, friendly, and marked by exchanges of praise for accomplishments. In noncohesive groups hostility and aggression surface, along with a tendency to criticize other group members (Deutsch, 1968; Shaw & Shaw, 1962).

Internal dynamics.   As cohesion increases, the internal dynamics of the group tend to intensify as well. Cohesive groups exert a stronger influence on their members than noncohesive groups, for people in such groups more readily accept the group's goals, decisions, and norms. Furthermore, pressures to conform are greater in cohesive groups, and individuals' resistance to these pressures is weaker. In an early study of communication patterns in cohesive dyads, for example, the researcher directly manipulated cohesiveness by telling the subjects that they would either enjoy being in the group, since care had been taken in assembling highly compatible teams, or that the dyad would not be cohesive, since the members were incompatible (Back, 1951). Subsequent analyses revealed that when the subjects discovered that they disagreed with their partner's interpretations of three ambiguous stimuli, the members of cohesive groups tried to exert greater influence over their partner than did the members of noncohesive groups. In addition, conformity to the partner's attempt to influence was also greater in cohesive dyads. The increases in the group's power to influence others during this stage is what prompted Tuckman (1965) to call this stage of development the "norming" stage.

The intensity of cohesive groups has its drawbacks; members of such groups sometimes become intolerant of any sort of disagreement, and harsh measures are taken to bring dissenters into line. Schachter (1951), for example, found that when groups were highly cohesive, anyone who went against the group consensus tended to be disliked by the members and to be assigned undesirable roles if allowed to remain within the group (see Chapter 6). Also, as noted later in this chapter, cohesiveness can lead to decreases in productivity, particularly if the group's norms discourage greater productivity. Cohesion can also increase negative group processes, including hostility, scapegoating, and rejection (French, 1941; Pepitone & Reichling, 1955).

Cohesiveness thus works as an *intensifier* of group processes. On the positive side, cohesiveness is associated with group stability, satisfaction, effective communication, positive personal consequences for members, and increased group influence. On the negative side, however, as groups become more cohesive, social pressures can become so intense that individual members are overwhelmed. Furthermore, given the right (or wrong) combination of circumstances, cohesiveness also decreases the quality of group performance and increases hostility and interpersonal rejection.

Performing: The Task-Performance Phase

In the summer of 1962 the Beatles entered a period of unparalleled productivity. Their albums began to sell in record numbers, and each new song soon moved to number one. Their concert tours were overwhelming successes in both England and the United States, and television appearances and a full-length feature movie soon followed. Lennon and McCartney composed dozens of songs that made millions of dollars in royalties, and eventually the group opened its own recording studio. The Beatles stopped touring in 1966, but they continued to record albums into 1970. Their albums routinely sold in the millions.

Few groups are productive immediately; instead, productivity must usually wait until the group matures. A. Paul Hare, after studying historical records of the Camp David conference of 1978 that brought together delegates from Egypt, Israel, and the United States, concluded that most of the positive outcomes were achieved during a two-day period near the end of the conference (Hare & Naveh, 1984). He reports a similar shift in performance in a group of factory workers assembling relay units, workshop participants, and the members of an anthropological expedition (Hare, 1967, 1982). Bales, too, after systematically coding the types of behaviors exhibited by group members, concludes that task-focused actions occur more frequently later in the group's life (Bales & Strodtbeck, 1951; Borgatta & Bales, 1953; Heinicke & Bales, 1953).

Even when the group's task is a therapeutic one, as is the case in encounter groups, training groups, and other types of growth groups, time is needed to achieve considerable change. In one study investigators observed and coded the behaviors displayed by adolescents in a program of behavioral change. These groups did not immediately start to work on self-development issues, nor did the group members try to help one another. Rather, the groups first moved through orientation, conflict, and cohesion-building stages before they began to make therapeutic progress (Hill, 1977; Hill & Gruner, 1973). In a similar investigation the members of a sensitivity-training group rated each session on a series of adjective pairs such as good/bad, labored/easy, and uncertain/definite. These ratings, when examined by the researchers, followed the general pattern suggested by Tuckman's stage theory: a period of mild tension followed by increased conflict that was resolved by the ninth session. Group members rated the next four sessions as smooth and comfortable, but as the group entered the work phase (sessions 13–15) the positive ratings dropped slightly, whereas ratings of the potency of the meetings increased (Stiles, Tupler, & Carpenter, 1982).

Not all groups reach this productive stage, unfortunately. If you have never been a member of a group that failed to produce, you are a rare individual indeed. In a study of neighborhood action committees only 1 of 12 groups reached the productivity stage; all the others were bogged down at the conflict or cohesion stages (Zurcher, 1969). An early investigation of combat units found that out of 63 squads, 13 could be clearly classified as effective performance units (Goodacre, 1953). An analysis of 18 personal-growth groups concluded that only 5 managed to reach the task-performance stage (Kuypers, Davies, & Hazewinkel, 1986; see also Kuypers, Davies, & Glaser, 1986). These studies and others suggest that time is needed to develop a working relationship, but time alone is no guarantee that the group will be productive (Gabarro, 1987). (See Focus 4-2).

- -
FOCUS 4-2: COHESIVENESS AND GROUP PERFORMANCE

Are groups that have passed through the earlier stages of group development more productive than those that bypass the orientation, conflict, and cohesion stages? The newly formed group, with its lack of cohesion and structure, may be able to perform tasks in which individual members' efforts are pooled, but tasks that require a high coordination of effort may prove difficult. Yet having suffered through a period of conflict followed by a growth of cohesion is no guarantee that the group will perform effectively.

In most cases groups that are very cohesive, like the Beatles, are highly successful; blessed by members who were committed to the group and its objectives, the Beatles overcame obstacle after obstacle to finally achieve their shared goal (Greene, 1989; Littlepage, Cowart, & Kerr, 1989). Yet cohesiveness does not always go hand in hand with productivity, because the group's goal may not necessarily be to maximize productivity. Consider the results of a major survey of 5871 factory workers in 228 groups. This study found that the more cohesive the group, the less the productivity levels varied among members; members of cohesive groups produced nearly equivalent amounts, but individuals in noncohesive groups varied considerably more in their productivity. Furthermore, fairly low standards of performance had developed within some of the highly cohesive groups, and thus productivity was uniformly low among these groups. In contrast, in cohesive groups with relatively high performance goals, members were extremely productive (Seashore, 1954). This evidence can be expressed in a hypothesis that predicts a link between cohesiveness and productivity: so long as group norms encourage high productivity, cohesiveness and productivity are positively related: the more cohesive the group, the greater its productivity. If group norms encourage low productivity, however, the relationship is negative (see Figure 4-3).

Schachter and his colleagues confirmed this hypothesis in an experimental study of female college students working in three-person teams on an assembly-line project (Schachter, Ellertson, McBride, & Gregory, 1951). First, half of the subjects were led to believe that they were members of cohesive groups, and the other subjects were convinced that their groups were noncohesive. Second, during the task, messages were ostensibly sent from one worker to another to establish performance norms. In some instances the messages called for increased production (positive messages), but in other instances the messages requested a slow down (negative messages). As expected, the impact of the messages was significantly greater in the cohesive groups than in the noncohesive groups. Furthermore, the decreases in productivity brought about by the negative messages were greater than the increases brought about by the positive messages. The implications of these findings are clear: cohesive groups are often more enjoyable, but they aren't always more productive.

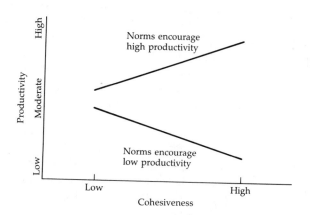

FIGURE 4-3. The cohesiveness/productivity relationship. If the group's norms encourage productivity, cohesiveness and productivity will be positively correlated. If the group standards for performance are low, cohesiveness will actually undermine productivity.

Adjourning: The Dissolution Stage

In George Harrison's words, "All things must pass." As the Beatles labored through the tortured 1960s, a growing distance replaced their prior inseparability. Brian Epstein, their manager, died of a drug overdose; Lennon married Ono; McCartney began to turn more to his wife, Linda, and away from Lennon and the others; Starr continued to be the goodnatured arbiter of disputes, but Harrison withdrew more and more to concentrate on his spiritual growth. Finally, in 1970 McCartney announced that he was leaving the group. The group that was once the Quarry Men, Johnny and the Moondogs, the Silver Beatles, but finally the Beatles, had disbanded.

A group's entry into the dissolution stage can be either planned or spontaneous. *Planned dissolution* takes place when the group accomplishes its prescribed goals or exhausts its time and resources. A baseball team playing the last game of the season, a wilderness expedition at the end of its journey, a party at 3 A.M., a jury delivering its verdict, and an ad hoc committee filing its report are all examples of groups that are ending as scheduled. *Spontaneous dissolution*, in contrast, results when an unanticipated problem arises that makes continued group interaction impossible. When groups fail repeatedly, their members or some outside power may decide that maintaining the group is a waste of time and resources. If the group fails to satisfy its members' social and interpersonal needs, members may abandon the group en masse and join other organizations. As social exchange theory maintains (see Chapter 3), when the number of rewards provided by group membership decreases and the costly aspects of our membership escalate, group members become dissatisfied. If the members feel that they have no alternatives or that they have put too much into the group to abandon it, then they may remain in the group even though they are dissatisfied. If, however, group members feel that other groups are available or that nonparticipation is preferable to participation in such a costly group, they will be more likely to let their current group die (Rusbult, 1983; Rusbult, Zembrodt, & Gunn, 1982; Thibaut & Kelley, 1959).

The dissolution stage can be stressful for members (Johnson, 1974; Mayadas & Glasser, 1985; Sarri & Galinsky, 1985). When dissolution is unplanned, the final sessions may be filled with conflict-laden exchanges among members, growing apathy and animosity, or repeated failures at the group's task. And even when it is planned, the members may feel distressed: their work in the group may be over, but they still mourn for the group and suffer from a lack of personal support. The members of the Beatles, for example, took the legal steps necessary to end their group, but like most members of dissolving business partnerships they probably experienced a wide range of negative feelings about the entire process: anxiety, feelings of inequity, and anger toward their former partners. Members of disbanding partnerships also tend to blame one another for the end of the group (Kushnir, 1984).

What can be done to minimize the stress associated with the adjourning stage? Experts suggest that the leader, before dissolution, should reduce the group's level of cohesion while stressing the independence of each individual member (Mayadas & Glasser, 1985). Negative feelings about the end of the group can also be alleviated by holding a series of debriefing sessions during which members review the accomplishments of the group, share concerns, and discuss plans for the future (Flapan & Fenchel, 1987).

Group Development: Summary and Implications

Over 100 stage models have been advanced by group dynamicists seeking to describe group development. Most, however, highlight the five stages identified by Tuckman in his model: forming (orientation), storming (conflict), norming (cohesion), performing (task performance), and adjourning (dissolution).

Tuckman's stage model, however, cannot be applied without qualification to all groups. His model is a **successive-stage** theory; it specifies the usual order of the phases of group development. Sometimes, however, development takes a different course. Interpersonal exploration is often a prerequisite for other interpersonal outcomes, and cohesion and conflict often precede effective performance, but this pattern is not universal. Some groups manage to avoid particular stages, others move through the stages but in a unique order, and still others seem to develop in ways that can't be described by Tuckman's five stages (Seeger, 1983). Also, the demarkation between stages is not clear-cut. When group conflict is waning, for example, feelings of cohesion may be increasing, but these time-dependent changes do not occur in a discontinuous, steplike sequence.

Many theorists also prefer **cyclical models** to the stage theory proposed by Tuckman (Hill & Gruner, 1973; Shambaugh, 1978). The cyclical models agree that certain issues tend to dominate group interaction during the various phases of a group's development, but they add that these issues can recur later in the life of the group. Bales's **equilibrium model,** for example, is based on the premise that group members strive to maintain a balance between accomplishing the task and enhancing the quality of the interpersonal relationships within the group (Bales, 1965). The group tends to oscillate between these two concerns, sometimes achieving high cohesiveness but then shifting toward a more work-centered focus:

> In the normal case of problem-solving, decision-making groups, after some period of concentration on Instrumentally Controlled behavior—task performance—people tend to "run out of gas," that is, they begin to turn in the Unfriendly (N), and then Emotionally Expressive (B) directions [see Bales & Strodtbeck, 1951]. From this point it is desirable (in my opinion) for the leader to help . . . bring the group behavior and imagery around to the Positive or Friendly direction again. After some period of reintegration of the Positive feelings of members toward each other and the group, another period of Instrumentally Controlled behavior may begin again. This is a kind

of optimum phase movement (not always realized) in task-oriented groups.
[Bales, Cohen, and Williamson, 1979, p. 107].

Bales thus argues that mature groups tend to shift back and forth between what Tuckman calls the norming and performing stages; a period
of prolonged group effort must be followed by a period of cohesion-cre-
ating interpersonal activity.

Tuckman's model, despite these theoretical caveats, summarizes much
of what we know about group development. Like most other groups the
Beatles did not meet one day and begin recording music. Rather, each
member had to get to know the others and become oriented toward the
group. Conflicts over the group's music and professional goals erupted
and had to be settled. Members had to learn to work together as a unit,
giving up personal goals to concentrate on the group's goals. The order of
these processes may differ among groups, and some groups may cycle repeatedly through some or all of these stages. At a general level, however,
group development tends to follow a predictable sequence.

GROUP SOCIALIZATION

In the spring of 1956 Pete Shotton and John Lennon formed a band called
the Quarry Men. When members dropped out, Lennon replaced them
with new recruits. One, a gifted guitarist named Paul McCartney, brought
his friend George Harrison to one of the group's performances; he would
soon join. But it wasn't until the summer of 1962 that Ringo Starr joined
the group. Starr replaced Pete Best, who was virtually driven from the
group by the others. Apart from his ability as a musician, which was considered to be subpar, Best was always aloof from the rest, never boisterous, never noisy, always controlled. Starr, whom the Beatles met while
playing in Hamburg, was chosen as much for his temperament as for his
skill.

The passage of time leaves its mark on a group and its members. As we
have already seen, developmental processes culminate in group-level
changes in levels of conflict, cohesion, and productivity. At the individual
level, each member's relationship to the group and to other members is
defined and redefined. When members leave the group, new members
must be recruited. When the group's leader steps down, others take on
the duties associated with the vacated role. When members fail to find a
place in the group, the group takes steps to expel them. Taken together,
these changes in the relationship between the individuals in the group
and the group itself are termed **group socialization.**

Socialization Processes

Can you remember a time when you joined an existing group? Perhaps
you took a job working for a small company or a fast-food restaurant. Or
you changed schools in the middle of the year when your family moved.

Have you ever been inducted into a fraternity or sorority, tried out for a sports team, moved into a new dormitory or apartment complex, or hovered for a time on the outskirts of a clique?

Our understanding of such situations owes much to the work of Richard Moreland and John Levine. These two group dynamicists have formulated a comprehensive model that describes how individuals are influenced by their passage through the group and how their passage, in turn, changes the group. Their model assumes that group socialization is intimately linked to three dynamic, reciprocal processes: evaluation, commitment, and role transition (Moreland, 1985, 1987; Moreland & Levine, 1982, 1984, 1988).

Evaluation. McCartney belonged to the group that evolved into the Beatles for 12 years. His entry and long-standing membership reflect his highly positive evaluation of the group and the group's positive evaluation of him. Initially, he was dissatisfied with the band's music, and many of the band members thought that he was pushy and quarrelsome. With changes in time and personnel, however, he and the group became quite satisfied with each other. Evaluation, then, is a reciprocal process: individuals appraise the group, and the group appraises them.

What factors influence evaluations? Social-exchange theory suggests that the exchange of rewards and costs is critical. If members receive or expect to receive relatively many rewards while suffering few costs, a positive evaluation is likely. Groups, too, will evaluate a member positively if the individual makes many contributions to the collective while exacting few costs (Kelley & Thibaut, 1978; Thibaut & Kelley, 1959). Both the group and each individual have a "general sense of the rewardingness" of their relationship (Moreland & Levine, 1982, p. 143).

One's assumptions about the value of groups in general can also influence the evaluation process. Consider new students entering college. Although some will decide to join an organization on campus, such as student government, a sorority, or a music club, others will avoid membership. Moreland and his colleagues found that students who had belonged to high school groups tried harder to find groups that would help them achieve their personal goals, provided those prior experiences had been positive. A student who was active in student government in high school, for example, was likely to investigate political parties on campus, but only if the high school experience had been rewarding (Pavelshak, Moreland, & Levine, 1986). Individuals with either little prior experience or negative experiences in groups avoided membership in groups (Bohrnstedt & Fisher, 1986; Gold & Yanof, 1985; Hanks & Eckland, 1978; Ickes, 1983, Ickes & Turner, 1983).

Commitment. The second process identified by Moreland and Levine, commitment, focuses on individuals' "enduring adherence" to the group and the group's adherence to its members (Kelley, 1983, p. 313). An individual who is committed to a group "is expected to stay in that relationship" for a relatively long period (Kelley, 1983, p. 287), and a group that is committed to its members strives to retain them. Importantly, commitment and a positive evaluation do not always occur together. One early member of the Beatles, Stu Sutcliffe, liked the group, but he wasn't committed to long-term membership. Conversely, McCartney felt that membership in the Beatles during the later years was unrewarding, but he still felt a strong sense of commitment to the band.

Commitment to a group is in many cases determined by the availability of alternative groups. Harrison, who barely knew how to play the guitar when he began performing, probably felt committed to the Beatles since other groups would not accept him as a member. Starr, on the other hand, had been a drummer for many groups, and hence his commitment was weaker. Members who feel that they have no alternative to remaining in the group are often the most committed.

Members also become more committed to a group the more they put into it. Although putting time, energy, and personal resources into a group raises the costs associated with membership, everyday experience suggests that people sometimes become more favorable toward their group the more they invest in it. Many groups require new members to pass elaborate initiation tests, on the premise that these personal investments strengthen the bond between the individual and the group. Similarly, people who join emotionally involving groups such as social movements or cults sometimes become more and more committed to the movement each time they make a personal investment in it (see Focus 4-3). Initiates in biker gangs, for example, must earn the right to wear the letters and emblems of their gang—their "colors"—by performing a variety of distasteful behaviors (Davis, 1982, p. 43):

> Gang members could defecate, urinate, vomit, spit, or pour liquids of any sort on the initiate's colors. The new member then donned his colors, which were to remain free from washing forever. . . . The initiation may also include the initiate's eating the carcass of a dead animal or parts thereof. He may also be required to consume large quantities of liquor or narcotics, or perform acts designed to shock the non-biker community.

. . . .
FOCUS 4-3: COSTS, COMMITMENT, AND THE PSYCHIC

Are devotees of sects, movements, or radical religious groups bound to these groups by their personal investments? Consider the group that formed around a psychic, Marion Keech. Keech asserted that she was receiving messages from the Guardians, whom she identified as the inhabitants of a planet named Clairon. Through these messages, Keech said, the Guardians warned her of the impending destruction of the world by flood. The Guardians, however, supposedly assured Keech that she and her followers would be rescued by flying saucer before the December 21 deadline.

As the 21st approached, the tension in the group waiting for the Guardians became unbearable. For weeks each member had supported the group's prophecy, often at the expense of friendships, finances, and public embarrassment. Some were college students who had let their grades go, since studying, they believed, was of little importance. Others had stopped paying their bills, quit their jobs, and severed relations with unbelieving family members and friends. The group members had changed their lives, and many felt that they could never reclaim their past ways of life. In the words of one member, "I've had to go a long way. I've given up just about everything. . . . I can't afford to doubt. I have to believe" (Festinger, Riecken, & Schachter, 1956, p. 168).

When December 21 came and went without any unearthly intervention, the group did not disband. Instead, Keech said that she had received a message that the dedication of the group had so impressed God that the Earth had been spared, and many of the members felt that they had helped save the world from a terrible flood. In the days after the disconfirmed prophecy the members seemed to become even more committed to their group, and they worked to recruit new members by publicizing the group's activities. Membership was costly, but each investment tied them more strongly to the group.

. . . .

Festinger's (1957) cognitive dissonance theory offers an intriguing explanation for the relationship between investment and commitment. Festinger and his colleagues, after studying the group described in Focus 4-3, concluded that the increased commitment that followed personal investment resulted from members' attempts to reduce the conflict among their beliefs about the group (Festinger, Riecken, & Schachter, 1956). Because the two cognitions, "I have invested in the group" and "The group has some cost-creating characteristics" are dissonant, Festinger contends these beliefs cause the members psychological discomfort. Although people can reduce cognitive dissonance in many ways, one frequent method is to emphasize the rewarding features of the group while minimizing the costly characteristics. By thinking more about the positive features of the group, individuals can reduce their uncertainty about its value.

Elliot Aronson and Judson Mills (1959) tested this intriguing hypothesis by manipulating the investments that individuals made before joining a group discussing topics related to sexual behavior. They randomly assigned female college students to one of three experimental conditions: a severe initiation condition, a mild-initiation condition, and a control condition. Subjects assigned to the severe initiation condition had to read aloud to the male experimenter a series of obscene words and two "vivid descriptions of sexual activity from contemporary novels." In the mild-initiation condition subjects read five sex-related but nonobscene words. In the control condition subjects were not put through any kind of initiation whatsoever.

At this point the subjects were told that their group was already meeting. The subjects couldn't interrupt the session, but they were given the opportunity to listen to the group discussion with headphones. What the subjects actually heard was a recorded group discussion that had been "deliberately designed to be as dull and banal as possible" (Aronson & Mills, 1959, p. 179). The participants discussed "dryly and haltingly" the sexual behavior of animals, mumbled frequently, uttered disjointed sentences, and lapsed into long silences.

Aronson and Mills expected that cognitive dissonance would be greatest for the people who had worked hardest to join the boring group. As predicted, when the participants evaluated the quality of the group discussion, the subjects from the severe-initiation condition were the most positive (see Figure 4-4).

Subjects in a conceptual replication of this study who were given electric shocks as an initiation also reacted more positively to the group (Gerard & Mathewson, 1966). Recent research suggests that the more favorable ratings that follow severe initiations may stem more from a desire to save face after making a faulty decision than from the psychic discomfort of cognitive dissonance, but the effect itself remains clear: people become more committed to their group after they invest in it (Schlenker, 1975).

Role transition.   The third and final socialization process is role transition, or changes in the behaviors enacted by individuals in and out of the

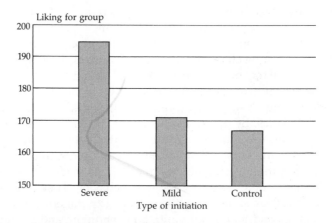

FIGURE 4-4. Group members' reactions to severe, mild, and no initiation. Ratings of the group discussion and the group members could range from highly negative (0) to highly positive (255). The average rating of 195.3 in the severe-initiation condition was significantly greater than the average ratings by subjects in the mild-initiation condition (171.1) or the control condition (166.7).

Source: Aronson & Mills, 1959

group. Moreland and Levine note that individuals usually move through a variety of roles, but they stress the importance of three: nonmember, quasi-member, and full member. Those who are not members of the group are considered *nonmembers*, but they "do not constitute a single, homogeneous social category" (Merton, 1957, p. 288). Some nonmembers are actually former members, whereas others have never been members. Some may be eligible for membership in the group but choose not to join, whereas others do not have the prerequisites of membership. And when nonmembers appraise the group, some are positive, some are negative, and some are simply indifferent (Fishbein, 1963). *Quasi-members* occupy a role that lies at the margins of the group, for they have either not yet been granted full membership or are being pushed out of the group by the others. *Full members*, in contrast, "are those who are most closely identified with the group and who have all the privileges and responsibilities associated with group membership" (Moreland & Levine, 1982, p. 149).

Like evaluation and commitment, role transition is a reciprocal process. Members cannot move from one role to another without the group's accepting and recognizing the move. Similarly, a group may try to relabel individuals' roles in a group, but unless they accept the role transition, they will not adhere to it. Because of the importance of mutual acceptance of transitions, groups often evolve systems of role change, rites of passage that amount to a public affirmation of a change in roles. Swearing in the president-elect, stripping dishonored military officers of their insignia, and giving the retiring employee a gold watch are all examples of rituals that punctuate a change in role (Garfinkel, 1956; Glaser & Strauss, 1971).

Over the course of his membership in the Beatles, McCartney moved through the roles of nonmember to full member and back to nonmember. Such transitions, however, are neither chaotic nor unpredictable. As the next section explains, socialization in groups seems to follow a stagelike pattern, with one transition providing the foundation for the next.

Stages of Socialization

Just as group development generally unfolds in an orderly way, so group socialization follows a cumulative, predictable sequence. Moreland and Levine (1982), drawing on studies of many types of groups—military units, self-help groups, church congregations, fraternities, classrooms, therapy groups, and work teams—conclude that members often move through five fundamental stages: investigation, socialization, maintenance, resocialization, and remembrance. During each stage the individual and the group evaluate each other, and the level of commitment also increases and decreases as the individual progresses through the socialization process. When members reach the transition point at the end of a stage, they experience a role transition and move into the next stage. This overall process is examined below and in Figure 4-5.

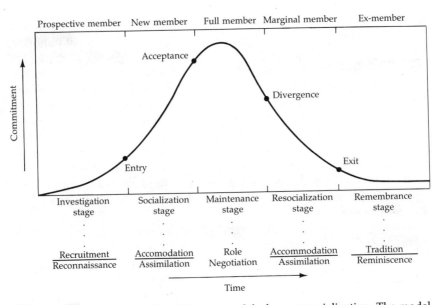

FIGURE 4-5. The Moreland and Levine model of group socialization. The model identifies five stages of socialization, demarcated by four transition points. Roles are listed across the top of the figure, and individual-level and group-level processes are shown at the bottom. The curved line represents a hypothetical individual's history of commitment in a group, but other patterns are equally likely.

Source: Moreland & Levine, 1982

Investigation. McCartney, before joining the Quarry Men, watched them perform several times and tried to decide if the band had any potential. The Quarry Men, too, hesitated for several weeks before accepting McCartney. Lennon, in particular, worried over the decision: "Up to that point, he had been the Quarry Men's undisputed leader. By admitting Paul, he would be creating a potential threat to that leadership. The decision was whether to remain strong himself or make the group stronger" (Norman, 1981, p. 44).

This cautious search for information is the hallmark of the *investigation* phase. During this period potential members engage in *reconnaisance;* they compare available groups with one another to determine which ones will best fulfill their needs. Groups, in turn, engage in *recruitment* as they try to estimate the value of each individual who is interested in joining them. In successful cases this mutual investigation ends when the group asks the candidate to join and the prospective member accepts. This transition point is termed *entry* (see Figure 4-5).

Socialization. The individual's move from prospective member to new member initiates the *socialization* process. In the group's eyes the initiate is a newcomer who must abandon old preconceptions in favor of the group's view. To the new member the group must be flexible enough to change to meet his or her particular needs. Again, socialization is a mutual process: through *assimilation* the individual accepts the group's norms, values, and perspectives, and through *accommodation* the group adapts to fit the newcomer's needs.

When this period of adjustment is completed, the *acceptance* transition point is reached, and the individual becomes a full member. This role transition point can be delayed, however, if the oldtimers react to the newcomer in negative ways. Newcomers, too, can prolong their assimilation into the group by remaining cautiously aloof or by misinterpreting other members' reactions. In a vivid illustration of this process Moreland (1985) arranged for groups of five unacquainted individuals to meet for several weeks to discuss various topics. To determine how people react when they think they are newcomers, he told two of the five that the group had been meeting for some time and that they were the only newcomers. Although the role of newcomer existed only in the minds of the two subjects, he found that they behaved differently than the others. Group members who thought that they were new to the group interacted more frequently and more positively with each other, they were less satisfied with the group discussion, and their descriptions of the group made reference to members' seniority. Thus, the belief that one is a newcomer who will be treated differently by the oldtimers can act as a self-fulfilling prophecy: the newcomers acted in ways that slowed their acceptance by the rest of the group.

Maintenance.   The socialization process does not end even when individuals become full-fledged group members. Even seasoned group members must adjust as the group changes through adding new members, adopting new goals in place old objectives, or modifying status and role relationships. Much of this *maintenance* phase is devoted to *role negotiation*. The group may, for example, require the services of a leader who can organize the group's activities and motivate members. The individual, in contrast, may wish instead to remain a follower in the group who is responsible for relatively routine matters. During this phase the group and the individual negotiate the nature and quantity of each member's expected contribution to the group.

Many group members remain in the maintenance period until their membership in the group reaches a scheduled conclusion. An employee who retires, a student who graduates from college, or an elected official whose term in office expires all leave the group after months or years of successful maintenance. In some cases, however, the maintenance process builds to a transition point that Moreland and Levine label *divergence*. The group may, for example, force individuals to take on roles that they do not find rewarding personally. Individuals, too, may fail to meet the group's expectations concerning appropriate behavior, and role negotiation may reach an impasse. When the divergence point is reached, the socialization process enters a new phase: resocialization.

Resocialization.   During resocialization the former full member takes on the role of a marginal member whose future in the group is uncertain. The individual sometimes precipitates this crisis, often in response to increased costs and dwindling rewards, waning commitment to the group, and dissatisfaction with responsibilities and duties. The group, too, can be the instigator, reacting to a group member who is not contributing or is working against the group's explicit and implicit purposes.

Moreland and Levine identify two possible outcomes of resocialization. The group and the individual, through accommodation and assimilation, can resolve their differences. In this instance *convergence* occurs, and the individual once more becomes a full member of the group. Alternatively, resocialization efforts can fail (see Figure 4-5). The group may conclude that the individual is no longer acceptable as a member and move to expel him or her. Similarly, the individual may reevaluate his or her commitment to the group and decide to leave. As a result, the divergence between the group and individual becomes so great that a final role transition is reached: *exit*.

Remembrance.   When the individual and the group finally reach a parting of the ways, one final task remains: the ex-member and the remaining group members review their shared experience during a period of *remembrance*. Former members *reminisce* about their time spent in the group. They may review their entry into the group, weigh their contributions and the outcomes of their membership, and make sense of their recent departure from the group. The group members, in contrast, discuss their former co-members by reviewing, for example, their commitment to the group, their contributions and actions while members of the group, and their reasons for leaving. If the group reaches a consensus on these issues, their conclusions become part of the group's *tradition*. This tradition often takes a negative tone, particularly when the individual's exit results from divergence during resocialization. This hostility toward individuals who leave the group may stem "from the threat to the group's values" that such individuals imply. The "ex-member is a living symbol of the inferiority imputed to the group's values" (Merton, 1957, p. 296), so the group tends to dismiss the contributions of such individuals.

Group Socialization: A Summary

How can McCartney's history with the Beatles be described? As Moreland and Levine's model suggests, group members' reactions to their group at any particular time are based on their evaluation of the value of membership, their commitment to the group, and their role in relationship to the group. McCartney, at the start of the investigation phase, did not admire the group nor was he himself committed to seeking membership. When he entered the group, however, his evaluation and commitment increased, and he spent many years in various roles within the group. Over time, however, incompatibilities created a gap between him and the others that resocialization could not heal; when the divergence became too great, he left the group. As with Tuckman's model of group development, an individual may not move through all the stages identified by Moreland and Levine, and the order may not follow that specified by the model. The model, however, yields considerable insight into the typical course that an individual follows from joining the group, to working in it, to leaving it.

ORGANIZATIONAL DEVELOPMENT

The management of the Harwood Manufacturing Corporation had a problem. The plant turned out a fairly basic product—pajamas—but production methods were modified frequently due to engineering advances and product alterations. Each modification, unfortunately, was met with protests and grievances from the line workers. It seemed to the women working in the factory that the management took pleasure in changing their jobs as soon as they had learned them perfectly. In consequence, turnover was high, productivity was down, and the amount of time needed for retraining after each production change was excessive.

Two group dynamicists, Lester Coch and John R. P. French, Jr., intervened to try to solve the problem (Coch & French, 1948). Approaching the problem from a developmental perspective, they devised three different training programs. Employees in the *no participation* program were not involved in the planning and implementation of the changes but were given an explanation for the innovations. Those in the *participation-through-representation* program attended group meetings where the need for change was discussed openly and an informal decision was reached. A subgroup was then chosen to become the "special" operators who would serve as the first training group. Employees in the third program, *total participation*, followed much the same procedures as those in the second method, but here all the employees, not a select group, were transferred to the training system.

The results of the innovation were impressive. The no-participation group improved very little, and hostility, turnover, and inefficiency within it remained high. In fact, 17% of these workers quit rather than learn the new procedure, and those who remained never reached the goals set by the management. The two participation conditions, in contrast, responded well. These workers learned their new tasks quickly, and their productivity soon surpassed prechange levels and management goals. Morale was high, only one hostile action was recorded, and none of the employees quit in the 40 days following the change. Furthermore, when the members of a control condition were run through a participation program several months later, they, too, reached appropriate production levels.

The Coch and French experiment is not the only example of a strategic attempt to promote effective change in groups and organizations. For instance, beginning in the late 1940s the executives at Texas Instruments, Inc., laid the foundations for what would become a billion-dollar-a-year enterprise. Showing remarkable insight into group processes, the management organized the employees into small groups whenever possible, took steps to build up team cohesiveness, and went to great lengths to establish clear goals based on realistic levels of aspiration (Bass & Ryterband, 1979). In the 1960s, in a related effort, the Banner Company, one of the largest packing manufacturers in the United States, systematically manipulated five organizational variables: emphasis on the work group, supportive supervision, participant leadership, organizational overlap among groups, and intensity of group interaction. These variables are highlighted in Rensis Likert's model of organizations (Likert, 1961). The study went on for several years, revealing consistent improvements in employee satisfaction, waste reduction, and turnover (Seashore & Bowers, 1970). At about the same time as the Banner project, the innovative management at the Harwood pajama plant began an elaborate series of changes designed to rework the organization of the recently purchased Weldon Company (Marrow, Bowers, & Seashore, 1967).

Because these efforts were generally quite effective, in recent years managers have been relying ever more heavily on group approaches to promote adaptive change in organizations. These approaches, which are collectively known as **organizational development** (or simply OD), often require assessing the organization's current stage of development, identifying future goals, and developing the means to achieve these organizational goals. If a company is having difficulty retaining employees, for example, the management may wish to interview workers and locate the source of the problem. If the executives of an international conglomerate become ensnared in petty squabbles during board meetings, they may hire a consultant who initiates a series of workshops to improve communication. If two companies are considering a merger, they may undertake elaborate planning to link the two organizations in the most profitable manner possible (Cole, 1987; French & Bell, 1984).

As Table 4-3 indicates, organizational-development consultants use a wide variety of strategies and techniques to promote growth (Buller, 1988; McGill, 1977; Varney, 1977). However, the three methods that are considered briefly below—survey feedback, process consultation, and team building—are among the most frequently encountered approaches to organizational development. Other methods, including T-group procedures and quality circles, are examined in more detail elsewhere (see Chapters 15 and 10, respectively).

Survey Feedback

Bill Busman was a personnel director, responsible for recruiting, training, and promoting employees in a wide range of positions. He was, therefore,

TABLE 4-3. A sampling of techniques used to promote
organizational development.

Method	Goal	Techniques
Survey feedback	Assessment of the organization's current state of development	Interviews, surveys, focus groups, structures and unstructured observation
Process consultation	Training group members to identify group processes (leadership, conflict) within the organization	Didactic instruction, role playing, structured process analysis, training in observational methods
Team building	Improving effectiveness by building cohesion, clarifying structure, and reducing conflict	Role analysis, interpersonal skill training, training in communication, retreats and workshops
Conflict diagnosis	Identifying sources of conflict within the organization and instituting conflict-management methods	Group discussions of conflict, intergroup conflict simulations, training in communication skills
Structure specification	Systematic analysis of group structure, including goals, procedures, roles, and implicit culture	Descriptive interviews, role-negotiation exercises, sociotechnical system design, job enrichment
Interpersonal skills training	Various activities that teach communication, leadership, and decision-making skills	Workshops, retreats, T-groups, short-term training sessions

well aware that a problem was developing on his staff. Recent months had seen an increase in turnover among the unit's secretaries and clerks, and despite several extensive conferences with office managers the source of the difficulty remained elusive. Losses in efficiency were growing more noticeable, and Busman realized that unless steps were taken to reverse the trend, upper-level management would soon be demanding answers.

In this type of situation an OD consultant might very well recommend using a strategy known as **survey feedback.** Developed in the 1950s by members of the Survey Research Center of the Institute for Social Research at the University of Michigan, the survey-feedback approach uses descriptive techniques to examine the organization's current stage of development (Mann & Likert, 1952). Initially, the consultant may gather information through observation, employee interviews, and surveys. Next, these findings are synthesized to form an overall picture of the organization that pinpoints both adequacies and inadequacies. These findings are then channeled back into the organization in the form of feedback, and in some instances the consultant develops a plan for changing the more problematic aspects of the organization.

Applied to Busman's problem, a survey-feedback analysis would begin by systematically assessing employees' attitudes toward their duties, their managers, and the organization as a whole. In a small company this poll may be taken by informally interviewing employees, but if the company is large and a wide sampling is required, the consultant may use a standard survey instrument such as the Management Diagnosis Chart (see Figure 4-6). This questionnaire, which was developed by Likert (1967), assesses several key dimensions of organizational climate, with higher scores reflecting smoother, more efficient functioning. After collecting an adequate sampling of employees' perceptions, the consultant typically summarizes these responses in an organizational profile. The average of employees' responses to each item is plotted on a diagnostic chart, which can be shared with the participating employees as well as the office managers. If a profile such as that graphed in Figure 4-6 is obtained, the OD consultant may conclude that the high turnover is being caused by poor leadership practices of the office managers, a lack of goal-oriented motivation among employees, and the company's centralized decision-making procedures. His or her recommendations for organizational development may therefore emphasize a more elaborate training program for corporate managers, a revitalized motivational system of group incentives and job enrichment, and a decentralization of procedures for setting goals.

Process Consultation

Suzanne Boss was delighted when she was promoted to director of the loan review section, but as the weeks went by, her delight turned into worry. The upper management had asked Suzanne to develop a revamped system for monitoring loan collateral, but the personnel she chose to complete the projection had already missed several deadlines. To spur the group's creativity, she scheduled weekly meetings to consider new ideas, but these sessions were characterized by so much irrelevant conversation and useless discussion of computer software that little was accomplished. Other problems were also surfacing in the unit, but she was not sure whether the fault lay with the staff, her leadership abilities, or the difficulty of the tasks facing the group.

OD experts called in to assist Boss in her diagnosis of the problem might decide to explore the unit's difficulties through **process consultation.** This approach, which has been most strongly advocated by Edgar Schein (1971), involves helping group members develop insight into the nature of their group's processes and their company's "culture of productivity" (Akin & Hopelain, 1986, p. 19). The consultant begins by observing the unit at work and takes note of patterns of communication and attraction, decision-making procedures, sources of power, informal social norms, the potency of in-group pressures, and varieties of intermember conflict. Once the consultant understands how the group is working, he or she discusses these observations with the unit. Through didactic instruction, role playing, and training in observational methods, the consultant and group members develop ways to improve the group's dynamics.

	Organizational variables	System 1	System 2	System 3	System 4	Item no.
Leadership	How much confidence and trust is shown in subordinates?	Virtually none	Some	Substantial amount	A great deal	1
Leadership	How free do they feel to talk to superiors about job?	Not very free	Somewhat free	Quite free	Very free	2
Leadership	How often are subordinates' ideas sought and used constructively?	Seldom	Sometimes	Often	Very frequently	3
Motivation	Is predominant use made of (1) fear, (2) threats, (3) punishment, (4) rewards, (5) involvement?	1, 2, 3, occasionally 4	4, some 3	some 3 and 5	5, 4, based on group	4
Motivation	Where is responsibility felt for achieving organization's goals?	Mostly at top	Top and middle	Fairly general	At all levels	5
Motivation	How much cooperative teamwork exists?	Very little	Relatively little	Moderate amount	Great deal	6
Communication	What is the usual direction of information flow?	Downward	Mostly downward	Down and up	Down, up, and sideways	7
Communication	How is downward communication accepted?	With suspicion	Possibly with suspicion	With caution	With a receptive mind	8
Communication	How accurate is upward communication?	Usually inaccurate	Often inaccurate	Often accurate	Almost always accurate	9
Communication	How well do superiors know problems faced by subordinates?	Not very well	Rather well	Quite well	Very well	10
Decisions	At what level are decisions made?	Mostly at top	Policy at top, some delegation	Broad policy at top, more delegation	Throughout but well integrated	11
Decisions	Are subordinates involved in decisions related to their work?	Almost never	Occasionally consulted	Generally consulted	Fully involved	12
Decisions	What does decision-making process contribute to motivation?	Not very much	Relatively little	Some contribution	Substantial contribution	13
Goals	How are organizational goals established?	Orders issued	Orders, some comments invited	After discussion, by orders	By group action (except in crisis)	14
Goals	How much covert resistance to goals is present?	Strong resistance	Moderate resistance	Some resistance at times	Little or none	15
Control	How concentrated are review and control functions?	Very highly at top	Quite highly at top	Moderate delegation to lower levels	Widely shared	16
Control	Is there an informal organization resisting the formal one?	Yes	Usually	Sometimes	No—same goals as formal	17
Control	What are cost, productivity, and other control data used for?	Policing, punishment	Reward and punishment	Reward, some self-guidance	Self-guidance, problem solving	18

FIGURE 4-6. A hypothetical profile of averaged responses to Likert's Management Diagnosis Chart. This abridged form of the instrument includes 18 questions focusing on leadership (1–3), motivation (4–6), communication (7–10), decision making (11–13), goals (14 and 15), and control (16–18).

Source: Likert, 1967

Applied to the example, process consultants may begin by observing the loan unit's weekly meetings. The consultants note such factors as where people sit around the conference table, who attends, who speaks to whom, and who offers task comments or socioemotional comments. They try to integrate this information in an overall portrayal of the group. The consultants then cautiously describe these dynamics to the group during their next meeting, and after much discussion the members may begin to understand the implications of their group's dynamics. The group will then agree to take special precautions, such as relocating offices to break up coalitions and regulating information flow through Boss's office, so that the efficiency of the unit can be improved.

Team Building

As he prepared for the weekly meeting, Arthur recalled how the previous session had been interrupted by a personal argument between two members, a 20-minute discussion of the company's new office furniture, and the loud snoring of one less-than-enthusiastic member. Overcoming an impulse to skip the meeting, Arthur arrived first despite being five minutes late. As others trickled in, they sat around the table in silence, and the few feeble attempts at conversation were short lived. Not too surprisingly, about a third of the members never showed up.

Arthur's group could profit from **team building.** This OD technique begins with the assumption that success in work groups results from a collaborative interdependence that develops through practice. The work-group-as-team analogy is fundamental to this approach, so in many ways team building in the workplace parallels team building in sports. For example, a game such as football—with its high interdependence among players and emphasis on group goals—requires elaborate teamwork if played with any degree of success. Players must practice continually until they function as a single unit, and the desire for personal success must be transformed into a desire for group success. The team's coach may create situations designed to foster a sense of team spirit, and he or she may encourage the players to formulate group goals, identify weaknesses in the team, and strive for cooperation and integration. Similarly, during team building in the work setting the manager/consultant acts as the coach by helping the group develop a sense of team unity. Just as athletes must learn how to pool their individual abilities and energies to maximize the team's performance, employees must learn to coordinate their efforts with those of the other group members. Group goals must be set, work patterns structured, and a sense of group identity developed. Individual members must learn how to coordinate their actions, and any strains and stresses in interpersonal relations need to be identified and resolved. Thus, team building emphasizes the analysis of work procedures, the development of positive member-to-member relationships, and the role of the manager as coach (Buller, 1986; Dyer, 1977; Hanson & Lubin, 1986; Orpen, 1986).

Applied to Arthur's group, team building may begin with a retreat or workshop held away from the work setting. This workshop lasts for several days to enable members to move past surface problems to more essential issues. A consultant runs the workshop, and she chooses to start things off with a discussion of the unit's problems. To show the group members that they can work together smoothly and efficiently, she utilizes special decisional procedures that stimulate productivity. As the day continues the results of the discussion are written on newsprint so that they can be posted around the conference room to remind participants that progress is being made. Once Arthur's group reaches agreement concerning the reasons for the group's difficulties—say, unclear goals, unstructured work procedures, and poor group decision-making skills—the consultant introduces specific activities designed to solve these problems. A structured goal-setting session is used to obtain members' agreement on a set of realistic objectives, and work procedures are reviewed and redesigned to make better use of the group's resources (Pritchard, Roth, Jones, Galgay, & Watson, 1988). To improve group-communication skills, the consultant arranges for the unit to work on tasks that are very similar to the activities that the group generally performs. A videotape is made of this activity to be critiqued later by the consultant and the group, and once specific limitations are noted, the group practices problem solving. Lastly, on the final day of the workshop the consultant asks the members to relax and open up by publicly voicing any gripes or dissatisfactions that they might have been suppressing thus far.

Organizational Development: A Summary
Team building, and survey feedback and process consultation as well, offer executives the means of controlling the rate and direction of corporate development. These methods, however, are not cure-alls. One review of 29 studies of team development, for example, concluded that the effectiveness of this OD method is not yet clear (Woodman & Sherwood, 1980). Other reviews have been similarly critical, and they suggest that OD should be integrated with (1) empirical procedures that will provide evidence of the effectiveness of the intervention, (2) programs that take individual-level socialization processes into consideration (Wanous, Reichers, & Malik, 1984), and (3) standard management practices (Buller, 1988). Although OD holds much promise, additional work is needed in this area before this promise can be fulfilled.

SUMMARY

Groups, as dynamic systems, change continually. *Group development*, or growth and change across the group's life span, operates at the group level. *Group socialization*, in contrast, is an individual-level process; over time the relationship between individuals in the group and the group itself changes. *Organizational development* suggests that the secret to achieving success in group settings lies in controlling both group development and group socialization.

Many theorists have described the typical course of development seen in groups, but most agree with Tuckman's so-called forming/storming/norming/performing/adjourning model.

1. *Orientation (forming) stage*. This stage is characterized by tentative interactions, tension, concern over ambiguity, growing interdependence, and attempts to identify the nature of the situation.

2. *Conflict (storming) stage*. Group members experience *conflict* when the actions of one or more of them are incompatible with, and resisted by, one or more of the other members. During this stage members often express dissatisfaction with the group, respond emotionally, criticize one another, and form coalitions. These negative processes, however, are a natural aspect of group development, As Bormann's *threshold theory* suggests, most groups experience periods of both *primary tension* and *secondary tension*.

3. *Cohesion (norming) stage*. The bonds linking the members to one another and to the group become stronger. When the group enters this stage, unity increases, membership stabilizes, the members report increased satisfaction, and the group's internal dynamics intensify.

4. *Task performance (performing) stage*. The group reaches a point at which it can perform as a unit to achieve desired goals. Not all groups reach this stage, for even highly cohesive groups are not necessarily productive.

5. *Dissolution (adjourning) stage*. The group is disbanded. A group's entry into the dissolution stage can be either planned or spontaneous, but even planned dissolution can create problems for members as they work to reduce their dependence on the group.

Tuckman's model is a *successive-stage theory*; it specifies the usual order of the phases of group development. *Cyclical models*, however, have also been proposed by theorists. Bales's equilibrium model, for example, maintains that a group can cycle through various stages repeatedly.

Just as groups develop, so individuals change as they pass through the group. Moreland and Levine's model of *group socialization* emphasizes three reciprocal processes:

1. *Evaluation*. Individuals appraise the group, and the group appraises the individual member. Evaluation is often based on the balance between rewards and costs and on one's assumptions about the value of groups in general.
2. *Commitment*. Individuals have an enduring adherence to the group, and the group adheres to its members. Commitment depends on the availability of alternative groups and the amount of investment the individual has made in the group.
3. *Role transition*. Individuals in and out of the group usually move through a variety of roles, including nonmember, quasi-member, and full member.

Just as group development generally unfolds in an orderly pace, so group socialization follows a predictable sequence: investigation, socialization, maintenance, resocialization, and remembrance.

The field of *organizational development* (or simply OD) is based on the idea that the processes of group development and group socialization can be controlled to maximize organizational effectiveness. OD interventions serve both diagnostic and prescriptive functions, and they include:

1. *survey feedback:* the assessment of the organization's current state of development through the use of interviews, surveys, focus groups, and structured and unstructured observation
2. *process consultation:* training group members to identify group processes (leadership, conflict) within the organization through didactic instruction, role playing, structured process analysis, and training in observational methods
3. *team building:* fostering cohesion, clarifying structure, and reducing conflict through the use of role analysis, interpersonal-skills training, communication training, retreats, and workshops

·5·

Group Structure

No pilot's announcement, no flashing lights, and no buzzing alarm warned the rugby team aboard the Fairchild F-227 that its chartered plane was too close to the snow-capped Andes peak named Tinguiririca. The sudden crash killed the pilot and flight crew, leaving the surviving passengers to fend for themselves. Their only shelter from the cold and snow was the broken fuselage. Food was scarce, they melted snow for their drinking water, and the only fuel for a fire came from a couple of wooden crates. Injured and exhausted, the group members argued intensely over the likelihood of a rescue. Some insisted that searchers would soon find them. Others maintained that they must climb down from the mountain. Some became so apathetic that they didn't care. At night the cries of the injured were often answered with anger rather than pity, for the severely cramped sleeping arrangements created continual conflict. And early one morning, as they were sleeping, an avalanche filled the cabin with snow, and many died before they could dig their way out.

The group escaped from the crash site after nearly three months. But the group that came down from Andes was not the same group that began the chartered flight; the pattern of relationships among the group members, or the group's structure, had been altered. The survivors began the ordeal without a leader but ended up with a plethora of "commanders," "lieutenants," and "explorers." Men who were at first afforded little respect or courtesy eventually earned considerable status within the group. Some of the men who were well liked before the crash became outcasts, and some who hardly spoke to the others became active communicators within the group. As the harsh environment taxed the group to the limit, new structures emerged that redefined who would lead, clean, and explore (role structure), who gave orders and who carried them out (authority structure), who was liked and who was treated with contempt (attraction structure), and who communicated frequently or only infrequently (communication structure).

Any group, whether one stranded in the Andes, one sitting around a conference table, or one playing soccer in a packed stadium, can be better understood by studying its **structure:** the underlying pattern of stable relationships among the group members. Just as physicists, when studying an unknown element, analyze its basic atomic structure rather than its superficial features, so group dynamicists look beyond the unique features of groups for evidence of these basic structures. Four of these key structural components—roles, authority, attraction, and communication—are examined in this chapter, but this listing doesn't exhaust all the ways in

110

which members are joined. Indeed, in later chapters we will examine a number of other structural properties of groups, including norms and reward structures (see Jones & James, 1979; and Scott & Scott, 1981, for reviews).

ROLES

On the day after the crash Marcelo, the captain of the rugby team, organized the efforts of those who could work. Two young men and and one of the women administered first aid to the injured. A subgroup of boys melted snow for drinking water, and another team cleaned the cabin of the airplane. These various positions in the group—leader, doctor, snow melter, cabin cleaner—are all examples of **roles:** sets of behaviors that are characteristic of persons in a particular social context (Biddle, 1979). When the passengers enacted particular roles in the group, they were engaging in a fairly standard set of behaviors, and others in the group generally responded to them in particular ways.

Roles within a group are, in some respects, similar to roles in a play. For dramatists roles describe the characters that actors portray before the audience. To become Romeo in Shakespeare's *Romeo and Juliet*, for example, the actor must perform certain actions and recite his dialogue accordingly. Similarly, roles in groups structure behavior by dictating the "part" that members take as they interact. Once cast in a role such as leader, outcast, or questioner, the group member tends to perform certain actions and interact with other group members in a particular way.

Just as some variability is permitted in theatrical roles, roles do not structure group members' actions completely. When an actor lands the role of Romeo, he memorizes the script and rehearses his actions. He must perform certain behaviors as part of his role; he wouldn't be Shakespeare's Romeo if he didn't fall in love with Juliet. He can, however, recite his lines in an original way, change his stage behaviors, or even ad lib. In social groups, too, different people can fulfill the same role in somewhat different ways, and so long as they do not stray too far from the role's basic requirements the group tolerates this variation. However, like the stage director who replaces an actor who presents an unsatisfactory Romeo, the group can replace members who repeatedly fail to play their part within the group. Indeed, roles often supersede any particular group members. When the role occupant departs, the role itself remains and is filled by a new member (Sarbin & Allen, 1968; Shaw & Costanzo, 1982; Stryker & Statham, 1985).

Role Differentiation

Group roles and dramatic roles share many similarities, but they differ significantly as well. Whereas playwrights deliberately create roles and directors select actors to portray these roles, roles in small groups develop over time. When the group forms, the participants typically consider themselves members, basically similar to one another. Yet gradually, in a process called **role differentiation,** various roles emerge. Among the Andes survivors this process proceeded very rapidly, as might have been expected from past research suggesting that differentiation is accelerated in groups that must cope with emergencies or deal with difficult problems (Bales, 1958). In this group along with leader, doctor, and cleaner emerged the role of "inventor," who created makeshift snowshoes, hammocks, and water-melting devices; "explorer," who was determined to hike down from the mountain, and "complainer," "pessimist," "optimist," and "encourager."

Researchers admit that the roles that emerge during this process are often unique to a particular group. Many believe, however, that some roles are more common than others and that certain types of roles will develop in virtually all groups. For example, the roles of Romeo and Juliet may be unique to Shakespeare's play, but a protagonist and antagonist are found in almost any play. Similarly, evidence indicates that group roles become increasingly differentiated over time into one of two basic categories. Some roles, such as explorer and inventor, are **task roles,** for their occupants are concerned with accomplishing the task at hand, organizing the group to attain goals, and providing support for all the other group members. Other individuals, like the encourager or optimist, adopt **socioemotional roles;** they regularly perform actions that help satisfy the emotional needs of the group members.

Task and socioemotional roles. Early theorists suggested that role differentiation usually begins with the majority of the members recognizing one or more individuals as leaders and the remainder as followers (see Hare, 1976). Among the Andes survivors, for example, Marcelo took on the leadership role, for his position as team captain generalized to the new situation. He organized work squads and controlled the rationing of their meager food supplies, and the rest of the members obeyed his orders. Like doctor and patient, teacher and student, or mother and daughter, Marcelo and his followers were *role partners* linked together in a reciprocal relationship.

Because most of Marcelo's leadership activities were centered on the performance of group tasks, he ably filled the role of *task specialist*: he motivated the group to work, assigned tasks to members, and provided guidance and advice (see Table 5-1). He did not, however, satisfy the group members' emotional needs. By the ninth day of the ordeal morale was sagging, and Marcelo began crying silently to himself at night. Yet, as if to offset Marcelo's inability to cheer up the survivors, several group members became more positive and friendly, actively trying to reduce conflicts and to keep morale high. For example, the only surviving woman, Liliana Methol, provided a "unique source of solace" for the young men she cared for, and she came to take the place of their absent mothers and sweethearts. One of the younger boys "called her his god-mother, and she responded to him and the others with comforting words and gentle optimism" (Read, 1974, p. 74).

TABLE 5-1. Task roles and socioemotional roles in groups.

Role	Function
	Task Roles
Initiator/contributor	Recommends novel ideas about the problem at hand, new ways to approach the problem, or possible solutions not yet considered
Information seeker	Emphasizes getting the facts by calling for background information from others
Opinion seeker	Asks for more qualitative types of data, such as attitudes, values, and feelings
Information giver	Provides data for forming decisions, including facts that derive from expertise
Opinion giver	Provides opinions, values, and feelings
Elaborator	Gives additional information—examples, rephrasings, implications—about points made by others
Coordinator	Shows the relevance of each idea and its relationship to the overall problem
Orienter	Refocuses discussion on the topic whenever necessary
Evaluator/critic	Appraises the quality of the group's methods, logic, and results
Energizer	Stimulates the group to continue working when discussion flags
Procedural technician	Cares for operational details, such as the materials, machinery, and so on
Recorder	Takes notes and maintains records
	Socioemotional Roles
Encourager	Rewards others through agreement, warmth, and praise
Harmonizer	Mediates conflicts among group members
Compromiser	Shifts his or her own position on an issue in order to reduce conflict in the group
Gatekeeper and expediter	Smooths communication by setting up procedures and ensuring equal participation from members
Standard setter	Expresses, or calls for discussion of, standards for evaluating the quality of the group process
Group observer and commentator	Points out the positive and negative aspects of the group's dynamics and calls for change if necessary
Follower	Accepts the ideas offered by others and serves as an audience for the group

(Source: Benne & Sheats, 1948)

The development of an emotionally supportive role in addition to the task-specialist role is consistent with studies conducted at the National Training Laboratories (NTL), an organization devoted to the improvement of groups. These studies suggest that a group generally requires the services of both a task specialist to help it work in the direction of its goals and a *socioemotional specialist* who intervenes regularly to reduce interpersonal strains and stresses within the group. As Table 5-1 indicates, specific duties often accompany each one of these two roles (Benne & Sheats, 1948).

Why differentiation? Why do task roles and socioemotional roles emerge in so many different groups? One answer, proposed by Bales and his colleagues, suggests that very few individuals can simultaneously fulfill both the task and socioemotional needs of the group (Bales, 1955, 1958; Parsons, Bales, & Shils, 1953). When task specialists try to move groups toward their goals, they must necessarily give orders to others, restrict the behavioral options of others, criticize other members, and prompt them into action. These actions may be necessary to reach the goal, but the group members may react negatively to the task specialists' prodding. Because most of the members believe the task specialist to be the source of the tension, "someone other than the task leader must assume a role aimed at the reduction of interpersonal hostilities and frustrations" (Burke, 1967, p. 380). The peacekeeper who intercedes and tries to maintain harmony is the socioemotional specialist.

Phillip E. Slater, in an investigation carried out in the 1950s, examined the emergence of these two roles by making use of Bales's IPA system of group observation (Slater, 1955). (Chapter 2 explained that Bales's system helps the observer identify certain specific types of behavior, such as agreeing with others, giving suggestions, asking for opinions, and showing tension. Table 2-1 lists the 12 behavior categories.) Half of the categories in the IPA focus on task-oriented behaviors, either direct attempts to solve specific problems in the group or attempts to exchange information via questioning. The remaining six categories are reserved for positive socioemotional behavior (solidarity, tension release, agreement) or negative socioemotional behavior (disagrees, shows tension, shows antagonism).

Slater used this system to record and compare the behaviors initiated by and received by the task specialist (labeled the "idea man" by Slater) and the socioemotional specialist (labeled the "best-liked man") in a number of groups. Just as Bales hypothesized, the individuals who occupied the two roles behaved very differently. The task specialist tended to dominate in the problem-solving area by giving more suggestions and opinions and by providing more orientation than the socioemotional specialist. The latter, however, dominated in the interpersonal areas by showing more solidarity, more tension release, and greater agreement with other group members. Moreover, when on the receiving end the task specialist tended to elicit more questions, displays of tension, antagonism, and disagreement, whereas the socioemotional specialist received more demonstrations of solidarity, tension reduction, and solutions to problems. Bales (1958) suggests that these data demonstrate that the two types of roles frequently exist simultaneously in groups, although alternative interpretations have been offered (Verba, 1961; Wilson, 1970).

Role Stress

The roles of Romeo and Juliet are not the only parts that must be played in Shakespeare's drama. Innumerable actors are needed for the supporting parts, such as guard, festival celebrant, and spectator. Such roles, although essential to the play, differ from the leading roles in terms of their relative complexity. Whereas Romeo is in many scenes, displaying many emotions, taking many actions, and reciting line after line of dialogue, the guard's actions are relatively few and limited in scope. The role of Romeo also includes many subsidiary roles such as lover, swordsman, devoted son, and friend, but the guard is basically just a guard.

Variation in the complexity of roles also occurs in groups; members expect the occupants of some roles to perform only one type of behavior, whereas a wide range of behaviors is required of others. Like the star of a play, those who enact complex roles often enjoy greater status in the group. Yet complex roles can create considerable stress for occupants, particularly when the behaviors associated with the role are poorly defined (role ambiguity) or inconsistent with one another (role conflict).

Role ambiguity.   When the the behavioral requirements associated with a particular role are unclear, the individual who is supposed to enact that role may experience **role ambiguity.** Imagine, for example, a young woman who has just been hired to fill a new position in a company, labeled assistant to the vice-president. She may wish to fulfill all her duties with dispatch and competency, but because the role is a new one, expectations associated with it may be unclear. As a result she constantly wonders if she is acting appropriately and she sometimes performs behaviors that others in the organization should be carrying out (see Focus 5-1).

Role conflict.   In some instances group members may find themselves occupying several roles at the same time, with the requirements of each role making demands on their time and abilities. If the multiple activities required by one mesh with those required by the other, the individuals who adopt these roles experience few problems. If, however, the expectations that define the appropriate activities associated with these roles are incompatible, **role conflict** may occur (Brief, Schuler, & Van Sell, 1981; Graen, 1976; Kahn, Wolfe, Quinn, Snoek, & Rosenthal, 1964; Van Sell, Brief, & Schuler, 1981).

Researchers have identified many varieties of role conflict, but two of the more problematic types are interrole conflict and intrarole conflict. **Interrole conflict** occurs when the person trying to enact two or more roles discovers that behaviors associated with one role are incompatible with those associated with the other roles. A woman who has been a member of a small production unit for several years, for example, may experience role conflict when she is promoted to a supervisory position; the behaviors required of her as manager may clash with the role of friend and workmate. Similarly, college students may find that the student role conflicts with another role, such as boyfriend, girlfriend, husband, or wife. If the student role requires spending every free moment in the library studying for exams, such roles as companion and friend will be neglected.

Intrarole conflict results from contradictory demands within a single role. A supervisor in a factory, for example, may be held responsible for overseeing the quality of production, training new personnel, and providing feedback or goal-orienting information. At another level, however, supervisors become the supervised, because they take directions from a higher level of management. Thus, the members of the team expect the manager to keep their secrets and support them in any disputes with the management, but the upper echelon expects obedience and loyalty (Katz & Kahn, 1978; Miles, 1976). In addition, role conflict can stem from differences in expectations held by the person enacting the role (the role taker) and people who are responding to that individual (role senders). For example, the newly appointed supervisor may assume that leadership means giving orders, maintaining strict supervision, and criticizing incompetence. The work group, however, may feel that leadership entails eliciting cooperation in the group, providing support and guidance, and delivering rewards. As Focus 5-1 indicates, such contrasting expectations would probably produce problems in the group's role relations.

· ·
FOCUS 5-1: ROLE STRESS IN THE WORKPLACE

The workplace, with its emphasis on efficiency and productivity, is stressful enough without adding problems of role ambiguity and conflict. Most businesses, however, are based on complex organizational structures that make conflicting demands on the occupants of various positions. If role ambiguity occurs, workers may experience uncertainty about their responsibilities, leading to such complaints as these (House, Schuler, & Levanoni, 1983, p. 336):

- I don't know what is expected of me.
- I work under unclear policies and guidelines.
- The planned goals and objectives are not clear.
- I don't know how I will be evaluated for a raise or promotion.

Role conflict, in contrast, occurs when employees experience "an incompatibility between job tasks, resources, rules or policies, and other people" (Nicholson & Goh, 1983, p. 149). Role conflict can prompt such complaints as these (House et al., 1983, p. 336):

- I work with two or more groups who operate quite differently.
- I often get myself involved in situations with conflicting requirements.
- I'm often asked to do things that are against my better judgment.
- I do things that are likely to be accepted by one person and not by others.
- I receive incompatible requests from two or more people.

Researchers have implicated both role ambiguity and role conflict as potential sources of low employee morale and job stress. In one study of accountants and hospital employees, for example, role stress was linked to feelings of tension, decreased job satisfaction, and employee turnover (Kemery, Bedeian, Mossholder, & Touliatos, 1985). Similarly, a large-scale review of 42 studies of role conflict obtained the findings presented in Table 5-2 (Fisher & Gitelson, 1983). The size of the relationships varied considerably across studies, but in general, increases in role ambiguity and conflict were associated with an increased desire to leave the organization and with decreases in commitment to the organization, involvement, satisfaction, and participation in decision making.

What can organizations do to help their employees cope with role stress? One solution involves making role requirements explicit; managers should write job descriptions for each role within the organization and provide employees with feedback about the behaviors expected of them. The workplace can also be designed so that potentially incompatible roles are performed in different locations and at different times. In such cases, however, the individual must be careful to engage in behaviors appropriate to the specific roles, because slipping into the wrong role at the wrong time can lead to considerable embarrassment (Gross & Stone, 1964). Some companies, too, develop explicit guidelines regarding when one role should be sacrificed so that another can be enacted, or they may prevent

TABLE 5-2. Average correlations among role ambiguity, role conflict, and work satisfaction.

Variable	Correlation with Role Ambiguity	Correlation with Role Conflict
Propensity to leave	.32	.29
Organizational commitment	−.34	−.25
Job involvement	−.26	−.15
Satisfaction with pay	−.12	−.20
Satisfaction with co-workers	−.22	−.31
Satisfaction with promotion	−.24	−.26
Satisfaction with supervision	−.37	−.37
Participation in decision making	−.51	−.28

(*Source:* Fisher & Gitelson, 1983, pp. 323–324)

employees from occupying positions that can create role conflicts. Ambiguity and conflict can reach epidemic levels in most organizations, but inventions aimed at restructuring the workplace offer a potential cure (Brief, et al., 1981; Sarbin & Allen, 1968; Van Sell, et al., 1981).

. . . .

AUTHORITY

The roles that emerged in the Andes group following the crash defined who would lead, explore, and care for the injured. The individuals who took on these roles, however, were not equal in terms of authority in the group. Fito Strauch, for example, was more influential than the other group members; when he gave orders, most of the others obeyed. Also, the group's explorers were afforded more authority than the rank-and-file members. These stable variations in dominance, prestige, and control among the group members reflect a second structural aspect of groups: **status relations, or authority relations.**

Status patterns are often hierarchical and centralized. Consider the Andes group, as depicted in Figure 5-1. Fito Strauch, joined by his two cousins, E. Strauch and Fernandez, headed up a coalition that controlled most of the group's activities. This triumvirate, moreover, was supported by its "lieutenants": a group of three younger men who made certain that the leaders' orders were enforced and who also carried out certain minor duties. Their requests carried less force than those of Fito Strauch, but they still commanded a fair amount of respect.

Below the lieutenants we find a special class of group members called the explorers. These individuals were the fittest and strongest and had been chosen to hike down the mountain in search of help. In preparing for their journey, they were given special privileges, including better sleeping arrangements and more clothing, food, and water. They were not leaders in the usual sense, but they could require lower echelon members to obey their orders. These lower ranking members fell into three clusters. The rank-and-file members included three men who, because of their youth and disposition, were considered to be childish and unstable. Their authority was equal to that of the four men who had received disabling injuries but somewhat greater than that of the two group members who were considered to be malingerers.

Figure 5-1 depicts the levels of authority that existed in the group: the power holders at the top of the hierarchy made more decisions, took more responsibility, and served as the foci for communication within the group. Below this top level was a second stratum of members who had less power than the leaders but more prestige than the occupants of lower echelons. As we move down the chain of command, authority diminishes and the number of occupants at each subordinate level increases. Hence, the lines of group authority formed a pyramid pattern like that of formally organized groups such as businesses and military organizations (Dale, 1952).

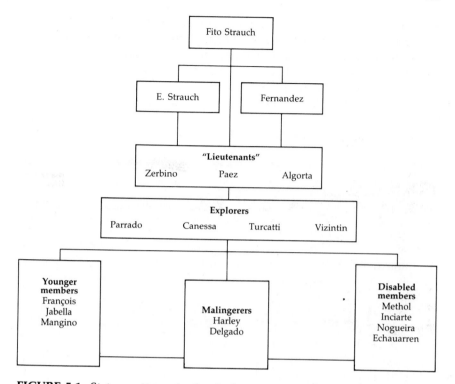

FIGURE 5-1. Status patterns in the Andes survivors (after the avalanche): an example of a hierarchical, centralized authority structure.

Status differences in groups violate our expectations of "equal treatment for all," but in the microsociety of the group, equality is the exception and inequality the rule. Initially, group members may start off on an equal footing. Over time, however, **status differentiation** usually takes place: certain individuals acquire the authority to coordinate the activities of the group, providing others with guidance and relaying communications (Bales, 1950; Fisek & Ofshe, 1970). How and why these status structures evolve is not completely known, but the two theories discussed below (expectation-states theory and dominance theory) offer potential answers.

Expectation States and Status

Joseph Berger and his colleagues trace the development of status differentiation back to group members' initial expectations. Their **expectation-states theory** assumes that status differences are most likely to develop when members are working collectively on a task that they feel is important. Because the group hopes it can successfully complete the project, group members intuitively take note of one another's status characteristics—that is, any personal qualities that they think are indicative of ability or prestige. Those who possess numerous status characteristics are implicitly identified and then permitted to perform more numerous and varied group actions, to provide greater input and guidance for the group, to influence others by evaluating their ideas, and to reject the influence attempts of others. (The basic propositions of the theory are discussed in Berger, Cohen, & Zelditch, 1972; Berger, Conner, & Fisek, 1974; Berger, Fisek, Norman, & Zelditch, 1977; Berger, Webster, Ridgeway, & Rosenholtz, 1986; Humphreys & Berger, 1981; and Ridgeway, Berger, & Smith, 1985.)

Expectation-states theorists believe that we generally take two types of cues into consideration when allocating status in our groups. First, we consider *specific-status characteristics*, qualities that attest to each individual's level of ability at the task to be performed in the given situation. On a basketball team, for example, height may be a specific status characteristic, whereas prior jury duty may determine status in a jury (Strodtbeck & Lipinski, 1985). In the Andes group the higher status explorers were chosen on the basis of several specific status qualities: strength, determination, health, and maturity.

Second, we also notice *diffuse-status characteristics*, any general quality of the person that the members think is relevant to ability and evaluation. Sex, age, wealth, ethnicity, status in other groups, or cultural background can serve as diffuse-status characteristics if people associate these qualities with certain skills, as did the members of the Andes group. Among the survivors age was considered to be an important diffuse characteristic, with youth being negatively valued.

Cecilia Ridgeway (1982, 1984), in an extensive review of status differentiation, concludes that expectation-states theory accurately describes how status is allocated in most cooperative groups. In such groups members are striving to accomplish their goals, and they are willing to confer status on those who will contribute skills and energy to that purpose. The end result is that people with positively evaluated specific-status and diffuse-status characteristics usually command more authority than those who lack status-linked qualities. (Berger et al., 1977; Fox & Moore, 1979; Greenstein, 1981; Greenstein & Knottnerus, 1980; Ridgeway, 1984; Ridgeway, et al., 1985; and Webster & Driskell, 1978, 1983, present reviews of the available evidence.)

Expectations-states theory also offers a cogent explanation for **status generalization:** "the tendency for external status characteristics to determine internal group structure" (Molm, 1986, p. 1363). Consider, for example, a jury with 12 members that includes

• Dr. Prof, a 40-year-old White female college professor who teaches in the college of business and who has written several books on management.
• Mr. Black, a 35-year-old Black executive with outstanding credentials and long experience in a leadership position
• Dr. White, 58-year-old male physician who has an active general practice.

Of these three individuals, whom would a group of White, middle-class jurors select to be the foreman?

Considerable evidence suggests that this hypothetical group would probably be biased against Dr. Prof and Mr. Black and biased in favor of Dr. White. All too often, both gender and race operate as diffuse status characteristics, for women and Blacks are given less status and authority in groups than are Whites and men. Thus, Dr. Prof and Mr. Black, despite their specific status credentials, may be disqualified from positions of status in the group by their diffuse, and completely irrelevant, status characteristics. In contrast, because Dr. White has a high-prestige occupation (physician), status generalization will work in his favor. Indeed, Dr. White poses little incongruency for the group, if the group members unfairly consider advanced age, white skin, and an M.D. degree to be positive features. Hence, Dr. White ends up as the group leader (see Lockheed & Hall, 1976; Lockheed, Harris, & Nemceff, 1983; Riordan, 1983; Webster & Driskell, 1978, 1983). (See Focus 5-2.)

Although specific- and diffuse-status characteristics have a considerable impact on status in groups, Ridgeway notes that status differentiation also results from competition among members. In a board meeting, for example, one executive may belittle the work of another. In the Andes group one of the men tried to gain control over the food supplies through deceit. In the classroom a student may try to stare down the instructor. As we will see in the next section, group members don't always apportion authority on the basis of status characteristics: sometimes individuals gain status by exhibiting aggressive or dominant interpersonal behaviors.

• •

FOCUS 5-2: OVERCOMING STATUS GENERALIZATION BIASES

Despite recent changes in sexist and racist attitudes in society, stereotypical biases still make gaining status in small groups a difficult task for women, Blacks, and other minorities. As a result, groups that are heterogeneous with regard to gender, race, ethnic background, and so on are often characterized by individual stress and group strain. Women and Blacks report dissatisfaction with their unfairly low status rankings, and often the rest of the group is uncertain about their status (Crosbie, 1979; Hembroff, 1982; McCranie & Kimberly, 1973). Group performance, too, can suffer as the group overlooks the valuable contributions offered by members who are competent but not considered worthy of high status (Kirchler & Davis, 1986).

These negative effects can be overcome, however. As a first step, individuals who possess status-limiting qualities must learn to look past their group's negative expectations. The lone Black member of an otherwise all-White group, for example, must be careful not to accept a low-status position if the group is biased (Cohen, 1982; Katz, 1970; Riordan & Ruggiero, 1980). Second, studies indicate that biases in status allocations can be overcome over time as women and minorities demonstrate their abilities at the group tasks (Cohen & Roper, 1972). Groups are often unfair, for women and minorities must put extra effort into their activities just to remain on a par with the advantaged white men. Eventually, though, they will find that they no longer need to continually prove themselves to the others (Hembroff & Myers, 1984; Markovsky, Smith, & Berger, 1984). Claiming the right to high status does not seem to be as effective as demonstrating that right through successful performance (Freeze & Cohen, 1973; Martin & Sell, 1985; Pugh & Wahrman, 1983).

Third, Ridgeway recommends that women and minorities can gain status in groups if they act in a group-oriented manner rather than a self-oriented way (Ridgeway, 1982). In her research she trained male and female confederates to adopt either a cooperative, friendly interaction style or an emotionally distant, self-absorbed style. As she predicted, men in otherwise all-female groups achieved high status no matter what style they exhibited. Women in otherwise all-male groups, in contrast, achieved high status only if they displayed a group-oriented motivation. These results are encouraging; although they indicate that status generalization continues to create biases in status differentiation, they also suggest that these biases are not an intractable aspect of mixed-gender and interracial groups.

. . . .

Dominance and Status

Consider the parallels between status patterns in human groups and the *pecking orders* seen in many nonhuman social species. The individual at the top of these status hierarchies, who is termed the alpha male or female, enjoys greater access to the group's resources. These high-ranking members maintain their position by threatening or attacking low-ranked members, who, in turn, manage to avoid these attacks by performing behaviors that signal deference and submissiveness. This system of dominance and submission places limits on the amount of conflict that occurs within the group and, hence, ensures individual and group survival (Mazur, 1973; Wilson, 1975).

Dominance theorists propose that humans, too, are influenced by behaviors that signal dominance and submissiveness. When people wish to gain greater authority over others, or convey their own lack of power, they often display behaviors that signal their interpersonal dominance or weakness (Lee & Ofshe, 1981; Mazur, 1983; Mazur et al., 1980; Ofshe & Lee, 1981). Anyone who has witnessed a boss giving orders to an errant subordinate, a student standing before an aggravated teacher, or a doctor discussing symptoms with a patient has undoubtedly seen these verbal and nonverbal interpersonal cues.

On the verbal side, higher status individuals' comments often hint at their wider experience, greater knowledge, and better judgment (Godfrey, Jones, & Lord, 1986). In a study group, for example, a high-status member may say "I've studied this theory before," "I know this stuff backwards and forwards," or "I think it's more important to study the lecture notes than the text." A low-status individual, in contrast, may lament that "I always have trouble with this subject" or "I'm not sure I understand the material." In general, high-status individuals tend to (1) tell other people what they should do, (2) interpret other people's statements, (3) confirm or dispute other people's viewpoints, and (4) summarize or reflect on the discussion. High-status people can also be presumptuous. As Focus 5-3 explains, they often maintain that they understand other group members' viewpoints even when they do not (Stiles, Waszak, & Barton, 1979).

. . . .
FOCUS 5-3: PROFESSORIAL PRESUMPTUOUSNESS

According to William B. Stiles, when high- and low-status individuals meet in interaction, the alpha woman or man often presumes an understanding of the low-status person's position. The power holder's claim to insight may be warranted, but in many cases such presumptuousness is unjustified (Stiles, 1978, 1981; Stiles, Putnam, & Jacob, 1982; Stiles, Orth, Scherwitz, Hennrikus, & Vallbona, 1984).

Stiles measures presumptuousness using the taxonomy shown in Table 5-3. In this coding system presumptuousness occurs whenever the speaker's statements contain relatively large amounts of the final four categories: *advisement* about what the other person should do, *interpretations* of

TABLE 5-3. A taxonomy for coding verbal statements.

Type of Statement	Definition	Example
Disclosure	Statement of personal information, feelings, opinions	• I'm bored. • I am a group dynamicist.
Question	A request for information	• Do you like my bow? • What's for breakfast?
Edification	A statement of information from an objective frame of reference	• The time is 11:11 A.M. • The next test will be very difficult.
Acknowledgment	An indication of recognition of another person	• Hello. • I heard that.
Advisement	A suggestion that another person should do something	• Drop that gun. • Read Chapter 5 closely.
Interpretation	Rephrasing or explaining another person's statements	• Your statements show how angry you are.
Confirmation	Stating agreement or disagreement with another's statements	• I think group dynamics is fun, too.
Reflection	Summarizing or repeating another's statements	• But last week you said you opposed the plan.

the other person statements, *confirmations* of the other's viewpoint, and *reflections* about the other's statements.

Stiles and his co-workers illustrated the utility of the coding system in one study by studying the presumptuousness of university teachers who were talking to their students (Stiles et al., 1979). When their classroom statements were coded, the professors were far more presumptuous than their students, for they made such remarks as "Try looking at the bottom of page 24," "I don't understand the point you're making," "Rephrase your question," and "In summarizing our discussion." This presumptuousness in the classroom is understandable, since the professor enjoys higher status than the student in this setting. Even in a sample collected during a comfortable ten-minute conversation, however, the professors continued to make presumptions about the other person's views. They may have wished to treat their students as equals, but their choice of words belied these egalitarian intentions.

• •

Nonverbal cues, too, are important indicators of status. Just as many primates communicate dominance through gestures, gaze, posture, and facial expressions, so a human in a group may lay claim to status through a firm handshake, an unwavering gaze, a relaxed but poised posture, and an unsmiling countenance (Leffler, Gillespie, & Conaty, 1982). In one illustrative study of nonverbal dominance cues, subjects read a summary of a personal-injury lawsuit and estimated how much money should be awarded to the plaintiff. All the subjects initially favored an award of at least $10,000. The subjects then watched a videotape of a man arguing that the plaintiff should receive a smaller award ($2000). Although the content of the man's arguments was held constant, his nonverbal behavior was varied across three conditions (paraphrased from Lee & Ofshe, 1981, p. 78):

1. *Deference-demanding condition.* The man spoke in a firm, rapid, and loud voice. His speech contained few hesitations, and he spoke without stumbling over his words. His posture appeared to be relaxed, he looked up as he spoke, and he periodically dropped his eyebrows to make a point. He wore a tie and sport-coat.

2. *Deferential condition.* The man spoke softly, slowly, and hesitantly. His speech contained pauses, and as he searched for words he occasionally said "umm" and "uh." He sat rigidly, made nervous movements (wringing his hands), and sometimes looked down when he spoke. He wore a T-shirt.

3. *Neutral condition.* The man spoke at a moderate rate, hesitated only occasionally, and did not mumble. He sat as if somewhat relaxed but did not use facial cues (such as eyebrows or eye contact) extensively when speaking. He was dressed in a sport-shirt.

As expected, the subjects who saw the deference-demanding speaker changed their initial decisions the most, dropping their award by an average of $4273. Those who saw the neutral speaker reduced their award slightly (an average of $2426), but subjects who listened to the deferential speaker actually increased their award by an average of $2843. Moreover, even though the occupation of the man was systematically varied across subjects, this external status cue had no impact on the subjects. Evidently, in some cases *how* something is said may be more important than *who* is saying it (Lee & Ofshe, 1981; see also Mohr, 1986; Sherman, 1983; Tuzlak & Moore, 1984).

ATTRACTION

The 19 Andes survivors took on many roles in their group, including hero, food preparer, explorer, and invalid. Status differences emerged as well, for some rose to positions of authority while others remained relatively powerless. Yet to describe the group in just these terms would be to miss a vital part of the social structure. The individuals were not just leaders and followers, powerful and powerless, they were also friends and enemies. Moreno, the developer of sociometry, maintains that the tendency to react to one another on a spontaneous, affective level imparts a unique quality to human groups. Our relationships with other group members take on many different shades—hate, condemnation, liking, friendship, love, and so on—but only rarely do we react neutrally to one another. Taken together, these relationships make up the group's **attraction relations,** or **sociometric structure** (Moreno, 1960).

Sociometric Differentiation

The sociometric structure of the Andes survivors changed gradually during the long ordeal. Figure 5-2 partially summarizes the results of this **sociometric differentiation** process by focusing on the relationship between the rank-and-file group members and the four explorers, Turcatti, Parrado, Vizintin, and Canessa. Nearly everyone admired Turcatti and Parrado; their warmth, optimism, and physical strength buoyed the sagging spirits of the others. Vizintin and Canessa, in contrast, "did not inspire the same affection" (Read, 1974, p. 141). They liked each other but had few other friends within the group. Mangino, one of the younger men, was an exception; he liked them both. Most of the others, however, quarreled with them constantly.

Attraction patterns like those in the Andes group are not a disorganized jumble of likes and dislikes but a network of stable social relationships (Doreian, 1986). Just as members of the group can be ranked from low to high in terms of status, so, too, can the members be ordered from least liked to most liked. Individuals in groups also fall into certain categories or clusters: popular individuals *(stars)* are singled out by virtually all the others to be the target of much affection; *isolates* are neglected by most of the group; *outcasts* are rejected by the majority of the group; and the average members are liked by several others in the group (Coie, Dodge, & Coppotelli, 1982; Newcomb & Bukowski, 1983). In the Andes group, for example, Parrado was admired by all; he was, sociometrically, the star of the group. Delgado, in contrast, was the group's outcast; he had no friends in the group, and the young men ridiculed him constantly for not doing his share of the work.

Figure 5-2 also indicates that attraction patterns among the Andes survivors tended to be *reciprocal*; Vizintin, for example, liked Canessa, and Canessa liked Vizintin in return. Such reciprocity of both liking and disliking is a powerful tendency in most settings; it has beeen documented repeatedly in a variety of groups, including football teams, police squads, psychotherapy groups, and classroom groups (Kandel, 1978; Newcomb, 1979; Segal, 1979; Wright, Ingraham, & Blackmer, 1984). Granted, exceptions to reciprocity sometimes occur. Individuals who have very low self-esteem, for example, may be less likely to reciprocate liking since they don't like themselves (Deutsch & Solomon, 1959; Newcomb, 1956; Regan, 1976). Some forms of attraction, such as respect, also tend to be less reciprocal than other forms of attraction, such as friendship (Segal, 1979). These exceptions to the reciprocity principle, however, are relatively rare.

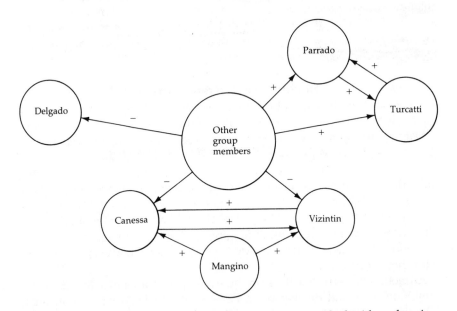

FIGURE 5-2. A sociogram of the Andes group. Lines marked with a plus sign indicate liking, lines marked with a minus sign indicate disliking, and arrows indicate the direction of the affect. As noted in Chapter 2, Moreno is generally given credit for developing this method for assessing group members' emotional reactions to one another.

Last, subgroups, or coalitions, often exist within the total group. In the Andes group Vizintin, Canessa, and Mangino formed a unified coalition within the larger group. Others rarely hesitated to show their disdain for the members of this subgroup, but these three were joined by strong bonds of attraction. In many cases these subgroups are more homogeneous than the total group. Members of the same racial category, for example, may join to form a coalition, or the group may separate naturally into all-male and all-female cliques (Hallinan, 1981; Hansell, 1984; Schofield & Whitley, 1983).

Determinants of Social Standing

Why did Parrado gain social standing in the group, and why was Delgado held in disregard? One's popularity, in large part, is determined by the interpersonal factors reviewed in Chapter 3: similarity, complementarity, reciprocity, personality qualities, and even physical attractiveness can influence one's sociometric ranking in a group. Parrado was similar to the others in age and background, and he possessed qualities that the others admired: he was optimistic, handsome, dependable, helpful, and strong. Delgado, in contrast, did not. Interaction with Delgado incurred considerable costs and yielded very few interpersonal rewards (Thibaut & Kelley, 1959).

In another group Delgado might have been well-liked, for he was quite articulate and socially skilled. In the Andes group, however, the fit between his personal qualities and the group was poor. As Lewin's concept of interactionism emphasizes, popularity cannot be predicted solely on the basis of the group members' personal qualities. Different groups value different attributes; the qualities that earn one popularity in a board room differ from those that predict sociometric standing on a baseball team or in a biker gang. Thus, predictions of social standing must take into account the *person/group fit*, the degree to which individuals' attributes match the qualities valued by the groups to which they belong.

The impact of person/group fit on social standing was aptly illustrated by a recent study of attraction structures in male adolescent groups (Wright, Giammarion, & Parad, 1986, study 1). Researchers began by asking the members to indicate whom they liked as a friend within their group. They also arranged for observers to record the behaviors displayed by each boy, with a particular focus on aggressive actions (displays of anger or physical aggression), withdrawal (plays by himself, is aloof), and prosocial behavior (helps others, shares). As the concept of person/group fit suggests, the investigators found that in nonaggressive groups popular boys displayed many prosocial behaviors and avoided aggressive behaviors. The popular boys in groups that were characterized by relatively high levels of hostility, fighting, and verbal abuse, in contrast, did not avoid aggressive behaviors; rather, they remained active in the group by avoiding such withdrawn activities as physical inactivity, failures to assert themselves, and displays of low confidence. These results, which are par-

TABLE 5-4. The correlations between group members' behaviors and their sociometric standing in nonaggressive and aggressive groups.

	Type of Group	
Behavior Category	Low Aggression	High Aggression
Aggression	− .34	.02
Withdrawal	− .03	− .51
Prosocial action	.34	.26

(Source: Wright, Giammarion, & Parad, 1986)

tially summarized in Table 5-4, suggest that popularity in one group does not guarantee popularity in another group; a sociometric star can become an outcast if the person/group fit is poor.

Maintaining Structural Balance

Why do some attraction patterns among members seem to occur only rarely, whereas other patterns are much more common? Fritz Heider's **balance theory** offers a possible answer. According to Heider, attraction relations in groups are balanced when they fit together to form a coherent, unified whole. A two-person group or subgroup, for example, is balanced only if liking (or disliking) is mutual. If Vizintin liked Canessa but Canessa disliked Vizintin, the dyad would be unbalanced, and the result would be structural strain (Cartwright & Harary, 1956, 1970; Heider, 1958; Newcomb, 1963).

The sociometric structures of larger groups also tend to be balanced. Consider, for example, the triad containing Vizintin, Canessa, and Mangino (see Figure 5-2). This subgroup is balanced because everyone in it likes one another; all bonds are positive. What would happen, however, if Mangino came to dislike Canessa? According to Heider, this group would be unbalanced, since the product of the three relationships (Vizintin likes Canessa, Mangino likes Vizintin, and Mangino dislikes Canessa) is negative. In general, a group is balanced if (1) all the relationships are positive or (2) an even number of negative relationships occur in the group. Conversely, groups are unbalanced if they contain an odd number of negative relations.

Because unbalanced sociometric structures generate tensions among group members, people are motivated to correct the imbalance and restore the group's equilibrium. Heider notes, however, that this restoration of balance can be achieved through either psychological changes in the individual members or interpersonal changes in the group. If, for example, Mangino initially likes only Vizintin and not Canessa, he may change his attitude toward Canessa when he recognizes the strong bond between Vizintin and Canessa. Alternatively, group members who are disliked by the other group members may be ostracized, as in the case of Delgado (Taylor, 1970). Lastly, because the occurrence of a single negative relationship within a group can cause the entire group to become unbalanced, large groups tend to include a number of smaller, better balanced cliques (Newcomb, 1981). The Andes group, for example, was somewhat unbalanced overall, but subgroups tended to be very harmonious (Cartwright & Harary, 1956, 1970; Mayer, 1975). As a result the group was high in cohesiveness.

COMMUNICATION NETWORKS

In the Andes group the three leaders stayed in close communication, discussing any problems among themselves before relaying their interpretations to the other group members. The other members usually routed all information to the threesome, who then informed the rest of the group. In contrast, the injured members were virtually cut off from communicating with the others during the day, and they occasionally complained that they were the last to know of any significant developments.

Regular patterns of information exchange among members of a group are called **communication networks.** Like the other forms of structure discussed earlier in this chapter, communication networks are sometimes deliberately set in place when the group is organized. Many companies, for example, adopt a hierarchical communication network that prescribes how information is passed up to superiors, down to subordinates, and horizontally to one's equals. Even when no formal attempt is made to organize communication, an informal communication network will usually take shape over time. Moreover, this network tends to parallel role, status, and attraction patterns. Take the Andes group as a case in point. Individuals who occupied certain roles—the explorers, the food preparers, and the lieutenants—communicated at much higher rates and with more individuals than individuals who occupied the malingerer and injured roles. Often, too, those with higher status initiated and received more information, as did those who were better liked within the group (Aiken & Hage, 1968; Bacharach & Aiken, 1977; Jablin, 1979; Shaw, 1964).

Initial analyses of communication networks were carried out with small groups in laboratories, but in recent years researchers have studied networks in many settings, including large business organizations, families, research and development units, university departments, and military units (for example, Craddock, 1985; Friedkin, 1983; Keller & Holland, 1983; Monge, Edwards, & Kirste, 1983; Tallman, 1970; Tutzauer, 1985). These empirical efforts, which are partially summarized below, attest to the powerful impact of networks on group performance and effectiveness and on members' level of satisfaction.

Centralization and Performance

The earliest systematic studies of communication networks were carried out in the 1950s by researchers at the Group Networks Laboratory at the Massachusetts Institute of Technology. A study conducted by Harold J.

Leavitt (1951) provides an excellent example of this approach. He seated men at a circular table but separated each individual from the others by means of a partition. He then gave each person a card bearing five of the following symbols: ○ △ ★ □ + ◇. The subjects' task was to identify the one symbol out of the six that was common to all the group members' cards.

Subjects could easily solve the problem by comparing all the cards, but Leavitt restricted the flow of communication. This manipulation was accomplished by opening particular slots in the partitions separating the participants. Leavitt examined four types of networks: the wheel, the chain, the Y and the circle (see Figure 5-3). In the *wheel* network one person in the group communicated with everyone, but the others communicated only with the individual located at the hub position. In the *chain* information was passed along sequentially, in the *Y* only one member could contact more than one other person, and in the *circle* all members could interact with two other persons. Leavitt found that in all but the circle group members tended to send information to the more central member, who integrated the data and sent back a solution. This summarizing of the data was most easily accomplished in the wheel, as all members could interact directly with the central member, whereas in the Y and chain the pooling process took longer (Bavelas, 1948, 1950; Bavelas & Barrett, 1951; Leavitt, 1951).

Leavitt's study, and subsequent research as well, has shown again and again that one of the most important features of a network is its *degree of centralization* (Shaw, 1964, 1978). Although this variable can be assessed mathematically by considering the relative number of links joining the positions in the network, for our purposes a broad distinction between centralized and decentralized patterns will suffice (Bavelas, 1948, 1950; Freeman, 1977; Grofman & Own, 1982; Moxley & Moxley, 1974). With centralized networks one of the positions is located at the "crossroads" of communications, as in the wheel and Y of Figure 5-3. As Leavitt's findings suggested, groups with this type of structure tend to use the hub position as the data-processing center, and its occupant typically collects information, synthesizes it, and then sends it back to others. In decentralized structures, like the circle or comcon (a network in which all individuals can communicate with one another), the number of channels at each position is roughly equal, so no one position is more central than another. These groups tend to use a variety of organizational structures when solving their problems, including the so-called *each-to-all pattern*, in which everyone sends messages in all directions until someone gets the correct answer.

The early MIT studies suggested that a centralized network was more efficient than a decentralized network. Leavitt, for example, found that individual and group error rates were lower in the centralized Y and wheel than in the more decentralized chain and circle. Other studies tended to support this conclusion, as centralized groups outscored decentralized groups in time taken to find a solution, number of messages sent, finding and correcting errors, and improvement with practice (Shaw, 1964, 1978). The only exceptions occurred when the simple tasks like that used by Leavitt were replaced with more complicated ones: arithmetic, sentence construction, problem solving, and discussion. When the task was more complex, the decentralized networks outperformed the centralized ones.

These contradictory results led Marvin E. Shaw to propose that network efficiency is related to *information saturation*. When a group is working on a problem, exchanging information, and making a decision, the

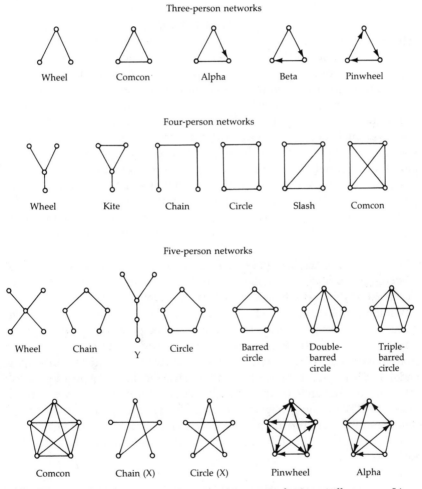

FIGURE 5-3. Some common communication networks in small groups. Lines without arrows are bidirectional. (The X-designation in the five-person groups indicates that members can communicate only with people seated across from them.)

Source: Shaw, 1964

central position in the network can best manage the inputs and interactions of the group. As work progresses and the number of communications being routed through the central member increases, however, a
saturation point can be reached at which the individual can no longer efficiently monitor, collate, or route incoming and outgoing messages. Shaw
notes that saturation can occur in a decentralized network, but it becomes
more likely when a group with a centralized structure is working on complex problems. Because the "greater the saturation the less efficient the
group's performance" (Shaw, 1964, p. 126), Shaw predicts that when the
task is simple, centralized networks are more efficient than decentralized
networks; when the task is complex, decentralized networks are superior.

Positional Effects

In the Andes group the malingerers, the younger men, and the injured often complained about the food, their living conditions, and their leadership. Their morale was low, but the rest of the group hardly noticed,
because they so rarely communicated with them directly.

These peripheral members' reactions are typical of people who find
themselves in the outlying positions in centralized communication networks. In such networks most of the group's actions are controlled by
whoever is in the central position, and that person can arbitrarily open
and close channels of communication. Whereas central-position occupants typically report that they are very much satisfied with the group
structure, the more peripheral members emphasize their dissatisfaction.
Indeed, the more removed the position is from the center of the network,
the less satisfied is the occupant. Shaw (1964) notes that since the number
of peripheral positions in a centralized network exceeds the number of
central positions, the overall level of satisfaction in a centralized group is
lower than the level of satisfaction in decentralized groups (Eisenberg,
Monge, & Miller, 1983; Krackhardt & Porter, 1986).

Position is linked not only to satisfaction and enjoyment but also to role
allocation. In Leavitt's study, for example, participants completed a questionnaire at the close of the session that included the item "Did your
group have a leader? If so, who?" The responses to this query concerning
leadership indicated that the individual in the most central position of the
network was chosen to be the leader by 100% of the group members in the
wheel, by 85% of the group members in the Y, and by 67% of the group
members in the chain. In contrast, leadership choices in the egalitarian
circle were approximately equally divided across all the different
positions.

Communication in Hierarchical Networks

For reasons of efficiency and control many organizations adopt hierarchical communication networks (Goetsch & McFarland, 1980). In such networks information can pass either horizontally, among members on the

same rung of the communication ladder, or vertically, up and down from followers to leaders and back (Jablin, 1979). Evidence indicates that upward communications are strikingly different from downward communications (Browning, 1978; Katz & Kahn, 1978). What type of information passes downward from superior to subordinate? Explanations of actions to be taken, the reasons for actions, suggestions to act in a certain manner, and feedback concerning performance are examples. Upward communications from subordinates to superiors, in contrast, include information on performance, insinuations about a peer's performance, requests for information, expressions of distrust, factual information, or grievances concerning the group's policies. These upward communications, moreover, tend to be fewer in number, briefer, and more guarded than downward communications. Indeed, in larger organizations the upward flow of information may be much impeded by the mechanics of the transferral process and by the low-status members' reluctance to send information that might reflect unfavorably on their performance, abilities, and skills (Bradley, 1978; Browning, 1978; Manis, Cornell, & Moore, 1974). As Focus 5-4 suggests, the low-status members' selective reticence may mean that good news will travel quickly up the hierarchy, whereas the top of the ladder will be the last to learn bad news (see Jablin, 1979, for a detailed review of communication in hierarchical organizations).

. . . .
FOCUS 5-4: THE MUM EFFECT AND COMMUNICATION IN HIERARCHIES

During the first few days after the Andes crash two of the survivors were assigned the job of monitoring newscasts on a small transistor radio. When they heard a broadcaster announce that the Uruguayan Air Force had canceled the search, one refused to tell the others, on the ground that it would destroy their hopes. The other insisted that they be told the truth, and when he dutifully relayed the information, they reacted with anger and bitterness.

This reluctance to tell the others bad news is one form of the MUM effect, keeping *m*um about *u*ndesirable *m*essages (Tesser & Rosen, 1975). According to research, individuals are reluctant messengers not only when the information describes personal inabilities or shortcomings but also when they are not at fault for the problems described. Apparently, people dislike being the bearer of bad tidings since they fear that the negative feelings the bad news creates will generalize from the message to the messenger. Studies conducted in work settings also suggest that individuals who are not satisfied with their jobs are more likely to distort information, apparently because they aren't interested in helping the organization achieve its long-range goals (O'Reilly, 1978).

. . . .

SYMLOG: AN INTEGRATIVE MODEL OF
GROUP STRUCTURE

In this chapter I have carried out a structural analysis of the Andes group. This analysis assumes that despite widespread differences among groups, all share a common structural core. In a sense examining group structures is like studying an individual's personality. We cannot directly see our friends' personalities, but we assume that their behavior depends partly on their basic traits and dispositions. Similarly, a structural analysis assumes that interaction among members follows a predictable, organized pattern because it is regulated by influential interpersonal structures.

Just as the structure of personality can be described in a variety of ways, so different theorists have stressed different structural qualities in their analyses of groups (Borgatta, Cottrell, & Mann, 1958; Carter, 1954; Mehrabian, 1980; Schutz, 1958; Triandis, 1978; Wish, Deutsch, & Kaplan, 1976). Three of the four structures examined in this chapter, however, are the ones that form the basis for Bales's **System of Multiple Level Observation of Groups,** or **SYMLOG.** As noted in Chapter 2, Bales and his associates at the Social Interaction Laboratory at Harvard University have spent years searching for regularities in group interaction (Bales, 1950, 1970, 1980, 1985; Bales, Cohen, & Williamson, 1979). Initially, they assumed that most of the variation in group behavior revolved around role structures. Hence, their initial system, Interaction Process Analysis (IPA), underscored the difference between task and socioemotional behavior. In time, however, Bales expanded his model to include two additional structural dimensions, status (dominance/submission) and attraction (friendly/unfriendly).

When these three dimensions are combined, they yield the cube pictured in Figure 5-4. To interpret this rather imposing theoretical model, begin by breaking down each dimension into three segments: for the status dimension the three segments are dominant (upward), submissive (down), and neutral; for attraction, they are friendly (positive), unfriendly (negative), and neutral; and for the role dimension they are instrumentally controlled (forward), emotionally expressive (backward), and neutral. Next, use the labels based on combinations of the letters of these reference directions to describe each person in the group (if a person is neutral on a particular dimension, the letter is simply omitted). For example, if someone acts in a dominant, unfriendly, emotionally expressive manner, then he or she would be located in the section on the front facet at the top-left-hand corner, labeled UNB. Similarly, a dominant, task-oriented person would occupy the position marked UF (upward/forward), a friendly, emotionally expressive person would be labeled PB (positive/backward), and so on.

SYMLOG has many uses. As a theoretical model it integrates the structural components discussed earlier in the chapter. The instrumentally controlled/emotionally expressive dimension focuses on role structure, the dominant/submissive dimension parallels status structure, and the friendly/unfriendly dimension pertains to attraction structure. Also, although communication structure is not considered explicitly, studies of task-performance groups indicate that individuals who are instrumentally controlled and friendly communicate more frequently with others, whereas those who are dominant tend to receive more communications from others (Bales et al, 1979; Stiles, 1980).

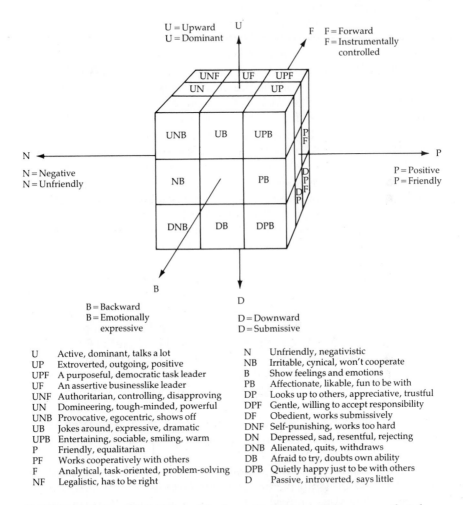

U = Upward
U = Dominant

F F = Forward
F = Instrumentally controlled

N = Negative
N = Unfriendly

P = Positive
P = Friendly

B = Backward
B = Emotionally expressive

D = Downward
D = Submissive

U	Active, dominant, talks a lot	N	Unfriendly, negativistic
UP	Extroverted, outgoing, positive	NB	Irritable, cynical, won't cooperate
UPF	A purposeful, democratic task leader	B	Show feelings and emotions
UF	An assertive businesslike leader	PB	Affectionate, likable, fun to be with
UNF	Authoritarian, controlling, disapproving	DP	Looks up to others, appreciative, trustful
UN	Domineering, tough-minded, powerful	DPF	Gentle, willing to accept responsibility
UNB	Provocative, egocentric, shows off	DF	Obedient, works submissively
UB	Jokes around, expressive, dramatic	DNF	Self-punishing, works too hard
UPB	Entertaining, sociable, smiling, warm	DN	Depressed, sad, resentful, rejecting
P	Friendly, equalitarian	DNB	Alienated, quits, withdraws
PF	Works cooperatively with others	DB	Afraid to try, doubts own ability
F	Analytical, task-oriented, problem-solving	DPB	Quietly happy just to be with others
NF	Legalistic, has to be right	D	Passive, introverted, says little

FIGURE 5-4. The SYMLOG model of group structure. Bales argues that three structural dimensions underlry differences among individuals in groups: dominance versus submission (or status), friendliness versus unfriendliness (or attraction), and instrumental control versus emotional expressiveness (or role orientation). When individuals are classified as either high, neutral, or low on these three dimensions, their position in the group's structure can be identified. Bales's model yields the 26 distinct positions identified by the labels listed under the cube.

Source: Bales, 1980

As a tool, when group members describe one another using the 26 sets of adjectives shown in Figure 5-4, SYMLOG yields insight into the way people in groups perceive one another. Moreover, when objective observers rate the group members using SYMLOG, it provides a visual summary of the group's structure (see Figure 5-5). Such an approach was exemplified in a recent study in which subjects rated the social behavior of such notable figures as Jesus, Hitler, Groucho Marx, and Henry Ford (the automobile magnate) on the sets of adjectives listed in Figure 5-4. The relative standing of each individual on each of the three dimensions (status, attraction, and role) was then determined by adding together appropriate items. The investigators discovered that the three dimensions of SYMLOG neatly summarized these ratings and that the classifications of these stimulus persons followed predictable patterns. For example, Hitler was viewed as UNF, Jesus was PF, Groucho was UPB, and Ford was UF. The investigators concluded that SYMLOG seems to measure group structures adequately, but they cautiously suggested that other dimensions not measured by SYMLOG may also be important (Isenberg & Ennis, 1981).

In the current context the SYMLOG model also provides a fitting conclusion to the structural analysis of the Andes group. Although SYMLOG ratings were never completed for the group members, Figure 5-5 presents a hypothetical map of the group's structure based on Bales's model. The vertical axis corresponds to the role-related behavior in the group. People like Fito Strauch and Fernandez rank near the instrumentally controlled end of this dimension because they were very task-oriented in the group, whereas Harley and Mangino are located near the emotionally expressive end of this dimension because they tended to express their feelings and emotions within the group. The horizontal axis pertains to attraction relations among the members. Parrado and Turcatti, for example, occupy positions at the friendly end of this dimension because they were both very popular within the group, whereas Delgado's and Canessa's low social standing places them at the unfriendly end. Bales uses the circles of varying size to illustrate the third structural dimension: dominance/submission. The larger the circle, the greater the group member's status in the group; hence, Fito Strauch is represented by a very large circle, whereas Harley (one of the malingerers) is represented by a very small circle.

By taking into account role, status, and attraction, the model yields an integrative and in-depth picture of the organization of groups. Admittedly, a number of theoretical and methodological questions concerning Bales's model remain to be answered (Breiger & Ennis, 1979; Fassheber & Terjung, 1985; Hare, 1985; Polley, 1984, 1986, 1987, 1989). Early analyses, however, are promising; they suggest that SYMLOG is a powerful conceptual and methodological tool that gives group dynamicists a clearer understanding of the unseen group structures that underlie recurring patterns of interpersonal behaviors in groups.

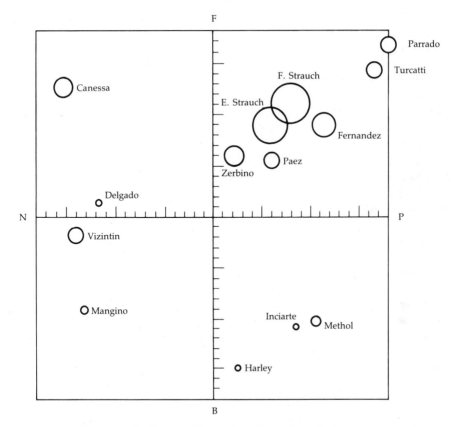

FIGURE 5-5. Hypothetical locations of a subset of the Andes group members in the three-dimensional space described by the SYMLOG rating system.

SUMMARY

Although we may be tempted to treat each of the many and varied groups we observe as unique social aggregates with unique features, certain *structures* are common to virtually all groups. These structures provide an underlying organization for the role, status, attraction, and communication relationships among members, and they influence a variety of group processes. Individuals who occupy particular *roles*, for example, generally perform certain types of behaviors in their groups. Many different roles can develop as group members interact with one another *(role differentiation)*, but most fall under one of two categories: *task roles* and *socioemotional roles*. Roles create stable patterns of behavior in groups, so disruptions in role relations can be stressful. One type of role stress, *role ambiguity*, occurs when the behaviors associated with a role are poorly defined. *Role conflict*, in contrast, occurs when group members occupy two or more roles that call for incompatible behaviors (interrole conflict) or when the demands of a single role are contradictory (intrarole conflict). Researchers have implicated both role ambiguity and role conflict as potential sources of low employee morale and job stress.

In most groups a stable pattern of variations in *status* or *authority* can also be discerned. As with roles, group members may start on an equal footing, but *status differentiation* processes usually result in certain individuals acquiring more authority than others. These differences seem to be caused by processes that are both rational and irrational, cooperative and competitive, and fair and unfair. One perspective, *expectation-states theory,* argues that differences in authority derive from members' status characteristics—that is, any personal qualities that the group members think indicate ability or prestige. Those who possess specific status characteristics that will increase the group's chances for success are afforded greater status, provided *status generalization* doesn't occur. In these instances group members unfairly allow irrelevant, diffuse status characteristics such as race, age, or ethnic background to influence the allocation of prestige.

A second approach to understanding status differentiation notes that in some instances people compete with one another for status in groups. Evidence indicates that group members' status allocations are strongly influenced by certain verbal and nonverbal behaviors. For example, individuals who speak rapidly without hesitating, advise others what to do, and confirm others' statements are often more influential than individuals who display cues that signal submissiveness.

Attraction relations (or *sociometric structure*), too, are neither arbitrary nor disorganized. Just as members of the group can be ranked from low to high in status, so can members be ordered from least liked to most liked. Attraction relations also tend to be reciprocal, and smaller subgroups, or coalitions, often exist within the group as a whole. *Sociometric differentiation* generally favors individuals who possess socially attractive qualities, such as cooperativeness or physical appeal, but social standing also depends on the degree to which individuals' attributes match the qualities valued by the groups to which they belong (person/group fit). As Heider's *balance theory* suggests, sociometric structures also tend to be balanced: they fit together to form a coherent, unified whole.

Lastly, the exchange of information among members of a group often follows a stable, predictable pattern. Although these *communication networks* may parallel formally established paths, most groups also have an informal network that defines who speaks to whom most frequently. A group's network, in addition to structuring communication, influences a variety of group and individual outcomes, including performance, effectiveness, and members' level of satisfaction. For example, evidence indicates that centralized networks are most efficient for simple tasks and that peripheral members are often dissatisfied in such networks. Also, more information generally flows downward in hierarchical networks than flows upward, and the information that is sent upward is often unrealistically positive.

In conclusion, four major structural dimensions organize interpersonal behavior in groups: role, status, attraction, and communication. Indeed, Bales highlights three of these four dimensions in his System of Multiple Level Observation of Groups, or *SYMLOG*. This model maintains that individuals in groups differ from one another in dominance and submissiveness, friendliness and unfriendliness, and instrumental control and emotional expressiveness. This model offers promising insights into the structures that underlie recurring patterns of interpersonal behaviors in groups.

·6·

Conformity and Influence

O n May 20, 1971, sheriff's deputies discovered the body of an elderly man in a shallow grave on a farm near Yuba City, California. When diggers found a second body near the first one, they expanded their search. Two weeks later the tally stood at 25: all older men, all brutally murdered, all buried in the lonely orchard during the preceding six months.

The police's prime suspect was Juan Corona, a Mexican citizen who worked in the area as a labor contractor. They arrested Corona and brought him to trial, building their case on hundreds of bits of evidence that implicated him and no one else. But was Corona guilty of one of the largest mass murders in U.S. history, or was he innocent? After five months of trial this question was put to a jury of Corona's peers: men and women, strangers to one another, chosen at random from the community, unschooled in legal principles, and unpracticed in group decision making. For eight days this jury reviewed the evidence, debated points of law, separated fact from innuendo, and argued over ethics. On January 18, 1973, they emerged from their deliberations with a guilty verdict.

How did the jury reach this decision? When the deliberations began, the jurors differed in their opinions about trial procedures, the law, and the defendant's guilt. But when their deliberations ended, the group had reached consensus. How did the group achieve this agreement? Why did the jurors who initially believed in Corona's innocence change their votes?

The answer lies in **social influence:** interpersonal processes that lead to changes in individuals' feelings, thoughts, or behavior. The lone individual is free to think and act as he or she chooses, but a group member loses some of that freedom. Groups influence their members; they sway their judgments, favor one interpretation of reality over another, and encourage certain behaviors while discouraging others. To create these effects, groups exert pressure on individuals that makes agreement with the norms of the group preferable to deviation from these rules. The person who strays too far from the group's idea of appropriate action, thought, or belief must be convinced of the value in the group's perspective and encouraged to return to the fold. As you will see in this chapter and the next, social influence can be a powerful force within groups.

CONFORMITY, NONCONFORMITY, AND INFLUENCE

According to Victor Villaseñor's (1977) account of the Corona trial, the jurors, listed in Table 6-1, took their work very seriously. They met at a large

TABLE 6-1. The Corona trial jurors.

Juror	Age	Occupation	Characteristics
Faye Blazek	66	Retired teacher	Well-educated; spoke with precision; backed up points with compelling arguments
Rick Bremen	26	Welder	Defended his points vehemently, often to the irritation of the other jurors
Frank Broksell	58	Retired toolmaker	Skeptical of the legal process; contributed only rarely
Larry Gallipeo	41	Ship construction	Quiet; maintained a casual, relaxed attitude during the deliberations
Matt Johnson	54	Retired sergeant	Easy-going, active contributor who diffused tension through laughter
Victor Lorenzo	45	Grocer	Reserved; contributed only when knowledgeable on the subject
George Muller	43	Employee at air base	Enthusiastic and outgoing; moderately involved in the discussion
Jim Owen	39	Shipyard inspector	Thoughtful contributor; offered appropriate and provocative insights
Ernie Phillips	53	Retired sergeant	Foreman of the jury; talkative and task-oriented; accepted by jurors
Donald Rogers	60	Retired machinist	Smoked a cigar, irritated others by speaking loudly, brusquely
Naomi Underwood	61	Retired clerk	Prior experience in jury duty; high-strung; raised issues that others felt were irrelevant
Calvin Williams	51	School janitor	Only Black on the jury; frequent participant; guided the group and maintained discussion norms

table for hour after hour, reviewing the evidence, sharing their own interpretations of that evidence, pointing out inconsistencies in one another's reasoning, and from time to time voting by secret ballot. By the second ballot the majority was leaning toward guilt, but on subsequent ballots the number favoring guilt and innocence fluctuated widely. Eight days of deliberation were needed before unanimity was reached.

This complex interplay of social influence is not unique to the Corona jury. Beneath the surface of most groups flows an undercurrent that pushes the group together, toward greater consensus, uniformity, homogeneity, or conformity. Other forces, in contrast, push members in divergent directions; they promote dissension, uniqueness, heterogeneity, and nonconformity. As these forces play against one another, the consensus within the group ebbs and flows; on one issue the group members may agree, but on the next they may be divided against one another.

Solomon E. Asch's studies conducted in the 1950s offer a gold mine of information about conformity and nonconformity in groups. Asch was not the first group dynamicist to investigate social influence in groups (Hollander, 1975, presents a historical overview). His studies, however, provided undeniable evidence of the power of groups (Asch, 1952, 1955, 1957). He began his work by telling male college students seated in a group-dynamics laboratory that he was studying vision. The subjects sat in a semicircle facing Asch's experimenter, who explained that on each of 18 trials he would show the group two cards. One card bore a single line that was to serve as the standard. The second card contained three numbered test lines (see Figure 6-1). The subjects were to pick the line that matched the standard line in length. Asch found that when making such judgments alone, few people made mistakes. One test line was always the same length as the standard line, so the correct answer was obvious.

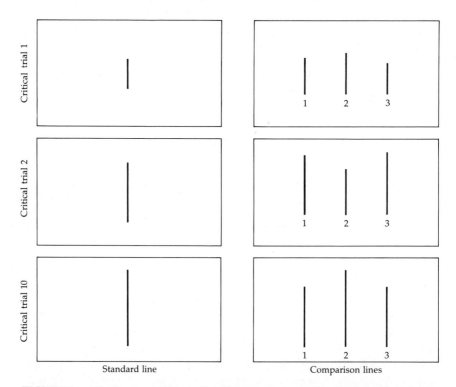

FIGURE 6-1. The lines used by Asch in his experiments. On 12 of the 18 trials the majority of the group members picked the incorrect comparison line. On the first of these 12 critical trials, the standard line was 3 inches long, and Comparison Line 3 was the correct answer. However, the group chose Line 1, which was actually 3 3/4 inches long. On the second critical trial the correct answer was 1, but the group unanimously answered with 2. The lines used in the tenth critical trial are also shown; the correct answer in this case was 2, but the group suggested 1.
Source: Asch, 1957

As the experiment got under way, the researcher displayed two cards and asked the subjects to state their answers aloud, starting at the left-hand side of the semicircle. As each person answered, it became apparent that everyone in the group had picked the right answer. This agreement held for the second trial as well, but on the third trial the first subject picked Line 1 even though Line 3 was a closer match to the stimulus. Then, as the other group members reported, each one followed the first subject's lead by selecting Line 1 as the correct answer. By the time the study was completed, the majority had made mistakes on 12 of the 18 trials.

These mistakes in judgment were planned in advance. Only one group member was an actual subject. All the others were trained confederates who deliberately made errors to see if the subject would conform to a unanimous majority's judgments. When the subject arrived, he was seated so that he would hear the reports of most of the other subjects before giving his own response. He would study the lines, identify the correct answer, but hear everyone else make a different selection. When his turn came, he could disagree with the other subjects' judgments, or he could conform by giving the incorrect answer.

Asch's initial findings were surprising. The task was very easy, but 76.4% of 123 men made at least one conforming response. On average, a subject gave the correct answer on about two-thirds of the test trials but conformed on the remaining 36.8% (4.4 out of 12). As Figure 6-2 shows, 29 of the subjects (23.6%) never conformed to the majority opinion, but 6 subjects (5%) conformed on all 12 critical trials.

In the years since Asch startled social scientists with his findings, group dynamicists have conducted hundreds of conformity studies using a variety of methods (see Focus 6-1). These findings indicate that individuals

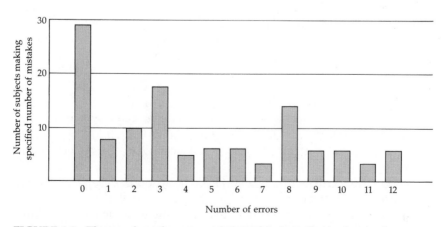

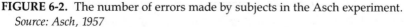

FIGURE 6-2. The number of errors made by subjects in the Asch experiment. *Source: Asch, 1957*

often conform to the incorrect opinions of a majority, but they also indicate the conditions that encourage nonconformity. Some of these factors are examined in Focus 6-1 below (see Allen, 1975; Hare, 1976; Kiesler & Kiesler, 1976; and Wolf, 1987, for reviews).

Forms of Social Response

When a subject in Asch's studies gave the same answer as the incorrect majority, was he going along with the group even though he knew the group was wrong? Not always. As Asch explains:

> Among the extremely yielding persons we found a group who quickly reached the conclusion: "I am wrong, they are right." Others yielded in order "not to spoil your results." Many of the individuals who went along suspected that the majority were "sheep" following the first responder, or that the majority were victims of an optical illusion; nevertheless, these suspicions failed to free them at the moment of decision [1955, p. 33].

Agreeing with other group members is not always a sign of conformity, just as nonconformity does not always signal independence. Conformity and nonconformity are two broad categories that include a variety of related, but distinct, social responses (Allen, 1965; Festinger, 1953; Kelman, 1961; Kiesler & Kiesler, 1976; Levine & Russo, 1987; Nail, 1986; Stricker, Messick, & Jackson, 1970; Willis, 1963).

• •
FOCUS 6-1: THE CRUTCHFIELD APPARATUS

Asch ingeniously captured the essentials of many group-decision settings in his studies: the groups were small, members could see one another, and they stated opinions aloud. The procedure, however, was inefficient: many confederates were required to study just one subject.

Richard S. Crutchfield (1955) solved this problem by designing an apparatus that could be used to assess conformity without confederates. In Crutchfield's laboratory the subjects made their judgments while seated in individual cubicles (see Figure 6-3). They flipped a small switch on a response panel to report their judgments to the researcher, and their answers would supposedly light up on the other group members' panels as well. Crutchfield, however, told each person in the group that he or she was to answer last, and he himself simulated the majority's judgments from a master control box. During the critical trials Crutchfield would lead subjects to think that all the other subjects were giving erroneous answers.

Although it sacrifices the face-to-face interaction between the subject and confederates, the Crutchfield apparatus is efficient: five or more subjects participate in a single session, and no confederate is needed. Using this technique, Crutchfield explored a number of personality factors that are related to conformity and nonconformity, and other researchers have also profitably applied the technique.

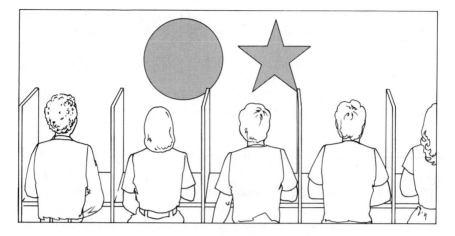

FIGURE 6-3. The Crutchfield apparatus. When asked a question—such as "Which one of the figures has a greater area, the star or the circle?"—subjects answered by flipping the appropriate switch in their booth. They thought that their answers were being transmitted to the experimenter and the other subjects, but in actuality the experimenter was simulating the majority's judgment from a master control panel.

Source: Wrightsman, 1977

· ·

Conformity. When people respond to group influence by changing their publicly stated position, one of at least two different processes may be occurring. First, the individual's private position may have changed to match the group's position. On the Corona jury, for example, Calvin initially voted for "not guilty" because he did not know if general circumstantial evidence, such as bloodstains in Corona's truck, should be considered as evidence pertaining to particular murders. He changed his vote when this point was clarified during the deliberations. This type of social response is known as **conversion** or **private acceptance** (see Table 6-2).

TABLE 6-2. Four types of social responses.

Public Position	Private Position	
	Agree	*Disagree*
Agree	Conversion, or private acceptance	Compliance
Disagree	Counterconformity, or anticonformity	Independence

Naomi, in contrast, never fully accepted the guilty verdict. As the deliberations wore on and she became exhausted, she reached the point at which she publicly favored guilt but privately was still uncertain. Similarly, many of Asch's (1952) subjects knew which answer was correct yet went along with the group because they did not want to seem out of step with the others, anger the experimenter, or appear stupid. This type of conformity is usually labeled **compliance**: public agreement paired with private disagreement.

Nonconformity.   Nonconformity, too, can involve one of two very different processes. First, people who refuse to bend to the will of the majority may be displaying **independence**: the public expression of ideas, beliefs, and judgments that are consistent with their personal standards. On ballot after ballot Jim refused to vote for a guilty verdict. Only at the very end, when he reconsidered his own moral values, did he change his opinion. Up to the end, however, he remained independent. Second, nonconformity can reflect **counterconformity** (or anticonformity): expressing ideas or taking actions that are the opposite of whatever the group recommends. Counterconformists privately agree with the group, but publicly they insist on disagreeing with others. On the Corona jury, Donald initially voted "not guilty" even though he was certain of Corona's guilt. He later explained that he had voted "not guilty" only because he wanted to be certain that the jury would review all the evidence thoroughly. Similarly, in a replication of Asch's study carried out in Japan, many of the subjects displayed anticonformity by deliberately making errors on the *neutral* trials of the experiment (Frager, 1970).

Table 6-2 summarizes these four types of social responses. When people react to group pressures, conformity can be labeled compliance, and nonconformity can be thought of as counterconformity. In the opposite situation, when the response is prompted by one's personal standards, conformity becomes private acceptance, and nonconformity, independence. These distinctions, however, are somewhat arbitrary. Despite the need to reach agreement on the meaning of these terms, the field of group dynamics appears to be populated by nonconformists rather than conformists, for no one seems to be willing to follow the recommendations of the various theorists who have made reasonable attempts to clarify the terminology. Indeed, much of the research does not allow us to make these distinctions, thus forcing the use of the more general terms. (The interested reader is referred to Nail, 1986, and Levine & Russo, 1987, for reviews.)

Majority Influence

On the sixth day of deliberations the jury was split 9-3 favoring guilt. Naomi looked around the table, wondering who else had voted "not guilty" and hoping that others would swing that way, too. But when the jury revoted later that day, the tally was 11-1. Naomi now realized that she was the only person who thought that Corona was innocent of the murders, and on the next ballot she changed her vote to guilty.

When it comes to social influence, size makes a difference. As the number of individuals in the group, in the majority, and in the minority changes, social influence waxes and wanes. Consider the most basic case: a lone individual who disagrees with the rest of the group. Asch investigated this situation by replicating his procedures with groups ranging in size from 2 to 16 members. As he expected, the larger the unanimous majority facing the lone individual, the greater the rate of conformity (1952, 1955). He also found that the impact of increasing group size seemed to level off when the group reached four. Adding more people to a majority of three didn't appreciably increase the majority's power to influence. This type of pattern is often called a *ceiling effect*.

The positive relationship between majority size and conformity has been confirmed in many studies, using both laboratory and field methods (Buby & Penner, 1974; Gerard, Wilhelmy, & Conolley, 1968; Milgram, Bickman, & Berkowitz, 1969; Nordholm, 1975; Reis, Earing, Kent, & Nezlek, 1976; Stang, 1976). The precise shape of the relationship between size and conformity, however, remains uncertain. Some researchers have confirmed Asch's ceiling effect. Sarah Tanford and Steven Penrod (1984), for example, have argued persuasively that few people conform when one other person disagrees with them but that conformity rises rapidly when the majority increases to two or three. The ceiling effect occurs after that point, with the result that increasing the number of people in the majority has little impact (see Figure 6-4).

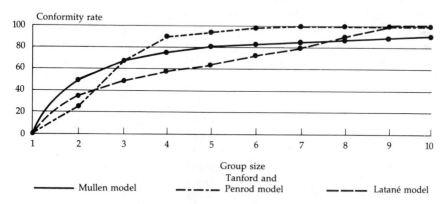

FIGURE 6-4. Three hypothesized relationships between group size and conformity. The Tanford and Penrod model is consistent with Asch's discovery of a ceiling effect; conformity rates stabilize once the group size reaches 4. Latané's psychosocial law of social impact argues that each person adds to the majority's impact but that the gain in impact decreases as the majority grows larger and larger. Mullen's model is based on the other/total ratio: social impact depends on the size of one's own subgroup relative to the size of the group as a whole.
Sources: Latané, 1981; Mullen, 1985; Tanford & Penrod, 1984

Bibb Latané and his colleagues have advanced an alternative hypothesis based on **social-impact theory** (Jackson, 1986; Jackson & Latané, 1981; Latané, 1981; Latané & Wolf, 1981; Williams & Williams, 1983; Wolf, 1987). According to Latané's psychosocial law of social impact, the first person who opposes the lone minority has the greatest social impact. Each additional person adds to the majority's impact, but the gain in impact decreases as the majority grows larger and larger. Latané expresses this idea in the following formula:

$$I = sN^t.$$

Applied to conformity, the formula states that the amount of social impact (I), will equal the impact of a single person on conformity (s) times the number of people in the majority (N), raised to a certain power (t). In the formula s represents the amount of conformity found when the majority consists of only one other person. In Asch's studies, for example, s would equal 3.6, the percentage of people who agreed with a "majority" of one. N is the number of people in the majority, and t is usually a number less than 1.

Brian Mullen, drawing on his **self-attention theory,** offers a third prediction concerning the relationship between conformity and group size (1983, 1985, 1986a, 1986b, 1986c, 1987b). Mullen proposes that group members are not always self-aware; they do not always monitor their behavior and determine whether it is consistent with the group's standards. Self-awareness increases, however, as the number of people in the majority becomes larger and the individual's subgroup becomes smaller. Imagine, for example, that Chuck disagrees with a group of five other people. If two more people join the group and both disagree with Chuck (bringing the total to seven), then he will become more self-aware. If, however, the two new people agree with Chuck, then he will become less self-aware. Mullen quantifies these predicted changes in self-awareness in his **other/ total ratio** (OTR), which states that self-awareness depends on the ratio of the number of other people in the majority (O) to the number of people in the minority (S), or:

$$OTR = \frac{O}{O + S}.$$

Applied to the example, when Chuck stands alone and disagrees with five other people, OTR would be $5/(5+1)$ or 5/6 (or .833). When two more people join the majority OTR would increase to $7/(7+1)$ or 7/8 (or .875). If, however, the two newcomers side with Chuck, then OTR would be $5/(5+3)$ or 5/8 (or .625).

The function described by OTR is also shown in Figure 6-4. According to this formulation, self-attention increases gradually as more people join the majority, and reaches its maximum value (near 1.0) when the individual stands alone on an issue·facing a large, unified majority. As in the psychosocial law of social-impact theory, Mullen argues that the impact of the first opposing individual has the greatest impact and that the impact of each additional individual becomes less and less. But Mullen's theory suggests that self-awareness mediates the relationship.

Which one of the three patterns shown in Figure 6-4 is most accurate? In all likelihood the answer depends on a number of situational factors. If the task is very simple, then possibly the Tanford and Penrod model is most accurate. In a situation like that studied by Asch, it takes several people disagreeing with you before you are ready to admit you are wrong. In contrast, when issues are complex, as in a jury trial, then the Latané model or the Mullen model may prove more predictive (Campbell, Tesser, & Fairey, 1986). Other factors, such as anonymity of responses, the group's cohesiveness and longevity, and concern for accuracy are also important determinants (Insko, Smith, Alicke, Wade, & Taylor, 1985; see Jackson, 1987, and Wolf, 1987, for reviews).

Minority Influence

The situation of one against many is a special case of minority/majority influence. Whereas the lone person stands little chance of resisting the influence of the majority, a minority coalition, even if it contains only two individuals, is more likely to withstand the majority's attempts at influence. Asch demonstrated this effect by telling one of the confederates to agree with the subject on some trials. As predicted, when someone else disagreed with the majority, conformity rates were cut to one-fourth their previous levels. Even an inaccurate ally helped subjects withstand conformity pressures. In yet another variation Asch arranged for some confederates to disagree with the majority but still give an incorrect answer. Subjects didn't agree with the erroneous nonconformist, but his dissent made it easier for them to express their own viewpoint (Asch, 1955).

Why are members of a minority coalition able to resist conformity pressures that would overwhelm them were they alone? First, the power of the majority is weakened when its unanimity is broken. A single dissenter's arguments can be dismissed as personal idiosyncrasies or biases, but several dissenters cast doubt on the majority's view (Morris & Miller, 1975a). Most subjects realize that the group will think that their nonconforming answer is strange and irrational. After all, "the correct judgment appeared so obvious that only perceptual incompetents, fools, or madmen could err" (Ross, Bierbrauer, & Hoffman, 1976, p. 149). A partner, however, makes their answer, and they themselves, seem more reasonable. Second, when people face the majority without a single ally, they bear the brunt of all the group's pressure; the influence pressures that are put on a single dissenter are just too great (Asch, 1955). Third, the larger the size of the minority coalition, the smaller the majority's coalition. A majority of 11 united against 1 has a greater social impact than a majority of 9 against 3 (Latané, 1981).

The minority can even succeed, in rare cases, in influencing the majority. Although the minority view lost in the Corona trial, the impact of a dissenting minority on the majority's opinion has been documented by several researchers, most notably Serge Moscovici and his colleagues. In his research Moscovici reverses the usual Asch situation by studying the reaction of the majority to the disagreeing judgments of a single confederate on a highly subjective task. Care is taken to make certain that the subjects don't attribute any special expertise or skill to the minority confederate, and elements in the situation suggest that the minority's responses are not caused by some personal idiosyncrasy. Moscovici reports that a minority of one or two members can sometimes considerably influence the majority's judgments, provided that (1) the minority's responses are highly consistent over time, (2) the majority is aware of this consistency, and (3) majority members believe that the consistency is an indication of the minority's confidence (Moscovici, 1976, 1980, 1985; Moscovici & Faucheux, 1972; Moscovici & Lage, 1976; Moscovici & Nemeth, 1974; Moscovici & Personnaz, 1980; Nemeth, 1986). (See Focus 6-2).

• •
FOCUS 6-2: MAJORITY/MINORITY INFLUENCE IN JURIES

The drama *Twelve Angry Men* captures the frustrations of a jury trying to reach a verdict in a murder trial. Eleven of the jurors agree in the first straw poll that the defendant is guilty. The majority attacks the lone holdout's position. The holdout, however, stands firm, and one by one the rest of the group members change their minds. The jury eventually returns a verdict of not guilty.

The plot of *Twelve Angry Men* is dramatic but unrealistic; in juries the minority rarely influences the majority. One study compared the first-ballot voting pattern with the jury's final verdict. When 7 to 11 jurors (a majority) favored guilt, in 90% of the cases the jury returned a verdict of guilty. If, in contrast, only from 1 to 5 voted "guilty" on the first ballot, then a not-guilty verdict occurred in 86% of the cases (Kalven & Zeisel, 1966). Other studies of the social-decision rules implicitly adopted by juries indicate that if a significant majority of the members (say, two-thirds) favor a verdict, the jury usually returns that verdict. (For reviews, see Davis, Bray, & Holt, 1977; Nemeth, 1980; and Penrod & Hastie, 1979.) As in the Corona trial once the first vote is taken and the majority's position is identified, the jurors not only reexamine the evidence but also begin pressuring the dissenting minority to adopt the majority decision (Hastie, Penrod, & Pennington, 1983).

Even though the majority tends to prevail in juries, the statistics in Table 6-3 show that staunch minorities can sometimes hang a jury or even persuade the majority to adopt its viewpoint. For example, in the Mitchell/ Stans Watergate-conspiracy trial the first vote was 8-4 in favor of a guilty verdict (Wrightsman, 1978; Zeisel & Diamond, 1976). However, one of the

TABLE 6-3. Outcomes of deliberations in juries with and without minority coalitions on the first vote.

Outcome	Number of Juries	Percentage
Total agreement on first ballot	69	31.0
Jury adopts majority's decision	127	56.5
Jury adopts minority's decision	6	2.5
Hung jury	13	5.6
Split 6-6 on first ballot	10	4.4

(Source: Penrod and Hastie, 1980)

members of the minority coalition, a vice president of a bank, had achieved a position of high status by doing favors for the other jurors such as paying for their small expenses and arranging for entertainment while the jury was sequestered. In time he managed to enlarge the size of the minority coalition until the jury's stance shifted to acquittal. In many cases the minority's success depends on its size (Penrod & Hastie, 1980). A lone dissenter will generally change his or her vote, but as the minority swells in size, its power increases exponentially. In fact, a computer model that simulates jury deliberations (DICE) assumes that a 3-person coalition in a standard 12-person jury will be relatively weak but a 4- or 5-person coalition will be fairly stable and influential (Hastie et al., 1983; Penrod & Hastie, 1980; Tanford & Penrod, 1983).

• •

Moscovici also suggests that whereas majorities influence members directly, often creating compliance, minorities influence members indirectly, creating *conversion* to the minority's position (Maass, West, & Cialdini, 1987; Nemeth, 1986). This influence occurs at a latent level, and it often becomes evident only when the group has completed its initial deliberations and moved on to another task. Researchers demonstrated this tendency in one study by asking five-person groups to make an award in a simulated personal-injury case. One of the five group members was a confederate, who consistently argued for an award of $3000, which was substantially below the $15,000 award favored by the majority. On the final vote the majority's position was unchanged, but when the subjects turned to a second case, they gave significantly smaller awards than subjects who had never been exposed to the minority (Nemeth & Wachtler, 1974).

Thus, when behavior is measured directly, the majority prevails. When an indirect measure is taken, however, the minority may prevail (Maass & Clark, 1984). The indirect impact of the minority may also extend to the level of perception. Moscovici exposed female subjects to a series of blue slides that were consistently labeled green by a confederate. On each trial the subject reported her judgment of the color (the direct measure) but was also asked to look at a blank white screen and report the color of the slide's afterimage (the indirect measure). Unknown to the subjects, the afterimage of blue is yellow/orange, whereas the afterimage of green is red/purple. Subjects' judgments of the color of the slides were not influenced by the minority, as Moscovici predicted. Their judgments of the afterimage, in contrast, changed; they saw more red/purple (Moscovici & Personnaz, 1980).

These findings are provocative and have generated considerable debate (Doms & Van Avermaet, 1980; Sorrentino, King, & Leo, 1980). When combined with other evidence, however, they suggest that "minorities tend to produce profound and lasting changes in attitudes and perceptions that generalize to new settings and over time . . . whereas majorities are more likely to elicit compliance that is confined to the original influence setting" (Maass et al., 1987, pp. 56–57). They also correct a bias that runs throughout much of the conformity literature. Researchers in this field have tended to focus on how a majority influences a minority while ignoring the reciprocal process of minority influence. This emphasis stems from the implicit assumption that group change comes about primarily through a one-way process of influence, with the majority members deciding the best course of action and persuading the disagreeing minority to get in line. Moscovici's findings, in contrast, cite a different source of social change, a consistent, determined minority leading the way during decision making. An even-handed perspective on the question of influence suggests that change in a group is a mutual process; the majority influences the minority, and the minority influences the majority (Maass & Clark, 1984; Maass et al., 1987; Moscovici, 1985; Nemeth, 1986, 1987; Spitzer & Davis, 1978; Tanford & Penrod, 1984; Wolf, 1985, 1987).

Status and Influence

Several people dominated the deliberations of the Corona jury. This subgroup included Ernie, the foreman, Faye, the retired teacher, and Jim, the shipyard inspector. Others participated, but these three commanded the most respect in the group. Is it a coincidence that the verdict they favored was the final verdict of the jury?

Low status and conformity. Fairly or unfairly, people who have high prestige or status are more influential than low-status members. In one study of this bias Fred L. Strodtbeck and his colleagues repeatedly selected sets of 12 individuals from a pool of eligible jurors, simulated the pretrial-interview process designed to eliminate biased jurors (voir dire), and assembled the group in the courtroom. A bailiff then played a recording of a trial and asked the group to retire to a jury room to decide on a verdict. Except for the use of a recording, the groups were treated exactly as actual juries are (Strodtbeck & Hook, 1961; Strodtbeck, James, & Hawkins, 1957; Strodtbeck & Mann, 1956).

As the concept of status generalization suggests, diffuse-status characteristics influence status allocations within groups (see Chapter 5). Juries favored people of high socioeconomic status (proprietors and clerical workers) over those of low socioeconomic status (skilled and unskilled workers) when choosing a foreman, even though no mention of occupation was made (Strodtbeck & Lipinski, 1985). High-status members also participated more frequently in the jury's discussions, often by offering more suggestions and providing more orientation to the task. Low-status members, in contrast, showed more agreement with others.

High-status members were also more successful in convincing the others that their judgments on the case were the most accurate. The correlation between private predeliberation opinion and the jury's final decision was .50 for proprietors, but it dropped all the way down to .02 for the laborers (Strodtbeck et al., 1957). Sex differences were also apparent, for women joined in the discussion less frequently than men (James, 1959; Strodtbeck et al., 1957). Furthermore, women's comments were more often socioemotional in nature, showing solidarity and agreement, whereas men's comments were more task-focused (Strodtbeck & Mann, 1956). Whether these differences have persisted is unclear, since research conducted in the mid-1970s using a mock jury both confirmed and disconfirmed the original Strodtbeck findings (Nemeth, Endicott, & Wachtler, 1976).

Status and idiosyncrasy credits.   The tendency for groups to react more favorably to high-status members prompted Edwin P. Hollander to develop his theory of idiosyncrasy credits. According to Hollander (1971, p. 573), **idiosyncrasy credits** are "the positive impressions of a person held by others, whether defined in the narrower terms of a small face-to-face group or a larger social entity such as an organization or even a total society." These credits accumulate during the course of interaction, typically as the member contributes to the progress of the group toward desired goals. Because high-status members have usually contributed more in the past and possess more valued personal characteristics, they have more idiosyncrasy credits. Therefore, if they do not conform, their actions are more tolerable to the other members (see, however, Focus 6-3). The low-status members' balance of credits is, in comparison, very low; hence, they are permitted a smaller latitude for nonconformity (Hollander, 1958, 1960, 1961, 1971, 1981).

· ·
FOCUS 6-3: WHEN DOES STATUS BECOME A LIABILITY?

One major exception to the general tendency to react less negatively to the nonconformity of high-status members occurs when the nonconformity is so extreme and damaging in its consequences that it completely bankrupts the store of idiosyncrasy credits. This phenomenon has been labeled **status liability,** because it occurs when dissenting high-status members are held especially responsible for their actions (Wiggins, Dill, & Schwartz, 1965).

Clear evidence of status liability was obtained in a study in which four-person groups worked on a task to try to earn a $50 prize (Wiggins et al., 1965). During the task a high-status group member or a medium-status group member was supposedly seen cheating, and in consequence the experimenter deducted a small, medium, or large number of points from the group's overall performance score. The small penalty did not signifi-cantly interfere with the group's performance, but the large penalty was hard to overcome. When the subjects later evaluated the cheater, evidence of the protective effects of idiosyncrasy credit surfaced in the low- and me-dium-penalty conditions: the low-status member was more disliked than the high-status member. However, status became a liability in the high-penalty condition. In this case the high-status cheaters were more dis-liked than the low-status members. Because status liability seems to occur whenever nonconformity results in extremely negative consequences, let innovative group leaders be warned: although nonconformity that helps the group will be merely tolerated, nonconformity that lowers the quality of the group's outcome may lead to rejection, negative sanctioning, and a loss of status (Giordano, 1983).

. . . .

The idiosyncrasy model suggests that influence levels in a group are in-creased by careful conformity to group norms during the early phases of group formation, followed by dissent when a sufficient balance of credit has been established (Stein, 1982). To examine this notion, Hollander ar-ranged for male engineering students to work in groups of five on a com-plex decisional task. One of the members was a confederate who systematically violated certain rules of procedure during the early phases of problem solving or later in the session. Hollander found that the con-federate's influence over the others tended to increase over time but that a confederate who prefaced his nonconformity with conformity exerted somewhat more influence than an early nonconformist. Similar findings were reported when children with well-developed leadership skills were placed in new groups (Merei, 1958). Those who tried to take over and change the group immediately were rejected, whereas those who worked within the group for a time before attempting innovations became suc-cessful influencers. Lastly, other researchers report that the greater the perceived competency and group-centered motivation of the individual, the greater the group's toleration of early nonconformity (Ridgeway, 1978; Wahrman & Pugh, 1972, 1974).

Hollander's advice about early conformity contrasts, to some extent, with Moscovici's recommendations concerning consistent nonconformity. Hollander warns that dissenters who challenge the majority without first earning high status in the group will probably be overruled by the majority, but Moscovici argues that consistent nonconformity will lead to innovation and change. Both tactics, however, may prove effective. One study contrasted the two approaches by asking groups of college students to discuss three issues. Each group included two confederates who took a minority viewpoint on all three issues (as Moscovici's model suggests) or on the last issue only (as Hollander's idiosyncrasy-credits approach argues). The investigators found that the minority members influenced the majority no matter what approach was taken. Hollander's aproach, however, was more influential in all-male groups (Bray, Johnson, & Chilstrom, 1982).

Men, Women, and Conformity

For centuries, American juries did not include women. Why? Many jurists argued that women could not hold fast to their private views or influence others, so they wouldn't contribute to the decision (see Table 6-4).

Do women conform more than men? Alice H. Eagly (1978, 1983), in a review of dozens of conformity studies, shows that women conformed more than men only in studies that involved face-to-face social pressure. In more anonymous, low-surveillance situations such as that developed by Crutchfield, differences between men and women are almost nonexistent. This conclusion has been confirmed in two separate reviews that combined the results of dozens of independent studies statistically (Cooper, 1979; Eagly & Carli, 1981).

A number of methodological, personal, and interpersonal factors combine to create this difference between men and women. Methodologically, much of the research examining conformity is biased in favor of men; by focusing on political or military issues, women suffered from "an information deficit relative to males" (Eagly, 1978, p. 97). Researchers have found that people who feel unskilled on a particular task are much more likely to conform to an incorrect majority opinion (Coleman, Blake, & Mouton, 1958; Endler & Hartley, 1973; Wiesental, Endler, Coward, & Edwards, 1976). Therefore, examining conformity in groups that were discussing male-oriented topics would make men seem less conforming. This hypothesis was supported in one study that asked men and women if they

TABLE 6-4. Changes in jury composition in the United States.

Date	Change
1879	U. S. Supreme Court rules that a West Virginia law excluding women from juries is constitutional.
1920	Women are given the right to vote but not the right to serve on juries.
1957	Civil Rights Act of 1957 gives women the right to serve on federal juries.
1975	U. S. Supreme Court rules that women cannot be excused from jury duty because of their gender.

agreed or disagreed with a series of feminine-oriented or masculine-oriented items (Sistrunk & McDavid, 1971). The results shown in Figure 6-5 indicate that gender-biased tasks may indeed account for the greater conformity of females; on masculine items males were less conforming than females, but on feminine tasks males were more conforming. On neutral items the sexes conformed at nearly equivalent rates (see also Goldberg, 1974, 1975; Javornisky, 1979; Karabenick, 1983; and Morelock, 1980).

Second, and more surprising, is the possibility that the sex difference may stem from researchers' tendencies to "design, implement, or report their studies in a way that results in an egotistical or flattering portrayal of the attributes of their own gender" (Eagly & Carli, 1981, p. 17). Since nearly two-thirds of the research on persuasion has been carried out by men, this own-sex bias has led to an overabundance of studies favoring men rather than women.

Sex differences in conformity have also been traced back to other male/female differences. Some researchers believe that women are superior to men in verbal skills so that their comprehension of persuasive messages is superior. Since comprehension is generally positively correlated with persuadability, differences in verbal skills actually mediate the sex difference in influenceability (Eagly, 1974; Eagly & Warren, 1976). Second, the difference may stem from sex-role socialization. In some cultures women are encouraged to adopt a feminine sex role that includes such characteristics as passivity, reliance on others, submissiveness, and a tendency to yield to the decisions of others. Men, in contrast, are taught to be independent, unemotional, and assertive. Hence, when women find them-

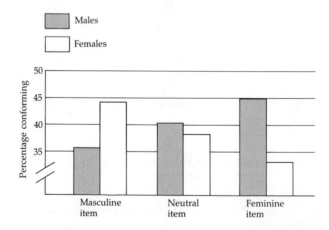

FIGURE 6-5. Sex differences in conformity. When a traditionally masculine task is used, women conform more than men. When the task calls for more feminine skills, men conform more than women. The sexes do not differ on gender-neutral tasks.

Source: Sistrunk & McDavid, 1971

selves in a conformity situation, they tend to yield to the majority; men, on the other hand, aggressively defend their viewpoints (Crutchfield, 1955, study 1; Gerard et al., 1968; Tuddenham, 1958, study 1). In support of this sex-role hypothesis, evidence indicates that women *and* men who adopt a feminine sex role conform more than men *and* women who adopt a masculine role or a role that combines elements of both masculinity and femininity (an androgynous sex-role orientation; see Bem, 1975, 1985). Moreover, as sex roles have changed in recent years, sex differences in conformity rates have become less robust (Eagly, 1978).

Lastly, interpersonal forces also contribute to this sex difference. Studies of status allocation reviewed in Chapter 5, for example, indicate that women are often accorded less status than men in groups. This sexist bias against women undermines their resistance to influence and weakens their power to influence others (Eagly, 1987). Eagly also notes that women, more so than men, agree with fellow group members so that the group's level of cohesiveness and harmony will be maintained (Eagly, Wood, & Fishbaugh, 1981). Men, in contrast, disagree with others so they can separate themselves from the rest of the group (Santee & Maslach, 1982; Maslach, Santee, & Wade, 1987). This final explanation is supported by a number of studies that suggest that women, in contrast to men, (1) vary their expressed opinions in order to match the views of attractive male partners (Zanna & Pack, 1975), (2) use opinion conformity as a self-presentational tactic (Braginsky, 1970; Tuthill & Forsyth, 1982), and (3) interpret conformity as a sign of competence rather than weakness (Santee & Jackson, 1982). Men, in contrast, have been found to be particularly nonconforming when their responses would be known to other group members (Eagly et al., 1981).

This final explanation of women's tendency to conform applies to the Corona jury. Of the two women in the group, one (Faye) agreed with the majority from the outset, but she was an opinion leader and major spokeswoman rather than a conforming follower. The second woman (Naomi), in contrast, never truly accepted Corona's guilt, but she eventually changed her vote to calm the conflict her dissent had created. As she exclaimed at the end of the deliberations, "Please, I'll change my vote. Just don't hate me" (Villaseñor, 1977, p. 241).

WHY CONFORM?

Many people think of conformity in a negative way. They assume that conformity is a spineless refusal to stand up for one's personal beliefs and is motivated by apathy or fear. This pejorative view of conformity, however, underestimates the complexity of conforming. Individuals in any group, including the Corona jury, change their behavior for a variety of reasons (Deutsch & Gerard, 1955; Kelley, 1952). A lack of personal conviction may be a factor, but other equally important causes should also be considered. Three basic factors examined here generally operate in concert to produce conformity: (1) normative influence, (2) informational influence, and (3) interpersonal influence.

Normative Influence

You attend a formal dinner and spend much of your time worrying about when to use each fork. At a fast-food restaurant you stand in line to order your food even though there are no directions or signs posted. When the traffic light turns red, you bring your car to a halt. You enter a public restroom but rush out when you discover that you have blundered into one reserved for the opposite sex.

Much of the conformity in these examples springs from what theorists call normative influence (Aronson, 1980; Deutsch & Gerard, 1955; Kelley, 1952). When you eat in a nice restaurant, you conform to the rules of proper etiquette. When nature calls, you use your gender's restroom. No one forces you to do so, but you feel better if you do. **Normative influence,** as we will see below, causes us to feel, think, and act in ways that are consistent with the group's norms.

The nature of norms.   The jurors in the Corona trial soon discovered that all the group members would have to adhere to certain rules if they were to reach a decision. Many of these rules governed speaking privileges. The foreman announced several of the rules at the outset of the deliberations, including (1) only one person speaks at a time, and speakers seek recognition by raising their hand; (2) a single statement may last no more than five minutes; and (3) all jurors must be present, or there will be no deliberations. Other rules were left unspoken, but they still influenced the group members: Treat others politely, No one should be pressured into agreeing with the majority, and The decision must be made gradually, without haste.

Social standards that describe what behaviors should and should not be performed in any social setting are known as **norms** (Rossi & Berk, 1985). They serve as guidelines by which group members regulate their own behaviors and thereby improve the coordination among interactants. *Prescriptive norms,* such as Treat others politely, describe desirable actions, whereas *proscriptive norms* identify negative behaviors: Do not make racist remarks and Do not make fun of Naomi were two proscriptive norms that emerged in the jury (Sorrels & Kelley, 1984).

Group norms, if written down, become the formal rules of the group, but in most instances norms are adopted implicitly. Groups rarely vote on which norms to adopt but, rather, gradually align their behaviors to match certain standards. As a consequence norms are often taken for granted so fully that members do not realize their existence until a norm has been violated. Norms thus imply evaluation; people who break the norms are considered "bad" and are open to sanction by the other group members. When one of the jurors spoke out of turn, Matt told him to "sit back, quiet down, and let's follow the basic rules Ernie laid down yesterday" (Villa-señor, 1977, p. 62). At another time Calvin glared at Rick, who had been waving his hand to be recognized, and complained "It's disturbing and rude to be waving like that" (p. 65).

The development of norms.

The jury's decision about Corona's guilt exemplifies the development of norms in a group. The jury faced a difficult task: it had to review the testimony of 117 witnesses and weigh 988 exhibits before passing judgment on Corona. As the group reviewed the evidence, a small subgroup began expressing its opinions publicly. Although the ballots were secret, those who voted "guilty" spoke out strongly in support of their position. Gradually, more of the group members began to favor a guilty verdict, and the seating arrangements of the table even shifted until the "not guilty" jurors were sitting together. Finally, one of the holdouts for innocence shifted to guilt, explaining that he had come to realize, with moral certitude, that Corona was responsible for the crimes. When the judge later asked each one of the group to give his or her personal decision on each count, every single juror said "guilty."

According to Muzafer Sherif, this type of change reflects the development of group standards that serve as frames of reference for behaviors and perceptions (M. Sherif, 1936, 1966; C. W. Sherif, 1976). A group facing an ambiguous problem or situation lacks internal consensus, but members soon structure their experiences until they conform to a standard accepted by the group. This standard can be pressed upon the group by an outside authority or a group leader, but Sherif notes that in most instances group norms develop through reciprocal influence. In the Corona jury individuals did not actively try to conform to the judgments of others but used the group consensus to revise their own opinions and beliefs. "When the external surroundings lack stable, orderly reference points, the individuals caught in the ensuing experience of uncertainty mutually contribute to each other a mode of orderliness to establish their own orderly pattern" (1966, pp. xii–xiii).

Sherif studied the development of norms by taking advantage of the *autokinetic effect*, the illusory movement of a stationary pinpoint of light in a dark room. Individuals, dyads, and triads were placed in the darkened room, shown a dot of light, and then asked to make a judgment about how far the dot of light moved. After repeated trials Sherif found that individuals making judgments by themselves established their own idiosyncratic average estimates, which varied from 1 to 10 inches. When people made their judgments in groups, however, their personal estimates blended with those of other group members until a consensus was reached. As Figure 6-6 shows, before joining the group, individuals varied considerably in their estimates; one subject thought the light moved an average of 7 inches on each trial, and the other two individuals' estimates averaged less than 1 inch and less than 2 inches. When these individuals were part of a group, however, their judgments converged over time in what Sherif called a *funnel pattern*; by the final session a norm of just over 2 inches had been formed.

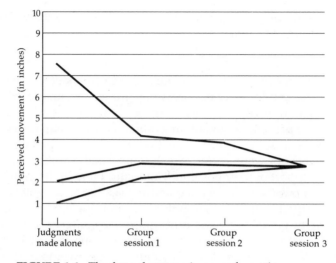

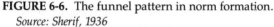

FIGURE 6-6. The funnel pattern in norm formation.
Source: Sherif, 1936

Some researchers use the autokinetic research as an example of compliance, but Sherif argues that the subjects internalized the group norm (Pollis, Montgomery, & Smith, 1975). To verify this internalization, Sherif disbanded the groups and had subjects make judgments alone. In these sessions the subjects still relied on the group norm (Sherif, 1966). Other researchers have even shown that such norms may eventually establish a life of their own (Jacobs & Campbell, 1961). When a confederate who made extreme judgments (15 inches) was placed in each group, this individual was able to deflect the rest of the group members' judgments upward so that a higher norm of movement was created in the group. Then, once this arbitrary standard had been created, the group confederate was removed from the group and replaced by a naive subject. The remaining group members retained the large-distance norm, however, and the newest group member gradually adapted to the higher standard. Old members were removed from the group and replaced with naive subjects, but the initiates continued to shift their estimates in the direction of the group norm. The arbitrary group norm eventually disappeared, but not before the group membership had been changed five or six times. Moreover, when a less extreme norm was established, the norm lasted indefinitely (MacNeil & Sherif, 1976).

Norms and conformity.   Norms can exert considerable influence in groups. At one level people feel compelled to act in accordance with group norms, because a variety of negative consequences could result from nonconformity. Violating group norms can create conflict within the group and can lead to losses in status, to rejection, or even to ostracism. This aspect of normative influence seems to be well summarized in the aphorism "To get along, you go along."

At another level, however, people obey norms in order to fulfill personal expectations about proper behavior. Norms are not simply external constraints but internalized standards; members feel duty bound to adhere to the norms of the group since, as loyal members, they accept the legitimacy of the established norms and recognize the importance of supporting these norms. As applied to a situation such as that studied by Asch or Sherif, these dualistic bases of normative social influence suggest that people conform because (1) they fear the negative interpersonal consequences—ostracism, ridicule, or punishment—that their nonconformity may produce and (2) they feel personally compelled to live up to others' expectations.

Normative influence accounts for many empirical relations evident in research. If normative pressures are weakened, perhaps because the majority cannot reach unanimous agreement on the correct responses (Allen, 1975; Morris & Miller, 1975a) or the stimulus is very ambiguous (Crutchfield, 1955), nonconformity becomes much more likely. Furthermore, if these normative pressures are heightened—perhaps by increasing the cohesiveness of the group (Festinger, Schachter, & Back, 1950), creating an expectation of future interaction (Lewis, Langan, & Hollander, 1972), or emphasizing the importance of maintaining a congenial group atmosphere (Reckman & Goethals, 1973)—conformity tends to increase. Lastly, the concept of normative social influence also explains why certain people, such as those with a high need for social approval, conform more than others (Tuddenham, 1959).

Informational Influence

Several jurors, before deliberating, were uncertain of Corona's guilt. The evidence pointed in his direction, but was the prosecution's case strong enough for a conviction? Before making up their minds, they often sought out the opinions of their fellow group members. The basic question "Do you think he did it?" was asked over and over in private conversations, and on the second day the group took a preliminary vote. The jurors knew that the vote was premature, because they still needed to review all the evidence, but "most of the jurors were anxious to know where everyone else stood before expressing their own views" (Villaseñor, 1977 p. 63).

Individuals often change their own personal position when they gain information about others' responses on the issue. This process, known as **informational influence,** occurs because other people are a valuable source of information about the social world. As social-comparison theory notes (see Chapter 3), one primary reason for joining a group is to gain information about the accuracy of one's own perceptions and beliefs (Festinger, 1954; Goethals & Darley, 1977). Through social comparisons people are able to construct meaningful and coherent definitions of social situations and validate their conclusions (Fazio, 1979). We often compare ourselves to others implicitly, and we overestimate the extent to which these others agree with us (Gerard & Orive, 1987; Orive, 1988a, 1988b). Alternatively, the comparison may take place explicitly, as when the Corona jury took its first vote. In either case we sometimes modify our own position once we process the information contained in others' responses.

Informational influence works by prompting a reinterpretation, or cognitive *restructuring*, of key aspects of the issue (Allen & Wilder, 1980; Campbell, Tesser, & Fairey, 1986). Within the Corona jury, for example, several jurors voted "innocent" because they did not know whether general circumstantial evidence should be considered as evidence pertaining to the specific murders. These jurors changed their vote when they realized that the majority was voting on all 25 murders taken together rather than on each single case.

In one study of restructuring researchers asked subjects to respond to a number of opinion items while seated in standard Crutchfield testing booths (Allen & Wilder, 1980). Although each statement was accompanied by information about the opinions of a previous group of participants, the subjects weren't asked to give their opinions on the items. Rather, they were asked to define certain phrases in the statements. The subjects were shown an item such as "I would never go out of my way to help another person," and then they learned that a four-person group had unanimously agreed with the statement, clearly an unexpected and unpopular response (Allen & Wilder, 1980, p. 1118). When the subjects were asked what the phrase "go out of my way" meant in the sentence, they reinterpreted it to mean "risk my life" rather than "be inconvenienced."

Both majorities and minorities make use of informational influence (Campbell et al., 1986; Wolf, 1987). For the majority informational influence is greatest when each person in the majority acts independently of the others. One investigator demonstrated this point by giving subjects information about others' judgments concerning a fictitious court case (Wilder, 1977, experiment 2). The subjects were told that these opinions represented either the judgments of people working independently or the judgments of people working as a group. As predicted, when the information was apparently coming from a single social entity—for example, a group of individuals working together—the magnitude of conformity was the same whether the group contained two members or six members. However, when the number of discrete social entities was increased (for example, from two independent individuals to six independent individuals or from one four-person group to two two-person groups), a ceiling effect became evident when the number of entities reached three (Gerard et al., 1968; Wilder, 1977).

Minorities, too, influence by conveying information (Wolf, 1985, 1987). Moscovici argues that the consistent minority is an innovative "creator of conflicts," which challenges the status quo of the group by calling for a reevaluation of issues at hand. Such a minority shakes the confidence of the majority and thereby forces the group to seek out new information about the situation. In one study of this process subjects were asked to identify all possible solutions to a series of puzzles. When working on this task alone, the subjects tended to select the most obvious solution. Also, when working in a group, most subjects went along with the majority's choice, even if that choice was not the best. If, however, a minority (two confederates) argued for a nonobvious solution, the subjects chose solutions that were both novel and correct. They did not accept the minority's proposal, as they had the majority's, but the minority did succeed in forcing them to reevaluate their original answer (Nemeth & Wachtler, 1983). Other evidence indicates that minorities often prompt group members to use more varied strategies in solving problems and to devise more creative solutions (Nemeth, 1986; Nemeth & Kwan, 1985, 1987). (See Focus 6-4).

· ·

FOCUS 6-4: MINDLESSNESS AND CONFORMITY

Informational influence occurs when individuals confront a puzzling situation and extract information from the responses that others are making. Yet people are not always rational information seekers. As Ellen Langer and her associates explain, in everyday social situations we often respond automatically; when **mindlessness** occurs, we just don't stop to think about what we are doing (Langer, Blank, & Chanowitz, 1978; Langer & Newman, 1979).

Langer and her associates demonstrated the impact of mindlessness on conformity in a field study conducted in a university library. A male or female experimenter approached adults who were using a photocopying machine and asked: "Excuse me. I have five pages. May I use the Xerox machine?" In the control condition no explanation for this request was offered, but in the real-information condition the experimenter explained "I'm in a rush." In a third condition a justification was given, but the explanation was essentially absurd: "May I use the Xerox machine, because I have to make copies?" Langer labeled this variation the placebic-information condition; the statement took the form of a justification, but it made little sense (Langer et al., 1978, experiment 1, p. 637).

Only 60% of the subjects complied with the request in the control condition, but over 90% agreed in the two other conditions. In a second variation of the study the request was increased from just 5 pages to 20 pages. In this instance the researchers found that compliance rates dropped dramatically and that people no longer mindlessly reacted to the placebic information. In this case compliance in the control and placebic-information conditions was equal (24%). This study and others reported by Langer and her associates suggest that people sometimes fail to consider the implications of conformity (see Folkes, 1985; Langer, Chanowitz, & Blank, 1985).

· ·

Interpersonal Influence

Just before a key vote by the jurors, Naomi interrupted the proceedings (Villaseñor, 1977, p. 149):

> "Wait. I got one thing to say. If Corona is so guilty, then why didn't the sheriff come and tell us that he knows Corona is guilty?"
>
> Everyone looked at Naomi. Victor and Matt, almost in unison, pushed back their chairs and lowered their heads, trying not to laugh. Frank and Larry looked at each other. Rogers yelled:
>
> "Because that's not evidence! That would be hearsay! Dammit, why don't you ask why God doesn't come down here and tell us everything about everybody, then we don't even need the jury system and we can all go home!"

More is going on here than normative influence and informational influence. The jury has detected a nonconformist in its midst, and it is exerting direct **interpersonal influence**, including persuasion, bargains, promises, and even the threat of rejection in an attempt to change her vote.

If Asch's procedure can be identified as the key study of the individual's reaction to the majority, then Schachter's 1951 study should be considered the corresponding classic on the majority's reaction to the individual. The theoretical framework for the study derived from a field study of social pressures in informal groups conducted by Schachter in collaboration with Festinger and Kurt Back. This project, which was sponsored by the Research Center for Group Dynamics, examined the relationship between attraction and opinion conformity in two housing developments reserved for married university students. One of the developments, Westgate, was a garden complex whose units were arranged in U-shaped courts. The second development, Westgate-West, featured 17 two-story buildings containing ten apartments each.

At the time of the study the tenants of both complexes were embroiled in a debate over the relative advantages and disadvantages of joining a tenant association. Nearly all the residents of Westgate-West favored the association. In Westgate, in contrast, opinions varied *among* courts, but agreement *within* each court was high. Festinger, Schachter, and Back reasoned that group pressures had created uniformity of opinion in the courts because their physical design promoted interaction among the residents who lived in each courtyard. Indeed, in Westgate individuals who expressed an opinion that deviated from their court's overall judgment lived in the more physically isolated units and were not as well liked as those who agreed with the majority opinion (Festinger et al., 1950).

Festinger and his colleagues explored these provocative findings in a number of subsequent studies (Back, 1951; Festinger, Gerard, Hymovitch, Kelley, & Raven, 1952; Festinger & Thibaut, 1971; Gerard, 1953). Schachter, for his dissertation, decided to examine how three key variables—group cohesiveness, topic relevance, and degree of opinion conformity—influenced attraction and rejection in laboratory groups. He invited men majoring in economics to join one of four clubs that would be (1) discussing case studies at the behest of a group of local lawyers, (2) advising a new national magazine on editorial policies, (3) screening movies for local theaters, or (4) evaluating material to be used by a local radio station. The potential subjects were asked to indicate their interest in two of these four possible clubs, and cohesiveness was manipulated by putting some of the subjects in clubs that interested them and others in clubs that did not interest them. Schachter assumed that people with common interests would be more cohesive than those with disparate interests.

The relevance of the topic to the group was manipulated in a more straightforward fashion. During what the participants thought was the organizational meeting of their clubs, the experimenter asked them to discuss a legal case. This case, which rather sympathetically described the problems of a young juvenile delinquent named Johnny Rocco, was relevant to the stated purposes of the case-study and the editorial club (it was purportedly the basis for a feature article on delinquency) but was irrelevant to those of the radio and movie clubs. Thus, Schachter created four different kinds of groups corresponding to his 2 × 2 factorial design:

1. high-cohesiveness/relevant issue groups
2. low-cohesiveness/relevant issue groups
3. high-cohesiveness/irrelevant issue groups
4. low-cohesiveness/irrelevant issue groups

Schachter also added three confederates to each of the five- to seven-member clubs. These paid participants played one of three roles: "mode," deviant, and "slider." The group members were to decide on a course of treatment for Rocco that could range from "love" (Position 1) to "punishment" (Position 7). Most of the subjects tended to offer fairly lenient recommendations, and the *mode* confederate supported the group consensus. If the group's opinion shifted in any direction, the mode went along with the group. The *deviant*, in contrast, adopted a position of extreme discipline (Position 7) and refused to change his opinion during the discussion. The *slider* also began by championing punishment but shifted his position during the course of the group meeting to agree with the majority of the members.

Schachter, drawing on Festinger's (1950) theory of informal communication, predicted that the group members would try to influence the unrelenting nonconformist through various forms of interpersonal persuasion, bargains, promises, and even threat of rejection. These reactions are examined below.

Interpersonal rejection.   Schachter felt that the nonconformist would be disliked by the other group members, but he also felt that the magnitude of this rejection would depend on the relevance of the nonconformity to the group's purposes and on the cohesiveness of the group. Schachter hypothesized that both these variables would lead to increases in group pressure in the direction of uniformity, so he predicted that rejection would be relatively greater in cohesive groups and in the groups working on a relevant task.

Schachter measured the group members' reactions to the deviant, slider, and mode by collecting sociometric rankings and asking for nominations to various committees. The sociometric data indicated that across all four experimental conditions, the deviant was given a more negative ranking than either the mode or the slider. In addition, this rejection was more pronounced in the more cohesive groups (see Table 6-5).

Subsequent studies have replicated this relationship between rejection and nonconformity, although these later studies frequently note that certain situational factors increase the magnitude of this relationship. Task relevance (Lauderdale, 1976; Wiggins, Dill, & Schwartz, 1965), cohesiveness (Emerson, 1954), interdependency (Berkowitz & Howard, 1959), behavior extremity (Hensley & Duval, 1976; Levine & Ranelli, 1978; Mudd, 1968), and the degree of threat posed by the dissenter (Lauderdale, Smith-Cunnien, Parker, & Inverarity, 1984) all work to increase rejection, whereas the facilitation of task performance through deviation (Kelley & Shapiro, 1954), apologies for deviation (Dedrick, 1978), group norms that encourage innovation (Moscovici, 1976), and prior conformity (Hollander, 1960; Katz, 1982) minimize the rejection of nonconformists. Overall, however, the general relationship between nonconformity and rejection appears to be a robust one. (See Levine, 1980, for a comprehensive review.)

Schachter's findings also hint at an intriguing tendency to reject even the slider (Emerson, 1954; Kiesler & Pallak, 1975). Although studies of interpersonal attraction suggest that disagreement doesn't always engender dislike (Dutton, 1973; Sigall, 1970), John Levine and his associates have found that a little dissent often leads to a little rejection (Levine, 1980; Levine & Ranelli, 1978; Levine & Ruback, 1980; Levine, Saxe, & Harris, 1976; Levine, Sroka, & Snyder, 1977). In one study the subjects watched a film portraying the case of a juvenile delinquent named Gary (Levine et al., 1976). Next, using a Crutchfield apparatus, the group members answered the item "Gary would benefit more from psychological help than from im-

TABLE 6-5. Sociometric rankings of paid participants in Schachter's study of deviancy.

Type of Group	Type of Task	Type of Nonconformist		
		Deviant	Mode	Slider
Cohesive group	Relevant task	6.44[1]	4.65	5.02
Noncohesive group	Relevant task	5.83	4.70	4.56
Cohesive group	Irrelevant task	6.41	4.68	4.44
Noncohesive group	Irrelevant task	5.67	3.83	5.03

[1]Higher scores indicate less liking.

(Source: Schachter, 1951)

prisonment" by flipping one of nine switches arranged in order from "very strongly disagree" (1) to "very strongly agree" (9).

During the course of the session the subjects voted on the issue five times, and the experimenters manipulated these responses to create six experimental conditions. Subjects in the control condition believed that the group was unanimous in its opinions on the issue. The rest of the subjects, in contrast, received information indicating that one of the group members was a nonconformist (see Figure 6-7). In the neutral/agree condition this individual initially expressed a neutral opinion but agreed with the majority by Vote 5. In the neutral/disagree condition just the reverse occurred: the nonconformist shifted from neutral to disagreement during the sessions. Subjects in the other conditions saw the nonconformist shift from disagreement to agreement, shift from agreement to disagreement, or consistently disagree with the majority on all five votes.

The subjects were asked to rate one of the other group members, and "by chance" all were asked to give their opinion of the nonconformist. These ratings, which are shown in Figure 6-7, suggest that a slider who eventually agrees with the majority's opinion will be liked slightly less

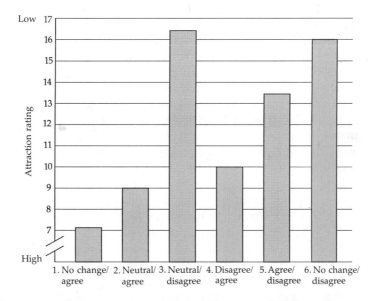

FIGURE 6-7. Attraction ratings for various types of sliders in groups. The conformist (Condition 1) and the slider who moved from neutrality to agreement (Condition 2) were the best liked. The slider who shifted all the way from nearly complete disagreement to nearly complete agreement (Condition 4) and the slider who actually moved away from the majority opinion (Condition 5) were rated as somewhat attractive. Lastly, the slider who moved from neutrality to disagreement and the constant dissenter were the most negatively evaluated of all partners.

Source: Levine, Saxe, and Harris, 1976

than a conformist. Moreover, if the slider initially expresses an extremely deviant attitude, subsequent conformity is not sufficient to overcome this negative first impression. Finally, demonstrating initial conformity and subsequently disagreeing does not shield one from interpersonal rejection, nor does steadfastly refusing to yield to the group's persuasive communications. Apparently most subjects interpreted such a refusal to yield as a sign of close-mindedness rather than independence.

Status and nonconformity.   Being liked was not all that was lost by the dissenters in the Schachter study. When he examined nominations to various internal committees within the groups, he found that deviants were assigned the lower status jobs. The executive and steering committees were of higher status, whereas members viewed the writing and recording duties of the correspondence committee with distaste. As expected, the deviants were elected to the correspondence committee more frequently than chance would dictate in nearly all groups (the exception was the low-cohesion/irrelevant task groups). Overall, this general tendency was more pronounced when the task was relevant rather than irrelevant to the groups' goals.

Influence and ostracism.   Schachter felt that the pressure put on the nonconformists would be evident in the frequency of communications directed at them by other group members. At first, communications would be fairly evenly distributed among the mode, deviant, and slider as the group members made public their various positions. As soon as it became obvious that the deviant and slider were in disagreement with the others, however, the bulk of the group's communications would involve these two participants. This focus on the dissenters would increase, he hypothesized, until (1) the dissenter capitulated to the majority opinion (as in the case of the slider) or (2) the majority concluded that the deviant would not budge from his position (as in the case of the nonchanging deviant). Schachter felt, however, that this latter reaction would probably occur only in cohesive groups that were working on a relevant task and, even then, for only those group members who strongly rejected the deviant. In these unique circumstances communication would be related to time spent deliberating in a curvilinear fashion: low initially, peaking at the halfway point, and then falling off as the session ended.

  Schachter tested these predictions by noting each comment made to the deviant, mode, and slider during the course of the meeting. These records indicated that communication with the deviant tended to increase throughout the course of the session, apparently as the group tried to identify the appropriate position to take on the issue. However, when subjects who eventually rejected the deviant on the questionnaire measures were studied separately from the others, Schachter found evidence of the hypothesized curvilinear relationship between time and communication in the high-cohesiveness/relevant-task cell of the design; in this specific instance the rate of communication peaked approximately 30 minutes into the discussion but dwindled in the final minutes. Surprisingly, the total amount of communication with the deviant was greatest in the low-co-hesiveness/irrelevant-task condition, the very group that should have evidenced few attempts at persuading the confederate to agree with the majority.

The ostracism of a nonconformist appears to occur only as a last resort (Berkowitz, 1971; Emerson, 1954; Mills, 1962). In most cases groups display an *inclusive reaction* to intractable nonconformists: communication between the majority and the minority is intensive and hostile, but long-term exclusion does not occur. If an *exclusive reaction* occurs, however, communication with the deviant dwindles along with overt hostility, but at a covert level the deviant is rejected by the majority members. According to this inclusion/exclusion hypothesis, the curvilinear relationship predicted by Schachter will occur only when certain behavioral and situational factors create an exclusive reaction among the group members (Orcutt, 1973).

Available evidence lends partial support to this inclusion/exclusion hypothesis. In most cases majority members send tremendous amounts of information to the most deviant members of their group unless the experimenter increases tendencies toward exclusion by telling the members that their group is extremely heterogeneous (Festinger et al., 1952; Festinger & Thibaut, 1951). In addition, although homogeneous groups are characterized by high rates of communication between modal members and deviants during the initial phases of interaction, when the modal members realize that the deviant will not be influenced, this communication level decreases. In such cases the group members seem to be "redefining their group boundary" by rejecting dissenters (Gerard, 1953). Even more conclusive findings came from a study of White women discussing the case of a Black juvenile delinquent (Sampson & Brandon, 1964). Each group included a confederate who espoused either a conforming or deviating opinion; this confederate was the opinion deviant. Each group also included a confederate who introduced herself either as a typical liberal college student or as a racist; this confederate was the role deviant. Content analysis of the subsequent group discussion revealed that, overall, hostile statements and requests for information were more frequently directed at the opinion deviant, whereas statements of solidarity were directed at the conformist. However, far greater differences were produced by the role-deviancy variable. As predicted, the announcement of a prejudiced attitude created an exclusive reaction. Rather than arguing with this nonconformist, the members excluded her from conversations, rated her very negatively on postexperiment evaluations, and in some cases even moved their chairs to avoid facing her (Sampson, 1971).

Influence in Groups: A Conclusion

The power of groups is great. We tend to think of ourselves as individualists who control our own actions and thoughts, but our groups often exert a strong guiding hand on our attitudes and behaviors. Recall, for example, the results of Newcomb's 1943 study of political attitudes, discussed in Chapter 2. He discovered that students changed their attitudes until their political preferences matched the attitudes of their fellow classmates and professors. More recently Chris S. Crandall (1988) documented similar normative, informational, and interpersonal influences in a study of bulimia, a pernicious cycle of binge eating followed by self-induced vomiting or other forms of purging. Bulimia tends to run in certain social groups, such as cheerleading squads, dance troupes, sports teams, and sororities (Crago, Yates, Beutler, & Arizmendi, 1985; Garner & Garfinkel, 1980; Squire, 1983). In explanation Crandall notes that such groups adopt norms that encourage binging and purging. Rather than viewing these actions as abnormal and a threat to health, the sororities that Crandall studied accepted purging as a normal means of controlling one's weight. He also found indirect evidence of interpersonal influence; to be popular in the group, one had to binge at the rate established by the group's norms. Also, as time passed, those who were not binging began to binge.

In sum, we strive to live up to the norms of our group and our society. When uncertain, we rely on our fellow group members for information. And when we stray from the golden mean, our group members pull us back through interpersonal influence. From Festinger and his colleagues (1950, p. 91): "If a person wants to stay in a group, he will be susceptible to influences coming from the group, and he will be willing to conform to the rules which the group sets up."

APPLICATION: UNDERSTANDING JURIES

The practice of asking a group of people to serve as the final arbiter of guilt and innocence has formed the foundations of judicial systems for centuries. As far back as the 11th century the neighbors of those accused of wrongdoing were asked both to provide information about the actions of the accused and to weigh the evidence. Witnesses and experts now provide the evidence, but the jury remains responsible for weighing the testimony of each person before rendering a verdict. (Hyman & Tarrant, 1975, and Moore, 1973, discuss the history of juries.)

Yet given what we know about conformity and nonconformity in groups, should the jury system currently in use in the United States and other Western countries be modified? Asch's studies tell us that people often conform and that even a correct minority often loses to an incorrect majority. As we have seen, normative, informational, and interpersonal influence are powerful forces in groups, and they can quash individuals' freedom to speak their minds. Juries are a time-honored tradition, but are they effective?

How Effective Are Juries?

Determining the effectiveness of juries as deciders of guilt or innocence is a complicated task, for we can never know when the jury has been correct or incorrect in condemning or freeing a defendant. If a clear criterion for determining guilt existed, juries would not be necessary in the first place. Several bits of evidence, however, provide partial support for the effectiveness of juries as decision makers.

First, jurors seem to take their role very seriously. As Villaseñor's account of the Corona jury vividly illustrates, jurors strive to reach the fairest decision possible (Hastie, Penrod, & Pennington, 1983). A jury expert, Rita James Simon, after studying the responses of more than 2000 jurors participating in a Chicago law project, concluded that

> the jurors spent most of their time reviewing the court record. By the time they finished deliberating they had usually considered every bit of testimony, expert as well as lay, and every point offered in evidence. The most consistent theme that emerged from listening to the deliberations was the seriousness with which the jurors approached their job and the extent to which they were concerned that the verdict they reached was consistent with the spirit of the law and with the facts of the case [1980, p. 52].

Second, juries do well when compared with judges' preferences. In a survey of nearly 8000 actual criminal and civil trials, judges and juries disagreed on only 20% of the cases; for criminal trials the jury was somewhat more lenient than the judge, but for civil trials the disagreements were evenly split for and against the defendant. Furthermore, 80% of these disagreements occurred when the weight of the evidence was so close that the judge admitted that the verdict could have gone either way. This concord between verdicts may explain why 77% of the judges surveyed felt that the jury system was satisfactory, 20% felt that it had disadvantages that should be corrected, but only 3% felt that the system was so unsatisfactory that its use should be curtailed (Kalven & Zeisel, 1966).

Lastly, jurors are hardly unbiased, rational weighers of evidence; the defendant's physical appearance, the lawyer's style of questioning, and the sequencing of evidence are just a few of the factors that bias jurors' decisions (Dane & Wrightsman, 1982; Hastie et al., 1984; Kaplan, 1982). These biases are largely controlled, however, by relying on group decisions rather than individuals' decisions. Simulations of juries suggest that the lone juror's initial biases and preferences have very little impact on the group's final decision, no matter what the size of the jury (Kerr & Huang, 1986).

Improving Juries

The judicial system is long on tradition, but in recent years several innovations have been suggested and even implemented (Saks, 1977). Many of these changes focus on juries and are designed to increase their effectiveness and efficiency. But do these changes make sense, given the findings of group dynamicists?

Jury size. In 1970 the U.S. Supreme Court returned a landmark ruling in the case of *Williams v. Florida* (National Center for State Courts [NCSC],

1976). Williams sought to have his conviction overturned on the ground that the deciding jury had included only 6 persons. The Supreme Court, however, found in favor of the State, ruling that a jury can function adequately with fewer than 12:

> To be sure, the number should probably be large enough to promote group deliberation, free from outside attempts at intimidation, and to provide a fair possibility for obtaining a representative cross-section of the community. But we find little reason to think that these goals are in any meaningful sense less likely to be achieved when the jury numbers six, than when it numbers twelve—particularly if the requirement of unanimity is retained. And certainly the reliability of the jury as a factfinder hardly seems likely to be a function of its size [*Williams v. Florida*, 1970, pp. 100–101].

Michael J. Saks, one of the leading researchers in the area of psychology and law, suggests that the Supreme Court should have taken group dynamics research into consideration before making its decision (Saks, 1977; Saks & Hastie, 1978). As he notes, modifying the size of a group leads to numerous other changes:

1. *Changes in communication patterns*. In two experiments Saks (1977) systematically manipulated the sizes of mock juries while coding the pattern and content of communications. Overall, he found that participation was more equally distributed among the members of small groups but that the larger groups communicated more, because they took longer to deliberate. As an incidental finding, he also reported that the members of the smaller juries rated one another more positively.

2. *Changes in representativeness*. Saks (1977) also notes that 6-person juries are not as representative of the community as 12-person juries. Although this loss was anticipated by the Supreme Court members in their ruling, Saks showed that the magnitude of the effect could be quite large. For example, if a community was 10% Black and 90% White, in all probability about 80% of the 12-person juries would include at least one Black, but only 40% of the 6-person juries would contain a Black.

3. *Changes in minority/majority pressures*. As noted earlier in this chapter, once the group reaches a certain size, conformity rates remain essentially constant as the group increases in size; this finding suggests that juries could include as few as four members. Conformity pressures may be greater in smaller juries, however, since the likelihood of finding a partner for one's minority coalition becomes smaller. The Court assumed that a 5-1 vote in a 6-person jury was essentially the same as a 10-2 split in 12-person group, but psychologically the situation is dramatically different. With the 10-2 vote one's opinion is buttressed by the presence of a dissenting partner, whereas in the 5-1 vote one must face the majority alone. As a result the likelihood of a hung jury is greater in larger juries (Kerr & MacCoun, 1985).

4. *Changes in conviction and acquittal rates.* From a practical standpoint differences in communication, representativeness, and majority/minority pressures are of secondary importance. Of primary interest is the impact of the change on conviction and acquittal rates, and evidence bearing on this consequence is encouraging. On the negative side many studies conducted to investigate this issue are methodologically flawed and, therefore, difficult to interpret (Davis & Stasson, 1988; Vollrath & Davis, 1980). On the positive side studies that yield interpretable data suggest that verdict differences between 6- and 12-member juries are slight (Padawer-Singer, Singer, & Singer, 1977; Saks, 1977). As the Supreme Court's ruling suggested, the impact of jury size may be negligible on the overall product of the deliberation.

Unanimity.   In 1972 three men were convicted, in separate trials, of assault, grand larceny, and burglary by the court system of Oregon. They appealed their case to the U. S. Supreme Court on the ground that their right to a fair trial had been violated because the votes of the juries had not been unanimous; in the first two trials the vote was 11-1 for conviction, and in the burglary trial the decision was 10-2. To the defendants' dismay, the Supreme Court ruled in favor of Oregon (*Apodoca v. Oregon*, 1972), concluding that the Sixth Amendment to the U.S. Constitution guarantees only that a "substantial majority of the jury" must be convinced of the defendant's guilt. Later in the ruling the Court suggested that 75% agreement constitutes an acceptable minimum for most juries.   .

From an empirical perspective the Court's conclusion was, in part, reasonable but, in part, unreasonable. First, the verdict preferred by the majority of the jurors on the first vote usually becomes the final verdict in a large percentage of the cases with or without a unanimity rule. The minority's opinion sometimes prevails, but in such cases the minority is usually so substantial that a 9-out-of-12 majority would not have been reached anyway. Also, studies of informal rules in juries suggest that despite the judge's instructions to deliberate to unanimity, most juries implicitly operate according to either a basic two-thirds or a 10-out-of-12 rule (Davis, Kerr, Atkin, Holt, & Meek, 1975; Davis, Kerr, Stasser, Meek, & Holt, 1977; Stasser, Kerr, & Bray, 1982).

Relaxing the requirement for unanimity, however, changes the decision-making process in juries. Juries that do not have to reach a unanimous decision render their judgments twice as quickly and are far less likely to come to a stalemate (Foss, 1981; Kerr et al., 1976). Saks and Hastie assert (1978, pp. 84–85), that the consequence of relaxing unanimity requirements will be that juries reach "decisions on the basis of weaker evidence; and this means that more errors of both types will occur: convictions when the correct decision is acquittal; acquittals when the correct decision is conviction." Saks and Hastie feel that "increased efficiency is purchased at some cost in accuracy" but that the magnitude of this inaccuracy is not yet clearly known.

Voir dire.   For a number of years the courts have selected jury members from a pool of potential participants through a process known as voir dire. **Voir dire,** which means "to speak truly," calls for verbal or written questioning of prospective jurors to uncover any biases or prejudices that may stand in the way of fairness and impartiality (Hans & Vidmar, 1982).

Until the 1970s voir dire was primarily left up to judges' discretion; defense lawyers could submit questions, but judges were free to omit them if they desired. However, in the face of certain Supreme Court rulings in which convictions were overturned because trial judges had disallowed defense participation in voir dire (for example, *Ham v. S. Carolina*, 1973), courts began opening up the procedure to defense attorneys. In consequence, defense lawyers began to use the voir dire process to identify sympathetic and antagonistic jurors. For example, defense attorneys used systematic jury-selection techniques when picking the panel to try the political activist Angela Davis, who was brought to trial in 1972 to face charges of murder and kidnapping. The defense attorneys spent 13 days selecting the 12 jurors and 4 alternates for the trial, and they based their choices on detailed analyses of each juror, prepared by a team of five psychologists. Davis was acquitted, but the impact of the jury selection procedures on the final verdict is not known.

Systematic jury selection based on elaborate pretrial research and intensified voir dire has sparked a controversy over the purposes of voir dire. Proponents of the technique argue that in many political and criminal trials, biases produced by unfair publicity, regional prejudices, and unrepresentative jury rosters must be controlled if the defendant is to receive just treatment. Critics, in contrast, feel that systematic selection is tantamount to jury rigging, since it produces lenient rather than fair juries and works to exclude certain types of people from juries (Wrightsman, 1978). Lawrence Wrightsman, an expert on psychology and the law, goes so far as to conclude that voir dire, when conducted by a lawyer, is not "in the best interests of justice" (1987, p. 243).

Wrightsman offers a solution to the problem. He suggests that voir dire questioning be carried out in the judge's chambers and that judges supervise the process. Voir dire is a useful way of identifying highly biased individuals, but it should not be a means of manipulating the composition of the jury. Wrightsman concludes that if voir dire is abused by lawyers, then it should be done away with altogether (Wrightsman, 1987).

SUMMARY

Groups change their members' thoughts, feelings, and behavior through various forms of *social influence*. Asch's research, for example, illustrates how groups encourage conformity and discourage nonconformity. When the majority of the members of a group made an obvious error, most subjects went along with the unanimous majority's judgments. On average, a subject gave a conforming answer on about one-third of the test trials.

Asch concluded that conformity, which includes both *conversion* (or *private acceptance*) and *compliance*, is more prevalent than the two basic forms of nonconformity, *independence* and *counterconformity* (or anticonformity).

When do individuals display conformity or nonconformity? Group and faction size often make a difference: the larger the unanimous majority facing the lone individual, the greater the rate of conformity. Asch himself found that this impact leveled off when the group size reached four (a ceiling effect), but Latané's *social impact theory* and Mullen's *self-attention theory* with its *other/total ratio* (OTR) offer alternative models. The size of the minority coalition is critical as well, and in some cases a minority can even succeed in influencing the majority. Moscovici, for example, finds that a consistent minority can influence the majority at a latent level. In juries, however, the minority rarely influences the majority.

Status and influence are also closely linked. People who are accorded high status in the group generally conform less than those who are low in status, and the concept of *idiosyncrasy credits* assumes that they are also protected from sanctions when they do display nonconformity. High-status individuals are, however, strongly sanctioned if *status liability* occurs.

Women conform more than men, albeit only in face-to-face groups. Eagly has identified a number of methodological, personal, and interpersonal factors that combine to create this difference. Several studies, for example, suggest that women use conformity to increase group harmony, whereas men use nonconformity to create the impression of independence.

Why do people conform? Three basic factors generally operate in concert to produce conformity. First, *normative influence* prompts us to feel, think, and act in ways that are consistent with our group's social standards. These standards, or *norms*, describe what behaviors should and should not be performed in any social setting. As Sherif's work shows, when individuals make judgments in groups, their judgments converge over time as a norm develops.

Second, *informational influence* takes place whenever we look to others for information. As social-comparison theory notes, people are a valuable source of information about our social world; the majority is influential because we assume that a large number of people can't all be wrong, and a minority is influential because it prompts us to reevaluate our position. When *mindlessness* sets in, however, we respond automatically without bothering to process relevant information.

Third, *interpersonal influence* includes persuasion, bargains, promises, and even the threat of rejection. Just as Asch's work stimulated many studies of conformity, Schachter's analysis of group rejection of a nonconformist initiated a line of research that testifies to the many consequences of nonconformity. These studies have shown that a nonconformist is generally less well liked by others in the group and that communication with an unyielding deviant eventually diminishes, at least when cohesive groups are working on relevant tasks. Even members who change their minds and conform are often rejected and stripped of status.

Despite these social influence pressures, available evidence suggests that juries are satisfactory vehicles for making legal decisions and that recent changes in the legal system have not substantially undermined this effectiveness. These innovations, which include reducing the number of jurors, relaxing the unanimity rule, and selecting jurors through more sophisticated *voir dire* procedures, do not seem to have dramatically changed the functioning of juries.

·7·

Power

Horror and disbelief were common reactions when over 900 members of the People's Temple committed mass suicide in a South American jungle village. The idea that so many people could commit suicide was appalling, and as journalists reported the gruesome details, incredulity grew into bafflement. Why would the group's leader, Jim Jones, formerly noted for his humanitarian acts of social reform, command his followers to take poison? Why did the group members obey his order when refusal could have had no worse consequences than obedience? What force is great enough to make parents give poison to their children?

Many traced the tragedy back to Jones—his childhood, his persuasiveness, and his irrational fears of persecution. Others emphasized the kind of people who joined the group—their psychological instability, their willingness to identify with the cause, and their religious fervor. Still others suggested a more fantastic explanation: did a divine power eradicate the Jonestown colonists for acts against nature? This chapter, in contrast, offers an explanation that is based on the concept of social power. Jones, like many other influential leaders, possessed an extraordinary **power**: the capacity to influence others, even when they try to resist this influence (Lewin, 1951).

THE NATURE OF POWER

Cartwright, a leading researcher and theorist in group dynamics, believes that few interactions advance very far before elements of power and influence come into play. Leaders who demand obedience from their followers, the person who agrees to help another provided the other reciprocates, and the boss who offers employees a bonus if they work overtime are all experiencing the dynamics of social power as they influence and are, in turn, influenced by others. Indeed, Cartwright concluded many years ago that "such concepts as influence, power, and authority (or their equivalents) must be employed in any adequate treatment of social interaction wherever it may take place" (1959, p. 183). Bertrand Russell stressed even more heavily the importance of power when he wrote that "the fundamental concept in social science is Power, in the same sense in which Energy is the fundamental concept in physics" (1938, p. 10).

But what is power? Definitions abound, but two themes are salient in most: "the ability to *exert* power, in the sense of controlling others and events, and the capacity to *defend* against power" (Hollander, 1985, p. 488).

John R. P. French and Bertram Raven (1959) suggest, for example, that power is the capacity to cause another person to behave in a certain way, no matter what that person's desires or defense. Max Weber defines power as "the probability that one actor within a social relationship will be in a position to carry out his own will despite resistance" (1947, p. 27). Other definitions cite similar themes: power is "control or influence over the actions of others to promote one's goals without their consent, against their will, or without their knowledge or understanding" (Buckley, 1967, p. 186); "the capacity to produce intended and foreseen effects on others" (Wrong, 1979, p. 21); and "the interaction between two parties, the powerholder and the target person, in which the target person's behavior is given new direction by the powerholder" (Kipnis, 1974, p. 9).

This theme of forces operating in opposition to each other is made even more salient in the equational definitions of power offered by Lewin and by French and Raven. According to Lewin's definition (1951, p. 336), the amount of power that Person A holds over Person B depends on the force that A brings to bear on B and on B's ability to resist A's pressure, or

$$\text{Power of A over B} = \frac{\text{(Maximum force A can induce on B)}}{\text{(Maximum resistance B can offer against A)}}.$$

French and Raven (1959) modified this formula slightly by proposing that the power of A over B is equal to the maximum force A can induce on B minus the maximum resistance B can offer against A.

These definitions, when applied to a specific group interaction, define the meaning of social power more precisely. All accounts of the Jonestown group, for example, agree that Jones was the hub of the entire organization and that he exerted a strong influence over the group even before the move to Guyana. His church was apparently well organized, for he surrounded himself with loyal followers who would support his sometimes eccentric decisions. His influence was so strong that he could mobilize large numbers of people in support of any political view he endorsed, and he managed to convince many of his followers to join him in his utopian Jonestown. In contrast, the members of the People's Temple offered little resistance to his pressures, for they never rebelled in spite of his demands for large donations, his threats of death, the marathon "conditioning" sessions he set up, and his use of corporal punishment. In terms of French and Raven's equation, the amount of resistance to subtract from Jones's forceful influence was zero; he was the all-powerful figure in the group.

Yet even if we accept that Jones was the primary powerholder in his group, we are still left with the task of explaining the source of his power. He was able to extract a deadly degree of obedience from his followers, but we have explained little if we are unable to describe the source of this power, the interpersonal bases of his control over the members of the People's Temple. Where exactly did his power come from?

Bases of Power

French and Raven (1959), in a brilliant analysis of power that has become a standard work in the field of small groups, explain the origin of power by focusing on five critical power bases. They point out that an individual's capacity to exert influence over other people often derives from one or more of the sources examined below (see Table 7-1).

Reward power.   Many of the initiates of the People's Temple joined because Jones offered them things they wanted but could not obtain for themselves. He drew members from all sectors of society, but he was adept in offering each member what he or she needed most. To the poor and elderly Jones provided security, economic support, and companionship. To those interested in progressive political reform he offered the means of effecting valued changes. To the gullible he provided miracles and faith healings, convincing many that he could cure cancer with the touch of his hand. His ability to mediate the distribution of positive or negative reinforcers lay at the heart of his **reward power.**

A wide range of rewards can function as reinforcers in groups: gold stars for students, salaries for workers, social approval for insecure friends, positive feedback for employees, food for the starving poor, freedom for prisoners, or even suicide for those who are leading tortured lives. Rewards, however, translate into power only when the following three conditions specified by social-exchange theory are met: (1) the rewards must be valued, (2) the group members must depend on the powerholder for the resource, and (3) the powerholder's promises must seem credible. Jones, for example, enhanced his reward power by offering members rewards and outcomes that they *valued*. When the group was forming, he promised his followers happiness and social reform; later, after the move to Jonestown, he rewarded them with meals of rice and beans. In addition, by isolating the settlement, he ensured that these needs could not be

TABLE 7-1. French and Raven's taxonomy of power bases.

Power Base	Definition
Reward power	The ability to mediate the distribution of positive or negative reinforcers
Coercive power	The capacity to dispense punishments to those who do not comply with requests or demands
Legitimate power	Authority that derives from the powerholder's legitimate right to require and demand compliance
Referent power	Influence over others that is based on their identification with, attraction to, or respect for the powerholder
Expert power	Power that derives from others' assumption that the powerholder possesses superior skills and abilities

(Source: French & Raven, 1959)

fulfilled by others, guaranteeing his followers' complete *dependence* on him alone. He recognized that the power of rewards is lost if group members can earn the reward through other means, such as joining another group or making a deal with another powerful group member. Where power-holders are the only source of valued commodities, their position becomes more secure. Last, many members felt that Jones was *credible;* they believed Jones's idealistic promises, and when disbelief came, it was too late. By this time he had managed to strengthen his position in the group by building his coercive power (Emerson, 1962, 1981).

Coercive power.   Accounts of the development of the People's Temple vividly describe Jones's growing reliance on physical and psychological punishment as a means of exacting obedience from his followers. Public beatings were common, and he sometimes conducted all-night prayer sessions designed to break the will of his congregation. He also threatened group members with death if they failed to obey him, and he warned them of the horrible consequences that would overtake those who refused to join him in Jonestown. Once in Guyana he used beatings, solitary confinement, denials of food and water, and long hours of labor in the fields as punishment.

Coercive power derives from one's capacity to dispense punishments to those who do not comply with requests or demands. Examples of coercive influence abound: Countries threaten other countries with attacks and economic sanctions. Employers threaten employees with the loss of pay, a transfer to an undesirable job, or even firing. Teachers punish mischievous students with an arsenal ranging from extra assignments to detention and suspension. Disagreeing friends insult and humiliate one another, gang members coerce other members through acts of physical violence, and religious leaders threaten members with loss of grace or ostracism. People also use coercion to influence fellow group members, although evidence suggests that most people prefer to use reward power rather than coercive power if both are available (Molm, 1987, 1988). Evidence also indicates that when two parties in conflict are equal in coercive power, they learn over time to avoid the use of their power (Lawler, 1986; Lawler, Ford, & Blegen, 1988).

Legitimate power.   When the police officer tells the bystander to move along, she hurries off down the street. When the lieutenant enters the room, the sergeant snaps to attention. The classroom quiets down when the professor reaches the podium. The office workers feign a tremendous outburst of activity when their boss enters the work area. The congregation contributes willingly under the watchful eye of the minister.

Several bases of power are involved in these examples, but at core these individuals are powerful because they have **legitimate power,** a socially sanctioned right to require and demand compliance. According to French and Raven, legitimate power is unlike the other bases, because it emphasizes the powerholder's right to command the target and the target person's duty to obey the powerholder. Legitimate power may be achieved by any one of a variety of means—appointment by a legitimizing agent, election by members of the group, qualification through possession of specified characteristics, and so on—provided that the method is supported by group norms as the appropriate means of gaining this position of authority.

As a base legitimate power is particularly potent because it springs from the group structure itself—roles, status, and norms—rather than from the delivery or withholding of valued resources. When individuals obey the commands of another because they hope to earn a reward or avoid a punishment, the reason for the obedience is transparently obvious. Take away the powerholder's control over the resources, and the base of power is gone. If the powerholder is a legitimate authority in the group, however, members obey because they personally accept the norms of the group; they voluntarily obey from an internalized sense of duty, loyalty, or moral obligation. As one power theorist (Wrong, 1979, p. 52) notes:

> Legitimate authority is more efficient than coercive or induced authority in that it minimizes the need for maintaining means of coercion in constant readiness, continual surveillance of the power subjects, and regular supplies of economic or non-economic rewards. For these reasons, naked (that is, coercive) power always seeks to clothe itself in the garments of legitimacy.

When power emanates from one's position within a legitimate political or social institution, followers are willing to overlook some of the powerholder's weaknesses and mistakes (Rasinski, Tyler, & Fridkin, 1985).

Jones's legitimate power emanated from his successful retention of prominent political and religious offices. He managed to ally himself with powerful political forces in the San Francisco area, and he soon won a series of accolades: a citation as Humanitarian of the Year, chairmanship of the San Francisco Housing Authority, and the Martin Luther King, Jr., Humanitarian Award. His credentials as an ordained minister legalized his right to lecture and preach, and a decision to join his congregation was tantamount to an agreement to follow his dictates.

Referent power.   French and Raven were struck by the power of the reference group. As noted in Chapter 2, a reference group provides its members with standards by which they can evaluate their own attitudes, beliefs, and behaviors. Conformity to one's reference group is partly due to the desire to secure rewards and avoid punishment, but group members also gain a sense of intrinsic personal satisfaction from identification with the reference group.

People we identify with, people who are attractive, and people we respect possess **referent power.** Like our reference groups, they serve as models for our self-evaluations. Identification with the powerholder is the key factor involved in this type of power, for the target admires, respects, and hopes to resemble the powerholder as much as possible. Attraction, too, is usually involved, since we rarely try to emulate people we dislike, and we sometimes become excessively concerned with pleasing and satisfying the referent powerholder. Some examples of referent power at work include a boy mimicking his older brother; the youngster who, in standing up to the neighborhood bully, earns the respect of his or her buddies; and soldiers following the example of bravery set by their leaders.

Applying the concept of referent power to Jonestown, we see that the bulk of this power resided in the hands of Jones himself. He offered the devoted a clear path to salvation, and they needed only to study his teachings and obey his orders to be saved. The strength of his personality, the simplicity of his ideology, and his willingness to act on his beliefs inspired a sincere trust among his followers, who eventually accepted him as the final source of truth and knowledge. Many group members came to love their leader fervently and made tremendous financial and emotional sacrifices in the hope of pleasing him. As one observer commented, "To his followers, Jones was a god whose power they could take into themselves merely by obeying him" (Allen, 1978, p. 121). Jones was truly a **charismatic leader** (see Focus 7-1).

. . . .
FOCUS 7-1: CHARISMA AS POWER
_____

The sociologist Max Weber, intrigued by the sheer magnitude of the power wielded by political leaders throughout history, introduced the term *charisma* to account for the almost irrational devotion that followers exhibit for their leaders. Originally, charisma referred to special power given by God to certain individuals. These individuals were capable of performing extraordinary, miraculous feats, and they were regarded as God's legitimate representatives on Earth (Weber, 1921/1946).

People sometimes use *charisma* incorrectly to refer to a charming, pleasant leader (for example, "Kennedy's good looks and warm smile made him a charismatic leader"). Weber, however, reserved the term to describe the tremendous referent and legitimate power of the "savior-leader." Charismatic leaders are nearly worshipped by their followers, who trust them absolutely. If the charismatic leader commands, the followers obligingly do their duty and obey (Tucker, 1977). Weber himself was struck by the charismatic leader's power to demand actions that contradict established social norms: "Every charismatic authority would have to subscribe to the proposition, 'It is written . . . but I say unto you . . . ' The genuine prophet . . . preaches, creates, or demands *new* obligations" (1968, p. 243; see also Cavalli, 1986; Lepsius, 1986).

Charismatic leaders such as Jones usually appear on the scene when a large group of people is dissatisfied or faces a distressful situation. The leader offers these people a way to escape their problems, and the masses react with intense loyalty. In the vivid words of the social critic Eric Hoffer (1951, p. 105), the charismatic leader

> personifies the certitude of the creed and justifies the resentment dammed up in the souls of the frustrated. He kindles the vision of a breathtaking future so as to justify the sacrifice of a transitory present. He stages the world of make-believe so indispensable for the realization of self-sacrifice and united action. He evokes the enthusiasm of communion—the sense of liberation from a petty and meaningless individual existence.

. . . .

Expert power. A successful real estate broker, tired of being repeatedly cheated out of his commission by owners and buyers who arranged property closings behind his back, decided early in his career to increase his power in such transactions by becoming an "expert from afar" (Ringer, 1973). He would fly to a prospective client's city in his jet, bringing his own office equipment, assistants, reference manuals, contracts, and reports. He always dressed impeccably, feigned an interest in the quality of the building construction, and seemed to know more about the real estate than the owners themselves. Eventually the buyer and seller would be so intimidated by the power of this expert that they wouldn't consider cheating him.

The broker relied on **expert power:** power that derives from our assumption that the powerholder possesses superior skills and abilities. Like the physician interpreting a patient's symptoms, a local resident giving directions to an out-of-towner, or a teacher dictating the correct spelling of a word for a student, the broker was able to transform his special knowledge into power.

The broker, as it turns out, really was an expert in his field, but according to French and Raven this fact was almost irrelevant; the key was his clients' belief in his special expertise (Kaplowitz, 1978). For example, how would you react if you were working with a partner on a series of simple judgment problems and this person repeatedly disagreed with your solution? In an experimental version of this situation, subjects worked in dyads on a series of problems. Half of the subjects were led to believe that their partner's ability on the task was superior to their own, and the rest were told that their partner possessed inferior ability. As the concept of expert power suggests, individuals who thought that their partners were experts accepted their recommendations an average of 68% of the time, whereas subjects paired with partners who they thought were inferior accepted their recommendation only 42% of the time (Foschi, Warriner, and Hart, 1985; see also Schopler & Layton, 1972a, 1972b).

Similarly, Jones's actual skills, abilities, and knowledge were less important than his followers' perceptions of their leader. Uninvolved analysts found it difficult to think of him as a religious or political expert, but his followers felt that he was the most knowledgeable religious figure of modern times. Of all the bases specified by French and Raven, Jones's expert power was probably the weakest, but he still managed to convince some members of his special expertise.

Power Tactics

French and Raven's theory of power argues that people draw power from five key sources; Jones was powerful because he controlled all five bases, and his followers were weak because they lacked a power base (French & Raven, 1959; Raven, 1965). When it comes to exerting influence in groups, however, these power bases do not translate directly into power tactics. During group interaction people can rely on additional, and much more specific, means of social influence that go beyond the five sources of influence described by French and Raven (Kipnis, 1984; Schein, 1985). A boss with coercive power may threaten people, but he may also use persuasion or charm. A duly elected leader may remind members of their duties, but she may also use logical arguments or promises to exact compliance. Powerful people may have more tactics at their disposal, but even a person without a power base can still influence others by using various power tactics (Dion & Stein, 1978; Donohue, 1978; Kipnis, 1984; Parsons, 1962; Tedeschi, Schlenker, & Bonoma, 1973; Wrong, 1979).

How do people get their way in groups? Several researchers have explored this question by asking people to describe the methods that they use to influence others in business, group, and interpersonal settings. Although the number of tactics that people report is enormous, most can be classified into one of the categories shown in Table 7-2. Several of these categories are consistent with French and Raven's theory of power bases.

TABLE 7-2. Twenty power tactics.

Tactic	Definition	Examples
Promise	Pledging to do or give something in the future	• I promise her a pay increase. • I offer him a bonus. • We tell them sales will increase.
Reward	Providing valued reinforcers	• I increase his pay. • I give her the day off. • I shower him with praise.
Threat	Warning of negative consequences in the future	• I threaten to cut her pay. • I tell him he might be fired. • I threaten legal action.
Punishment	Imposing negative consequences	• I cut her pay. • I reprimand her. • I punch him.
Bullying	Using strong threats, insults, or violence	• I yell at her. • I criticize his work. • I curse until she does it.

(continued)

TABLE 7-2. *(continued)*

Tactic	Definition	Examples
Discussion	Using rational argument or explanation	• I give her supporting reasons. • I explain why I favor the plan. • We talk it over.
Request	Stating what should be done or asking for compliance	• I say what I want. • I tell her what I expect. • I ask her to do it.
Demand	Forcefully asserting oneself; insisting on compliance	• I demand that she do it. • I insist that he stop. • I give the order.
Instruction	Teaching; demonstrating by example	• I explain how to do it. • I set an example.
Persuasion	Using coaxing, convincing arguments	• I talk him out of it. • I persuade her to do it. • I develop a strong presentation.
Negotiation	Bargaining; making compromises; trading favors	• I work out a deal. • We compromise. • I drop a demand if she does.
Pressure	Using group influence	• I appeal to the boss. • I turn the group against her. • I get others to take my side.
Claiming expertise	Demonstrating or claiming superior knowledge or skill	• I rely on my experience. • I let them know I'm an expert. • I bury them in technical details.
Persistence	Continuing in one's influence attempts or repeating a point	• I reiterate my point. • I don't give up. • I don't take no for an answer.
Fait accompli	Doing what one wants without gaining approval	• I do it anyway. • I take whatever action I want. • I send it on without approval.
Manipulation	Lying; hinting; deceiving	• I lie about it. • I get her to think it's her idea. • I drop a hint.
Supplication	Entreating; asking for humbly or earnestly	• I plead. • I cry. • I act helpless.
Ingratiation	Deliberately increasing one's attractiveness	• I try to seem cooperative. • I flatter him. • I try to be seductive.
Evasion	Avoiding the issue or the person who would disapprove	• I keep it from him. • I don't let her know about it. • I call in sick.
Disengagement	Withdrawing from the setting; breaking off the interaction	• I go on strike. • I ignore him until he does it. • I leave.

When people must influence others, they often report using promises, rewards, threats, punishment, and expertise. Other tactics, however, supplement those suggested by French and Raven. They include discussion, making requests and demands, instruction, persuasion, negotiation, applying group pressure, persistence, presenting a fait accompli, manipulation, supplication, ingratiation, evasion, and disengagement. (Table 7-2 is a compilation of power tactics identified in a number of research studies, including Belk et al., 1988; Buss, Gomes, Higgins, & Lauterbach, 1987; Cowan, Drinkard, & MacGavin, 1984; Dillard and Fitzpatrick, 1985; Falbo, 1977; Falbo & Peplau, 1980; Howard, Blumstein, & Schwartz, 1986; Instone, Major, & Bunker, 1983; Kipnis, 1984; Kipnis & Consentino, 1969; Marwell & Schmitt, 1967; Offermann & Schrier, 1985; Wheeless, Barraclough, & Stewart, 1983; Wilkinson & Kipnis, 1978; and Wiseman & Schenck-Hamlin, 1981.)

These various methods differ from one another in certain interesting ways. Toni Falbo and David Kipnis, two leading theorists in the field of power, both highlight (1) directness (or strength), (2) rationality, and (3) bilaterality in their theoretical analyses (Falbo, 1977; Falbo & Peplau, 1980; Kipnis, 1984).

1. Directness. *Direct tactics* are explicit, overt methods of influence; threats, demands, and faits accomplis (simply going ahead and doing what you want to do despite objections) are all direct methods. *Indirect tactics,* in contrast, involve covert manipulation and indirect influence. When we drop hints, use ingratiation, or evade the issue, we are using indirect methods. Kipnis (1984) uses the terms *strong* and *weak* rather than *direct* and *indirect*.

2. Rationality. Tactics that emphasize reasoning, logic, and good judgment are the *rational tactics;* bargaining and persuasion are examples. Others, such as ingratiation and evasion, are *nonrational tactics* of influence, because they rely on emotionality and misinformation.

3. Bilaterality. Some tactics are interactive, involving give-and-take on the part of both the influencer and the target of the influence. Such *bilateral tactics* include persuasion, discussion, and negotiation. *Unilateral tactics,* in contrast, can be enacted without the cooperation of the target of influence. Such tactics include demands, faits accompli, evasion, and disengagement.

These dimensions help us make predictions about when a particular tactic will be used to influence someone. Kipnis and his colleagues, for example, report that managers use a variety of strong and weak methods to influence subordinates but, when dealing with superiors, rely heavily on rational methods such as persuasion and discussion. Kipnis also finds that those who are higher in status or authority in the group are more likely to use direct (strong) power tactics, whereas those who are low in status rely on indirect (weak) power tactics (Kipnis, 1984; Kipnis, Schmidt, Swaffin-Smith, & Wilkinson, 1984). A little boy, for example, may use relatively weak methods when trying to influence his father but stronger methods when interacting with his peers (Cowan et al., 1984). Also, the more the target of the influence resists, the greater the likelihood that the influencer will shift from a weak tactic to a strong tactic (Kipnis, 1984; Michener & Burt, 1975a; Wilkinson & Kipnis, 1978). The choice of tactic also depends on one's goals (Canary, Cody, & Marston, 1986), the target person's expected reaction (Ansari & Kapoor, 1987), and the amount of conflict already present in the group (Cheng, 1983).

Individual differences in personality and gender also shape our use of the different influence methods in Table 7-2. When Falbo examined the relationship between reported strategy and personality traits, she found that people who were very concerned with being accepted and liked by their fellow group members tended to use indirect/rational tactics rather than direct/nonrational ones. In contrast, those who espoused a Machiavellian, manipulative philosophy when dealing with others tended to use indirect/nonrational tactics as opposed to direct/rational ones. Last, those who tended to conform to others' judgments (as assessed by a standard Asch situation paradigm; see Chapter 6) reported using rational methods more than nonrational ones. Gender also plays a role in the selection of power tactics. One laboratory study examined the impact of gender on power tactics by placing men and women in supervisory positions over three workers. Two workers were highly productive, but a third was not; he or she didn't work very hard and often complained about the assignment. As expected, the supervisors used more influence tactics with the noncompliant employee, including both rewarding and coercive methods. Female supervisors, however, made fewer attempts at influence than men and used a more limited range of tactics. They promised fewer pay raises and threatened more pay deductions than men, and they were more likely to criticize subordinates (Instone, Major, & Bunker, 1983). Also, studies of intimate heterosexual relationships suggest that men tend to use bilateral and direct tactics, whereas women report using unilateral and indirect methods (Falbo & Peplau, 1980; Belk et al., 1988). Moreover, in a study of heterosexual, gay male, and lesbian couples, people partnered with men tended to rely on relatively weak influence tactics, including manipulation and supplication. Women who did not work outside the home were most likely to use strong influence tactics, such as bullying and demands. Men were more likely to use disengagement, and if heterosexual they also used bargaining (Howard, Blumstein, & Schwartz, 1986; cf. Koberg, 1985).

THE METAMORPHIC EFFECTS OF POWER

Using power to sway others is like using a drug to combat an illness. Drugs cure our bodily ailments, but all too often they cause unwanted side effects. Similarly, power may result in influence, but often at an interpersonal cost. Once used, power's side effects reverberate through the group, creating changes in both those it influences and those who exercise the influence.

Reactions to the Exercise of Power

The members of the People's Temple reacted to Jones's demands in many ways. Some became so angry that they left the group. Others remained in the group but withdrew from many of the church-sponsored activities. Some, however, accepted their punishment passively or even joined with Jones to inflict harm on others. Each attempt at influence by Jones had **metamorphic effects** on the members: it changed their behavior, their beliefs, their emotions, and even their view of themselves (Kipnis, 1974, 1984).

Compliance and change. When the boss asks, the leader orders, the police officer demands, a child begs, a lover smiles, or a friend suggests, we often respond to their influence by yielding. As many theorists have noted, dominance and submissiveness are complementary social responses. When one person acts in a dominant fashion, the other tends to become submissive. When one person seems weak, the other will become strong. This **complementarity hypothesis** has been confirmed in a wide variety of interpersonal settings, including groups (Carson, 1969; Giffort & O'Connor, 1987; Kiesler, 1983; Strong et al., 1988).

But even though we often overtly follow the dictates of the powerholder, we do not always personally accept this change at the covert level. Herbert Kelman (1958, 1961) maintains that in most cases coercive and reward power generate only **compliance.** We do not agree with the powerholder's views and we do not want to obey, but we comply anyway. Hence, coercive powerholders must maintain close surveillance over the group if they wish to be effective. Jones, for example, relied on strict surveillance to prevent escapes from the Jonestown colony.

In contrast, forms of influence that depend on the relationship between the powerholder and the target of influence result in **identification.** Again, we may not completely accept all that the powerholder says, but we "adopt the induced behavior because it is associated with the desired relationship" (Kelman, 1958, p. 53). Identification is the most likely reaction to ingratiation, manipulation, supplication, and disengagement.

Some tactics, however, stimulate **internalization;** discussion, instruction, persuasion, and negotiation are all ways to change the target's personal opinions and behaviors. When internalization occurs, the individual "adopts the induced behavior because it is congruent with his value system. He may consider it useful for the solution of a problem or find it congenial to his needs" (Kelman, 1958, p. 53).

Attraction and interpersonal relations. We simply do not like people who control us by using direct and irrational tactics. Falbo (1977), in addition to identifying these power dimensions, also explored group members' reactions to various power tactics. She arranged for people who reported using such tactics as discussion, negotiation, persistence, threat, and evasion to meet in same-sex groups of three to five persons to discuss the topic "What I plan to get out of college." After this discussion the participants rated one another on such characteristics as friendliness, consideration, and desirability as a group member.

Falbo found that evaluations of liking and willingness to join in another discussion were more closely associated with the rationality of influence than with the directness of influence. People who claimed that they influenced others through discussion, persuasion, and expertise were most favorably evaluated, whereas those who emphasized manipulation, evasion, and threat received the most negative evaluations. Moreover, people who used (or at least, reported using) indirect/rational strategies such as persuasion or ingratiation were rated as more considerate and friendlier than people who used direct/nonrational strategies such as threats and faits accomplis.

These findings suggest that different power tactics influence attraction and acceptance into the group in different ways, but we should accept these conclusions with caution; no evidence is available to indicate whether the people actually used the tactic they described in their self-reports. The results of other studies, however, are generally consistent with Falbo's findings (French, Morrison, & Levinger, 1960; Litman-Adizes, Fontaine, & Raven, 1978; Pandey & Singh, 1987; Shaw & Condelli, 1986). For example, in one study subjects rated the attractiveness of a manager who used either coercive, reward, legitimate, referent, or expert power to influence a subordinate. As Figure 7-1 indicates, the subjects gave the most positive evaluations to the referent powerholder and the most negative evaluations to the coercive powerholder (Shaw & Condelli, 1986).

Conflict.   The likelihood of conflict within the group increases with the use of certain types of influence. Coercive influence tactics, such as threats and punishments, are tolerated by group members when the group is successful (Michener & Lawler, 1975), the leader is trusted (Friedland, 1976), or the use of such tactics is justified by the group's norms (Michener & Burt, 1975b). Often, however, such tactics generate anger

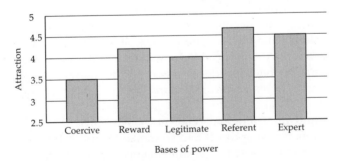

FIGURE 7-1. Ratings of attraction (from 1 to 7) for managers who used the influence tactics described in the French-Raven theory of power.
Source: Shaw & Condelli, 1986

and hostility (Johnson & Ewens, 1971; Mulder et al., 1964). Studies of *reciprocity* in groups indicate that when people are rewarded by a powerholder, they tend to reciprocate with cooperation; if, in contrast, powerholders employ coercion, they are met with malevolence and animosity (Schlenker, Nacci, Helm, & Tedeschi, 1976). Moreover, even when mildly coercive methods are used, such as threats, people often overreact and respond with even stronger threats. This escalating pattern sets in motion an upward spiral of conflict (Youngs, 1986). Hence, although coercive powerholders may be successful in initial encounters, influence becomes more difficult in successive meetings as the target's anger and resistance to pressure grow. (We will return to the issue of conflict and influence in Chapter 12.)

The conflict created by coercive influence can disrupt the entire group's functioning. Consider, for example, the use of power in the classroom. Evidence indicates that many teachers rely more heavily on coercion than on other bases of power when trying to regulate students' actions, but this coercion causes rather than solves disciplinary problems (Kounin, 1970). In one study strong, coercive tactics such as physical punishment, displays of anger, and shouting not only failed to change the target student's behavior but also led to negative changes in the classroom's atmosphere (Kounin & Gump, 1958). When the misbehaving student was severely reprimanded, the observing students would often become more disruptive and uninterested in their schoolwork, and negative, inappropriate social activity seemed to spread from the trouble spot throughout the classroom. This disruptive contagion, which the investigators labeled the **ripple effect,** was found to be especially strong when the reprimanded students were powerful members of the classroom authority structure or when commands by teachers were vague and ambiguous. On the basis of these findings the researchers suggested that teachers avoid the ripple effect by relying on other influence bases, including reward power, referent power, and expert power.

Rebellion and defiance.   When an individual or group abuses power, in some cases the targets of influence will rebel. The targets of influence may respond by escaping from the powerholder's region of control or by applying influence in return. They may also strive to form a **revolutionary coalition,** a subgroup that opposes the powerholder's demands (Lawler, 1975; Lawler & Thompson, 1978, 1979). In one analysis of this process subjects worked in three-person groups under the direction of a leader who was appointed to that post because he or she had outscored them on a bogus test of ability. The leader then proceeded to keep over half of the money earned by the work, giving the subjects less than one-fourth. When the leader had personally decided how to apportion payment, 58% of the subjects revolted by forming a coalition with the other low-status subject. When the leader was not responsible for the payment scheme, only 25% revolted (Lawler & Thompson, 1978).

Counterconformity, discussed in Chapter 6, also becomes more likely when coercive methods are used to force group members into changing their position. Such strong social-influence methods can create **reactance,** the feeling that one's freedom to choose is being threatened by others. When reactance occurs, individuals strive to reassert their sense of freedom by deliberately disagreeing with others (Brehm, 1976; Brehm & Brehm, 1981). In one study in which teammates had to make a choice between two alternatives marked 1-A or 1-B, 73% chose 1-A if the partner said "I prefer 1-A," but only 40% chose 1-A if the partner demanded "I think we should both do 1-A" (Brehm & Sensenig, 1966). Similarly, in a later study 83% of the members of a group refused to go along with a group participant who said "I think it's pretty obvious all of us are going to work on task A" (Worchel & Brehm, 1971).

Motivation.   The use of coercive and reward power can, in some instances, alter the target person's level of intrinsic motivation. For example, suppose subordinates maintain a high level of productivity because their work is intrinsically satisfying to them; they enjoy it for personal, internal reasons. If a supervisor begins making rewards and punishments contingent on the level of production, however, the workers may, in time, come to work to earn rewards and avoid punishments rather than to experience the enjoyment they once felt spontaneously. By introducing external motivators—rewards, promises, threats, or punishments—the supervisor has destroyed the potency of intrinsic motivators. Hence, when the extrinsic motivators are withdrawn or the powerholder fails to maintain surveillance, the productivity levels drop off (Condry, 1977; Deci & Ryan, 1985).

Self-blame.   In extreme instances when a powerholder inflicts tremendous suffering and misfortune on people, the latter may respond by blaming themselves for their misery. Since most people intuitively "believe that their environment is a just and orderly place where people usually get what they deserve" (Lerner & Miller, 1978, p. 1030), they tend to think that those who suffer must have done something to deserve their misfortunes. When we ourselves are the victims, however, this same belief in a just world produces self-blame and self-derogation. For example, the residents of the Jonestown colony totally accepted Jones as their spiritual leader, and yet he punished and abused them. To make sense of their suffering at the hands of their supposed savior, they may have assumed that they themselves were responsible for their misfortunes. In blaming themselves instead of Jones, they may have felt so deserving of their fate that they chose to suffer rather than escape suffering. These feelings of self-condemnation may account for their willingness to take their own lives (Clark, 1971; Comer & Laird, 1975; Fanon, 1963; Gamson, 1968; Kipnis, et al,1976). (Focus 7-2 examines how people in the workplace react to the exercise of power.)

· ·

FOCUS 7-2: USING SOCIAL INFLUENCE TO GET RESULTS

Mr. Dithers in the comic strip *Blondie* is a terrible boss. Why? Because he uses power indiscriminately. He is painfully directive, a little Napoleon who never gives employees a voice in deciding their outcomes. He revels in his power over the helpless Dagwood, who seems to live in fear, insecurity, and frustration. Almost exclusively, Mr. Dithers relies on coercive, direct tactics rather than rewarding or rational tactics. These are precisely the qualities that people mention when asked to describe their worst boss (Lombardo & McCall, 1984).

Bosses who, like Mr. Dithers, rely on their coercive power to influence subordinates create problems for themselves. Reviews of research suggest that the use of coercive power is negatively associated with employees' productivity, satisfaction with their supervisors, and job satisfaction. In contrast, strategies that require expert power and referent power generally increase productivity, satisfaction, and commitment to the organization (Podsakoff & Schriesheim, 1985; Yukl, 1981).

Gary Yukl, after reviewing dozens of studies of power tactics used in business and industry, concludes that individuals must be aware of the methods they use to influence others and that they should take steps to build their bases of power within the group. His suggestions to people who want to improve their management methods are summarized in Table 7-3 (p. 196).

· ·

Changes in the Powerholder

In 1976 Jones fought for the improvement of housing and for progressive political change in the San Francisco area, and his followers worked diligently toward the goals outlined by their leader. In 1978 he was accused of human-rights violations, physical assault, and illicit sexual practices while many of his followers were laboring in the fields in Guyana. In this short period his power had reached dramatic levels, but with this power came strange changes in his behavior and perceptions. Were these changes in Jones unique, or were they evidence of the metamorphic effects of power?

As Kipnis has pointed out, the influence of power on the powerholder has been described and discussed in philosophical, historical, and dramatic works through the ages (Kipnis, 1974). In their tragedies the Greeks often dramatized the fall of heroes who, swollen by past accomplishments, conceitedly compared themselves to the gods. Greek myth is replete with tales of temptations to seek too much power, as in the case of Icarus, whose elation at the power of flight caused his death. In our own century we find examples of political thinkers who, like Jones, began their careers envisioning utopian societies but became cruel and inhuman dictators when they achieved positions of power. The impact of gaining

TABLE 7-3. Guidelines for building and using power in industrial and
organizational settings.

Power Base	Guidelines
Coercive power	• Inform subordinates about rules and penalties. • Administer discipline consistently and promptly. • Provide sufficient warning before resorting to punishment. • Get the facts before using reprimands or punishment. • Stay calm, and avoid appearing hostile. • Maintain credibility. • Use appropriate punishments. • Administer warnings and punishments in private.
Reward power	• Make certain to verify compliance. • Make certain the request is feasible. • Use an attractive incentive. • Deliver on all promises. • Make only proper and ethical requests.
Legitimate power	• Make polite requests. • Make requests in a confident tone. • Make clear requests, and check for comprehension. • Make sure that requests appear legitimate. • Explain the reasons for a request. • Follow proper channels. • Exercise authority regularly. • Insist on compliance, and check to verify it. • Be responsive to subordinate needs.
Reference power	• Allow time for loyalty to develop. • Show consideration for subordinates' needs. • Treat all subordinates fairly. • Spend time in face-to-face interaction. • Select subordinates who will identify with you. • Act as a role model for subordinates.
Expert power	• Promote an image of expertise. • Maintain credibility. • Act confident and decisive. • Keep informed. • Recognize subordinate concerns. • Avoid threatening the self-esteem of subordinates.

(Source: Yukl, 1981, pp. 44–58)

power seems to be aptly summarized by Lord Acton's maxim "Power
tends to corrupt, and absolute power corrupts absolutely."

But what are some of the consequences of acquiring power that have
been corroborated through scientific research? To begin at the most fundamental level, researchers have found that people who are delegated
power in experimental situations tend to use their power to control others.
For example, Kipnis (1972) arranged for advanced business students to
participate as managers in a simulated manufacturing company after telling them that their performance would be a good indicator of their lead-

ership potential in other executive situations. In one condition the subjects were given a good deal of reward power and coercive power over their subordinates; they could award bonuses, cut pay, threaten and actually carry out transfers to other jobs, give additional instructions, or even fire a worker. The subjects in the second condition could use only persuasion or extra instructions to influence their subordinates.

The procedure was designed so that the managers could not actually see their workers but were kept informed of their production levels by an assistant, who brought in the finished products from the four workers. This arrangement was chosen so that Kipnis could carefully control the level of productivity of the fictitious workers (all performed adequately) and also provide a reason for the use of an intercom system in giving orders to subordinates. These communications were surreptitiously recorded, and subsequent analyses revealed that the powerful managers initiated roughly twice as many attempts at influence as the nonpowerful managers and that the difference between the two types of managers became more apparent as the sessions progressed. In addition, the powerful and nonpowerful managers used different power tactics: the powerless ones relied on persuasion, whereas the powerful ones coerced or rewarded their workers. Other studies have yielded similar support for the idea that people with power tend to make use of it (for example, Deutsch, 1973; Kipnis & Consentino, 1969), but they also suggest that the magnitude of this effect depends on many other factors (Bedell & Sistrunk, 1973; Black & Higbee, 1973; Goodstadt & Hjelle, 1973; Michener & Burt, 1975a).

Once power has been used to influence others, changes in powerholders' perceptions of themselves and of the target of influence may also take place. In many instances the successful use of power as a means of controlling others leads to self-satisfaction, unrealistically positive self-evaluations, and overestimations of interpersonal power (Erez, Rim, & Keider, 1986; Kipnis, 1974; Raven & Kruglanski, 1970; Sorokin & Lundin, 1959). In the Kipnis simulation described above, for example, subjects were asked if their subordinates were performing well because of the workers' high self-motivation levels, their manager's comments and suggestions, or their desire for money. Analyses showed that the high-power managers felt that their workers were only in it for the money (which the manager could control), whereas the low-power managers felt that the workers were "highly motivated." In fact, in the powerful-manager condition the correlation between the number of messages sent to the workers and the manager's agreement with the statement "My orders and influence caused the workers to perform effectively" was quite strong ($r = .65$) (Kipnis, 1974). Other studies have also revealed this tendency for powerful individuals to assume that they themselves are the prime cause of other people's behavior (Kipnis, Castell, Gergen, & Mauch, 1976).

Devaluation of the target of the influence attempt also tends to covary with increased feelings of control over people. In a classic study of power dynamics in a mental hospital, Alvin Zander and his colleagues found that psychiatrists tended to underestimate the abilities of the psychologists they supervised (Zander, Cohen, & Stotland, 1959). Although the psychologists believed themselves to be capable of developing diagnoses and conducting therapy, the psychiatrists considered them qualified only to conduct psychological testing. Evidence also suggests that powerholders tend to (1) increase the social distance between themselves and the nonpowerful, (2) believe that the nonpowerful are untrustworthy and in need of close supervision, and (3) devalue the work and ability of the less powerful (Kipnis, 1972; Sampson, 1965; Strickland, 1958; Strickland, Barefoot, & Hockenstein, 1976). This tendency to derogate the target person while simultaneously evaluating oneself more positively works to widen the gap between group members who have varying degrees of power.

In some cases powerholders' inflated views of their power and control over the group can tempt them into overstepping the bounds of their authority. In 1937, for example, Franklin D. Roosevelt was elected president of the United States by an overwhelming majority and subsequently went about increasing the powers of the presidency beyond those specified in the U.S. Constitution. This reaction to increased power brought on by overwhelming support from the group has been labeled the **mandate phenomenon** (Clark & Sechrest, 1976). In one experimental analysis of this process in small groups, researchers told male college students that they would be working on a learning task while being exposed to a nauseating smell. The researchers explained that various odors were used in the research, ranging from ones that cause nausea in 10% of the population to ones that cause nausea in 90% of the population. Groups were instructed to elect a leader who was to pick the smell the group would be exposed to, but they were promised that the fouler the odor, the more money they would receive. Elections were then held, and three conditions were established:

1. Mandate condition: the leader was told that he had been unanimously selected to be the leader.
2. Majority condition: the leader believed that he had won just enough votes to get the position.
3. Control condition: the leader was told that he had been randomly selected.

In the final stage of the research the leaders were asked to select the odor that the group would have to tolerate. Consistent with mandate-phenomenon predictions, individuals who felt that they had the overwhelming support of their group selected more noxious odors than either the leaders elected by simple majority or the subjects in the control condition.

Lastly, several sources suggest that acquiring power stimulates the powerholder into acquiring more power. Because the possession of power may provide the means to achieve many goals, power eventually becomes so closely associated with valued outcomes that people seek it for its own sake (Cartwright & Zander, 1968). Hence, we find that once in power, individuals take steps to protect their sources of influence. This protective aspect of power translates into a small group version of Michels's (1915/1959) *iron law of oligarchy:* individuals in power tend to remain in power. Eventually, too, powerholders may become preoccupied with seeking power, driven by a strong motivation to acquire greater and greater levels of interpersonal influence (McClelland, 1975, 1985; Winter, 1973). This need for power (*n* Power), which was described in Chapter 3, is a prominent personality characteristic in individuals who rise to positions of authority in organizations and politics. Evidence also indicates, however, that when those who are high in power motivation cannot exercise that power, they experience increased tension and stress (McClelland, 1985). Under such conditions they also exaggerate the amount of conflict that exists in the group and overlook group members' efforts at cooperation (Fodor, 1984, 1985).

OBEDIENCE TO AUTHORITY

We have seen that power permeates many aspects of group life but that to understand its effects we must consider its sources and forms. Given this background, we are now ready to explore the question first raised at the beginning of this chapter: why did the people of Jonestown obey?

Obedience in the Laboratory

Stanley Milgram began his studies of obedience in the early 1960s (Milgram, 1963, 1965, 1974). He was interested in adults' reactions to authorities, so he solicited subjects through newspaper advertisements and direct mailings to local residents. The announcement, which is shown in Focus 7-3, described the research as a scientific "study of memory and learning" to be conducted at nearby Yale University. His subjects, in most variations, were males between the ages of 25 and 50.

. . . .
FOCUS 7-3: ANNOUNCEMENT OF THE MILGRAM EXPERIMENT

We will pay you $4.00 for one hour of your time

Persons Needed for a Study of Memory

- We will pay five hundred New Haven men to help us complete a scientific study of memory and learning. The study is being done at Yale University.
- Each person who participates will be paid $4.00 (plus 50¢ carfare) for approximately one hour's time. We need you for only one hour: there are no further obligations. You may choose the time you would like to come (evenings, weekdays, or weekends).

• No special training, education, or experience is needed. We want:

Factory workers	Professional people
City employees	Telephone workers
Laborers	Construction
Barbers	workers
Businessmen	Salespeople
Clerks	White-collar workers
	Others

• All persons must be between the ages of 20 and 50. High school and college students cannot be used.
• If you meet these qualifications, fill out the coupon below and mail it now to Professor Stanley Milgram, Department of Psychology, Yale University, New Haven. You will be notified later of the specific time and place of the study. We reserve the right to decline any application.

(Source: Milgram, 1974)

• •

When subjects arrived at the impressively appointed laboratory, they met the experimenter, a 30ish man with a crew cut and dressed in a gray technician's coat, and a fellow subject. This participant, who looked to be in his late 40s, was actually a confederate; he deliberately acted in a friendly, nervous way.

In a matter-of-fact voice the experimenter explained the study by noting that several scientific theories had suggested that punishment facilitated learning, even though little systematic research on the issue had ever been conducted. Continuing, he explained that the study at hand was designed to fill this gap. One person would play the role of Teacher by reading a series of paired words (for example, *blue box, nice day, wild duck,* and so on) to the other person, who would play the role of Learner. The Teacher would check the Learner's ability to recall the pairs by reading the first word in the pair and several possible answers (for example, *blue: sky, ink, box, lamp*). Failures would be punished by an electric shock.

After thus describing the procedure, the experimenter assigned the subject and the confederate to the roles of Teacher and Learner by asking them to draw slips of paper from a hat. The subject did not know that both slips said *Teacher.* Next, subjects were led into the next room, where the confederate was strapped into a chair that was designed "to prevent excessive movement during the shock." The Learner sat quietly while an electrode was attached to his wrist but finally asked if the shocks were dangerous. "Oh, no," said the experimenter, "although the shocks can be extremely painful, they cause no permanent tissue damage" (Milgram, 1974, p. 19). The confederate, of course, did not actually receive shocks.

Leaving the Learner strapped in his chair, the subject and experimenter returned to the room containing the shock generator. This bogus machine, which Milgram himself fabricated, featured a row of 30 electrical switches. The switch at the far left indicated that it was 15 volts; the next switch was 30, the next was 45, and so on all the way up to 450 volts. To add authenticity, Milgram labeled the voltage levels, from left to right, "Slight Shock," "Moderate Shock," "Strong Shock," "Very Strong Shock," "Intense Shock," "Extreme Intensity Shock," and "Danger: Severe Shock." The final two switches were marked "XXX." The rest of the face of the shock generator was taken up by dials, lights, and meters that flickered whenever a switch was pulled.

The experimenter administered a sample shock of 45 volts to each subject, supposedly to give them an idea of the punishment magnitude. The study then began in earnest. Using a microphone to communicate with the Learner, the Teacher read over the list of pairs and then began "testing" his memory. Each time the Teacher read a word and the alternatives, the Learner indicated his response by pushing one of four numbered switches that were just within reach of his bound hand. His response lit up on the subject's control panel. Subjects were to deliver one shock for each mistake and increase the voltage one step each time.

The sessions proceeded smoothly for a time, but because the confederate deliberately made mistakes, the shock level rapidly reached an alarming intensity. Although subjects began with just a 15-volt jolt, each failure moved them closer and closer to XXX, 450 volts. At the 300-volt level the Learner also began to protest the shocks by pounding on the wall, and after the next shock of 315 he stopped responding altogether. Most subjects assumed that the session was over at this point, but the experimenter told them to treat a failure to respond as a wrong answer and to continue the delivery of shock. When subjects balked, the experimenter would use a sequence of **prods** to goad the subject into action (Milgram, 1974, p. 21):

Prod 1: "Please continue" *or* "Please go on."
Prod 2: "The experiment requires that you continue."
Prod 3: "It is absolutely essential that you continue."
Prod 4: "You have no other choice; you must go on."

Milgram used variations of this paradigm to examine subjects' reactions to the experimenter's orders. The situation, although extremely realistic from the subjects' perspective, was carefully engineered to create a laboratory analog to a real-world obedience dilemma. The experimenter, although making no claim to special expertise, acted with self-assurance and poise. He gave orders crisply, as if he never questioned the correctness of his own actions, and he seemed surprised that the Teacher would try to terminate the shock sequence. Yet from the participants' point of view, this authority was requiring them to act in a way that might be harmful to another person. When they accepted the $4.50 payment, they implicitly agreed to carry out the experimenter's instructions, but they were torn between this duty and their desire to protect the Learner from possible harm. Milgram designed his experiment to determine which side would win this conflict.

Milgram's Findings

Milgram realized that his subjects would find the obedience conflict a challenge to their loyalties, but he believed that very few would deliver shocks past the 300-volt level. Although the experimenter was an authority, the failure of the Learner to respond could only mean that he wished to quit or was seriously hurt, so Milgram felt confident that most people would break off the shocks when the pounding on the wall began. In fact, Milgram polled a number of psychological researchers and psychiatrists on the subject, and their predictions are summarized by the line in Figure 7-2 marked "Psychologists' predictions." None of these 39 "experts" felt that subjects would shock to the 450-volt level; they predicted that most would quit at the 150-volt level.

Their expectations, however, proved incorrect. Of the 40 individuals who served as Teachers in the experiment, 26 administered the full 450 volts to the helpless Learner. None broke off before the 300-volt level, and several of the eventually disobedient subjects gave one or two additional shocks before finally refusing to yield to the experimenter's prods. The

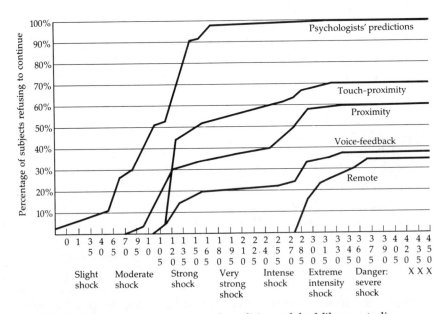

FIGURE 7-2 Obedience rates in several conditions of the Milgram studies.
Source: Milgram, 1974

comments made by the subjects during the shock procedure and their obvious psychological distress revealed that they were unwilling to go on but
felt unable to resist the experimenter's demands for obedience.

Over a period of several years Milgram studied the responses of nearly
1000 people in a series of replications and extensions of his original study.
In these later researches, some of which are discussed below, different aspects of the setting were systematically manipulated, allowing him to assess their influence on obedience rates. Although he continued to search
for the limits of obedience, again and again his subjects buckled under the
pressure of the experimenter's power.

Proximity of the "victim."   Reasoning that the high rate of obedience
observed in the original study could have occurred because the Teacher
heard only an ambiguous pounding coming from the other room, Milgram ran three additional conditions that varied the number of cues concerning the Learner's suffering:

1. Voice-feedback: Complaints from the Learner could be heard
through the walls. He grunted when shocked at levels below 120 volts,
and at that point he began to complain about the pain. At 150 volts he cried
out: "Experimenter, get me out of here! I won't be in the experiment any
more! I refuse to go on!" (Milgram, 1974, p. 23). He continued screaming
and demanding release until the 300-volt level, when he refused to answer
any more questions.

2. Proximity: the Learner sat in the same room as the Teacher, voicing
the same complaints used in the voice-feedback condition.

3. Touch-proximity: The Learner could be shocked only if he put his
hand on a shock plate, and he refused to do so once the shocks reached
the 150-volt level. At this point, the experimenter ordered the subject to
hold the Learner's hand down on the plate while giving the shocks (the
Teacher was protected from the shock).

The results of these three conditions are presented in Figure 7-2, along
with the obedience rates from the original condition (the remote condition). Obedience declined as the proximity of the Learner increased, dropping from 65% obedience in the remote condition to 62.5% in the voice-
feedback condition, 40% in the proximity condition, and 30% in the touch-
proximity condition.

Limiting the experimenter's power.   To examine the sources of the experimenter's power, Milgram manipulated the experimenter's surveillance capabilities, prestige, expertise, and legitimacy. In one variation the
situation (as in most of the later studies) was nearly identical to the voice-
feedback condition, except that the experimenter left the room after going
over the instructions. He continued giving orders by telephone, but when
the experimenter could not maintain visual surveillance, only 20% of the
participants were obedient to the 450-volt level. In fact, many subjects as-

sured the experimenter that they were administering increasingly large shocks with each mistake when they were actually delivering only 15 volts.

To remove another source of power that derived from the link between the study and prestigious Yale University, Milgram moved the research to an office building in nearby Bridgeport:

> The experiments were conducted in a three-room office suite in a somewhat rundown commercial building located in the downtown shopping area. The laboratory was sparsely furnished, though clean, and marginally respectable in appearance. When subjects inquired about professional affiliations, they were informed only that we were a private firm conducting research for industry [Milgram, 1974, pp. 68–69].

With the prestige component of the experimenter's authority eliminated, obedience dropped to 48%, still a surprisingly large figure given the questionable research setting.

Focusing on the experimenter's legitimate power, Milgram added a second confederate, who was to record information at what had formerly been the experimenter's desk. The experimenter explained the study, as in other conditions, but gave no instructions about shock levels before being called away. The confederate, however, filled the role of the authority; he suggested that shocks be given in increasingly strong doses and ordered the subject to continue giving shocks when the Learner started to complain. In this instance obedience dropped to 20%, but when the accomplice began giving shocks at the point the subject had refused to continue, very few subjects were willing to intervene. The majority (68.75%) simply stood by and watched as their fellow subject enthusiastically "electrocuted" the screaming Learner.

Lastly, in a particularly creative episode the experimenter agreed to take the role of the Learner to supposedly convince a reluctant subject that the shocks weren't harmful. However, after the experimenter made a mistake and received a 150-volt shock he shouted "That's enough gentlemen." However, the confederate, who had been watching the procedure, gleefully insisted: "Oh, no, let's go on. Oh, no, come on, I'm going to have to go through the whole thing. Let's go. Come on, let's keep going" (Milgram, 1974, p. 102). Although the confederate demanded continuation, in all cases the subject released the experimenter; obedience to the ordinary person's command to harm the authority was nil (see Focus 7-4).

• •

FOCUS 7-4: AUTHORITY AND UNIFORMS

Doctors have their white coats and black bags; police officers, their crisp uniforms, shiny badges, and guns; fire fighters, their hats and boots. Do these uniforms serve as signs of authority, suggesting that the orders of the wearer should be obeyed even if he or she is acting outside the normal limits of authority? To find out, Leonard Bickman compared subjects' obedience to a man dressed in a sport coat and tie with obedience to a uniformed guard who resembled a police officer in all respects except that he was not carrying a gun. These two types of authorities wandered about Brooklyn ordering people to do such things as pick up litter ("Pick up this bag for me!") and donate money to a motorist ("This fellow is overparked at the meter but doesn't have any change. Give him a dime!"). Bickman found that far more people obeyed the guard than the civilian.

The use of a uniform to increase authority has its limits, however. When Bickman tested people's reactions to a different sort of uniform—an experimenter dressed up as a milk-delivery person—obedience equaled that found in the civilian condition. Apparently, not all uniforms elicit equal amounts of respect, perhaps because only police uniforms imply that the wearer can back up her or his threats with coercive power (see also Bushman, 1984, 1988; Geffner & Gross, 1984; Sackhoff & Weinstein, 1988; Sigelman & Sigelman, 1976).

. . . .

Group effects.   Milgram also demonstrated some interesting effects of other group members' behaviors on subjects' obedience. In one variation the subject merely recorded information and performed other ancillary tasks while an accomplice actually pulled the shock switches. In this variation 92.5% obediently fulfilled their tasks without intervening. If, however, the accomplice refused to administer shocks and the experimenter required the subject to take over, only 10% of the subjects were maximally obedient. Also, if two experimenters ran the research but one demanded continued shocking while another argued for stopping the shocks, all the subjects obeyed the commands of the benevolent authority.

Similar findings were obtained in an obedience study conducted with Australian college students (Kilham & Mann, 1974). Because the researchers assumed that in many cases orders are passed down from superiors to subordinates through the chain of command, the basic Milgram experiment was modified to include the roles of "transmitter," who relayed orders, and "executant," who actually delivered the shocks. As predicted, transmitters were more obedient than executants (54% versus 28%). In addition, in this study men were more obedient than women. Other studies, however, have found either no differences between men and women (Milgram, 1974) or heightened obedience among women (Sheridan & King, 1972).

Explaining Obedience

The obedience observed in Milgram's studies has been interpreted in a variety of ways. According to one explanation, the subjects were irritated by the Learner's slow progress and therefore punished him for his failure. This possibility points to the frustration of the Teacher caught between a demanding experimenter, a dim-witted Learner, and an aggression-eliciting shock machine. Yet the extreme reluctance evidenced by nearly all the subjects during the procedure suggests that their actions were not motivated by a desire to inflict pain. As Milgram reports,

> many subjects showed signs of nervousness in the experimental situation, and especially upon administering the more powerful shocks. In a large number of cases the degree of tension reached extremes that are rarely seen in sociopsychological laboratory studies. Subjects were observed to sweat, tremble, stutter, bite their lips, groan, and dig their fingernails into their flesh [1963, p. 375].

Indeed, the distress of the subjects was so great that the publication of the study sparked a controversy over the ethics of social-psychological research (Baumrind, 1964; Forsyth, 1981; Milgram, 1964, 1977; Miller, 1986; Schlenker & Forsyth, 1977).

A related explanation focuses on other characteristics of the subjects. Just as many people, when first hearing of the Guyana tragedy, wondered "What strange people they must have been to be willing to kill themselves," when people are told about Milgram's findings they react with the question "What kind of evil, sadistic men did he recruit for his study?" Indeed, research has shown that people tend to blame the subjects for their obedience, attributing their actions to their personal characteristics rather than acknowledging the powerful situational forces at work in the experimental situation (Ross, 1977; Safer, 1980). Furthermore, when asked if they would have obeyed in the same circumstances, most people respond they would have stopped at around the 150-volt level. None of the individuals polled answered that they would actually have delivered 450-volt shocks (Milgram, 1974), even though Milgram's findings suggest otherwise (see Focus 7-5).

· ·

FOCUS 7-5: UNDERSTANDING THE CAUSES OF OBEDIENCE

Why do we underestimate our own obedience? Why do we react to reports of major political scandals, criminal actions, and atrocities by faulting the morality of those involved? According to Stephen West and his colleagues, these errors stem from our mistaken attributional assumptions (West, Gunn, & Chernicky, 1975). Although dispositional factors are no doubt involved in such events, their causal role is often overestimated. Indeed, even when people are strongly pressured to obey, as in the Milgram experiment, other people tend to overlook these social determinants of actions to conclude that personality defects caused them to obey. This bias is known as the **fundamental attribution error** (Milgram, 1974; Ross, 1977; Sabini & Silver, 1983; Safer, 1980).

To test this idea, West's research group contacted students in criminology classes and asked them to burglarize a local office building. The experimenter was known by all those contacted to be a private detective, and he presented an elaborate plan backed up by aerial photographs, maps of police routes, blueprints, and so on. However, before people were asked to join the team, four different experimental conditions were established:

1. Immunity: the burglary was sponsored by a government agency (the IRS) to acquire tax records; if caught, the "agents" would receive immunity from prosecution.
2. No immunity: the project was sponsored by the IRS, but immunity could not be guaranteed.
3. Reward: participants were told that a rival company would pay to get information from the target company's safe; the subject's share would be $2000.
4. Control: subjects were told that the burglary would just be a test to see if the plan would work.

As Figure 7-3 shows, far more subjects agreed to participate in the immunity condition than in the other three, but the subjects' explanations for their agreement to participate are of particular interest.

West tested for the fundamental attribution error by asking people who complied to give a reason for their decision. They then compared these responses to the reasons given by observers who had read a full description of the procedures. As expected, the subjects emphasized environmental causes (for example, "The private investigator put pressure on me"), whereas observers favored dispositional causes (for example, "He seemed to be the kind of person who doesn't care about honesty").

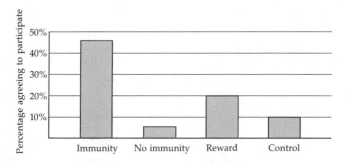

FIGURE 7-3 The percentage of subjects in each condition who agreed to take part in a burglary.
Source: West, Gunn, & Chernicky, 1975

. . . .

Milgram, as might be anticipated, rejects explanations based on personal characteristics. He believes that his results stem from the unique power of the researcher in a scientific investigation. First, his power to reward was high, because he gave out the payment and also because he was an important source of positive evaluations; subjects wanted to win a favorable appraisal from this figure of authority. Second, the experimenter used coercive power in his prods; "The experiment requires that you continue," "It is absolutely essential that you continue," and "You have no other choice, you must go on" all warn of possible negative consequences for disobedience. Third, many subjects felt that when they agreed to participate in the study, they were entering into a verbal contract that required obedience. In consequence, the experimenter had a legitimate right to control their actions, and the Learner had no right to quit the study. Fourth, the experimenter also relied on referent power. The subjects respected Yale and recognized the importance of scientific research; so they trusted the researchers to do the "right thing." Lastly, very few of the subjects knew much about electricity or its effects in such a unique situation; because they considered the experimenter to be an expert, they believed him when he said "Although the shocks may be painful, there is no permanent tissue damage" (Milgram, 1974, p. 21). In sum, Milgram succeeded in constructing a situation in which the authority boasted all five forms of power: reward, coercive, legitimate, referent, and expert.

Milgram also notes that when subjects agree to take part in a study, they become part of a social hierarchy. They no longer act in an autonomous state in which they fulfill their own purposes and goals but, rather, are in what Milgram calls the **agentic state**; that is, they become agents of a higher authority (Milgram, 1974). In the obedience research their role as Teacher requires them to pay attention to instructions, carefully monitor their own actions, and try to carry out the orders of the authority. Although they may question the punishment of the Learner, they tend to accept the authority's definition of the situation as a nonharmful one. Also, they feel little responsibility for what is happening to the Learner, since they are only following orders. Disobedience, if it comes, arises only when the effects of obedience become so negative that inner beliefs about the value of human life overwhelm the external pressures of the situation. In the agentic state obedience is easy; disobedience, in contrast, is achieved only with great difficulty and at a considerable psychological cost (Milgram, 1974; see Hamilton, 1986; Silver & Geller, 1978; Staub, 1985).

Conclusions about Obedience

A number of sources, reacting to the seemingly pessimistic implications of Milgram's findings, have argued that the laboratory groups he investigated were unique and that obedience to an experimenter's demands bears little similarity to "real" obedience as it occurs in naturally occurring groups (Orne & Holland, 1968; Patten, 1977). Milgram, however, believes that in any instance of obedience to a malevolent authority—such as the Nazi campaign to exterminate the Jews, the My Lai episode in the Vietnam War, or the kamikaze suicides of World War II—the same processes he observed in his laboratory are at work. In the case of Jonestown the members were used to following the orders of an absolute authority; they had reached an agentic state. They had no responsibility for their own destiny and looked to Jones for definitions and order. He emphasized loyalty and self-discipline and extolled the virtues of death for a noble cause. Eventually, when he called for the "ultimate sacrifice," his followers could only obey.

SUMMARY

Power, to a group dynamicist, is the capacity to influence others, even when these others try to resist this influence. Although many factors determine who exerts power and who can defend against this influence, French and Raven's analysis of power bases emphasizes five sources of power:

1. *Reward power* is the ability to mediate the distribution of positive or negative reinforcers. This power base is strongest when the rewards are valued, the group members depend on the powerholder for the resource, and the powerholder's promises seem credible.
2. *Coercive power* is the capacity to dispense punishments to those who do not comply with requests or demands.
3. *Legitimate power* stems from an authority's legitimate right to require and demand compliance.
4. *Referent power* is based on group members' identification with, attraction to, or respect for, the powerholder. As with reference groups, group members gain a sense of intrinsic personal satisfaction from identification with the referent powerholder. *Charismatic leaders* generally possess both legitimate and referent power.
5. *Expert power* derives from group members' assumption that the powerholder possesses superior skills and abilities.

Extending these bases of power, recent researchers such as Kipnis and Falbo have identified a number of specific tactics that can be utilized to influence others. These tactics, which include promises, rewards, threats, punishment, expertise, discussion, requests and demands, instruction, persuasion, negotiation, group pressure, persistence, faits accomplis, manipulation, supplication, ingratiation, evasion, and disengagement, differ from one another in terms of directness (or strength), rationality, and bilaterality. Which tactic we use to influence others depends on both the nature of the setting (for example, our status relative to the target and the target's prior compliance) and our personal qualities (for example, personality traits and gender).

The exercise of power and influence leads to direct and indirect consequences for both the target of the influence and the influencer. As the *complementarity hypothesis* suggests, coercive, powerful influence tactics often lead to submissive, passive reactions in the target. Such methods, however, usually generate *compliance* rather than *identification* or *internalization*. These latter two reactions are more likely when rational methods of influence are used. Coercive methods have also been linked to a number of dysfunctional group processes, including (1) dislike and rejection, (2) anger and reciprocal conflict, (3) *revolutionary coalitions*, (4) *reactance*, (5) reductions in intrinsic motivation, and (6) self-blame.

Kipnis notes that power influences both the target *and* the powerholder. In his studies of the metamorphic effects of power he finds that people who are given coercive power will use this power and that once it is used, the powerholders tend to overestimate their control over others and devalue these targets. Powerholders who are very secure in this position may also overstep the bounds of their authority in a process termed the *mandate phenomenon*, or they may become so enamored of power that they are preoccupied with gaining it and using it.

The concept of power offers insight into the too-human tendency to obey authorities. In a classic analysis of obedience Stanley Milgram told adults to give painful and potentially deadly electric shocks to a confederate. He found that 65% of his subjects obeyed, apparently because they felt powerless to refuse the orders of the authority. Although some observers feel that the personal characteristics of Milgram's subjects prompted them to obey (the *fundamental attribution error*), Milgram argues that when the individual enters an *agentic state*, disobedience to authority is achieved only with great difficulty, whereas obedience is easy.

·8·

Leadership

Alice Bertemes runs the Farmers Cooperative Grain Elevator in Tauton, Minnesota. The co-op stores and sells corn and oats, soybeans, flax, rye, barley, and wheat for hundreds of local farmers and also produces feed from these grains. Bertemes's job includes supervising the day-to-day operation of the elevator and storage tanks, buying and selling feed, fertilizer, and chemicals, and managing all fiscal aspects of the co-op. She also supervises a staff of five and disburses profits to the shareholders annually.

Bertemes began working for the co-op as a bookkeeper. The co-op at that time was struggling; storage facilities were limited, most of the equipment was antiquated, and only a handful of the farmers in the area used the elevator. Part of the problem stemmed from mismanagement, but as bookkeeper she had little opportunity to get directly involved in running the facility. When the manager quit, however, she took over the elevator on a trial basis. Today, as a result of her efforts, the co-op is prospering. Before her promotion the co-op was losing money, and the number of shareholders had dropped to about 150. But she revitalized the operation by replacing equipment, expanding facilities, and adding new members. At present the co-op makes over a million dollars a year and has around 1500 shareholders. (Alice Bertemes's work at the co-op is discussed in Wetherby, 1977, pp. 12–21.)

Bertemes is a leader. She took responsibility for solving the co-op's problems; she settled disputes among co-op members and convinced them to work together to achieve desired goals; and she persuaded banks to lend the co-op money. She succeeded where others had failed. But her success, and the success of others like her, raises many questions about the complicated and intricate interpersonal process we call leadership. First, what ingredients did Bertemes, as the co-op manager, use to motivate her employees, ensure the smooth functioning of the business, and attract new shareholders? What do leaders do? Second, why was Bertemes herself chosen to be the manager of the co-op? Was she just the next in line for promotion, or did she emerge as the leader because of her special characteristics? Third, why did she succeed where her predecessors had failed? This chapter examines these three basic questions in an attempt to clarify the nature of leadership.

THE NATURE OF LEADERSHIP

Leadership has long intrigued observers of human behavior. Presumably, ever since the first cave dweller told the rest of the group "We're doing this

212

all wrong. Let's get organized" people have been trying to understand the leadership process. Leadership seems to be an inevitable element of life in groups, a necessary prerequisite for coordinating the behavior of group members in pursuit of common goals. Indeed, leadership may be one of the few universals of human behavior. Anthropological evidence indicates that "there are no known societies without leadership in at least some aspects of their social life" (Lewis, 1974, p. 4; see also Mann, 1980; Zamarripa & Krueger, 1983).

But what is leadership? Is it power over other people? Is it a special talent that the lucky possess and that the unlucky can never hope to gain? Is it something that can be distilled into a set of maxims? As a prelude to our review of the research, we will explore what leadership is and what it is not. (Several excellent reviews of leadership are available for those who require additional information: Barrow, 1977; Bass, 1981; Gibb, 1969; Hollander, 1978, 1985; Stogdill, 1974; and Yukl, 1981.)

Misconceptions about Leadership

The political scientist James McGregor Burns (1978, p. 2) asserts that leadership is "one of the most observed and least understood phenomena on earth." Other experts have also expressed dismay at the prevalence of misunderstanding about leadership, complaining for example, that most people "don't have the faintest concept of what leadership is all about" (Bennis, 1975, p. 1), that "the nature of leadership in our society is very imperfectly understood," and that the "many public statements about it are utter nonsense" (Gardner, 1965, pp. 3, 12). Overall, these notables conclude that commonsense conclusions about leadership are based more on myth than on reality (Cribbin, 1972).

To lead is to control.   Many people, including some prominent political leaders, assume that good leaders are capable of manipulating, controlling, and forcing their followers into obedience. Hitler, for example, defined leadership as the ability to move the masses, whether through persuasion or violence, and Ho Chi Minh once said that a good leader must learn to mold, shape, and change the people just as a woodworker must learn to use wood (see Focus 8-1). However, to refer to leaders—be they kings, presidents, bosses, or chairpersons—as individuals who influence others through domination and coercion seems incorrect. Instead, the term *leader* should be reserved for those who act in the best interests of a group with the consent of that group. Leadership is a form of power, but power *with* people rather than *over* people; it represents a reciprocal relationship between the leader and the led: "Leadership, unlike naked power-wielding, is thus inseparable from followers' needs and goals" (Burns, 1978, p. 19).

. . . .

FOCUS 8-1: POLITICIANS LOOK AT LEADERSHIP

To use people is like using wood. A skilled worker can make use of all kinds of wood, whether it is big or small, straight or curved.

Ho Chi Minh

Leadership is the ability to decide what is to be done, and then to get others to want to do it.

Dwight D. Eisenhower

I must follow the people. Am I not their leader?

Benjamin Disraeli

To be a leader means to be able to move masses.

Hitler

A leader is a man who has the ability to get other people to do what they don't want to do, and like it.

Harry S. Truman

I want to be a President who is a Chief Executive in every sense of the word—who responds to a problem, not by hoping his subordinates will act, but by directing them to act.

John F. Kennedy

The [leader is the] last person in the world to know what the people really want and think.

James A. Garfield

[A leader is] one who implants noble ideals and principles with practical accomplishments.

Richard M. Nixon

The true leader must submerge himself in the fountain of the people.

Lenin

. . . .

The born leader.   Henry Ford, the amazingly successful founder of a major automotive empire, once remarked that asking " 'Who ought to be Boss?' is like asking 'Who ought to be the tenor in the quartet?' Obviously, the man who can sing tenor."

Ford was suggesting that the ability to lead stems from a collection of naturally developing qualities within the person. He thought that leadership was a talent, like singing or dancing, that existed in some people but not in others. Because this talent derives from inborn characteristics, the "born follower" cannot develop this skill, and situational factors have little impact on leadership. Group dynamicists, however, now believe that the born-leader idea exaggerates the strength of the relationship between one's personal qualities and one's leadership potential. Certain personality variables are associated with effective leadership, but for the most part leadership "is an achievement, not a birthright or happy accident of heredity" (Cribbin, 1972, p. 14).

The formula for leadership.   Scholars and laypeople are constantly offering prescriptive suggestions to leaders. Niccolo Machiavelli, perhaps the first management consultant, advised the careful ruler to gain the friendship and support of the populace. Many popular authorities argue that since group members begrudge leaders their power, leadership duties should be shared with group members. Management specialists offer workshops that promise to teach participants how to lead, books on leadership are filled with sage advice about what makes for good leadership, and aspiring leaders can even purchase videotapes that spell out "excellence in management."

These proposals, in trying to distill leadership into simple *do* and *don't do* lists, assume that some formula exists for predicting leadership effectiveness. Yet current research tells us that generalizations about leadership tend to be overgeneralizations. Well-liked leaders are often effective leaders, but many outstanding leaders are actively disliked by their subordinates. Sharing leadership democratically may be effective in some instances, but this strategy may backfire in others. In general, blanket statements about leadership tend to overlook the need to make certain that one's leadership actions fit the given situation. A person with one set of skills may do a marvelous job when leading a problem-solving group, but these skills lead to disastrous consequences when applied elsewhere. (For an opposing view, see Blake & Mouton, 1982.)

Leadership is the answer.   People often assume that the leader determines the group's destiny. But when the losing team wishes the coach would be changed, the members of an ineffective committee privately blame the chairperson, or the workers blame their boss, they are overlooking their own contribution to group performance. The idea that a good leader will cure all the group's ills is a myth, for group performance depends on the interaction between the leader and the rest of the group members (Gemmill, 1986).

Leadership: A Working Definition

Pointing out what leadership is not is far easier than pointing out what it is. The term is used in a variety of contexts and has been accused of a multitude of scientifically reprehensible crimes: excessive ambiguity, an overbroad scope, significant overlap with other descriptive terms, and doubtful theoretical utility (Pfeffer, 1977; Katz & Kahn, 1978; Grimes, 1978; and Miner, 1975, respectively). Given this disagreement, it is unlikely that all theorists and researchers would accept any one definition of leadership. However, some sort of working definition of the concept will prove useful in guiding our analysis of leaders and leadership.

Toward this end consider this *interactional definition:* **leadership** is a reciprocal, transactional, and transformational process in which individuals are permitted to influence and motivate others to promote the attaining of group and individual goals. This definition is cumbersome, but it emphasizes several key features noted by many previous definers.

1. Leadership is a *reciprocal* process. Any aspect of the leader, group member, or setting can influence, and be influenced by, every other variable in the system. An interactional view assumes that leadership is a fluid, dynamic process involving continual adjustments among the three elements (Barrow, 1977; Cartwright & Zander, 1968; Hollander, 1985).

2. Leadership is a *transactional* process. The leader/member relationship is a form of social exchange; leaders and group members trade their time and energy in exchange for valued monetary and social rewards (Burns, 1978; Hollander & Julian, 1969; Pigors, 1935).

3. Leadership is often a *transformational* process. The transformational leader heightens group members' motivation, confidence, and satisfaction by uniting members and changing their beliefs, values, and needs (Bass, 1985a, 1985b; Bass, Avolio, & Goldheim, 1987).

4. Leadership is a *cooperative* process of legitimate influence rather than sheer power (Grimes, 1978). In a small group, for example, the individual who influences others the most is often designated the leader (Hollander, 1985). The right to lead is, in most instances, voluntarily conferred on the leader by some or all members of the group (Kochan, Schmidt, & DeCotiis, 1975).

5. Leadership is an adaptive, *goal-seeking* process, for it organizes and motivates group members' attempts to attain personal and group goals (Katz & Kahn, 1978).

This working definition fits Bertemes. She was appointed to the position by the Board of Directors of the co-op, and she can be removed by the board at any time. Yet through the years she has earned the respect of the shareholders, who rely on her to safeguard their farm products. She works closely with the farmers, directs the processing of the grains, responds to questions, and rarely makes decisions by fiat. For Bertemes, leadership is reciprocal, transactional, transformational, cooperative, and efficient.

Leadership: A Behavioral Definition

Opportunities for attaining a leadership role abound in everyday life. For example, you may attend the organizational meeting of a club and find yourself elected chair of one of the committees. You may be promoted at your job from a production position to one that involves some supervisory responsibilities. Your fraternity or sorority may elect you its president.

But what would you do if you became the leader in one of these groups? How would you behave? What behaviors would be part of your role as leader? Naturally, your answer to these questions would depend, in part, on the kind of group you were leading: work group, discussion group, recreational group, and so on. Researchers, however, have found similarities in leaders' behaviors in many different types of groups. In the Ohio State University Leadership Studies, for example, investigators first developed a list of nine key types of behavior that seemed to characterize military and organizational leaders (initiating new practices, interacting informally with subordinates, representing the group, integrating group action, and so on; see Hemphill, 1950). Second, they designed a questionnaire to measure these behaviors and asked a large number of group members to rate their leader using the instrument. Third, a statistical technique known as factor analysis was used to eliminate overlapping and irrelevant behaviors, and the original nine were narrowed down to four factors, or dimensions: consideration, initiating structure, production emphasis, and sensitivity (Halpin & Winer, 1952). Of these four factors the first two seemed to be the most important dimensions; together they accounted for over 80% of the variation in followers' ratings of their leaders.

The Ohio State University Leadership Studies are not unique. A host of studies argues that the behaviors that make up the role of leadership fall into two general clusters, relationship behaviors and task behaviors (see Table 8-1). **Relationship behaviors** address the feelings, attitudes, and satisfactions of the members of the group and therefore correspond closely to the functions fulfilled by the socioemotional specialist (Bales, 1958; see Chapter 5). Even in groups that exist to complete tasks or solve problems, leaders must often take steps to meet the members' personal needs. Boosting morale, increasing cohesiveness, reducing interpersonal conflict, establishing leader/follower rapport, and illustrating one's concern and consideration for group members all go into relationship leadership (Lord, 1977).

Task behaviors, in contrast, pertain to the problem at hand rather than the personal satisfactions of the group members. Leaders must also lead; they must guide the group in the direction of successful goal attainment. Defining problems for the group, establishing communication networks, providing evaluative feedback, planning, motivating action, coordinating members' actions, and facilitating goal attainment by proposing solutions and removing barriers are key aspects of task leadership (Lord, 1977).

These two dimensions were incorporated by the Ohio State researchers in their **Leader Behavior Description Questionnaire,** or LBDQ (Kerr, Schriesheim, Murphy, & Stogdill, 1974; Stogdill, 1974). To complete this measure, group members rate their leader on a series of items such as those presented in the right-hand column of Table 8-1. The totals from the

TABLE 8-1. The two basic dimensions of leadership behavior.

Conceptual labels	Definition	Sample behaviors
Relationship Leadership		
-Relationship-oriented -Socioemotional -Supportive -Employee-centered -Relations-skilled -Group maintenance	Involves actions that maintain positive interpersonal relations in the group; entails friendliness, mutual trust, openness, and willingness to explain decisions	-Listens to group members -Is easy to understand -Is friendly and approachable -Treats group members as equals -Is willing to make changes
Task Leadership		
-Task-oriented -Goal-oriented -Work-facilitative -Production-centered -Administratively skilled -Goal-achievement	Involves actions that promote task completion; entails regulating behavior, monitoring communication, and reducing goal ambiguity	-Assigns tasks to members -Makes attitudes clear to the group -Is critical of poor work -Sees to it that the group is working to capacity -Coordinates activity

(Sources: Halpin & Winer, 1952; Lord, 1977)

two separate subscales are assumed to measure the two dimensions of leadership. These dimensions have also been noted by other independent researchers. Although the labels vary—supportive versus work-facilitative (Bowers & Seashore, 1966), employee centered versus production-centered (Likert, 1967), relations-skilled versus administratively skilled (Mann, 1965), or group-maintenance versus goal achievement (Cartwright & Zander, 1968)—the two basic dimensions surface with remarkable consistency.

These two elements of leadership also emerge when leaders talk about their work. As Bertemes explains, much of her work requires establishing a rapport with the farmers: "You have to communicate with your patrons. It takes a lot of time. You have to explain markets to them. They want to know what the market is doing, so you have to talk with them"(Wetherby 1977, p. 16). At the same time, however, she takes care of the daily operation of the co-op, produces feed, purchases fertilizer and chemicals, reviews farm prices before selling the grains, prepares financial statements, and runs the annual shareholders' meeting. Her position requires a wide range of behaviors, but most of them fall into either the relationship category or the task category (see Focus 8-2).

• •

FOCUS 8-2: THE LEADERSHIP BEHAVIORS OF MANAGERS

Studies of military, business, educational, and political leaders suggest that the leadership role involves a mix of task behaviors and relationship behaviors. Yet as Ralph M. Stogdill explains, these two clusters are "not sufficient to describe all the complexities of leader behaviors" (1974, p. 143). Similarly, Henry Mintzberg (1975, 1980), in his provocative analysis of what managers actually do within the organization, argues that the manager's role requires leadership behaviors that go well beyond those specified in most training manuals or formal job descriptions (see also Hackman & Walton, 1986; Luthans, Welsh, & Taylor, 1988; Paolillo, 1987). Mintzberg's list of managerial behaviors includes:

1. figurehead: acting as the representative of the group at social functions or ceremonies
2. motivator and trainer: guiding the development of group members by providing feedback, training, and motivational messages
3. liaison: making and maintaining contacts with individuals outside of the immediate group
4. monitor: seeking out information about group and organizational performance by contacting others, reviewing records, attending meetings, and so on
5. disseminator: relaying information to subordinates through memorandums, meetings, presentations, and so on
6. spokesperson: providing information about the group to individuals outside the immediate work group
7. entrepreneur: identifying business opportunities, expanding to new areas, and solving production problems with creativity and vision
8. disturbance handler: solving problems as they arise, including conflicts within the group, production problems, and so on
9. resource allocator: making budgeting decisions, including allocating funds for new projects and distributing personnel to organization units
10. negotiator: mediating disputes between group members, handling labor problems, and bargaining with outsiders

· ·

LEADERSHIP EMERGENCE

Recall some of the groups discussed in earlier chapters. Why, for example, was John Lennon the Beatles' leader? Why did the Strauches rise to positions of authority among the Andes survivors? Why was Kennedy elected president? Why did Bertemes emerge as the manager of the co-op? If you have ever wondered how in the world a particular person ever became a group leader, then you, too, have been puzzled by the process of leadership emergence.

To understand **leadership emergence,** we must examine two interrelated processes. First, we must ask why a group like the Beatles or the co-op requires a leader. In many cases groups function well without a leader, whereas in other circumstances the role of leader emerges. What factors determine when the leadership role will emerge? Second, given the emer-

gence of the role, who will fill that role? Was Bertemes's emergence unpredictable, or did she possess characteristics that prompted the board
members to select her to run the co-op?

When Does a Leader Emerge?

In many formally organized groups—juries, committees, conferences,
workshops, or business meetings—the leadership role is explicitly built
into the structure of the group. Yet in groups with no formally defined
structures, the role still seems to emerge with remarkable regularity (see
Chapter 5). Informal gatherings such as parties, study groups, discussion
groups, or spectators at a sporting event may initially start off as leaderless
groups, but in time someone steps up to fill the role. The question is
"When does a group require the services of a leader?"

One particularly active researcher in the area, John K. Hemphill, relates
the need for a leader to a number of situational factors, including the
group's size and the type of task confronting it. According to Hemphill, as
a group becomes larger, it begins to encounter problems of coordination,
administration, and communication that can be easily ameliorated by a
leader. Therefore, members of large groups are more open to attempts by
possible candidates to gain leadership. Hemphill (1950) tested this hypothesis by comparing the behaviors of large-group leaders with those of
small-group leaders, and he found evidence of a greater reliance in the
larger groups on the leader to make rules clear, keep members informed,
and make group decisions. In a later review of other variables Hemphill
(1961) also suggests that leaders appear in groups when (1) members feel
that success on the group task is within their reach, (2) the rewards for
success are valued, (3) the task requires group rather than individual effort, and (4) an individual with previous experience in the leadership role
is present in the group.

Other researchers have noted that the likelihood of leadership roles
emerging increases when the group faces a stressful situation, or a crisis
(Hamblin, 1958; Helmreich & Collins, 1967; Mulder & Stemerding, 1963).
College students in one study worked in three-person groups on an easy
task. This task was changed during the second phase, however, and the
group uniformly performed poorly. The situation posed a crisis because
the experimenter told the failing groups that their performance was being
compared with that of high school students who had earlier worked on
the task and performed it easily. Faced with the possibility of an embarrassing failure on a task that the younger groups had mastered, the subjects tended to centralize the structure of their groups. During this crisis,
substantive, directive comments became localized around one group
member, who was soon replaced by another high influencer if the group's
performance did not improve. During a crisis individual group members
apparently tend to prefer the structure and support provided by a leader,
but they expect the leader to help them deal successfully with the stressful
situation (Hamblin, 1958).

A final determinant of the need for a leadership role is the presence or absence of **leadership substitutes** in the group (Kerr & Jermier, 1978). Although leadership does occur widely in many groups, substitutes for leadership tend, in some cases, to "negate the leader's ability to either improve or impair subordinate satisfaction and performance" (Kerr & Jermier, 1978, p. 377). When a number of these substitutes are in evidence in a situation, leadership is both unnecessary and unlikely (Childers, Dubinsky, & Gencturk, 1986).

These substitutes are summarized in Table 8-2, which lists characteristics of the group members, the group task, and the group situation that tend to neutralize relationship leadership, task leadership, or both. As the table shows, when a group is composed of competent individuals with a great need for independence, a sense of professional identity, and a disdain for the rewards that their work supervisors can offer, both relationship and task leadership are neutralized. In contrast, only task leadership becomes unnecessary when the group members can work on problems that are unambiguous, routine, and clearly evaluable. Lastly, formal, inflexible, and unambiguous group structures tend to neutralize task-oriented leadership, whereas group cohesiveness, low reward power, and spatial distance make both types of leadership unnecessary.

TABLE 8-2. Substitutes for leadership.

	Will tend to neutralize	
Characteristic	*relationship leadership*	*task leadership*
Of the group member		
1. Has ability, experience, training, knowledge		X
2. Has a need for independence	X	X
3. Has a "professional" orientation	X	X
4. Is indifferent to group rewards	X	X
Of the task		
5. Is unambiguous and routine		X
6. Is methodologically invariant		X
7. Provides its own feedback concerning accomplishment		X
8. Is intrinsically satisfying	X	
Of the organization		
9. Is formalized (has explicit plans, goals, and areas of responsibility)		X
10. Is inflexible (has rigid, unbending rules and procedures)		X
11. Has highly specified and active advisory and staff functions		X
12. Has closely knit, cohesive work groups	X	X
13. Has organizational rewards not within the leader's control	X	X
14. Imposes spatial distance between superior and subordinate	X	X

(Source: Kerr & Jermier, 1978)

In an imaginative exploration of these substitutes, researchers asked respondents to complete a questionnaire that measured each of the substitutes for leadership listed in Table 8-2. (For example, to measure Item 1 the subjects reported their degree of agreement with the item "Because of my ability, experience, training, or job knowledge, I have the competence to act independently of my immediate superior in performing day-to-day duties"; see Kerr & Jermier, 1978.) However, rather than answering as they themselves felt, the subjects were to respond from the viewpoint of a character in one of three well-known nationally televised programs: Mary Richards in the *Mary Tyler Moore Show,* Hawkeye Pierce in *MASH,* and Archie Bunker in *All in the Family* (this study was conducted when the character of Archie worked at the loading dock of the plant). Although the researchers pointed out that the limitations of this role-playing procedure required that the findings be interpreted with caution, their results did suggest that the presence of certain leadership substitutes corresponded to the absence of task and relationship leader roles. For example, Mary Richards, as depicted on the program, appears to derive a good deal of intrinsic satisfaction from working on the various tasks that make up her job. Furthermore, her work group seems to be fairly cohesive, and the members express a strong degree of professionalism and respect for one another. According to Table 8-2, these features of the situation should serve as substitutes for relationship-oriented leadership; as the researchers conclude, "on the show she does seem happy in her work despite the erratic attempts at warmth and collegiality displayed by her superior [Lou Grant]" (1978, p. 387). For Hawkeye Pierce, in contrast, his high personal skill and knowledge obviate the need for task leadership, but the combat situation depicted on the program undermines his professionalism and intrinsic satisfaction with the role of surgeon. Hence, these findings suggest that Pierce would benefit from relationship-oriented leadership. These predictions were confirmed.

Who Will Lead?

Why did Bertemes rise to a position of leadership within the co-op? She did not have a high school education, she was not trained in management, and she was a woman seeking work in an area that was dominated by men. Yet when the manager resigned after only three years with the co-op, the Board of Directors hired her to run the plant.

Leaders gain their central positions through a variety of means, but group dynamicists assume that a number of specifiable factors determine which individual in a group will eventually become the leader. These factors include a number of physical characteristics, such as height, age, and gender, as well as such personal qualities as intelligence and personality.

Physical characteristics.   Are physical attributes related to leadership emergence? As Ralph Stogdill noted in reviews of research published in

1948 and 1974, the correlation between *height* and leadership varies from −.13 to +.71, but the average is about .30. Group members seem to associate height with power, but the relationship is not so strong that height is a prerequisite for leadership. History is filled with Napoleons who have managed to reach positions of leadership despite being short.

Stogdill also concluded that leaders tend to *weigh* more than their followers, but he found that the link between *age* and leadership emergence was a bit more complicated. Studies of informal discussion groups find little relationship between leadership and age, but political and business leaders are often older than their subordinates. It apparently takes time to climb up the organizational hierarchy. Fewer than a tenth of a percent of the corporate executives listed in the *Register of Corporations, Directors, and Executives* are under 30 years of age (Stanton & Poors, 1967), and 74% are 50 or older. As Stogdill notes, "Organizations tend to rely upon administrative knowledge and demonstration of success that comes with experience and age" (1974, p. 76). Further, if group members assume that age is an indicator of wisdom, experience, and sagacity, they are likely to prefer a leader who is older rather than younger.

Gender.   Bertemes is something of an exception. Although the gender gap in leadership has narrowed in recent years, it has not closed. Increasing numbers of women now hold jobs in what were once male-dominated fields, but their rise to upper-level management and leadership positions in these fields has been slow. This bias occurs in both small-group and organizational contexts (Bass, 1981, chap. 30; Dion, 1985; Hollander, 1983, 1985). Studies of the gradual emergence of leaders in small, unstructured discussion groups, for example, tend to find men outnumbering women in the leadership role (Bartol & Martin, 1986; Eagly, 1983). In several studies of mixed-sex groups, women displayed fewer leadership actions than men (Craig & Sherif, 1986), and both leaders and subordinates perceived the female leaders to be less dominant than male leaders (Snodgrass & Rosenthal, 1984). Evidence also suggests that the lone man in an otherwise all-female group often becomes the leader, whereas the lone woman in an otherwise all-male group has little influence (Crocker & McGraw, 1984). The tendency for men to dominate women in informal discussion groups was obtained even when the men and women were all deemed to be androgynous (Porter, Geis, Cooper, & Newman, 1985).

Several studies suggest that even women who are interpersonally dominant cannot escape the constraints of this gender bias (Fleischer & Chertkoff, 1986; Megargee, 1969; Nyquist & Spence, 1986). Researchers first tested their subjects to determine their usual level of dominance. They then created dyads that included one person who was highly dominant and one who was low in dominance. In same-sex dyads the dominant individual became the leader 73% of the time. In mixed-sex dyads the dominant man became the leader 90% of the time, but the dominant woman became the leader only 35% of the time (Nyquist & Spence, 1986).

The bias is not, however, irremediable. When groups are warned before the discussion about the tendency to favor men, men and women share leadership equally (Porter et al., 1985). Also, men and women respond differently depending on the type of task being attempted. As noted in Chapter 6, researchers have found sex differences in conformity when tasks require skills and abilities that are traditionally linked to one gender. Similarly, men tend to assume the leadership role when the group tasks are "masculine," whereas women emerge as leaders when groups work on tasks that are "feminine" (Wentworth & Anderson, 1984).

Intelligence. Stogdill (1948, 1974) cites 48 studies of the link between intellectual ability and leadership. Although the average correlation is small, on the order of .25 to .30, small-group and managerial leaders tend to score higher than average on standard intelligence tests, make superior judgments with greater decisiveness, be more knowledgeable, and speak more fluently. Leaders typically do not, however, exceed their followers in intellectual prowess by a wide margin (Simonton, 1985). Groups appear to prefer leaders who are more intelligent than the average group member, but too great a discrepancy introduces problems in communication, trust, and social sensitivity. Although highly intelligent individuals may be extremely capable and efficient leaders, their groups may feel that large differences in intellectual abilities translate into large differences in interests, attitudes, and values. Hence, although high intelligence may mean skilled leadership, a group prefers to be "ill-governed by people it can understand" (Gibb, 1969, p. 218).

Personality traits. Early leadership researchers believed that leaders possess certain personality traits that set them apart from others. This *trait view,* which in its strongest form assumed that some people were natural-born leaders, faded in popularity as researchers reported a series of failures to find any consistent impact of personality on behavior across a wide variety of situations. After conducting hundreds of studies, several reviewers concluded that the correlation between personality traits and leadership was too small to serve much predictive purpose (Mann, 1959; Stogdill, 1948).

In retrospect this rejection of the personality/leadership relationship was premature. Stogdill, who first reviewed the literature in 1948, later concluded that his early review had been too pessimistic. After painstakingly reviewing 163 studies in 1970, Stogdill concluded that leaders, relative to followers, were higher in achievement orientation, adaptability, ascendancy, energy level, responsibility taking, self-confidence, and sociability. Similarly, Robert Lord and his colleagues recently used meta-analytic methods to statistically pool the results of dozens of studies of the relationship between personality traits and leadership emergence (Lord, De Vader, & Alliger, 1986). This analysis indicated that intelligence, masculinity/femininity, and dominance were all significantly related to leadership perceptions. David Kenny and Stephen Zaccaro (1983), too, conclude that between 49% and 82% of the variance in leadership emergence can be attributed to some stable characteristic. They speculate that this characteristic, rather than being a traditional personality trait, may actually involve the ability to perceive the needs and goals of a constituency and to adjust one's personal approach to group action accordingly. They, too, warn us not to reject the notion that personality determines leadership emergence. (This trait model will be examined further in this chapter's section on the effectiveness of leaders.)

Task abilities. Possessing skills and abilities that (1) are valued by the other group members or (2) increase the group's chances for achieving success also gives an individual an edge during leadership emergence. In a review of 52 studies of characteristics typically ascribed to the leader, Stogdill (1974) found that the most frequently suggested factor (appearing in 35% of the studies cited) emphasized technical, task-relevant skills. Groups are more accepting of leaders who have previously demonstrated task ability (Goldman & Fraas, 1965) and are more willing to follow the directions of a task-competent person than those of an incompetent person (Hollander, 1965). Furthermore, although high task ability facilitates leadership, low task ability seems to be an even more powerful factor in disqualifying individuals from consideration as leaders (Palmer, 1962). Even marginal group members who frequently violate group norms can become leaders if their task abilities significantly foster the attainment of goals (Hollander, 1964).

Field studies of leadership in organizational and military settings also suggest that individuals who possess valued skills are more often recognized as leaders. The successful head of the accounting department, for example, is usually recognized as a better accountant than his or her subordinates or other, less well-regarded managers (Tsui, 1984). Studies of ratings of military leadership ability also find that physical ability and task-performance skills are highly correlated with leadership emergence (Rice, Instone, & Adams, 1984). Bertemes's emergence as a leader was probably due to her skills. Her talent for accounting earned her the job of bookkeeper, but she was also an expert at organizing the efforts of her subordinates and communicating to the farmers. As a result she was able to function effectively as the co-op's manager.

Participation rates. The relationship between task skills and leadership is heartening, for it suggests that groups tend to favor leaders who are qualified for that role. In contrast, studies of the relationship between participation rate and leadership are more disappointing, for they suggest that the person who talks the most in the group is the most likely to emerge as leader (Burke, 1974; Stein & Heller, 1979, 1983). The data are surprising: the correlation between leadership emergence and most personal characteristics usually averages in the low .20s, but the correlation between participation rate and leadership is .65 (Stein & Heller, 1979).

Furthermore, what counts is the sheer quantity of the participation rather than the quality. People who make many useless remarks are more likely to emerge as leaders than individuals who make relatively few useful remarks. In a demonstration of this effect researchers manipulated both the quantity and quality of the statements of a trained confederate in a problem-solving group (Sorrentino & Boutillier, 1975). While the four-person all-male group was working to solve the experimental tasks, the confederate systematically offered either many comments or few comments that were either high in quality (they promoted success on the tasks) or low in quality (they promoted failure on the tasks). When the subjects later rated, on five-point scales, the confederate's confidence, interest in the problem, competence, influence over others, and contributions to solving the task, only his quantity of comments significantly influenced his ratings of confidence and interest. Furthermore, although the subjects viewed the confederate as more competent and more influential when he interjected high-quality rather than low-quality comments, the effects due to quantity were still stronger. The only dependent variable that was strongly influenced by the quality of comments was the rating of his contribution to solving the problem.

Why pick leaders based on the sheer quantity of their remarks? This tendency may stem from our assumption that the individual who is actively involved in the group discussion is interested in the group and is willing to take responsibility for its performance. Low participation rates, in contrast, imply that the individual has little interest in the group or its problems: "Quality is not positively related to leadership unless the competent person demonstrates his willingness to share his resources with the group members and is perceived as seriously trying to contribute to the group's goals" (Sorrentino & Boutillier, 1975, p. 411). These perceptions can apparently be best fostered by participating at high levels (Sorrentino & Field, 1986).

Leadership Emergence: A Cognitive Model

Does this maze of relationships between leadership emergence and age, height, weight, personality traits, gender, and so on follow any discernible pattern? A number of leadership experts believe that a *cognitive approach* to leadership emergence best accounts for these results. According to this view, most people intuitively assume that leaders possess certain qualities. Are leaders intelligent or unintelligent? outgoing or introverted? understanding or insensitive? cooperative or inflexible? strict or undisciplined? Group members readily answer these questions by drawing on their intuitive beliefs about leaders. These cognitive structures, which have been termed **implicit leadership theories** (Lord et al., 1986) or **leader prototypes** (Foti, Fraser, & Lord, 1982), guide the way in which people perceive and evaluate their fellow group members. If someone in the group acts in ways that match the group members' leadership theories, that person is more likely to emerge as the leader (Lord, Foti, & De Vader, 1984). Consider, for example, the gender bias described earlier. This bias against women may result from sexism, a negative attitude toward women. But the bias may also be produced by implicit leadership theories that erroneously suggest that men make better leaders than women (Binning, Zaba, & Whattam, 1986, Jacobson & Effertz, 1974; Nye, 1988; Nye & Forsyth, 1987; Rosen & Jerdee, 1973, 1978).

Implicit leadership theories, in addition to influencing who emerges as the group leader, may also explain certain biases that pervade subordinates' evaluations of their leaders (Ilgen & Fujii, 1976; Lord, Binning, Rush, & Thomas, 1978; Rush, Thomas, & Lord, 1977). If group members believe that dominance is a key aspect of leadership, for example, they may mistakenly remember their leader acting dominantly and forget the times when their leader engaged in submissive behavior (Cronshaw & Lord, 1987; Lord, 1985; Lord & Alliger, 1985; Lord et al., 1984). Lord and his colleagues illustrated the biasing effects of implicit leadership theories in one study by arranging for raters to watch a videotape of a group interaction. After the tape they asked the observers to identify behaviors that the leader had or had not performed. Lord found that the raters were less accurate, were less confident, and took longer to respond when trying to judge behaviors that were part of their leadership theories but had not been performed by the leader they had watched. He also found that the raters were less accurate but more confident when rating the leader on traits that were not part of their leadership theories (Foti & Lord, 1987).

Lord also believes that when researchers ask subordinates to describe their leaders, these ratings reflect the subordinates' implicit leadership theories more than their leaders' actions (Lord, 1985; Phillips & Lord, 1986). Why, asks Lord, do so many studies indicate that leadership has two sides, one focusing on relationships and one focusing on the task? Because, he answers, followers' implicit leadership theories include these two components. Lord and his colleagues have found that the implicit leadership theories adopted by laypeople match the explicit leadership theories developed by group dynamicists, and he worries that the distinction between task and relationship may rest more in group members' minds than in leaders' actual behaviors.

In sum, although leadership emergence can be related back to certain characteristics of individuals in the group, cognitive processes seem to be critical as well. Most members believe that their leaders should be intelligent, extraverted, masculine, interpersonally sensitive, dominant, conservative, and well-adjusted, so these are the characteristics possessed by most emergent leaders (Lord et al., 1986). For those who are interested in becoming the leaders in their groups, the best advice that researchers can offer is to fulfill the expectations of the group members as closely as possible. If the members expect the leader to have Characteristics X, Y, and Z, the successful candidate for leadership must be able to convince the others that he or she has these characteristics. If, however, you wish to avoid leadership (as many people do), you should perform actions that can only be interpreted as evidence against your possession of Characteristics X, Y, and Z (see Focus 8-3).

· ·

FOCUS 8-3: HOW TO AVOID LEADERSHIP IN SMALL GROUPS

B. Aubrey Fisher (1980, pp. 223–224) offers some tongue-in-cheek principles that, if followed carefully, guarantee a position of low status in a group:

Rule 1: Be absent from as many group meetings as possible.

Rule 2: Contribute to the interaction as little as possible.

Rule 3: Volunteer to be the secretary or the record keeper of your group's discussions.

Rule 4: Indicate that you are willing to do what you are told.

Rule 5: Come on strong early in the group discussion.

Rule 6: Try to assume the role of joker.

Rule 7: Demonstrate your knowledge of everything, including your extensive vocabulary of big words and technical jargon.

Rule 8: Demonstrate a contempt for leadership.

· ·

LEADER EFFECTIVENESS

Alexander the Great governed from a centralized position where he could monitor every important aspect of his huge empire. The Strauch cousins, who emerged as the leaders in the group stranded in the Andes, helped their fellow members survive the brutal winter. General George Patton inspired those under his command by displaying high levels of personal confidence, sureness, and an immense strength of character. Bertemes turned the failing grain elevator into a highly profitable, thriving enterprise.

These individuals were not simply leaders; rather, they were effective leaders. But what was the source of their effectiveness? Did they possess certain skills and abilities that set them apart from others, ensuring their success as leaders or military commanders? Or did they respond to the particular situation, the pawns of social forces that were the real determinants of their apparent success (Simonton, 1980, 1987)?

In the 19th century the historian Thomas Carlyle asserted that many prominent political figures were great geniuses who shaped the times in which they lived. According to this *great leader theory* of history (Carlyle called it the great-man theory), some individuals possess certain characteristics that destine them to greatness. Thus, he concluded that history could be best studied by considering the contributions of the few great men and women. The Russian novelist Leo Tolstoy took a contrasting viewpoint by emphasizing the role that situational factors play in determining history. To Tolstoy such leaders as Alexander and Napoleon came to prominence because the spirit of the times—the *Zeitgeist*—was propitious for the dominance of a single individual, and the qualities of the person were largely irrelevant to this rise to power. Tolstoy thus concluded that the conquests and losses of military leaders such as Napoleon were caused not by their decisions and skills but by uncontrollable aspects of the historical situation (Carlyle, 1841; Tolstoy, 1869/1952).

When researchers began examining leadership in small groups, they realized that these two viewpoints explained leadership in completely different terms. If, as Carlyle's great-leader theory suggested, leaders are unique individuals with special characteristics, we should be able to predict their effectiveness by considering these traits. If Tolstoy's *Zeitgeist* view is correct, leadership depends on the situation: the nature of the task, the composition of the group, the group structure, and so on.

As is so often the case when two seemingly incompatible explanations for the same phenomenon are carefully analyzed, group dynamicists soon discovered that both theories contained elements of truth. Early studies of the **trait model** found few traits that were consistently related to leadership effectiveness, but some individuals did possess a style of interaction that made them more effective in that role; these "great leaders" performed well in many different groups working on a variety of tasks (Borgatta, Couch, & Bales, 1954). However, as a scaled-down version of Tolstoy's **situational model** would predict, even a superior leader in one situation sometimes turned out to be an inferior leader when observed in a different context.

Recognizing the kernel of truth in both the trait and the situational models of leadership, theorists worked to forge new models of leadership effectiveness that took into account the *interaction* between the leader's qualities, group members' qualities, and situational characteristics. Several of these **interactional models** of leadership are examined below. (For more detailed reviews, see Chemers, 1983, 1987; Hollander, 1985; and Yukl, 1981.)

Fiedler's Contingency Model

Fred Fiedler called his theory the **contingency model** because he assumed that leadership effectiveness was *contingent on* both the personal characteristics of the leader and the nature of the group situation (Fiedler, 1978, 1981). He began his program of research in 1951 by studying a large number of groups that produced an outcome that could be evaluated, worked together as a team, and had an appointed, elected, or emergent leader. By noting when these interacting groups prospered and failed, he was able to specify both the leadership variables and the situational variables that influenced this outcome. His theory, which was derived from these findings rather than from logic or intuition, pinpointed two key sets of factors, the leader's motivational style and the leader's control in the problem-solving situation.

The leader's motivational style.   Early in his research Fiedler recognized that leaders vary in their approach to motivating their subordinates and that these differences influence their effectiveness. *Relationship-motivated leaders*, he argued, try to find acceptance within their groups. Such leaders seek to establish strong interpersonal links with the other members of their groups, and they are concerned more with these relationships than with completing the task. In contrast, the *task-motivated leader* concentrates on completing the task as the primary goal of the group.

These hypotheses are consistent with other research into leader behavior that was reviewed earlier in the chapter, but Fiedler's method of assessing motivational style is unique. Rather than basing his estimates on group members' ratings of the leader, he asks leaders to complete an indirect measure of motivational style known as the **Least Preferred Co-worker Scale** (LPC Scale). Respondents are told to think of the one individual with whom they have experienced the *most difficulty* in working with at some time. This person, dubbed the least preferred co-worker, is then evaluated on the scales in Focus 8-4:

> An individual who describes the LPC in very negative, rejecting terms (low LPC score, i.e., less than 57) is considered task-motivated. . . . In effect, the individual says, "If I cannot work with you, if you frustrate my need to get the job done, then you can't be any good in other respects." The relationship-motivated individual who sees his or her LPC in relatively more positive terms (high LPC score, i.e., about 63 and above) says, "Getting a job done is not everything. Therefore, even though I can't work with you, you may still be friendly, relaxed, interesting, etc., in other words, someone with whom I could get along on a personal basis." Thus, high LPCs are relationship motivated, while low LPCs are task motivated [Fiedler, 1978, p. 61].

· ·

FOCUS 8-4: THE LEAST PREFERRED CO-WORKER (LPC) SCALE

Think of a person with whom you can work least well. He or she may be someone you work with now or someone you knew in the past. This co-worker does not have to be the person you like least but should be the person with whom you had the most difficulty in getting a job done. Describe this person by circling one of the numbers between each pair of adjectives:

Pleasant	: 8 7 6 5 4 3 2 1 :	Unpleasant
Friendly	: 8 7 6 5 4 3 2 1 :	Unfriendly
Rejecting	: 1 2 3 4 5 6 7 8 :	Accepting
Tense	: 1 2 3 4 5 6 7 8 :	Relaxed

Distant	: 1 2 3 4 5 6 7 8 :	Close
Cold	: 1 2 3 4 5 6 7 8 :	Warm
Supportive	: 8 7 6 5 4 3 2 1 :	Hostile
Boring	: 1 2 3 4 5 6 7 8 :	Interesting
Quarrelsome	: 1 2 3 4 5 6 7 8 :	Harmonious
Gloomy	: 1 2 3 4 5 6 7 8 :	Cheerful
Open	: 8 7 6 5 4 3 2 1 :	Guarded
Backbiting	: 1 2 3 4 5 6 7 8 :	Loyal
Untrustworthy	: 1 2 3 4 5 6 7 8 :	Trustworthy
Considerate	: 8 7 6 5 4 3 2 1 :	Inconsiderate
Nasty	: 1 2 3 4 5 6 7 8 :	Nice
Agreeable	: 8 7 6 5 4 3 2 1 :	Disagreeable
Insincere	: 1 2 3 4 5 6 7 8 :	Sincere
Kind	: 8 7 6 5 4 3 2 1 :	Unkind

To calculate your score, add up the numbers you have circled for each of the adjective pairs. According to Fiedler (1978), if your score is 56 or less, you are a low-LPC leader. If your score is 63 or above, you are a high-LPC leader. If your score falls between 56 and 63, you don't fit either category.

. . . .

Situational control.   Just as leadership style is the key *personal* variable in Fiedler's theory, *situational control* is the key *situational* factor in the model. If leaders can control the situation, they can be certain that decisions, actions, and suggestions will be carried out by the group members. Leaders who have trouble gaining control, in contrast, cannot be certain that the group members will carry out their assigned duties.

What factors determine control? Fiedler highlights three: leader/member relations, task structure, and position power.

1. *Leader-member relations.* The quality of the relationship between the leader and the group is the most important determinant of situational control. If the group is highly cohesive and relatively conflict free, the leader will be less concerned with peacekeeping and monitoring interpersonal behavior. Further, when group members are loyal to their leaders and acknowledge their ability, the leaders can be confident that their suggestions and requests will be heeded.

2. *Task structure.* The clarity of the task is the second most important determinant of situational control. When task structure is high, the group's tasks are straightforward and have only one right solution whose correctness is easily checked. Tasks that are unstructured, in contrast, are am-

biguous, admit to many correct solutions, and offer no "right" way of reaching the goal.

3. *Position power.* The final situational-control variable, position power, refers to the leader's power over the other group members. In some groups, such as military units, work departments, and committees, leaders have more power relative to their subordinates. They can control rewards, punishments, salaries, hiring, evaluation, and task assignment. In contrast, in such groups as informal discussion sessions, classroom groups, and social gatherings, the leader has relatively little power.

Situational control is determined by all three of these variables. As leader/member relations deteriorate from good to bad, as the task structure shifts from high to low, and as the leader's position power becomes weaker, the leader's control diminishes. As shown in Figure 8-1, groups that fall into Octant I are highly favorable for the leader, because relations are good, the task is highly structured, and the leader's position power is strong. But as we move from Octant I to Octant VIII, the situation grows less favorable for the leader. In this last type of group the relations are poor, the task is unstructured, and the leader has little power.

The contingency-model predictions.   Once the group is classified into one of the eight octants shown in Figure 8-1 and the leader's motivational style has been assessed via the LPC Scale, Fiedler can then offer predictions about leadership effectiveness. Overall, his model predicts that the low-LPC leader (task-motivated) will be most effective in situations that are either highly favorable or unfavorable, whereas the high-LPC leader (relationship-motivated) will be most effective in the middle-range situations (see Figure 8-1). Consider, for example, two hypothetical antiaircraft artillery crews labeled A and B (Fiedler, 1964). In both crews the leaders enjoy a strong position power, because their authority is determined by rank. In addition, task structure is high in both crews, because the same sequence of decisions must be made for each target. In Crew A, however, the commander is well-liked, whereas in Crew B the commander is disliked. According to the contingency model, Crew A would be located in Octant I because leader/member relations are good, the task is structured, and position power is strong. Crew B, however, falls into Octant V, because the leader/member relations are poor. Thus, two different types of leadership would be appropriate for the two crews: for A the low-LPC leader would be most effective, but for B the high-LPC leader would be superior. Supporting this prediction, Fiedler (1955) found that LPC scores were negatively correlated with effectiveness for artillery squads such as Crew A ($r = -.34$), but positively correlated with effectiveness for such crews as B ($r = .49$).

Validational studies of the model.   Fiedler's theory of leadership effectiveness is a data-based model; its predictions are derived from research findings rather than deducted from theoretical generalizations.

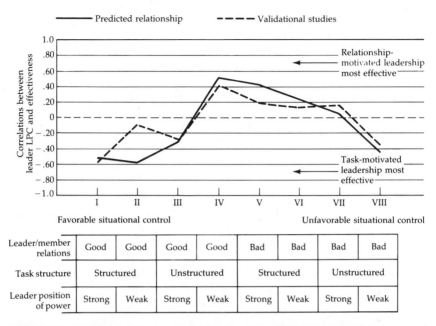

FIGURE 8-1. The predicted and obtained relationship between LPC score and leadership effectiveness in eight group situations. The horizontal axis represents the eight octants that define situational control. Octant I corresponds to the most controllable and favorable situation, and Octant VIII corresponds to the least controllable and least favorable setting. The vertical axis indicates the predicted relationship between LPC scores and task performance. If the correlation is greater than 0 (positive), effectiveness is positively related to LPC; that is, relationship-motivated leaders are more effective. If the correlation is smaller than 0 (negative), effectiveness is negatively related to LPC; task-motivated leaders are more effective.

Source: Fiedler, 1978

Therefore, he felt that before the model could be deemed acceptable, additional studies were needed to validate the original conclusions.

In 1971 Fiedler reviewed the results of dozens of validational studies. As the dashed line in Figure 8-1 indicates, these studies tended to track quite closely the earlier findings. Overall, the task-motivated, low-LPC leader was more effective than the relationship-motivated, high-LPC leader in the favorable or unfavorable octants: I, II, III, and VIII. This effect was reversed in the intermediately favorable octants:IV, V, VI, and VII (Fiedler, 1967, 1971a, 1971b, 1978). The only exception to this overall confirmation of the model occurred in Octant II. In this cell many validational studies yielded positive correlations between LPC and effectiveness (Graen, Orris, & Alvares, 1971). Fiedler believes that the inconsistency in the findings related to this octant may stem from the difficulty in simultaneously establishing good leader/member relations, a structured task, and low leader power. Furthermore, a recent investigation that focused specifically on Octant II groups reports a significant negative correlation, as the original formulation predicted ($r = -.55$: Schneier, 1978).

Other recent validational studies have been less uniform in their support for the model. Although many of the experimental studies support the model (e.g., Chemers & Skrzypek, 1972), others do not (Graen et al., 1971; Vecchio, 1977). Also, whereas some experts in the area feel that the model's predictions are accurate in all eight of the octants, (Strube & Garcia, 1981, 1983), others feel that predictions hold only in certain octants (Peters, Hartke, & Pohlmann, 1985; Nathan, Hass, & Nathan, 1987; Vecchio, 1983). Indeed, several critics have argued that the correlations obtained by Fiedler in his initial investigations should be interpreted cautiously because they do not reach conventional levels of statistical significance (Ashour, 1973a, 1973b; McMahon, 1972; Nathan et al., 1987).

Implications and conclusions.   Like most other theories Fiedler's approach to leadership possesses both strengths and weaknesses. On the negative side some studies have failed to support the theory, and because most of the research relied on correlational designs, cause/effect conclusions may be inappropriate. Although LPC and situational control may combine to determine effectiveness, it is possible that effectiveness may actually cause changes in LPC and situational control. The LPC scale is often the butt of criticisms. Like any other psychological instrument the LPC should be both reliable (internally and temporally consistent) and valid (an accurate index of the construct it is supposed to assess). Unfortunately, the LPC has been modified many times, and some critics have suggested that the different versions are incompatible and, in general, unreliable (Schriesheim, Bannister, & Money, 1979). Although a precise conceptual understanding of an LPC score has been sought for 25 years, the theoretical meaning of the instrument remains uncertain (Schriesheim & Kerr, 1977).

The behavioral processes that account for the predicted relationship between a leader's motivational style, situational control, and effectiveness are also unclear. Why should liking for a co-worker influence a leader's ability? Why would a task-motivated leader do well in unfavorable settings? Why would a relationship-motivated leader do poorly when conditions are favorable for leadership? Fiedler has answered some of these questions in his *motivational hierarchy hypothesis* (Fiedler, 1972, 1978; Fiedler & Chemers, 1974). This hypothesis assumes that leaders seek a series of goals but that some goals have a higher priority than others. Moreover, high- and low-LPC leaders possess different priorities: the high-LPC leader gives greatest priority to establishing and maintaining satisfying interpersonal relations within the group, but the low-LPC leader stresses successful completion of tasks. Therefore, in an unfavorable situation the low-LPC leader is concerned with driving the group toward task completion and wastes no time trying to improve group relations. The high-LPC leader, on the other hand, concentrates on trying to reestablish satisfying interpersonal relations in a hopelessly irretrievable situation. Hence, the high-LPC leader is ineffective. In a favorable situation, in contrast, leaders become reasonably certain that their number one priority can be reached, so they can shift their focus toward a lower order priority (Fiedler 1978). In such settings low-LPC leaders become more interpersonal, whereas high-LPC leaders become inappropriately task-oriented. This hypothesis, however, has not yet been subjected to an extensive test (Beach, Mitchell, & Beach, 1975; Green & Nebeker, 1977; Meuwese & Fiedler, 1965).

On the positive side the contingency model takes into account both personal factors (LPC score) and situational factors (situational control) in predicting effectiveness, and the model is supported by a wealth of empirical data collected from a wide variety of groups. Also, a leadership training program derived from the theory, called Leader Match, has proven useful. Although many different programs and techniques have been developed to "train" effective leaders, the results of these procedures are typically disappointing (Stogdill, 1974). Fiedler, however, suggests that these programs fail because they place too much emphasis on changing the leaders: making them more supportive, more decisive, more democratic, and so on. In contrast, he suggests that the situation should be engineered to fit the leader's particular motivational style. He calls his training program Leader Match, because he teaches enrollees to modify their group situation until it matches their personal motivational style (Fiedler, Chemers, & Mahar, 1976). Investigators have tested the effectiveness of this innovative training program, and in general they conclude that the procedure is remarkably successful (Burke & Day, 1986; Csoka & Bons, 1978; Fiedler, 1978). Trained leaders are typically rated as more effective in the group than untrained leaders, apparently because they can change their group's situational favorability.

Given these conflicting appraisals of the model's adequacy, no immutable conclusions can be offered. The contingency model continues to be modified as new research findings come to light, and evidence suggests that much progress is being made. Recent studies support the model (for example, Chemers, Hays, Rhodewalt, & Wysocki, 1985) and affirm the utility of the LPC scale (R. W. Rice, 1978a, 1978b, 1979). As Focus 8-5 indicates, however, leadership experts are still substantially divided on the question of the model's validity, and more research will be needed before a final verdict can be rendered.

. . . .

FOCUS 8-5: EVERYBODY CAN'T BE RIGHT

Many people think that science should provide answers to questions in absolute, right-or-wrong terms. But in most cases scientific questions must be debated and argued for some time until a general consensus is reached. As Robert W. Rice notes, when researchers discuss the contingency model, they tend to take sides, with partisanship often determining one's appraisal of the value of the model.

PRO-CONTINGENCY VIEWS

- The contingency model seems at this point to retain its viability as an instigator of research [Chemers, 1983, p. 16]. Although the last 10 to 15 years have spawned many alternative approaches to leadership, the leader-oriented contingency paradigms continue to be productive. [Chemers, 1987, p. 259].
- I believe that the model does have some ability to predict group performance on the basis of the leader's LPC score and an appropriate analysis of situational factors [Rice, 1978b, p. 1202].
- [The] claim that the model lacks empirical validity, contains fatal methodological flaws, and is theoretically inadequate is refuted by the available data [Fiedler, 1973, p. 366].
- The model is capable of directing meaningful research, but only as long as traditional research procedures designed to safeguard internal and external validity are carefully exercised [Shiflett, 1973, p. 429].
- The model was found to be extremely robust in predicting group performance. . . . The model as a whole was overwhelmingly supported [Strube & Garcia, 1981, p. 307, p. 316].

OPPOSING VIEWS

- [Available research] casts grave doubts on the plausibility of the contingency model. . . . The model has lost the capability of directing meaningful research [Graen et al., 1970, p. 295].
- The evidence concerning the LPC instrument does not support its continued use. LPC lacks sufficient evidence of construct, content, predictive, and concurrent validity, and test-retest reliability [Schriesheim & Kerr, 1977, p. 31].
- Clearly the contingency model is based on a simplistic scheme that omits essential linkages intervening between leader's traits and group outcomes [Ashour, 1973a, p. 352].
- Fiedler's Contingency Model and its related research have serious empirical, methodological and theoretical problems [Ashour, 1973b, p. 375].
- Analysis of the model in terms of logic and methodology has revealed serious questions which must be answered if the model's potential is to be realized [McMahon, 1972, p. 708].
- Contrary to Strube and Garcia's (1981) conclusion that "the model as a whole was overwhelmingly supported" (p. 316), the results of the present meta-analysis present a mixed set of findings concerning the Contingency Theory [Peters et al., 1985, p. 281].

Perhaps both sides in the dispute should heed the suggestion of Abraham K. Korman:

> Theory, contingency or otherwise, is to help and guide research, not to control it. We should not become so invested in any theory, particularly our own, that it "strangles" us and we ignore the major goal of our work, the understanding of behavior [1974, p. 195].

. . . .

Theories of Leadership Style

Fiedler's contingency model, and the LPC Scale as well, assumes that leaders are either relationship motivated or task motivated. Several other leadership theories, in contrast, assume that leaders can deal with both relationship and task concerns and that leadership effectiveness depends on the balance between these two basic ingredients (for example, Bowers & Seashore, 1966; Hersey & Blanchard, 1977; House, 1971; Kerr et al., 1974; Likert, 1967; Misumi, 1985; Reddin, 1970; Yukl, 1981). A sampling of these models is examined below.

The Managerial Grid.   Robert Blake and Jane Mouton (1964, 1978, 1980), drawing on the Ohio State Leadership Studies, hypothesize that leadership style depends on how one answers two basic questions: "How important is the production of results by the group?" and "How important are the feelings of people?" To some leaders their key goal is achieving results. For others positive feelings in the group are so important that they emphasize teamwork and personal satisfaction. Others may feel that both these goals are important.

Blake and Mouton summarize these differences in leadership style in their **Managerial Grid,** which is presented in Figure 8-2. Both dimensions, concern for people and concern for results, are represented as nine-point scales ranging from "low concern" to "high concern." Although in theory a person's orientation could fall at any of 81 possible positions on the grid, Blake and Mouton emphasize the five orientations located at the four corner positions and one in the very center. Apathetic, impoverished 1,1 leaders aren't interested in either their subordinates' feelings or the production of results; they are hardly leaders at all. The 9,1 individual (high on concern for production, low on concern for people, located in the lower right corner of the grid) is a taskmaster who seeks productivity at any cost. The 1,9 leader, in contrast, adopts a "country-club" approach that makes subordinates feel comfortable and relaxed while in the group. The "middle-of-the-roader," located at 5,5, tries to balance both performance and morale but sometimes sacrifices both when results and individuals' feelings come into conflict. Last, the 9,9 values both people and products highly and, therefore, tackles organizational goals through teamwork: "a high degree of shared responsibility, coupled with high participation, involvement, and commitment" (Blake & Mouton, 1982a, p. 41).

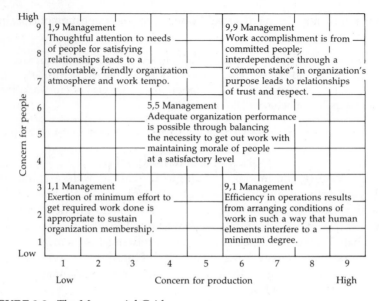

FIGURE 8-2. The Managerial Grid.

Source: Robert R. Blake and Jane Srygley Mouton, The New Managerial Grid. Houston: Gulf Publishing Company, Copyright © 1978, p. 11. Reproduced by permission.

Blake and Mouton are not contingency theorists; they feel that the 9,9 leadership style is the "one best style" to use when leading people (1982a). In their initial studies they found that managers who adopted the 9,9 style were far more successful in their careers than managers who adopted other methods (1964). They also note that studies conducted in educational, industrial, and medical organizations support the utility of the 9,9 leadership style, as do the favorable results of their management training system (Blake & Mouton, 1980, 1982, 1985, 1986). These results are impressive, but many experts still question their strong claim that the 9,9 style works in all situations (Kerr et al., 1974; Larson, Hunt, & Osborn, 1976; Nystrom, 1978; Quinn & McGrath, 1982).

Situational-leadership theory.   Paul Hersey and Kenneth Blanchard also describe leadership in terms of the relationship and task dimensions. Unlike Blake and Mouton's grid, however, their **situational-leadership theory** rejects the notion that the high-relationship/high-task leader (the 9,9) will be effective in all groups and all situations. Rather, it suggests that groups benefit from leadership that meshes with the needs of their members (Hersey & Blanchard, 1976, 1977, 1982).

To a large extent the fit between leadership style and group members' needs is determined by the maturity of the group, with maturity defined as "the capacity to set high but attainable goals, willingness and ability to take responsibility, and education and/or experience of an individual or a group" (1976, p. 96). In this sense, then, maturity has little to do with age; what counts is the group's experience in working on a particular problem. Newly formed groups, groups beginning a new project, or groups with many new members are all immature, whereas groups that function as a team are mature.

The predictions of the situational model are shown in Figure 8-3. As this graph indicates, immature group members will work most effectively with a high-task/low-relationship leader (Quadrant 1). As a group matures and begins working adequately on the task, however, the leader can increase relationship behavior and adopt a high/high style (Quadrant 2). Still later in the group's development, the leader can ease off on both types of leadership, starting first with task emphasis. In moderately mature groups the high-relationship/low-task style is most effective (Quadrant 3), and in fully mature groups a low/low, or laissez-faire, style is appropriate (Quadrant 4). Thus, an effective leader must display four different leadership styles as the group moves through its life cycle: telling, selling, participating, and delegating (Hersey & Blanchard, 1977).

Hersey and Blanchard recognize that most people have a preferred style of leadership, but they argue that flexibility rather than consistency is the hallmark of effective leadership. To assess this flexibility, they ask individuals to describe, in a questionnaire, the leadership methods they would use in hypothetical situations that call for a variety of leadership styles. This instrument is call the Leader Effectiveness and Adaptability Description (the LEAD).

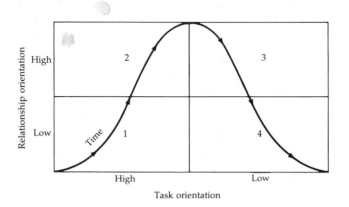

FIGURE 8-3. The Hersey and Blanchard situational theory of leadership. According to this theory, leaders must be flexible. When the group forms, they must use a Quadrant 1 style of leadership (high-task/low-relationship orientation), but must change over time to other styles of leadership as the group matures.

Source: Hersey & Blanchard, 1976

Some critics, including Blake and Mouton (1982a), argue that the situational model puts too much emphasis on matching the maturity of the members; these experts call for a careful balancing of task and relationship orientation at all developmental levels (Nicholls, 1985). But the initial results are promising. In one investigation, as the model predicts, newly hired employees needed and appreciated greater task structuring from their manager than did veteran employees (Vecchio, 1987). Also, while the LEAD instrument has been criticized on methodological grounds, it seems to function well as a method of assessing rigidity in leadership style (Graeff, 1983; Hersey, 1985; Lueder, 1985a, 1985b). Lastly, the training model based on the approach has become extremely popular, and it forms the basis for the "one-minute-management" approach to leadership in organizational settings (Blanchard & Johnson, 1981; Carew, Parisi-Carew, & Blanchard, 1986).

⋮ Participation Theories of Leadership

The chief executive officer asks the Board of Directors for input before making a final judgment. A small-business owner studies company productivity levels before deciding to make some organizational changes. Factory workers elect representatives who negotiate with the owners over a wage increase. A group of college students get together with their professor and vote on the topic they will research in the coming semester.

Studies of **participatory leadership** examine the impact on the group's performance of group members' participation in making decisions. At one end of the participation continuum the group members decide the issues in question. At the other end the leader alone weighs the available information and makes the decision. Between these two extremes are instances in which the leader makes the decision after receiving various amounts of information from the other group members. The question the leader must ask in each situation is clear: "What point along this continuum is the most effective in terms of productivity and satisfaction?"

The issue of group-member participation in decision making was first made salient to group dynamicists by Kurt Lewin, Ronald Lippitt, and Ralph White in their classic studies of authoritarian, democratic, and laissez-faire leadership (Lewin, Lippitt, & White, 1939; White & Lippitt, 1960, 1968). As noted briefly in Chapter 2, these researchers arranged for 10- and 11-year-old boys to meet after school to work on various hobbies. In addition to the boys each group included a man who adopted one of three leadership styles:

1. The authoritarian or *autocratic leader* took no input from the members in making decisions about group activities, did not discuss the long-range goals of the group, emphasized his authority, dictated who would work on specific projects, and arbitrarily paired the boys with their work partners.

2. The *democratic leader* made certain that all activities were first discussed by the entire group. He allowed the group members to make their own decisions about work projects or partners and encouraged the development of an egalitarian atmosphere.

3. The *laissez-faire leader* rarely intervened in the group activities. Groups with this type of atmosphere made all decisions on their own without any supervision, and their so-called leader functioned primarily as a source of technical information.

In some cases the boys were rotated to a different experimental condition so that they could experience all three types of participation.

When the behaviors of the boys in the three conditions were compared, a number of differences in efficiency, satisfaction, and aggressiveness seemed to be apparent. As Figure 8-4 reveals, autocratic groups spent as much time working on their hobbies as the democratic groups, but the laissez-faire groups worked considerably less. When the leader left the room, however, work dropped off dramatically in the autocratic-led groups, remained unchanged in the democratic groups, and actually increased in the laissez-faire groups. Furthermore, members of groups with an autocratic leader displayed greater reliance on the leader, expressed more critical discontent, and made more aggressive demands for attention. Democratic groups tended to be friendlier and more group oriented. Overall, the boys preferred democratic leaders to the other two varieties.

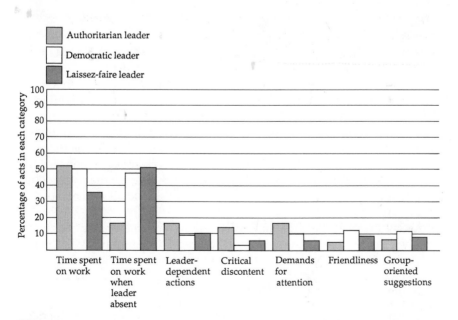

FIGURE 8-4. Findings in Lewin, Lippitt, and White's study of three leadership types.

Source: White & Lippitt, 1960

Although these findings seem to recommend the democratic-leadership approach over the two alternatives, the findings of Lewin, Lippitt, and White were not as clear cut as Figure 8-4 implies. Several of the groups reacted to the autocratic leader with hostility, negativity, and scapegoating, but others responded very passively to their authoritarian leaders. In these latter groups productivity was quite high (74%) when the leader was present, but it dropped to 29% when he left the room. Aggression, very apparent in some of the autocratic-led groups, was replaced in these others by apathy and acceptance of the situation. Although the group became aggressive if the autocratic leader was replaced with a more permissive one, when he was present the group members worked hard, demanded little attention, only rarely engaged in horseplay, and closely followed his recommendations. Apparently, the relationship between participation and effectiveness is not a simple one.

Following the lead of Lewin, Lippitt, and White, a plethora of investigators studied the participation issue, but to an extent the original results—complete with the contradictory conclusions—still hold. Indeed, Stogdill (1974), after reviewing more than 40 studies of various leadership methods that ranged along the participation/no-participation continuum, concluded that no single participatory technique was more frequently associated with increases in productivity than another. Although several studies indicated that productivity decreased when group members participated in decisions, the majority of the research found no differences stemming from centralizing of decisions. Stogdill goes on to note that satisfaction with the group seems to be highest in democratic groups as opposed to autocratic and laissez-faire groups. Even this conclusion, however, fails to hold when groups expect an autocratic leader (Foa, 1957) or when the group is very large (Vroom & Mann, 1960).

Victor Vroom has recently offered a sophisticated solution to this problem of contradictory findings regarding group-member participation in leadership (Vroom, 1973, 1974, 1976; Vroom & Yetton, 1973). According to Vroom, participation in decision making increases the satisfaction and effectiveness of the group only in certain situations. He calls his theory a normative model of leadership because it makes clear suggestions for the prospective leader. He recommends that leaders use the theory to determine how much involvement in decisions they should allow members.

A taxonomy of leadership methods.   Vroom begins by identifying five key types of leadership methods (see Figure 8-5). Beginning at the leader-centered, authoritarian end of the continuum and ranging to the group-centered, democratic end, we find the following methods of leadership (paraphrased from Vroom & Yetton, 1973, p. 13):

1. Autocratic I (AI): The leader solves the problem or makes the decision, using information available to him or her at that time.
2. Autocratic II (AII): The leader obtains necessary information from members and then decides on the solution to the problem. In getting the

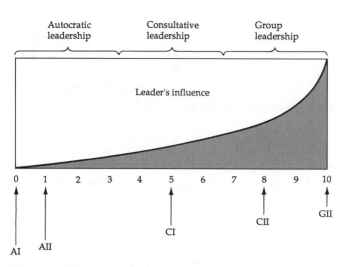

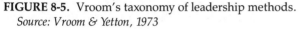

FIGURE 8-5. Vroom's taxonomy of leadership methods.
Source: Vroom & Yetton, 1973

information, the leader may not tell the group members what the problem is. The role played by the members is one of providing information rather than suggesting or evaluating alternative solutions.

3. Consultative I (CI): The leader shares the problem with relevant group members individually, getting their ideas and suggestions without bringing them together as a group. Then the leader makes the decision, which may not reflect the group members' influence.

4. Consultative II (CII): The leader discusses the problem with the members as a group, collectively obtaining their ideas and suggestions. Then the leader makes the decision, which may not reflect the group members' influences.

5. Group II (GII): The leader discusses the problem with the members as a group. Together, the leader and members devise and evaluate alternatives and attempt to reach agreement (consensus) on a solution. The leader's role is much like that of the chairperson of a committee. The leader does not try to influence the group to adopt a particular solution and is willing to accept and carry out any solution that is supported by the entire group.

Other leadership methods are, of course, possible (for example, delegative, or Group I, leadership), but Vroom emphasizes these five.

Which leadership method, when?   Vroom's normative model, like Fiedler's model, is a contingency theory; it argues that no single leadership method will be best in all situations. In general, leaders should probably meet with the group whenever a major decision is to be made, but in some situations this democratic approach may prove ineffective, time con-

suming, and dissatisfying to members. In these instances a more autocratic type of leadership may be the most successful approach. The key
issue thus focuses on the leadership-method/situation contingency:
which leadership approach in which situation?

In answer, Vroom and his colleagues list a number of rules of thumb to
follow when selecting a leadership method (Vroom, 1976; Vroom & Jago;
1978; Vroom & Yetton, 1973). These rules are proscriptive rather than prescriptive, for they identify methods to avoid rather than ones to adopt.
Also, whereas some of these rules are designed to protect the quality of
the decision the group is making, others are designed to ensure the acceptance of the decision by the group. They include (paraphrased from
Vroom & Jago, 1978, pp. 151–162):

1. Leader-information rule: Do not use AI if the quality of the decision is
   important and if you do not have enough information or expertise to
   solve the problem alone.
2. Goal-congruence rule: Do not use GII if the quality of the decision is
   important and if subordinates are not likely to pursue the organizational goals in their efforts to solve this problem.
3. Unstructured-problem rule: Do not use AI, AII, or CI if finding a high-
   quality decision is important, if you lack sufficient information to solve
   the problem alone, and if the problem is unstructured. In such situations input is needed from the group.
4. Acceptance rule: Do not use autocratic methods (AI or AII) if acceptance of the decision by subordinates is critical to effective implementation and if it is not certain that an autocratic decision will be accepted.
5. Conflict rule: Do not use AI, AII, or CI when the conditions noted by
   the acceptance rule above hold *and* disagreement among subordinates
   is likely. In such instances methods that require the resolution of differences should be used.
6. Fairness rule: Do not use autocratic or consultative methods when the
   quality of the decision is unimportant but acceptance of the decision is
   critical and not certain to result from an autocratic decision.
7. Acceptance-priority rule: Do not use autocratic or consultative methods if acceptance is critical but not likely to result from an autocratic
   decision and if subordinates are motivated to pursue organizational
   goals.

Does the normative model work? Available evidence, although scant, is
supportive. Vroom and his colleagues, for example, report that when expert managers read a case study of a leadership decision and then make a
recommendation about an appropriate leader method, their suggestions
coincide with the predictions of the normative model (Hill & Schmitt,
1977; Jago, 1978; Vroom & Yetton, 1973). More research, however, is
needed to examine the impact of each of the five key methods in each situation specified by Vroom (Field, 1979; Hill & Schmitt, 1977; Vroom &
Jago, 1978).

· ·
FOCUS 8-6: SEX DIFFERENCES IN LEADERSHIP EFFECTIVENESS

True or False?

1. Men are more effective leaders than women.
2. Men are task leaders whereas women are relationship leaders.
3. People prefer to work for men rather than for women.

When it comes to leadership, how do the sexes differ from each other? Although this was once a moot question, because females were traditionally denied access to positions of leadership, long-overdue changes in the role of women in contemporary society have resulted in an increasing number of female leaders. Historically, women became leaders through heredity (queens, heads of family businesses) or marriage, but as we move into the 1990s the number of women who are hired, appointed, promoted, and elected to leadership positions is rising.

How do these female leaders differ from their male counterparts in terms of effectiveness, style, and acceptance by subordinates? First, available evidence finds that men and women are equally effective as leaders (Bass, 1981; Brown, 1979; Hollander, 1983). For example, one review of 32 empirical studies found that in some laboratory studies male leaders outperformed female leaders, but studies conducted in actual managerial settings generally found no gender differences (Brown, 1979).

Second, do men and women adopt different leadership styles? As early as 1956, researchers suggested that men in groups tended to provide orientation, opinions, and directions designed to lead the group toward goal attainment, whereas women emphasized group solidarity, reduction of group tension, and avoidance of antagonism (Strodtbeck & Mann, 1956). Despite the many changes in perceptions of women and men during the years since that study, men still tend to be task oriented, whereas women are still friendlier and more interpersonally oriented (Forsyth, Schlenker, Leary, & McCown, 1985; Leary, Robertson, Barnes, & Miller, 1986; Wood, 1987). These sex differences in group behavior, however, may not translate into sex differences in leadership style. Men tend to be task oriented, but when they become leaders they may add relationship-oriented actions to their behavioral repertoires. Similarly, when women become leaders they may become more task oriented. To explore this hypothesis Alice Eagly and Blair Johnson (in press) reviewed over 150 studies that compared the leadership styles adopted by men and women. As they expected, relative to men women performed more relationship-oriented actions in laboratory groups and they also described themselves as more relationship oriented on questionnaires. The sexes did not differ, however, in studies conducted in organizational settings (Dobbins & Platz, 1986). Indeed, as managers women tended to be both task and relationship oriented, whereas men were primarily task oriented (Stratham, 1987). The only difference between men and women that emerged consistently across studies concerned participation: women used a democratic style whereas men were more autocratic.

Lastly, do people prefer to work for men rather than for women? As noted earlier in this chapter, in many cases individuals express a preference for male bosses. Evidence indicates that many people assume that men make better leaders than women (Ferber, Huber, & Spitze, 1979; Jacobson & Effertz, 1974; Rosen & Jerdee, 1973, 1978) and that they even give men higher evaluations when male and female leaders perform the same behaviors (Brown & Geis, 1984; Geis, Boston, & Hoffman, 1985). Recent studies of these biases, however, are also encouraging. A field study conducted with cadets at the U.S. Military Academy found no male favoritism (Rice, Instone, & Adams, 1984), as did surveys conducted in managerial settings (Kushell & Newton, 1986; Tsui & Gutek, 1984). Subordinates are often more satisfied when their leader adopts a democratic style or a relationship-oriented style, but gender per se has little impact on evaluations (Kushell & Newton, 1986). In addition, evidence suggests that group members' perceptual biases are minimized when they know how effectively the group and the leader have performed in the past (Dobbins, Stuart, Pence, & Sgro, 1985; Izraeli, Izraeli, & Eden, 1985; Wood & Karten, 1986).

As the roles enacted by men and women in contemporary society continue to change, new questions and confrontations will emerge. These issues require careful thought and scrutiny, and in many cases they are best clarified by examining available evidence objectively rather than by relying on intuition and folklore. If we take such an approach to studying women and leadership, we must conclude that the available literature suggests that the variables specified by the theories examined in this chapter, not gender, determine leadership effectiveness.

• •

Predicting Leadership Effectiveness: Some Conclusions

Our initial question, "What made Alice Bertemes such an effective leader?" has been answered by different theorists in different ways. Fiedler's model, noting Bertemes's good relationship with the farmers, the high amount of structure in the task, and her secure position power, would predict that her task-motivated management style matched the situation she faced. Alternatively, the leadership style theorists might suggest that she was a master at providing both the farmers and her staff with clear goals and objectives while also maintaining positive relationships within the co-op. This explanation is consistent with studies of women who are leaders in organizational settings (see Focus 8-6). Last, Vroom's normative model would suggest that she knew when to include others in the decision-making process and when to make decisions on her own.

These explanations of leadership, although they stress different processes, are similar in many respects. Virtually all explicitly consider the interaction between the leader's characteristics and the nature of the leadership situation. They may emphasize different leader characteristics (for example, the leader's motivation, style, or method) and different features of the situation (such as situational control, group maturity, or attributes of the problem), but all take note of the interaction among leaders, members, and settings when predicting effectiveness.

These theories offer insights into leadership, but the light they cast is often too dim. More attention should be paid to developing measures of effectiveness and style that are not open to alternative interpretations. Also, theorists must continue to integrate the various theories of leadership into more coherent frameworks (Chemers, 1987; Yukl, 1981). Although the progress is impressive and continuing, the goal of understanding leadership has not yet been reached.

SUMMARY

In some respects specifying what leadership is not is easier than specifying what it is. It is not necessarily power to manipulate or control others, an inborn talent, a skill that can be learned by following a few guidelines, or the key to group success. An interactional approach, however, defines *leadership* as a reciprocal, transactional, and transformational process in which individuals are permitted to influence and motivate others to promote the attaining of group and individual goals. At the behavioral level leadership usually requires *relationship behaviors* that improve interpersonal relations within the group and *task behaviors* that help the group complete its tasks. The *LBDQ*, or *Leader Behavior Description Questionnaire*, assesses both components.

Leadership emergence in groups depends both on the need for the leader role itself and on the qualities of the individuals available to fill that role. Groups generally require leaders when interpersonal processes need improvement or the efforts of individual members must be better coordinated. But whenever features of the situation fulfill these functions, it is likely that these *leadership substitutes* will make the leadership role unnecessary. Many factors determine who emerges as the leader in the group, including physical characteristics such as height, weight, age, and gender; intelligence; personality traits; task abilities; and participation rates. Apparently, leadership emergence depends to a large extent on group members' perceptions. The cognitive approach to leadership emergence suggests that individuals who act in ways that match the group members' *implicit leadership theories* or *leader prototypes* are likely to emerge as leaders.

For centuries observers of the human condition have sought to understand why some leaders succeed and others fail. Although earlier approaches adopted either a *trait model* or *situational model*, most modern theories are *interactional models* that base predictions on the reciprocal relationships among the leader, the followers, and the nature of the group situation. Fiedler's *contingency model*, for example, bases its predictions on the leader's particular motivation styles—task motivated or relationship motivated—as measured by the *LPC (Least Preferred Co-worker) Scale*. By taking into consideration the leader/member relations, the task structure, and the leader's power, Fiedler's theory predicts that task-motivated (low-LPC) leaders are most effective in situations that are either extremely unfavorable or extremely favorable, whereas relationship-motivated leaders are most effective in intermediate situations.

Fiedler assumes that task and relationship orientation are the endpoints of a single dimension, whereas several leadership-style theorists assume that effectiveness depends on the balance between these two basic ingredients. The *Managerial Grid* proposed by Blake and Mouton, for example, assumes that people vary in their concern for others and their concern for results and that individuals who are high on both dimensions (9,9) are the best leaders. *Situational-leadership theory,* as proposed by Hersey and Blanchard, takes an opposing position by suggesting that groups benefit from leadership that meshes with the maturity level of the group.

Taking a different approach, other theorists have extended the early findings of Lewin, Lippitt, and White regarding the effects of autocratic, democratic, and laissez-faire leaders by asking when *participatory leadership* is effective. Vroom's normative model is one of the most sophisticated answers to this question, for it compares the effectiveness of autocratic, consultative, and group-centered leaders in many situations. This theory, like Fiedler's model and other theories examined in the chapter, is a contingency theory because it is based on the assumption that leadership effectiveness is contingent on the leader's characteristics and the nature of the situation.

·9·

Performance

In May 1927 five young women working in the Hawthorne Plant of the Western Electric Company volunteered to take part in an experiment. All were experienced "operators"; they built telephone relay switches out of an assortment of clamps, pins, screws, coils, and electronics parts. The women were told that the company's executives wanted to learn more about their employees and so they had set up an observation room where a small subgroup could be studied for an extended period. The Relay Test Room group would consist of the five operators, who actually assembled the units, a layout operator, who stocked parts, an inspector, who checked and approved each relay, and at least one observer.

The operators weren't selected for their dedication to the company or for their special expertise as operators. Operator 1, although a hard worker in the regular shop, did not take any special interest in the experiment; her outside interests, including her family and fiancé, distanced her from the others. Her closest friend in the group was Operator 2. Operator 2 enjoyed the special attention received in the Test Room, but she was not particularly motivated by it. She often rejected the influence attempts of her supervisor and the other group members. Operator 3 was the most outgoing member of the group; she was "naturally gregarious, lively, and fond of a joke" (Whitehead, 1938, p. 155). Operator 4 came from a very cohesive family, and during the first years of the study she kept to herself. Over time, however, she began to adjust to the situation, and she became good friends with one of the other operators. Operator 5 was a little older than the other workers. She wasn't as productive as some operators, but she "worked faithfully for her pay, she never showed petulance, and she thoroughly appreciated the real advantages of the Test Room" (Whitehead, 1938, p. 156).

The Relay Test Room was part of an impressive project carried out by industrial psychologists with the cooperation of executives at Western Electric. The project lasted for five years, and during all that time researchers monitored the operators' rates of production and observed their interactions. Initially, the investigators were convinced that changes in productivity depended on such factors as the weather, the number of rest breaks, the workers' physical health, and vacations. Soon, however, they were forced to conclude that group processes, not aspects of the physical work setting, were the principal determinants of productivity (Mayo, 1933; Roethlisberger & Dickson, 1939; Whitehead, 1938).

This chapter examines some of these processes in an attempt to explain why the Relay Test Room, and groups in general, are sometimes productive and sometimes unproductive. Although people seem to invariably answer the question "How can we get the job done" with "Let's form a group," groups are often the object of criticisms. We use groups to pursue goals, discuss problems, concoct plans, forge products, and perform tasks, but at the same time we grumble about the time they waste and the inadequacy of their products. Here we will consider some of the processes that operate in groups that may influence their effectiveness. This chapter examines processes that come into play as soon as one individual enters the presence of another, as well as interpersonal processes that increase and decrease productivity. Chapter 10 extends this analysis by concentrating on how groups formulate decisions.

Before beginning, we should note that all too often the study of group performance summons up images of strictly task-oriented groups: staid executives debating across a conference table, workers adding to a product as it passes along an assembly line, or laborers pooling their efforts to move a heavy object. Granted, performance is a crucial aspect of these groups, but even groups with social goals must often be productive and solve problems. People at a party may need to discover why the stereo isn't working or decide if more ice will be needed before the stores close. A group of conferees, when their work is done, may need to choose a restaurant for dinner or coordinate their travel across town. A coterie headed to the beach must decide who brings the food, the drinks, the towels, and the chairs. This chapter focuses on a task-oriented group, but remember that issues of group performance are relevant to many other kinds of groups.

SOCIAL FACILITATION

The assembly of the relays, at least in the eyes of the management, was a strictly individual project. The operators sat at their own benches and had all the necessary tools and materials within easy reach. The work, although repetitive, called for a high degree of skill; operators had to remember where each part went and cull faulty parts from their supplies when they ran across them. The task also demanded manual dexterity, for assembling a single relay required over 30 different movements of each hand (Whitehead, 1938).

A novice could turn out only 25 to 30 completed relays an hour, but an expert could build as many as 50, even when the relay pattern was changed frequently. The operators in the Test Relay Room, however, surpassed this rate on a regular basis. Although Operators 1 and 2 rarely turned out more than 50 per hour, the others soon reached an average rate of 65 relays per hour. Indeed, when two of the operators exchanged seats during a later phase of the project, these two operators increased their speeds in step with each other, until, during one week, both averaged at least 80 relays per hour (Whitehead, 1938, p. 157).

The assembly task lies at the interface of individual performance and group performance. Like riding a bicycle, reading, working homework problems, or driving a car, the assembly task can be performed by individuals working either in isolation or in the presence of others. Such a task does not create interdependence, because it can be accomplished without direct interaction with others. These types of performance situations, however, are of fundamental importance because they signal a shift from a nonsocial, purely individualistic orientation and toward a social, group-dynamics focus.

Coaction, Audiences, and Performance

The study of the performance of individuals when alone and when in the presence of others dates back to 1898 and an early social scientist named Norman Triplett. A bicycling enthusiast, Triplett noticed that cyclists achieved different speeds during races, when paced by motor-driven cycles, and when racing against the clock (see Figure 9-1). Triplett, intrigued by the invariably better times reported for races, decided to conduct what is generally recognized as one of the first social-psychological laboratory experiments. He tested the hypothesis that people work more effectively when others are present by arranging for 40 children to play a simple game in pairs or alone. As was the case with the cyclists, the children's times were better when they played the game in pairs. Triplett had experimentally created **social facilitation:** the enhancement of performance when another person is present (Allport, 1920; Dashiell, 1930; Travis, 1925).

Social facilitation occurs in both coaction settings and in audience settings. In Triplett's work the children worked on the same task in the same room, but they did not interact with one another. This type of situation is a **coaction task.** Eating alone in a fast-food restaurant, taking a test in a

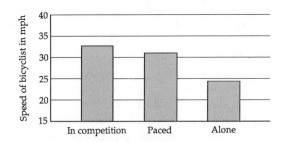

FIGURE 9-1. The average speeds of bicyclists in three types of races: in competition with other cyclists, alone, and paced by another cyclist.
Source: From Triplett, 1898

classroom, riding a bicycle with a friend, or studying in the reading room of the library are all everyday instances of coaction. An **audience task,** in contrast, involves an individual who performs a task in front of a passive spectator. One of the first scientific demonstrations of social facilitation in the presence of a passive spectator occurred in, of all places, an exercise laboratory. By the turn of the century studies of muscular exertion and exercise had become feasible through the development of the ergograph, a device that precisely recorded how far an individual, working at the upper limit of his or her capacity, could move a weight. People who worked the ergograph typically reached a uniform level of performance that remained fairly constant across time, but one researcher noticed that this rate improved when an observer was present in the room. When he unexpectedly returned to his lab one night a subject whose performance had been constant for several days of testing changed. Although the ergograph did not detect any increase in the amount of effort being expended, the subject was still able to move the weight a greater distance. The investigator concluded that the presence of a spectator was facilitating (Meumann, 1904).

Despite these early discoveries of social facilitation for both coaction and audience tasks, subsequent investigations yielded a more checkered pattern of results. Floyd H. Allport's early studies of what he called "co-working" or "co-feeling," groups, for example, did not always yield evidence of social facilitation (Allport, 1920, p. 159). He arranged for his subjects to complete certain tasks twice, once while alone in a small testing cubicle and once with others at a table. In an attempt to reduce pressures toward competition he cautioned his subjects not to compare their scores with one another, and he also told the participants that he himself would not be making comparisons. Despite the absence of competition between coactors, however, Allport found a slight but consistent improvement in the coacting condition as compared with the isolation condition. For example, when given a word and asked to write down as many of their associated thoughts as possible, 14 of the 15 subjects generated more associates in the coaction condition. Similar effects were found when participants crossed out vowels in newspaper articles, performed multiplications, and thought up arguments to disprove points made in passages taken from philosophical works. On these more complex tasks Allport also found evidence of detrimental effects of coaction. Subjects still produced more in the group setting, but their products tended to be lower in quality. Likewise, other researchers sometimes reported gains in performance through coaction (Carment, 1970; Dashiell, 1930; Weston & English, 1926) but sometimes reported evidence of performance decrements (Burwitz & Newell, 1972; Martens & Landers, 1972; Travis, 1928).

Studies of the effects of a passive audience on individual performance also tended to be inconsistent. In one experiment 22 college students were asked to hold a pointer over a small target that was attached to a rotating disk (the pursuit-rotor task). When they performed the task before an audience of advanced undergraduates, their tracking of the target was better than when they performed alone (Travis, 1925). Yet in another study of 60 subjects trying to learn lists of nonsense syllables, the subjects required fewer repetitions of the list when they were working alone than when they were working before an audience (Pessin, 1933). As was the case for co-action studies and research with animals, working before an audience was sometimes but not always facilitating. Hence, the major question became "When does the presence of others help, and when does it hurt?"

When Does Facilitation Occur?

These contradictory findings puzzled group dynamicists for many years, so much so that interest in social facilitation dwindled in the 1940s and 1950s. Then, in an article published in 1965, Robert B. Zajonc integrated the divergent results by drawing a distinction between dominant and non-dominant responses. Zajonc noted that some behaviors are easier to learn and perform than others. These **dominant responses** are located at the top of the response hierarchy, so they dominate all other potential responses. Other behaviors may be present in the organism's behavioral repertoire, but these **nondominant responses** are less likely to be observed.

With the distinction between dominant and nondominant responses in mind, Zajonc turned to the other pieces of the puzzle. First, he pointed out that extensive studies of many organisms had repeatedly demon-strated that increases in arousal, activation, motivation, or drive level en-hance the emission of dominant responses while impeding the performance of nondominant responses. Second, he reexamined previ-ous studies of social facilitation and found that the presence of others nearly always facilitates well-learned or instinctual responses. Third, he noted that when inhibiting effects of coaction or observation are reported, they almost always occur for novel, complicated, or unpracticed tasks.

Putting these facts together, Zajonc concluded that social facilitation oc-curs for simple tasks that require dominant responses and that social im-pairment occurs for complex tasks that require nondominant responses. For example, one of the replications of Allport's initial studies with the word-association task did not find improvement in the coaction condition (Travis, 1928). The studies used nearly identical procedures, but the par-ticipants in the later study were all stutterers. Because verbal production is not an easily performed, dominant response for these individuals, the presence of an audience impeded their performance. The distinction also accounts for some of the speed shown by the women working in the Relay Test Room. The presence of both coactors and an audience was facilitating because all of the operators were experts. If they had been novices (as was the case when new operators joined the group near the end of the study), social facilitation would have been unlikely (see Focus 9-1).

• •
FOCUS 9-1: OF MICE, MEN, AND COCKROACHES

Social facilitation is not limited to *Homo sapiens:* puppies, chickens, mice, rats, monkeys, armadillos, ants, and opossums are on the list of species that show signs of increased performance in the presence of other members of their species (Clayton, 1978). Even the lowly cockroach will work harder when surrounded by other cockroaches. Zajonc and his colleagues taught 32 female cockroaches (*Blatta orientalis*) to run a maze or a simple runway task. Some roaches performed alone, others were with coacting pairs, and still others were watched by other cockroaches (the cockroach spectators watched from their side of a plastic barrier). Both facilitating and inhibiting effects were obtained, just as Zajonc expected. As Table 9-1 indicates, for the simple runway task the presence of an audience or coactor improved performance; for the more complicated maze task the presence of an audience or coactor impaired performance (Zajonc, Heingartner, & Herman, 1969).

TABLE 9-1. The average number of seconds taken by cockroaches to escape from a bright light.

	Condition	
Task	Alone	Coaction
Simple (runway)	40.6	33.0
Complex (maze)	110.4	130.0

(*Source:* Zajonc, Heingartner, & Herman, 1969)

• •

The bulk of the experimental studies of social facilitation fall easily into place when viewed from the parsimonious perspective suggested by Zajonc. For example, when Charles Bond and Linda Titus (1983) carried out a comprehensive review of this area, they identified 241 studies of social facilitation that involved nearly 24,000 human subjects. After statistically combining the results of these studies, they concluded that the presence of others did not improve the quality of performance even for simple tasks but that it did increase the rate of productivity. They also found that, for complex tasks, the presence of others decreased both quantity and quality. They also noted that the gains that occurred when people worked together on simple tasks were not as great as the losses that occurred when people worked on complex tasks. (For other reviews see Baron, 1986; Geen, 1980; Geen & Gange, 1977; Guerin, 1986; Guerin & Innes, 1982; Suenaga, Andow, & Ohshima, 1981; and Zajonc, 1980.)

Why Does Facilitation Occur?

Even though the *when* of social facilitation is now fairly well understood, considerable debate still rages over the *why* of social facilitation. Triplett (1898), for example, offered a number of explanations for his observations of cyclists. Perhaps, he suggested, the pacing machine or lead rider creates a partial vacuum, and followers are pulled along with less effort. Similarly, maybe the lead rider or the pacing machine breaks the wind resistance and makes the followers' job easier. Also, the presence of other riders may buoy up the spirits of the competitors, encouraging them to expend greater effort. His laboratory study, however, eliminated most of these explanations and suggested, instead, that the presence of others is psychologically stimulating.

But what is the source and nature of this mysterious "psychological stimulation?" Researchers disagree, but most highlight one of three basic processes: arousal, apprehension about evaluation, and information processing.

Arousal.   When Zajonc first outlined his predictions concerning *compresence* (his term for the "state of responding in the presence of others"), he hypothesized that the "mere presence" of a member of the same species raised the performer's arousal level by touching off a basic alertness response (1965, 1980). Given the primary importance of social stimuli in the life of many organisms, Zajonc believes that compresence arouses the individual "simply because one never knows, so to speak, what sorts of responses—perhaps even novel and unique—may be required in the next few seconds" (1980, p. 50). This drive-induced arousal functions to facilitate performance, provided the task calls for dominant responses.

Although other theorists have sometimes suggested that the typical concomitants of compresence—heightened competitiveness, fear of evaluation, distraction, imitation, and so on—actually mediate social facilitation, Zajonc considers these processes to be ancillary effects of only incidental relevance to the basic phenomenon. He uses the phrase *mere presence* to reinforce the idea that social facilitation refers only to the drive-arousal effects of compresence.

Evaluation apprehension.   Nickolas B. Cottrell (1972) contends that the alertness response identified by Zajonc is not sufficient to account for social facilitation. According to Cottrell, in the young organism the mere presence of another organism is motivationally neutral, for it neither increases nor decreases alertness, arousal, or drive. In time, however, the individual learns that the receipt of rewards and punishments often covaries with the presence of others. The

> individual learns to anticipate subsequent positive or negative outcomes whenever others are merely present and not overtly doing anything that has motivational significance for him. It is these anticipations, elicited by the presence of others, that increase the individual's drive level [Cottrell, 1972, p. 277].

Other theorists share Cottrell's conviction that our concern about evaluation is responsible for the facilitating and impairing effects of audiences and coactors (Henchy & Glass, 1968; Weiss & Miller, 1971). Self-presentational theory, for example, suggests that in many cases this **evaluation**

apprehension stems from the fear that a failing performance will damage our public image. When others are watching, errors are a source of embarrassment, so we often work more slowly and are reluctant to answer (Bond, 1982; Miyamoto, 1985; Sanders, 1984).

Distraction.   In contrast to both of these motivational theories of social facilitation, several theorists believe that the presence of others changes our capacity to process information adequately. Self-awareness theory, for example, suggests that when we are acting before an audience, we may become so self-focused that our performance is impaired (Carver & Scheier, 1981; Duval & Wicklund, 1972; Mullen & Baumeister, 1987). Also, when in the presence of people who are unfamiliar to us, we may have to monitor what they are doing (Guerin, 1983; Guerin & Innes, 1982).

However, distraction does not always translate into poorer performances. Distraction interferes with the attention given to the task, but at the same time it creates response conflicts that can be overcome with greater effort. Therefore, on simple tasks the interference effects are inconsequential compared with the improvement brought about by the conflict, and performance is thus facilitated. On more complex tasks the increase in drive is insufficient to offset the effects of distraction, and performance is therefore impaired. This **distraction conflict** explanation has been supported in several investigations (Baron, 1986; Groff, Baron, & Moore, 1983; Sanders, 1981a; Sanders & Baron, 1975; Sanders, Baron, & Moore, 1978).

A Multifactor Model of Social Facilitation

These three analyses of social facilitation, despite their differing emphases, have all been at least partially supported empirically. The mere-presence hypothesis has been supported on three counts. First, even when the companion refrains from attending to the individual in any way, social facilitation still occurs (Berger, 1981; Schmitt, Gilovich, Goore, & Joseph, 1986; Towler, 1986; Worringham & Messick, 1983). Second, one has difficulty applying the concept of apprehension or distraction to certain organisms, such as cockroaches or chickens, that have shown effects of compresence. Third, although one may wonder if any task is completely neutral, activities that involve little threat of evaluation—eating, drinking, getting dressed—still show social facilitation effects. This effect was demonstrated in one study by arranging for subjects to (1) take off their shoes, (2) don a pair of large socks and shoes, (3) put on a lab coat that tied in the back, and later (4) remove the coat, shoes, and socks and (5) put on their own shoes. Tasks 1 and 5 were both highly familiar activities, and Tasks 2, 3, and 4 were novel actions, so Zajonc's model predicts that the presence of others would speed up the performance of 1 and 5 while slowing down the performance of 2 through 4. The results supported this hypothesis (Markus, 1978).

The primary hypothesis that derives uniquely from Cottrell's theory—that any stimulus increasing the organism's apprehension over future rewards or punishments should increase drive levels—has received only limited support (Bond & Titus, 1984). However, evidence does indicate that increasing evaluation apprehension prompts individuals to perform dominant rather than nondominant responses (Cohen, 1979, 1980). Also, situational factors that decrease evaluation apprehension, such as allowing for private responses and having unevaluative audiences, often eliminate social facilitation effects (Cottrell et al., 1968; Henchy & Glass, 1968; Martens & Landers, 1972; Sasfy & Okun, 1974).

The distraction/conflict model, too, has been verified in a number of studies. As the model predicts, working with others appears to be somewhat distracting; people forget key aspects of the task when they complete it in the presence of others rather than alone (Sanders, Baron, & Moore, 1978; Gastorf, Suls, & Sanders, 1980). Second, social facilitation effects tend to be stronger when subjects' attention is divided between the task and the other people who are present. If people are present but do not draw the subjects' attention, facilitation does not occur (Groff et al., 1983; Sanders et al., 1978). Last, a recent review of the literature indicates that subjects who are distracted in some way outperform control subjects provided the task is quite simple (Baron, 1986).

In sum, the experts still disagree about the ultimate cause of the social-facilitation effect: some favor the mere-presence perspective (Markus, 1981; Zajonc, 1980), others prefer the evaluation-apprehension notion (Geen, 1981; Shaw, 1981), and still others advocate the distraction/conflict hypothesis (Baron, 1986; Sanders, 1981a, 1981b). However, given the amount of research testifying to the impact of each factor, researchers have begun to reject the idea that any one approach is better than the others. Instead of trying to discover which theory subsumes the others, these investigators have realized that in any given situation variables deriving from arousal, evaluation apprehension, and distraction may be equally important, making it necessary to take them all into consideration when making predictions (Bond & Titus, 1983; Geen, 1980, 1981; Geen & Bushman, 1987; Sanders, 1981a).

Furthermore, despite these theoretical uncertainties, the conclusions of social facilitation research may still be fruitfully applied to many everyday situations (see Focus 9-2). For example, Zajonc's distinction between dominant and nondominant tasks suggests that the presence of others interferes with learning, because learning implies that the dominant responses are not the correct ones, but will facilitate performance once the behavior becomes routine. This hypothesis applies to all sorts of behaviors, including learning athletic skills, acquiring a second language, memorizing and reciting a speech, developing clinical skills, or even studying for a test (Berger, Carli, Garcia, & Brady, 1982; Ferris & Rowland, 1983; MacCracken & Stadulis, 1985; Schauer, Seymour, & Geen, 1985).

· · · · · · · · ·.. ·
FOCUS 9-2: THE CHAMPIONSHIP CHOKE

If having an audience helps when we are performing simple, well-practiced tasks, what is the impact of highly appreciative, supportive audiences? Will they spur us on to even greater accomplishments? Or will the pressure they heap on us be so great that we collapse and fail?

Roy Baumeister and his colleagues believe that supportive audiences have a paradoxical effect: they motivate us to do well, but at the same time they undermine our performance by making us too self-conscious. As a result we become so concerned with doing well that even smooth, well-learned actions are disrupted, and our performance plunges. In short, we "choke" (Baumeister, 1984, 1985; Baumeister & Showers, 1986; Baumeister & Steinhilber, 1984; Mullen & Baumeister, 1987).

Baumeister illustrated the paradoxical effects of audiences in a study of professional athletes. As a rule the team that is playing on its home field beats the visiting team (Altman, 1975; Edwards, 1979; Greer, 1983). When the game is so important that the pressure to win becomes too great, however, the home team's performance deteriorates. Baumeister found that the records from both baseball's World Series games and basketball's season-ending championship games confirmed that the team playing at home in the decisive game of these tournaments usually loses rather than wins (Baumeister, 1985). In the World Series, for example, the champion must win four of seven games. Because pressure to win is lower during the first two games, Baumeister found, playing at home is an advantage; home teams have won 60.2% of these games. In the final, and decisive, game, in contrast, the visiting teams have won 59.2% of the time. Baumeister also found that in the early games the home team averaged only .65 errors per game, whereas in the later games this average jumped to 1.31.

Baumeister's studies illuminate an important exception to the facilitative effects of an audience. Even when the performer is highly skilled at the task and has practiced the activity for years, an audience that has high expectations can be a hindrance rather than a help (Baumeister, Hamilton, & Tice, 1985).

· ·

Zajonc goes so far as to advise students to avoid trying to learn difficult materials in study groups, since such an arrangement may interfere with their acquisition of information. Instead he recommends that the student should

> study all alone, preferably in an isolated cubicle, and arrange to take his examinations in the company of many other students, on stage, and in the presence of a large audience. The results of his examination would be be-

yond his wildest expectations, provided, of course, he had learned his material quite thoroughly [Zajonc, 1965, p. 274].

INDIVIDUAL VERSUS GROUP PERFORMANCE

The Relay Test Room group was a success. After a few weeks in their new environs, the women began to reach new heights of productivity, and some increased their performance by as much as 25%. They easily outstripped the employees working individually in the main shop.

Not all groups, however, are as fortunate as this one. Despite the widespread use of groups in government, industry, education, and the private sector, they are the object of surprisingly consistent criticisms. People often complain about time wasted in groups and swap jokes such as "An elephant is a mouse designed by a committee," "Trying to solve a problem through group discussion is like trying to clear up a traffic jam by honking your horn," and "Committees consist of the unfit appointed by the unwilling to do the unnecessary." It is as if all agree with Carl Jung, who said that whenever "a hundred clever heads join a group, one big nincompoop is the result."

Is a group more or less capable than a single individual? No simple answer can be offered to this question. However, much of the research suggests that the key to the puzzle lies in the way in which individual inputs are combined. When people work, solve problems, or make decisions individually, their performance depends strictly on their personal resources, including their talent, skill, and effort. When groups work, in contrast, performance depends on individuals' resources *plus* the interpersonal processes that determine how these resources are combined. Do too many cooks spoil the broth? Or are two heads better than one? It depends on the social combination rule used to combine their wisdom (Davis, 1973; Laughlin, 1980; Shiflett, 1979; Stasser, Kerr, & Davis, 1980; Steiner, 1972).

Task Demands and Social-Combination Processes

Ivan Steiner compares social-combination rules to a recipe used in baking a cake. Just as the recipe lists all the ingredients needed and the step-by-step procedures to follow in combining them, **social-combination rules** specify "what is to be done when, but also who should do each part of the total task" (Steiner, 1976, p. 402). Steiner notes that "for many tasks there are no ready-made recipes, or the available recipes do not specify appropriate actions very clearly," but in most cases the nature of the task itself will require a particular type of social-combination process (1972, p. 402). A group that is assembling relays, for example, must combine members' products in ways that differ from the combination process used by a team playing baseball or workers mining coal. Moreover, groups tend to be more effective than individuals on certain types of tasks but less effective on others.

Steiner calls the combination processes dictated by the problem or group activity the **task demands.** These demands, he suggests, vary depending on the *divisibility* of the task, the *type of output* desired, and the *combination rules* required to complete the task (see Table 9-2).

1. Divisibility. *Divisible tasks* can be broken down into subtasks that can be assigned to different members. Building a house, planting a garden, or working a series of math problems by assigning one to each group member are all divisible tasks, since the entire task can be split into parts. *Unitary tasks*, however, cannot be divided: only one painter is needed for a small closet in a house, only one gardener can plant a single seed, and only one person need solve a simple math problem.

2. Type of output desired. With *maximizing tasks*, quantity is what counts. In a relay race, a tug-of-war, or a wooden-block-stacking problem, the ultimate judgment of task performance rests on the sheer quantity; the emphasis is on maximal production. In contrast, performance on *optimizing tasks* is dependent on a predetermined set of criteria; a good performance is one that most closely approximates the optimum performance. Examples of optimizing tasks include estimating the number of beans in a jar or coming up with the best solution to a problem.

3. Social-combination processes. Several methods can be used to combine individual inputs. *Additive tasks* involve adding or summing individual inputs to yield a group product. *Compensatory tasks* require a "statisticized" group decision derived from the average of individual members' solutions (Lorge, Fox, Davitz, & Brenner, 1958). *Disjunctive tasks* require a single specific answer to an either/or, yes/no problem. *Conjunctive tasks* are completed only when all the group members perform some specific action. Lastly, on *discretionary tasks* the group members are free to choose the method by which they will combine their inputs.

These three basic dimensions can be used to describe any particular task the group attempts. A tug-of-war, for example, is unitary, maximizing, and additive. Assembling a motor in a production line is divisible, optimizing, and, in some instances, conjunctive. Playing softball is unitary, maximizing, and additive for the team at bat but divisible and optimizing for the team in the field. Making a complex decision would probably be divisible, optimizing, and discretionary. (For other analyses of group tasks see Carter, Haythorn, & Howell, 1950; Hackman & Morris, 1975; Laughlin, 1980; McGrath, 1984; and Shaw, 1963, 1981.)

Predicting Potential Group Performance

In Steiner's theory task classification is important because different types of tasks require different sorts of resources: skills, abilities, tools, materials, equipment, time, and so on. If the members possess these resources, the group may be successful. If they lack the requisite resources, failure is likely. The potential productivity of any group can thus be calculated by

TABLE 9-2. A summary of Steiner's typology of tasks.

Question	Answer	Task Type	Examples
Can the task be broken down into sub-components, or is division of the task inappropriate?	Subtasks can be identified.	Divisible	Playing a football game, building a house, preparing a six-course meal
	No subtasks exist.	Unitary	Pulling on a rope, reading a book, solving a math problem
Which is more important, quantity produced or quality of performance?	Quantity	Maximizing	Generating many ideas, lifting the greatest weight, scoring the most runs
	Quality	Optimizing	Generating the best idea, getting the right answer, solving a math problem
How are individual inputs related to the group's product?	Individual inputs are added together.	Additive	Pulling a rope, stuffing envelopes, shoveling snow
	Group product is average of individual judgments.	Compensatory	Averaging individuals' estimates of the number of beans in a jar, weight of an object, room temperature
	Group selects the product from pool of individual members' judgments.	Disjunctive	Questions involving yes/no, either/or answers such as math problems, puzzles, and choices between options
	All group members must contribute to the product.	Conjunctive	Climbing a mountain, eating a meal, relay races, soldiers marching in file
	Group can decide how individual inputs relate to group product.	Discretionary	Deciding to shovel snow together, opting to vote on the best answer to a math problem, letting leader answer question

(Source: Steiner, 1972, 1976)

determining the type of task at hand, using this information to deduce the resources needed by the group members, and then observing the group to determine whether the members possess these resources. In the following subsections this basic approach to group performance is applied to groups performing additive, compensatory, disjunctive, conjunctive, and discretionary tasks.

Additive tasks. As Table 9-2 indicates, **additive tasks** are divisible and maximizing, for they require the summing together of individual group members' inputs to maximize the group product. In consequence, so long as each group member can perform the simple individualistic task required—such as pulling on a rope, cheering at a football game, clapping after a concert, or raking leaves in a yard—the productivity of the group will probably exceed the productivity of the single individual. As we will see later in this chapter, people in groups don't always work hard at additive tasks; as the saying goes, "Many hands make light work." They still, however, outperform a solitary individual (Latané, Williams, & Harkins, 1979).

Compensatory tasks. Referring back to Steiner's typology in Table 9-2, we find that **compensatory tasks** are those that require the averaging together of individual judgments to yield the group's product. Although very few tasks are strictly compensatory, in the sense that they can only be performed by the averaging of individual inputs, groups often choose to use compensatory methods to solve problems. If a finance committee must decide how much money to allocate for Project X, the chairperson can simply telephone the members and ask for their personal estimates. If he then takes the average of each member's suggestions, he is using a compensatory approach.

Marvin E. Shaw, after reviewing a number of studies that compared the quality of group judgments reached through compensatory methods and individual judgments, concludes that the bulk of the evidence indicates that judgments yielded by the averaging process are more accurate than those of individuals (Shaw, 1981). For example, in one of the earliest studies in this area (Knight, 1921), college students estimated the temperature of their classroom. Naturally, some people overestimated the temperature, and others underestimated; thus, the "group" judgment, which was an average of those offered, was more accurate than the judgments made by 80% of the individuals. Note, however, that when a later researcher allowed a single individual to make multiple estimates and then averaged these estimates together, he, too, found that the average was superior to the individual judgment (Stoop, 1932). Multiple judgments, but not a group, were the only prerequisites for improved accuracy.

Disjunctive tasks. Interest in **disjunctive tasks**—problems that require an either/or answer—is often traced back to Marjorie E. Shaw's 1932 study.

She arranged for four-person, same-sex groups to work at tasks like those shown in Focus 9-3. All were unitary (they could not be profitably broken down into subtasks), optimizing (a "best answer" was sought), and disjunctive (only one answer could be turned in as the group's solution). Across all these tasks, groups outperformed individuals, although (1) time costs were greater in groups and (2) groups rarely outperformed their best member.

• •
FOCUS 9-3: DISJUNCTIVE PUZZLES
_____

Disjunctive tasks come in two varieties: Eureka and non-Eureka. When we are told the answer to a Eureka problem, we are very certain that answer offered is correct. It fits so well, we react with an "Aha!" or "Eureka!" The answers to non-Eureka problems, in contrast, are not so satisfying. Even after arguing about them, we often wonder if the recommended answer is the correct answer. Examples of both types of problems are listed below, and their answers are given on page 266.

1. What is the next letter in the following sequence?

O T T F F S S

2. A man bought a horse for $60 and sold it for $70. Then he bought it back for $80 and again sold it for $90. How much money did he make in the horse-trading business? (*Source:* Maier & Solem, 1952)

3. Three missionaries and three cannibals are on one side of a river. They want to cross to the other side by means of a boat that can only hold two persons at a time. All the missionaries but only one cannibal can row. For obvious reasons, the missionaries must never be outnumbered by the cannibals, under any circumstances or at any time, except where no missionaries are present at all. How many crossings will be necessary to transport the six people across the river? (*Source:* Shaw, 1932)

4. Isaac is staying at a motel when he runs short of cash. Checking his finances, he discovers that in 23 days he will have plenty of money, but until then he will be broke. The motel owner refuses to let Isaac stay without paying his bill each day, but since Isaac owns a heavy gold chain with 23 links, the owner allows Isaac to pay for each of the 23 days with one gold link. Then, when Isaac receives his money, the motel owner will return the chain. Isaac is very anxious to keep the chain as intact as possible, so he doesn't want to cut off any more of the links than absolutely necessary. The motel owner, however, insists on payment each day, and he will accept no advance payment. How many links must Isaac cut while still paying the owner one link for each successive day? (*Source:* Marquart, 1955)

• •

Shaw, after watching her groups work on these problems, concluded that groups were better than individuals at detecting errors and rejecting incorrect suggestions. Later researchers, however, have pointed to the group's greater resources. Since disjunctive tasks require only one answer, groups stand a better chance of including a member who knows the correct answer (Marquart, 1955). In a game like Trivial Pursuit, for example, Donna may know about sports, and John may be familiar with literature, so they outperform a single individual by drawing on each other's resources. Hence, groups tend to outperform individuals, and larger groups tend to outperform smaller ones (Davis, 1973; Littlepage, West, Beard, Robeson, & Bryant, 1988; Lorge & Solomon, 1955; Smoke & Zajonc, 1962; Thomas & Fink, 1961).

This prediction, however, assumes that truth wins: that once the group members are told the correct answer by one group member, they will adopt it as the group solution. Clearly, however, the **truth-wins rule** does not always operate in groups (Bray, Kerr, & Atkin, 1978). Donna may be certain that the answer to the question "Who hit the game-winning home run in the 1960 World Series?" is Bill Mazeroski, but her team may not accept her solution. Similarly, when 67 groups discussed the horse-trading problem shown in Focus 9-3, many groups included a member who knew the correct answer, but many of these groups nonetheless adopted the wrong solution. In this case truth lost because knowledgeable members had a difficult time persuading their fellow members to adopt their solutions. In fact, some people later changed their answers to match the incorrect solution advocated by their groups (Maier & Solem, 1952).

We can untangle these contradictory findings by considering the two essential steps involved in solving disjunctive problems. First, someone in the group must suggest the correct answer. Second, the members of the group must adopt the answer as the group solution. If both these steps do not occur, the group will be unable to answer the problem correctly. For some tasks the second step occurs almost automatically; the solution, once proposed, is so satisfyingly correct that the group immediately endorses it. Therefore, *truth wins*. Such problems are typically called *Eureka tasks*, or insight problems (see Focus 9-3). For non-Eureka tasks, such as the horse-trading problem, the correctness of the answer is less obvious, so the second step is much more difficult. For these problems, the group will be successful only when a significant proportion of the group knows the correct answer. For non-Eureka tasks the **truth-supported-wins rule** applies (Hastie, 1986; Laughlin, 1980; Laughlin & Adamopoulos, 1980; Laughlin & McGlynn, 1986; Stasser, Kerr, & Davis, 1980).

Conjunctive tasks.   Fairly clear predictions can be made about the performance of groups working on unitary conjunctive tasks. Because all group members must complete (or at least contribute to) **conjunctive tasks,** groups invariably perform at the level of the group member with the poorest performance! The speed of a group of mountain climbers moving up the slope is determined by the slowest member. The trucks in a convoy can move no faster than the slowest vehicle. Research has confirmed this logical consequence of conjunctive tasks (Frank & Anderson, 1971; Steiner, 1972).

Often, however, conjunctive tasks are divisible; they can be broken down into subcomponents that can be performed by individual members. Building an automobile, for example, can be construed as the creation of many subproducts that, once combined, yield the final product. Groups can function more effectively once the task is divided, provided members can be matched to tasks that coincide with their ability levels and interests. If the least competent member is matched with the easiest task, a more satisfying level of performance may be obtainable. If the least competent member is matched with a difficult subtask, of course, performance will decline still further. (See Steiner, 1972, chap. 3, for a detailed review of group performance on divisible tasks.)

Discretionary tasks. The final category of tasks identified by Steiner includes any task that group members can perform using their own preferred combination procedures. How, for example, would a group estimate the temperature of the room in which they were working? One simple method would involve averaging individual judgments. Alternatively, members could determine whether anyone in the group was particularly good at such judgments and then use this person's answer as the group solution. In any case, the temperature-judging task is **discretionary,** because members themselves can choose the method for combining individual inputs. Discretionary tasks are examined in more detail in Chapter 10.

· ·

SOLUTIONS TO THE PROBLEMS IN FOCUS 9-3

1. The answer to this Eureka problem is E. The letters are the first letters of the first eight digits: One, Two, Three, Four, Five, Six, Seven, and Eight.

2. This non-Eureka puzzle is known as the Horse-Trading Problem. The answer is $20.

3. The missionary/cannibal problem is a non-Eureka problem. The entire process requires the following 13 crossings of the missionaries (M1, M2, and M3), the two nonrowing cannibals (C1 and C2), and the cannibal who can row (RC).

1. M1 and C1 cross	5. M1 and M2 cross
2. M1 returns	6. M1 and C1 return
3. RC and C2 cross	7. RC and M1 cross
4. RC returns	8. M1 and C2 return

9. M1 and M3 cross   12. RC returns
10. RC returns   13. RC and C2 cross
11. RC and C1 cross

4. The chain puzzle is a Eureka problem. Many groups answer 11, since that would involve cutting only every other link. The correct answer, however, is 2. If the 4th and 11th links are cut, all the values from 1 to 23 can be obtained by getting "change" back from the motel owner. Separate links (the 4th and the 11th) are given on Days 1 and 2, but on Day 3 the 3-link unit is given to the owner, who returns the separate links. These links are then used to pay on Days 4 and 5, but on Day 6 the 6-link unit is used, and the owner returns the others as change. This process can be continued for 23 days.

• •

Two Heads Are Better, Sometimes

Do groups deserve their reputation as time-wasters that produce poorly and decide badly? The evidence suggests that, in comparison with individuals, groups often excel. Their effectiveness, however, depends in large part on the type of task being attempted. As Table 9-3 indicates, groups clearly outperform the most skilled individual when the task is an additive one, and groups generally perform better than the average group member on many other kinds of tasks (compensatory, disjunctive-Eureka, divisible-conjunctive with matching, and discretionary; see Focus 9-4).

TABLE 9-3. A summary of the potential productivity of groups working on various tasks.

Type of Task	Productivity Effect
Additive	Better than the best: the group exceeds the performance of even the best individual member.
Compensatory	Better than most: the group exceeds the performance of a substantial number of the individual members.
Disjunctive: Eureka	Equal to the best: the group equals the performance of the most capable member.
Disjunctive: non-Eureka	Less than the best: the group equals the performance of the most capable member but often falls short.
Conjunctive: unitary	Equal to the worst: the group equals the performance of the least capable member.
Conjunctive: divisible	Better than the worst: performance will be superior if subtasks match members' capabilities.
Discretionary	Variable: performance depends on the combination rules adopted by the group.

(Source: Steiner, 1972, 1976)

Note, however, that these predictions describe the group's *potential* level of productivity. Groups working on additive tasks, in principle, will out-perform an individual. Groups that include one person who knows the correct answer have the potential to solve a disjunctive problem. Steiner argues, however, that groups rarely reach their full potential because pro-cesses unfold within them that detract from their proficiency. These per-formance-inhibiting processes are examined in the next section.

· ·

FOCUS 9-4: SEX DIFFERENCES IN GROUP PERFORMANCE

Would the Relay Test Room group have performed any differently if it had been an all-male group rather than an all-female group? Until recently studies of sex differences in group performance yielded no clear-cut an-swer. In some, when all-male and all-female groups worked on various types of tasks the men outperformed the women (Bouchard, Barsaloux, & Drauden, 1974; Hoffman & Maier, 1961). In others, in contrast, the all-fe-male groups outstripped the all-male groups (Kerr, 1983; Laughlin & McGlynn, 1967) or the sexes did not differ at all (Shaw & Harkey, 1976).

Wendy Wood (1987), however, offers some fresh insight into these seemingly inconsistent findings. After reviewing 52 studies of sex differ-ences in group performance she identified two key factors that determine which sex excels: task content and interaction style. First, in the studies that favored all-male groups the content of the task was more consistent with the typical skills, interests, and abilities of men rather than women. Groups of men were better at tasks that required mathematical expertise or physical strength, whereas groups of women excelled on verbal tasks. Second, Wood also suggested that sex differences in performance are in-fluenced by the differing interaction styles that men and women often adopt in groups. Because men more frequently enact a task-oriented in-teraction style whereas women enact an interpersonally oriented interac-tion style, men outperform women (to a small extent) when success is predicated on a high rate of task activity and women outperform men when success depends on a high level of social activity (Wood, Polek, & Aiken, 1985).

These findings suggest that men would not have outperformed the women in the Relay Test Room. Although the task required manual dex-terity, the women were all experts. Also, although men show a slight ten-dency to excel at tasks that require maximal productivity, positive social activities within the group were responsible for the high level of motiva-tion maintained by the workers. If the group had become too task-ori-ented, this source of motivational encouragement may have been lost.

· ·

PRODUCTIVITY LOSSES IN GROUPS

The operators in the Relay Test Room were more productive than their co-workers in the main plant, but this high level of productivity did not mean that they were maximally productive. During any given week some members of the groups would reach their usual levels of productivity, whereas others (especially Operators 1 and 2) would work below their maximum efficiency. As a result the group produced more than individuals working in isolation, but the difference wasn't overwhelming.

Why didn't the Relay Test Room women reach their full potential as a working group? Ivan Steiner (1972) draws on the concept of **process losses** to provide an answer. According to Steiner, group productivity depends on the resources of the group members and the demands of the task. If groups have sufficient resources (skills, ability, time, and so on) and the task is easy, the group has the potential to succeed. Steiner adds, however, that any prediction based only on task demands and member resources is optimistic, because it does not take into account group processes that detract from the group's proficiency. His "law" of group productivity predicts that

$$\text{Actual productivity} = \text{Potential productivity} - \frac{\text{Losses owing to}}{\text{faulty process.}}$$

Thus, even when a group includes highly skilled members who possess all the resources they need to accomplish their tasks, faulty group processes may prevent them from succeeding. In this section we will consider some of these problematic processes and how they influence performance in interacting groups.

Social Loafing in Groups

Max Ringelmann was a French agricultural engineer who, in the late 19th century, studied the productivity of horses, oxen, men, and machines in various agricultural applications. Should you plow a field with two horses or three? Can five men turn a mill crank faster than four? Ringelmann answered these questions by carrying out some of the first experimental studies in social psychology (Ringelmann, 1913). (Kravitz and Martin, 1986, present an excellent summary and interpretation of Ringelmann's work.)

One of Ringelmann's most startling discoveries pertained to the loss of productivity in groups working on additive tasks—problems that require the summing together of individual group members' inputs to yield a group product. Such tasks include competing in tugs-of-war, applauding at a concert, cheering at a sporting event, or teaming up to lift a heavy object. The work in the Test Relay Room was, in part, an additive task: group productivity was determined by adding together each worker's output.

As noted earlier, groups have an easy time with additive tasks, particularly when their performance is compared with that of individuals. A group of five persons making relays can easily outperform a single person, just as a team pulling a rope is stronger than a single opponent or an audience applauding makes more noise than an individual. Ringelmann found, however, that even though a group outperforms an individual, this productivity on additive problems does not mean that the group is working at maximum efficiency. When he had individuals and groups pull on a rope attached to a pressure gauge, groups performed below their capabilities (Moede, 1927). If two persons working alone could each pull 100 units, could they pull 200 units when they pooled their efforts? No, their output reached only 186. A three-person group did not produce 300 units, but only 255. An eight-person group managed only 392. Groups certainly outperformed individuals, but as more and more people were added, the group became increasingly inefficient (see Figure 9-2). The tendency for groups to become less productive as group size increases is now known as the **Ringelmann effect** (Ingham, Levinger, Graves, & Peckham, 1974; Steiner, 1972).

Why might a group of people working on an additive task fail to be as productive as they could be? Ringelmann suggested two interrelated mechanisms. First, **coordination losses** caused by the "the lack of simultaneity of their efforts" interfere with performance (1913, p. 9). Individuals, when working on additive tasks, have difficulty combining their inputs in a maximally effective fashion; on a task such as rope pulling they tend to pull and pause at different times, resulting in a failure to reach

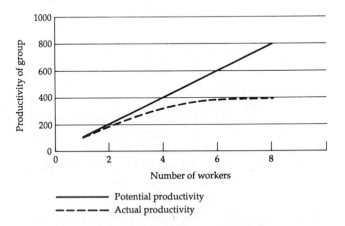

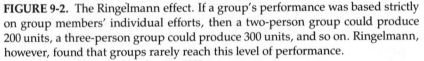

FIGURE 9-2. The Ringelmann effect. If a group's performance was based strictly on group members' individual efforts, then a two-person group could produce 200 units, a three-person group could produce 300 units, and so on. Ringelmann, however, found that groups rarely reach this level of performance.

Source: Adapted from Ringelmann, 1913

their full productive potential. Ringelmann notes that work groups often sing songs in an attempt to better coordinate their efforts.

Second, Ringelmann speculated that people may not work so hard when they are in groups. After watching a group of prisoners turning the crank of a flour mill, he noted that their performance was "mediocre because after only a little while, each man, trusting in his neighbor to furnish the desired effort, contented himself by merely following the movement of the crank, and sometimes even let himself be carried along by it" (p. 10; translation from Kravitz & Martin, 1986, p. 938). This reduction of effort by individuals when working in groups is called **social loafing** (Williams, Harkins, & Latané, 1981).

Ringelmann's insightful speculations have been confirmed experimentally. In one study Bibb Latané, Kip Williams, and Stephen Harkins told subjects that they were examining "the effects of sensory feedback on the production of sound in social groups." So their job was to shout as loudly as they could while wearing blindfolds and headsets that played a stream of loud noise. Consistent with the Ringelmann effect, groups of subjects made more noise than individuals, but the group performance failed to reach its maximum. When the subjects were tested alone, they averaged a rousing 9.22 dynes/cm2 (about as loud as a pneumatic drill). In dyads, each subject worked at only 66% of capacity, and in six-person groups, at 36%. This drop in productivity is charted in Figure 9-3 (Latané, Williams, & Harkins, 1979; experiment 2, p. 826; see also Harkins, Latané, & Williams, 1980; Williams et al., 1981).

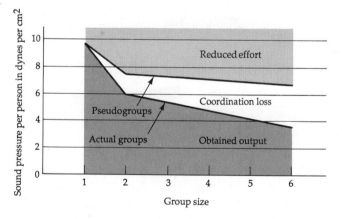

FIGURE 9-3. Two factors cause the Ringelmann effect: coordination losses and social loafing. The darker-shaded area represents the amount of noise produced by people working alone, in dyads, and in six-person groups. The area below the line marked "Pseudogroups" represents losses caused by faulty coordination. The area above that line signifies losses due to social loafing.

Source: Latané, Williams, & Harkins, 1979

Latané and his colleagues separated out the relative impact of coordination losses and social loafing by testing noise production in "pseudogroups." In these conditions, subjects were led to believe that either one other subject or five other subjects were cheering with them, but in actuality they were working alone (the blindfolds and headsets made this deception possible). Thus, any loss of production obtained in these conditions couldn't be due to coordination problems, because there weren't any other group members shouting. Instead, any decline in production could only be blamed on reduced effort brought about by social loafing. Figure 9-3 summarizes their findings. When subjects thought that one other person was working with them, they shouted only 82% as intensely, and if they thought that five other persons were shouting, they reached only 74% of their capacity. These findings suggest that even if work groups are so well organized that virtually all losses due to faulty coordination are eliminated, individual productivity might still be below par due to social loafing.

Avoiding Productivity Losses in Groups

Social loafing is not limited to groups that must exert physical effort. Loafing appears to be a pervasive aspect of groups, for it has been documented in groups working on such tasks as maze performance, vigilance exercises, creativity problems, job-selection decisions, typing, swimming, and even brainstorming. The effect also seems to apply equally to men and women, to people of all ages, and to groups in many different cultures (see Jackson & Williams, in press, for an extensive review). Given the scope of the problem, investigators have begun to identify ways to reduce this harmful consequence of group membership. Some of their suggestions are summarized below.

Identifiability and evaluation. Several studies suggest that social loafing is minimized when each member's contribution to the group project can be clearly identified (Hardy & Latané, 1986; Kerr & Bruun, 1981; Williams et al., 1981). In one study Williams, Harkins, and Latané (1981, experiment 1) once more asked subjects to make noise when alone or in groups. In one condition all the subjects shouted at the same time. In the pseudogroup condition the subjects shouted alone but thought that the others were shouting too. In the third condition the subjects once again thought that others were shouting with them, but they were also told that their individual contributions would be identifiable. As in earlier studies, subjects in dyads and six-person groups worked at only 59% and 31% of their peak efficiency, respectively, and productivity remained low even when coordination losses were eliminated (69% for dyads and 61% for six-person groups). When output was identifiable, however, this loafing was virtually eliminated.

Why does identifiability limit loafing? Social-loafing researchers suggest that when other members or an audience know an individual's outcomes, this evaluative pressure facilitates rather than impedes his or her performance. But when one's contributions are unidentified, the presence of others reduces evaluative pressures, and social loafing becomes more likely (Harkins & Jackson, 1985; Harkins & Szymanski, 1987; Jackson & Latané, 1981; Szymanski & Harkins, 1987; Williams et al., 1981). Harkins and Jeffrey Jackson illustrated the importance of evaluation by asking the members of a four-person group to generate as many ideas as possible for using a common object. The subjects did not discuss their task out loud but simply wrote their ideas on slips of paper. Some of the subjects thought that their ideas were individually identifiable, whereas others thought that their ideas were being collected in a common pool. In addition, some subjects believed that everyone was devising uses for the same object, but others thought that each group member was working with a different object. In this study loafing occurred only when the subjects believed that their individual outputs were not comparable and thus could not be evaluated. Thus, evaluation, rather than identifiability per se, may be the key to controlling social loafing (Harkins, 1987).

Involvement. Evidence indicates that when groups are working on interesting, involving, or challenging tasks, their members are much less likely to loaf (Brickner, Harkins, & Ostrom, 1986; Harkins & Petty, 1982; Zaccaro, 1984). In one investigation college students were asked to generate arguments either for or against a plan to make all seniors pass a comprehensive final examination before they were permitted to graduate. To manipulate involvement, some of the subjects were told that the plan was being considered for immediate implementation at their own university (high involvement), whereas others were told that the plan was being considered by another university (low involvement). As predicted, the only subjects who loafed were unidentifiable and uninvolved in the issue being discussed. If the plan pertained to them, they offered numerous thoughts even when unidentified (Brickner et al., 1986).

Trust in co-members. Norbert Kerr's (1983) work on the **free-rider effect** suggests yet another way to minimize social loafing. Kerr notes that in some groups people get a free ride; they do not do their share of the work, yet they still share equally in the group's rewards. Kerr suggests that this reduced effort sometimes occurs because group members worry that their co-workers are also holding back. Rather than look like a "sucker" by working harder than the others, group members reduce their efforts to match the level that they think other group members will be expending. In an experimental verification of this free-rider effect, Kerr found group members did not reduce their efforts if they believed that their partner was both capable and willing to contribute to the group. Similarly, Jackson and Harkins (1985) found that group members who thought their partner would loaf reduced their own efforts to establish an equitable division of labor. Those who believed that their partner would be expending maximum effort, however, did not loaf even when unidentifiable.

Personal responsibility.   When individuals join groups, their feeling of personal responsibility sometimes decreases; this process is known as **diffusion of responsibility** (Latané & Darley, 1970). Studies of bystanders witnessing an emergency, mobs, decision-making groups, and even diners at restaurants all suggest that reductions in responsibility can lead to failures to contribute to group goals (see Latané, 1986, and Leary & Forsyth, 1987, for reviews).

Steps can be taken, however, to minimize responsibility diffusion. Kerr, for example, believes that the free-rider effect noted above is caused, in part, by the feeling that one plays a relatively small or even negligible part in the group. Particularly in larger groups individuals feel that they are dispensable, a small cog in a larger machine that will continue to function even if they do not (Kerr, 1983; Kerr & Bruun, 1981, 1983; Kerr & Sullaway, 1983). If individuals think that their efforts will have an impact on the final decision or product, they are less likely to reduce their efforts (Kerr & Bruun, 1983).

Conclusions and Applications

Working in groups sets the stage for both social facilitation and social loafing. The presence of others motivates us and hence often improves our work on simple problems, but if our personal contributions to the total group effort can't be identified and evaluated, social loafing can wipe out these gains. The implications of these findings are significant. In many situations individuals work with others on projects, yet their own individual contribution to the group goal is unclear or hazy. When evaluation and identifiability are low, social loafing may limit the quality of the group's product.

Brainstorming groups provide a clear example of the detrimental, but often unrecognized, effects of social loafing. **Brainstorming** is by far the best-known group technique for finding novel or creative solutions. Alex F. Osborn, an advertising executive, developed brainstorming to stimulate ideas via group discussion. He complained of constantly having to struggle for new ideas for his advertising campaigns, so he developed four basic rules to follow to ensure group creativity (Osborn, 1957):

1. Expressiveness: Express any idea that comes to mind, no matter how strange, wild, or fanciful. Don't be constrained or timid; freewheel whenever possible.
2. Nonevaluation: Don't evaluate any of the ideas in any way during the generation phase. All ideas are valuable.
3. Quantity: The more ideas, the better. Quantity is desired, for it increases the possibility of finding an excellent solution.

4. Building: Because all ideas belong to the group, members should try to modify and extend others' ideas whenever possible. Brainstorming is conducted in a group so that participants can draw from one another.

Brainstorming is a popular creativity technique even though the bulk of the empirical evidence weighs against Osborn's method (Lamm & Trommsdorff, 1973; Mullen & Johnson, 1989). Initial studies conducted in the late 1950s found positive effects of brainstorming, but these investigations "stacked the deck" against individuals; group members were told to follow Osborn's four basic brainstorming rules, whereas individuals weren't given any special rules concerning creativity (Cohen, Whitmyre, & Funk, 1960; Meadow, Parnes, & Reese, 1959). When individuals working alone were better informed about the purposes of the study and the need for highly creative responses, they tended to offer more solutions than individuals working in groups. In one study, for example, four-person groups came up with an average of 28 ideas in their session, whereas four individuals working alone suggested an average of 74.5 ideas when their ideas were pooled. The quality of ideas was also lower in groups; when the researchers rated each idea on creativity, they found that individuals had 79.2% of the good ideas (Diehl & Stroebe, 1987; see also Bouchard, Barsaloux, & Drauden, 1974; Bouchard, Drauden, & Barsaloux, 1974; Bouchard & Hare, 1970; Dunnette, Campbell, & Jaastad, 1963; Taylor, Berry, & Block, 1958).

These studies offer a clear recommendation: do not use groups to generate ideas unless one or more of the following special precautions are taken:

1. The four rules suggested by Osborn are useful, but group members should be trained to follow them. Those who have not practiced brainstorming methods usually generate only mediocre ideas (Bouchard, 1972b).
2. Recording ideas individually, after the group session, often improves the results of brainstorming (Bouchard, 1972b; Philipsen, Mulac, & Dietrich, 1979).
3. All talking should be stopped periodically to allow group members to think silently. Evidence indicates that the more pauses and silences that occur during brainstorming, the higher the quality of the ideas (Ruback, Dabbs, & Hopper, 1984).
4. Record all ideas in full view of participants, and take turns if the quantity of ideas offered is low (Osborn, 1957; Rickards, 1974; see Focus 9-5).
5. In some cases a skilled discussion leader can help the group reach high levels of creativity. One such approach, termed **synectics,** involves identifying group members' goals, wishes, and frustrations; using analogies, metaphors, and fantasy; and using distracting activities and role-playing exercises. (See Gordon, 1961; Prince, 1970, 1975; and Ulschak, Nathanson, & Gillan, 1981, for a more detailed description of synectics.) Studies of groups that employ such techniques have found

that such groups are superior to traditional brainstorming groups (Bouchard, 1972a; Bouchard et al., 1974).

Many of these recommendations are incorporated in the **nominal-group technique,** which is described in Focus 9-5.

. . . .
FOCUS 9-5: THE NOMINAL GROUP TECHNIQUE

Researchers interested in the effects of group interaction on performance often include *nominal groups* in their studies, for control purposes. The members of these groups don't actually interact, but when their products are summed or averaged, their performance can be compared with those of the interacting groups. Thus, these aggregates are groups "in name only" (hence the designation *nominal*), but they often perform quite well when the task involves generating ideas.

The major drawback to their use, of course, is that feedback, resolution of disagreements, and commitment to the final decision are less likely if members never have the opportunity to interact with one another. Recognizing the benefits of both nominal groups and interacting groups, André L. Delbecq and Andrew H. Van de Ven developed an approach to decision making that includes elements of both types of groups (Delbecq & Van de Ven, 1971; Delbecq, Van de Ven, & Gustafson, 1975; Van de Ven & Delbecq, 1971). This special procedure, which they have named the *nominal-group technique* (NGT), involves four basic phases:

Step 1: The group-discussion leader introduces the problem or issue in a short statement that is written on a blackboard or flipchart. Once members understand the statement, they silently write ideas concerning the issue, usually working for 10 to 15 minutes.

Step 2: The members share their ideas with one another in a round-robin; each person states an idea, which is given an identification letter and written beneath the issue statement, and the next individual then adds his or her contribution.

Step 3: The group discusses each item, focusing primarily on clarification.

Step 4: The members rank the five solutions they most prefer, writing their choices on an index card. The leader then collects the cards, averages the rankings to yield a group decision, and informs the group of the outcome.

Delbecq and Van de Ven suggest that at this point the group leader may wish to add two additional steps to further improve the procedure: a short discussion of the vote (optional Step 5) and a revoting (optional Step 6) (Delbecq et al., 1975).

Evidence suggests that NGT is an effective alternative to traditional brainstorming (Gustafson, Shukla, Delbecq, & Walster, 1973; Van de Ven, 1974). Van de Ven (1974), for example, found that when groups discuss issues that tend to elicit highly emotional arguments, NGT groups produce more ideas and also report feeling more satisfied with the process than unstructured groups. The ranking/voting procedures also provide for an explicit mathematical solution that fairly weights all members' inputs and provides a balance between task concerns and socioemotional forces. By working alone during Step 1, members can generate many ideas without fear of sanctions by their fellow conferees. Then, in the interaction phase, the group is able to hash out differences and misunderstandings, all the while becoming committed to the final decision. The approach, however, is not without its drawbacks: certain materials are needed, NGT meetings typically can focus on only one topic, and members sometimes feel uncomfortable in following the highly structured NGT format.

. . . .

PRODUCTIVITY GAINS IN GROUPS

By the winter of 1927 the Relay Test Room workers had increased productivity well beyond the standards set by operators working in the main department. The observers couldn't help noticing, however, that two of the group members were not very involved in the experiment or in the group. When they were transferred out of the group and two new women took their place, productivity skyrocketed. In the main shop workers averaged 50 relays per hour, but in the Relay Test Room the rate reached over 70 units per hour (Whitehead, 1938).

Despite problems with coordination loss and social loafing, the Relay Test Room group surpassed all expectations. Steiner's law argues that productivity in groups is equal to potential productivity minus losses owing to faulty process, but the Relay Test Room group reached beyond these limits, suggesting that the more appropriate "law" might be

$$\frac{\text{Actual}}{\text{productivity}} = \frac{\text{Potential}}{\text{productivity}} - \frac{\text{Losses due to}}{\text{faulty process}} + \frac{\text{Gains from}}{\text{group process.}}$$

This possibility has prompted many group dynamicists to suggest ways to push actual productivity beyond the limits specified in Steiner's law. Richard Hackman (1983, 1987), for example, draws on his extensive analyses of performing groups to offer a number of suggestions for maximizing productivity in groups. Some of these suggestions are examined below. (Other excellent analyses of group performance are offered by Gist, Locke, & Taylor, 1987; Gladstein, 1984; Goodman, Ravlin, & Schminke, 1987; Guzzo, 1986; Pearce & Ravlin, 1987; Tjosvold, 1986; and Zander, 1971, 1977, 1982, 1985.)

The Normative Model of Group Effectiveness

Interpersonal relations among group members is a topic of little relevance to any manager who assumes that people work solely to make money.

Such a viewpoint, which was popularized in the early decades of this century by the so-called scientific-management theories (Taylor, 1923), is based on the premise that human beings, like reluctant donkeys, must be goaded into action by promises of financial carrots. This philosophy of human nature presumes that although people don't enjoy working, they will labor simply to avoid the more unpleasant alternative of starvation. In consequence, early managerial methods emphasized financial incentives directly tied to production, close supervision of workers to prevent loafing, and clear, simple goals set by management rather than workers.

Modern approaches to productivity, however, recognize the impact of interpersonal processes on performance. These interpersonal approaches, which can be traced back to industrial research projects conducted in such places as the Relay Test Room, assume that a strict focus on situational factors overlooks many important determinants of behavior, such as motivations, attitudes, satisfactions, aspirations, and personal goals. Whereas workers were once thought of as the mere "adjuncts of machines" (March & Simon, 1958), contemporary approaches focus on group-level processes, including the cohesiveness of the work group (Chapter 4), the level of teamwork (Chapter 4), group structure (Chapter 5), and leadership (Chapter 8).

Hackman's **normative model of group effectiveness** describes some of the factors that must be considered when designing effective work groups (Hackman, 1983; Hackman & Morris, 1975; Hackman & Oldham, 1980). The model, which is shown in Figure 9-4, takes a systems approach to group performance. Rather than assuming that variables are linked to one another in simple, one-to-one relationships, Hackman identifies several categories of input variables that set the stage for group work, key processes that facilitate or inhibit performance, and a variety of outputs that result from group activity.

Take a moment and apply the model to the Relay Test Room, looking first at the box labeled *organizational context*. Hackman argues that a change in the reward, education, or information system in the organization will lead to changes in the "process criteria of effectiveness," which includes the group members' level of effort, their knowledge, and their selection of performance strategies. Focusing on the reward system, all of the 100-plus assemblers at the Hawthorne Plant were paid on a group-piecework system. The more relays assembled by the group members during the week, the more they were paid, and individuals who worked at a consistently faster rate were paid more than the slower workers. This same system applied to the Relay Test Room workers, except that the group numbered only 5 rather than 100. This reward system was very motivating for the workers, and it increased their "level of effort brought to bear on the group task." (It did not, however, influence the "amount of knowledge or skill applied to the task work" or create a change in task-performance strategies.) At the output level this reward system increased

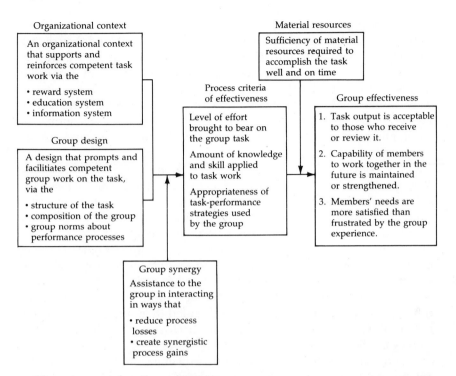

FIGURE 9-4. Hackman's normative model of group effectiveness. He identifies two sets of input variables that have a major impact on performance: organizational context and group design. These two factors, as moderated by synergy, determine the level of effort, the knowledge, and the task-performance strategies used by the group. These process criteria determine group effectiveness, provided sufficient material resources are available to accomplish the task.

Source: Hackman, 1987

productivity, strengthened the bonds among members, and left members feeling "more satisfied than frustrated by the group experience."

Now, turn to the *group design* box. As research and Figure 9-4 indicate, the structure of the task, the composition of the group, and group norms have a very large impact on performance. The Relay Test Room, for example, was not particularly impressive during the initial months. Operators 3, 4, and 5 all enjoyed the Relay Test Room, but the supervisor repeatedly reported problems in getting Operator 1 and Operator 2 to co-operate with the team. Because both of them could speak Polish and the others couldn't, they would talk about the others in that language. They also began ridiculing Operator 3 and Operator 4 for working so rapidly.

During this period the group adopted norms that did not encourage productivity. The women had been told "to co-operate with management and to work with a good will, but they were not to force output in any way" (Whitehead, 1938, p. 26). In fact, Operators 1 and 2 repeatedly said "We were told to work like we feel, and we do" (p. 104), and they did not try to set any records. But when two new women replaced them, the norms changed. One of the new operators pounded high-production norms into the fabric of the group by constantly encouraging members to work harder and harder. Speed and high production became highly prized by the group, and those who did not comply with this norm were constantly berated. As a result, the level of effort increased, and productivity jumped.

Lastly, consider the third factor that Hackman includes in his model: **synergy.** According to Hackman, group process sometimes results in gains in energy and effectiveness that go beyond what would be expected given the organizational context and the task design. Synergistic gains can be seen in the Relay Test Room group. When the two new operators joined the group, these five individuals were transformed into a single unit. They began to forget about their own outcomes and worry more about the group. When fellow group members urged them to work harder, they did. When they were asked not to take a day off, they canceled their vacation plans. When the researchers presented them with weekly performance feedback, they took pleasure in discovering that the group was doing well. They came to think of themselves as group members first and as individuals second. As one member explained, "It isn't so much the money we care about as it is being considered the best and fastest group" (p. 134).

Outlook for the Future

Hackman's normative model, in focusing on the manipulable aspects of the group and the organization, offers suggestions for designing and building effective work groups. If group members don't seem to be expending sufficient effort, for example, adjustments may be needed in the organizational context. If the group members identify challenging, specific performance objectives, if their rewards increase, and if group incentives replace individual ones, their level of effort may rise. Alternatively, the group can be redesigned, so that members "experience their work as meaningful," "feel collectively reponsible for the products they create," and "know, on a more or less continuous basis, how they are doing" (Hackman, 1983, p. 26).

The efforts of Hackman, Steiner, and other group dynamicists offer hope that in the future groups will function more effectively than they do at present. The task of understanding group performance has only begun, however. As Steiner writes, although "much of the work of the world is done by crews, teams, and committees, and although society often dispenses rewards to effective social units rather than to effective individuals," researchers have not yet determined "what makes groups perform well or poorly" (1986, p. 282). Group performance is not the bemusing puzzle it once was, but "the questions that are yet to be raised almost certainly outnumber those that have been formulated and researched" (Steiner, 1986, p. 283).

SUMMARY

Across the gamut of human experience we find example after example of group performance: people making decisions, solving problems, completing tasks, and attaining valued goals by working with others in groups. In these, and in all the thousands of other varieties of group performance, interdependent individuals are pooling their personal efforts to reach specifiable goals.

But are groups effective vehicles for achieving goals? Triplett's 1898 study of *social facilitation* suggests that people work more efficiently when other people are present. This effect occurs in both coaction and audience settings, depending on the difficulty of the task to be attempted. As Zajonc notes, social facilitation usually occurs only for simple tasks that require *dominant responses*, whereas social impairment occurs for complex tasks that require *nondominant responses*.

Why social facilitation occurs is not completely clear. Zajonc's *compresence* hypothesis argues that the mere presence of a member of the same species raises the performer's arousal level by touching off a basic alertness response. Cottrell's *evaluation-apprehension* hypothesis proposes that the presence of others increases arousal only when individuals feel that they are being evaluated. And the *distraction/conflict* hypothesis emphasizes the mediational role played by distraction, attentional conflict, and increased motivation. Available evidence suggests that these three processes, as well as others, combine to create social facilitation.

Is a group more or less capable than a single individual? No simple answer can be offered to this question, but Steiner argues that in many cases group effectiveness depends on the *task demands* of the activity being attempted. These task demands depend on the task's divisibility (divisible versus unitary), the type of output desired (maximizing versus optimizing), and the *social combination rule* used to combine individual members' inputs. Although the group's ability to perform any task successfully depends on members' resources and the processes utilized to combine these resources, Steiner argues that groups generally do well on *additive tasks*. *Compensatory* and *disjunctive tasks* also find the group outperforming most of the individual members, although performance on disjunctive tasks can be undermined if the solution, once suggested, is not so obviously correct that the group readily accepts it. *Conjunctive tasks*, because they require inputs from all members, can be a problem for groups, and the effectiveness of groups working on *discretionary tasks* covaries with the method chosen to combine individuals' inputs. Thus, two heads can be better than one, but it depends on the task.

Why don't groups reach their full potential as determined by task demands and member resources? Steiner notes that some loss in productivity is caused by faulty group process. These *process losses* were described as early as 1913 by Ringelmann, who discovered that groups become less productive as they increase in size. This *Ringelmann effect* is caused by *coordination losses* and by *social loafing*, the reduction of individual effort when people work in a group. Social loafing appears to be a pervasive aspect of work groups, but it can be limited by identifying individuals' inputs, increasing evaluation, involving members in the task, increasing trust, and controlling *diffusion of responsibility* among members. Also, although special methods such as *brainstorming* may minimize social loafing, groups should take steps to avoid social loafing beyond the expressiveness, nonevaluation, quantity, and building rules recommended by Osborn. The *nominal-group technique* (NGT), for example, seems to offer all the advantages of traditional brainstorming while avoiding its disadvantages.

Can groups reach beyond the limits set by their resources and task demands to reach extraordinary levels of productivity? Some theorists are optimistic. Hackman's *normative model of group effectiveness*, for example, describes some of these productivity-enhancing features. According to Hackman, two sets of input variables have a major impact on performance: organizational context and group design. These two factors, depending on the degree of *synergy* in the group, determine the level of effort, the knowledge, and the task-performance strategies used by the group. These process criteria determine group effectiveness, provided sufficient material resources are available to accomplish the task.

·10·

Decision Making

The date is April 4, 1961. A group of experts handpicked by President John F. Kennedy discusses a plan for invading Cuba. The proposal, which originated in the Central Intelligence Agency, argues that a small squad of well-trained commandos could capture and defend a strip of land in the Bahía de Cochinos (Bay of Pigs) on the southern coast of Cuba. It could then launch raids against Fidel Castro's army and encourage civilian revolt in Havana.

The group has been working on the plan for several months. Rather than simply approving or rejecting the CIA's original plan, the committee decides to improve it. The committee members work well together, and a strong feeling of unity and cohesiveness pervades the group. Mutual respect for others' opinions is quite high, because the qualifications of each member are unquestioned. Secretary of State Dean Rusk has years of experience in crafting foreign-policy decisions. Secretary of Defense Robert McNamara is a onetime faculty member of the Harvard Business School, a statistician, and a researcher into rational approaches to decision making. Other members, including Douglas Dillon, secretary of the treasury; McGeorge Bundy, a special assistant to Kennedy for national security affairs; and Arthur Schlesinger, Jr., a historian, are known for their objectivity and skill as decision makers (see Figure 10-1). Under Kennedy's leadership the group detects several minor flaws in the CIA's strategy, and it irons them out with dispatch. Discussion is carefully controlled by Kennedy, and norms concerning who can ask questions, the order of questioning, and even the proper phrasing for comments and inquiries are rarely broken. The group deals with problems like a smoothly functioning machine.

Today the members listen as Senator J. William Fulbright, an invited guest, makes a brief speech. Fulbright condemns the plan eloquently, arguing that the invasion would be risky and might have an irreparable impact on U.S. foreign relations. When he is finished, Kennedy thanks the senator and then begins to take a straw poll of the committee members' opinions. Three members voice their approval of the invasion, but one suggests that something should be done to disguise U.S. involvement in the action. This remark sparks an extensive discussion, and many ideas are offered. When the discussion winds down, the president adjourns the meeting. The straw poll is never completed, and the Bay of Pigs invasion takes place on April 17, 1961. Irving Janis, after conducting a thorough analysis of the event, described the decision as one of the "worst fiascoes ever perpetrated by a responsible government" (1972, p. 14).

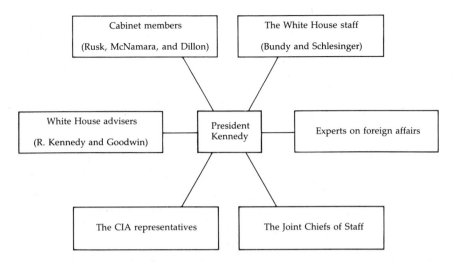

FIGURE 10-1. The members of the ad-hoc advisory committee that planned the Bay of Pigs invasion.

The advisory committee was not unique. Like many other groups, it faced a problem needing a solution. To make their decision, the members sought out information from available sources, weighed alternatives, and considered the ramifications of their actions. When their alternatives were narrowed down to two—invade or do not invade—they made a decision as a group. In the first section of this chapter we will examine the steps that are generally involved in group decision making, beginning with recognition of a problem or question and ending with a solution.

But the advisory committee was typical in another way. Like so many other groups, it made the wrong decision. The Watergate cover-up, the marketing of Thalidomide, the launching of the space shuttle Challenger in freezing temperatures, and the design of safety features at the Union Carbide plant in Bhopal, India, all resulted from group decisions. In examining how groups like the advisory committee function, we will look for the sources of its errors and for ways in which these mistakes could have been avoided. Two particularly important biases that operate in groups, groupthink and polarization, are examined in the second and third sections of this chapter.

THE ANATOMY OF GROUP DECISION MAKING

In January of 1961 the CIA gave the newly inaugurated Kennedy a "nutshell briefing" on its plans to invade Cuba (Janis, 1989). The CIA had been training Cuban exiles for several months, and now it needed the president's approval to launch the attack. To the president's credit, rather than acting on the basis of such limited information, he created the special ad hoc advisory committee.

This committee's deliberations over the next few months followed a pattern that is relatively common in decision-making groups. Although no two groups reach their decisions in precisely the same way, the stages shown in Figure 10-2 appear consistently in many groups. During the initial **orientation** stage the group identifies the problem to be solved, the choice that must be made, or the conflict that requires resolution. Next, during the **discussion** stage, the group gathers information about the situation and, if a decision must be made, identifies and considers options. In the **decision** stage the group chooses its solution by reaching a consensus, bargaining, voting, or through some other social decision process. Lastly, **implementation** must occur, and the impact of the decision is assessed (Dewey, 1910; Fisher, 1980; Guzzo, 1986; Hoffman, 1982; Mintzberg, 1979; Penrod & Hastie, 1980; Simon, 1976; Zander, 1982).

Orientation

How did the advisory committee begin its work? Kennedy had been in office for only two days, so his staff of advisers needed to take some time to develop an *orientation* to the group and to the problem. Members were introduced to one another, the problem facing the group was defined, and the steps to be taken in solving the problem were addressed.

As in most groups this orientation period was very brief. Although evidence indicates that groups that spend time getting oriented make better decisions, group members rarely show much interest in process planning.

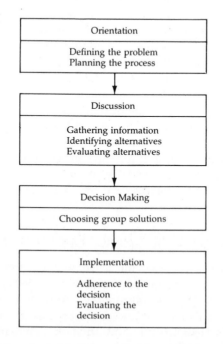

FIGURE 10-2. A rational model of group decision making.

In one study of 100 discussions recorded in task-oriented groups, fewer than 1.5 orientation statements were made per group. In fact, many groups never even discussed strategies, and when someone did raise the issue, additional comments from other group members were unlikely to follow (Hackman & Morris, 1975). Other studies have found that group members (1) when first presented with a task tend to start working on the problem immediately rather than considering process-related issues (Varela, 1971); (2) often believe that planning activities are less important than actual task activities, even when they are cautioned that proper planning is critical (Shure, Rogers, Larsen, & Tassone, 1962); and (3) assume that discussing process is a waste of time, because they will rely on whatever procedure was used previously (Hackman & Morris, 1975).

Yet controlling process by good planning generally has positive effects. When groups in one study worked on a role-playing problem involving survival on the moon, the only factor that distinguished successful groups from failing groups was the number of strategy-planning remarks made during the group discussion (Hirokawa, 1980). In a study of six conferences in which panels of experts evaluated new medical technologies, participants were more satisfied when the decisional procedures had been discussed in advance (Vinokur, Burnstein, Sechrest, & Wortman, 1985). Similarly, in a project that experimentally manipulated the use of process planning, groups were more productive when they were encouraged to discuss their performance strategies before working on a task requiring intermember coordination (Hackman, Brousseau, & Weiss, 1976). Process planning also leads to more positive ratings of group atmosphere, increments in verbal interaction, greater satisfaction with leadership, and flexibility in performing tasks (Hackman & Morris, 1975).

Discussion

During the *discussion* stage the group gathers and processes information relevant to the decision (see Figure 10-2). Relying primarily on discussion among members, the group identifies alternative courses of action and seeks out new information that it can use to evaluate these alternatives. If it is working effectively, the group will consider both the positive and negative consequences of the alternatives it identifies and will reconsider options that it initially dismissed as unacceptable. The group must also plan to carry out the decision and develop strategies for monitoring its impact. The group considers all information, even if it conflicts with the group's initially preferred course of action. Patrick Laughlin calls this process **collective induction.** Laughlin notes that the group first uses discussion to develop an hypothesis, generalization, or explanation of the situation at hand. Once one or more hypotheses are formulated, the group tests its ideas by exchanging personal opinions, pooling available information, or gathering evidence (Laughlin, 1980, 1988; Laughlin & Futoran, 1985; Laughlin & Shippy, 1983).

Just as the orientation period is essential to effective decision making, so the amount of time spent in active discussion influences the quality of the group's decision (Harper & Askling, 1980; Katz & Tushman, 1979; Lanzetta & Roby, 1960; Laughlin, 1988). In one study the researchers carefully monitored group members' communications while working on a problem that could be solved only by properly sequencing individuals' responses. Although some subjects were better trained than others to perform the task, the group's utilization of essential resources through discussion proved to be the best predictor of success (Lanzetta & Roby, 1960). Similarly, a detailed case study of groups working on projects for a college class found that the overall rate of discussion was higher in the successful groups, and that participation rates and product quality were positively correlated (Harper & Askling, 1980). Lastly, Laughlin (1988) reports that the exchange of information through discussion enhanced group problem-solving, particularly when the exchange focused more on evidence rather than hypotheses.

Unfortunately, groups do not always use discussion to their advantage (Stasser & Titus, 1987). According to Janis and Leon Mann, group members, when faced with a decision, are often "beset by conflict, doubts, and worry, struggling with incongruous longings, antipathies, and loyalties," and they cope with this decisional conflict by relying on a variety of discussion-limiting strategies (Janis & Mann, 1977, p. 15):

1. Procrastination: Rather than spending its time studying alternatives and arguing over their relative merits, the group postpones the decision.
2. Bolstering: The group quickly but arbitrarily formulates a decision without thinking things through completely, and then it bolsters the preferred solution by exaggerating the favorable consequences and minimizing the importance and likelihood of unfavorable consequences.
3. Avoiding responsibility: The group denies responsibility by delegating the decision to a subcommittee or by diffusing accountability throughout the entire assemblage.
4. Ignoring alternatives: The group engages in the fine art of muddling through (Lindblom, 1965) by considering "only a very narrow range of policy alternatives that differ to only a small degree from the existing policy" (Janis & Mann, 1977, p. 33).
5. "Satisficing": Members accept as satisfactory any solution that meets only a minimal set of criteria instead of working to find the best solution. Although superior solutions to the problem may exist, the "satisficer" is content with any alternative that surpasses the minimal cutoff point.
6. Trivializing the discussion: The group avoids dealing with larger issues by focusing on minor issues. (This tendency supports the Law of Triviality discussed in Focus 10-1.)

Janis and Mann argue that these psychological strategies may help the group members cope with their conflict about making the decision but that they undermine **vigilant information processing.**

· ·

FOCUS 10-1: THE LAW OF TRIVIALITY

The British humorist C. Northcote Parkinson is best known for the law that bears his name: work expands so as to fill the time available for its completion. He has also argued for the validity of a Law of Triviality: the time a group spends discussing any issue will be in inverse proportion to the consequentiality of the issue (Parkinson, 1957, paraphrased from p. 24). Providing a fictitious example, he describes a finance committee dealing with Item 9 on a long agenda, a $10-million allocation to build a nuclear reactor. Discussion is terse, lasting about $2\frac{1}{2}$ minutes, and the committee unanimously approves the item. However, when the group turns to Item 10, the allocation of $2350 to build a bicycle shed to be used by the office staff, everyone on the committee has something to say. As Parkinson explains:

> A sum of $2350 is well within everybody's comprehension. Everybody can visualize a bicycle shed. Discussion goes on, therefore, for forty-five minutes, with the possible result of saving some $300. Members at length sit back with a feeling of achievement [p. 30].

· ·

Decision Making

By early April the advisory committee was ready to make its decision. The members had spent $2\frac{1}{2}$ months examining the CIA's plan, and even though many questions remained unanswered, the group could delay no longer. Word of the plan had leaked to the press, and the group was worried that Castro would shore up his defenses if he suspected anything. So at that fateful April meeting the members reached their decision: first by voting, and then by discussing the issue until they reached a consensus.

As the group reaches a point at which members feel that they have sufficient information to make a decision, some sort of **social-decision scheme** must be used to combine individual preferences into a collective decision. Some groups adopt *explicit* social-decision schemes; a jury, a fraternity, or a committee may decide issues by calling for a show of hands or by following Robert's Rules of Order (see Focus 10-2). In other groups, in contrast, the social-decision schemes remain *implicit;* the group members reach a decision without going through any formal procedure such as voting. Instead, members simply state their opinions until some consensus is reached. Some common social-decision schemes are delegation, averaging, voting, and discussion to unanimity. (See Davis, 1969, 1982; Kerr,

1982; Laughlin, 1980; and Stasser, Kerr, & Davis, 1980, in press, for reviews; Wood, 1984).

• •
FOCUS 10-2: ROBERT'S RULES OF ORDER

For a number of years Henry M. Robert, an army engineer, had been irritated by the chaos and confusion that characterized many of the meetings he attended. Realizing that a solution to this problem lay in the development of a set of rules for standardizing meetings, he published Robert's Rules of Order in 1876. Patterned after the operating principles of the U. S. House of Representatives, Robert's Rules explicate not only "methods of organizing and conducting meetings, the duties of officers, and the names of ordinary motions" but also such technicalities as how motions should be stated, amended, debated, postponed, voted on, and passed (Robert, 1915/1971). For example, no fewer than 7 pages are used to describe how the group member "obtains the floor," including suggestions for proper phrasings of the request, appropriate posture, and timing. More complex issues, such as the intricacies of voting, require as many as 20 pages of discussion.

Robert's Rules are the traditionally adopted regulations for many groups, and they are certainly useful in structuring the group's decision-making process. But they are not without certain drawbacks. Robert purposely designed them to "restrain the individual somewhat," for he assumed that "the right of any individual, in any community, to do what he pleases, is incompatible with the interests of the whole" (1915/1971, p. 13). In consequence, the rules promote a formal, technically precise form of interaction, sometimes at the expense of openness, vivacity, and directness. Additionally, the rules can create a win/lose atmosphere in the group, for members expect to debate differences and to solve these disagreements through voting rather than through a discussion to consensus. Lastly, groups using the rules can become so highly structured that little room is left for group development, interpersonal adjustment, and role negotiation. Because, in a sense, the rules take the dynamics out of group dynamics, group members should remain ever mindful of their weaknesses as well as their strengths.

• •

Delegating decisions.   In some cases an individual or a subgroup within the group makes the decision for the entire group. Under a *dictatorship* scheme the chairperson or some other authority makes the final decision with or without input from the group members. Similarly, when an *oligarchy* rules, a coalition of powerful individuals within the group speaks for the entire group. Other forms of delegation include asking an expert to provide an answer or forming a subcommittee made up of a few members to study the issue and reach a conclusion (Smoke & Zajonc, 1962).

All these methods are similar in that they take some of the decision-making power away from the members, who may feel that their inputs have been ignored. However, the amount of time saved sometimes justifies delegated decisions, particularly when tasks are routine or extremely technical or group commitment to the decision is of little importance. Often the group is relieved not to be consulted about such simple matters as "How many paper clips should we order?" or technical questions like "What is the best type of photocopying equipment now on the market?"

Averaging individual inputs. In some cases groups make decisions individually (either before or after a group discussion), and these private recommendations are averaged together to yield an overall conclusion. For example, to choose among five possible candidates for a job opening, each member of the hiring committee could rank the candidates from 1 (the best) to 5, and the group could then average these rankings. As noted in Chapter 9, averaging ensures that all group members have a voice in the decision, and individual errors or extreme opinions are canceled out during the averaging process. If this procedure is used without discussion, however, the decision may be an arbitrary one that fails to satisfy any of the group members, all of whom may end up feeling little responsibility for implementing it.

Voting. Many groups follow parlimentary procedures, such as Robert's Rules of Order, and vote on choices. Depending on the group and the issue, the number of votes needed varies from a simple majority to unanimity. Like an averaging procedure, voting closes discussion on the issue and so provides a mechanism for making a clear-cut decision. When the vote is close, however, some members of the group may feel alienated and defeated. In consequence, they become dissatisfied with membership and are less likely to follow through on the decision (Castore & Murnighan, 1978). A voting method can also lead to internal politics as members get together before meetings to apply pressures, form coalitions, and trade favors to ensure the passage of proposals they favor. Also, if the vote is taken publicly, individuals may conform to previously stated opinions rather than expressing their personal views (Davis, Stasson, Ono, & Zimmerman, 1988). Voting is one of the most frequently used social-decision schemes, yet it is not without certain liabilities.

Consensus. Some of these problems with voting are reduced if unanimity is required before the decision is accepted. This complete-consensus scheme seems to be the ideal procedure, because all the group's resources are fully utilized and the in-depth discussion binds members both to the group and to the decision itself. No one in the group occupies a position of a minority whose ideas lose out in the final ballot, and the high levels of communication among members lead to improved effectiveness in the future.

Unfortunately, consensus carries many prerequisites that are not necessarily met in all group situations. Reaching a consensus invariably takes a good deal of time, and if rushed the strategy can misfire. Often, too, although the group may explicitly claim to be using the unanimity scheme, the implicit goal may be something less than unanimity. When nine people on a jury all favor a verdict of guilty, for example, the three remaining jurors may hold back information that they believe would cause dissent within the group. As a result, in groups operating under a unanimity scheme, initial biases and errors are often perpetuated rather than corrected (Stasser & Titus, 1985).

Thus, a consensus-decision scheme is not necessarily superior to the other schemes described above (Hirokawa, 1984; Rawlins, 1984; Stumpf, Freedman, & Zand, 1979). In general, groups prefer to reach a consensus on questions that require sensitive judgments, such as issues of morality, but on intellectual problem-solving tasks a majority-rules voting scheme finds considerable acceptance (Kaplan & Miller, 1987). In fact, evidence indicates that group members feel satisfied with any procedure so long as they agree with the final decision. Even a dictator's judgment satisfies group members when it coincides with their own (Miller, Jackson, Mueller, & Schersching, 1987).

Implementation

Even when the die is cast and the decision made, two significant pieces of work remain undone. First, the decision must be implemented. If a union decides to strike, it must put its strike plan into effect. If a city planning commission decides that a new highway bypass is needed, it must take the steps necessary to begin construction. If an advisory committee approves an invasion plan, its members must mobilize the necessary military forces. Second, the quality of the decision must be evaluated. Was the strike necessary? Did we put the highway where it was needed the most? Was it really such a good idea to invade Cuba?

When the group evaluates its decision, the decision-making process becomes a cycle rather than a sequence with a start and a finish. Kennedy's advisory committee, for example, could not ignore the low quality of its decision; no amount of rationalization could explain away the havoc the invasion had wreaked. In reaction, Kennedy and his advisers investigated the debacle (Janis, 1972, 1982, 1989). This inquiry, after identifying the problem (orientation), appraised a range of alternative explanations (discussion). Some of these explanations partly exonerated the advisory committee. However, as we will see in the next section of this chapter, most of the evidence suggested that the group was at fault. After weighing the evidence, Kennedy decided what aspects of the group should be changed (decision), and he later instituted these changes (implementation). As a result the group functioned much more efficiently.

Quality circles provide a second example of the cyclical nature of decision making in groups. These small, self-regulated decision-making groups usually include five to ten employees who perform similar jobs within the organization. The groups are often led by a supervisor who has been trained for the role, but participation in the circle is voluntary, and no monetary incentives are offered to those involved (Crocker, Chiu, & Charney, 1984; Deming, 1975).

The concept of quality circles can be traced to the work of W. Edwards Deming (1975), who was a managerial consultant in Japan in the post–World War II years. Deming insisted that the primary goal of any company should be quality in products and service and that failures to achieve quality should not be tolerated. Moreover, he raised two objections to the widespread use of inspection systems for detecting defective products. First, each time a defective item is manufactured, materials, equipment, and time are wasted. Second, inspection systems implicitly reinforce the idea that some slippage in quality is expected and will be tolerated. Deming offered a different means of maintaining quality: give production personnel the responsibility for identifying and solving problems that are creating the losses in quality.

Thus, the quality circle was born, and it quickly became a standard feature in many businesses. Although quality circles vary greatly in size and procedures, most follow the decision-making sequence described earlier. Initially, the group must identify problems in the workplace that are undermining productivity, efficiency, quality, or job satisfaction. Next, the group spends considerable time discussing the causes of the problems and suggesting possible solutions. A cause-and-effect diagram, like the one shown in Figure 10-3, is often used to assist the group members in identifying the source of the difficulty. Eventually, decisions are made

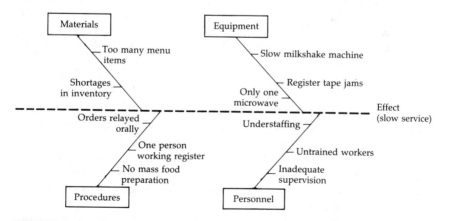

FIGURE 10-3. An example of a cause-and-effect (or fishbone) diagram. The four basic categories of causes for most industrial problems—materials, procedures, equipment, and personnel—are shown as spines flowing toward the problem to be solved. Subcauses are shown by connecting them to each of the primary causes. In this example the reasons for slow service in a fast-food restaurant are considered.

about changes (usually by consensus), and these changes are implemented and evaluated. If the changes do not have the desired effect, the process is repeated. At all steps the group members make use of simple graphics, such as line charts, pie figures, or bar charts, as well as statistical data pertaining to productivity.

Quality circles have many advocates, but most experts agree that their indirect effects are as powerful as their direct effects. A group of workers trained to identify problems in their workplace are doing more than just maintaining quality control by careful monitoring. They are also working together, as volunteers, to improve their job environment. They are taking responsibility for their own performance, and they often become more committed to their group, their job, and their company. The problems that were targeted by the group disappear, but so do other problems such as turnover, absenteeism, and low motivation. Thus, the quality circle offers a means of increasing teamwork and employee involvement in the workplace (Drucker, 1981).

GROUPTHINK

Janis, after reading historical accounts of the Bay of Pigs invasion, found himself puzzling over many questions: How could such a disastrous decision have been reached? Why didn't anyone object to the patently obvious shortcomings of the plan? Why did this group make such a faulty decision even when its deliberations had followed the usually effective pattern of orientation, discussion, decision making, and implementation?

As he became more intrigued by this defective decision, Janis began to collect other examples of people in groups reaching wrong conclusions. In the realm of politics and military planning he found that many of U.S. history's most profound blunders—the failure to defend Pearl Harbor from Japanese air attack, the escalation of the Vietnam War, the Watergate burglary—had resulted from the decisions of groups. In the newspapers he read of ordinary citizens seriously misjudging issues—for example, a complacent community that ignored warnings of a mining disaster until it was too late or a committee that approved placing a coal-storage facility so close to a school that its accidental collapse killed all the town's school-age children. Lastly, in reviewing his own experiences and observations in many kinds of groups—infantry platoons, air crews, therapy and encounter groups, seminars, and experimental groups—he recalled a number of instances in which group members had sacrificed effective decisional processes during the course of group discussions.

In his book *Victims of Groupthink,* Janis (1972, 1982) relied on case-study methods to develop an explanation for these groups' failures. After studying a number of groups whose gross errors of judgment virtually doomed their plans to failure, he concluded that the errors had stemmed from a process he termed **groupthink:** a distorted style of thinking that renders group members incapable of making a rational decision. According to

Janis (1982, p. 9), groupthink is "a mode of thinking that people engage in when they are deeply involved in a cohesive in-group, when the members' strivings for unanimity override their motivation to realistically appraise alternative courses of actions." During groupthink, members try so hard to agree with one another that they make mistakes and commit errors that could easily be avoided.

Symptoms of Groupthink

To Janis groupthink is a "disease" that infects healthy groups, rendering them inefficient and unproductive. And like the physician who searches for symptoms that signal the onset of the illness, Janis has identified a number of symptoms that occur in groupthink situations (Janis, 1972, 1979, 1982, 1989; Janis & Mann, 1977; Longley & Pruitt, 1980; Wheeler & Janis, 1980). These symptoms are examined below.

Personal pressure.   As noted in Chapter 6, pressures to conform are present to some degree in nearly all groups. When groupthink occurs, however, these pressures become very powerful. Tolerance for any sort of disagreement seems virtually nil, and in some cases exceedingly harsh measures are taken to bring those who dissent into line. In the ad hoc advisory committee a taboo emerged that censured criticism, and members who broke this norm were subjected to pressure. If someone criticized the plan, the president would ask the CIA representatives for their comment; they invariably dismissed the complaints as groundless.

Self-censorship.   Even in the absence of direct pressure, most of the group members kept a tight rein on their own negative comments. Many of the members of the group privately felt uncertain about the plan, but their discomfort over expressing their doubts openly prompted them to remain silent. In some instances they would raise questions by sending private memorandums to the president before or after a meeting, but when the group convened, the doubting Thomases sat in silence. As Schlesinger later wrote:

> In the months after the Bay of Pigs I bitterly reproached myself for having kept so silent during those crucial discussions in the Cabinet Room, though my feelings of guilt were tempered by the knowledge that a course of objection would have accomplished little save to gain me a name as a nuisance. I can only explain my failure to do more than raise a few timid questions by reporting that one's impulse to blow the whistle on this nonsense was simply undone by the circumstances of the discussion [1965, p. 225].

Mindguards.   Janis coined the term *mindguard* to refer to self-appointed vigilantes who protect group members from information that they think will disrupt the group. As a *gatekeeper* the mindguard diverts controversial information away from the group by "losing" it, "forgetting" to mention it, or deeming it irrelevant and thus unworthy of the group's attention. Alternatively, the mindguard may take dissenting members aside and pressure them to keep silent. The mindguard may use a variety of strategies to achieve this pressure: requesting the change as a personal favor, pointing out the damage that might be done to the group, or informing the dissenter that in the long run disagreement would damage his or her position in the group (Uris, 1978). But whatever the method the overall goal is the same: contain dissent before it reaches the level of group awareness.

Many of the members of the advisory committee took the role of mindguard, including Kennedy, Rusk, and the president's brother, Robert. President Kennedy, for example, withheld memorandums condemning the plan from both Schlesinger and Fulbright. Similarly, Rusk suppressed information that his own staff had given him. One extreme example of this mindguarding occurred when Rusk, unable to attend a meeting, sent Undersecretary of State Chester Bowles. Although Bowles was "horrified" by the plan under discussion, President Kennedy never gave him the opportunity to speak during the meeting. Therefore, he later followed bureaucratic channels by voicing his critical misgivings in a memorandum to his superior, Rusk. Rusk, however, kept silent during the next committee meeting and informed Bowles that the plan had been revised. Ironically, Bowles was fired several weeks after the Bay of Pigs defeat.

Apparent unanimity.   Public unanimity of opinion was commonplace in the advisory committee. Almost from the outset the entire group seemed to agree to a man that the basic plan presented by the CIA was the only solution to the problem and in later discussions appeared to just be "going through the motions" of debate. Retrospective accounts revealed that many of the group's members objected to the plan, but these objections never surfaced during the meetings. Instead, a "curious atmosphere of assumed consensus" (Schlesinger, 1965, p. 250) characterized discussion, as each person wrongly concluded that everyone else liked the plan. As Janis (1972, p. 39) explains, the group members played up "areas of convergence in their thinking, at the expense of fully exploring divergences that might disrupt the apparent unity of the group." Apparently, the members felt that it would be "better to share a pleasant, balmy group atmosphere than be battered in a storm."

Illusions of invulnerability.   Feelings of assurance and confidence engulfed the group. The members felt that their plan was virtually infallible and that their committee could not make major errors in judgment. The atmosphere in the new group could almost be described as euphoric, for members felt that such a powerful group of men would be invulnerable to dangers that could arise from bad decisions or ill-considered actions. As Janis notes, such feelings of confidence and power may help athletic teams or combat units reach their objectives, but the feeling that all obstacles can be easily overcome through power and good luck tends to cut short clear, analytic thinking in decision-making groups.

Illusions of morality.   Although groups are capable of reaching admirable levels of sophistication in moral thought, during groupthink this capability is unrealized (McGraw & Bloomfield, 1987). The plan to invade Cuba could unsympathetically be described as an unprovoked sneak attack by a major world power on a virtually defenseless country. But the decision makers never questioned the morality of their plan. They seemed to lose their principles in the group's desire to bravely end Castro's regime. Although the means used to defeat the spread of communism may have been considered questionable, the group felt that the ends certainly justified them; the cause of democracy was offered as justification enough for the planned attack. In this regard the advisory committee was similar to many other U.S. administrative groups that suffered from groupthink. Phillip Tetlock, after reviewing the public statements of politicians who had served on committees that made poor decisions, found that the faulty decision makers tended to make relatively more positive statements about their own country and causes (Tetlock, 1979).

Biased perceptions of the out-group.   The members of the advisory committee shared an inaccurate and negative opinion of Castro and his political ideology, and this opinion often found expression during the group discussions. Castro was depicted as a weak leader, an evil communist, and a man too stupid to realize that his country was about to be attacked. His ability to maintain an air force was discredited, as was his control over his troops and the citizenry. The group participants' underestimation of their enemy was so pronounced that they sent a force of 1400 men to fight a force of 200,000 and expected an easy success. The group wanted to believe that Castro was an ineffectual leader and military officer, but this oversimplified picture of the dictator turned out to be merely wishful thinking.

Although Tetlock found little evidence of this devaluation of the out-group in his work, a study of one groupthink crisis, the decision to escalate the Vietnam war, found a consistent theme in American justifications for U.S. intervention. In many of President Lyndon B. Johnson's speeches on the subject he depicted the North Vietnamese as "savages" who were driven by an irrational desire to subjugate others by military force (Ivie, 1980).

Defective decision-making strategies.   The decisions made in groupthink situations can be described in many different ways, but none of them is complimentary. Words like *fiasco, blunder, failure, error,* and *debacle* are fair descriptors, for groupthink leads to decisions that are so inadequate that they seem to ask disaster to strike.

Janis notes that these fiascoes are a logical outgrowth of the poor decision-making strategies so symptomatic of groupthink. In Kennedy's advisory group, for example, discussion focused on two extreme alternatives—either endorse the Bay of Pigs invasion plan or abandon

Cuba to communism—while ignoring all other potential alternatives. In addition, the group lost sight of its overall objectives as it was caught up in the minor details of the invasion plan, and it failed to develop contingency plans. Lastly, the group also actively avoided any information that pointed to limitations in its plans while seeking out facts and opinions that butressed its initial preferences. The group members didn't make a few small errors. They committed dozens of blunders.

Causes of Groupthink

Did these conformity pressures, illusions, misperceptions, and faulty decision-making strategies cause the group's error? Janis suggests that these faulty processes undoubtedly contributed to the faulty judgments (Janis, 1989), but he continues to feel that they were *symptoms* of the problem rather than actual *causes*. The causes of groupthink, which are considered below, include cohesiveness, the isolation of the group, the style of the leader, and the stress on the group to reach a good decision (Janis, 1972, 1979; Janis & Mann, 1977).

Cohesiveness.   The members of the Bay of Pigs advisory committee probably felt that they were fortunate to belong to a group that boasted such high morale and esprit de corps. Problems could be handled without too much internal bickering, personality clashes were rare, the atmosphere of each meeting was congenial, and replacements were never needed, because no one ever left the group. However, these benefits of cohesiveness did not offset one fatal consequence of a closely knit group: group pressures so strong that critical thinking degenerated into groupthink.

Of the many factors that contribute to the rise of groupthink, Janis emphasizes cohesiveness above all others. He admits that cohesive groups are not necessarily doomed to be victims of groupthink, but he points out that a "high degree of *group cohesiveness* is conducive to a high frequency of *symptoms of groupthink*, which, in turn, are conducive to a high frequency of defects in decision-making" (Janis, 1972, p. 199). Cohesiveness, when it reaches high levels, limits the amount of dissent in the group to the point that internal disagreements—so necessary for good decision making—disappear. In fact, evidence indicates that when someone does manage to disagree with the rest of the members of a group, he or she is likely to be ostracized when the group is high in cohesiveness rather than low (Cartwright, 1968; Schachter, 1951). Certainly, noncohesive groups can also make terrible decisions—"especially if the members are engaging in internal warfare"—but they cannot experience groupthink (Janis, 1982, p. 176). Only in a cohesive group do the members refrain from speaking out against decisions, avoid arguing with others, and strive to maintain friendly, cordial relations at all costs.

Measures of cohesiveness were, of course, never collected for the advisory committee. Archival evidence, however, suggests that cohesiveness was high in the group. First, the majority of the men on the committee were close personal friends and, at minimum, confessed to a profound respect for one another. Second, later comments and memoirs are replete with laudatory evaluations of the group, suggesting that attitudes toward the group were exceptionally positive. Third, identification with and commitment to the group and its goals were quite high, for all the members were proud to proclaim their membership in such an elite body. The magnitude of this identification is suggested by the frequent use of *we* and *us* in the following remark made by Robert Kennedy as he described the group (quoted in Guthman, 1971, p. 88; italics added):

> It seemed that with John Kennedy leading *us* and with all the talent he had assembled, nothing could stop *us*. *We* believed that if *we* faced up to the nation's problems and applied bold, new ideas with common sense and hard work, *we* would overcome whatever challenged *us*.

Lastly, the group retained all its members for the duration of the decision-making process, testimony to the strength of the forces working to keep members from leaving the group.

Isolation. The advisory committee carried out its discussion in secret under the belief that the fewer people who knew of the plan, the better. The committee did not need to report its conclusions to anyone, including Congress, so there was no final review of the decision before putting the plan into action. This isolation also meant that very few outsiders ever came into the group to participate in the discussion, and thus the committee was virtually insulated from criticisms. Therefore, although many experts on military questions and Cuban affairs were available and, if contacted, could have warned the group about the limitations of the plan, the committee closed itself off from these valuable resources.

Leadership. President Kennedy's *style of leadership* in conducting the problem-solving sessions is another aspect of the group situation that contributed to groupthink. By tradition, the advisory-committee meetings, like cabinet meetings, were very formal affairs that followed a rigid protocol. The president could completely control the group discussion by raising only certain questions and asking for input from particular conferees. Open, free-wheeling discussion was possible only at the suggestion of the president, but since he tended to follow traditions while also suppressing any dissenting opinions, the group really never got down to the essential issues. His tendency to make his opinion clear at the outset of each meeting also stultified discussion. Also his procedures for requiring a voice vote by individuals without prior group discussion paralleled quite closely the methods used by Asch (1952) to heighten conformity pressures in discussion groups.

Decisional stress. Janis notes that our tendency to make use of coping mechanisms such as procrastination or bolstering actually becomes stronger when we must make major decisions. The insecurity of each individual can be minimized if the group quickly chooses a plan of action, with little argument or dissension. Then, through collective discussion, the group members can rationalize their choice by exaggerating the positive consequences, minimizing the possibility of negative outcomes, and concentrating on minor details while overlooking larger issues. Naturally, these stress-reduction tactics increase the likelihood of groupthink (Callaway, Marriott, & Esser, 1985). (See Focus 10-3.)

• •
FOCUS 10-3: DECISION MAKING IN THE COCKPIT

In 1982 a B-737 crashed into the 14th Street Bridge while taking off from National Airport in Washington, D.C. The crash was traced to a mechanical problem: the pilot, misled by an ice-jammed thrust indicator, had set the engine thrust too low to achieve a safe takeoff. But faulty group decision-making processes also contributed to the crash. During the takeoff the copilot noticed that the plane was not reacting properly, and he repeatedly advised the captain. The copilot's warnings, however, were so subtle that the captain ignored them (Foushee, 1984; Foushee & Helmreich, 1988).

Flying a large aircraft is a complex task, but crews generally perform this task with remarkable skill. During emergencies, however, they operate under the conditions that Janis argues can lead to poor decision making. First, the crew is isolated in the cockpit, receiving information from dispatchers and controllers but relying mostly on instrument information and crew members' judgments. In some cases crashes and near misses have occurred because the group did not seek additional information or ignored warnings from controllers. Second, the chain of command in aircraft crews is so entrenched that crew members are often reluctant to correct a captain's errors, and captains often ignore warnings from the crew. The crash of a DC-8 in 1978 was caused by this problem. The crew, while checking a malfunctioning instrument, ignored their dangerously low level of fuel. The flight engineer reported the low fuel to the captain, but he dismissed the warning. The National Transportation Safety Board (NTSB), after investigating this crash, concluded that "the stature of a captain and his management style may exert subtle pressure on his crew to conform to his way of thinking. It may hinder interaction and adequate monitoring and force another crewmember to yield his right to express an opinion" (1979, p. 27).

Third, when significant problems occur during the flight, the group may overlook alternatives in seeking a solution. During emergencies the captain often takes complete manual control of the aircraft, but flying the aircraft is so demanding that it draws his or her attention away from the initial problem. As a result, pilots tend to "develop 'tunnel-vision' and often lock-in on the most obvious hypotheses which are often at least partially incorrect" (Foushee, 1986, p. 3).

The problem of poor crew performance is a significant one. Estimates suggest that between 65% and 80% of all airplane transport crashes (both passenger and freight) that occurred in the United States in the last ten years resulted from faulty group decision-making processes rather than mechanical problems (Cooper, White, & Lauber, 1979). To deal with this problem, many airlines are beginning to shift their focus from individual proficiency to group proficiency. In some cases crews are trained using flight simulators, and their reaction to planned emergencies are studied and corrected. Also, steps are being taken to change the top-down communication pattern of the cockpit so that crew members have more input during the flight. By addressing group processes rather than individual skills, these training programs should improve problem solving and increase safety.

• •

Predicting the Emergence of Groupthink

Janis maintains that you need not worry too much if only one of these causes of groupthink is operating in your group. For example, if your group is highly cohesive but its meetings are held in public, are run by an impartial leader, and have low decisional stress, groupthink probably won't occur. If two or more of these factors are present, however, the likelihood of groupthink becomes much greater.

This model of groupthink has been supported in a number of case studies and archival analyses (Hensley & Griffin, 1986; Herek, Janis, & Huth, 1987; Janis, 1985; Manz & Sims, 1982; Tetlock, 1979). Janis and his colleagues, for example, identified 19 international crises that were initiated or resolved by top-level U.S. leaders. Next, using an elaborate content-analysis system, they calculated the number of symptoms evidenced by each group. As predicted, the higher the number of symptoms, the more unfavorable the outcome of the group's deliberations ($r = .62$) (Herek et al., 1987).

Experimental evidence, although limited, also supports the model (Callaway & Esser, 1984; Flowers, 1977; Moorhead, 1982; Moorhead & Montanari, 1986; Leana, 1985). In one study John A. Courtright (1978) manipulated both cohesiveness in the group and the degree to which the group's discussion was constrained. Several steps were taken to increase cohesiveness, including giving the members more time to interact with one another before considering the issue and telling them that they would be extremely compatible. To ensure low cohesion in the other groups, the members were told that the attempt to bring together compatible people had failed and that there was no reason to expect group members to like one another very much. To manipulate the second potential cause of groupthink—constraints imposed on the group's discussion—Courtright created three conditions:

1. a *freeing condition*, in which group members were told that sufficient time was available to fully discuss the issue and that "the best solutions usually come from vigorous competition among a large number of incompatible ideas" (p. 233)
2. a *limiting condition*, in which the instructions suggested that little time was left for discussion and that "the best solutions usually come when one good idea cooperatively evolves from a small number of initial ideas" (p. 233)
3. a *no-instructions condition* that served as a control group

The results of the study provided partial support for Janis's model. Courtright predicted that the groups in the freeing condition would formulate better decisions when they were cohesive but that this relationship would reverse when discussion was limited by time and cooperation restraints. In this condition cohesive group members would tend to agree more with one another, disagree less with one another, and formulate poorer decisions. These predictions did not hold when Courtright examined the number of solutions offered or the degree of agreement within the group, but the predicted pattern did emerge when he analyzed the frequency of disagreement among members and the quality of the solutions (see Figure 10-4).

Other studies, however, suggest that the leader's style may play a larger role in creating groupthink than Janis initially proposed (Moorhead, 1982). In one investigation that used a role-playing technique, the subjects were told to make a controversial personnel decision (Flowers, 1977). To manipulate leadership style, the leader of the group had been previously trained to adopt either an *open* style or a *closed* style of leadership. Open leaders didn't describe their solution to the problem until the other members had made their recommendations, they encouraged open discussion, and at two times during the meeting they said: "The most important thing, I think, is that we air all possible viewpoints in order to reach a wise decision. Now, what does each of you think should be done?" (Flowers, 1977, p. 891). In contrast, the closed leaders described their solution before yielding the floor to the other participants, limited discussion whenever possible, and at two times during the meeting said: "The most important thing, I think, is that we all agree on our decision. Now, what I think should be done is . . . " The cohesiveness of the groups was also manipulated by examining two types of teams, those composed of strangers and those composed of friends.

Content analysis of tape recordings of the problem-solving sessions focused on two primary dependent variables, the number of solutions proposed during the 30- to 45-minute period and the number of facts that emerged during the group discussion. As expected, the leader's behavior

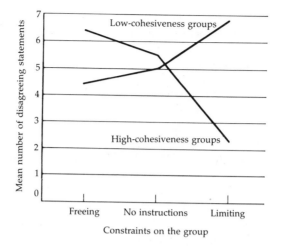

FIGURE 10-4. Mean number of disagreeing statements in the six experimental conditions of the Courtright experiment. As predicted, disagreement among cohesive group members tended to be greatest in the freeing condition, less in the no-instruction condition, and least in the limiting condition—the very group that, theoretically, should have suffered from groupthink. Furthermore, these relationships tended to reverse in the low-cohesiveness condition, although the overall differences were not as pronounced.
Source: Courtright, 1978.

produced obvious effects during the discussion. The number of solutions proposed was higher in the open-leader condition than in the closed-leader condition (the respective means were 6.5 and 5.1), and prior to the reaching of a solution more facts were mentioned in the open-leadership group than in the closed-leadership group (the means were 15.5 and 8.2). Little support was found for Janis's cohesiveness prediction (see also Leana, 1985).

These findings provide some support for the adequacy of Janis's prediction, but several qualifications apply. First, the usual limitations of generalizing from laboratory studies of college students to policy-making groups are particularly relevant in this instance. Second, given the inconsistent effects of cohesiveness on the development of groupthink, more research is needed before any firm conclusions can be drawn. Third, evidence also suggests that although symptoms and causes may be conceptually distinct, at a group-process level both are involved in the production of groupthink (Moorhead & Montanari, 1986).

Preventing Groupthink

For 13 days in October 1962 the world swayed on the brink of nuclear holocaust. The Soviet Union, perhaps at the request of a Cuban government frightened by the misguided Bay of Pigs invasion, was rapidly constructing a missile base in Cuba. To resolve this crisis President Kennedy once again called together his top advisers, to form the Executive Committee of the National Security Council. Though it was somewhat larger than the Bay of Pigs advisory group, many of the same individuals attended its meetings. For five days these men considered the issues, debated possible solutions, and disagreed over strategies. They finally recommended a plan that involved a naval blockade of all Cuban ports. Although the Soviet Union denounced the naval quarantine as piracy, ships believed to be carrying nuclear armaments were successfully directed away from Cuba. Eventually, the Cuban missile crisis was resolved, as the Russians agreed to dismantle the launching sites and the Americans promised never to invade Cuba.

The parallels between the Bay of Pigs invasion and the resolution of the Cuban missile crisis are obvious. To a large extent both decisions were formulated by the same people, meeting in the same room, guided by the same leader, and working equally hard under similar time pressures. Both crises occurred in the same area of the world, involved the same foreign powers, and could have led to equally serious consequences. Yet despite these similarities, the Executive Committee worked with admirable precision and effectiveness. Members thoroughly analyzed a wide range of alternative courses of action, deliberately considered and then reconsidered the potential effects of their actions, consulted experts, and made detailed contingency plans in case the blockade failed to stop the Russians. Clearly, this group, in contrast to its unfortunate predecessor, avoided the pitfall of groupthink. Janis (1972) feels that three sets of factors led to this beneficial about-face: limiting a premature seeking of concurrence, correcting group members' misperceptions, and utilizing effective decision techniques.

Limiting premature seeking of concurrence.   As noted earlier in this chapter, Kennedy did not take his Bay of Pigs failure lightly. In the months following the defeat, he explored and corrected the causes of his group's poor decision. As a result his new group was prepared to deal with the Cuban missile crisis. No norm of conformity was given the slightest opportunity to develop, and each person in the group was able to express doubts and worries openly. Rules of discussion were suspended, agendas were avoided, and new ideas were welcomed. Although pressures to conform surfaced from time to time during the discussion, the members felt so comfortable in their roles of skeptical critical thinkers that they were able to resist the temptation to go along with the consensus. In fact, the group never did reach 100% agreement on the decision to turn back Soviet ships.

The atmosphere of open inquiry can be credited to changes designed and implemented by Kennedy. Essentially, he dropped his closed style of leadership to become an open leader as he (1) carefully refused to state his personal beliefs at the beginning of the session, instead waiting until others had let their views be known; (2) required a full, unbiased discussion of the pros and cons of each possible course of action; (3) convinced his subordinates that he would welcome healthy criticism and condemn "yea-saying" (see Focus 10-4); and (4) arranged for the group to meet without him on several occasions. Although some observers interpreted his refusal to rule the meetings with an authoritarian hand as a sign of weakness, the results more than justified Kennedy's open leadership approach.

· ·
FOCUS 10-4: USING A DEVIL'S ADVOCATE

The term *devil's advocate* originated centuries ago during investigations of proposals for sainthood in the Roman Catholic Church. Because such decisions were critically important to the church and its members, the deciding panel felt that explicit, formalized procedures should be used to guarantee examination of both supporting and detracting evidence. Hence, the position of devil's advocate was developed to ensure that someone would explore and present any information that might lead to the disqualification of the candidate for sainthood. The technique is now utilized by many legal, corporate, academic, and parliamentary decision-making bodies with positive results (Herbert & Estes, 1977).

During the Executive Committee discussions and in private meetings, Kennedy encouraged his brother Robert to play the role of the devil's advocate by trying to find fault with any argument that might be offered as valid. Accordingly, the younger Kennedy continually raised questions about undiscussed consequences and potentially ruinous oversights, a practice that did not earn him popularity in the group. However, the undeniable benefits of Robert Kennedy's argumentativeness—forcing discussion of both sides of any proposal while motivating members to present their ideas more carefully—outweighed the harmful effects of increased interpersonal conflict. Furthermore, Janis suggests that the stresses created by having to disagree continually with one's coparticipants can be reduced if (1) the devil's advocate is careful to present his or her arguments in a low-key, nonthreatening manner; (2) the leader publicly and unambiguously assigns the role; and (3) the role is shifted from one group member to another.

· ·

To further break down pressures to conform unthinkingly to the majority opinion, Kennedy arranged for the members to meet separately in two subgroups. The committee members had practiced this approach on other policy-issue decisions, and they were satisfied that it yielded many benefits: arbitrary agreement with the views of the other subgroup was impossible, the lower level staff members felt more at ease expressing their viewpoints in the smaller meetings, and the presence of two coalitions in the subsequent combined meetings virtually guaranteed a spirited debate. Generalizing this approach to other situations, Janis and his colleague Daniel D. Wheeler suggest that organizations that rely on groups for decision making should use this duplicating process:

> If groupthink takes over in one of the groups, the contrasting recommendation from the other group might serve as a caution. A new or combined group can explore the reasons for the difference and make a single recommendation. If the two groups agree in their findings, it is less likely that either group has overlooked or ignored any of the important considerations. The decision can be implemented with more confidence than if only a single group had worked on it [Wheeler & Janis, 1980, p. 207].

Correcting misperceptions and errors.   Janis's image of people as reluctant decision makers does not quite match the Executive Committee members. The participants fully realized that *some* course of action had to be taken, and they resigned themselves to their difficult task. Their decisional conflict was fanned by doubts and worries over questions that they could not answer, and at times they must have been tempted to ease their discomfort by overestimating American superiority, belittling the Russians, and denying the magnitude of the dangers. Yet through vigilant information processing they succeeded in avoiding these misperceptions, illusions, and errors.

No trace of the air of confidence and superiority that permeated the planning sessions of the Bay of Pigs invasion was in evidence during the Executive Committee meetings. The men knew that they, and their decision, were imperfect and that wishful thinking would not improve the situation. President Kennedy repeatedly told the group that there was no room for error, miscalculation, or oversight in their plans, and at every meeting the members openly admitted the tremendous risks and dangers involved in taking coercive steps against the Russians. Each solution was assumed to be flawed, and even when the blockade had been painstakingly arranged, the members developed contingency plans in case it failed.

Members also admitted their personal inadequacies and ignorance and, therefore, willingly consulted experts who were not members of the group. No group member's statements were taken as fact until independently verified, and the ideas of younger, low-level staff members were solicited at each discussion. Participants also discussed the group's activities with their own staffs and entered each meeting armed with the misgivings and criticisms of these unbiased outsiders.

Lastly, instead of assuming that the Russians' actions justified any response (including full-scale invasion of Cuba), the committee discussed the ethics of the situation and the proposed solutions. For example, although some members felt that the Russians had left themselves open to any violent response the Americans deemed appropriate, the majority argued that a final course of action had to be consistent with "America's humanitarian heritage and ideals" (Janis, 1972, p. 157). Illusions of morality and invulnerability were successfully minimized along with biased perceptions of the out-group.

Using effective decision techniques. The Executive Committee is not an example of an effective decision-making body simply because its solution to the missile crisis worked. Rather, just as the decision methods used by the Bay of Pigs advisory committee ensured their failure, the Executive Committee's use of effective, time-proven decision-making techniques increased its chances of success. For example, an early push to agree on a military intervention as the best solution was quickly rejected by the majority of the members, who instead insisted that other alternatives be explored. This demand led to an expanded search for alternatives, and soon a list that ran from a "hands-off" policy to full military involvement was developed. The ten most seriously discussed alternatives were these:

1. doing nothing
2. exerting pressure on the Soviet Union through the United Nations
3. arranging a summit meeting between the two nations' leaders
4. secretly negotiating with Castro
5. initiating a low-level naval action involving a blockade of Cuban ports
6. bombarding the sites with small pellets, rendering the missiles inoperable
7. launching an air strike against the sites with advance warning to reduce loss of life
8. launching an air strike without advance warning
9. carrying out a series of air attacks against all Cuban military installations
10. invading Cuba

Once this listing of alternatives was complete, the men focused on each course of action before moving on to the next. They considered the pros and cons, fleshed out unanticipated drawbacks, and estimated the likelihood of success. During this process, outside experts were consulted to give the members a better handle on the problem, and contingency plans were briefly explored. Even those alternatives that had initially been rejected (for example, doing nothing) were resurrected and discussed, and the group invested considerable effort in trying to find any overlooked detail. When a consensus on the blockade plan finally developed, the group went back over this alternative, reconsidered its problematic aspects, and meticulously reviewed the steps required to implement it. Messages were sent to the Russians, military strategies were worked out to prevent any slip-ups that would escalate the conflict, and a graded series of actions was developed to be undertaken should the blockade fail. Allies were contacted and told of the U.S. intentions, the legal basis of the intervention was established by arranging for a hemisphere blockade sanctioned by the Organization of American States, and African countries with airports that could have been used by Russia to circumvent the naval blockade were warned not to cooperate. To quote Robert Kennedy, "Nothing, whether a weighty matter or a small detail, was overlooked" (1969, p. 60).

GROUP POLARIZATION

The Bay of Pigs plan that the newly elected President Kennedy was asked to approve was a risky one; success depended on certain key factors falling into place, but a victory would earn the United States many rewards. Kennedy faced a host of complicated questions: Are the risks too great? Do the positive consequences of a successful attack justify the risks involved? Should steps be taken to reduce the risks and thereby ensure victory? Naturally, he could have answered these questions without consulting anyone, but he decided instead to form a group to explore these issues. Although historians cannot say why he relied on a group, he may have acted on the intuitively appealing notion that groups have a moderating impact on individuals. He may have assumed that a group, if faced with a choice between a risky alternative (such as "Invade Cuba") and a more moderate alternative (such as "Use diplomatic means to influence Cuba"), would prefer the moderate route. Unfortunately for Kennedy, for his advisers, and for the members of the attack force, groups' decisions actually tend to be more extreme than individuals' decisions. Groups don't urge restraint; instead, they *polarize* opinions.

The Risky-Shift Phenomenon

At about the time that Kennedy's advisory committee was grappling with the problems inherent in the invasion plan, group dynamicists were initiating studies of the effects of group discussion on decision making. Although several of these investigations suggested that groups do indeed offer more conservative solutions than individuals (for example, Atthowe, 1961; Hunt & Rowe, 1960), in others a surprising shift in the direction of greater riskiness was found (Stoner, 1961; Wallach, Kogan, & Bem, 1962). For example, in one of the most frequently cited projects male and female college students responded to 12 story problems individually and in small groups (Wallach et al., 1962). All the problems used in the investigation followed the same basic form, each one describing a hypothetical situation in which an individual had to choose between one of two possible courses of action. Unfortunately for the decision maker, the alternative that offered the more desirable rewards was also the course of action least likely to be carried out successfully. The question put to the subject after reading each situation was "What would the probability of success have to be before you would advise the character in the story to choose the riskier course of action?" Focus 10-5 presents the first story item from this Choice-Dilemmas Questionnaire along with the format used to measure subjects' responses (Wallach et al., 1962).

. . . .
FOCUS 10-5: THE CHOICE-DILEMMAS QUESTIONNAIRE

Mr. A, an electrical engineer, who is married and has one child, has been working for a large electronics corporation since graduating from college five years ago. He is assured of a lifetime job with a modest, though adequate, salary and liberal pension benefits upon retirement. On the other hand, it is very unlikely that his salary will increase much before he retires. While attending a convention, Mr. A is offered a job with a small, newly founded company which has a highly uncertain future. The new job would pay more to start and would offer the possibility of a share in the ownership if the company survived the competition of the larger firms.

Imagine that you are advising Mr. A. Listed below are several probabilities or odds of the new company proving financially sound. Please check the *lowest* probability that you would consider acceptable to make it worthwhile for Mr. A to take the new job.

—— 1. The chances are 1 in 10 that the company will prove financially sound.
—— 2. The chances are 3 in 10 that the company will prove financially sound.
—— 3. The chances are 5 in 10 that the company will prove financially sound.
—— 4. The chances are 7 in 10 that the company will prove financially sound.
—— 5. The chances are 9 in 10 that the company will prove financially sound.
—— 6. Place a check here if you think Mr. A should not take the new job no matter what the probabilities.

. . . .

To test for changes following group discussion, the investigators followed a fairly simple procedure. First, the subjects filled out and turned in their answers to the choice dilemmas. Second, they discussed the items in five- or six-person groups in an attempt to reach a unanimous decision concerning the degree of tolerable risk. Third, the group members were instructed to separate and once more answer the questions to determine if the change induced by the group setting had any carryover effects. In addition, (1) a control condition was included in which the subjects merely filled out the questionnaire twice without an intervening discussion, and (2) some subjects were contacted several weeks after the session and asked to complete the questionnaire again.

Table 10-1 contains the results of the investigation. In adding together choices from all 12 items, the investigators found that the mean of prediscussion individual decisions was 66.9 for males and 65.6 for females. The

TABLE 10-1. Shifts toward risk following group discussion.

Comparison	Males	Females
Individual pretest versus group decision	−9.4[a]	−9.4
Individual pretest versus individual posttest	−10.4	−8.2
Individual pretest versus individual delayed posttest	−12.3	—

[a] Negative scores indicate a shift in the direction of greater risk.

(Source: Wallach, Kogan, and Bem, 1962)

mean of the group's consensual decision, however, was 57.5 for males and 56.2 for females, a shift of 9.4 points in the direction of greater risk. As Table 10-1 reveals, this shift also occurred when individual judgments were collected after the group discussion and when the individual post-discussion measures were delayed two to six weeks (the delayed posttests were collected from male subjects only). Lastly, participants in the no-group-discussion control condition shifted very little.

The finding that groups seem to make riskier decisions than individuals was promptly dubbed the **risky-shift phenomenon,** and in the decade from 1960 to 1970 hundreds of studies were conducted in an attempt to better understand this rara avis. These studies demonstrated that the risky shift was not limited to the types of decisions required on the Choice-Dilemmas Questionnaire but that group discussion seemed to in-tensify all sorts of attitudes, beliefs, values, judgments, and perceptions (Myers, 1982). The shift was reliably demonstrated in many countries around the world (for example, Canada, the United States, England, France, Germany, and New Zealand) and with many kinds of group par-ticipants (Pruitt, 1971a). Although commentators sometimes wondered about the generality and significance of the phenomenon (Smith, 1972), laboratory findings were eventually bolstered by field studies (Lamm & Myers, 1978).

Polarizing Effects of Discussion

During this research period, however, some investigators hinted at the possibility of the directly opposite process: a *cautious shift*. For example, when the early risky-shift researchers examined the amount of postdis-cussion change revealed on each item of the Choice-Dilemmas Question-naire, they frequently found that group members consistently advocated a less risky course of action than did individuals on one particular item (Wallach et al., 1962). Intrigued by this anomalous finding, subsequent re-searchers wrote additional choice dilemmas, and they too, occasionally found evidence of a cautious shift. Then in 1969 researchers reported ev-idence of individuals moving in *both* directions after a group discussion, suggesting that both cautious and risky shifts were possible (Doise, 1969; Moscovici & Zavalloni, 1969).

Somewhat belatedly, group dynamicists realized that risky shifts after group discussions were a part of a more general process. When people discuss issues in groups, there is a tendency for them to decide on a more extreme course of action than would be suggested by the average of their individual judgments, but the direction of this shift depends on what was initially the dominant point of view. After examining dozens of risky-shift studies in this light, David G. Myers and Helmut Lamm summarized the many findings in terms of the **group-polarization hypothesis:** the "average postgroup response will tend to be more extreme in the same direction as the average of the pregroup responses" (Myers & Lamm, 1976, p. 603; see also Lamm & Myers, 1978).

This group-polarization hypothesis can be applied to the item from the Choice-Dilemmas Questionnaire shown in Focus 10-5. Imagine two groups containing four individuals whose opinions vary in terms of preference for risk. As Figure 10-5 indicates, when the average choice of the group members before discussion is closer to the risky pole of the continuum than to the cautious pole (as would be the case in a group composed of Persons A, B, C, and D), a risky shift will occur. If, in contrast, the group is composed of Persons C, D, E, and F, a cautious shift will take place, because the pregroup mean of 6.5 falls closer to the cautious pole. This example is, of course, something of an oversimplification, because the shift depends on distance from the psychological rather than the mathematical midpoint of the scale. As Myers and Lamm (1976) note, on choice dilemmas an initial pregroup mean of 6 or smaller is usually sufficient to produce a risky shift, whereas a mean of 7 or greater is necessary to produce a cautious shift. If the pregroup mean falls between 6 and 7, shifting is unlikely.

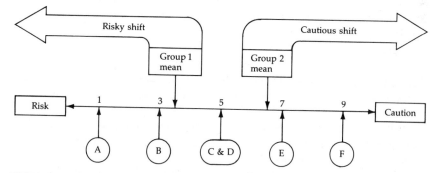

FIGURE 10-5. Group polarization processes. Imagine that Group 1 includes Person A (who chose 1), Person B (who chose 3), and Persons C and D (who both chose 5); the average of pregroup choices would be (1 + 3 + 5 + 5)/4, or 3.5. Because this mean is less than 5, a risky shift would probably occur in Group 1. If, in contrast, Group 2 contained Persons C, D, E, and F, their pregroup average would be (5 + 5 + 7 + 9)/4 or 6.5. Because this mean is closer to the caution pole, a conservative shift would probably occur in the group.

What Causes Polarization?

Group dynamicists have been prolific in their attempts to explain the causes of risky shifts, cautious shifts, and polarization in groups. Briefly tracing the theoretical roots of current perspectives on the issue, we find that the earliest period of research (which focused almost exclusively on risky shifts) generated a number of explanations:

1. Diffusion-of-responsibility theory: Group members, feeling that they have less personal responsibility for the negative consequences of excessively risky decisions when the decision is a group effort, experience less anxiety over recommending a risky course of action.

2. Leadership theories: Shifts occur because high-risk takers tend to exercise more influence over the group members due to their greater persuasiveness, confidence, assertiveness, and involvement in the discussion.

3. Familiarization theory: As individuals discuss the problems with others, they become more familiar with the items; as familiarity increases, uncertainty decreases, creating a willingness to advocate more risky alternatives.

4. Value theories: Since taking risks and dares is a positively valued attribute in many cultures, participants prefer to think of themselves (and prefer to be seen by others) as willing to take a chance; when members discover that others in the group favor riskier alternatives, they change their original positions to agree with the riskiest group member.

Although most theorists came to endorse the "value" perspective (for example, Clark, 1971; Dion, Baron, & Miller, 1970; Myers & Lamm, 1975, 1976; Pruitt, 1971a, 1971b; Vinokur, 1971), two schools of thought later developed *within* this general approach. One approach, based on **social-comparison theory,** argues that group members are trying to accomplish two interrelated goals during discussions. First, they are attempting to evaluate the accuracy of their own position on the issue by comparing it with others. Second, they are trying to make a favorable impression within the group. When these two motives combine, the result is a tendency to describe one's own position in somewhat more extreme terms (Goethals & Zanna, 1979; Myers, 1978; Myers & Lamm, 1976; Sanders & Baron, 1977). **Persuasive-arguments theory,** in contrast, stresses the information obtained during discussion. If that discussion exposes the individual to persuasive arguments that favor position A, the person will shift in that direction. If the discussion generates more pro-B arguments, however, the individual will shift in that direction (Burnstein & Vinokur, 1973, 1977; Vinokur & Burnstein, 1974, 1978).

Both of these theories have been supported by researchers. For example, a number of studies have shown that polarization occurs when people have been exposed to others' positions but not to their arguments (Blascovich, Ginsburg, & Howe, 1975, 1976; Blascovich, Ginsburg, & Veach, 1975; Goethals & Zanna, 1979; Myers, 1978). These studies suggest that knowledge of group norms is sufficient to generate a shift. However, evidence also supports the persuasive-arguments theory. Studies indicate, for example, that the direction of polarization in a group depends on the preponderance of arguments for risk and caution possesed by individual members. If individuals can muster more arguments for risk, a risky shift occurs. If, in contrast, their discussion generates more arguments favoring caution, a cautious shift results (Burnstein & Vinokur, 1975; Kaplan & Miller, 1983; Vinokur & Burnstein, 1974, 1978).

The empirical success of these perspectives has prompted several theorists to suggest that the two processes combine to produce polarization (Isenberg, 1986; Kaplan & Miller, 1983). Social comparison theory, with its emphasis on self-presentational attempts to match or exceed the group norm, reflects the operation of normative influence in the group. Persuasive-arguments approaches, in contrast, emphasize informational influence processes (Kaplan & Miller, 1983). As noted in Chapter 6, normative and informational influence generally occur together, so it is likely that social comparison and persuasive argumentation also work together to create polarization.

Polarization and Groupthink

Although Janis does not emphasize polarization as a major antecedent of faulty group decision making, he clearly hints at this possibility when he writes that "members show interest in facts and opinions that support their initially preferred policy and take up time in their meetings to discuss them, but they tend to ignore facts and opinions that do not support their initially preferred policy" (1972, p. 10). In agreement with Janis's viewpoint Lamm and Myers (1978) cite a number of studies in which subjects, after engaging in group discussions, became more aggressive, made more extreme and unreasonable demands, became more competitive, and formulated more negative appraisals of out-group members. For example, in one particularly relevant study college students, army officers, and ROTC cadets made decisions about how the U.S. armed forces should best deal with an international conflict involving the United States and another world power. Each of the hypothetical problems centered on a potential military crisis, and the decision makers were asked to select one course of action from a list of six alternatives ranging from bilateral negotiation to the use of nuclear weapons. Consistent with the polarization hypothesis, the "dovish" college students shifted in the direction of less militaristic responses after group discussion, and the "hawkish" army officers advocated even more forceful tactics. The ROTC cadets, who began at an intermediate position on the six problems, shifted very little (Semmell, 1976).

SUMMARY

In office buildings executives hold conferences to solve problems of management and production; in courthouses juries weigh evidence to determine guilt and innocence; in schools teachers work together to plan the curriculum. In these and in thousands of other similar settings interdependent individuals make decisions through groups.

Although no two groups reach their decisions in precisely the same way, four stages appear consistently in many groups. During the *orientation* stage the group identifies the problem to be solved and plans the process to be used in reaching the decision. During the *discussion* stage the group engages in *collective induction*: it gathers information about the situation, identifies and weighs options, and tests its assumptions. To be effective at this stage, the group must engage in *vigilant information processing* of all important information rather than relying on protective strategies that limit discussion (for example, procrastination, bolstering, avoiding responsibility, and the like). During the decision period groups rely on an implicit or explicit *social-decision scheme* to combine individual preferences into a collective decision. Common schemes include delegating, averaging inputs, voting with various proportions needed for a decision, and consensus. Lastly, *implementation* must occur, and the impact of the decision must be assessed. *Quality circles* exemplify the cyclical nature of this decisional sequence.

Not all groups are effective decision makers. As Janis argues, fiascoes and blunders such as the decision to invade Cuba at the Bay of Pigs occur when group members strive for solidarity and cohesiveness to such an extent that any questions or topics that could lead to disputes are avoided. Janis calls this process *groupthink*. In describing the symptoms of groupthink, he emphasizes interpersonal pressure, self-censorship, mindguards, apparent unanimity, illusions of invulnerability, illusions of morality, biased perceptions of the out-group, and defective decision-making strategies. But when considering the causes of groupthink, he focuses on cohesiveness, isolation, leadership, and decisional stress. Turning to ways to prevent poor decision making, Janis notes that groups need not sacrifice cohesiveness in order to avoid the pitfall of groupthink. Rather, he recommends limiting premature seeking of concurrence, correcting misperceptions and errors, and improving the group's decisional methods.

Poor decisions can also be caused by the polarizing influence that groups sometimes have on their members. Although common sense suggests that groups are more cautious than individuals, early studies carried out using the *Choice-Dilemmas Questionnaire* found that group discussion generates a shift in the direction of the more risky alternative (the *risky-shift phenomenon*). When researchers later found evidence of cautious shifts as well as risky ones, they concluded that the responses of groups tend to be more extreme than individual members' responses (the *group-polari-*

zation hypothesis). Researchers are continuing their efforts to understand group polarization, but the available evidence suggests that the effect is caused by two processes: (1) the desire to evaluate one's own opinions by comparing them to others' (*social-comparison theory*) and (2) exposure to other members' pro-risk or pro-caution arguments (*persuasive-arguments theory*).

·11·

Environmental Processes

In 1965 a group of ten volunteers lived for 15 days in a 12-foot by 57-foot steel cylinder on the floor of the Pacific Ocean. As willing guinea pigs in a U.S. Navy project called Sealab II, they tested the limits of human endurance by carrying out salvage operations and tests of equipment 200 feet beneath the ocean's surface. Visibility was only 10 to 20 feet, and on warm days the water temperature reached only 50 degrees. When outside of the cylinder they performed difficult and time-consuming tasks while trying to avoid the attacks of scorpion fish. Inside the capsule they found relief from the cold and danger, but even there they had to cope with discomfort, noise, and the inevitable irritation produced when ten men live in a space about the size of a trailer.

Sealab was an attempt to circumvent some of the problems associated with working underwater. Even though specialized breathing equipment allows humans to venture beneath the surface for extended periods, divers must be careful to ascend to the surface slowly, or they can experience the bends: cramping, paralysis, or death caused by too-rapid decompression. The longer and deeper the dive, the more time needed for decompression. Sealab's solution to this problem was to provide divers with an underwater shelter where they could work, rest, and recuperate before going back out. Since the men didn't surface, they wouldn't need to spend time going through decompression. Sealab is diagrammed in Figure 11-1.

The Sealab project demonstrated that people can adapt to undersea living. The social psychologists Roland Radloff and Robert Helmreich (1968) kept detailed records of the men's daily interactions, and these records tell us much about the group's dynamics, including its structure, leadership, and performance. Time and again these analyses indicated that life in Sealab was determined in large part by the subtle and not-so-subtle interplay between the group and its unique environment. Like any other group the Sealab divers did not exist in a neutral, passive void but in a fluctuating environment that was sometimes too hot, too cold, too impersonal, too intimate, too big, too little, too noisy, too quiet, too restrictive, or too open but rarely just right. The steel cylinder was little more than a "hole in the ocean," but it was the group's *environment:* the setting for all the group's interactions (Radloff & Helmreich, 1968, p. 1).

Many disciplines, including environmental psychology, ethology, human ecology, demography, and ecological psychology, affirm the important impact of environmental variables on human behavior (Fisher, Bell, & Baum, 1984; Darley & Gilbert , 1985; Stokols & Altman, 1987). This chapter, in reviewing work that pertains to groups, begins by examining group

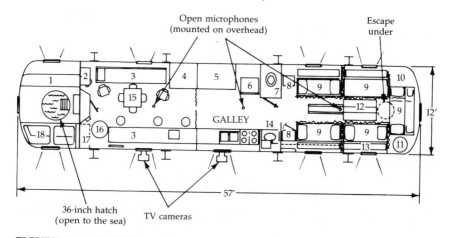

FIGURE 11-1. Sealab II, as viewed from above. Because the pressure inside the cylinder equaled the water pressure, the hatch remained open at all times. 1. Stowage area for swimming gear. 2. Television. 3. Lab bench. 4. Fan housing. 5. Electrical equipment. 6. Refrigerator. 7. Toilet. 8. Locker. 9. Berths. 10. Stowage area. 11. Carbon dioxide can. 12. Table. 13. Bench. 14. Lavatory. 15. Table and chairs. 16. Water heater. 17. Storage. 18. Shower.
Source: Radloff and Helmreich, 1968.

and individual territoriality. Next, the spatial behavior of groups and their members is examined, with a particular focus on personal space and seating patterns. The chapter closes with a brief look at several environmental stressors that can undermine members' satisfaction and group performance, including crowding, temperature, and noise.

TERRITORIALITY

When the men first swam through the Sealab's access hatch, they entered an empty cylinder filled with equipment and supplies. But within days this physical space was transformed into the group's territory. Each man chose a bunk and stowed his personal gear in his own locker. They explored the waters outside the habitat, and soon a trip outside seemed like a "walk across the street." They also put up signs reading "Welcome to the Tiltin' Hilton" (the floor of the cylinder was tilted). By the end of the 15 days the men felt at home in the capsule. As one diver explained: "You know that the Pacific Ocean is a mighty big place and you got a 36 inch hole that's home. There ain't no place you can go but there, 'cause you know you're gonna die if you go up" (Radloff & Helmreich, 1968, p. 1). They also reacted negatively when another team of divers came to take their place: "When those guys came down there for the third team, I thought they were intruding. And I hated to see them come in because I realized that was the end" (p. 113).

Like so many animals—birds, wolves, lions, seals, geese, and even seahorses—human beings are territorial: they develop proprietary orientations toward certain geographical locations and defend these areas against intrusion by others. A person's home, a preferred seat in a classroom, a clubhouse, a football field, and the Sealab are all **territories,** because they are specific areas that an individual or group claims, marks, and defends against intrusion by others.

When people establish a territory, they generally try to control who is permitted access. As Irwin Altman notes, however, the degree of control depends on the type of territory (see Table 11-1). Control is highest for **primary territories:** areas that are maintained and "used exclusively by individuals or groups . . . on a relatively permanent basis." (Altman, 1975, p. 112). Access is strictly controlled. Individuals maintain only a moderate amount of control over their **secondary territories.** These areas are not owned by the group members, but because they use the area regularly they come to consider it "theirs." The divers, for example, did not own Sealab, but they became so accustomed to it that it seemed like home to them. Similarly, college students often become very territorial about their seats in a class (Haber, 1980, 1982). Control over **public territories** is even more limited. Occupants can prevent intrusion while physically present, but they relinquish all claims when they leave. A bathroom stall or a spot on the beach can be claimed when occupied, but when the occupant leaves another person can step in and claim the space.

Many fascinating issues concerning territory have been raised in recent years as researchers question its instinctual basis (Ardry, 1970), its role in mating and reproduction (McBride, 1964), and the differences between territories established by nonhuman species and those of *Homo sapiens*

TABLE 11-1. Three types of territories.

Type of Territory	Examples	Degree of Control and Use by Occupants	Duration of User's Claim to Space
Primary	A family's home, a clubhouse, a bedroom, a dorm room, a study	*High:* Occupants control access and are very likely to actively defend this space.	*Long term:* Individuals maintain control over the space on a relatively permanent basis, ownership is often involved.
Secondary	A table in a bar, a seat in a classroom, a regularly used parking space, the sidewalk in front of your home	*Moderate:* Individuals who habitually use a space come to consider it "theirs." Reaction to intrusions is milder.	*Temporary but recurrent:* Others may use the space, but must vacate area if occupant requests.
Public	Elevator, beach, telephone booth, playground, park, bathroom stall, restaurant counter	*Low:* Although occupant may prevent intrusion while present, no expectation of future use exists.	*None:* The individual or group uses the space on only the most temporary basis and leaves behind no markers.

(Altman, 1975; Edney, 1975). However, group dynamicists' interest in territoriality is more circumscribed. First, both research and everyday experience tell us that groups, as social entities, often establish territories. Second, once in a group, the individual members tend to establish areas that they consider theirs, and the study of these areas provides clues to status hierarchies and privacy needs in groups. Both group territories and individual territories within groups are examined below. (Brown, 1987, thoroughly reviews much of the work on human territoriality.)

Group Territories

Territoriality is, in many cases, a group-level process. Instead of an individual claiming an area and defending it against other individuals, a group will lay claim to its turf and prevent other groups from using it. South American howler monkeys, for example, live together in bands of up to 20 individuals, and these groups forage within a fairly well-defined region. The bands themselves are cohesive and free of internal strife, but when another group of howlers is encountered during the day's wandering, a fight begins. Among howlers this territorial defense takes the form of a "shouting match" in which the members of the two bands simply howl at the opposing group until one band, usually the invader, retreats. Indeed, boundaries are rarely violated, because each morning and night the monkeys raise their voices in a communal, and far-carrying, howling session (Carpenter, 1958).

Human groups have also been known to territorialize areas. Classic sociological analyses of gangs, for example, often highlighted the tendency for young men to join forces in defense of a few city blocks that they consider to be their turf (Thrasher, 1927; Whyte, 1943; Yablonsky, 1962). Many gangs took their names from a street or park located at the very core of their claimed sphere of influence and sought to control areas around this base. In one study of gangs in Philadelphia, researchers found that part of this defense involved the strategic placement of graffiti on the buildings, signs, and sidewalks of the claimed area. Researchers found that the number of graffiti mentioning the local gang's name increased as one moved closer and closer to the home base, suggesting that the graffiti served as territorial markers warning intruders of the dangers of encroachment. This marking, however, was not entirely successful, for neighboring gangs would occasionally invade a rival's territory to spray-paint their own names over the territorial marker of the home gang or, at least, to append a choice obscenity. In fact, the frequency of graffiti attributable to outside groups provided an index of group power and prestige, for the more graffiti written by opposing gangs in one's territory, the weaker was the home gang (Ley & Cybriwsky, 1974b).

Human groups also maintain secondary and public territories. People at the beach, for example, generally stake out their claim by using beach towels, coolers, chairs, and other personal objects (Edney & Jordan-Edney, 1974). These temporary territories tend to be circular, and larger groups command bigger territories than smaller groups. Groups also create territories when they interact in public places, for in most cases nonmembers are reluctant to break through group boundaries. Although the area around a group of people may not be marked in any distinctive way, most people feel that it is rude to walk through a group of conversing people even if the group has little legitimate right to the space it occupies (Knowles, 1973; Knowles & Basset, 1976).

Group-level territoriality can lead to both negative and positive consequences. On the negative side observers have noted that serious conflicts can arise over territories. Altman (1975), for example, describes a neighborhood in New York City that contained both Jewish and Irish Catholic residents. These two groups maintained relatively exclusive territories except during certain sanctioned times. The location of the parochial and public schools necessitated travel across the other group's territory twice a day, so during these times the usual territorial rules were suspended. Altman notes, however, that even though passage through the rival territory was permissible during the specified times, the neighborhood children typically seemed ill at ease and circumspect as long as they were off their own turf. Another example of intergroup conflict is discussed in Focus 11-1.

· ·
FOCUS 11-1: STREET CORNERS AS TERRITORIES

The Norton Street corner boys were a group of young men who lived near a particular intersection in Boston. As noted in Chapter 2, the corner boys were extremely territorial, for much of their free time was spent hanging out on their corner. They also maintained and protected their turf from invasion. As Doc, their leader, explains:

> Once a couple of fellows in our gang tried to make a couple of girls on Main Street. The boy friends of these girls chased our fellows back to Norton Street. Then we got together and chased the boy friends back to where they came from. They turned around and got all Garden Street, Swift Street, and Main Street to go after us. . . . It usually started this way. Some kid would get beaten up by one of our boys. Then he would go back to his street and get his gang. They would come over to our street, and we would rally them. . . . I don't remember that we ever really lost a rally. Don't get the idea that we never ran away. We ran sometimes. We ran like hell. They would come over to our street and charge us. We might scatter, up roofs, down cellars, anywhere. We'd get ammunition there. . . . Then we would charge them—we had a good charge. They might break up, and then we would go back to our end of the street and wait for them to get together again. . . . It always ended up by us chasing them back to their street. We didn't rally them there. We never went looking for trouble. We only rallied on our own street, but we always won there [Whyte, 1943, p. 5].

Doc's allusion to his gang's remarkable success rate when fighting on the home ground is consistent with studies that have examined the superiority of the home team over the visiting team in sporting events (Edwards, 1979). Provided the pressure of performance is not overwhelming, the home team usually has a considerable edge over an opponent (Altman, 1975; Greer, 1983; see Chapter 9).

. . . .

On the positive side, studies of territoriality in prisons (Glaser, 1964), naval ships (Heffron, 1972; Roos, 1968), neighborhoods (Newman, 1972), and dormitories (Baum & Valins, 1977) suggest that people feel far more comfortable when their groups can territorialize their living areas. The Sealab divers, for example, became more satisfied with their work and interpersonal relations as their feelings of territoriality increased. Similarly, an experimental study of groups that territorialize the rooms in which they work with signs and decorations found that members felt that the rooms belonged to the group, considered the rooms more pleasant, reported less arousal, and assumed that the rooms could hold fewer people than unclaimed rooms (Edney & Uhlig, 1977).

Andrew Baum, Stuart Valins, and their associates report particularly striking findings concerning the benefits of group territories. They conducted a series of studies of college students who were randomly assigned to one of two types of dormitories. Many lived in the more traditionally designed corridor-style dorm, which featured 17 double-occupancy rooms per floor. A long corridor ran the entire length of the floor and provided the sole means of access to each room. Further, bathrooms and lounges were shared by all 34 residents of the floor and could be reached only by walking through public corridors. In contrast, the suite-style dorms featured two or three bedrooms clustered around a common lounge and bathroom. Access to these facilities was controlled by the residents of the adjoining bedrooms, and the outside corridor was used only when leaving the building or visiting another suite. Hence, the group living in a suite of rooms maintained a fairly well-defined territory, including a private space shared by two roommates as well as the bathroom and lounge controlled by the suitemates. The only territory available to the two-person groups living in the corridor-style dormitories was a small bedroom (Baum & Davis, 1980; Baum, Davis, & Valins, 1979; Baum, Harpin, & Valins, 1976; Baum & Valins, 1977).

Baum and Valins found that these two types of living conditions produced a range of consequences for the students. Although nearly equal numbers of individuals lived on any floor in the two types of designs, students in the corridor-style dormitories reported feeling more crowded, complained of their inability to control their social interactions with others, and emphasized their unfulfilled needs for privacy. Suite-style residents, on the other hand, developed deeper friendships with their suite mates, worked with one another more effectively, and even seemed more sociable when interacting with people outside the dormitory. Baum and Valins concluded that these differences stemmed from the corridor-style residents' inability to territorialize areas that they had to use repeatedly—the bathrooms, lounges, and hallways. Given the overall design of the dorm and the large number of residents per floor, the only defensible spaces available to corridor-style residents were the bedrooms. Although this limited territory enhanced the cohesiveness of the dyads sharing each room, the design did little to enhance interpersonal relationships among neighbors. The suite-style residents, however, could territorialize and control frequently used spaces with much greater success.

Territoriality within Groups

Territoriality also operates at the level of each individual in the group. Although the navy group, as a whole, claimed Sealab as home, each member of the team had his own bunk and his own locker within the steel cylinder. These individual territories are critical, for a number of reasons (Altman, 1975; Edney, 1976). First, they help group members maintain their *privacy* by providing them with a means of reducing contact with others. As Altman (1975) notes, depending on the situation, people prefer a certain amount of contact with others, and interaction in excess of this level produces feelings of crowding and invasion of privacy. The student in the classroom who is distracted by a jabbering neighbor, employees who are unable to concentrate on their jobs because of their noisy office mates' antics, and the wife who can't enjoy reading a novel because her husband is playing the stereo too loudly are all receiving excessive inputs from a fellow group member. If they moderated their accessibility by successfully establishing and regulating a territorial boundary, they could achieve a more satisfying balance between contact with others and solitude.

Territories also work as *organizers* of group members' relationships (Edney, 1976). Once we know the location of others' territories, we can find—or avoid—them with greater success. Furthermore, because we often grow to like people we interact with on a regular basis, people with contiguous territories tend to like one another (Moreland, 1987). Territories also work to regularize certain group activities—such as preparing and eating food, sleeping, or studying—by providing a place for these activities. Lastly, territories define what belongs to whom; without a sense of territory the concept of stealing would be difficult to define, because one could not be certain that the objects carried off actually belonged to someone else.

In addition to these privacy and organizing functions, territories also help individual group members define and express a sense of personal *identity*. If you enter someone's territory—an office, a dorm room, a bedroom, or a desk in a classroom—you are likely to find evidence of self-definition through marking (see Table 11-2). Office walls often display posters, diplomas, crude drawings produced by small children, pictures of loved ones, or little signs with trite slogans, even when company regulations specifically forbid such personalizing markings. Although such decorations may seem insignificant to the chance visitor, to the occupant

TABLE 11-2. Categories for wall decorations in dormitory rooms.

Category	Decorations
Entertainment or equipment	Bicycles, skis, radios, stereos or components, climbing gear, tennis racquets
Personal relations	Pictures of friends and family, flowers, snapshots of vacations, letters, drawings by siblings
Values	Religious or political posters, bumper stickers, ecology signs, flags, sorority signs
Abstract	Prints or posters of flowers, kittens, landscapes; art reproductions
Reference items	Schedules, syllabi, calendars, maps
Music or theater	Posters of ballet, rock, or musical groups; theater posters
Sports	Ski posters, pictures of athletes, motorcycle races, magazine covers, mountain-climbing or hiking posters
Idiosyncratic	Handmade items (macramé, wall hangings, paintings), plants, unique items (stolen road signs, bearskins)

(Source: Vinsel, Brown, Altman, & Foss, 1980)

of the space they have personal meaning and help turn a drab, barren environment into home.

In an investigation of this function of personal territories, a team of researchers at the University of Utah photographed the walls over the beds of students living in campus dormitories. As an incidental finding they discovered that most of these decorations fit into one of the categories listed in Table 11-2. More importantly, however, they also found that students who eventually dropped out of school seemed to mark their walls more extensively—particularly in the categories of personal relations and music and theater—than students who stayed in school. Although "stay-ins" used fewer markers, their decorations revealed greater diversity, cutting across several categories. Whereas a dropout's wall would feature dozens of skiing posters or high school memorabilia, the stay-in's decorations might include syllabi, posters, wall hangings, plants, and family photos. The researchers concluded that the wall decorations of dropouts "reflected less imagination or diversity of interests and an absence of commitment to the new university environment" (Hansen & Altman, 1976; Vinsel, Brown, Altman, & Foss, 1980, p. 1114).

Territory and dominance. Imagine the surprise of John W. Scott when he discovered the first known mating ground of the North American sage grouse (Scott, 1942). Assembling in groups of 400 to 500 members, the males would arrive well in advance of the hens to secure their individual territories within the selected clearing. All the cocks were able to secure small areas, but the hens considered only some of these territories to be valuable ones. So as the hens arrived, they crowded into the territory of the number one male (often labeled the alpha male) and patiently waited their turn. Hens ignored cocks who didn't secure and defend one of these coveted locations, so birds without territories were unable to mate.

Observers of human groups have likewise noted that the sizes of territories and their locations in the choice areas occupied by the group seem to match the dominance hierarchy of the group. As one informal observer has noted, in many large corporations the entire top floor of a company's headquarters is reserved for the offices of the upper echelon executives and can only be reached by a private elevator (Korda, 1975). Furthermore, within this executive area offices swell in size and become more lavishly decorated as the occupant's position in the company increases. Substantiating these informal observations, a study of a large chemical company headquarters, a university, and a government agency found a clear link between office size and status (Durand, 1977). The correlation between size of territory and position in the table of organization was .81 for the company, .79 for the agency, and .29 for the university.

The link between territory and dominance in small groups, in contrast, tends to be more variable. Several studies suggest that territory size increases as status increases (Esser, 1973; Sundstrom & Altman, 1974). Other studies, however, indicate that territory size seems to *decrease* as status in the group increases (Esser, 1968; Esser, Chamberlain, Chapple, & Kline, 1965). Eric Sundstrom and Altman (1974) suggest that these contradictory results occur because territorial boundaries are more fluid in small groups. In one study they conducted at a boys' rehabilitation center, they asked each subject to rank the other boys in terms of ability to influence others. In addition, an observer passed through the residence bedrooms, lounge, TV area, and bathrooms regularly and noted whenever (1) a boy limited his space usage to a few areas or (2) an area was used exclusively by a single boy. Lastly, the boys evaluated each area in order to determine which territories were more desirable than others.

Sundstrom and Altman found evidence of the territory/dominance relation, but the strength of this relation varied over time. During the first phase of the project the high-status boys maintained clear control over certain areas, whereas the low-status residents used many areas with equal frequency. In addition, the areas claimed by the high-status boys tended to be more desirable (the best seats in front of the television set), whereas the territory available to the low-status boys was unsatisfying (too close to the supervisor's desk). This period of tranquillity ended, however, when the supervisors removed two of the most dominant boys from the group, replacing them with two who would eventually rise to prominent positions. During this second phase of the study territorial behavior was disrupted as the boys competed with one another for both status and space, and the group was wracked by fighting, teasing, and other forms of misbehavior. By the end of the tenth week, however, the group had quieted back down, although certain highly dominant members continued to be disruptive. When formal observations were finally terminated, available evidence suggested that the group's territorial structures were once more beginning to stabilize.

These findings suggest that dominance/territory relations, like most group processes, are dynamic. In many small groups the higher status members possess larger and more aesthetically pleasing territories, but chaotic intermember relations or abrupt changes in membership can create discontinuities in territorial behavior. In addition, the hostility that surfaced in the group when spatial claims were disputed suggests that territories can work as tension reducers by clarifying the nature of the social situation and increasing opportunities for maintaining privacy.

Territory and stress.   During the International Geophysical Year (1957–1958) several countries sent small groups of military and civilian personnel to outposts in Antarctica. These groups were responsible for collecting various data concerning that largely unknown continent, but the violent weather forced the staff to remain indoors most of the time. Equipment malfunctioned regularly, radio contact was limited, and water rationing restricted bathing and laundering. As months went by and these conditions remained, interpersonal friction often surfaced, and the group members found themselves arguing over trivial issues. The members summarized their group malaise with the term *antarcticitis:* lethargy, low morale, grouchiness, and boredom brought on by their unique living conditions (Gunderson, 1973).

These Antarctic groups are by no means unique, for accounts of sailors confined in submarines (Weybrew, 1963), the divers living in Sealab (Helmreich, 1974; Radloff & Helmreich, 1968), astronauts in a spacecraft (Fraser, 1966), and work teams on large naval ships (Weiler & Castle, 1972) report evidence of stress produced by these environmental circumstances of isolation (Harrison & Connors, 1984). Although technological innovations make survival in even the most hostile environments possible, groups living in these space-age settings must learn to cope with problems of interpersonal adjustment. However, evidence also indicates that just as group-level territories help members cope with stressful events, so individual territories promote adaptation to the situation.

Some of the best evidence bearing on the effects of isolation on small-group dynamics comes from a series of laboratory studies conducted by Altman, William Haythorn, and their colleagues at the Naval Medical Research Institute in Bethesda, Maryland (see Altman, 1973, 1977, and Haythorn, 1973, for summaries). In one project pairs of men worked in a 12-foot by 12-foot room equipped with beds, a toilet cabinet, a table and chairs. They worked for several hours each day at various tasks but were left to amuse themselves with card games and reading the rest of the time. The men in the isolation condition never left their room during the ten days of the experiment; matched pairs in a control condition were permitted to eat their meals at the base mess and sleep in their regular barracks.

Territoriality was a powerful influence in these groups. The control groups seemed to establish few mutually exclusive areas of use, but the members of isolated groups quickly claimed particular bunks as theirs. Furthermore, this territorial behavior increased as the experiment progressed, with the isolated pairs extending their territories to include specific chairs and certain positions around the table. Not all of the groups, however, benefited by establishing territories. In some of the groups, territories structured the group dynamics and eased the stress of the situation, but in other dyads, these territories worked as barricades to social interaction and exacerbated the strain of isolation. Overall, withdrawal and time spent sleeping increased across the ten days of the study, whereas time spent in social interaction decreased. Other measures revealed worsened task performance and heightened interpersonal conflicts, anxiety, and emotionality for isolates who drew a "psychological and spatial 'cocoon' around themselves, gradually doing more things alone and in their own part of the room" (Altman & Haythorn, 1967, p. 174).

Altman and his colleagues followed up these provocative findings in a second experiment by manipulating three aspects of the group environment: (1) availability of privacy (half of the groups lived and worked in a single room, and the remaining groups had small adjoining rooms for sleeping, napping, reading, and so on); (2) expected duration of the isolation (pairs expected the study to last either 4 days or 20 days); and (3) amount of communication with the "outside world" (short music broadcasts, news programs, and taped questions and answers taken from the adviser column of *Playboy* magazine were played to some of the pairs). Although the study was to last for eight days for all the pairs, more than half terminated their participation early. Altman explains this high attrition rate by suggesting that the aborting groups tended to "misread the demands of the situation and did not undertake effective group formation processes necessary to cope with the situation" (1973, p. 249). On the first day of the study these men tended to keep to themselves, never bothering to work out any plans for coping with what would become a stressful situation. Then, as the study wore on, they reacted to increased stress by significantly strengthening their territorial behavior, laying increased claim to particular areas of the room. They also began spending more time in their beds, but they seemed simultaneously to be increasingly restless. Access to a private room and an expectation of prolonged isolation only added to the stress of the situation and created additional withdrawal, maladaptation, and eventual termination (Altman, Taylor, & Wheeler, 1971).

Groups that lasted the entire eight days seemed to use territoriality to their advantage in structuring their isolation. On the first day they defined their territories, set up schedules of activities, and agreed on their plan of action for getting through the study. Furthermore, the successful groups tended to relax territorial restraints in the later stages of the project and thereby displayed a greater degree of positive interaction. As described by Altman (1977, p. 310),

> The epitome of a successful group was one in which the members, on the first or second day, laid out an eating, exercise, and recreation schedule; constructed a deck of playing cards, a chess set, and a Monopoly game out of paper . . .

In essence, the men who adapted "decided how they would structure their lives over the expected lengthy period of isolation." Thus, although territorial behavior worked to the benefit of some of the groups, the last-minute attempts of some of the faltering groups to organize their spatial relations failed to improve their inadequate adaptation to the isolation.

SPATIAL BEHAVIOR

The anthropologist Edward T. Hall argues that much of our behavior is shaped by a "hidden dimension." Although this dimension rarely captures our attention, it indirectly structures much of our daily transactions (Hall, 1966). In Sealab, for example, this dimension determined where the divers sat during their meals. It placed limits on how many men could work on their equipment in the area around the diving hatch. This dimension even influenced the divers as they swam side by side in the murky water outside of the habitat. What is this hidden dimension? Space.

Personal Space

Imagine yourself standing in the center of a fairly large room, facing the doorway. As you watch, a stranger appears in the threshold and begins walking toward you with a slow, deliberate step. As the distance between you and the stranger diminishes and the stranger shows no sign of stopping, you begin to experience a vague sense of discomfort. Yet you feel you have no right to complain, at least until the stranger gets "too close." But what is "too close?" Ten feet? five feet? two feet? so close you can tell the color of the stranger's eyes? so close you can smell the stranger's breath, or hear his or her stomach rumbling? so close the two of you can touch each other?

Most researchers refer to the distance that people like to keep between themselves and others as **personal space.** Often likened to an invisible bubble that surrounds the individual, personal space provides a boundary that limits the amount of physical contact among people. This boundary tends to extend farther in the front of the person than behind, but the individual is always near the center of the bubble. Personal space, in clear contrast to territoriality, is portable, a psychological shell that people carry with them from situation to situation. However, just as territorial encroachments create stress, arousal, and defensive reactions, personal space is actively maintained and defended. When someone violates our personal space, we tend to take steps to correct this problem (Aiello, 1987).

Personal space has been studied by researchers for a number of reasons: the manifestations of interpersonal positioning in everyday interactions are readily apparent, the concept is intuitively appealing, and in some respects personal space is easily measured. The term *personal space* is something of a misnomer, however, since the process actually refers to distances people maintain between one another; hence, it is an *interpersonal* space (Patterson, 1975). Some people seem to require more space than others, but as we will see, our need for space is largely determined by interpersonal factors, including the nature of the group situation and the characteristics of the individuals with whom we are interacting. (Aiello, 1987; Altman, 1975; Altman & Chemers, 1980; Evans & Howard, 1973; Hayduk, 1978, 1983; and Knowles, 1980 provide detailed reviews of the literature on personal space.)

Spatial behavior and intimacy.   Group members' space requirements vary depending on the situation: 2 inches was "just right" when the divers were working side by side taking measurements, but they needed much more space when eating dinner in the recreation area. Hall, in describing these variations, proposes the four **interpersonal zones** shown in Table 11-3. The *intimate zone* is appropriate for only the most involving and personal behaviors, such as lovemaking and whispering. The *personal zone*, in contrast, is reserved for a wide range of small-group experiences, such as discussions with friends, interaction with acquaintances, and conversation. More routine transactions are conducted in the *social zone*. Meetings held over large desks, formal dining, and professional presentations to small groups generally take place in this zone. The *public zone* is reserved for even more formal meetings, such as stage presentations, lectures, or addresses. Virtually all interactions in the Sealab group took place in either the personal zone or the social zone (Hall, 1966).

As Hall's theory of interpersonal zones suggests, small distances tend to be associated with friendlier, more intimate interpersonal activities. As a result cohesive groups occupy smaller spaces than noncohesive gatherings (Evans & Howard, 1973), extraverted people maintain smaller distances from others than do introverts (Patterson & Sechrest, 1970); people who wish to create a friendly, positive impression usually choose smaller distances than less friendly people (Evans & Howard, 1973); and groups of friends tend to stand closer to one another than groups of strangers (Edney & Grundmann, 1979).

Space needs also vary depending on the level of intimacy desired by the interactants. According to an **equilibrium model of personal space,** group members control the intimacy of the group's interaction by adjusting their personal space, body orientation, and eye contact. If group members feel that a low level of intimacy is appropriate, they may sit far apart, make little eye contact, and assume a relatively formal posture. If, in contrast, the

TABLE 11-3. Hall's four interpersonal zones.

Zone	Distance	Activities	Zone Characteristics
Intimate	Touching to 18 inches	Procreation, massage, comforting, accidental jostling, handshake, slow dancing	Sensory information concerning other is detailed and diverse; stimulus person dominates perceptual field.
Personal	18 inches to 4 feet	Friendly discussions, conversations, car travel, watching television	Other person can be touched if desired, but also avoided; gaze can be directed away from the other person with ease.
Social	4 feet to 12 feet	Dining, meetings with business colleagues, interacting with a receptionist	Visual inputs begin to dominate other senses; voice levels are normal; appropriate distance for many informal social gatherings.
Public	12 feet or more	Lectures, addresses, plays, dance recitals	All sensory inputs beginning to become less effective; voice may require amplification; facial expressions unclear.

(Source: Hall, 1966)

members are relaxing and discussing personal topics, they may move close together, make more eye contact, and adopt more relaxed postures (Argyle & Dean, 1965; Patterson, 1975, 1976, 1982). Group members, by continually adjusting their nonverbal and verbal behavior, can thereby keep the intimacy of their interactions at the level they desire (Burgoon, 1983; Kaplan, Firestone, Klein, & Sodikoff, 1983).

Gender.   Would the amount of personal space maintained by the divers in Sealab have differed if they had been women? Probably, for studies suggest that women's personal spaces tend to be smaller than men's (Hayduk, 1983). Relative to men, women allow others to get closer to them, and they approach other people more closely. Women also take up less space, by sitting with arms close to their sides and by crossing their legs, whereas men enlarge their personal space by assuming expansive, open positions (Mehrabian, 1972). In one study of same-sex pairs the researchers first photographed pairs of adults as they were walking along a city street and then asked the couple to describe the nature of their relationship (Heshka & Nelson, 1972). When personal space sizes were later calculated by examining the photographs, the investigators discovered that women needed less space when they were close friends, but that men's spatial needs weren't related to intimacy. Similarly, a study of mixed-sex dyads indicated that the reduced distance separating interacting friends was largely due to women's moving closer to the men rather than men's moving closer to the women (Edwards, 1972).

Status.   As logic and experience suggest, the type of relationship linking interactants plays a particularly significant role in determining personal space. A study of 562 U.S. Navy personnel, for example, found that subordinates conversing with superiors required more space than conversing peers (Dean, Willis, & Hewitt, 1975). In addition, many studies suggest that when we are with friends rather than strangers or mere acquaintances, our personal space needs become relatively small. This effect occurs in both same-sex and mixed-sex dyads, although the effect is sometimes seen only in women (Hayduk, 1983).

Culture.   Hall (1966) argues that many of our distance norms are specific to our particular culture or subculture. We learn what distance is proper in various situations and are surprised when we find that other countries and cultures have established very different norms. According to Hall, people who grow up in *contact cultures* of the Mediterranean, Middle East, and Latin America learn to prefer strong sensory involvement with others, and so they seek direct social contact whenever possible. In contrast, residents in such *noncontact countries* as the United States, England, and Germany try to limit their spatial openness with others. Given that all the divers in Sealab had been reared in the United States, they shared similar norms about how much distance should be maintained. If, however, the dive teams had included members from different cultural backgrounds, misunderstandings might have further complicated life in Sealab.

Seating Arrangements

Group members can be found in all sorts of spatial configurations, including densely packed clusters, single-file lines, irregularly shaped circles, and disorganized clumps (see Focus 11-2). These configurations, however, are often determined by the seating arrangements available to the group. In Sealab, for example, when four divers ate a meal at the table, they sat equidistant from one another at the four sides of the table. When conversing, they often sat side by side on the lab benches. When they were resting, distance from one another was determined by the location of the berths. As Robert Sommer (1967) notes, seating arrangements play a large role in creating the "small group's ecology." Although often unrecognized or simply taken for granted, seating pattern influences interaction, communication, and leadership in groups.

• •

FOCUS 11-2: GROUP SPACES

Just as individuals are protected from unwanted social contact by their invisible bubble of personal space, so groups seem to be surrounded by a sort of "shell," or "membrane," that forms an invisible boundary for group interaction. Various labels have been used to describe this form of spatial behavior: **group space** (Edney & Grundmann, 1979), *interactional territory* (Lyman & Scott, 1967), *temporary group territory* (Edney & Jordan-Edney, 1974), *jurisdiction* (Roos, 1968), and *group personal space* (Altman, 1975). No matter what it is called, evidence indicates that this boundary often effectively serves to repel intruders.

Eric Knowles examined the impermeability of groups by placing two or four confederates in a hallway (Knowles, 1973). Subjects who wished to move through this space were forced either to walk between the interactants or to squeeze through the approximately 2.5-foot space between the group and the hallway wall. Knowles found that 75% of the passersby chose to avoid walking through the group, but this figure dropped to about 25% in a control condition in which the interacting individuals were replaced by waste barrels. Other studies show that people begin invading group space if the distance between interactants becomes large (Cheyne & Efran, 1972) or the group is perceived to be a crowd rather than a single entity (Knowles & Basset, 1976). Furthermore, mixed-sex groups whose members are conversing with one another seem to have stronger boundaries (Cheyne & Efran, 1972), as do groups whose members are either (1) laughing and joking or (2) angrily arguing (Lindskold, Albert, Baer, & Moore, 1976).

In a related study Knowles and his colleagues discovered that group space also seems to increase as the number of group members grows (Knowles et al., 1976). Knowles observed solitary individuals walking along the right wall of a tunnel that connects two buildings on the University of Wisconsin campus. As they approached the alcove diagrammed in Figure 11-2 (p. 334), the subjects could see that the alcove was empty or occupied by one, two, three, or four confederates. An observer positioned in the opposite alcove recorded the deflection of the subject away from the experimental alcove. Knowles discovered that subjects actively avoided the alcove when it was occupied by a group but that the magnitude of the deflection was limited, in part, by their unwillingness to cross to the opposite side of the hallway.

• •

Seating patterns and social interaction.   Groups will behave very differently if their seating pattern is sociopetal rather than sociofugal. **Sociopetal** patterns promote interaction among group members by heightening

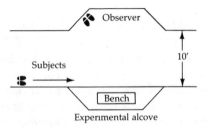

FIGURE 11-2. The experimental space used to study the deflection of passersby away from groups of varying sizes.
Source: Knowles, Kreuser, Haas, Hyde, & Schuchart, 1976

eye contact, encouraging verbal communication, and facilitating the development of intimacy. **Sociofugal** arrangements, in contrast, discourage interaction among group members and can even drive participants out of the situation altogether. Sociopetal environments might include a secluded booth in a quiet restaurant, a park bench, or five chairs placed in a tight circle, whereas sociofugal environments include classrooms organized in rows, movie theaters, waiting rooms, and—as Sommer laments—airports:

> In most terminals it is virtually impossible for two people sitting down to converse comfortably for any length of time. The chairs are either bolted together and arranged in rows theater-style facing the ticket counters, or arranged back-to-back, and even if they face one another they are at such distances that comfortable conversation is impossible. The motive for the sociofugal arrangement appears the same as that in hotels and other commercial places—to drive people out of the waiting areas into cafes, bars, and shops where they will spend money [1969, pp. 121–122].

Group members generally prefer sociopetal arrangements (Batchelor & Goethals, 1972; Giesen & McClaren, 1976; Sommer, 1969). This preference, however, depends in part on the type of task undertaken in the situation (Ryen & Kahn, 1975; Sommer, 1969). Sommer found, for example, that college students' preferences varied when they were conversing, cooperating on some task, competing, or coacting on individual tasks. As Figure 11-3 shows, corner-to-corner and face-to-face arrangements were preferred for conversation, and side-to-side seating was selected for cooperation. Competing pairs either took a direct, face-to-face orientation (apparently to stimulate competition) or tried to increase interpersonal distance, whereas coacting pairs preferred arrangements that involved a visual separation. As one student stated, such an arrangement "allows staring into space and not into my neighbor's face" (Sommer, 1969, p. 63). Similar choices were found with round tables.

These differences in preference parallel differences in behavior. In one study conducted with dyads, for example, the subjects were seated in chairs that directly faced each other, were adjacent to each other (simulating sitting together on a couch), or were placed at a 90-degree angle to each other (Mehrabian & Diamond, 1971). By coding verbal and nonverbal behaviors through a one-way mirror, the researchers were able to conclude that the 90-degree orientation increased affiliative tendencies, whereas the face-to-face arrangement led to a greater degree of relaxation. In related research comparing circle seating with L-shaped seating, the circle was associated with feelings of confinement but fostered greater interpersonal attraction (Patterson, Kelly, Kondracki, & Wulf, 1979; Patterson, Roth, & Schenk, 1979). People seated in the L-shaped groups, on the other hand, engaged in more self-manipulative behaviors and fidgeting, and they paused more during group discussions. Overall, the positive effects of the circle arrangement relative to the L arrangement were stronger in female groups than in male groups.

Gender effects.   Women and men diverge, to a degree, in their preferences for seating arrangements, for men prefer to position themselves across from those they like, and women prefer adjacent seating positions (Sommer, 1959). Obversely, men prefer that strangers sit by their side, whereas women feel that strangers should sit across from them. This difference in preference can lead to confusion in mixed-sex dyads. In one study of this problem solitary women and men working at a library table were approached by a same- or opposite-sex confederate who sat next to them or across from them (Fisher & Byrne, 1975). A measure of attraction,

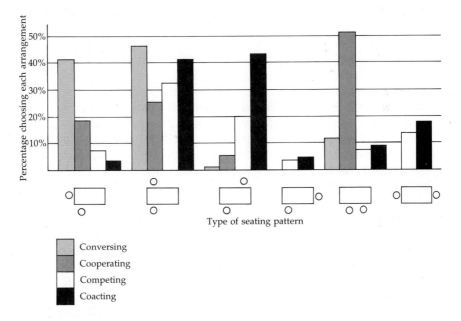

FIGURE 11-3. Seating preferences at rectangular tables.
Source: Sommer, 1969

affect, crowding, and perceptions administered after the confederate left indicated that men were the least favorably disposed toward the stranger who sat across from them but that women reacted more negatively to the stranger who sat next to them. Elaborating on some possible implications of these findings, the researchers note:

> A female who wants to befriend an unknown male may be surprised to find that a nonthreatening (to her) eyeball-to-eyeball approach causes consternation and alarm. In the same way, a male who attempts to ingratiate himself with an unknown female by sitting down beside her in a nonthreatening (to him) position may be surprised to find that he elicits a "Miss Muffet" reaction [Fisher & Byrne, 1975, pp. 20–21].

Clearly, group members should be sensitive to the possibility that their spatial behaviors will be misinterpreted by others and should be willing to make certain that any possible misunderstandings will be short lived.

Communication patterns.   Bernard Steinzor's early studies of face-to-face discussion groups indicate that spatial patterns also influence communication rates in groups. Although at first he could find few significant relationships between seat location and participation in the discussion, one day while watching a group he noticed a participant change his seat to sit opposite someone he had argued with during the previous meeting. Inspired by this chance observation, Steinzor (1950) reanalyzed his findings and discovered that individuals tended to speak *after* the person seated opposite them spoke. In explanation he reasoned that we have an easier time observing and listening to the statements of people who are seated in a position that is central to our visual field, so that their remarks serve as stronger stimuli for our own ideas and statements. The tendency for members of a group to comment immediately after the person sitting opposite them is now termed the **Steinzor effect.** The phenomenon appears to occur primarily in leaderless discussion groups, for later research suggests that when a strong leader is present, group members direct more comments to their closest neighbor (Hearn, 1957).

The head-of-the-table effect.   Researchers have also been able to provide confirmation for the intuitively appealing notion that the leadership role is closely associated with the chair at the head of the table (Sommer, 1967). For example, Sommer (1969) found that people appointed to lead small discussion groups tended to select seats at the head of the table, just as other available evidence indicates that the occupants of this exalted position, relative to those in the so-called ordinary seats, tend to possess more dominant personalities (Hare & Bales, 1963), talk more frequently, and often exercise greater amounts of interpersonal influence (Strodtbeck & Hook, 1961). Although many factors could account for this intriguingly consistent spatial relation, Sommer emphasizes two explanations: perceptual prominence and the social meaning associated with sitting at the head of the table. Looking first at prominence, Sommer suggests that in many groups the chair at the end of the table is the most salient position in the group and that the occupant of this space can therefore easily maintain greater amounts of eye contact with more of the group members, can move to the center of the communication network, and (as the Steinzor effect suggests) can comment more frequently. In the Western cultures where most studies of leadership have been conducted, the head chair at a table has been virtually defined as *the* most appropriate place for the leader to sit. Sommer is careful to note that this norm may not hold in other societies, but in most Western cultures leadership and the head of the table go hand in hand.

Each of these factors seems to play a role in the leadership/head-of-the-table relationship. Examining the role of perceptual prominence, investigators arranged for five-person groups to hold a discussion while seated at a rectangular table (Howells & Becker, 1962). They manipulated salience by having two persons sit on one side of the table and three on the other side. Although no one sat in the end seat, the investigators made specific predictions about who should emerge as the leader if eye contact and control of communication were important causal factors. Whereas those seated on the two-person side of the table could maintain easy eye contact with three of the group members, those on the three-person side could best focus their attention on only two members. Therefore, those on the two-person side should be able to influence others more and, hence, be the more likely leaders. As predicted, 70% of the leaders came from the two-person side, and only 30% came from the three-person side.

In another study the tendency for people to automatically associate the head-of-the-table location with leadership was examined by arranging for a confederate to voluntarily choose or be assigned to the end position or some other position around a table (Nemeth & Wachtler, 1974). These confederates then went about systematically disagreeing with the majority of the group members on the topic under discussion, and the extent to which the subjects altered their opinions to agree with the deviant was assessed. Interestingly, the deviants succeeded in influencing the others only when they had freely chosen to sit in the head chair. Apparently, disagreeing group members sitting at the "normal" locations around the table were viewed as "deviants," whereas those who had the confidence to select the end chair were viewed more as "leaders" (Riess, 1982; Riess & Rosenfeld, 1980).

ENVIRONMENTAL STRESS

The Sealab divers lived in a world filled with **stressors:** environmental conditions that threatened their well-being (Baum, Singer, & Baum, 1982; Evans & Cohen, 1987). When they were outside their habitat, their breathing gear sometimes malfunctioned, leaving them temporarily without oxygen. Scorpion fish were plentiful, and many of the divers were stung by this poisonous fish. The water was icy, and visibility was so poor that a diver could get lost just 40 feet from Sealab. Inside, conditions were not much better. Their habitat was too crowded, and the men often couldn't work because other divers were in their way. Equipment was also very noisy, to the point that it interfered with communication. The tilt of the floor also made cooking and eating difficult, the canned food was tasteless, and the relative humidity in the cylinder was too high for comfort.

These stressors directly influenced the nature and quality of social life in Sealab. In most cases, to understand a group's dynamics we need to consider the people in the place rather than the place itself. However, when the group must function in a place that is too crowded, is too noisy, and has temperatures that are uncomfortably high or low, the physical environment begins to control the outcome of these social interactions (Harrison & Connors, 1984; Suedfeld, 1987).

Crowding

John B. Calhoun's classic studies of overcrowded rats still offer some of the best evidence of the deleterious impact of crowding on social behavior. Calhoun (1962) began his work by establishing a rat colony in a quarter-acre pen. He allowed the animals to breed freely, supplied them with plenty of food and water, and protected them from predation. Despite these unlimited supplies Calhoun found that the population stabilized at around 150 rats. Most of the rats lived in subgroups of 10 to 12 members, and groupings with more rats tended to show signs of aggression and disruptive behavior.

Calhoun next increased the size of the population by building a pen that was divided into four sections. If one colony lived in each section, the optimal population level would be 40 to 50 rats, but Calhoun arranged the pens so that during feeding times 60 to 80 rats would congregate in one of the sections. Calhoun observed that these high-density conditions created what he called a **behavioral sink:** a significant distortion of many aspects of rat behavior, including disruption of courting rituals, mating, nest building, territoriality, aggression, and rearing practices. He also found that as conditions in the behavioral sink deteriorated, members of the colony tended to die off rapidly.

Studies of human groups corroborated Calhoun's suspicions about the detrimental effects of high density. When survey researchers examined urban living patterns, they found that as population density increases, infant mortality rates, incidence of venereal disease, mental illness, and juvenile delinquency all increase (Gove, Hughes, & Galle, 1983; Galle, Gove, & McPherson, 1972). Studies carried out in a number of naturalistic settings, including prisons, hospitals, naval ships, and dormitories, also suggested that high density often culminates in a number of negative processes (see Baum & Paulus, 1987, for a review). One study of prisons found that high density was associated with increased rates of death, suicide, disciplinary infractions, and psychiatric problems, whereas decreases in density were linked to reductions in inmate-on-inmate assaults, suicides, and mutilations (Cox, Paulus, & McCain, 1984). Similarly, researchers have found that "tripling"—putting three students in dormitory rooms designed for only two—leads to a number of problems, including interpersonal rejection, feelings of helplessness, and problems adjusting to college (Aiello, Baum, & Gormley, 1981; Baum & Davis, 1980; Baum & Valins, 1979).

The empirical evidence also suggests, however, that high density does not always lead to feelings of crowding and other negative interpersonal outcomes. As Daniel Stokols (1972, 1978) notes, **density** refers to a characteristic of the environment—literally, the number of people per unit of space. **Crowding,** in contrast, refers to a psychological, experiential state that sometimes but not always corresponds to physical density. Although the density of a given situation, such as a party, a rock concert, or Sealab, may be very high, interactants may not feel crowded at all. Yet two persons sitting in a large room may still report that they feel crowded if they expected to be alone, are engaged in some private activity, or dislike each other intensely. High density can be debilitating, but its effects depend on a number of other factors: overload, controllability, arousal, the intensity of the group situation, and interference.

Overload.   Picture the inside of Sealab at about 4 P.M. As the video cameras look on, some of the men inside are talking, others are readying their diving gear, others may be calculating data for reports, and someone is probably preparing the evening meal. The intercom sounds intermittently, giving announcements and orders for the following day. A school of fish appears in one of the viewing ports, and the men crowd around to catch a glimpse before the school flashes away into the murky water. The smell of the ocean emanating from the open hatch is strong, but it cannot mask the the cooking odors and the smell of the men who have labored all day underwater.

High-density environments are often stimulating environments. So long as this stimulation is not excessive, then few ill effects should occur. When the stimulation reaches extremely high levels, however, **overload** can occur: group members are overwhelmed by the amount of incoming information. Because this overstimulation is psychologically stressful, it can provoke a negative reaction to the situation. In addition, evidence suggests that when group members experience overload, they often use various coping methods to reduce this stimulation. An overloaded Sealab diver, for example, might have compensated by reducing his contact with others, limiting the amount of information he received, avoiding conversations, staying in his bunk, or simply ignoring certain types of inputs (Baum, Calesnick, Davis, & Gatchel, 1982; Greenberg & Firestone, 1977; Milgram, 1970; Saegert, 1978).

Control.   The divers dreaded the end of their 15 days, not just because the interesting project was over but also because it meant they had to enter the personnel transfer capsule (PTC). In Radloff and Helmreich's words (1968, p. 77):

> The PTC was barely large enough to accommodate the ten men. Conditions inside it were very cramped. Once the men were all in, and had put on their football helmets and tightened their seat belts (used in order to reduce the possibility of head injuries should the capsule suddenly lurch), the hatch was sealed. It was then hauled to the surface on a cable dangling from the end of a crane on the support vessel. . . . During these operations, when the PTC was in the air swinging free, it could have collided with the support vessel or its structures, the cable could have failed, or the tackle might have slipped dropping the PTC onto the deck or back into the sea.

If the PTC had sprung open during this operation, all the men would have died from decompression.

The trip in the densely packed PTC must have been particularly stressful because the men had no control over what was happening to them. Just as a sense of high personal control helps people cope with a range of negative life events, including failure, divorce, illness, and accidents, a loss of personal control often leads to a range of negative psychological and emotional consequences (Thompson, in press). The concept of control as applied to crowding suggests that high-density situations are unsettling because they undermine our sense of control over our own personal behavior, our ability to understand and process information, and our group's success in reaching sensible decisions (Baron & Rodin, 1978; Rodin, 1976; Rodin & Baum, 1978; Schmidt & Keating, 1979; Sherrod & Cohen, 1979).

Research conducted by Judith Rodin and her colleagues illustrates how a sense of control protects group members from some of the negative effects of high density (Rodin, Solomon, & Metcalf, 1978, experiment 2). Groups of six men were established in either a small laboratory room or a large one (14.04 square meters versus 5.94 square meters) and asked to perform tasks. One problem was a 15-minute discussion of censorship, and the second involved blindfolding members one at a time and letting them wander about within a circle formed by the rest of the group. To manipulate control, one of the subjects was designated the *coordinator;* he had responsibility for organizing the group, dealing with questions concerning procedures, and blindfolding members for the second task. A second subject, the *terminator,* was given control over ending the discussion and over each member's turn in the center of the circle.

After completing the two tasks, the group members answered a series of questions concerning their perceptions of the room. Significantly, group members who could control the group tasks through coordination or termination were not as bothered by the high-density situation as the four group members who were given no control over the situation. Feeling "in control" partially ameliorated the effects of high density, for even when interacting in the small room, the coordinators and terminators tended to downplay the magnitude of the crowding. (Focus 11-3 discusses another study conducted by Rodin and her colleagues to further test the effects of controllability on crowding.)

· ·

FOCUS 11-3: THE UPS AND DOWNS OF CROWDING

Imagine yourself standing with eight other people in a small enclosure that measures only about 6 feet by 4 feet. The enclosure has no windows and no pictures on the walls, but the lighting is so bright that you can see every pore on the nose of the person standing next to you. The air in the booth is both stale and noncirculating, so you can easily tell what cologne the man on your left is wearing, the brand of soap used by the woman on your right, and the type of pizza the person behind you had for lunch. Not one of the occupants says a word, but instead all stand in silence staring at a point in the wall just above the door.

Amazingly, people willingly enter such noxious environments every day, for our imaginary enclosure is nothing more than a well-loaded elevator. Although some people simply cannot adjust to the experience and hence resign themselves to long climbs up and down stairs, most learn to cope with the momentary crowding by concentrating on the background music, carefully avoiding others' eyes, scrutinizing the floor-indicator lights, or reading any available sign with feigned interest. In addition—as Rodin and her colleagues suggest, some individuals cope by situating themselves near the control panel that contains the push buttons for the various floors (Rodin et al., 1978, experiment 1). According to these researchers, such a position increases one's feeling of control in the situation and, hence, makes the elevator ride less distressing. Seeking evidence for this hypothesis, these investigators arranged for four confederates to enter an elevator in the Yale University Library whenever a lone individual arrived to use the elevator. These confederates then carefully jockeyed the subject into either the corner opposite the control panel or the corner in front of the control panel. Another member of the research team then trailed the subject when he or she left the elevator, and under the ruse of collecting information for an architecture class, administered a questionnaire that contained several items concerning the elevator. Consistent with control theory, passengers who had been able to manipulate the floor-selection buttons felt that the elevator was less crowded than those who had not been able to reach the buttons.

· ·

Arousal. Physiologically speaking, what happens to people when they find themselves in high-density situations? In many cases they become aroused: their heart rate and blood pressure increase, they breathe faster, and they sometimes perspire more (Evans, 1979; Middlemist, Knowles, & Matter, 1976; Walden & Forsyth, 1981). This arousal is not always stressful, however. If the intruder is a close friend, a relative, or an extremely attractive stranger, closeness can be a plus (Willis, 1966). Similarly, if we believe that the other person needs help or is attempting to initiate a friendly relationship, we tend to react positively rather than negatively (Baron, 1978; Murphy-Berman & Berman, 1978).

Several theorists argue that **attributions** play a key role in mediating reactions to high density (Patterson, 1976, 1982; Worchel, 1978). Stephen Worchel, for example, believes that when individuals experience arousal in high-density settings, they search the environment for a plausible explanation of this arousal. If they attribute the arousal to others standing too close, then they will conclude "I feel crowded." If, in contrast, they explain the arousal in some other way—"I'm fearful," "I drank too much coffee," "I'm in love," and so on—they will not feel crowded (Worchel, 1978; Worchel & Teddlie, 1976; Worchel & Yohai, 1979).

Several facts lend support to Worchel's position. First, as he argues, interpersonal distance, not room size, is related to crowding. He tested this idea by placing groups in large or small rooms and seating the members either close together or far apart (Worchel & Teddlie, 1976). Significantly, only people seated close together felt crowded. Second, the link between personal-space violations and arousal was confirmed in a study of men micturating in a public restroom (Middlemist, Knowles, & Matter, 1976). Reasoning that arousal would lead to a general muscular contraction that would delay micturation and reduce its duration, the researchers set up a situation in which men using wall-mounted urinals were joined by a confederate who used either the next receptacle (*near condition*) or one located farther down the wall (*far condition*). When onset times and duration for men in the near and far condition were compared with those same times for men in a no-confederate control condition, the researchers found that personal-space invasion significantly increased general arousal.

Worchel also reports that crowded individuals who mistakenly attribute their arousal to some other cause do not feel as crowded as people who do not make misattributions (Worchel & Yohai, 1979). Participants in this study were seated in chairs placed either 20 inches apart or touching at the legs. The five-person groups were told to work on a variety of tasks and were told that during their work subliminal noise would be played in the room. For one-third of the groups the experimenter stated that although the noise was below conscious hearing level, it was detectable subconsciously and would lead to stressful, discomforting effects. To another third of the groups the experimenter explained that the noise would be undetectable consciously but would have relaxing and calming effects. The final third of the subjects were given no explanations concerning the effects of the subliminal noise. After this manipulation the groups worked on tasks but were not actually exposed to any noise.

The results shown in Table 11-4 confirm Worchel's predictions. As expected, subjects seated close together generally reported feeling more crowded than subjects seated far apart. The important exception, however, occurred when subjects were led to believe that the subliminal noise would have arousing side effects. These subjects felt no more crowded than those seated far apart.

Intensity.   Jonathan Freedman summarizes his theory of crowding in the first few pages of his book *Crowding and Behavior:*

> Based on research over a period of five or six years by myself and a number of other investigators, we have concluded that crowding does not generally have negative effects on people and that, indeed, it can have either good or bad effects depending upon the situation [1975, p. vii].

Essentially, if something in the situation makes the group interaction unpleasant, high density will make the situation seem even more unpleasant. If the situation is a very pleasant one, however, high density will make the good situation even better. Freedman labels this basic idea the **density-intensity hypothesis,** for it suggests that crowding (what he calls high density) merely intensifies whatever is already occurring in the group situation (Freedman, 1975, 1979).

Freedman has tested this notion by placing groups of people in large or small rooms and then manipulating some aspect of the group interaction to create unpleasantness or pleasantness. In one investigation groups of six to ten high school students sat on the floor of either a large room or a small room. Each delivered a speech and then received feedback from the other group members. By prearrangement Freedman made certain that in some groups the feedback was always positive, whereas in other groups the feedback was always negative. When the subjects later rated the room and their group, people in the little room reported feeling more crowded than those in the big room, but density interacted with pleasantness of the situation such that liking for the group was (1) highest in the high-density/positive-feedback condition but (2) lowest in the high-density/negative-feedback condition. Furthermore, Freedman found that these effects were clearest for all-female groups as opposed to all-male or mixed-sex groups (see also Storms & Thomas, 1977, experiment 3).

TABLE 11-4. Perceptions of crowding by those seated close together and far apart.

Interpersonal Distance	Arousing Noise	Relaxing Noise	No Explanation
Close	4.3[1]	7.1	6.7
Far	3.4	2.7	3.1

[1] 1 = not crowded; 10 = very crowded.

(Source: Worchel & Yohai, 1979)

Interference.   One clear difference distinguishing studies that find no ill effects of crowding (for example, Freedman, Klevansky, & Ehrlich, 1971) and those that do (say, Paulus, Annis, Seta, Schkade, & Matthews, 1976) centers on the interactive quality of the group task. In Freedman's research the subjects sat in crowded and uncrowded rooms and worked on many different memory, reasoning, concentration, and creativity tasks, but all of these problems were individualistic. The subjects never had to interact with the others in their group, and the crowding caused no interference. In contrast, other studies have required the participants to complete interactive tasks that are more difficult to solve under crowded circumstances (such as Heller, Groff, & Solomon, 1977; Paulus et al., 1976).

Researchers demonstrated the importance of interference in creating crowding by deliberately manipulating both density and interaction. Six- to eight-member groups of men were given a task to perform in either a small laboratory room or a large one. The task itself involved correctly collating eight-page booklets, and to add an incentive, the experimenter promised the participants a bonus for each booklet correctly assembled. The order of the pages was not constant, however, but was determined by first selecting a card that had the order of pages listed in a random sequence (for instance, 3 5 8 7 6 1 2 4). In the low-interaction condition the task was simple, because each person was given all eight stacks of pages and a set of sequence cards. In the high-interaction condition all group members shared the same eight stacks, which were located all around the room. Furthermore, because each sequence differed from the last, subjects constantly had to walk around the room in unpredictable patterns. In fact, the subjects often bumped into one another while trying to move from one stack to another (Heller et al., 1977).

The interference created in the high-interaction condition did, indeed, lead to decrements in task performance—provided density was high. When the researchers checked the booklets for collating errors, they discovered that crowded/high-interaction groups incorrectly collated their booklets more than 12% of the time. This error rate dropped to less than 6% in the uncrowded/high-interaction condition and to about 4% in the two low-interaction conditions. These results, as well as those discussed in Focus 11-4, suggest that performance suffers when high density interferes with a group's ability to complete a task (McCallum, Rusbult, Hong, Walden, & Schopler, 1979; Morasch, Groner, & Keating, 1979; Paulus et al., 1976; Sundstrom, 1975).

• •
FOCUS 11-4: THE RIGHT NUMBER FOR THE JOB

The ecological psychologist Roger Barker argues that in some cases individuals fit their environment like a glove. A small family may move into a home that is neither too big for it nor too small. A fast-food restaurant may use a system of guide chains and multiple cash registers to handle large numbers of customers efficiently. A high-use highway may have reversible lanes and computer-controlled traffic lights. Barker uses the word **synomorphy** to describe this fit between the setting and its human occupants (Barker, 1968, 1987; Barker et al., 1978).

Allan Wicker draws on the concept of synomorphy to explain how groups can still perform adequately even in crowded conditions (Wicker, 1979, 1987). To choose a common example, consider workers in an office in a small business, university, or government agency who are responsible for typing papers and reports, answering the telephone, duplicating materials, and preparing paperwork on budgets, schedules, appointments, and so on. If the number of people working in the office is sufficient to handle all these activities, then the setting is synomorphic, or *optimally staffed*. (Wicker uses the phrase *optimally manned*.) If telephones are ringing unanswered, reports are days late, the photocopy machine is broken and no one knows how to fix it, the office lacks "enough people to carry out smoothly the essential program and maintenance tasks" and is *understaffed* (Wicker, 1979, p. 71). Lastly, if the number of group members exceeds that needed in the situation—if the flow of work is so slight that the staff has little to do, the number of typewriters available is insufficient, only one duplicating machine is available so users must wait their turn, and the desk of the new staff member hasn't yet arrived—*overstaffing* exists (Sundstrom, 1987).

Wicker's staffing theory predicts that the adequacy of staffing in a work setting will have effects on a number of individual and group variables, some of which are listed in Table 11-5 (p. 346). Significantly, the theory hypothesizes that overstaffed groups may not perform inadequately—after all, so many extra people are available to carry out the basic functions—but overstaffing can lead to dissatisfaction with task-related activities and heightened rejection of other group members (Arnold & Greenberg, 1980). Supporting this prediction, Wicker and his associates found that the members of four-man groups, when placed in an overstaffed situation (too few tasks to keep all members active), reported feeling less important, less involved in their work, less concerned with performance, and less needed. These effects were reversed in the understaffed groups (Wicker, Kirmeyer, Hanson, & Alexander, 1976).

• •

Conclusions. All of the theoretical frameworks just described seek to explain crowding in small groups, albeit in somewhat different ways. Although one could try to single out the one theory that best accounts for crowding, more likely each theory adds something that is overlooked by the others. In Sealab, for example, the divers were certainly overstimulated, and the constant, inescapable danger probably led them to experience a loss of personal control. The close conditions in the habitat

TABLE 11-5. Group members' responses to inadequately staffed work settings.

Members of understaffed groups will tend to:	Members of overstaffed groups will tend to:
Show strong, frequent, and varied actions in carrying out goal-related behavior	Perform tasks in a perfunctory, lackadaisical manner
Act to correct inadequate behavior of others	Show a high degree of task specialization
Be reluctant to reject group members whose behavior is inadequate	Demonstrate little concern for the quality of the group product
Feel important, responsible, and versatile as a result of their participation	Exert little effort in helping others in the group
Be concerned about the continued maintenance of the group	Feel cynical about the group and its functions
Be less sensitive to and evaluative of individual differences among group members	Evidence low self-esteem, with little sense of competence and versatility
Think of themselves and other group members in terms of the jobs they do rather than in terms of personality characteristics	Focus on personalities and idiosyncrasies of people in the group rather than on task-related matters

(Source: Wicker, 1979)

probably also led to crowding-induced arousal, but many of them attributed their feelings to the danger and felt a sense of excitement. Most truly enjoyed this challenging experience, so the crowding may even have intensified their positive reaction. They did, however, complain when they interfered with one another as they were entering and leaving through the hatch. Thus, "at present it is not possible to point to one theory as reflecting most accurately all of the processes underlying the broad range of crowding-related phenomena we have considered" (Baum & Paulus, 1987, p. 561).

Temperature

One of the minor miseries of social life occurs when people must work in a room that is too hot or too cold. Although a wide range of temperatures—from the mid 60s to the mid-80s is rated as "comfortable" by most people, temperatures that fall outside this range cause discomfort, irritability, and reduced productivity (Baron, 1978; Bell, 1981; Parsons, 1976). In a study that specifically focused on group members' reactions to temperature (Griffitt & Veitch, 1971), 3 to 16 people were assembled to work on tasks in a room at normal temperature (72.4°F) or a hot room (93.5°F). When later questioned about the experience, the overheated group members reported feelings of aggression, fatigue, sadness, and discomfort, whereas subjects in the normal-temperature room reported feeling more elated, vigorous, and comfortable. Studies also suggest that extremes in temperature can reduce interpersonal attraction (Griffitt, 1970), interfere with successful task performance (Parsons, 1976), cause severe physical dysfunctions (Folk, 1974), and contribute to increases in aggressive behavior (Anderson, 1989; Baron, 1978). Also, one of the concomitants of high temperatures in groups is exposure to others' body odors, an experience that most people find to be objectionable (McBurney, Levine, & Cavanaugh, 1977).

Noise

Sealab was a noisy place. An air-filtering system ran for several hours each day and virtually obliterated all conversation. The cylinder also contained a variety of machinery and communication devices and was constantly filled with the sound of air tanks being loaded and unloaded. Also, for technical reasons the air inside the habitat had a high helium content. As anyone who has ever sucked the helium out of a balloon and then tried to talk knows, helium changes the tone and pitch of the voice. Hence, the men sounded like chipmunks.

Noise has been linked to distraction, irritation, and psychological stress (Cohen & Weinstein, 1981). In a close-up study of noise researchers arranged for people to work on simple and complex tasks while listening to tape-recorded noise. The noise tape, which was specially prepared by superimposing several sounds, included two people conversing in Spanish, one person speaking Armenian, and the operating sounds of a mimeograph machine, a desk calculator, and a typewriter. Although the investigators began their research by assuming that people would be unable to work effectively while bombarded with this cacophony, they obtained little evidence of the debilitating consequences of noise. The subjects succeeded in adapting psychologically to the noise: although they had at first been distracted, in time they became so inured to the stimulus that they no longer even noticed it (Glass & Singer, 1972; Glass, Singer, & Pennebaker, 1977). These findings suggest that a group working in a noisy setting may eventually be able to surmount the problems posed by their excessive environmental stimulation, like a family Sommer (1972, p. 28) describes:

> When friends of mine first moved into a house about 10 miles from Sacramento airport, they were bothered by the noise and billowing black smoke spewing from the jets during takeoff. But when I visit their house now, I am the only one who is disturbed by the noise and black clouds. My friends have adapted to them; conversation continues as the jets roar by, and drinks are poured without a shudder.

Delving deeper into the problem, these researchers found that people cannot always adapt successfully to noise. Extremely loud sound, for example, is difficult to ignore, and if exposure is prolonged, significant hearing loss can occur. Aperiodic noise also tends to lead to greater discomfort, particularly if it is unpredictable and the group is working on a complex task. Thus, if people are working diligently on a hard problem while a pneumatic drill is in use in the street outside the building, fewer negative effects of the noise will be felt if the drill is in continuous use rather than switched off and on with no warning. Also, uncontrollable noise is particularly aggravating; indeed, when group members believe that they can control the noise, satisfactions, arousal levels, and stress tend to be relatively unaffected. If the group members feel that nothing can be done to reduce the volume of noxious ambient noise, negative consequences—including headaches, nausea, argumentativeness, irritability, and poor task performance—are more likely (Glass et al., 1977).

Sealab Stresses: A Look Back

When people gather in groups at specific locations, they often experience a number of other stressors in addition to overcrowding, uncomfortable temperatures, and noise. For example, the group may have to wait for the arrival of a tardy, but important, member. The lighting in the room may be bright and glaring or subdued and diffuse. The air in the place may feel uncomfortably hot, too still, odorous, dusty, or smoky. All of these features of the room and many, many others can generate stress among group members.

Yet, as was the case with the Sealab divers, groups are capable of overcoming the limiting conditions created by these environmental stressors. Some groups may not survive in a hostile environment, but others respond to stress by becoming better organized, more cohesive, and more efficient (Harrison & Connors, 1984; Suedfeld, 1987). In the words of the divers themselves (Radloff & Helmreich, 1968):

> Maybe we were all welded together a little bit by the fact that it was a dangerous situation and maybe that makes men better friends [p. 108].

> If we hadn't had a real compatible group there might have been a lot of hard feelings. Everybody was cooperative. They all worked and helped each other as much as possible. I think it was a real good group [p. 82].

> That was the hardest I have every worked in my life. And it is the busiest I have ever been. I would go back right now [p. 79].

SUMMARY

Because groups exist in a physical setting, members' interactions are often influenced by such environmental factors as territory, spatial distances, seating arrangements, and environmental stressors. Like many other animals humans establish *territories*: geographical locations that an individual or group defends against intrusion by others. Many variations in territories have been noted by researchers, but Altman distinguishes between *primary territories, secondary territories*, and *public territories*. At the group level, territories can be as well established as the turfs of urban gangs or as transitory as the territories surrounding individuals engaged in interaction, but the consequences of territorial processes are often far reaching. Individuals' territories within a group also influence group dynamics, for they fulfill important privacy, organizing, and identity functions within the group. Territoriality also influences dominance and members' ability to cope with periods of prolonged isolation.

Studies of *personal space* suggest that group members prefer to keep a certain distance between themselves and others. Smaller spaces are associated with greater intimacy, so space requirements tend to increase as the situation becomes less intimate. Hall describes four *interpersonal zones: intimate, personal, social, and public.* The *equilibrium model of personal space* predicts that individuals will moderate their distances to achieve the desired level of intimacy, but researchers have also found that variations in space are linked to the gender, status, and cultural background of the interactants. Studies of *group space,* similarly, suggest that groups seem to be surrounded by a sort of shell that forms an invisible boundary for group interaction.

As Sommer notes, seating arrangements make up an important part of the ecology of a small group. *Sociopetal* spaces tend to encourage interaction, whereas *sociofugal* seating patterns discourage interaction. Although people generally prefer interaction-promoting sociopetal patterns, these preferences vary with the type of task being attempted and the gender of the interactants. Across a wide variety of groups, however, seating arrangements significantly influence patterns of attraction, communication, and leadership. For example, in many groups individuals tend to speak immediately after the person seated opposite them (the *Steinzor effect*), and leadership is closely associated with sitting at the end of the table (the head-of-the-table effect).

Features of the environment that surround the group can function as *stressors:* extremes in density, temperature, and noise can in some cases lead to psychological stress and distraction and can undermine performance. Looking first at crowding, Calhoun's analysis of a *behavioral sink* argues that high density can lead to significant distortions of many aspects of behavior, at least in rats. Studies of humans, in contrast, draw a distinction between *density*—the number of people per unit of space—and *crowding*—the psychological reaction to high physical density. Crowding is exacerbated by a number of factors, including *overload,* a low sense of personal control, cognitive processes that prompt individuals to make *attributions* about the causes of their arousal, group members' overall evaluation of the high-density setting (the *density-intensity hypothesis*), and the degree to which others interfere with task performance. People also react more negatively when they must work in a situation in which the number of people present is not compatible with the characteristics of the physical setting. Such settings lack *synomorphy,* because they are either understaffed or overstaffed.

Extremes in temperature and noise are also stressful. High temperatures seem to be linked with losses of attention as well as a number of other unpleasant consequences, including discomfort, irritability, and reduced productivity. Noise, too, has been linked to irritation and psychological stress, particularly if it is unpredictable and the group cannot control its source.

·12·

Conflict

In 1977 Steve Wozniak and Steven Jobs founded a company called Apple Computers, Inc. Their first product, the Apple II, hit the mark exactly, and the tiny company grew rapidly into a multinational corporation with billions of dollars in sales. Because Wozniak preferred to work on technical development, and Jobs had little experience in corporate management, they hired John Sculley to be the chief executive officer (CEO). Sculley gradually reorganized the company to create three divisions: an Apple II division, a division run by Jobs that was responsible for developing the Macintosh (Mac) computer, and a marketing and sales division that handled all the company's products.

The company's success continued, and Jobs and Sculley became close friends. Sculley, like most other people, was impressed by Jobs's brilliance and zeal, and Jobs felt that Sculley was a wizard at organizing and managing. But in the spring of 1985 the company began to falter. Apple's stock plunged, orders for both Apple IIs and Macs dwindled, and IBM's share of the business market grew. The board of directors began pressuring Sculley to intervene in the management of the Mac division, but Jobs refused to recognize Sculley's authority. Jobs and Sculley began bickering openly, and their partnership began to crumble. In April of 1985 Sculley decided that "we could run a lot better with Steve out of operations" (Gelman et al., 1985, p. 47) and Jobs began taking steps to replace Sculley as CEO.

The conflict escalated. Jobs first approached Sculley privately and asked him for more time to bring the Mac division back in line. When Sculley refused, Jobs called together many of the top personnel at Apple and asked them to join him in a fight against Sculley. He also contacted the members of the board and began to shift them against Sculley as well. Sculley countered by calling an executive committee meeting for the morning of May 24. Everyone at the meeting was tense, and emotions ran strong when Jobs and Sculley accused each other of ruining Apple. But Sculley won the committee's endorsement, and Jobs was transferred to a nonmanagement position. Later that year Jobs resigned from the company he had founded.

The conflict between Jobs and Sculley was not an anomaly. Group members rarely agree with one another completely, and in many cases these disagreements can escalate into conflicts. Perhaps one of the more talkative members of the group is bluntly told to "let somebody else say something for a change." One group member may be committed to Plan X, but another member may just as strongly endorse Plan Y. The competence of the group's leader may be challenged by a rival leader. Whatever the issue, as the problem grows, the group spends more and more of its time discussing it. Disputants may begin by explaining their position on the issue, but eventually they begin criticizing the others' position. Persuasion gives way to arguing, emotions take the place of logic, and the once unified group splits up into factions and coalitions. Conflict, if unrelieved, can be fatal to the group.

This chapter and the next examine some basic questions about the causes and consequences of conflict. Drawing on the Sculley/Jobs incident and on available research, we begin by exploring some of the factors that can turn group members into adversaries and the perceptual, cognitive, and interpersonal factors that exacerbate conflict. We also examine the tendency for groups to break up into coalitions and review some of the strategies for resolving conflict. Thus, this chapter focuses on conflicts that occur within groups—**intragroup conflict**—and leaves the analysis of conflict between groups—**intergroup conflict**—to Chapter 13.

SOURCES OF CONFLICT IN GROUPS

The Latin word *conflictus*, a "striking together with force," implies disagreement, discord, and friction among members of a group: interaction in which words, emotions, and actions "strike together" to produce disruptive effects. When conflict occurs in a group, the actions or beliefs of one or more members of the group are unacceptable to—and hence are resisted by—one or more of the other group members.

Intragroup conflict has many causes. Some theorists prefer to emphasize communication difficulties, others organizational structures, and others social and psychological factors (Blake & Mouton, 1984; Fraser & Hipel, 1984; Pruitt & Rubin, 1986; Tjosvold, 1986). Unfortunately, all these factors interact to produce conflict, making a complete listing of potential problem areas impossible. Once we admit that the list is incomplete, however, we can concentrate on three mechanisms that can change disagreements into conflicts: competition over scarce resources, the use of threatening, contentious influence strategies, and the personal characteristics of the individuals involved.

Competition

When Sculley first joined Apple, he and Jobs worked together on various projects. But as the Macintosh project ran into snags, Jobs began to pour all the company's resources into the Mac rather than the industry-leading Apple II model. Sculley wanted the Mac to be the machine of choice for businesses, but Jobs wanted it to be the most technologically advanced computer ever built. When Sculley insisted that the Mac be modified and that more resources be devoted to the Apple II, Jobs refused to cooperate. The two were no longer working together to solve Apple's problems. Instead, they had become competitors: for Sculley to succeed, Jobs would have to fail, and if Jobs succeeded, Sculley would fail.

Conflict often arises because group members compete for desired goals and resources. As the group dynamicist Morton Deutsch explains, when a situation involves **competition,** the success of any one member of the group means that someone else in the group must fail. Deutsch (1949b) calls this form of interaction "contrient interdependence." In contrast, conflict becomes less likely when the success of any one group member will improve the chances of success for the other members. This form of interaction is termed **cooperation,** or "promotive interdependence" (Deutsch, 1949b).

In some of his earliest work Deutsch observed the impact of contrient and promotive interdependence on subgroups of students in an introductory psychology class (Deutsch, 1949a, 1949b). Students assigned to cooperative groups were told that the group's performance would determine their individual grades. All groups would supposedly be compared, and members of those that did well would get high grades, whereas members of those that did poorly would get low grades. In the competition groups, however, students were told that their ranking in their group would determine their course grades. The individual who did the best in their group would get the highest grade, whereas the individual who did the worst would get the lowest grade. Hence, members of cooperative groups sought promotively interdependent goals, and those in competitive groups sought contriently interdependent goals.

As Deutsch predicted, the cooperative groups evidenced more friendliness during the meetings, their members were more encouraging toward one another, and the contributions of others were more positively evaluated. Members of competitive groups, in contrast, reported less dependency on others, a weaker desire to win the respect of others, and greater rejection by the group (Deutsch, 1949a, 1949b, 1973, 1980, 1985). (See Focus 12-1.)

· ·

FOCUS 12-1: COOPERATIVE LEARNING ENVIRONMENTS

Classrooms, like groups, can be structured to promote either competition or cooperation. In some classrooms students can earn good grades only if other students earn poor grades; grading "on the curve" involves a mild form of competition, because students' performances are judged against the average student performance. In classes based on cooperation students can succeed only if the other members of the class (or subgroup) succeed.

The relative benefits of each of these classroom practices are still being debated, but empirical evidence increasingly ranks cooperative classrooms over individualistic, or competitive, classrooms. Although the findings are not uniform, a recent review of more than 120 studies conducted in educational and performance settings concluded that "cooperation is considerably more effective than interpersonal competition and individualistic effort" (Johnson, Maruyama, Johnson, Nelson, & Skon, 1981, p. 47) and that competition helps only when students cooperate in small groups competing against other groups. David W. Johnson, a leading researcher in this area, goes so far as to predict that an "emphasis on positive goal interdependence among students not only will create the supportive, accepting, and caring relationships vital for socialization but will also promote achievement, perspective-taking ability, self-esteem, psychological health, liking for peers, and positive attitudes toward school personnel" (1980, p. 40). He feels that given the divergent effects of cooperation and competition shown in Table 12-1, teachers should make learning a cooperative enterprise (see also Cotton & Cook, 1982; Johnson, Johnson, & Maruyama, 1984; Johnson, Johnson, & Smith, 1986; McGlynn, 1982; Slavin, 1983, 1986).

TABLE 12-1. Characteristics of Cooperative and Competitive Learning Environments.

Characteristic	Cooperative Classroom	Competitive Classroom
Interaction	High	Low
Communication	Effective	Minimal, misleading, or threatening
Peer support and influence	Helpful, supportive, and achievement-oriented	Unhelpful, unsupportive, and competition-oriented
Conflict management	Integrative, egalitarian	Ineffective, win/lose oriented
Learning outcomes	Higher-order, conceptual	Factual, uncreative
Atmosphere	Friendly	Hostile
Commitment to learning	High	Low
Utilization of resources	Efficient, sharing	Inefficient, individualistic
Fear of failure	Decreased	Increased

(Source: Johnson, 1980)

Other researchers, too, have found that cooperative situations tend to be friendly, intimate, and involving, whereas competitive situations are viewed as unfriendly, nonintimate, and uninvolving (King & Sorrentino, 1983). One researcher, for example, carried out a long-term observation of two employment agencies that varied in competitiveness. In one the personnel considered the successful placement of an applicant a team success, and thus cooperation was high. In the second agency, however, personnel competed by working alone and keeping job information from one another. Naturally, conflicts, anxiety, and ineffectiveness were more pronounced in the second agency (Blau, 1954). (See Schmitt, 1981, for a more detailed review of this area.)

Evidence also suggests, however, that few situations involve pure co-operation or pure competition; more commonly, the motive to compete is mixed with the motive to cooperate. Sculley, for example, wanted to gain control over the Mac division, but he also needed Jobs's help with product development. Jobs, in contrast, valued Sculley's organizational expertise, but he felt that Sculley misunderstood the company's goals. Thus, the men found themselves in a **mixed-motive situation:** they were tempted to compete and cooperate at the same time.

Social psychologists have often used a specialized laboratory technique known as the **prisoner's dilemma game,** or PDG, to study confict in mixed-motive situations. This procedure takes its name from a hypothetical quandary that ensnares two prisoners (Luce & Raiffa, 1957). The two imaginary criminals, John and Steve, are being interrogated by police detectives in separate rooms. The police are certain that the two committed a crime, but they need a confession to be sure of a conviction. Therefore, they try to turn the two into competitors by telling them that the other is about to confess. John's and Steve's choices are shown in Figure 12-1:

1. If John confesses and Steve does not, John will get no sentence at all, but Steve will get ten years.
2. If Steve confesses but John does not, Steve will be set free, but John will be locked away for ten years.
3. If both confess, a five-year sentence will be arranged.

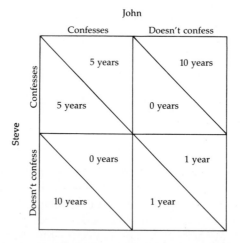

FIGURE 12-1. The prisoner's dilemma. This chart, or matrix, summarizes the problem that the two imaginary prisoners face. Each prisoner has two choices: confess or don't confess. These choices are shown along the sides of the matrix. The numbers within each cell of the matrix correspond to the outcomes that the two prisoners can receive. In each cell John's outcomes are shown above the diagonal line, and Steve's outcomes are shown below the diagonal. For example, if John confesses but Steve does not confess, John will receive 0 years, but Steve will receive 10 years.

4. If neither confesses, both will be tried on a minor charge that carries the light sentence of one year.

The dilemma for the prisoners is obvious. By confessing, the prisoner will end up with either no sentence or an intermediately long sentence, but by remaining silent the prisoner will get either one year or ten years. Should John and Steve gamble that their partner will remain silent or give in to the pressure and confess?

In the experimental version of this dilemma the prisoners are subjects, and the years become points or money. If you are a participant in such a study, you and one other person will be taken to separate cubicles. Once seated you are told that you can win money by picking one of two options, labeled A and B. If you choose the "right" option, you will get anywhere from 50 cents to $1. If you pick the "wrong" option, you can lose as much as $1.

To complicate things, you are also told that neither A nor B will always be the "right" solution, because you are not playing the game alone. The person you waited with (Person X) is in the next room, and X will also be choosing between A and B in the hope of earning some money. The researchers explain that each turn of the game will have one of four outcomes shown in Figure 12-2:

1. If you choose A and X chooses A, both of you will earn 50 cents.
2. If you choose A and X chooses B, you will lose $1, but X will earn $1.

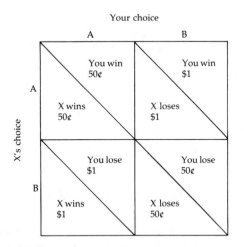

FIGURE 12-2. Another example of a prisoner's dilemma game matrix. The subjects' task is simple: pick either A or B. In each cell, your outcomes are shown above the diagonal line, and Subject X's outcomes are shown below. For example, if Subject X chooses A and you choose A, you both earn 50 cents. If one of you chooses A and the other chooses B, however, the one who picks A loses money, and the one who picks B wins money. A is the cooperative choice, whereas B is the competitive choice.

3. If you choose B and X chooses A, you will earn $1, but X will lose $1.
4. If you choose B and X chooses B, you will both lose 50 cents.

The situation is more complicated than it first seems. Certainly you would like to get the $1, but to do so you must choose B. However, X (who you must assume wants the money too) must also choose B to get the $1. Unfortunately, when you pick B and X picks B, you will both lose 50 cents. So, rather than trying for the whole $1, you begin thinking that both you and X should choose A, thereby earning 50 cents each. But what if X, a stranger whom you have no way of communicating with, "cheats" and picks B while you pick A? Then you'll lose $1, and X will win $1. But what if you pick B but X tries to cooperate and therefore picks A? What if . . . ?

The PDG is an artificial procedure that oversimplifies the complexities of conflict in groups. (See Rapoport, 1985; Schlenker & Bonoma, 1978; and Wrightsman, O'Connor, & Baker, 1972, for reviews and critiques.) But the game provides clear data concerning the competition/conflict link. Players can maximize their own winnings by exploiting a partner who cooperates. In addition, if the other person attempts to maximize his or her profit by making competitive responses, the participant will again be better off (or, at least, will lose the least) if this competition is answered with competition. However, mutual competition means that both parties lose money, whereas mutual cooperation maximizes the group's joint winnings. Thus, the group would benefit the most from cooperation, but any shade of doubt about the trustworthiness of the partner will evoke competition and conflict (Brickman, Becker, & Castle, 1979; Deutsch, 1958, 1960, 1973, 1980). Moreover, competition breeds competition rather than cooperation. As Deutsch (1973, p. 193) explains, once individuals' choices in the PDG were "out of phase—e.g., one choosing cooperatively and the other not— it was extremely difficult for them to get together again. Thus if Person I chose cooperatively and Person II chose uncooperatively, Person I might get angry and choose uncooperatively while Person II would choose cooperatively." As a result, the PDG is a social trap: competition seems advantageous initially, but if the players compete against each other, the long-term consequences are ruinous (see Focus 12-2).

. . . .
FOCUS 12-2: SOCIAL TRAPS

Consider the "tragedy of the commons." A group of shepherds all use a common grazing land. The land can support many sheep, so the system works smoothly. However, several selfish members of the community want to maximize their personal profit, so they add animals to their own flocks. Others notice the extra sheep, so they, too, add to their flocks. Soon the commons is overgrazed, and all of the sheep die from starvation (Hardin, 1968).

What happens when group members who are supposed to share a resource begin to compete for this resource? In many cases the situation becomes a **social trap**: the individuals are tempted to act in their own self-interest to the detriment of the group's overall needs (Platt, 1973). In the commons dilemma extra sheep earn the individuals extra profit, but in the long run increasing the size of the flocks will exhaust the available resources. The shepherds are tempted by the short-term gains of competition, but if they succumb, they will incur long-term losses (Hardin, 1968).

Many laboratory studies have examined social traps by simulating the tragedy of the commons. A group of four or five people are given the chance to draw as many tokens as they want from a pool of available tokens, but all are informed that after each round of "harvesting" the pool regenerates in direct proportion to the number of tokens remaining in the pool. If members quickly draw out all the tokens, the pool is permanently exhausted; cautious removal of only a small number of tokens ensures replenishment of the resource. Nonetheless, group members often act in their own self-interest by drawing out all the tokens, even when they understand the nature of social traps and realize that the pool is quite small (Brewer & Kramer, 1986; Dawes, 1980; Edney, 1980; Messick & Brewer, 1983; Schroeder, Irwin, & Sibicky, 1988).

How can groups escape from this social dilemma? Both experience with the situation and maintaining communication among members appear to be critical factors (Allison & Messick, 1985a; Edney & Bell, 1984). In one illustrative study triads harvested from a large or small pool. Members of half of the groups were allowed to communicate with one another, but the rest could not. The differences between these groups were striking. Over 80% of the groups that could not communicate ruined their pool within a minute; the members harvested so much that the pool was empty in no time. Even when the pool was large, the noncommunicating groups still had problems with overharvesting. Many of these groups realized the long-term negative consequences of overharvesting, but they did not manage their resources as well as the communicating groups. These results suggest that groups can avoid traps if their members can plan a strategy for dealing with the situation through face-to-face communication (Brechner, 1977).

• •

Contentious Influence Strategies

In his autobiography Sculley (1987, pp. 241–242) describes the day he told Jobs that he wanted him to step down as manager of the Mac division. Sculley recalls that he wracked his mind for some alternative but eventually decided that Jobs must go. So he went to Jobs's office and told him about his decision. Jobs was "stunned," "incensed and outraged," and told Sculley that he was ruining the company. Sculley responded by telling Jobs "I have lost confidence in your ability to run the Macintosh division."

As noted in Chapter 7, we can influence people in dozens of different ways. We can promise, reward, threaten, punish, bully, discuss, instruct, negotiate, manipulate, supplicate, ingratiate, and on and on (Table 7-2 presents a detailed listing). Some of these tactics, however, are more contentious than others. Threats, punishment, and bullying, for example, are all contentious tactics, because they are direct, nonrational, and unilateral. When one uses such interpersonal strategies, the likelihood of group conflict becomes greater.

Sculley, in threatening Jobs with a demotion, chose a contentious method of dealing with the company's dwindling profits and his problems in working with Jobs. Unfortunately, as Deutsch and Robert Krauss (1960) document in their classic investigation of threats, such tactics tend to increase hostility, counterthreats, and unwillingness to compromise. They conducted their study by asking pairs of women to play a simple "trucking game." Each participant was to imagine herself the owner of a trucking company—Acme or Bolt—that carried merchandise over the roads portrayed in Figure 12-3. Each time Acme's truck reached her designated destination, she would earn 60 cents minus any "operating costs," 1 cent for each second taken up by the trip. Bolt was rewarded on a similar contract.

The subjects soon discovered that they had a problem. Ideally, each company would travel on the main road, labeled Route 216 on the map, to cut operating expenses to a minimum. Unfortunately, a stretch of this highway was only one lane, and the rules of the game stipulated that this section was too narrow to allow the trucks to pass each other. When trucks encountered each other along this route, one player had to back up to her starting position to let the other through. Of course, the problem could have been avoided by taking the winding alternate route, but this path was so long that the extra time taken during transit meant that operating costs would cut deeply into profits.

All the pairs played the same basic game, but some were provided with the power to threaten their opponents, and others were not. In the *unilateral-threat condition*, Acme was told that a gate, which only she could open and close, was located at the fork in Route 216. When the gate was closed, neither truck could pass this point in the road, making control of the gate a considerable benefit to Acme. If Bolt attempted to use the main route, all Acme had to do was close the gate, forcing Bolt to back up and enabling Acme to reopen the gate and proceed quickly to her destination. Thus, when only Acme possessed the gate, Bolt's profits were greatly threatened. In the *bilateral-threat condition* both sides had the use of gates located at the ends of the one-lane section of Route 216, and in the *control condition* no gates were given to the players.

Deutsch and Krauss found that subjects who could not threaten each other soon learned to resolve the conflict over the one-lane road. Most of these pairs took turns using the main route, and on the average each subject playing the game in the control condition made a $1 profit. Winnings

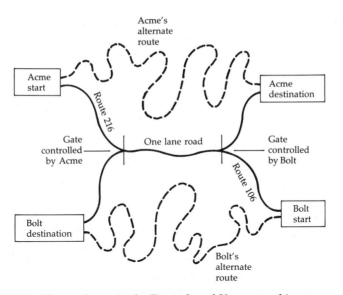

FIGURE 12-3. The road map in the Deutsch and Krauss trucking game.
Source: Deutsch, 1973

dwindled, however, when one of the players was given a gate. Subjects in the unilateral-threat condition lost an average of $2.03. Bolt's losses were twice as great as Acme's, but even Acme lost more than a dollar at the game. Conflict was even worse when both Acme and Bolt had gates. In the bilateral-threat condition both players usually took the longer route because the gates on the main route were kept closed, and losses in this condition averaged $4.38.

On the basis of these findings Deutsch and Krauss concluded that the capacity to threaten others sets up a conflict situation and that the actual use of threats serves to intensify the conflict. Subsequent investigations have supported this conclusion, and in general they indicate that earnings are highest when neither side can threaten the other. More surprisingly, these studies also suggest that if one party can or does threaten the other party, the threatened party will fare best if he or she *cannot* respond with a counterthreat (for example, Borah, 1963; Deutsch & Lewicki, 1970; Froman & Cohen, 1969; Gallo, 1966). More recent research, however, suggests that equally powerful opponents, over time, learn to avoid the use of their power. Provided fear of retaliation is high, individuals will not attack each other (Lawler, Ford, & Blegen, 1988).

In sum, influencing others by using threats may cause the situation to become "dynamically competitive" as "each party employs counterthreats and counterdemands in response to the other's threats in an escalatory cycle" (Milburn, 1977, p. 131). This conclusion suggests that the commonsense rule that open communication in groups that are experiencing conflicts curbs conflict should be qualified: if group members are exchanging threats and demands, communication will increase rather than decrease conflict. When Deutsch and Krauss let subjects in the bilateral-threat condition communicate, messages typically emphasized threats and did little to reduce conflict (Deutsch, 1973). Other studies, too, suggest that communication among participants is detrimental, because these initial messages are often inconsistent, hostile, and contentious (McClintock, Stech, & Keil, 1983; Pilisuk, Brandes, & van den Hove, 1976; Stech & McClintock, 1981). Evidence also indicates that communication can be beneficial if the subjects have been trained to use communication appropriately (Krauss & Deutsch, 1966) or if threats—such as those based on the gates in the trucking game—are not permitted (Smith & Anderson, 1975).

Interpersonal Orientation

Extensive reviews of the previous research conclude that many group-member characteristics are related to conflict, but general conclusions are still difficult to formulate. As Kenneth Terhune (1970) points out in his detailed analysis of personality and conflict, researchers encounter difficulties in (1) generalizing from findings based on laboratory studies to more complex, nonlaboratory conflicts, (2) accurately assessing the critical personal characteristics of group members, (3) measuring conflict behaviors, and (4) capturing and understanding the interaction between situational and personal characteristics. As a result about all that Terhune can conclude is that the relationship between "personality and conflict is complicated" (Terhune, 1970, p. 225; see also Hare, 1976; Rubin & Brown, 1975; Tedeschi, Schlenker, & Bonoma, 1973).

One variable that is consistently stressed more than others is the **interpersonal style** of interacting group members. Both Jobs and Sculley, for example, were tough-minded entrepreneurs who sought to maximize their gains whenever possible. Jobs has been described as the "John McEnroe of American capitalism: arrogant, self-centered, and too wealthy for his own good" (Samuelson, 1985, p. 59). Sculley had the reputation for being a tough manager who preferred to deal with problems by restructuring the group (Sculley, 1987). Did their interpersonal styles contribute to the conflict?

Researchers have conceptualized and operationalized interpersonal style in a variety of ways, but most draw a broad distinction between *cooperators* and *competitors* (Apfelbaum, 1974; Blake & Mouton, 1984; Brenner & Vinacke, 1979; Hermann & Kogan, 1977; Kelley, 1968; Rubin & Brown, 1975, Swap & Rubin, 1983). Cooperators tend to be accommodative, interpersonally sensitive, and concerned that everyone in the group benefits. A cooperator, for example, would argue that "when people deal with each other, it's better when everyone comes out even" and, if playing a game with a child, would "try to arrange it so that no one really wins or loses" (Brenner & Vinacke, 1979, p. 291). A competitor, in contrast, deals with conflict by confronting it and overwhelming it at all costs. Such a person views group disagreements as win/lose situations and finds satisfaction in forcing his or her ideas on the others; concession and compromise are only for losers. A competitor believes that "each person should get the most he can" and plays to win even when playing a game with a child (Brenner & Vinacke, 1979, p. 291).

As you would expect, when individuals with differing interpersonal orientations meet in a group, the result is often conflict. The competitor's style is often abrasive, spurring cooperative members to react with criticism and requests for fairer treatment. Competitors, however, rarely modify their behavior in response to these complaints, because they are relatively unconcerned with maintaining smooth interpersonal relations. Hence, competitors often overwhelm cooperators, who sometimes respond by becoming competitive themselves. Also, when two competitors meet, the result is often an intense conflict like that seen at Apple; when the interaction is complete and one of the individuals has won, the loser often withdraws from the group altogether (Cummings, Harnett, & Stevens, 1971; Harnett, Cummings, & Hamner, 1973; Shure & Meeker, 1967). (See Focus 12-3.)

• •
FOCUS 12-3: GENDER DIFFERENCES IN COMPETITIVE SETTINGS

You are about to meet a man and a woman. One of them is self-centered, competitive, forceful, active, and assertive. The other is group-centered, cooperative, accommodative, and interested in maintaining harmony. Which one is the woman, and which is the man?

Common sex-role stereotypes generally assume that men are more competitive than women. Stories of executives conjure up images of individuals who are driven, ruthless, self-seeking, and male. Yet, experimental studies of cooperation and competition suggest that women are just as competitive as men—if not more so (Deaux, 1976; Nemeth, 1973). In one study, for example, 140 same-sex pairs and 70 mixed-sex pairs played the PDG. Unexpectedly, the paired men tended to make more joint cooperative choices, whereas paired women tended to make more joint competitive choices. Moreover, men seemed to vary their strategies more to match the actions of their partner, whereas women's strategies remained more constant.

The greater competitiveness of women in the PDG is not a particularly stable finding. One review of previous work found that in 21 experiments women were more competitive, but 27 other studies suggested that women were less competitive (Rubin & Brown, 1975). This instability may reflect differences in men's and women's definitions of competition and cooperation (Buss, 1981; Deaux, 1976; Stockard, van de Kragt, & Dodge, 1988). Men often select the cooperative choice not because they want to help their partner but because they realize that this choice will maximize their profit. Women, in contrast, make choices that are consistent with the nature of the interpersonal setting. If, for example, their partner is attractive, they tend to make cooperative choices. If they do not like their partner, they are likely to compete (Kahn, Hottes, & Davis, 1971). As Kay Deaux (1976, p. 99) explains, "men seem to be more oriented toward the game itself, attempting to develop tactics that will guarantee them the largest financial payoff. . . . Women on the other hand seem less concerned with the game itself and more concerned with the interpersonal setting."

• •

THE CONFLICT PROCESS

Early in 1985 Sculley and Jobs began moving toward a showdown, pushed into conflict by the competitive nature of their interdependence, their reliance on contentious tactics of influence, and their competitive interpersonal orientations. As the dispute worsened, the combatants' exchanges become increasingly hostile, persuasive influence was dropped in favor of threats, and compliments were replaced by insults. By spring the men were trapped in a **conflict spiral:** each new dispute led to more conflict, which in turn led to more conflict. The conflict escalated, seemingly uncontrolled. Here we consider a host of perceptual, cognitive, and interpersonal factors that contributed to this escalation process.

Attributions and Misperceptions

When Sculley told Jobs that he was replacing him, Jobs must have asked himself many questions: Was Sculley only worried about the success of Apple, or was he trying to make Jobs the scapegoat for the company's troubles? Would Sculley follow through on his threat, or was he trying to increase his control over the Mac division? Was Sculley playing fairly, or was he using devious, illicit methods to oust Jobs?

Jobs's understanding of the conflict situation was shaped by his answers to such questions. According to **attribution theory,** which is a social-psychological explanation of how people make inferences about the causes of behaviors and events, people continually formulate intuitive causal hypotheses about events that transpire in the group (Heider, 1958). During conflict, interactants make attributions about their associates' motives and intentions, and these inferences steer their interpretation of the stituation. When group members argue, for example, they must determine why they disagree. If members conclude that their disagreement stems merely from the group's attempts to make the right decision, the disagreement will probably not turn into true conflict. If, however, participants attribute the disagreement to others' incompetence, belligerence, or argumentativeness, a simple disagreement can escalate into conflict (Horai, 1977; Messé, Stollak, Larson, & Michaels, 1979).

If group members' attributions were always accurate, they would help interactants understand one another better and thereby function as conflict reducers. Unfortunately, perceptual biases regularly distort individuals' attributional inferences. One bias occurs when attributors assume that other people's behavior is caused by personal (dispositional) rather than situational (environmental) factors (Ross, 1977). If, for example, Jobs fell prey to this so-called **fundamental attribution error,** he would blame Sculley's personality, beliefs, attitudes, and values for the conflict rather than pressure from the board of directors, shareholders, or Jobs's own actions.

Because of the fundamental attribution error, group members are predisposed to misinterpret the behavior of other group members (Kelley, 1979; Orvis, Kelley, & Butler, 1976). Moreover, the distortion is minimal when the group interaction is pleasant or interactants are careful to empathize with one another, but the effect grows stronger during conflict (Regan & Totten, 1975; Rosenberg & Wolfsfeld, 1977). Researchers in one study compared the attributions of *active observers*—those who not only observed others but also interacted with others—to the attributions of *passive observers*—individuals who were not actually part of the group. During the experiment the active observers played the PDG with a simulated partner who consistently chose either cooperative or competitive responses. When these two sets of observers later estimated the extent to which the behavior of the partner was a good indicator of personality, active observers made more dispositional attributions than passive observers—provided their partner had competed. In other words the bias was greatest during conflict (Miller & Norman, 1975; see also Cunningham, Starr, & Kanouse, 1979; Messé et al., 1979; Murata, 1982).

These findings and others suggest that people tend to assume the worst about other group members. In one study subjects played a PDG-like game with a partner whose behavior was either (1) competitive (he or she maximized personal gains while minimizing the partner's gains), (2) cooperative (maximized joint gains), (3) individualistic (ignored the partner's gains but maximized personal gains), or (4) altruistic (ignored personal gains but maximized the partner's gains). When asked to describe their partner's motives, subjects were most accurate when playing an individualistic or competitive person and least accurate in interpreting cooperation and altruism. Apparently, group members had difficulty believing that their associates were behaving in an altruistic manner but readily believed the suggestion that their behaviors revealed conflict (Maki, Thorngate, & McClintock, 1979). Similarly, Harold Kelley and Anthony Stahelski (1970a, 1970b, 1970c) found that people who tend to compete with others are less accurate in their perceptions than individuals who tend to cooperate. When cooperators play the PDG with other cooperators, their perceptions of their partner's strategy are inaccurate only 6% of the time. When competitors play the PDG with cooperators, however, they misinterpret their partner's strategy 47% of the time, mistakenly believing that the cooperators are competing (see Focus 12-4).

Commitment

Sculley and Jobs shared the same goal: to make Apple successful. Yet, the two were committed to different positions on how this success could be achieved. Sculley, with his marketing background, insisted that Apple build machines that fit consumers' needs. Jobs, in contrast, wanted the Macintosh to be the most elegant, efficient, and simple machine ever built.

• •

FOCUS 12-4: ATTRIBUTIONS OF RESPONSIBILITY FOR GROUP ENDEAVORS

When a group runs into problems, members often search for the cause. The board of directors at Apple blamed Jobs's devotion to the Mac for the company's economic misfortunes. The 1988 Oakland Athletics blamed the Los Angeles Dodgers' camaraderie and their own bad luck for their loss in the World Series. NASA scientists blamed the engineers who had designed the Challenger's O-rings for the disaster (Hirokawa, Gouran, & Martz, 1988).

In most cases group members' explanations are *group-serving:* they attribute the problems to factors outside of the group and, therefore, protect the group from blame (Norvell & Forsyth, 1984). During conflict, however, members tend to blame one another for the group's misfortunes. These *self-serving* attributions include attempts to deny responsibility ("It's not my fault we failed"), blaming other group members ("You really blew that one"), emphasizing one's own competence ("Personally speaking, I did very well"), and withdrawing from the group ("I'm not gonna play with you losers").

Naturally, group-serving tactics tend to unite the group, whereas self-serving tactics can result in interpersonal conflict and the loss of cohesion (Leary & Forsyth, 1987). For example, in one study two teams competed in a game situation (Shaw & Breed, 1970). Certain members of each team were confederates of the researcher, and they systematically blamed one of the actual subjects for the team's losses. Unfairly accused group members, relative to others who had escaped blame, were less satisfied with their teams, belittled their teammates' abilities, and preferred to work with other groups on future tasks.

Similar consequences of self-serving reactions in the face of failure were obtained when investigators assigned college students to small groups working on a simulated survival exercise. After the subjects learned whether their group had succeeded or failed at the task, they rated their personal responsibility for the outcome and rated others' responsibility, too. The subjects then evaluated other group members who had apparently claimed high, moderate, and low responsibility for the outcome. As shown in Figure 12-4, group members who blamed others for failure or tried to claim the lion's share of responsibility after success were not well liked (Forsyth, Berger, & Mitchell, 1981).

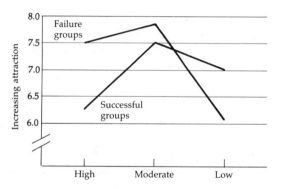

FIGURE 12-4. Consequences of self-serving and group-serving attributions. When the group failed, the self-serving members who claimed low responsibility were liked significantly less than the more group-serving members who claimed moderate or high responsibility. Conversely, when the group did well, individuals who claimed all the credit were liked the least, and those who claimed moderate responsibility were liked the most.

(Source: Forsyth, Berger, & Mitchell, 1981)

• •

Commitment frequently results when people defend their viewpoints against attack (Staw & Ross, 1987). First, attitude researchers have found that when we must persuade others, we often search out supporting arguments. If this *elaboration* process yields further consistent information, we become even more favorable toward our position (Petty & Cacioppo, 1986). Second, when people take a public position on an issue, they often feel that they will appear soft, weak, or inconsistent if they back down. Group members may realize that they are wrong, but to *save face* they continue to argue against their opponents (Brown, 1977; Felson, 1981; Stults & Messé, 1985). Third, once committed, individuals begin to *rationalize* their choice by overestimating the brilliance of their own solution, rejecting the veracity of information that conflicts with their stance, and increasing their dedication to their original position (Batson, 1975). Last, if we feel that other people in the group are attacking our position, we may experience *reactance* (Brehm, 1976; Brehm & Brehm, 1981). As noted in Chapter 7, when reactance occurs we often become even more committed to our original position.

Entrapment

When commitment becomes very extreme, it can lead to **entrapment:** "a special form of escalation in which the parties expend more of their time, energy, money, or other resources in the conflict than seems appropriate or justifiable by external standards" (Pruitt & Rubin, 1986, p. 122). Allan Teger's (1980) studies of "dollar auctions" vividly document the entrapment process. Using both naturally occurring groups and laboratory groups, Teger tells participants that he will auction off a dollar bill to the highest bidder. Interactants are instructed to offer bids, just as in an auction, but one unique rule is added: although the highest bidder gets to keep the dollar bill, the second highest bidder not only gets nothing but also must pay the amount he or she bid. In all the groups, members are at first reluctant to compete under these rules, but soon the bids begin to climb over 50 cents toward the $1 mark. As the stakes increase, however, the group members realize that quitting will be very costly, and thus they become trapped in the confrontation (Brockner & Rubin, 1985; Brockner, Shaw, & Rubin, 1979).

Why is this situation so problematic? Consider the predicament of two hypothetical group members, John and Steve. All other players have dropped out, and Steve has just bettered John's 80-cent bid by 10 cents. John would like to quit, but he would be out 80 cents, and Steve would be making 10 cents. So John raises his bid to $1 to avoid the loss of his 80-cent investment. Steve now faces a similar dilemma, for he will lose 90 cents if he gives up. Therefore, even though he feels somewhat foolish offering more money than the bill is actually worth, Steve bids $1.10. As this example shows, entrapment can be very costly; Teger has found that the bidding nearly always exceeds $1, and on occasion it has even gone as high as $20.

Arousal and Aggression

As conflict escalates, anxiety and tension become more dominant (Blascovich, Nash, & Ginsburg, 1978; Van Egeren, 1979). Even when group members begin by discussing their points calmly and dispassionately, as they become locked into their positions, emotional expressions begin to replace logical discussions. Unfortunately, this emotional arousal often exacerbates the conflict.

Evidence of this conflict-stimulating effect of emotional arousal comes from studies of the **arousal/aggression hypothesis.** This hypothesis is based on early studies of the link between frustration and aggression (Berkowitz, 1962, 1978, 1983, 1989). When group members are unable to attain the goals they desire because of some environmental restraint or personal limitation, they sometimes experience frustration. This frustration, in turn, produces a readiness to respond in an aggressive manner that boils over into hostility and violence if situational cues that serve as releasers are present. Recent research indicates that many unpleasant and noxious conditions, including competition, insults, failure, and stress, can set the stage for aggressive conflict. These aversive events work by creating a heightened emotional arousal, which is often subjectively labeled anger. This arousal, then, is the motivation driving the subsequent aggressive actions (see Berkowitz, 1989; Ferguson & Rule, 1983; Zillmann, 1983).

John R. P. French, in an early laboratory study of conflict in groups (1941), demonstrated the link between arousal and aggression by examining the reactions of 16 groups as they worked on a series of insoluble problems. Although all groups showed signs of increased hostility, French also found systematic differences in their reactions to their difficulties. In groups composed of subjects who had never interacted before the meeting, frustration led to deep divisions in the groups. The polarization was so intense that half of these groups either split up into subgroups to work on the problems or forced one or more of their members to leave the group and sit in a corner! When the group members knew one another before the meeting, however, the frustration did not produce as much separation between members, but interpersonal aggression—such as overt hostility, joking hostility, scapegoating, and domination—was relatively high. Indeed, in one group of "friends" the rates of aggression escalated so quickly that observers lost track of how many offensive remarks were made; they estimated that the number surpassed 600 comments during the 45-minute work period.

Reciprocity

Conflict-ridden groups may, at first consideration, seem to be aimless and normless, with hostility and dissatisfaction spinning out of control. James Tedeschi and his colleagues, however, believe that conflict is often sustained by the **norm of reciprocity**. Reciprocity suggests that when people who help you later need help, you are obligated to return their favor. However, *negative reciprocity* implies that people who harm you are also deserving of harm themselves. The converse of "You scratch my back and I'll scratch yours" is "An eye for an eye, a tooth for a tooth" (for example, Tedeschi, Gaes, & Rivera, 1977; Tedeschi, Smith, & Brown, 1974). If one group member criticizes the ideas, opinions, or characteristics of another, the victim of the attack will feel justified in counterattacking unless some situational factor legitimizes the aggression of the former. Indeed, laboratory studies involving two partners delivering electric shocks to each other typically find that partners return what they themselves received. If the opponent gives you one shock, you return one shock; if the other zaps you with seven shocks, seven shocks are meted out in return (Berkowitz & Geen, 1962; Buss, 1961).

The norm of reciprocity also explains a phenomenon that Harold Kelley and Anthony Stahelski have labeled **behavioral assimilation**: the eventual matching, or assimilation, of the behaviors displayed by interacting group members. Kelley and Stahelski (1970a, 1970b, 1970c) arranged for individuals to play the PDG with other subjects who chose either cooperative responses or competitive responses. If individuals who had begun by cooperating played cooperative partners, they remained cooperative. If their partners began competing with them, behavioral assimilation occurred, and the previously cooperative players became competitive. Moreover, negative reciprocity (competing with competitors) was stronger than positive reciprocity (cooperating with cooperators). Individuals who had begun by competing with others tended to continue competing even when they were faced with highly cooperative partners. The norm of positive reciprocity dictates that these competitors should have met this cooperation with reduced competition, but Kelley and Stahelski found little evidence of cooperative behavioral assimilation. Although other research has shown that negative reciprocity is minimal if cooperatively oriented individuals have the opportunity to withdraw from the interaction or can communicate their "good" intentions to their partners (Garner & Deutsch, 1974; Miller & Holmes, 1975), other findings have confirmed the greater strength of negative reciprocity (Carroll, 1987; Schlenker & Goldman, 1978). (See Focus 12-5.)

. . . .

FOCUS 12-5: WHY DO CONFLICTS SPIRAL?

If interactants followed the norm of reciprocity perfectly, helping would always be met with helping, a mild threat would elicit a mild threat in return, and an attack would lead to a counterattack. As George A. Youngs, Jr., (1986) notes, however, exact reciprocity occurs only when individuals precisely match the quantity and quality of rewards or punishments they received. In many cases interactants follow the norm of rough reciprocity: they give too much (overmatching) or give too little (undermatching) in return.

Youngs believes, to simplify somewhat, that conflict spirals occur when reciprocity is rough rather than exact. To investigate this hypothesis, he arranged for women to play a conflict game with a confederate. Before some trials the subjects were given the opportunity to send a warning to their partner: "If you do not make Choice 1 on the next round, I will take ____ points from your total," and subjects could fill in the blank with the size of the fine. If the partner did not comply, the subjects could act on the warning, but the fine did not have to match the warning.

Young found clear evidence of reciprocity: the more often the confederate sent threats, the more often the subjects sent threats; when the confederate's threats were large, the subjects' threats were large; and confederates who exacted large fines triggered large fines from subjects. This reciprocity, however, was rough rather than exact. At low levels of conflict the subjects tended to overmatch threats and punishments, and at high levels of conflict they tended to undermatch their threats. Young suggests that the overmatching that occurs initially may serve as a strong warning, whereas the undermatching at high levels of conflict may be used to send a conciliatory gesture.

. . . .

Coalition Formation

Although the initial disagreement may involve only two group members, these persons, by forming **coalitions,** marshal the forces of the group against one another, compelling previously neutral members to identify with one faction or the other. Similarly, even when members initially express many different views, with time these multiparty conflicts are reduced to two-party blocs through coalition formation (Mack & Snyder, 1957). Because coalitions play a key role in the conflict process, we will examine this topic in detail in the next section.

COALITIONS

When Jobs learned that Sculley was going to follow through with his threat to have him removed as the director of the Mac division, Jobs tried to persuade each member of the board to side with him in the dispute. His goal was to form a powerful coalition that would block Sculley's plans and swing the vote of the board in his favor. Unfortunately for Jobs his coalition was not strong enough to overcome Sculley's supporters.

Coalitions exist in most groups, but when conflict erupts, group members often use them to shift the balance of power in a self-serving direction. Coalitions vary in many respects, but in most cases

1. They involve participants who disagree on many fundamental issues but decide to ignore these differences until the problem at hand can be settled. As in politics, where certain coalitions involve "strange bedfellows," coalitions in small groups sometimes involve the unlikeliest of allies (Murnighan, 1978).

2. They form to promote the attainment of certain goals or the achievement of specific outcomes. For a time the members of the subgroup share a common goal and stand to profit more by forming a coalition than by remaining independent (Caplow, 1956; Pearce, Stevenson, & Porter, 1986).

3. They tend to be temporary, because members may abandon one alliance to form more profitable ones. Furthermore, once the goals of the coalition are accomplished, the participants' differences again become evident, making cooperation more difficult (Gamson, 1964).

4. They occur in mixed-motive situations. Although allies may wish to compete with one another, no single individual has enough power to succeed alone. Hence, while the coalition exists, the competitive motive must be stifled (Gamson, 1964).

5. They involve an adversarial element. Individuals in the coalition work not only to ensure their own outcomes but also to worsen the outcomes of noncoalition members. Coalitions form with people and against other people, as Thibaut and Kelley (1959, p. 205) point out: "By coalition we mean two or more persons who act jointly to affect the outcomes of one or more other persons."

These qualities explain why coalitions are associated with group conflict. Forming a coalition is, in most cases, a contentious influence strategy that increases competition, rather than cooperation, among members. In business settings, for example, the dominant coalition can control the organization, yet it often works outside the bounds of the formal group structure (Cyert & March, 1963; Pearce, et al., 1986; Stevenson, Pearce, & Porter, 1985). Those who are excluded from a coalition react with hostility to the coalition members and seek to regain power by forming their own coalitions. Thus, coalitions must be constantly maintained through strategic bargaining and negotiation (Murnighan, 1986). Because coalitions have such a major impact on group conflict, the conclusions of empirical studies of alliances within groups are examined in detail here.

Research on Coalition Formation

Just as researchers study competition and conflict using the PDG, coalition formation has been investigated in many cases using a "convention" or "legislative" role-playing paradigm. Groups of three or more subjects are assembled in the laboratory and told that they will be forming coalitions in order to win some points. After the concept of a coalition is defined, resources are allocated to each member. As defined by William Gamson, resources are "weights controlled by the participants such that some critical quantity of these weights is necessary and sufficient to determine the decision" (1964, p. 82). In one study of four-person groups (Murnighan, Komorita, & Szwajkowski, 1977) 17 votes were distributed unevenly among group members; one person was given 8 votes, another 7, and the remaining two people received 1 vote each. Although this distribution seemed to give the person with 8 a considerable edge, a majority of the votes—at least 9—was required to earn the payoff (100 points, which could be converted to money at the end of the experiment). This procedure might be termed a 9(8-7-1-1) game, where 9 is the number of votes needed to win and 8-7-1-1 is the allocation of resources to the four people in the group. In this situation four winning coalitions are possible: 8-7, 7-1-1, and 8-1.

Since none of the members of the group has enough power (votes) to win alone, the researcher invites them to contact one another to try to form a coalition. Although the mode of communication varies from study to study, subjects typically either pass written messages, make suggestions to the researcher, or bargain in face-to-face interactions. In most cases the experiment involves a series of trials in which subjects offer to join with others in a coalition while simultaneously suggesting that the payoff be divided in a particular way. These coalition and payoff negotiations are repeated on each trial, and this paradigm therefore contains two basic dependent variables: the type of coalition formed (for example, 8-7 or 7-1-1) and the manner in which the payoff is distributed. (As an example of the latter variable, when an 8-1 coalition forms, does the person with 8 votes get 85% of the prize while the person with 1 vote gets only

15%?) The following subsections describe the conclusions drawn from detailed reviews of these types of studies (Baker, 1981; Miller & Crandall, 1980; Miller & Komorita, 1986b; Murnighan, 1978).

The cheapest winning solution.   Coalitions form when no single individual has sufficient resources to control the group decisions (Komorita & Meek, 1978; Murnighan, 1978). In most instances, however, these coalitions contain only the minimum number of individuals necessary to win, with all superfluous parties being excluded from the subgroup. In the 9(8-7-1-1) game, for example, a coalition of 8-1-1 is very unlikely, because the 8-1 coalition alone is sufficient for success. Gamson calls the 8-1 coalition the *cheapest winning solution:* it reaches the decision point (9 votes) but does so by the smallest margin possible.

Smaller is better.   Georg Simmel (1950) long ago pointed out that a coalition of two tends to be more stable and more cohesive than a coalition of three or more. In dyads information and decisions can be exchanged more rapidly and accurately, whereas in larger coalitions more complex group structures are needed to make decisions and to exchange information. Also, because coalitions can be formed within the larger coalitions, confidence and trust among participants in large coalitions are almost always more uncertain. Studies conducted in laboratories give strong support to Simmel's prediction (Shears, 1967; Komorita & Meek, 1978), but coalitions in naturally occurring groups tend to be somewhat larger than necessary (Kravitz, 1981; Nachmias, 1974; Nicholson, Cole, & Rocklin, 1986).

Weakness is strength.   Paradoxically, individuals with fewer resources are often preferred partners in winning coalitions. Although people whose resources are so minimal that they are no help in achieving success are rarely chosen for coalition membership, the person who has just enough to tip the coalition's total resources over the top is typically the most popular partner (Caplow, 1968). First, the weaker individual may be more likely to realize that success can be attained only through a coalition with others who are more powerful. Second, stronger individuals tend to find weaker individuals more attractive partners, because they hope the weaker persons—realizing that they add only a small fraction to the coalition's total resources—will be satisfied with only a fraction of the payoff.

Strength is weakness.   Given the hypothesis that "weakness is strength," it also stands to reason that strength will be a weakness. Study after study has demonstrated that the individual with the greatest resources and power tends to be more frequently excluded from coalitions than weaker, less-well-off members (Gamson, 1964; Murnighan, 1978). First, those with few resources tend to avoid powerful partners because (1) their relatively large contributions to the coalition's resources entitles them to a bigger piece of the payoff pie and (2) they may attempt to manipulate or exploit members of the coalition who possess fewer resources (Komorita & Ellis, 1988). Second, those with large resources frequently do not realize that they need to join a coalition. Although their power exists only as long as the others don't unite against them, powerful persons often mistakenly believe their power base to be safe and incontrovertible.

Norms of reward.   Coalitions could use a variety of rules to determine how their winnings should be divided among members, but in most cases division is based on either an equity norm or an equality norm. According to the **equity norm** (also called the *parity norm*), coalition members should receive outcomes in proportion to their inputs. For example, a person with 20% of the votes in a coalition should receive only 20% of the payoff that the coalition earns by succeeding, whereas the individual with 80% of the resources should receive 80% of the payoff. The **equality norm,** in contrast, recommends that all group members, irrespective of their inputs, should be given an equal share of the payoff. Even though a person contributes only 20% of the coalition's resources, he or she should receive as much as the person who contributes 80%. In many cases the members of coalitions negotiate for payoffs, with weaker members arguing in favor of equality and stronger members arguing for equity (Murnighan, 1985).

Sex differences.   Women and men differ in coalition situations. As previous summaries of sex differences have noted, women don't always form the cheapest winning solution, they divide up payoffs based on equality rather than equity, they are less likely to exclude the powerful person from the coalition, and they more often refrain from taking full advantage of the weakness of others. In explaining these differences, Gamson (1964) proposes that women tend to adopt an *anticompetitive norm* in coalition situations. Men readily accept the situation as a mixed-motive problem that calls for competition with and exploitation of those who are excluded from the coalition, but women tend to coordinate their behavior with the needs of the rest of the group. Therefore, women strive to maintain smooth intermember relations as the men maximize their payoffs. Although any group could adopt an anticompetitive norm, women seem to accept this norm more readily than men (Miller & Crandall, 1980; Vinacke, 1971).

Theoretical Analyses of Coalitions
Consider for a moment the choice you might make if placed in a coalition-formation study. Assuming that the researcher has adopted a three-person game 9(8-7-2) and that you are the 2, would you seek an alliance with 7 or 8? If both indicated that they would accept you in a coalition, whom would you side with? How would you react if, after forming a liaison with 7, you discovered that he or she was willing to give you only 20% of the payoff? Would you abandon the alliance and join 8? How would you feel if 7 and 8 formed a coalition, leaving you with no payoff at all? How would

you go about breaking up their alliance and forming one of your own? To understand more fully how most people answer such questions, researchers have developed theoretical models to explain when and why certain types of coalitions are likely to form. Because of the wealth of such theories (Murnighan's 1978 review mentions 14!), coverage in this text must be limited, and several excellent models drawn from game theory, social psychology, and political science will unfortunately not be discussed. Still, the following brief overview of three perspectives—minimum-resource theory, minimum-power theory, and bargaining theory—will help convey the general direction of theory and research in this important area.

Minimum-resource theory. Gamson's minimum-resource theory is based on two fundamental assumptions: (1) people in group situations will behave hedonistically and will thus be motivated to maximize their power, outcomes, and payoffs by forming coalitions; and (2) individuals' expectations concerning the division of the coalition's payoff will conform to an equity norm (Gamson, 1961a, 1961b, 1964). Table 12-2 applies these two assumptions to a 9(8-7-2) triad. A coalition between any two group members will be sufficient to win the payoff. If the payoff is divided according to a equity norm, however, the coalition yielding the highest payoffs for two of the group members is the 7-2 combination. Therefore, the theory predicts that this coalition is the most likely one to form, because both 7 and 2 should prefer this alliance to one with person 8. This approach is called **minimum-resource theory** because it predicts the most likely coalition to be the grouping that is sufficient to win but involves partners with the fewest resources. (A similar theoretical position, first suggested by Theodore Caplow [1956, 1968], proposed that individuals in a group will form coalitions that maximize their control over the remaining group members. However, because Caplow felt that power typically derives from control over resources, his approach makes predictions that are for the most part identical with those of minimum-resource theory.)

Minimum-power theory. **Minimum-power theory** synthesizes Gamson's resource theory and a mathematical model derived from game theory (Shapley, 1953). The theory begins by suggesting that prior resources are an inadequate indication of a person's power in a coalition situation.

TABLE 12-2. Equity-norm payoffs predicted by minimum-resource theory in a 9(8-7-2) coalition situation.

Coalition	Total Votes	Payoff to 2	Payoff to 7	Payoff to 8
7-8	15	0	7/15	8/15
2-8	10	2/10	0	8/10
2-7	9	2/9	7/9	0

In the example triad—9(8-7-2)—any one of the three members possesses the power to turn a losing coalition into a winning one when a two-person liaison is formed. Even the lowly 2, who controls just 12% of the total resources, can still significantly determine the outcome by joining with one of the other group members in a coalition. In a sense, all three individuals have equal power, even though their resources differ.

Because the minimum-power theory is based on the concept of individuals' power rather than resources, to make it a viable approach we need a systematic way of calculating the power of each group member. Theorists typically solve this problem by calculating *pivotal power*: the power of an individual to turn a winning coalition into a losing one or a losing coalition into a winning one (Miller, 1980c). Pivotal power can be estimated by calculating the number of times a person can change a winning coalition into a losing one by withdrawing, and then dividing this number by the total number of possible coalitions. In the example of three persons (2, 7, and 8 votes), we find that all three are equal in terms of pivotal power; there are only three possible coalitions, and in each one both partners are pivotal— that is, completely necessary for the success of the coalition (Murnighan et al., 1977). Hence, all three have a pivotal power of 2/3, or .66.

Minimum-power theory also assumes that the equity norm determines payoff allocations, but it predicts that the payoff will be in proportion to pivotal power. Thus, the theory predicts that the most likely coalition to form will be one that wins but contains individuals with the smallest amounts of pivotal power. Forming a liaison with a person who commands a great deal of pivotal power makes little sense, because the equity norm suggests that a powerful person will expect, and deserve, a greater payoff than a coalition member with little pivotal power.

Bargaining theory. Samuel S. Komorita and his colleagues have developed **bargaining theory,** a model that emphasizes the importance of bargaining, concessions, objections, and threats. As applied to our example triad, the approach assumes that 2, 7, and 8, before beginning negotiations, calculate the payoffs of each possible liaison. For example, person 8, in considering a coalition with 7, could expect to receive 53% of the payoff, but by joining with 2 this payoff could be increased to 80% (see Table 12-3). This expectation is based solely on the equity norm, however, and bargaining theory suggests that 8 will also estimate payoffs by using the equality norm: equal payoffs to all coalition members irrespective of input or power. Hence, 8 also thinks that a link with either 2 or 7 will yield 50% of the payoffs if rewards are apportioned based on an equality norm. Although 8 would prefer that rewards be allocated based on the equity norm—since in each case this norm yields a higher payoff—he or she realizes that the actual distribution will fall somewhere in between these two expectations. As shown in Table 12-3, 8's expectation for the 7-8 coalition falls between 50% and 53%, and his or her expectation for the 2-8 coalition ranges from 50% to 80% (Komorita & Chertkoff, 1973; Komorita & Kravitz, 1983; Komorita & Meek, 1978; Komorita & Miller, 1986).

TABLE 12-3. Payoff expectations predicted by bargaining theory in a 9(8-7-2) coalition situation.

Individual	Coalition	Equity	Equality	Average Expectation
	7-8	8/15 (53%)	1/2 (50%)	31/60 (51.5%)
8	2-8	8/10 (80%)	1/2 (50%)	13/20 (65%)
	7-8	7/15 (47%)	1/2 (50%)	29/60 (48.5%)
7	2-7	7/9 (78%)	1/2 (50%)	23/36 (64%)
	2-8	2/10 (20%)	1/2 (50%)	7/20 (35%)
2	2-7	2/9 (22%)	1/2 (50%)	13/35 (36%)

On the basis of these mental calculations, 8 will probably prefer a co-alition with 2, because it will yield a payoff that most closely approximates that desired (based on averaging the payoffs suggested by the equity and equality norms). Person 8 may, however, be able to negotiate with 7 and 2 to increase his or her payoff. Although 2, as the individual with the weak-est position in terms of resources, will probably "demand" that the payoff be distributed on the basis of equality, 8 may note that unless 2 agrees to an equitable distribution, he or she will be left out of the coalition and therefore receive no payoff whatsoever. Using this threat, 8 may success-fully extract a promise of high rewards if a coalition is formed with 2 rather than with 7. Komorita's theory is also unique in its consideration of the importance of forming a liaison with a person who won't be tempted to break off the coalition and defect to the other side. For example, if 2 de-cides to form a coalition with 7, since 7 promises to divide the payoff on a 65%-35% basis, 8 will probably try to talk 2 into leaving the 7-2 coalition. As time goes on, 8 may be willing to make certain concessions to 2 so that 2's payoffs begin to more closely approximate their original expectations as based on the equality norm (50%). According to Komorita, the possi-bility of later bargaining and concessions suggests that (1) people will pre-fer to join with others who, because of the resource distribution, will not be tempted to defect, and (2) over a long period of time (or trials), payoff distributions may change as members of the coalition must increase the rewards given to those members who are being tempted away from the subgroup. Thus, bargaining theory, unlike the other two approaches, ex-plains changes that might take place in payoff allocations.

Comparing the Theories

A *crucial experiment* is one of the most exciting and informative types of studies in any scientific field. In such an experiment the researcher care-fully sets up the conditions in which the hypotheses of two or more rival theories can be compared in the hope of determining which model is more adequate. Although for a number of empirical, logical, and philosophical reasons no experiment can be truly crucial, studies that test the predic-tions of several theories at once can nevertheless be dramatic in the amount of information they yield (Forsyth, 1976).

In the area of coalition behaviors, several recent studies have compared predictions derived from the more prominent coalition theories to determine which can best stand the test (Komorita & Meek, 1978; Komorita & Moore, 1976; Komorita & Nagao, 1983; Miller, 1980a, 1980b, 1980c; Murnighan et al., 1977; Nail & Cole, 1985). In one project (Komorita & Moore, 1976) four-person groups were instructed to choose others as partners in order to achieve a winning coalition. The resources were allocated on a 10-9-8-3 basis, and a two-thirds majority (20 votes) was needed to win. Hence, only three-party coalitions could successfully win the prize of 100 points, which was to be converted into money at the end of the experiment. The predictions of the three theories—minimum-resource, minimum-power, and bargaining—are presented in Table 12-4. First, minimum-resource theory assumes that (1) the person with 10 votes will be left out of the coalition, since the subgroup can succeed with just the 9-vote individual; and (2) payoffs based on the equity norm will be 9/20 (45 points), 8/20 (40 points), and 3/20 (15 points). Second, minimum-power theory considers all four possible coalitions to be equally likely, since all the individuals have the same amount of pivotal power. Since power is equal, payoffs should also be equal: 33 points for everyone. Third, bargaining theory predicts a 9-8-3 coalition but also predicts that payoff allocations will change over time. On the first trial the payoff distribution should represent the average of an equity norm and an equality norm (for example, for the person with 9 votes the equity norm suggests a 45-point payoff, but the equality norm recommends 33 points. The average of these two payoffs is 39 points). By the end of the study, however, payoffs to the weaker members should gradually increase, as the high-resource members are forced to bargain with the low-resource members to keep them in the coalition.

The results of the study are quite complex, but in general they seem to lend the most support to bargaining theory. On the first trial the 9-8-3 coalition occurred most frequently (9 out of 20 times), but this tendency was not statistically significant. Although this "no difference" is consistent with minimum-power theory, the reward allocations in these 9-8-3 coalitions averaged 40-37-23, an almost perfect match of the bargaining-theory

TABLE 12-4. A test of three theories of coalition formation in a 20(10-9-8-3) resource situation.

Theory	Predicted Coalition	Predicted Division of Payoff
Minimum-resource	9-8-3	45-40-15
Minimum-power	Any	33-33-33
Bargaining (first trial)	9-8-3	39-37-24
Bargaining (final trial)	9-8-3	36-34-30

predictions. Furthermore, by the end of all the trials the tendency to form the 9-8-3 coalition was highly significant, and the distribution of payoff points had gradually changed to again match the overall prediction of bargaining theory: although the final distribution of 34-35-31 could have been predicted by either bargaining or minimum-power theory, the minimum-resource theory prediction of 45-40-15 seems to be fairly inaccurate.

Despite these findings favorable to bargaining theory, other studies find that a variety of factors influence coalition formation, including the number and size of available coalitions (Komorita & Miller, 1986; Kravitz, 1987; Kravitz & Iwaniszek, 1984), the manner in which subjects acquired their points (Miller & Wong, 1986), group members' experience in forming coalitions (Miller & Komorita, 1986a; Urruti & Miller, 1984), and the availability of strategies that do not require coalitions (Komorita, Hamilton, & Kravitz, 1984). Indeed, as Gamson (1964, p. 92) pointed out in his review, the varying results of the many empirical investigations seem to support just one theory: the utter-confusion theory. However, as research efforts continue, the various strengths and weaknesses of the theories are becoming better known. Undoubtedly at some point in the future our theoretical explanations of coalition formation will become more unified.

CONFLICT RESOLUTION

In one way or another, conflicts are resolved. In the case of Apple Computers, Sculley imposed his solution on Jobs, and Jobs responded by withdrawing from the organization. Sculley moved Jobs to another building, took him out of company decision making, and publicly stated that the "company's reorganizational plans included absolutely no operating role" for Jobs (Uttal, 1985, p. 24). Jobs struggled to define his role in the company, but he eventually decided to leave. He explained in an interview (Lubenow & Rogers, 1985, p. 51):

> John felt that after the reorganization, it was important for me to not be at Apple for him to accomplish what he wanted to accomplish. And, as you know, he issued that public statement that there was no role for me there then or in the future, or in the foreseeable future. And that was about as black-and-white as you need to make things. Probably a little more black-and-white than it needed to be.

Imposition and *withdrawal*, however, are only two of many modes of dispute resolution (see Table 12-5). Sculley, rather than taking active steps to solve the company's problems, could have remained *inactive* in the hope that the problems would resolve themselves. Jobs could have *yielded* to Sculley by giving up control of the Mac division voluntarily, or the two could have reached a *compromise* that required mutual concessions (Blake and Mouton, 1964; Burke, 1970; Filley, 1976; Pruitt, 1983; Pruitt & Rubin, 1986; Sternberg & Soriano, 1984).

TABLE 12-5. Some common modes of conflict resolution.

Mode	Similar Terms	Description
Imposition	Win/lose, forcing, contending	One party is forced to accept the other party's position.
Withdrawal	Escape, retreat	One party leaves the group.
Inaction	Avoidance, wait-and-see	One or both parties do as little as possible.
Yielding	Smoothing, lose/win, conceding	One party withdraws his or her demands.
Compromise	Lose/lose, mutual concessions	Parties locate an alternative that stands somewhere between their positions
Problem solving	Win/win, confrontation, integrative bargaining	Parties identify the source of the conflict and agree on a solution.

Alternatively, Jobs and Sculley could have resolved the conflict through *problem solving*. Rather than battling it out until one side wins and the other loses, problem solvers strive to identify the issues underlying the dispute and then work together to identify a solution that is satisfying to both sides (Pruitt & Rubin, 1986). Instead of competing with the other party, problem solvers reestablish trust by refusing to reciprocate competition and hostility. Problem solvers also rely on negotiation rather than persuasion, argument, or contentious methods of influence. Lastly, if necessary, they rely on others to mediate the conflict so that a fair solution can be reached. These three facets of problem solving—instilling trust, negotiating, and third-party intervention—are examined below. (Approaches that can be used to reduce conflict between groups are considered in Chapter 13.)

Instilling Trust

During one particularly nasty board meeting Jobs and Sculley exchanged harsh words. As Sculley (1987, pp. 251–252) recalls the incident, Jobs told him "You really should leave this company. I'm more worried about Apple than I have ever been. I'm afraid of you." Sculley, obviously angered, answered, "I made a mistake treating you with high esteem. . . . I don't trust you, and I won't tolerate a lack of trust."

Trust lies at the core of successful problem solving. Whereas consistent cooperation among people over a long period generally increases mutual trust, for a group that has been wracked by disagreement, confrontation, and escalating conflict, mutual trust becomes much more elusive (Haas & Deseran, 1981). As Svenn Lindskold explains, when people cannot trust one another, they often compete simply to defend their own best interests. Such competition, however, is self-defeating in the long run, for it initiates a cycle of distrust and competition. Writes Lindskold (1978, pp. 772–773): "If the other party could only be trusted to be cooperative in search of the mutually beneficial solution, then the cycle could be reversed, and both parties could gain rather than lose."

But how can trust, once lost, be regained? Communication, consistency, and cooperative initiatives are critical (Deutsch, 1973; Lindskold, 1978). First, group members should communicate their intentions in specific terms and make explicit references to trust, cooperation, and fairness when appropriate (Lindskold, 1986; Lindskold, Han, & Betz, 1986; Swingle & Santi, 1972). Second, to be viewed as objectively credible, they must make certain that their behavior matches their announced intentions. If they say they will give up their claim to a resource, they must follow up on their word. Third, group members should respond cooperatively to other members who act competitively, even when they know in advance that the noncooperators plan to compete (Brickman et al., 1979). If these others then continue to engage in conflict-generating behavior, the reciprocating response should match theirs. This strategy, which is known as *tit for tat*, is effective because even individuals who are acting to promote their own interests will cooperate when they realize that continued conflict is self-defeating (Axelrod & Hamilton, 1981; Boyd & Lorberbaum, 1987; Orkin, 1987). Such individuals will exploit the person who always cooperates, but they will learn to cooperate if others demonstrate their willingness to compete if necessary (Sermat, 1964; Soloman, 1960). Individuals who follow a tit-for-tat strategy are viewed as "tough but fair," whereas those who cooperate with a competitor are viewed as weak, and those who consistently compete are considered unfair (McGillicuddy, Pruitt, & Syna, 1984).

Negotiation

Negotiation is a reciprocal communication process that is used to identify a basis of agreement between two parties in a conflict. Through discussion the two parties examine specific issues, explain their positions, and exchange offers and counteroffers. Haggling illustrates the "negotiation minuet" (Fisher & Ury, 1981):

Customer: How much do you want for this car?
Seller: We just got it in this week. It was owned by a guy who only used it to drive to church. I guess you could have it for $2,000.
Customer: That's way overpriced. I've seen this model advertised for under $1,400.
Seller: But this car's in cream-puff condition. It's worth $1,900 if it's worth a penny.
Customer: I'll give you $1,500.
Seller: The car cost us much more than that; $1,750 cash, and it's yours.
Customer: $1,600, but you have to put new tires on it.

As this example illustrates, negotiation often involves a series of recurring steps in which Party A offers a proposal and Party B answers with an alternative. This sequence of offer/counteroffer is repeated over and over until a mutually satisfying solution is obtained. (For reviews see Druckman, 1977, 1987; Pruitt, 1981, 1987; Pruitt & Rubin, 1986; and Rubin & Brown, 1975.)

Negotiation takes many different forms. In some cases it amounts to little more than simple bargaining or mutual compromise. Both parties retain their competitive orientation and take turns making small concessions until some equally dissatisfying middle ground is reached. In contrast, **integrative negotiation,** or *principled negotiation,* occurs when the parties work together to find a solution that will benefit both sides (see Focus 12-6). Like the decision-making sequence described in Chapter 10, integrative negotiation begins with the group identifying the problem clearly. The discussants then gather information about the situation and propose as many alternative solutions to the problem as they can. Next, the group chooses a solution, preferably by consensus rather than by making mutual concessions. When this integrative method is used, negotiation combines many interpersonally advantageous elements: open communication between disputants (Deutsch, 1973); mutual cooperation in seeking a solution (Worchel, 1979); and conflict fractionation: the breaking down of the general conflict into smaller, specific issues that can be dealt with one at a time (Fisher, 1964).

. . . .

FOCUS 12-6: PRINCIPLED NEGOTIATION

Negotiators come in two common varieties: soft and hard. Soft bargainers see negotiation as too close to competition, and they worry that the process will ruin the group's cohesiveness. So they choose a gentle style of negotiation: they make offers that are not in their best interests, they yield to others' demands, they avoid any confrontation, and they maintain their friendship. Hard bargainers, in contrast, use tough, competitive tactics during negotiations. They begin by taking an extreme position on the issue, and then they make small concessions only grudgingly. The hard bargainer uses contentious strategies of influence and says such things as "Take it or leave it," "This is my final offer," "This point is not open to negotiation," "My hands are tied," and "I'll see you in court."

Roger Fisher and William Ury, drawing on studies and conferences conducted as part of the Harvard Negotiation Project, advocate a third approach to negotiating: principled negotiation. First, to prevent misunderstandings and misperceptions, principled negotiators focus on the problem rather than the intentions, motives, and needs of the people involved. Many of the negative consequences of conflict can be avoided simply by avoiding the misperceptions and entrapment processes described earlier. Second, rather than identifying and defending *positions,* principled negotiators try to identify the *issues* underlying the positions taken by disputants. Positional bargaining, Fisher and Ury (1981, p. 5) argue, is too dangerous:

> When negotiators bargain over positions, they tend to lock themselves into those positions. The more you clarify your position and defend it against attack, the more committed you become to it. The more you try to convince the other side of the impossibility of changing your opening position, the more difficult it becomes to do so. Your ego becomes identified with your position.

Third, Fisher and Ury recommend that negotiators explore a number of alternatives to the problems they face. During this phase the negotiation is transformed into a group problem-solving session, with the two parties working together in search of creative solutions and new information that the group can use to evaluate these alternatives (see Chapter 10). Lastly, rather than allowing the final choice among alternatives to be dictated by power, pressure, self-interest, or an arbitrary decisional procedure, Fisher and Ury's principled negotiators base their choice on objective criteria. Such criteria can be drawn from moral standards, principles of fairness, objective indexes of market value, professional standards, tradition, and so on, but they should be recognized as fair by both parties. Table 12-6 (p. 384) summarizes these recommendations, and it contrasts the principled negotiator to soft and hard negotiators (Fisher, 1983).

. . . .

Third-Party Intervention

A final conflict-reduction technique introduces a third party into the negotiation process. Although in many conflict situations the uninvolved group members may stand back and let the disputants "battle it out," impasses, unflagging conflict escalation, or the combatants' entreaties may cause other group members or outside parties to help clarify the source of the problem and thus resolve the conflict (Carnevale, 1986a, 1986b; Pruitt & Rubin, 1986; Raiffa, 1983; Rubin, 1980, 1986).

Third parties, in general, facilitate conflict reduction by performing a number of important functions. First, they reduce hostility and frustration by giving both sides an opportunity to express themselves while controlling contentiousness. Second, if communication breaks down or the two disputants begin to misunderstand each other, the third party can correct the problem. Third, they help disputants save face by providing a graceful means of accepting concessions and by taking the blame for these concessions. Fourth, they can formulate and offer proposals for alternative solutions that both parties find acceptable. Fifth, the third party can manipulate aspects of the meeting, including its location, seating, formality of communication, time constraints, attendees, and the agenda. Last, third parties can guide the disputants through the process of integrative problem solving described earlier (Carnevale, 1986a; Folberg & Taylor, 1984; Raven & Rubin, 1976).

TABLE 12-6: Three approaches to negotiation.

The Soft Negotiator	The Hard Negotiator	The Principled Negotiator
Stress that the participants are friends.	Stress that the participants are adversaries.	Stress that the participants are problem solvers.
Make the goal agreement.	Make the goal victory.	Make the goal a wise outcome reached efficiently and amicably.
Make concessions to cultivate the relationship.	Demand concessions as a condition of the relationship.	Separate the people from the problem.
Be soft on the people and the problem.	Be hard on the problem and the people.	Be soft on the people, hard on the problem.
Trust others.	Distrust others.	Proceed independently of trust.
Change your position easily.	Dig in to your position.	Focus on interests, not positions.
Make offers.	Make threats.	Explore interests.
Disclose your bottom line.	Mislead as to your bottom line.	Avoid having a bottom line.
Accept one-sided losses to reach agreement.	Demand one-sided gains as a price of agreement.	Invent options for mutual gain.
Search for a single answer: the one they will accept.	Search for the single answer: the one you will accept.	Develop multiple options to choose from; decide later.
Insist on agreement.	Insist on your position.	Insist on using objective criteria.
Try to avoid a contest of will.	Try to win a contest of will.	Try to reach a result based on standards independent of will.
Yield to pressure.	Apply pressure.	Reason and be open to reason; yield to principle, not pressure.

(Source: Fisher & Ury, 1981)

In general, third parties are effective, particularly in situations involving intense conflict (Hiltrop & Rubin, 1982). Jeffrey Rubin (1980), after reviewing the results of a number of studies dealing with the processes and effectiveness of third-party interventions, summarized his conclusions as follows:

1. Third parties help opponents conciliate without embarrassment and thereby promote more rapid and effective conflict resolutions (p. 380).
2. Traditional third-party intervention techniques (for example, mediation, arbitration, and counseling) that are effective when conflict intensity is low may prove to be ineffectual and even exacerbating when conflict intensity is high (p. 383).

3. The parties to a conflict may view third-party intervention as an unwelcome and unwanted intrusion; disputants may wish to resolve the conflict on their own accord (p. 385).

The effectiveness of third parties also depends on their power relative to the disputants. Go-betweens, moderators, facilitators, diplomats, advisers, mediators, or judges are all third-party intervenors, but they vary considerably in terms of power (LaTour, 1978; LaTour, Houlden, Walker, & Thibaut, 1976). In an *inquisitorial* procedure the third party simply questions the two parties and then hands down a verdict that the two parties must accept. In *arbitration* the disputants present their arguments to the third party, who then bases his or her decision on the information they provide. In a *moot* the disputants and the third party discuss, in as open and informal a meeting as possible, the problems and possible solutions. Although these third parties cannot make any binding decisions, they facilitate communication, make suggestions, and enforce standing rules. When the third party has no power to enforce participation or make recommendations, the intervention is known as *mediation*. Satisfaction with the use of a third party depends on how well the intermediary fulfills these functions, but research suggests that people most prefer arbitration, followed by a moot, then mediation, and lastly inquisitorial procedures (LaTour et al., 1976; cf. Lind, Kurtz, Musante, Walker, & Thibaut, 1980).

The Value of Conflict

Disagreeing is a natural consequence of joining a group. As noted in Chapter 4, observers of all types of groups have documented clashes among members and invariably conclude that group conflict is as common as group harmony (Bales, Cohen, & Williamson, 1979; Bennis & Shepard, 1956; Tuckman, 1965). As sociological conflict theory suggests, the dynamic nature of the group ensures continual change, but along which change come stresses and strains that surface in the form of conflict (for example, Dahrendorf, 1958, 1959). Although in rare instances group members may avoid all conflict because their actions are perfectly coordinated, in most groups the push and pull of interpersonal forces inevitably exerts its influence.

Conflict, then, is a valuable group process. Insofar as conflict is resolved successfully, it has stabilizing functions and becomes an integrating component of the relationship. Interdependency among members and the stability of a group cannot deepen until intragroup hostility has surfaced, been confronted, and resolved. Low levels of conflict in a group could be an indicator of positive interpersonal relations, but more likely the group members are burying conflict or are too uninvolved in the group to care. Conflict also preserves a group by providing a means of venting interpersonal hostilities (Bormann, 1975; Thibaut & Coules, 1952).

Rather than eliminating all sources of divisiveness, groups must manage conflict. When group members find themselves arguing with others, they should confront the problem and work together to solve the dispute.

If the conflict reaches the escalation stage, members must control their hostilities, break the conflict spiral, and regain a cooperative outlook. And through integrative negotiation, group members should generate new and creative solutions to their problems. Conflict, when properly managed and resolved, is a valued resource rather than a problem that must be eliminated.

SUMMARY

In contrast to *intergroup conflict*, which involves two or more groups, *intragroup conflict* occurs when the actions or beliefs of one or more members of the group are unacceptable to—and hence are resisted by—one or more of the other group members. In many instances conflict in a group occurs because members must compete for limited resources. Deutsch, a leading researcher in the area, notes that such *competition* creates contrient interdependence among members, whereas *cooperation* leads to promotive interdependence. *Mixed-motive situations*, like the *prisoner's dilemma game* (*PDG*) and *social traps*, stimulate conflict because they tempt individuals to compete rather than cooperate. Once individuals begin to compete in such situations, cooperation is difficult to reestablish. The use of contentious influence strategies, such as threats and punishments, also tends to heighten conflict, particularly if all parties in the confrontation have the capacity to threaten one another. Also, although the relationship between the personal characteristics of members and group behavior is complicated, people who adopt a competitive *interpersonal style* tend to generate more conflict than cooperators, and men and women often respond to competitive and cooperative situations differently.

Once conflict begins, it often intensifies before it begins to abate. This *conflict spiral* is produced by a host of factors, including misperceptions, commitment, entrapment, arousal, reciprocity, and coalitions. First, *attribution theory* suggests that conflict is exacerbated by members' tendency to misperceive others and to assume that the other party's behavior is caused by personal (dispositional) rather than situational (environmental) factors. This *fundamental attribution error* is particularly strong during conflict, with the result that people tend to assume the worst about other group members. Second, when individuals defend their viewpoints in groups, attitude elaboration, the need to save face, rationalization, and reactance can all combine to increase their commitment to their position. Third, if this commitment becomes overcommitment, *entrapment* can occur. Fourth, because conflict is often arousing, the *arousal/aggression hypothesis* predicts that group members will be ready to respond in an aggressive manner. Fifth, the *norm of reciprocity*, by sanctioning the matching of competition with competition, is partly responsible for the *behavioral assimilation* seen when a cooperative individual must work with a competitive one.

Lastly, although conflict may be confined during the initial stages, when *coalitions* form, the rest of the group is often drawn into the fracas. Coalitions represent a unique form of intragroup conflict. Forming a coalition is, in most cases, a contentious influence strategy that increases competition rather than cooperation among members. Through the use of simulation experiments in which subjects form coalitions in order to win points, researchers have found that coalitions tend to (1) include only the minimum number of members necessary (the "cheapest winning solution"), (2) be small rather than large, (3) include relatively weak members, (4) exclude relatively powerful members, (5) base division of resources on either the *equity norm* or the *equality norm,* and (5) differ depending on the gender of the individuals in the group. Because coalition formation and the distribution of resources gained through the joint venture are often determined by bargaining, concessions, objections, and threats, *bargaining theory* seems to offer a better explanation of coalition processes than either *minimum-resource theory* or *minimum-power theory.*

Fortunately, conflicts can be resolved in a number of ways, including imposition, withdrawal, inactivity, yielding, compromise, and problem solving. Instilling trust, *negotiation* (including *integrative negotiation*), and third-party interventions are all problem-solving methods, for they require group members to identify the issues underlying the dispute and then work together to identify a solution that is satisfying to both sides.

·13·

Conflict Between Groups

O n two midsummer days in 1954 a bus drove through Oklahoma City picking up excited 11-year-old boys to take them off to camp. They were "normal, well-adjusted boys of the same age, educational level, from similar sociocultural backgrounds and with no unusual features in their personal backgrounds" (Sherif, Harvey, White, Hood, & Sherif, 1961, p. 59). Their parents had paid a $25 fee, signed some consent forms, and packed them off to a camp situated in the Sans Bois Mountains in southeastern Oklahoma. The camp was in Robbers Cave State Park, which took its name from a cave that legend claimed had been used by desperadoes during the frontier era.

Robbers Cave, however, was not your everyday summer camp. All of the boys had been hand picked by a research team that included Muzafer Sherif, O. J. Harvey, Jack White, William Hood, and Carolyn Sherif. The Sherifs and their colleagues had spent more than 300 hours interviewing the boys' teachers, studying their academic records, reviewing their family backgrounds, and unobtrusively recording their behavior in school and on the playground. The parents knew that the camp was actually part of a group-dynamics research project, but the boys themselves had no idea that they were subjects in the **Robbers Cave Experiment.**

The staff brought the children to camp in two separate trips and strictly segregated the two groups for one week. During that week the boys camped, hiked, swam, and played sports while group norms, roles, and intragroup structures developed naturally. Leaders and captains for the baseball teams emerged as status hierarchies formed, and territories within the camp were quickly established (see Figure 13-1). The two groups made up names and slogans for their groups—the Rattlers and the Eagles—and stenciled these names on their shirts and painted them onto flags. Group norms developed as both groups standardized certain rules about their games, meals, and camping activities. By the end of this first stage of the research the staff members, who were actually the unobtrusive data collectors, noted clear increases in group-oriented behaviors, cohesiveness, and positive intragroup attitudes. The following excerpt describes a good example:

> At the hideout, Everett (a non-swimmer when camp started) began to swim a little. He was praised by all and for the first time the others called him by his preferred nickname. Simpson yelled, "Come on, dive off the board!" All members in the water formed a large protective circle into which Everett dived after a full 2 minutes of hesitation and reassurance from the others.

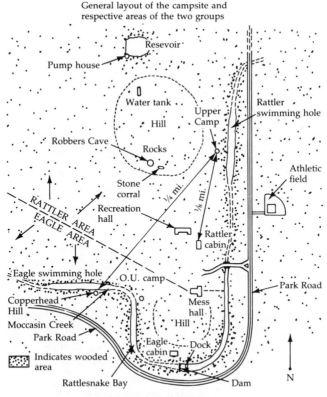

General layout of the campsite and
respective areas of the two groups

Robbers Cave State Park Area

FIGURE 13-1. The Robbers Cave campsite.
Source: Sherif, Harvey, White, Hood, & Sherif, 1961

While he repeated the performance, little Barton, a frightened non-swim-
mer, plunged forward and started swimming a little too. He was called to
the board and he too jumped in. Allen, a swimmer who was afraid to go off
the board, now followed. Harrison, on the bank with an injured hand, was
assured by the others that when his hand was healed they would all help
him "so that we will *all* be able to swim" [p. 79].

The researchers had planned to create conflict between the Rattlers and
the Eagles, but hostilities developed without any encouragement from the
staff. As soon as each group realized that it was sharing the camp facilities
with another group, references to "those guys," "they," and "outsiders"
became increasingly frequent. Both teams wanted to compete with the
other group and asked the staff to set up a tournament. Of course, a series
of competitions between the two groups was exactly what the staff had in
mind, so it held a tournament that included baseball games, tugs-of-war,

tent-pitching competitions, cabin inspections, and a (rigged) treasure hunt.

At first, the tension between the two groups was limited to insults, name calling, and teasing. Soon, however, the intergroup conflict escalated into full-fledged hostilities. After losing a bitterly contested tug-of-war, the Eagles sought revenge by taking down a Rattler flag and burning it. The next day, when the Rattlers discovered the charred remains of their flag, they

> went to the Eagles and asked if they burned the flag, which they admitted. The Rattlers followed . . . Simpson, calling invectives; Martin worked his way close to the Eagle flag, grabbed it and ran down the road with some other Rattlers and with Mason (Eagle) in hot pursuit.
>
> In the meantime, on the field, the Eagles ran for the Rattlers' second flag which they had left on the field. The remaining Rattlers tried to get it, but the Eagles tore it up. Swift (Rattler) grabbed Craig and held him in a wrestling hold, asking which Eagle had burned the flag. Craig said they all had. Simpson (R) had gotten Cuttler (E) down in a fist fight, and the physical encounters had to be stopped [pp. 105–106].

Next the Rattlers sought revenge by attacking the Eagles' cabin during the night. Dressed in dark clothes and with faces blackened, they swept through the Eagles' cabin, tearing out mosquito netting, overturning beds, and carrying off personal belongings. (The Rattlers even got away with a pair of blue jeans belonging to the Eagle leader; they turned them into a flag and on each leg painted "The Last of the Eagles.") The angered Eagles, who wanted to reciprocate that evening with a raid, were deterred by the staff because they were planning to use rocks. But when the Rattlers went to breakfast the next day, the Eagles struck:

> After making sure that the Rattlers were in the mess hall, they started off, armed with sticks and bats, and led by Cutler who had balked at participating in a raid the previous night. The Eagles messed up the Rattlers' cabin, turning over beds, scattering dirt and possessions, and then returned to their cabin where they entrenched and prepared weapons (socks filled with rocks) for a possible return raid by the Rattlers [p. 108].

The Eagles won the overall tournament by a slim margin and were awarded a trophy, knives, and medals. But later that night

> The Rattlers raided while the Eagles were gone, messing up beds, piling personal gear in the middle of the cabin, setting loose boats at the dock, and absconding with the prize knives and medals. When the Eagles found what had happened, they rushed to the Rattler cabin shouting invectives. Mason (E) was in the lead, furious and ready to fight. . . . The Rattlers told the Eagles that if they would get down on their bellies and crawl, they would return the prize knives and medals they had taken. Mason (E) begged the Rattlers to take out their two big boys and fight, which the Rattlers refused to do. Martin (R) got into a fist fight with Lane (low status E). Mills (R) was scuffling with Clark (E) [pp. 110–111].

The staff had to intervene to prevent the boys from seriously injuring one another. They moved the two groups to different parts of the camp, amid shouts of "poor losers," "bums," "sissies," "cowards," and "little babies."

In just two weeks the researchers at the Robbers Cave camp had managed to change a group of "normal" boys into two gangs of scheming, physically assaultive hellions. Why did this change occur? What factors in the situation were contributing to the animosity between the two groups? Perhaps even more important, how could the conflict between the two groups be reduced? This chapter focuses on the Robbers Cave Experiment in an attempt to answer these questions about intergroup conflict. In seeking a better understanding of this phenomenon, we will examine four general areas: (1) the factors that lead to tension between groups, (2) changes that take place within the group during conflict with other groups, (3) perceptual processes that exacerbate that conflict, and (4) ways to reduce group conflict.

SOURCES OF INTERGROUP CONFLICT

Two drug gangs attack each other with semiautomatic rifles in a struggle over territory. Striking miners attack police officers and state troopers when they try to move the strikers' picket lines. University students complain that faculty members aren't committed to teaching and assign grades unfairly, and the faculty believes that students are intellectually lacking. Inner-city Blacks attack Whites when several police officers accused of killing a Black robbery suspect are not sent to jail. Since Israel was established, to be an Israeli has meant that you hate Arabs, and to be an Arab has meant that you hate Israelis.

Intergroup conflict occurs at all levels of social organization, from fighting between gangs to organized disputes in industrial settings to riots stemming from breakdowns in racial relations to conflicts between nations. Although conflict between groups is one of the most complicated phenomena studied by social scientists, the goal of greater understanding and the promise of reduced tension remain enticing. The natural starting point for such an investigation is the deceptively simple query "What causes intergroup conflict?" (For more detailed analyses of the causes and consequences of conflict between groups, see Brewer & Kramer, 1985; Condor & Brown, 1988; Stephan, 1985; Tajfel, 1982; Taylor & Moghaddam, 1987; and Worchel & Austin, 1986.)

Competition

On the ninth day of the Robbers Cave Experiment the Rattlers and the Eagles saw the tournament-prize exhibit for the first time: the shining trophy, medals for each boy, and—best of all—four-bladed camping knives. The boys *wanted* these prizes, and nothing was going to stand in their way. From then on all the group activities revolved around the ultimate goal of winning the tournament. Unfortunately, although both groups aspired to win the prizes, success for one group meant failure for the other. The groups were now enemies who had to be overcome if the prizes were to be won.

Realistic conflict theory maintains that intergroup conflict is caused by competition among groups over limited resources. This theory notes that the things that people value, including food, territory, wealth, power, natural resources, and energy, are so limited that if the members of one group manage to acquire a scarce commodity, the members of another group will go without it. Naturally, groups would prefer to be "haves" rather than "have-nots," so they take steps to achieve two interrelated outcomes: attaining the desired resources and preventing the other group from reaching its goals (Campbell, 1965; LeVine & Campbell, 1972). Competition-based theories of conflict have been invoked to explain class struggles (Marx & Engels, 1947), rebellions (Gurr, 1970), international warfare (Deutsch, 1985; Streufert & Streufert, 1986), racism (Bobo, 1983; Kinder & Sears, 1981, 1985), tribal rivalries in East Africa (Brewer & Campbell, 1976), and even the development of culture and social structure (Simmel, 1955; Sumner, 1906).

Available evidence is generally consistent with the assumptions of realistic-conflict theory, for groups in competition are usually groups in conflict (Horwitz & Rabbie, 1982; Rabbie & Horwitz, 1969; Rapoport & Bornstein, 1987; Taylor & Moriarty, 1987; Worchel, Andreoli, & Folger, 1977). Robert Blake and Jane Mouton, for example, studied competition and conflict by assigning executives attending a two-week management-training program to small groups that worked on a series of problem-solving tasks. Although the researchers never explicitly mentioned competition, the participants knew that a group of experts would decide which group had produced the most adequate solution. Many viewed the project as a contest to see who was best, and they wholeheartedly accepted the importance of winning. Leaders who helped the group beat the opponent became influential, whereas leaders of losing groups were replaced. The groups bonded tightly during work and coffee breaks, and only rarely did any participant show liking for a member of another group. In some cases hostility between the two groups became so intense that the "experiment had to be discontinued" and special steps taken to restore order, tempers, and "some basis of mutual respect" (Blake & Mouton, 1984, 1986, p. 72; Blake, Shepard, & Mouton, 1964). These findings and others suggest that the mere anticipation of competition between groups seems to be sufficient to spark intergroup hostility (Rabbie, Benoist, Oosterbaan, & Visser, 1974).

We should note that the tendency for competition between groups to foster intergroup conflict parallels the link between competition and intragroup conflict examined in Chapter 12. Competition may play a larger role in generating intergroup conflict, however, because groups are more competitive than individuals (Carnevale, Pruitt, & Seilheimer, 1981;

Insko et al., 1987; McCallum et al., 1985; Rabbie, Visser, & van Oostrum, 1982). Chet Insko and his colleagues examined the greater competitiveness of groups by having individuals or groups play the prisoner's dilemma game. As Chapter 12 explains, this mixed-motive game offers players a choice between cooperative responding and competitive responding. Insko found that the individuals he studied weren't particularly competitive. When individuals played other individuals, they averaged only 6.6% competitive responses over the course of the game. Similarly, when three independent, noninteracting individuals played three other independent individuals, competition remained low (7.5%). But when an interacting triad played another interacting triad, 36.2% of their choices were competitive ones, and when triads played triads but communicated their choices through representatives selected from within the group, competition rose to 53.5% (Insko et al., 1987). These remarkable effects suggest that even though individual group members may prefer to cooperate, when they join groups this cooperative orientation is replaced by a competitive one.

Categorization and Identity

At Robbers Cave, conflict began to develop between the two groups even before the idea of a competitive tournament was mentioned. Indeed, the Rattlers and Eagles had not even seen each other when the boys began to refer to "those guys" in a derogatory way (Sherif et al., 1961, p. 94):

> When the in-group began to be clearly delineated, there was a tendency to consider all others as out-group. . . . The Rattlers didn't know another group existed in the camp until they heard the Eagles on the ball diamond; but from that time on the out-group figured prominently in their lives. Hill (Rattler) said "They better not be in our swimming hole." The next day Simpson heard tourists on the trail just outside of camp and was convinced that "those guys" were down at "our diamond" again.

The Sherifs suggested that the conflict between the two groups resulted from their competitions, but this explanation cannot fully account for the almost automatic rejection of members of the other group. Is it possible that group membership per se, even in the absence of any competition, is sufficient to produce intergroup conflict?

Henri Tajfel and his colleagues answer this question in the affirmative. Tracing conflict back to **social-categorization** processes, Tajfel maintains that people learn to understand their social environments by classifying objects, both animate and inanimate, into categories. This categorization process assumes that although many different kinds of people exist in the world, all can ultimately be fitted into various perceptual categories. Moreover, even though the perceiver may make use of a wide range of possible categories for classifying people, two very basic social categorizations are *member of my group* and *member of another group* (Jones, 1983; Wilder, 1986a, 1986b).

Social categorization plays a fundamental role in helping us understand the world around us (Fiske & Taylor, 1984). Tajfel and John Turner believe, however, that social categorization sows the seeds of conflict by creating a cognitive distinction between "us" and "them": the "mere perception of belonging to two distinct groups—that is, social categorization per se— is sufficient to trigger intergroup discrimination favoring the in-group" (1986, p. 13; see also Billig & Tajfel, 1973; Tajfel, 1978a, 1978b, 1978c, 1981, 1982; Turner, 1981, 1982, 1983, 1987).

Tajfel and his colleagues tested this hypothesis in what they call the *minimal-group paradigm*. First, researchers randomly assign participants to one of two groups, although the participants themselves are told that the division is based on some irrelevant characteristic such as art preference. Next, the subjects read over a series of booklets asking them to decide how a certain amount of money is to be allocated to other participants in the experiment. The names of the individuals are not given in the booklets, but the subject can tell which group a person belongs to by looking at his or her code number. Tajfel calls the result a minimal group because (1) members of the same group never interact in a face-to-face situation, (2) the identities of in-group and out-group members remain unknown, and (3) no one gains personally by granting more or less money to any partic- ular person. In essence, the groups are "purely cognitive"; they exist only in the minds of the subjects themselves.

Tajfel's research revealed a systematic in-group bias even in this mini- mal-group situation. Participants did not know one another, they would not be working together in the future, and their membership in the so- called group had absolutely no personal or interpersonal implications. Yet the subjects not only awarded more money to members of their own group, but they seemed to try actively to keep money from members of the other group. Indeed, the in-group bias persisted even when the re- searcher went to great lengths to make it clear that assignment to a group was being done on a random basis and that giving money to the out-group would not cause any monetary loss for any in-group member. Tajfel con- cluded that it was the categorization process itself, rather than feelings of similarity, competition, a common bond, or the like, that stimulated con- flict with the other group (Tajfel & Turner, 1986).

Tajfel's research provoked a search for the causes of in-group favoritism in minimal groups that is still continuing (Aschenbrenner & Schaefer, 1980; Bornstein et al., 1983; Brewer, 1979; Brewer & Kramer, 1985). Many researchers, however, now believe that **social-identity theory** offers an ex- planation for Tajfel's results. This theory, which draws heavily from prior social-psychological theorizing, is based on three basic assumptions: First, as the concept of social categorization maintains, we can readily dis- tinguish between in-group members and out-group members. Second, we are motivated to maintain a positive social identity. Third, we derive much of our social identity from our group identities. These three as- sumptions, taken together, suggest that we favor members of our own group in order to maintain and protect our own social identity. If our self-esteem is shaken by a personal setback, our group provides us with re-assurance and identity (Meindl & Lerner, 1984). By praising our own group more than others, we bolster our own self-esteem. By comparing our qualities to the qualities possessed by members of the out-group, we find evidence of our superiority (Crocker, Thompson, McGraw, & Inger-man, 1987; Lemyre & Smith, 1985; Oakes & Turner, 1980; Turner, Sachdev, & Hogg, 1983). This explanation, although speculative, certainly accounts for the boys' actions at Robbers Cave. Their pride in themselves and in their own group seemed to rise with each derogatory comment they made about the out-group.

Contentious Influence Strategies

The final source of conflict between the Eagles and the Rattlers is perhaps the most obvious one. The existence of two groups in the camp and the competitive tournament may have set the stage for conflict, but the neg-ative intergroup exchanges—insults, humiliations, threats, and destruc-tion of personal property—were the elements that sparked the explosion of hostilities. On the first day of the tournament the Rattlers harassed and insulted the Eagles. The Eagles retaliated by burning the Rattlers' team flag. When the Rattlers discovered their loss, they confronted the unre-penting Eagles. The Rattlers then burned the Eagles' flag, and the Eagles then tore up the second Rattler flag. Physical attacks began at that point, and from then on intergroup conflict remained at high levels.

As with intragroup conflicts, a relatively minor disagreement can spiral into a full-fledged conflict when individuals rely on contentious influence tactics, such as insults, threats, and physical attack (see Chapter 12 and Focus 13-1). The infamous Hatfield/McCoy feud, for example, began with the theft of some hogs by Floyd Hatfield (O. K. Rice, 1978). The McCoys countered by stealing hogs from another member of the Hatfield clan, and soon members of the two families began taking potshots at one another. By 1890 more then ten men and women had lost their lives as a direct re-sult of interfamily violence. Likewise, studies of gangs indicate that many street fights stem from some initial negative action that, in reality, may pose little threat to the offended group. The target of the negative action, however, responds to the threat with a counterthreat and the conflict spi-rals. Battles resulting in the death of gang members have begun over an ethnic insult, the intrusion of one group into an area controlled by another group, or the theft of one gang's property by another gang (Gannon, 1966; Yablonsky, 1959). Large-scale intergroup conflicts, such as race riots and warfare between countries, have also been caused by gradually escalating hostile exchanges (Goldberg, 1968; Holsti & North, 1965; North, Brody, & Holsti, 1964).

A spiral model of conflict intensification accurately describes the un-folding of violence at Robbers Cave. The conflict began with minor irrita-tions and annoyances but built in intensity. The mildest form of rejection—verbal abuse—began when the groups met for the tournament. Insults were exchanged, members of the opposing team were given demeaning names, and verbal abuses ran high. Next, the groups began to actively avoid contact with each other, and intergroup discrimination also developed. The groups isolated themselves from each other at meals, and the boys expressed the belief that it was wrong for the other team to use the camp facilities or be given an equal amount of food. Last came the acts of physical violence—the raids, thefts, and fistfights. Thus the conflict at Robbers Cave built in a series of progressively more dangerous stages from verbal abuse to avoidance to discrimination and finally to physical assault (Allport, 1954; Streufert & Streufert, 1986).

• •
FOCUS 13-1: COERCIVE POWER AND CONFLICT
BETWEEN GROUPS

Social evolutionists argue that one of the first steps in the development of complex forms of intergroup relations occurs when one group tries to dominate other groups. This domination, in some cases, is purely economic. By manufacturing desirable goods or performing valuable services, the group can become the center of a developing trade system (Service, 1975). Alternatively, however, domination can occur through military subjugation. Rather than gaining power through manufacturing and trade, the group can achieve it through coercion and force (Carneiro, 1970).

Chet Insko and his colleagues have contrasted these two means of achieving power in a fascinating simulation of intergroup relations. Inkso and his co-workers created a miniature economic system complete with three groups, multiple generations, a communication network, products, and a trading system. Each group included four individuals, but membership was always in flux because the senior member of each group was replaced by a new member every 20 minutes. To simulate commerce, each group made products by folding pieces of paper into shapes such as birds, boxes, boats, and hats. To communicate, groups elected a representative who exchanged messages and traded products with the other groups. To stimulate trading, groups were paid more money if they sold sets containing several shapes rather than just their own group's product; a set of 4 different shapes, for example, was worth as much as set of 16 of the same shapes. Thus, the groups often tried to trade some of their products for shapes made by the other groups (Inkso et al., 1980, 1983).

The research team created two experimental conditions to examine the impact of coercive, exploitive power on productivity and intergroup relations. In one condition, which can be termed the *economic-power condition*, one of the groups was advantaged economically because it could make two types of shapes instead of only one: Group A made birds, Group C made boxes, but Group B made both boats and hats. Thus, Group B was the center of all bargaining and trading efforts. In a second condition Group B was even more powerful, for it had the right to confiscate any products it desired from the other groups. In addition, in this condition the subjects were led to believe that the members of Group B were better problem solvers than the members of the other groups. This second condition can be called the *coercive-power condition*. (Insko referred to these conditions as the Service condition and the Carneiro condition, respectively.)

These differences in power had a dramatic effect on productivity and intergroup relations. When Group B had only economic power, all three groups reached very high levels of productivity (see Figure 13-2). Group B, with its superior products, turned out nearly 100 products during the final generation of the experiment, and Groups A and C weren't far behind, with an average of about 70 products. But when Group B had coercive power, performance dropped. Even though Group B could confiscate products from the other groups and make more valuable sets, the other groups reacted very negatively to this exploitation. As time passed and Group B continued to steal their work, the members of other groups held strikes and work slowdowns and sabotaged their products. Men, in particular, were more likely to strike back against the oppressive Group B members. Eventually, so little was left that B could not confiscate

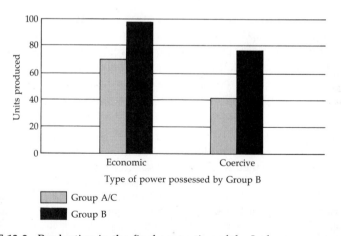

FIGURE 13-2. Production in the final generation of the Insko cross-generational simulation. Because Group B was economically advantaged in both conditions, it always made more money than either Group A or Group C (the rate shown for A and C is their average productivity). However, when Group B used coercion, productivity dropped considerably. In fact, Groups A and C, when working with an economically powerful Group B, were almost as productive as a Group B that used coercion.

Source: Insko et al., 1983

enough products to make much profit. The Group B members also sabotaged themselves. As the "idle-rich" hypothesis suggests, Group B members spent less time working when they could confiscate others' work.

These results suggest that, as with intragroup conflict, one sure way to create conflict is to give one group more coercive power than the other (Deutsch & Krauss, 1960). Apparently, when it comes to power, more is not always better.

• •

CONFLICT AND INTRAGROUP PROCESSES

Intergroup conflict does more than simply turn allies into opponents. Once competition, categorization, and contentious interpersonal exchanges fan the fire of hostility, a set of changes begins to unfold within the warring groups. These changes often leave the group more cohesive, more differentiated from the other group, and more satisfied with its accomplishments.

Conflict and Cohesion

Lewis Coser (1956), intrigued by the changes that groups undergo when they enter into conflicts with other groups, rejected the conclusion that social conflict is always pernicious. He was particularly struck by the marked tendency for conflict between groups to trigger a rapid rise in "internal cohesion" (1956, p. 87). At Robbers Cave, for example, as the competitions progressed the two groups became more tightly organized. The attitudes of each group toward the other became more and more negative, but the cohesiveness of each unit became increasingly stronger. Although every defeat was associated with initial dejection and internal bickering, the groups were quickly able to channel this animosity in the direction of the opponent. As time passed, the groups became better organized, and the group structure solidified. As the observers noted:

> The afternoon of the first day was spent by both groups in intensive preparation for other events. The Rattlers had cabin clean-up, practiced for tug-of-war, and washed their Rattler shirts which they decided to wear at every game. Mason delivered a *lecture* to the Eagles on how to win, and the group practiced at tug-of-war for 45 minutes. Mason had organized a cabin-cleaning detail before lunch, insisting on full participation, although prior to the tournament he himself had shown no interest at all in such chores. Later in the tournament, Mason was to urge his group to practice other activities in which he personally had little interest, such as the skits. When he felt they were not trying hard enough, his usual procedure was to declare he was going home, even starting for the door [p. 103].

Intergroup conflict does not invariably lead to increased cohesion (Tyerman & Spencer, 1983), nor is intergroup conflict a prerequisite for intragroup cohesion (Goldman, Stockbauer, & McAuliffe, 1977). In general, however, Coser's speculations concerning the solidifying effects of cohesion have been confirmed empirically: rises in intergroup conflict tend to go hand in hand with increases in intragroup cohesion (Dion, 1973, 1979; Kahn & Ryen, 1972; Ryen & Kahn, 1975; Wilson & Miller, 1961; Worchel, Lind, & Kaufman, 1975).

Group Differentiation

Coser also suggested that "conflict serves to establish and maintain the identity and boundary lines of groups" (1956, p. 38). As the conflict between the Eagles and the Rattlers escalated, each group tended to emphasize the major distinctions between the two combatants. The groups began to isolate themselves from each other and asked that they be allowed to eat separately. Unique group norms also began to develop, and if one group adopted a style of action, this behavior was soundly rejected by the other. For example, the Rattlers cursed frequently; to distinguish themselves from those "bad cussers," the Eagles adopted the norm of no profanity. Later their leader decided that the Rattlers were such poor sports that "the Eagles should not even talk to them anymore" (p. 106). Proprietary orientations toward certain portions of the camp also developed, along with mottoes, uniforms, and secret passwords.

Such differentiation is typical during intergroup conflict. Rather than noting shared similarities, the groups tend to emphasize their differences (Sherif, 1966). Competing groups also distance themselves from one another, whereas cooperating groups minimize distances (Ryen & Kahn, 1975). Members of competing groups even take pains to display nonverbal postures that are different from those displayed by members of the other groups (LaFrance, 1985) or try to speak differently from the out-group members. When people from different cultures find themselves in conflict, they often adopt a dialect, accent, or language form that is unique to their in-group and foreign to the out-group (Giles, 1977; Giles & Johnson, 1981).

In-Group/Out-Group Bias

In *Folkways* the sociologist William Graham Sumner (1906, p. 12) writes that intergroup conflict creates changes in members' perceptions of themselves (the in-group) and others (the out-group):

> The insiders in a we-group are in a relation of peace, order, law, government, and industry to each other. Their relation to all outsiders, or others-groups, is one of war and plunder. . . . Sentiments are produced to correspond. Loyalty to the group, sacrifice for it, hatred and contempt for outsiders, brotherhood within, warlikeness without—all grow together, common products of the same situation.

We don't just segment people into the categories "member of my group" and "member of another group" and then stop. Once they are categorized, we view people in our group (in-group members) more favorably

than those outside our group (out-group members). At the group level
this tendency is called the **in-group/out-group bias;** among larger social
groups, such as tribes, ethnic groups, or nations, the bias is termed **ethnocentrism** (Sumner, 1906).

In-group/out-group attraction.   The in-group/out-group bias is really
two biases combined: a tendency to favor our own group, its members,
and its products and a tendency to derogate another group, its members,
and its products (Brewer, 1979; Coser, 1956; Hinkle & Schopler, 1986). At
Robbers Cave in-group favoritism went hand in hand with with out-group
rejection. When asked to name their friends, Eagles picked Eagles and
Rattlers picked Rattlers (see Focus 13-2). Also, when the boys described
members of their own group and members of the other group using such
adjectives as "brave," "friendly," and "sneaky," the boys tended to use
the more negative characteristics to describe the out-group but rated their
own group more favorably (see Figure 13-3).

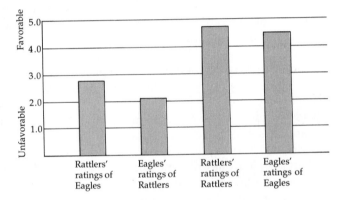

FIGURE 13-3. Patterns of attraction in the Robbers Cave groups.
Source: Sherif, Harvey, White, Hood, & Sherif, 1961

FOCUS 13-2: FRIENDSHIP AND INTERGROUP CONFLICT

Although the Robbers Cave Experiment is the best known of the Sherifs'
field studies of intergroup conflict, this project was actually the third in a
series. The first experiment, conducted in 1949 in a camp in northern Con-
necticut, roughly followed the procedures of the Robbers Cave study
(Sherif & Sherif, 1953). The teams in that study called themselves the Red
Devils and the Bull Dogs, and conflict was dispelled by (1) breaking up the
two groups during meals and other camp activities and (2) staging a softball game between the entire camp and a team from another camp. A 1953
study (Sherif, White, & Harvey, 1955) was designed to test hypotheses

concerning status and estimates of task performance but had to be aborted when the two groups, the Panthers and the Pythons, realized that the camp administration was creating the intergroup friction.

All three studies provide evidence of in-group/out-group bias, but the findings obtained in the Red Devils/Bull Dogs study are particularly striking (Sherif & Sherif, 1953). Unlike the campers at Robbers Cave, the boys were not separated into groups until a full week of campwide activities had been held. During that time friendships formed, and the researchers deliberately placed friends in different groups during the second week. Thus, when groups were formed many of the Red Devils had friends on the Bull Dog team, and many Bull Dogs accepted Red Devils as friends.

Intergroup conflict, however, virtually obliterated these original friendships. Boys who continued to interact with members of the out-group were branded traitors and threatened with bodily harm unless they broke off their friendships. One member of the Bull Dogs who did not completely identify with the group was partially ostracized, and eventually his parents had to remove him from the camp. A Red Devil who suggested that the two groups get together for a party was punished by the Red Devil leader. This observational evidence was buttressed by the sociometric-choice data collected before and after the groups were formed. As Figure 13-4 shows, before intergroup conflict most of the boys reported that their best friends were members of what would eventually become

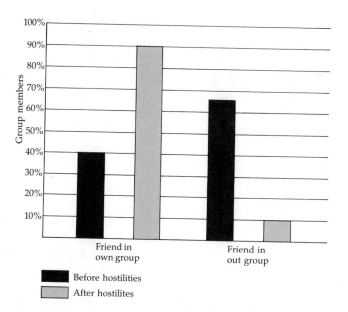

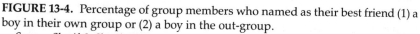

FIGURE 13-4. Percentage of group members who named as their best friend (1) a boy in their own group or (2) a boy in the out-group.
Source: Sherif & Sherif, 1953

the out-group. Later, however, friendship choices were generally limited to members of one's own group.

· ·

These biases in in-group/out-group attraction have been confirmed in a number of other studies, but many suggest that in-group favoritism is stronger than out-group rejection (Coser, 1956, p. 55). Coser, for example, points out that in-group favoritism during conflict is valuable, for it increases group cohesion and morale. At Robbers Cave, for example, both the Eagles and the Rattlers became more tightly organized. Although each failure of the group was followed by a brief period of internal strife, the groups soon countered with increased organization, strengthened leadership, and demands for stricter conformity to group norms. Coser adds, however, that out-group hostility is not a necessary consequence of conflict. Rejection helps the group carry out aggressive actions against the opposing group, but out-group hatred, rejection, and contempt do not always covary with in-group cohesion, acceptance, and attraction. Marilynn Brewer's more recent reviews of empirical evidence agree with Coser's conclusions, for they indicate that conflict creates "the perception that one's own group is better, although the outgroup is not necessarily deprecated" (Brewer, 1979, p. 322; see also Brewer, 1986).

Brewer suggests that the expression of out-group hostility depends on a number of situational factors, including the similarity of in-group and out-group members, anticipated future interactions, the type of evaluation being made, and the competitive or cooperative nature of the intergroup situation. Consider, for example, results reported by Stephen Worchel and his colleagues (Worchel et al., 1977). Group members worked in one of two small groups on "industrial" tasks for money. Subjects in *competitive* groups were told that only the best team would earn the prize money. In the *cooperative* groups the instructions stated that if the two groups managed to perform well, both would receive the reward; if not, both would fail. Lastly, *independent* groups were told that each session involved two groups rather than one simply for the sake of convenience. The groups would be evaluated separately, and the outcomes of one would in no way influence the other.

When the task was completed, half the groups were told that they had succeeded, but the other half were told that they had failed. All the subjects then indicated their liking for members of the other group on a 31-point scale. As expected, the subjects rated their own groups more favorably; the average was about 25 on the 31-point scale. The ratings of the out-group were lower, between 19 and 20, when the two groups were cooperating or working independently, and considerably lower (the average was 15) when the groups were competing. This out-group rejection was even more pronounced if the groups later experienced a second failure. Other studies have confirmed this effect, suggesting that in-group favoritism is stronger than out-group rejection and that out-group rejection is intensified by failure (Dion, 1973, 1979; Kahn & Ryen, 1972; Ryen & Kahn, 1975; Wilson & Miller, 1961).

In-group/out-group performance evaluations. The two sides of in-group/out-group bias are also evident when group members judge the quality of their group products. A rock band not only thinks that its music is very good but also considers a rival group's music to be inferior. One ethnic group prides itself on its traditions and also views other groups' traditions with disdain. One team of researchers thinks its theory explains intergroup conflict, and it criticizes other researchers' theories as inadequate.

The Sherifs illustrated the bias in evaluations of intergroup performance by asking the Eagles and Rattlers to judge the products of in-group and out-group members. After the tournament the boys were asked to compete in a bean-collecting game to win $5. The simple task involved picking up beans scattered on the ground within a one-minute time limit. The beans were then collected from the boys and exhibited on a screen via an overhead projector, and the boys from both groups estimated the number of beans shown. The boys thought that the projector was showing the beans they had collected, but in actuality they were being shown the same 35 beans over and over in slightly different configurations.

The boys' biases are evident in the data presented in Table 13-1. Rattlers overestimated the number of beans collected by Rattlers and slightly underestimated the number of beans supposedly collected by Eagles. The estimates provided by the Eagles were inflated for both in-group and out-group members, but the error was much greater for in-group evaluations. Subsequent laboratory studies have found similar biases in groups evaluating their own and others' products, but they also suggest that the magnitude of the bias depends on a host of situational factors, including the group's outcomes, the way evaluations are measured, and ambiguity about performance standards (Hinkle & Schopler, 1986).

CONFLICT AND INTERGROUP PERCEPTIONS

In his classic treatise *The Nature of Prejudice*, Gordon W. Allport (1954, p. 226) writes that "realistic conflict is like a note on an organ. It sets all prejudices that are attuned to it into simultaneous vibration. The listener can

TABLE 13-1. Average number of beans estimated by the two groups.

Group Judging	Group Being Judged		Mean Differences
	Rattlers	Eagles	
Rattlers	38.4	34.7	3.69
Eagles	39.6	46.8	7.24

(Source: Sherif, Harvey, White, Hood, & Sherif, 1961)

scarcely distinguish the pure note from the surrounding jangle." He is suggesting that conflict, even if rooted in objective characteristics of the situation, will eventually create subjective biases that will further divide the opposing factions. As noted earlier, the Eagles could reasonably blame the Rattlers for their losses, but their reactions went far beyond the simple rejection of a competitor. Each defeat strengthened their biased favoritism for their own group and their dislike of the other group. Eventually, when the groups confronted each other, they could no longer see boys like themselves but only stereotyped images of an unfair opponent. These biases, as we will see below, only served to exacerbate the conflict.

Stereotypes and Categorization Biases

As noted earlier in the chapter, social categorization makes it possible for us to distinguish between the members of our group and the members of other groups. When an Eagle met another boy on the trail, for example, social categorization prompted him to classify the other boy as either an Eagle or a Rattler. If he recognized him as a fellow Eagle, he probably expected the boy to be friendly, helpful, and brave. If a Rattler, he expected the boy to be unfriendly, aggressive, and deceitful.

These expectations are based on **stereotypes:** cognitive generalizations about the qualities and characteristics of the members of a particular group or social category. In many ways stereotypes function as cognitive labor-saving devices by helping us make rapid judgments about people based on their category memberships (McCauley, Stitt, & Segal, 1980; Miller, 1982). Stereotypes, however, come with some built-in biases, for they usually paint a picture of the out-group that is too simplistic, too extreme, and too uniform. First, studies of the *complexity bias* indicate that whereas our conception of the in-group tends to be complex and extremely differentiated, our out-group stereotype is often simplistic and nonspecific. A Rattler, for example, may say that the Eagles burned his flag because they were cowards, whereas he would stress the unique qualities of each Rattler when explaining his own group's actions (Linville, 1982; Linville & Jones, 1980; Park & Rothbart, 1982).

Second, our out-group stereotypes are too extreme; judgments about out-group members are often polarized, whereas our appraisals of our fellow group members are more guarded. This *extremity bias* was in evidence in one investigation in which college-age men read a favorable or unfavorable story about an out-group member (an elderly person) or an in-group member (a young person). When they later rated the character in the story, their evaluations were more extreme when judging a member of the out-group. Relative to the in-group member, the out-group member was rated more positively when the story was favorable but more negatively when the story was unfavorable (Linville, 1982).

Third, whereas most of us are quick to point out the many characteristics that distinguish us from our fellow group members ("Why I'm not like them at all!"), when we evaluate members of out-groups we tend to underestimate their variability ("They all look the same to me"). If you were an Eagle, for example, you would describe the Rattlers as poor sports who cheated whenever possible. When describing the Eagles, in contrast, you might admit that a few of the members were sissies and that maybe one Eagle liked to bend the rules, but you would probably argue that the Eagles were so heterogenous that sweeping statements about their typical qualities couldn't be formulated (Quattrone, 1986). Studies of a variety of in-groups and out-groups—women versus men, physics majors versus dance majors, Sorority A versus Sorority B, Princeton students versus Rutgers students, Canadians versus Indians, and Blacks versus Whites— have documented this so-called *out-group/homogeneity bias:* the tendency for people to assume that the out-group is much more homogeneous than the in-group (Judd & Park, 1988; Katz & Braly, 1933; Park & Rothbart, 1982; Quattrone & Jones, 1980; Tajfel, Sheikh, & Gardner, 1964; cf. Simon & Brown, 1987).

These mistaken beliefs about complexity, extremity, and variability can, in some cases, lead to other inferential errors. Because we assume that all the out-group members are the same, we sometimes base our judgments on the *law of small numbers:* if a few members of the out-group behave in a certain way or possess a particular characteristic, we assume that its members act that way or have those qualities. In one study of this bias, male students at Rutgers and Princeton watched a videotape of another student making a simple decision (choosing to join a group, selecting some music to listen to, or picking a problem to work on). Half the observers were told that the person was from their own college, but the other half were led to believe that the actor was from the rival university. As anticipated, when the subjects were asked to estimate how many men at Princeton and Rutgers would have made similar choices, they relied on the law of small numbers when making judgments about the out-group. They assumed that more students from the rival university would make the same choice as the stimulus person (Quattrone & Jones, 1980). Similar results were obtained in a study in which subjects watched a videotape of people stating their opinions concerning whom should be blamed in a civil court case. The experimenter pointed out that the people in the tape were strangers to one another and had reached their decisions individually. After the portion of the tape was played in which Person 1 stated her attitude, observers were asked to make an estimate of Person 3's attitude on the case. When told that the four women were an aggregate of individuals rather than a group, only 23% of the subjects felt that Person 3 would agree with Person 1. If told that the four women were a group, 50% felt that the women's opinions would match (Wilder, 1978a). (See Focus 13-3.)

· ·

FOCUS 13-3: THE GROUP-ATTRIBUTION ERROR

Scott Allison and his associates have examined a related bias, which they call the *group-attribution error:* the "tendency to assume that group decisions reflect group members' attitudes," irrespective of the proportion of individuals who favored the decision or the particular procedures used in making the decisions (Allison & Messick, 1985b, p. 563, 1987; Worth, Allison & Messick, 1987). They documented this effect by telling their college-student subjects that an election had recently been held at their college or at another college to determine how much funding should be given to the college's athletic programs. Half of the students were told that the students had voted to increase funding, whereas the others were told that the students had voted for decreased funding. The subjects were then asked to estimate the opinion of the "typical student" at the college where the vote had been taken. Although it makes sense to assume that the randomly chosen person's opinion will match the group's opinion, this logic should apply equally to the in-group and to the out-group. Yet as Figure 13-5 indicates, the subjects relied more heavily on the voting results when estimating an out-group member's opinion than when estimating an in-group member's opinion (Allison & Messick, 1985b).

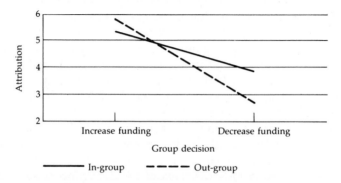

FIGURE 13-5. Attributions of attitude to an in-group or out-group member whose group voted either to increase funding of athletics or to decrease funding.
Source: Allison & Messick, 1985b

. . . .

Confirmatory Biases

When we see people through eyes clouded by stereotypes, we jump to simple conclusions when the facts require complexity, we make extreme judgments when uncertainty is the only rational alternative, and we look at diversity and see uniformity. Yet only rarely do we notice these errors, for our stereotypes are protected by **confirmatory biases** that serve to affirm their validity.

Perceptual distortions.   Walter Lippmann (1922, p. 99), who first used the word *stereotype* in this sense, argued that the stereotype resists disconfirmation because "it stamps itself upon the evidence in the very act of securing the evidence." In an early study of this tendency researchers showed Whites ambiguous pictures of Blacks and Whites interacting (All-port & Postman, 1947). After putting the picture away, the investigators asked the subjects to make up a story about what they had seen. As expected, prejudiced individuals' stories often suggested that the Whites and Blacks were arguing or fighting with each other, and they usually blamed the Black for starting the dispute. In a more recent study White college students who observed a staged argument between a Black and a White in which one person shoved the other described the push as "violent" when the perpetrator was Black, but "playing" or "dramatizing" when the perpetrator was White (Duncan, 1976). Stereotypes apparently resist disconfirmation because we reinterpret the evidence until we see what we expected (Darley & Gross, 1983).

Memory distortions.   Stereotypes also influence our memory, for our recall of information that is consistent with our stereotypes is often superior to our recall of stereotype-inconsistent information. If we think that Rattlers are vulgar, for example, we will be more likely to remember the time that one swore during the baseball game rather than the time that one said a prayer. If we think that Eagles are poor sports, we will forget the times that they cheered for us after one of the games (Markus & Zajonc, 1985).

Myron Rothbart and his associates have examined these memory biases experimentally in a number of studies (Howard & Rothbart, 1980; Park & Rothbart, 1982; Rothbart , Fulero, Jensen, Howard, & Birrell, 1978; Rothbart, Evans, & Fulero, 1979). In one study the subjects were first given a bogus test that indicated which group they belonged to, either underestimator or overestimator. Next, they were asked to read over a series of self-descriptive statements supposedly written by underestimators and overestimators. Some of the behaviors were positive ("I took two disadvantaged kids on a one-week vacation" or "I saved enough money to spend a year traveling in Europe") and some were negative ("I had two brief affairs with other people while I was married" and "I spread rumors that my roommate was dishonest"). These statements were written on separate cards that were organized into two decks of 48. One deck was labeled *overestimators*, and the other was labeled *underestimators*. The subjects then completed some filler tasks for ten minutes before their memory for the statements was tested. They were given the randomly ordered decks and asked to sort them into the two original piles. Although memories for positive behaviors committed by the in-group and out-group members were equal and unbiased, memories for negative behaviors were distorted. Subjects remembered more of the negative behaviors associated with the out-group and fewer of the negative behaviors associated with the in-group (Howard & Rothbart, 1980).

This memory bias may explain **illusory correlations:** tendencies to overestimate the strength of the relationship between unrelated characteristics in the out-group (McArthur & Friedman, 1980). Because we expect out-group members to engage in negative behavior and we remember the times that they acted negatively rather than positively, we feel vindicated in thinking that membership in the out-group and negative behaviors are correlated (Hamilton & Rose, 1980).

Self-fulfilling prophecies.   Interpersonal processes also insulate our stereotypes from disconfirmation. When we interact with others, we tend to evoke new behaviors in those people that are consistent with our stereotypical expectations. Allport illustrates this process when he describes an Irishman and a Jew who

> encounter each other in casual contact, perhaps in a small business transaction. Neither has, in fact, any initial animosity toward the other. But the Irishman thinks, "Ah, a Jew; perhaps he'll skin me; I'll be careful." The Jew thinks, "Probably a Mick; they hate the Jews; he'd like to insult me." With such an inauspicious start both men are likely to be evasive, distrustful, and cool [1954, p. 252].

Allport's anecdote suggests that stereotypes can function as **self-fulfilling prophecies.** If a Rattler thinks that an Eagle is aggressive, he may keep his distance from the Eagle. Even if the Eagle is trying to be friendly, he will probably be put off by the Rattler and so seem less friendly. The Rattler naturally interprets this change as further evidence of the Eagle's negative intentions and becomes more hostile. This cycle of expectation and behavioral confirmation continues until the prophecy of conflict is fulfilled (Cooper & Fazio, 1986; Darley & Fazio, 1980).

The self-fulfilling nature of stereotypes has been demonstrated in studies of attraction (Snyder, Tanke, & Berscheid, 1977), racism (Word, Zanna, & Cooper, 1974), and sexism (Skrypnek & Snyder, 1982), but a study of conflict conducted by Mark Snyder and William B. Swann (1978) is particularly relevant here. They asked pairs of men to compete in a simple reaction-time game. The subjects were seated in separate rooms and told to press a switch as soon as a signal light came on; the first to press his switch would be declared the winner on that particular trial. Subjects could also use a "noise weapon" on some trials: they could deliver a blast of noise to their opponent that ranged in intensity from very mild to very distracting and irritating. Before play began one subject (A) was given false information suggesting that his opponent (B) was either a hostile or a nonhostile individual. Subject B was unaware of this information, but he was subtly encouraged to attribute his behavior during the experiment to his personal dispositional characteristics or to the situation. As predicted, subject A used louder noise levels when he thought B was hostile. In addition, behavioral confirmation occurred: subject B, although unaware of A's false prophecy, used higher noise levels when he was labeled hostile. Snyder and Swann also found that B, when labeled hostile and encouraged to make internal attributions, continued to use louder noises when he played a new opponent who had not been given any expectations.

Thus, A's erroneous prophecy was fulfilled as the target became more aggressive, and the aggressiveness transferred to a new situation and a new interaction partner. Snyder and Swann (1978, pp. 158, 161) concluded that their study demonstrated that "a perceiver's initially erroneous beliefs about a target individual may initiate a chain of events that channel subsequent social interaction in ways that cause the behavior of the target to confirm the perceiver's beliefs. . . . Beliefs can and do create social reality."

Perceptual Biases and Images

Categorization biases and stereotypes sustain a number of attributional and perceptual biases. Although our personal view of the world is shaped by private analysis and introspection, our groups influence us in many ways; they provide us with support for shared beliefs, encourage particular values and attitudes, and guide our perceptions of the social and physical world (Cooper & Fazio, 1986; Triandis, 1986). During conflict, however, these shared perceptions become less and less accurate. As a result shared beliefs about the opponent, the other group's motives, and its capabilities emerge to further exacerbate conflict (Hewstone, 1988; Hewstone & Brown, 1986; Stephan, 1985).

The diabolical-enemy image.   Ralph White has examined how shared group perceptions influence conflict, particularly at the international level (White, 1965, 1966, 1969, 1970, 1977). According to White, one of the more frequently occurring misperceptions develops when group members transform members of the other group into the "enemy." At Robbers Cave, for example, members of the two groups tended to belittle, humiliate, and derogate out-group members. Although the only difference between the two sets of boys was their group identification—Rattler or Eagle—the boys acted as if the out-group members came from a different world. They were the "enemies," "bums," "bad guys," and "those damn campers" rather than opponents in a simple contest. They considered the out-group members capable of doing practically anything to win the prize, and they were certain that the others would cheat if they got the chance. No out-group boy could be trusted to tell the truth, and the group as a whole was believed to be continually planning to raid the other team's cabin, invade its sacrosanct swimming and camping areas, destroy its foodstuffs, and steal its property.

White contends that such *diabolical-enemy images* are prevalent in more widespread conflicts. In general, the other side is dehumanized and branded with various uncomplimentary labels—"terrorists," "queers," "rednecks," "geeks," and "chauvinist pigs." Furthermore, because in-group members assume that the other group is composed of evil, immoral, nearly inhuman barbarians, they tend to associate malevolent intentions with even the most benevolent actions on the out-group's part. Even Hitler, who should have realized that other countries were only reacting to his aggressive international policies, felt that his aggressions were motivated by atrocities committed by Poland, the encirclement of Germany by communists, a conspiracy led by the Jews to destroy the German republic, and France's willingness to launch air attacks against German industry.

The moral-group image.   The Sherifs report no evidence suggesting that the boys at Robbers Cave ever considered their aggressions against the other team to be "wrong." Poor sports etiquette, verbal derision, destruction of others' property, theft, vandalism, and physical violence were all condoned as actions taken against the enemy. The boys felt that their own group had the right to seek victory at all costs and that the home group's actions were somehow more *moral* than those of the other team. The Eagles even held prayer meetings before each contest to ask for God's help in vanquishing their foe; several boys were certain that their success was the result of divine intervention.

As the in-group/out-group bias suggests, groups use a double standard when evaluating their own actions and those of another group. When the other group *attacks* us, we *retaliate*. When we refuse to yield to *threats* (which the other side called *requests*), we are *courageous*, though they consider us *stubborn*. Pride in our own group is *nationalism*, though the other group takes it as evidence of *ethnocentrism*. We offer them *concessions*, but they interpret them as *ploys*. Examining such perceptual differences in Arabs' and Israelis' attributions concerning the cause of the major Middle East wars of 1948, 1956, 1967, and 1973, White (1977, p. 205) found that both sides believed the other side to have been the aggressor in all four wars. In two of these wars (1956, 1967) the Arabs believed that Israel had simply attacked without provocation. In the remaining two (1948, 1973) the Arabs admitted that they had initiated hostilities but believed that they had been forced to do so by the expansionistic policies of Israel. Conversely, the Israelis felt that the 1948 and 1973 wars were "instances of naked, obvious Arab aggression" and that the 1956 and 1967 battles had been indirectly caused by the threats and malevolent intentions of the Arabs. Similar biases have been found when students in the United States are asked to evaluate actions performed by their country and by the Soviet Union (Oskamp & Hartry, 1968) and when Whites' and Blacks' judgments of ambiguously aggressive action committed by either a Black and a White are compared (Sagar & Schofield, 1980). People judge actions that their own group performs positively, but they negatively evaluate these same actions when they are performed by the out-group.

The virile-group image.   When the groups at Robbers Cave were first told about the tournament, their members expressed total confidence in their ability to beat the opposing team. To admit otherwise would, of course, have suggested that the in-group was not as good as the other group. The group members had an image of power and toughness to live up to, and they were determined to demonstrate their strength and ability. According to White, such sentiments are typical during conflicts between groups. Indeed, in many instances groups seem to be more concerned with being—and appearing—strong and victorious rather than right and peaceful. These virile self-images, naturally, can get the group into difficulties, because they can create overconfidence that might eventually lead to the overextension of the group's resources.

Mirror images.   The distorted images that create misperceptions when two groups come into conflict are common to both groups. That is, just as Group A thinks of Group B as evil and deceptive, B thinks of A as wicked and treacherous. Just as A thinks of its actions as benevolent and peaceful, B thinks of its own actions as tranquil and benign. Lastly, both A and B believe that they can win any challenge to their might. This tendency for conflicting groups to adopt the same distorted picture of each other has been called **mirror-image thinking** (Bronfenbrenner, 1961). In the Arab/Israeli conflict, for example, both sides assume their opponent to be the aggressor, intent on war and destruction, unwilling to make any concession for peace, and motivated by selfish desires and deeply ingrained hatred (White, 1977). As a result the two sides continue to misunderstand each other completely, and the conflict continues to escalate. As White laments,

> There is supreme irony in this mirror-image type of war. It seems utterly ridiculous that *both* sides should be fighting because of real fear, imagining the enemy to be a brutal, arrogant aggressor, when actually the enemy is nerving himself to fight a war that he too thinks is in self-defense. Each side is fighting, with desperate earnestness, an imagined enemy, a bogey-man, a windmill [1969, p. 29].

RESOLVING INTERGROUP CONFLICT

The Robbers Cave researchers were left with a problem. The manipulations of the first two phases of the experiment had worked very well, for the Rattlers/Eagles War yielded a gold mine of data about intergroup conflict. Unfortunately, the two groups now despised each other, and certainly conscientious social scientists could not turn their back on these groups without trying to undo some of the negative interpersonal effects of the study. Therefore, the Sherifs and their colleagues felt compelled to seek a method through which harmony and friendship could be restored at the Robbers Cave campsite.

Intergroup Contact
The Robbers Cave researchers first tried to reduce the conflict by encouraging **intergroup contact.** Hoping that contact between the groups would disprove many of the boys' mistaken assumptions, negative stereotypes, and biased perceptions, the Sherifs arranged for the Rattlers and Eagles to join in seven pleasant activities such as eating, playing games, viewing

films, and shooting off firecrackers. Unfortunately, contact had little impact on the hostilities. During all these events the lines between the two groups never broke, and antilocution, discrimination, and physical assault continued unabated. When contact occurred during meals, "food fights" were particularly prevalent:

> After eating for a while, someone threw something, and the fight was on. The fight consisted of throwing rolls, napkins rolled in a ball, mashed potatoes, etc. accompanied by yelling the standardized, unflattering words at each other. The throwing continued for about 8–10 minutes, then the cook announced that cake and ice cream were ready for them. Some members of each group went after their dessert, but most of them continued throwing things a while longer. As soon as each gobbled his dessert, he resumed throwing [p. 158].

The failure of contact to alleviate conflict is not surprising. Although contact's supposed curative effects provide the basis for such social policies as school integration, foreign-student exchange programs, and the Olympics, contact leaves much to be desired as a means of reducing intergroup conflict. Studies of desegregated schools, for example, indicate that such contact between Blacks and Whites doesn't reduce racial prejudice (Gerard, 1983; Schofield, 1978). Studies carried out in industrial settings find little relationship between interdepartmental contact and interdepartmental conflict (Brown, Condor, Matthews, Wade, & Williams, 1986). Investigations of college students studying in foreign countries reveal that they become increasingly negative toward their host countries the *longer* they remain in them (Stroebe, Lenkert, & Jonas, 1988). Laboratory studies, too, suggest that contact alone is not sufficient to undo intergroup hostility (Stephan, 1987; Worchel, 1986). Indeed, even before they initiated the contact, the Sherifs predicted that a "contact phase in itself will not produce marked decreases in the existing state of tension between groups" (Sherif et al., 1961, p. 51).

Intergroup Cooperation

When simple contact between the group members failed to ease their animosity, the Sherifs took the contact situation one step further. Rather than placing the two groups together and allowing them to interact, the researchers forced the boys to work for **superordinate goals.** Because superordinate goals can be achieved only if the two groups work together, the Sherifs assumed that they would foster intergroup cooperation. Hence, like feuding neighbors who unite when a severe thunderstorm threatens to flood their homes or warring nations, in a recurring science-fiction theme, that pool their technological skills to prevent the collision of the earth with an asteroid, the Rattlers and the Eagles might be reunited if they sought goals that could not be solved by a single group working alone.

The staff created these superordinate goals by staging a series of crises. They secretly sabotaged the water supply and then asked the boys to find the source of the problem by tracing the water pipe from the camp back to the main water tank, located about three-quarters of a mile away. The boys became quite thirsty during their search and worked together to try to correct the problem. Eventually they discovered that the main water valve had been turned off by "vandals," and they cheered when the problem was repaired. Later in this stage the boys pooled their monetary resources to rent a movie that they all wanted to see, worked together to pull a broken-down truck, prepared meals together, exchanged tent materials, and took a rather hot and dusty truck ride together.

After six days of cooperation the tensions between the groups had been fairly well wiped out. When it came time to return to Oklahoma City, several of the group members asked if everyone could go in the same bus:

> When they asked if this might be done and received an affirmative answer from the staff, some of them actually cheered. When the bus pulled out, the seating arrangement did not follow group lines. Many boys looked back at the camp, and Wilson (E) cried because camp was over [p. 182].

Through the power of superordinate goals the Robbers Cave Experiment had a happy ending.

Why did contact between the Rattlers and the Eagles fail to unite the groups, whereas creating superordinate goals cured the conflict? A growing body of research argues that the key ingredient missing in all the contact situations was *cooperation*. The two groups had been competitors for the preceding week, and no explicit attempt was made to change the norms from a situation emphasizing competition to one calling for cooperation. Indeed, little payoff was afforded those group members who did try to work with out-group members, for they earned no special rewards and were usually criticized by their fellow group members. Without cooperation the two groups continued to perceive each other as opponents who must be rejected and defeated. Without cooperation they continued to discriminate against the out-group, view it with distrust, and even resort to aggression and verbal abuse (Bodenhausen, Gaelick, & Wyer, 1987; Riordan & Riggiero, 1980). The Sherifs' superordinate goals were effective because, unlike the simple contact situations they created, the emergencies forced the two groups to cooperate.

Superordinate goals are by no means the only way to achieve cooperation between groups. In the years since the Robbers Cave Experiment, researchers have identified a number of ways to achieve cooperation that go beyond the development of superordinate goals. Some of these methods are discussed below.

The common enemy.   In their 1949 research the Sherifs united the hostile Red Devils and Bull Dogs by pitting a softball team made up of members from both groups against an outside camp (Sherif & Sherif, 1953). This *common-enemy approach* was partially successful in that during the game the boys cheered one another on and, when the home team won, congratulated themselves without paying heed to group loyalties. By introducing the third party, the common-enemy approach forced the two groups to cooperate while also providing a *scapegoat* for group members' frustrations and animosity.

The Sherifs point out, however, that although combining groups in opposition to a common enemy works for a short time (during the actual competition or crisis), once the enemy is removed the groups tend to return to the status quo ante bellum. In fact the 1949 groups were never successfully reunited despite the experimenters' extended efforts. Also, the use of a common enemy to create cooperation actually enlarges a conflict; in the Sherifs' research the tension that had divided a single camp came to divide two different camps. At the international level this method would amount to solving the disagreements between the Soviet Union and the United States by forming a Soviet/American alliance to attack China.

Mutual conciliation. The Sherifs found that creating trust and cooperation between groups that had previously disagreed can be extremely difficult. In their 1949 research the camp administrators frequently urged the boys to sit together at dinner, cooperate when playing games, and help each other with camp chores, but despite these encouragements the in-group cliques remained. In explanation, Svenn Lindskold (1978, 1979, 1986) suggests that the barriers to reducing intergroup conflict can be overcome only gradually. Given the misunderstandings, misperceptions, reciprocated hostility, and general distrust between groups, interactants often find that attempts at cooperation are misinterpreted by the opponents as attacks.

As noted briefly in Chapter 12, Lindskold believes that mutual trust can be regained if group members communicate their desire to cooperate, engage in behaviors that are consistent with cooperative intentions, and initiate cooperative responses even in the face of competition. These guidelines provide the basis of the **Graduated and Reciprocal Initiative in Tension Reduction (GRIT)** model, shown in Table 13-2. This model was initially developed by Charles Osgood (1979) as a guide to international disarmament negotiations. The first three stages call for adequate communication between the groups in the hope of establishing the "rules of the game." The next three stages are designed to increase trust between the two groups as the consistency in each group's responses demonstrates credibility and honesty. Lindskold suggests that these phases are crucial to overwhelm the skepticism of the opponents as well as the tendency for other parties to assume that the concessions are merely "smokescreens" or propaganda tactics. The final four steps are necessary only in extremely intense conflict situations in which the breakdown of intergroup relations implies a danger for the group members. In the example used in the table—military conflict—the failure to stem the conflict could have disastrous consequences. Hence, each side must make concessions at a fixed rate while at the same time maintaining retaliatory capability.

TABLE 13-2. GRIT: Graduated and Reciprocal Initiative in Tension Reduction.

GRIT Point	Relevant Principles	Example
1. A general statement sets the stage for reciprocation.	Statement creates framework for interpreting subsequent actions; forces consistency in actions through commitment; activates third-party interest; must be a voluntary action.	Leader of Country X announces an important plan to change relations with Country Y.
2. Each unilateral initiative is publicly announced.	Anouncements work against misinterpretation due to communication breakdown; explain relationship to entire plan; contain no moralizing.	Leader of X announces that a satellite-destroying laser weapon will not be developed.
3. Reciprocation is invited but not demanded.	Actions are nonmanipulative; demonstrate vulnerability; prevent reactance in other group.	Country X notes it would welcome similar moves from Country Y but will take its action regardless.
4. Each initiative is carried out exactly as described.	Credibility is built as promises are kept.	Country X destroys preliminary model of laser weapon.
5. Initiatives are continued even without reciprocation.	Credibility is further reinforced; reciprocity norms pressure for concessions.	X relinquishes certain air bases; halts nuclear tests even though Y takes no action.
6. Initiatives are unambiguous and can be verified.	Open communication between parties is stressed; caution to make certain that publicity is not excessive.	Country X invites representatives of the world press to evaluate its initiatives.
7. Initiatives must be risky and meaningful, but retaliatory capacity is retained.	Conciliation, though not the only available strategy, is chosen; aggression and retaliation remain possible; attack capability maintained but not used.	X offers major concessions but retains nuclear superiority over Y.
8. Retaliation to aggression is precise.	Overretaliation is avoided to limit possibility of conflict spiral; norm of reciprocity makes precise retaliation admissible.	Y establishes a missile base too close to X; X blockades the base until the missiles are removed.
9. Initiatives are diversified.	Diversified attempts are made at cooperation to establish communication, trust, and increased conciliation.	X makes concessions concerning not only arms but also human-rights issues and X/Y trade.

(continued)

TABLE 13-2. *(continued)*

GRIT point	Relevant principles	Example
10. Any reciprocation in future initiatives is matched.	Any conciliation from the other group must be bilateral; each conciliation should be followed by an equal or more important initiative.	Y also destroys its laser weapon, and X follows by halting construction of its latest strategic bomber.

(Source: Lindskold, 1978)

Although the GRIT proposal may seem to be overly elaborate and therefore inapplicable to all but the most intense conflicts, the model does clarify the difficulties inherent in establishing mutual trust between parties that have been involved in a prolonged conflict. Although some of the stages are not applicable to all conflicts, the importance of clearly announcing intentions, making promised concessions, and matching reciprocation are relevant to all but the most transitory conflicts. Furthermore, case studies (Etzioni, 1967), simulations (Crow, 1963), and experiments (Lindskold, 1986; Lindskold & Aronoff, 1980) have lent considerable support to the recommendations of the GRIT model for inducing cooperation. At minimum the model offers a good deal of promise as a guide for better relationships between groups.

Minimizing social-categorization biases.   Norman Miller and Brewer have recently argued that cooperation works, in part, because it eliminates competition, reduces frustration among group members, and promotes positive group interaction. They add, however, that these changes are only secondary benefits of cooperation among groups. Drawing on a series of studies of conflict reduction in cooperative classrooms, they argue that cooperation reduces conflict because it reverses some of the pernicious consequences of "us" versus "them" thinking, including ingroup favoritism, out-group rejection, and stereotyping (Brewer & Miller, 1984; Miller & Brewer, 1986a, 1986b). (See Focus 13-4.)

· ·
FOCUS 13-4: REDUCING PREJUDICE THROUGH COOPERATIVE LEARNING

Why do desegregated schools so often fail to eliminate racial and ethnic prejudices? Many researchers argue that although such schools bring students from various groups into contact, they rarely promote cooperation between these groups (Amir, 1969, 1976; Cook, 1985; Schofield, 1978; Worchel, 1986). Studies of racially integrated schools, for example, indicate that Blacks interact primarily with Blacks and Whites interact primarily with Whites (Brewer & Miller, 1984). Many school systems contribute to this problem by grouping students on the basis of their prior academic experiences, and as a result educationally deprived students (who are typically Black) are segregated from students with stronger academic backgrounds (Schofield, 1978).

These studies argue that desegregation must be supplemented by educational programs that encourage cooperation among members of different racial and ethnic groups. One technique that has yielded promising results involves forming racially mixed teams within the classroom. The Jigsaw method (Aronson, Stephan, Sikes, Blaney, & Snapp, 1978), Teams/Games/Tournaments (TGT) (DeVries, Edwards, & Fennessey, 1973), and Student Teams Achievement Divisions (STAD) (Slavin, 1983, 1986) are all similar in that they force students to work together to learn course material. In the **Jigsaw method,** for example, students from different racial or ethnic groups are assigned to a single learning group. These groups are then given an assignment that can be completed only if each individual member contributes his or her share—that is, provides a piece of the overall puzzle. In general, a unit of study is broken down into various subareas, and each member of a group is assigned one of these subareas; students must then become experts on their subjects and teach what they learn to other members of the group. In a class studying government, for example, the teacher might separate the pupils into three-person groups, with each member of the group being assigned one of the following topics: the judiciary system (the Supreme Court of the United States), the duties and powers of the executive branch (the president's office), and the functions of the legislative branch (Congress). In developing an understanding of their assigned topic, the students would leave their three-person groups and meet with their counterparts from other groups. Thus, everyone assigned to study one particular topic, such as the Supreme Court, would meet to discuss it, answer questions, and decide how to teach the material to others. Once they had learned their material, these students would then rejoin their original groups and teach their fellow group members what they had learned. Thus, the Jigsaw class utilizes both group-learning and student-teaching techniques.

Studies of classrooms that use cooperative learning groups show some promising results. When reviewers combined the results of 31 separate studies statistically, they found that in-group/out-group hostility was reduced in cooperative classrooms (Johnson, Johnson, & Maruyama, 1984). In a similar type of review Miller identified a number of factors that increase the effectiveness of these innovative programs. These variables include (1) structuring the task so that each group member makes a contribution, (2) randomly assigning students to roles within the group, and (3) making certain that all groups contain an equal number of representatives from the group being merged. He also found that the procedures used to assign grades—either giving the entire group the same grade or giving grades to individuals in the group—had little impact on the success of the intervention, nor did the degree to which each individual's contribution was made public (Miller & Davidson-Podgorny, 1987).

. . . .

Miller and Brewer thus believe that the positive effects of cooperative contact between groups can be further enhanced by setting limits on the categorization process. Studies by Worchel and his colleagues, for example, indicate that intergroup conflict is reduced when similarities between the in-group and the out-group are accentuated and dissimilarities are minimized (Worchel, Axsom, Ferris, Samaha, & Schweitzer, 1978). David Wilder, too, found that *individuation* of out-group members was an an effective method of reducing in-group/out-group biases (Wilder, 1978b). In one experiment the out-group (Group B) acted as a jury making decisions that were clearly detrimental for another group (Group A). Later, the members of Group A were given the opportunity to allocate payment to members of both groups. Results indicated that members of A were strongly biased against members of B unless they had information that someone in B had disagreed with his or her fellow group members; that is, the decisions of Group B had not been unanimous because one out-group member had consistently dissented. In other studies Wilder found that the harmful effects of categorization biases could also be controlled by diminishing the boundaries between the groups, by stressing qualities shared by both groups, by removing out-group cues, and by diminishing members' dependence on their groups as a source of positive social identity (Wilder, 1986b).

Negotiation. Intergroup conflict can also be resolved through bargaining and *negotiation*. Emphasizing rationality, this approach involves meetings of parties to discuss their grievances and recommend solutions. Both sides draw up a list of problems that are sources of dissatisfaction. Next, the two groups together consider each issue and seek a solution that is satisfying to both sides. When one issue is solved, the negotiations proceed to the next item on the agenda.

Negotiation, however, is often only competition disguised as cooperation. The two parties refuse to accept each other's arguments, insist on maximizing their own interests, and use contentious bargaining tactics like those shown in Table 13-3. Given these limitations, most experts recommend the use of *integrative-negotiation* methods like those discussed in Chapter 12. Integrative negotiation requires cooperative problem solving: the identification of solutions that are mutually satisfying to both sides in the dispute (Pruitt & Rubin, 1986). Unlike competitive bargaining, integrative negotiation opens communication between disputants, encourages cooperation, and fractionates the general conflict into smaller, specific issues that can be dealt with one at a time (Fisher, 1964).

Representation. Although disputes between very small groups can be negotiated directly, in most cases this arrangement is impractical. Au-

TABLE 13-3. A sampling of contentious intergroup-bargaining strategies.

Strategy	Description
Good-guy/bad-guy ploy	Several members of the negotiation team take a harsh stance toward members of the other group. They make unreasonable demands and behave obnoxiously, refusing to make even the smallest concessions. Others on their team then put on a show of trying to reason with them.
Dancing	A member of the negotiation team speaks for long periods without saying anything intelligible or relevant.
Heckling	Members of the other group are rattled by insulting them, making excessive noise while they speak, joking around, or threatening them.
Last-chancing	One team announces "All right, this is my last and final offer. Take it or leave it."
Log rolling	When negotiators on each side have a list of grievances, they make concessions back and forth; when A gives in on one issue, B gives in on the next. Log rolling becomes contentious when bargainers add items to their list of demands just to use them as concessions during negotiations.
Scrambling eggs	When negotiations go poorly, teammates may deliberately try to confuse the issue by misinterpreting others, expressing themselves badly, and dragging in irrelevant issues.
Tiger team	A group of experts is brought in to unfreeze deadlocked negotiations or try to reclaim ground lost earlier.

thority is usually delegated to a group representative who meets with a representative from the other side in a discussion of the issues. Unfortunately, although the advantages of group representation are numerous, disadvantages are also often involved. On the positive side of the ledger representatives are often skilled in negotiations and therefore work more effectively toward acceptable solutions. Second, with just a few participants fewer communications problems crop up, and issues can be considered rapidly and efficiently. Third, when negotiators take their roles seriously, they often strive to seek the best solution while controlling their emotions, keeping the overall problem in perspective, and refusing to commit themselves to positions that the rest of their group may reject. On the negative side representatives may lack the power to make a final decision and therefore must continually consult their group before any concession can be made. Second, the group members may become dissatisfied with their negotiators and refuse to support the solutions that they may have spent long hours negotiating. Group members are often shocked when they discover that their representative has made agreements with the other side and then take steps to replace the "traitor" with a more "loyal" representative (Blake & Mouton, 1986). Lastly, the negotiators may become so concerned with presenting themselves as tough, dogged bargainers that they become hopelessly deadlocked even when a solution is, in fact, possible (Brown, 1977).

With as many positive features as negative, the use of representatives to solve conflicts may not always be a successful strategy. Indeed, in the Sherifs' 1949 study an informal attempt by one of the Bull Dog leaders to negotiate with the Red Devils ended in *increased* anatgonism:

> Hall . . . was chosen to make a peace mission. He joined into the spirit, shouting to the Bull Dogs, "Keep your big mouths shut. I'm going to see if we can make peace. We want peace."
>
>   Hall went to the Red Devil cabin. The door was shut in his face. He called up that the Bull Dogs had only taken their own [belongings] . . . and they wanted peace. His explanation was rejected, and his peaceful intentions were derided. He ran from the bunkhouse in a hail of green apples [Sherif & Sherif, 1953, p. 283].

Conclusions and Limitations

Worchel (1986, p. 292), after reviewing dozens of field and laboratory studies of intergroup-conflict resolution, ends by recommending the promotion of cooperation, since it leads to "increased communication, greater trust and attraction, greater satisfaction with the group product, greater feelings of similarity between group members, more helpfulness, and more coordination of effort and division of labor." Cooperation, he concludes, "may just be the panacea for what ails groups."

Worchel also notes, however, a number of situational factors that can limit the benefits of cooperation. First, in all likelihood several cooperative encounters will be needed before conflict is noticeably reduced. In the Robbers Cave research a whole series of superordinate goals was required to reduce animosity. In a more direct test of the importance of multiple cooperative encounters (Wilder & Thompson, 1980), students from two colleges worked together on problems, sometimes with students from their own schools but sometimes with students from the other school. The results indicated that a cooperative encounter led to increased liking for members of the out-group only when it occurred twice. Students who worked with the out-group just once or not at all rated the members of the out-group more negatively (the mean on a 9-point scale was 5.9) than students who worked with the out-group twice (this mean was 7.0). Similar findings have been obtained in studies of desegregated schools. A long period of favorable intergroup contact may reduce prejudice, but if this favorable contact is followed by an equally long period in which contact is not encouraged, groups inevitably drift apart once again (Schofield & Sagar, 1977).

Second, if the cooperative venture ends in failure for both groups, the magnitude of the resulting intergroup attraction will almost certainly be reduced. As a reinforcement position would suggest, when cooperating groups manage to succeed, the "warm glow of success" may generalize to the out-group and create greater intergroup attraction. If the group fails, however, the negative effect associated with a poor performance will spread to the out-group. In addition, if the cooperative encounter ends in failure, each group may blame the other for the misfortune, and inter-group relations may further erode (Worchel, 1986). The problem of failure was aptly demonstrated in one study in which groups that had previously competed were asked to work together to solve a problem (Worchel et al., 1977). Half the groups failed during the cooperative phase, and the other half succeeded. As predicted, when the intergroup cooperation ended in failure, out-group members were still rejected. Other studies have repli-cated this effect and indicate that unless some excuse for the failure exists, a disastrous performance during cooperation will only serve to further alienate groups (Blanchard, Adelman, & Cook, 1975; Blanchard & Cook, 1976; Blanchard, Weigel, & Cook, 1975; Cook 1978, 1984; Mumpower & Cook, 1978; Weigel & Cook, 1975; Worchel & Norvell, 1980).

SUMMARY

The results of the *Robbers Cave Experiment*, a field study of *intergroup conflict* conducted by Muzafer and Carolyn Sherif and their colleagues, shed con-siderable light on the causes of, consequences of, and possible solutions to conflict between groups. Although tensions between groups arise from many sources, three key factors precipitated the conflict at Robbers Cave. First, as *realistic-conflict theory* maintains, competition contributed signifi-cantly to the conflict. Second, as Tajfel maintains, *social-categorization* (the mere existence of two separate groups of campers) may have been suffi-cient to create the conflict. Relying on *social-identity theory*, he notes that favoring the in-group over the out-group helps members maintain and protect their social identities. Third, as with intragroup conflicts, the use of contentious influence tactics by the groups, such as insults, threats, and physical attack, undoubtedly stimulated the spiraling conflict.

In addition to recording the growing antipathy between the groups, the Sherifs also noted a number of consequences of the conflict. Some of these consequences occurred at an intragroup level. Over time the groups be-came more cohesive; more clearly differentiated; more favorable toward the in-group, its members, and its products; and more negative toward the other group, its members, and its products (the *in-group/out-group bias*, or *ethnocentrism*). Although other research suggests that in-group favorit-ism is stronger than out-group rejection, both forms of in-group/out-group bias emerged at Robbers Cave.

Conflict also led to distorted perceptions of the other group that, in gen-eral, exacerbated animosity. Many of these processes reflect the group members' reliance on *stereotypes*, for their judgments were distorted by the following biases:

1. Complexity bias: conceptions of the in-group tend to be complex and extremely differentiated, whereas the out-group stereotype is simplis-tic and nonspecific.

2. Extremity bias: judgments about out-group members are often polarized, whereas appraisals of in-group members are more guarded.
3. Out-group–homogeneity bias: the out-group is assumed to be much more homogeneous than the in-group.
4. Law of small numbers: the behaviors and characteristics exhibited by a small number of out-group members are generalized to all members of the out-group.
5. Group-attribution error: group decisions are assumed to reflect individual group members' attitudes, irrespective of the particular procedures used in making the decisions.

Confirmatory biases also served to reaffirm the validity of group members' stereotypes by introducing perceptual distortions, memory distortions, *illusory correlations*, and *self-fulfilling prophecies*. Various forms of *mirror-image thinking*, including the diabolical-enemy image, the moral-group image, and the virile-group image, also distorted intergroup perceptions.

Fortunately the Sherifs were successful in reducing the conflict between the two groups. Although their first attempt—encouraging *intergroup contact* by providing opportunities for the groups to perform interesting activities together—failed, they were much more successful when they established cooperation between the groups by prompting the boys to work toward *superordinate goals*. Other methods could have been utilized, such as the common-enemy approach, enouraging mutual conciliation by following the suggestions of the *Graduated and Reciprocal Initiative in Tension Reduction (GRIT)* model, minimizing social-categorization biases, creating cooperative learning groups based on the *Jigsaw method*, negotiation, or representation, but introducing the multiple superordinate goals was sufficient to reduce conflict at the Robbers Cave campsite.

·14·

Crowds and Collective Behavior

It is the evening of December 3, 1979. Nearly 8000 people are waiting to get into Cincinnati's Riverfront Coliseum to hear a concert by one of rock's most successful bands, the Who. Seating isn't reserved, and the most dedicated fans arrived early in the afternoon so that they could get seats down near the stage. But they've been joined now by thousands of others, and the throng is packed so tightly that whenever someone near the fringe is pushed forward, it causes ripples that spread through the rest of the group. Pranksters move about the perimeter, shoving at its edges and laughing as the shove passes like a wave through the group (see Figure 14-1).

The doors open at 7:30, and the eager crowd surges forward. A crowd of 8000 is loud, but above the din the concertgoers hear the band warming up. As those on the periphery push forward, people near the doors are picked up off the ground and borne along by the tide of other human beings. The ticket takers work as fast as they can, but the back of the group is moving faster than the front, and the flow jams. People near the clogged doors are trapped, and as one person is crushed into the next, breathing becomes a struggle. Some lose consciousness and fall to the concrete floor. Those around them try to pull them back to their feet, but the rest of the

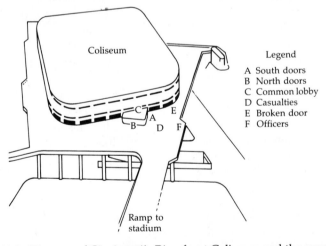

FIGURE 14-1. Diagram of Cincinnati's Riverfront Coliseum and the surrounding plaza. An estimated 8000 people were in the area leading from the ramp to the doors.

Source: Johnson, 1987

crowd sees the open doors and hears only the beckoning music. They push forward relentlessly, and the helpers fall or are pushed past those who have fallen.

Eleven people die in the crowd, and many others are injured. An emergency-room supervisor comments that "the bodies were marked with multiple contusions, bruises and the victims had suffered hemorrhages" (Richmond News Leader, December 5, 1979, p. 14). Survivors' descriptions revealed the gruesome details:

> "People were hitting other people, and a girl fell down in front of me. I helped her up finally." . . . "All of a sudden, I went down. . . . I couldn't see anything. My face was being pressed to the floor. I felt I was smothering." . . . "I saw people's heads being stepped on. I fell and couldn't get up. People kept pushing me down." . . . "People just didn't seem to care. I couldn't believe it. They could see all the people piled up and they still tried to climb over them just to get in" [Richmond *News Leader,* December 5, 1979, p. 14].

> "I screamed with all my strength that I was standing on someone. I couldn't move. I could only scream" [Johnson, 1987, p. 368].

This tragedy is a grim example of **collective behavior:** spontaneous and often atypical actions performed by individuals when they become part of a large group. In earlier chapters we focused on the rational, adaptive functions of groups as decision makers, problem solvers, and conflict resolvers. But Cincinnati and the world saw the darker side of human groups that night outside the Who concert, the side that surfaces spontaneously as the members commit violent actions and inflict unspeakable suffering, the side that myths and folk tales often emphasize and exaggerate when human nature is described as part human and part beast, part Dr. Jekyll and part Mr. Hyde.

Following a tradition that dates back to the 1800s, this chapter tries to separate myth from fact to better understand collective behavior. We begin by examining the characteristics of large, spontaneous groups, including crowds, mobs, rioters, and social movements. Next, we review both classic and contemporary theoretical analyses of collective behavior, beginning with the arguments that Gustave Le Bon presented in his book *The Crowd* and ending with a relatively new theory that seeks to explain why individuals lose their sense of individuality in groups (deindividuation theory).

CROWDS AND COLLECTIVES

The term *collective,* if taken literally, would describe any aggregate of two or more individuals and, hence, would be synonymous with the term *group* (Blumer, 1951). In practice, however, theorists use this term only to describe larger, more spontaneous social groups. A baseball team, a company's board of directors, or a family at a meal are all groups, but we typically wouldn't call them *collectives* because they are too small, too organized, and too stable. Collectives, in contrast, tend to be large and relatively unorganized. They also lack a specific set of procedures for selecting members and identifying goals, and they are usually temporary. A list of collectives, then, would include various types of *crowds:* audiences at a movie, street throngs watching a building burn, lines of people (queues) waiting to purchase tickets, lynch mobs, and panicked groups fleeing from danger. The list would also include *collective movements* of individuals who, although dispersed over a wide area, display common shifts in opinion or actions. These two types of collective behavior are examined in more detail below (Blumer, 1951; Turner & Killian, 1987).

Crowds

The throng of concertgoers massed outside the Riverfront Coliseum was a **crowd:** an aggregate of individuals who share a common focus and are concentrated in a single location. The individuals who are walking along a city block occupy a common location, but they don't become a crowd unless something happens—a fire, a car collision, or a mugging, for example—to create a common focus of attention (Milgram & Toch, 1969).

Theorists have been careful to note the great diversity of crowds (Blumer, 1946; Brown, 1954; Milgram & Toch, 1969). Whereas some are hostile, others are fearful; some remain stationary, whereas others move about collectively; some watch events passively, whereas others take part actively (see Table 14-1). Although "no taxonomy seems fully adequate to the task of naming all crowd phenomena," the types examined below are among the most common kinds of crowds: casual crowds, audiences, mobs, and crowds that panic (Milgram & Toch, 1969, p. 515).

TABLE 14-1. Some common types of crowds.

Type	Characteristics	Examples
Casual crowd	A temporary gathering of individuals in a public place who share a common focus of interest	Bystanders watching a street mime, witnesses to a car accident
Audience	Spectators at an exhibition, performance, or event, usually bound by certain conventions of appropriate behavior	Theatergoers, sports fans, parade watchers
Mob	An active, mobile crowd whose members are often emotionally aroused and ready to engage in aggressive behavior	Lynchers, rioters, gang members, hooligans
Panic	A crowd whose members feel threatened by danger or the loss of a scarce resource	Participants in bank panics, mass hysteria, emergency evacuations

Casual crowds.   Shoppers in a mall are just individuals until a woman spanks her small child when he cries too loudly. Suddenly, the hundred pairs of eyes of an instantly formed crowd focus on the woman, who hurries out the door.

A **casual crowd** is a group of otherwise unrelated individuals who, while going about their own personal business, (1) end up in the same general vicinity and (2) share a common experience (Blumer, 1946; Brown, 1954). Although such crowds are often short-lived, even these fleeting collectives possess boundaries that limit their size and extent. These boundaries are relatively permeable at the edges of the crowd, where individuals are allowed to enter and exit freely, but permeability diminishes as one moves nearer the center of the crowd. Also, roles, status hierarchies, and other group stuctures may not be very evident within such crowds, but close probing usually reveals some underlying structure. Casual crowds, for example, often form around *crowd crystals,* one or more individuals who, by drawing attention to themselves or some event, prompt others to join them (Canetti, 1962). Subgroups also exist in these crowds, for in many cases the people who populate public places are part of small groups rather than lone individuals. At the Who concert, for example, groups of friends waited together for the concert to begin, and these subgroups remained intact even during the fatal crush at the entrance doors. Evidence also indicates that those who occupy central positions in casual crowds are likely to be more actively involved in the experience than those who are content to remain on the fringes (Milgram & Toch, 1969).

Stanley Milgram and his colleagues examined the formation of casual groups by watching 1,424 pedestrians walking along a busy New York City sidewalk. As the pedestrians passed by one section of the sidewalk, they encountered one or more confederates who were gazing at the sixth floor of a nearby building. These confederates acted as crowd crystals by watching the building for one minute before gradually dispersing. Meanwhile, a camera filmed the passersby to determine how many looked up at the building or stopped and joined this casual group. If we define crowd membership as (1) occupying the same vicinity and (2) sharing the same focus of attention, the results in Figure 14-2 indicate that even a small group of three persons was sufficient to trigger the formation of a casual crowd. If, in contrast, we require that passersby actually stop walking and stand with the confederates before we consider them part of the crowd, then the larger the crowd, the greater the likelihood that others will join it (Milgram, Bickman, & Berkowitz, 1969).

Audiences.   Crowds of individuals who deliberately gather in a particular area to observe some event or activity are called **audiences,** or **conventional crowds.** Unlike the members of casual crowds, individuals in audiences join these crowds deliberately, and they are also bound more by

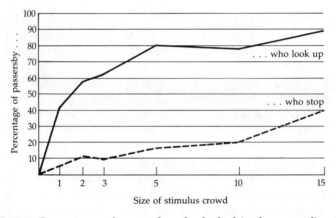

FIGURE 14-2. Percentages of passersby who looked in the same direction as a group of confederates or who actually stopped walking and stood with the confederates.

Source: Milgram, Bickman, & Berkowitz, 1969

social conventions that dictate their location and movements (Blumer, 1946). They enter the area via aisles or pathways and occupy locations that are determined by seating arrangements or by custom. While observing, they may perform a variety of behaviors, including clapping, cheering, shouting, or questioning, but these actions are usually in accord with the norms of the particular setting. Moreover, when the event or performance has ended, the crowd disperses in an orderly fashion (Hollingworth, 1935). (See Focus 14-1.)

• •
FOCUS 14-1: QUEUES AS CROWDS
_____

The waiting line, or **queue,** is a very special type of crowd. Like the casual crowd, the queue includes strangers who will probably not meet again. But like the members of a conventional crowd, those in this group have joined deliberately to achieve a particular goal, and as members of the crowd they are bound by certain norms of behavior (Mann, 1969, 1970). Queues are an interference, for they prevent us from immediately achieving our goal of purchasing tickets, services, or other commodities, but they also protect us from late-arriving competitors for these commodities. Milgram and his colleagues write:

> As in the case of most social arrangements, people defer to the restraints of
> the form, but they are also its beneficiary. The queue thus constitutes a clas-
> sic illustration of how individuals create social order, on the basis of a ru-
> dimentary principle of equity, in a situation that could otherwise degenerate
> into chaos. [Milgram, Liberty, Toledo, & Wackenhut, 1986, p. 683].

But what prevents the queue from breaking down into a mob? Milgram and his colleagues note that in addition to environmental supports such as ushers, rails, and ropes, queues are also protected by norms of civility. People in many cultures implicitly obey norms concerning queues and are ready to challenge those who try to violate the norm.

In a study of this process Milgram arranged for both male and female accomplices to break into 129 queues waiting outside of ticket offices and the like in New York City. Working either alone or in pairs, the accomplices would simply say "Excuse me, I'd like to get in here" and then insert themselves in the line. In an attempt to determine who is most likely to enforce the norm, Milgram also included either one or two passive confederates in some of the queues he studied. These individuals, who were planted in the line in advance, stood directly behind the point of intrusion (Milgram et al., 1986).

Objections occurred in nearly half of the lines studied. In a few cases (10.1%) queuers used physical action, such as a tap on the shoulder or a push. In 21.7% of the lines the reaction was verbal, such as "No way! The line's back there. We've all been waiting and have trains to catch" and "Excuse me, it's a line." In another 14.7% of the lines, queuers used dirty looks, staring, and hostile gestures to object to the intrusion nonverbally. Objections were also more prevalent when two persons broke into the line rather than one, and they were least prevalent when two confederates separated the intruders from the other queuers (see Figure 14-3). Overall, 73.3% of the complaints came from people standing behind the point of intrusion, compared with only 26.6% from people standing in front of the intrusion. These findings suggest that self-interest, as well as the normative force of the queues' rules, mediated reactions to the queue breakers' actions.

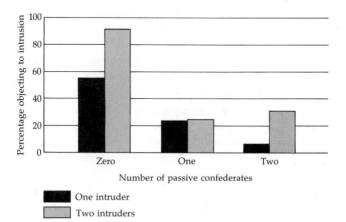

FIGURE 14-3. Percentage of groups in which objections to intrusions occurred. *Source: Milgram, Liberty, Toledo, & Wackenhut, 1986*

Mobs.   A hostile crowd of emotionally charged individuals is a **mob.**
Mobs tend to form when some negative event, such as a crime, a catastro-
phe, or a controversial action, draws a group of people together. As these
individuals discuss the event, they become more angry and more certain
that some corrective action must be taken. Unless the situation is diffused,
the mob becomes volatile, unpredictable, and capable of violent action. It
is in the mob that impulse replaces reason. Leonard Doob puts it very
strongly, calling a mob "a device for going crazy together" (1952, pp. 292–
293). He adds that "after a mob disbands, many of the participants may
report that they 'lost their heads.' In the light of 'pure reason' they may
be shocked by the ways in which they behaved."

Examples of mobs abound. Lynch mobs, for example, terrorized Black
men in the Southern United States until only recently. As Roger Brown
(1965) reports, the first documented lynch mob occurred in the United
States in 1882. Lynchings grew more and more numerous, until by 1950
lynch mobs had killed over 3000 victims. Virtually all the victims were
Black, and many of the killings were savagely brutal. Similarly aggressive
actions were observed in Los Angeles in 1943 when U.S. sailors roamed
through the city streets in search of Mexican-Americans wearing zoot
suits (a style featuring long suit coats and pleated trousers with tight
cuffs). Once located, the "zooters" were surrounded, insulted, and brutally beaten. In some cases the sailors forced their victims to strip (Turner
& Surace, 1956).

Riots can be construed as mobs on a grander scale. In 1969 when the
police force of Montreal went on strike for 17 hours, riots broke out all over
the city. As expected, professional crimes skyrocketed, but the noncri-
minal population also ran amok. A heterogeneous crowd of the impoverished, the rich, and the middle class rampaged along the central
business corridor, looting and vandalizing. Fires were set, 156 stores were
looted, $300,000 worth of glass was shattered, 2 people were killed, and
49 were wounded. Despite the violence observers commented that the entire incident seemed "carnival-like" (Clark, 1969). Race riots, although
clear examples of intergroup conflict (see Chapter 13), also display many
moblike qualities. Rioting in Detroit in the 1960s, for example, was precipitated by a police raid on a "blind pig" (a private drinking and gambling
establishment). A crowd gathered during the arrests, and looting began
after a window was broken by one spectator. Police then swept through
the streets in considerable force to quell the disorder. Blacks responded
with a series of firebombings, and officials asked that the state police and
national guard be brought in to control the mob. Rumors of sniping activity, the removal of restraints concerning the use of firearms, the lack of
clear organization, and a desire for revenge prompted police violence,
which in turn led to more widespread rioting (Goldberg, 1967).

Crowds that panic.   Other crowds are charged with a different emotion: fear. During catastrophes, such as fires, floods, or earthquakes,

crowds of people sometimes seek escape en masse from the dangerous situation. If the situation is seen as so dangerous that the only safe course of action is escape but the escape routes are very limited, a crowd **panic** can occur (Strauss, 1944). Members, fearing personal harm or injury, struggle to escape from the situation and from the crowd itself (Canetti, 1962, pp. 26–27):

> The individual breaks away and wants to escape from it because the crowd, as a whole, is endangered. But because he is still stuck in it, he must attack it. . . . The more fiercely each man "fights for his life" the clearer it becomes he is fighting *against* all the others who hem him in. They stand there like chairs, balustrades, closed doors, but different from these in that they are alive and hostile.

Panics often result in staggering losses of life. In 1903, for example, a panic at Chicago's Iroquois Theater killed nearly 600 people. When a small fire broke out backstage, the management tried to calm the audience. But when the lights shorted out and fire was visible behind the stage, the crowd stampeded for the exits. Some were burned or died by jumping from the fire escapes to the pavement, but many more were killed as fleeing patrons trampled them. As one observer described the panic:

> In places on the stairways, particularly where a turn caused a jam, bodies were piled seven or eight feet deep. Firemen and police confronted a sickening task in disentangling them. An occasional living person was found in the heaps, but most of these were terribly injured. The heel prints on the dead faces mutely testified to the cruel fact that human animals stricken in terror are as mad and ruthless as stampeding cattle. Many bodies had the clothes torn from them, and some had the flesh trodden from their bones [Foy & Harlow, 1928].

The incident in Cincinnati, from all objective reports, was more panicky crowd than mob. Although the news media described the crowd as a drugged-crazed stampede bent on storming into the concert, police interviews with survivors indicate that the crowd members in the center of the crush were trying to flee *from* the dangerous overcrowding rather than *to* the concert. Also, although some individuals in the crowd were clearly fighting to get out of the danger, good Samaritans in the crowd helped others to safety (Johnson, 1987).

Collective Movements

In 1929 as the United States plunged into the depression, people had little time or money to spend playing golf. But several entrepreneurs set up "miniature golf courses" in cities, and the idea took hold of the nation with a vengeance. Minature golf spread over the entire country, and some were saying that the game would replace all sports as the country's favorite form of recreation. The craze died out within six months (LaPiere, 1938).

On Halloween night in 1938 Orson Welles broadcast the radio program *The War of the Worlds*. General panic prevailed as listeners, taking the dramatization at face value, reacted by warning relatives, taking defensive precautions, contemplating suicide, and fleeing from the "invaded areas" (Cantril, 1940).

In 1943 Mrs. D. J. Mullane, a contestant on a radio program called *Truth or Consequences,* missed her question. Her penalty, the announcer explained, was that she would collect pennies as service to the nation's war effort. He also suggested that listeners should each send Mrs. Mullane a penny, and gave her address on the air. Within weeks she had received over 200,000 letters and well over 300,000 pennies. Many of the letters included personal messages, thanking Mrs. Mullane for her patriotism and wishing her good luck (Winslow, 1944).

In 1953 Victor Paul Wierwille taught his first course in the Power For Abundant Living. Two years later he founded a religious movement called The Way, and began spreading his unique brand of Christianity via radio broadcasts, magazines, classes, books, and meetings. By 1983 the Way had grown to include over 2,600 community groups (called "twigs") with an average number of 10 members per twig. Estimates indicate that in any single year 14,000 new recruits take at least one course based on The Way's religious teaching (Melton, 1986).

Not all collective phenomena transpire at close distances. As in these examples, individuals who are physically dispersed may still be similarly influenced and act in novel and often atypical ways. Such curious phenomena are variously termed **collective movements,** *mass movements,* or *dispersed collective behavior,* although this terminology is by no means formalized or universally recognized (Genevie, 1978; Smelser, 1962). But like crowds, collective phenomena come in many varieties, including fads, crazes, fashions, rumors, and social movements.

Fads, crazes, and fashions.   A **fad** is an abrupt, but short-lived, change in the opinions, behaviors, or lifestyles of a large number of widely dispersed individuals. Fads are remarkable both because they influence so many people so rapidly and because they disappear without leaving any lasting impact on society. Hula Hoops, the Twist, discos, breakdancing, Rubik's cube, "Baby on Board" stickers, video-games, trivia games, and *Wheel of Fortune* captured the imagination of many Americans, but within months their popularity dwindled. **Crazes** are similar to fads in most respects, except that they are just a bit more irrational, expensive, or widespread. Cabbage Patch Doll mania, streaking (running naked) on college campuses, the rapid proliferation of car telephones, and the widespread use of cocaine all qualify as crazes. Last, fads that pertain to styles of dress or manners are generally termed **fashions.** Clamdiggers gave way to hip-huggers, which were supplanted by bellbottoms, which lost out to blue jeans. Ties and lapels expand and contract, women's hemlines move up and down, and last season's "power" color is this season's embarrassment (Ragone, 1981).

Rumors and mass hysteria.   Rumors play an integral part in a variety of collective phenomena, including riots, panics, and crazes. Future rioters, for example, often mill about for hours swapping stories about injustices before taking any aggressive actions. Panics and crazes, too, are often sustained by rumors, particularly when the mass media perpetuate hearsay in news reports and announcements (Allport & Postman, 1947; Milgram & Toch, 1969).

Ralph L. Rosnow (1980), extending earlier theories of rumors, argues that two conditions tend to influence the spread of rumor: the degree of anxiety that individuals are experiencing and their uncertainty about the true nature of the situation. He argues that just as individuals often affiliate with others in threatening situations, "ambiguous or chaotic" situations tend to generate rumors. By passing rumors, individuals convey information (albeit false) about the situation. Rumors also reduce anxiety by providing, in most cases, reassuring reinterpretations of the ambiguous event (Walker & Berkerle, 1987). After the Three Mile Island nuclear power plant accident, for example, rumors circulated so rampantly that a rumor control center had to be opened to supply more accurate information. Rosnow, after studying this incident, maintains that even though many of the rumors were preposterous, they gave people a sense of security in a time of great anxiety (Rosnow & Kimmel, 1979; Rosnow, Yost, & Esposito, 1986).

Rumors also provide the basis for **mass hysteria:** the spontaneous outbreak of atypical thoughts, feelings, or actions in a group or aggregate, including psychogenic illness, common hallucinations, and bizzare actions (Pennebaker, 1982; Phoon, 1982). In June 1962, for example, workers at a garment factory began complaining of nausea, pain, disorientation, and muscular weakness; some actually collapsed at their jobs or lost consciousness. Rumors spread rapidly that the illness was caused by "some kind of insect" that had infested one of the shipments of cloth from overseas, and the owners began making efforts to eradicate the bug. No bug was ever discovered, however, and experts eventually concluded that the "June Bug incident" had been caused by mass hysteria (Kerckhoff & Back, 1968; Kerckhoff, Back, & Miller, 1965). Similarly, in 1954 rumors that windshields were being damaged by nuclear fallout began circulating in the Seattle area. The rumors escalated into a mild form of mass hysteria as reporters devoted much attention to the issue, residents jammed police telephone lines reporting damage, and civic groups demanded government intervention. Subsequent investigation revealed that no damage at all had occurred (Medalia & Larsen, 1958). (See Focus 14-2.)

• •

FOCUS 14-2: MASS PSYCHOGENIC ILLNESS IN THE WORKPLACE

In 1974 a team of researchers from the National Institute for Occpuational Safety and Health were called to a garment plant in the Southwestern

United States to investigate the cause of an epidemic of nausea, dizziness, and fainting among nearly one-third of the plant workers. Despite the severity of the symptoms, no toxic agent could be found, and the researchers were forced to conclude that the illness "involved psychogenic components, e.g., stress or anxiety" (Colligan & Murphy, 1982, p. 34).

This outbreak of a contagious psychogenic illness in an industrial setting is not an isolated incident. Although such incidents are difficult to document conclusively, researchers recently identified 23 separate cases that involved large numbers of individuals afflicted with "physical symptoms . . . in the absence of an identifiable pathogen" (Colligan & Murphy, 1982, p. 35). Over 1200 people were affected by these outbreaks, with most reporting symptoms that included headaches, nausea, dizziness, and weakness. Many were women working in relatively repetitive, routinized jobs, and the illness often spread through friendship networks.

Because of the scarcity of information, experts are reluctant to offer recommendations to prevent the problem. Some suggest that as soon as the possibility of a physical cause is eliminated, medical experts should tell workers that their problems are caused by stress rather than physical illness. An alternative, however, lies in removing the negative environmental conditions that encourage such epidemics. Research indicates that in many of the cases the affected employees work under very stressful conditions. In some instances the outbreaks occur when employees have been told to increase their productivity or have been working overtime. Poor labor/management relations have also been implicated, as have negative environmental factors, such as noise, poor lighting, and exposure to dust, foul odors, or chemicals. These findings suggest that psychogenic outbreaks can be reduced by improving working conditions (Colligan, Pennebaker, & Murphy, 1982).

· ·

Social movements.   A deliberate, organized attempt to achieve a change or resist a change in a social system is termed a **social movement.** Although such movements often arise spontaneously in response to some societal ill, social movements are more organized than other types of collectives, and members are more likely to share common goals (Killian, 1984). As noted in Chapter 3, social movements often form when a substantial number of individuals are dissatisfied with the current situation and decide to pool their efforts in a unified response. Mothers Against Drunk Drivers, the Moral Majority, the Unification Church, the feminist movement, the Way, and the civil-rights movement of the 1960s are all examples of social movements. (See McAdam, McCarthy, & Zald, 1988, and Zald & McCarthy, 1987, for detailed reviews of social movements.)

THEORETICAL VIEWPOINTS

Over the years investigators have succeeded in building a number of defensible theories of collective behavior. Such theories help us put our empirical questions and observations into a conceptual perspective, and there follows a review of the basic assumptions of several major approaches to collectives. Although many other viewpoints could be examined here, I have chosen to focus on Le Bon's crowd-psychology theory, convergence theory, and emergent-norm theory. (More extensive theoretical analyses are presented in Miller, 1985, McPhail & Wohlstein, 1983, and Turner & Killian, 1987.)

Le Bon's Crowd Psychology

> Should a horse in a stable take to biting his manger the other horses in the stable will imitate him. A panic that has seized on a few sheep will soon extend to the whole flock. In the case of men collected in a crowd all emotions are very rapidly contagious, which explains the suddenness of panics [Le Bon 1895/1960, p. 126].

Although scientific accounts of people immersed in crowds appeared as early as 1837 (Milgram & Toch, 1969), a more concerted effort to investigate such phenomena did not begin until after Le Bon published his classic study *The Crowd* in 1895. Le Bon was fascinated by large groups, but he also feared their tendency to erupt into violence. Perhaps because of these biases, he concluded that a crowd of people could, in certain instances, become a unified entity that acted as if guided by a single *collective mind*. Writes Le Bon (1895/1960, p. 27, italics added):

> Whoever be the individuals that compose it, however like or unlike be their mode of life, their occupations, their character, or their intelligence, the fact that they have been transformed into a crowd puts them in possession of a sort of *collective mind* which makes them feel, think, and act in a manner quite different from that in which each individual of them would feel, think, and act were he in a state of isolation.

According to the notion of the collective mind, no matter what the individual qualities of the people in the group, once immersed in a crowd they will *all* act in ways that are impulsive, unreasonable, and extreme. Once people fall under the "law of the mental unity of crowds," they act as the collective mind dictates.

Le Bon was a physician, and so he viewed the collective mind as a kind of disease that began at one point in the group and then spread throughout the rest of the crowd. Relying on observational data only, Le Bon concluded that emotions and behaviors could be transmitted from one person to another just as germs can be passed along, and he felt that this process of **contagion** accounted for the tendency for group members to behave in very similar ways (Wheeler, 1966).

The occurrence of contagion in groups is quite common. For example, how often have you caught yourself struggling to stifle a yawn after the person sitting next to you has just yawned broadly? Or have you noticed that one person laughing in a crowd will stimulate laughter in others? Do you recall how in lectures the question-and-answer sessions following the talks always begin very slowly but soon snowball as more and more questioners begin raising their hands? Le Bon believed that such contagion processes reflected the heightened suggestibility of crowd members, but other processes may be at work as well. Because many crowd settings are ambiguous, social-comparison processes may prompt members to rely heavily on other members' reactions when they interpret the situation (Singer, Baum, Baum, & Thew, 1982). Contagion may also arise in crowds through imitation, social facilitation, or conformity (Chapman, 1973; Freedman & Perlick, 1979; Nosanchuk & Lightstone, 1974; Tarde, 1903).

Herbert Blumer combines these various processes when he argues that contagion involves *circular reactions* rather than *interpretative reactions* (Blumer, 1946, 1951, 1957). During interpretative interactions group members carefully reflect on the meaning of others' behavior and try to formulate valid interpretations before making any kind of comment or embarking on a line of action. During circular reactions, however, the group's members fail to examine the meaning of others' actions cautiously and carefully and therefore tend to misunderstand the situation. When they act on the basis of such misunderstandings, the others in the group also begin to interpret the situation incorrectly, and a circular process is thus initiated that eventually culminates in full-blown behavioral contagion.

If we apply this view to a panic situation as an example, one person in the group may set off the contagion by acting excited, hostile, or fearful. As this source person seems to panic, others nearby assume that "something" is occurring, and they themselves begin to grow nervous. The source of the panic then reacts to the others' nervousness by becoming even more panicky, and the others, in turn, react to the source's behavior by becoming more excited. This spiral of intensifying reactions then multiplies throughout the group until all members are gripped in panic. Indeed, even uninvolved bystanders can become entrapped, for contagion sometimes "attracts and infects individuals, many of whom originally are detached and indifferent spectators and bystanders. At first, people may be merely curious about the given behavior or mildly interested in it. As they catch the spirit of excitement and become more attentive to the behavior, they become more inclined to engage in it" (Blumer, 1946, p. 176).

Convergence Theory

All movements, however different in doctrine and aspiration, draw their early adherents from the same types of humanity; they all appeal to the same types of mind [Hoffer 1951, p. 9].

What could the members of such widely disparate and internally heterogeneous collectives as the following possibly have in common: Blacks rioting in Watts, zealots eagerly confessing their sins during a religious crusade, gangs of shoppers rampaging through a department store searching for bargains, and Korean students throwing rocks at soldiers during a protest rally? According to **convergence theory,** a great deal, because in all these instances individuals join the group because they possess particular personal characteristics. Although these predisposing features may be latent or virtually unrecognizable, they are the true causes of the formation of both large and small collectives. Such aggregates are not merely haphazard gatherings of dissimilar strangers but, rather, represent the convergence of people with compatible needs, desires, motivations, and emotions. By joining in the group, the individual makes possible the satisfaction of these needs, and the crowd situation serves as a trigger for the spontaneous release of previously controlled behaviors. Although the list of predisposing characteristics differs from one perspective to the next, all convergence theories are similar in that they seek to "identify the latent tendencies in people that will cause them to act alike, the circumstances that will bring people with such tendencies together, and the kinds of events that will cause these tendencies to be released" (Turner & Killian, 1972, p. 19).

Sigmund Freud's theory of group formation, discussed in Chapter 3, is in many respects a convergence theory because Freud felt that people join collectives to satisfy repressed unconscious desires that otherwise would never be fulfilled (Freud, 1922). He was very much impressed with Le Bon's description of the changes that overtake the individual immersed in a crowd, but he believed that Le Bon had failed to recognize the role of unconscious needs. Accordingly, Freud extended his psychoanalytic theory to group situations by suggesting that even though individuals may experience sexual impulses, aggressive tendencies, and a strong desire to escape from danger, psychological mechanisms hold those libidinal tendencies in check. In the group situation, however, control over behavior is transferred to the leader or other group members, and each person is thus freed from the bonds of restraint and guilt. As a result, formerly repressed needs come to motivate behavior, and atypical actions become more likely. Indeed, later writers (Martin, 1920; Meerloo, 1950) extended the psychoanalytic perspective by suggesting that different kinds of groups are formed to satisfy different needs. In this view mobs satisfy latent aggressive tendencies, flights of panic satisfy a primitive need to flee from danger, and orgies fulfill deep-seated sexual passions.

Emergent-Norm Theory

An individual may know perfectly well what his parents, teachers, and preacher say is right and wrong, *and yet violate this without feelings of guilt if his fellows do not condemn him* [Sherif & Sherif, 1964, p. 182].

The third approach to collective behavior to be considered here was developed by Ralph Turner and Lewis Killian in response to certain shortcomings they attributed to both convergence theory and contagion theory (Turner, 1964; Turner & Killian, 1972). They argue that most crowds are not as homogeneous as convergence theories suggest, for group members typically differ from one another in terms of attitudes, motivations, emotions, and so on. Indeed, Turner and Killian reject one of the fundamental assumptions of most collective-behavior theories—that crowds are extremely homogeneous—and conclude that the "mental unity of crowds" is primarily an illusion. Crowds, mobs, and other collectives only *seem* to be unanimous in emotions and actions, since the members all adhere to norms that are relevant in the given situation. Granted, these **emergent norms** may be unique and sharply contrary to more general societal standards, but as they emerge in the group situation, they exert a powerful influence on behavior. Although emotions and actions can spread throughout the group, as contagion theories suggest, in many instances bystanders merely stand around without ever becoming actively involved.

Turner and Killian apply their **emergent-norm theory** to many types of collective actions, but their case-study analysis of a weekend religious retreat is especially informative. This particular retreat, which took place in California, proceeded along fairly typical lines for several days as the members met in small Bible-discussion groups, listened to short sermons, and sang hymns. The attendees also gathered at night to talk over their feelings about God and their church, and again these meetings followed a routine pattern as the members made matter-of-fact statements about their goals and satisfactions. Toward the end of the retreat, however, one well-known member of the group gave a long, emotional commentary on her relationship to God and eventually broke down as she sobbed about her selfishness and unworthiness. During her testimony the atmosphere of the group was marked by tension, for unlike some denominations, hers did not encourage such confessions, and hence they rarely occurred. Yet when the woman finished, a second person stood and gave a similarly emotion-laden oration, and others soon followed: "One after another individuals would arise, confessing everything from cheating on exams to fornication, each apparently outdoing the preceding in describing the intensity of his sinfulness" (Hamilton, 1972, p. 17).

Turner and Killian believe that a confession norm emerged during the retreat and that many of the group members conformed to this norm by publicly admitting their shortcomings. Many realized that public confessions were clearly contrary to the doctrines of the church, but they remained silent during the proceedings and thereby lent implicit support to the emergent norm. As in the conformity studies reviewed in Chapter 6, a powerful but incongruous norm developed in the group and became the standard for behavior (Asch, 1952; Sherif, 1936). Thus, although the actions—when viewed from a more objective perspective—may have seemed out of control and very strange, for the retreat participants they were consistent with the emergent norms.

Application: The Baiting Crowd

The three perspectives on collective behavior—contagion, convergence, and emergent-norm theory—are in no sense incompatible. Although each approach emphasizes different mechanisms, to achieve a fuller understanding of collective behaviors we need to draw from all of them. For example, consider the behavior of *baiting crowds*, groups of people who urge on a person threatening to jump from a building, bridge, or tower (Mann, 1981).

Applying the three theories, the convergence approach suggests that only a certain "type" of person would be likely to bait the victim to leap to his or her death. These shouts could then spread to other bystanders through a process of contagion until the onlookers were infected by a norm of callousness and cynicism that made their actions seem consistent with the structure of the setting. Hence all three processes—as well as others—may contribute to baiting, as an archival study conducted by Leon Mann suggests. Although Mann was unable to determine whether the baiters in a crowd possessed any identifying personality or demographic characteristics (as convergence theory would suggest), he did note that baiting became more likely as crowd size increased. This effect, which is generally consistent with contagion theory, may be due to the "greater probability that in a large crowd at least one stupid or sadistic person will be found who is prepared to cry 'Jump!' and thereby provide a model suggestible for others to follow" (Mann, 1981, p. 707). In addition, Mann reports evidence of an antilife norm in several of the crowds in which members not only encouraged the victim to "end it all" but also jeered and booed as rescuers attempted to intervene. (See Focus 14-3.)

Mann's study also indicated that other variables—such as the anonymity of the crowd, the dehumanization of the victim, and frustration due to waiting—influenced baiting. Although these factors are not inconsistent with the processes emphasized by collective-behavior theorists, they lie at the core of another perspective on atypical group behavior known as **deindividuation theory.** This theory is reviewed in the next section.

• •

FOCUS 14-3: FANS AS MOBS

The positive consequences of team sports for both participants and spectators are numerous and undeniable. For participants team sports provide exercise, enhance fitness, give pleasure, and teach teammates to work with others. For the spectator watching sports can be a stimulating and entertaining form of recreation that is as involving as it is satisfying. (For reviews see Sloan, 1979, and Zillmann, Sapolsky, & Bryant, 1979.)

Unfortunately, sporting events are also often marked by fans' violence. For example, in Peru 293 people were murdered or trampled to death during a soccer game in 1964. In 1971, 66 fans were crushed when they tried to jam through a stadium exit in Scotland. In 1974 the Cleveland Indians had to forfeit a game to the Texas Rangers because the hometown fans attacked the Rangers' players (Leonard, 1980). In 1989, 93 people died during a stampede at kickoff time in Sheffield, England.

The theories of collective behavior examined in this chapter offer insight into these incidents. First, as the concept of *contagion* suggests, when a foul is committed on the field or a limited act of violence occurs in the stands, this event triggers similar events in other areas of the crowd (Boire, 1980; Leonard, 1980). Second, *convergence* factors may be operating.

Not only are most of the spectators avid fans, but those that are prone to violence during the games often share other characteristics as well. Analyses of soccer spectators in England, for example, indicate that most are young men between the ages of 16 and 30, that they are from working-class backgrounds, and that they tend to tolerate the use of aggression to solve interpersonal problems (Coalter, 1985; Dunning, Maguire, Murphy, & Williams, 1982; Dunning, Murphy, & Williams, 1986). Third, the *norms* of the situation may condone or even promote violence by the fans. Studies of violence at British soccer matches suggest that *hooliganism* is considered a normal part of the event and is often sustained by sensationalized coverage in the mass media (Dunning et al., 1986; Mann, 1979).

Unfortunately, because of the nature of sports events, these instances of collective behavior may be difficult to prevent through direct physical means. Although some changes in the structure of the sporting stadium or arena and increases in "crowd-control personnel" may help to limit fans' attacks on players, mobs continue to become unruly. From a group-dynamics perspective a more effective approach would entail altering the norms of the sporting situation to emphasize respect among players and fan restraint. If the emergent norms in sports did not condone aggression, violence would be less frequent.

· ·

DEINDIVIDUATION THEORY

Leon Festinger, Albert Pepitone, and Theodore Newcomb (1952) coined the term **deindividuation** to describe how individuals can become so "submerged in the group" that they feel as though they no longer stand out as individuals. This feeling, they argued, could create a "reduction of inner restraints" and, in the extreme, atypical actions. In their initial test of this process Festinger, Pepitone, and Newcomb arranged for all-male groups to discuss their families. They assumed that young men would be reluctant to criticize their parents if they felt identifiable but that more negative opinions would be expressed by those who felt deindividuated. As expected, when subjects were later asked to recall which member of the group made a particular statement, those who made many errors also tended to express more negative attitudes toward their parents ($r = .57$).

Although several other researchers extended these initial results (for example, Singer, Brush, & Lublin, 1965; Ziller, 1964), much of the subsequent research has been stimulated by Philip Zimbardo's *process model* of deindividuation. Drawing on anecdotal observations, systematic small-group research, and prior theorizing in collective behavior, Zimbardo divides deindividuation into three interrelated components. As summarized in Figure 14-4, he begins by specifying the conditions of deindividuation, features of the group situation such as anonymity and responsibility that stimulate or retard the onset of the process. Next, he

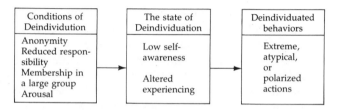

FIGURE 14-4. A process model of deindividuation.

describes the deindividuated state, a subjective experience in which the individual group members experience "a lowered threshold of normally restrained behavior" (1969, p. 251). Lastly, he examines a series of deindividuated behaviors that represent the outputs of the process. Although Zimbardo notes that deindividuation can result in a range of positive outcomes, for the most part he emphasizes antisocial behaviors such as violence, destruction, and hostility. In the sections that follow each of these aspects of the deindividuation process—inputs, the deindividuated state, and outcomes—are examined in turn. These sections rely heavily on Zimbardo's process model, but his view is also supplemented by findings drawn from more recent research (Diener, 1980; Prentice-Dunn & Rogers, 1983).

Conditions of Deindividuation

What factors set the stage for the loss of individuality in groups? Rather than offering a single-factor explanation, such as contagion, psychodynamic needs, or norms, Zimbardo identifies a number of social-psychological causes in his explanation of deindividuation. In examining the Who concert, for example, Zimbardo would begin by reviewing features in the specific situation that could have contributed to the creation of a state of deindividuation. These factors, which are shown in the left-hand portion of Figure 14-4, include members' anonymity, their feelings of responsibility in the group, the size of the group, and arousal induced by overcrowding, alcohol consumption, and marijuana use.

Anonymity. Zimbardo felt that anonymity was a variable of paramount importance in the deindividuation process. Although anonymity can be achieved in a variety of ways—wearing disguises, using an alias, avoiding acquaintances, or joining a group whose members are very similar to one another—these methods are equivalent in that they prevent identification: "others can't identify or single you out, they can't evaluate, criticize, judge, or punish you" (Zimbardo, 1969, p. 255). If group members are conforming to societal laws and norms simply because they fear legal reprisals and social sanctions, anonymity eases the likelihood that those in authority will locate and punish them for engaging in strange or illegal activities (Dodd, 1985; Ley & Cybriwsky, 1974a).

Both laboratory and field studies suggest that anonymity and atypical action go hand in hand. Members of anonymous groups, for example, are more likely to use obscene language, break conventional norms governing conversation, express themselves in extreme ways, criticize one another, and perform embarrassing behaviors (Cannavale, Scarr, & Pepitone, 1970; Lindskold & Finch, 1982; Mathes & Guest, 1976; M. J. White, 1977). One team of researchers illustrated these effects of anonymity by asking their female participants to wear old clothes or more formal attire (dresses) to their study. Once they arrived, those in old clothes were given oversized white lab coats to wear throughout the experimental session. The researchers felt that wearing lab coats would create a feeling of anonymity and that anonymous subjects would be more likely to display atypical behaviors. Consistent with this hypothesis, when the subjects wearing lab coats discussed the topic of pornography in four-woman groups, they (1) used more obscenities, (2) interrupted one another more frequently, (3) reported liking the group more, and (4) allowed fewer seconds of silence to pass during the discussion than the identifiable subjects. When a more neutral topic was discussed (attitude toward the value of a liberal education), no differences between the two conditions were obtained (Singer, Brush, & Lublin, 1965).

Other investigators have also found that anonymity leads, in some cases, to increased aggression (Donnerstein, Donnerstein, Simon, & Ditrichs, 1972; Mann, Newton, & Innes, 1982; Mathes & Kahn, 1975; Page & Moss, 1976). Zimbardo (1969), under an elaborate pretense, asked his all-female groups to give 20 electric shocks to another woman. To manipulate anonymity, subjects in the unidentifiable condition wore large lab coats (size 44) and hoods over their heads, and they were not permitted to use their names. They were also assured that they could not be identified. Subjects in the identifiable condition, in contrast, were greeted by name and wore large name tags, and the experimenter emphasized their uniqueness and individuality. To manipulate the characteristics of the person getting the shocks (the victim), before the shock session Zimbardo played a tape of an interview with the victim. This interview was contrived to make the woman seem attractive—"nice, accepting, altruistic, sweet" (p. 266)—or unattractive—"obnoxious, self-centered, conceited, and critical" (p. 266).

The groups were seated in a darkened room and watched the victim through a one-way mirror. Each subject was required to depress a switch on signal, and the experimenter emphasized the group's responsibility for the action. When the switch was depressed, the target would jump from the pain of the electric shock. Indeed, halfway through the 20 trials the target—who was actually a confederate and received no shocks—pretended to react so severely that her hand ripped out of the restraints. At that point the experimenter strapped her hand down again, and 10 more shock trials were carried out. This entire procedure was then repeated with the second victim; the order (nice versus obnoxious victim) was counterbalanced across groups.

The results of this intriguing study provided some support for Zimbardo's belief that feelings of anonymity stimulate aggressive behavior. Although identifiability was unrelated to the number of shocks given (the average was 17 of 20), the unidentifiable subjects held their switches down nearly twice as long as the identifiable subjects (.90 of a second versus .47 of a second). In addition, identifiable subjects tended to be more influenced by the targets' characteristics than were the unidentifiable subjects. The nonanonymous subjects administered shorter and shorter shocks to the nice victim over trials, whereas the anonymous subjects gradually increased the length of the shocks they gave (these trends were not statistically significant). Also, the correlation between shock duration and ratings of the target was significant for identifiable subjects ($r = .67$), but nonsignificant for unidentifiable subjects ($r = .10$), suggesting that the anonymous subjects were unaffected by the characteristics of the victim. Hence, this study not only attests to the importance of low identifiability but also lends some support to Zimbardo's assumption that the aggressive actions of deindividuated group members are not under stimulus control.

Field studies have also implicated anonymity as a key contributor to deindividuated actions. Mann (1981), in his study of baiting crowds, found that most of these crowds gather at night, when anonymity is easier. Studies of people communicating by computer find that these anonymous users often engage in a practice called *flaming;* they express their ideas and opinions far more strongly than is appropriate (Kiesler, Siegel, & McGuire, 1984; McGuire, Kiesler, & Siegel, 1987). Also, anthropological evidence suggests that aggressive groups are more likely to engage in anonymity-enhancing rituals than nonviolent groups (Watson, 1973). Through the use of the Human Relations Files maintained by anthropologists, ethnographers, and sociologists, a number of cultures were classified as either high or low in violence. Violent cultures were those that engaged in such practices as headhunting, the torturing of captives, fighting to the death in battles, and mutilation; low-violence cultures were those that spared prisoners or engaged in only minor raids on neighboring groups. Cultures that instituted a "specific change in appearance of the individual before battle" (p. 343) were also noted, as were those that featured no changes. Results indicated that 92.3% of the highly aggressive cultures (12 of 13) featured rituals that disguised the appearance of warriors, whereas only 30% of the low-aggression cultures (3 of 10) featured similar rituals.

Responsibility.   Group members' feeling of responsibility for their actions is another important input variable, with the occurrence of deindividuation increasing in likelihood as factors in the situation limit feelings of personal accountability. If an authority who demands compliance is present, for example, group members may feel that they are not personally responsible for the consequences of their actions (Milgram, 1974). In addition, if the consequences are somehow separated from the act itself—

as when a bombardier presses a bomb-release switch, a technician in an underground bunker launches a missile aimed at a site a thousand miles away, or the person you are shocking remains unseen and unheard—a sense of responsibility for the negative consequences is lessened.

Personal responsibility is also minimized whenever **diffusion of responsibility** occurs in the group. As researchers investigating helping behavior, productivity, and other group processes have noted, people in groups sometimes feel that they have less personal responsibility when other people are present. Consider the well-publicized case of Kitty Genovese, who in 1964 was stabbed to death on the street outside her New York City apartment. Police estimated that 38 people heard her cries for help, but no one intervened directly or even called the police. Their slow response gave the murderer, who had initially fled the scene, time to return to finish off his victim. Apparently, the "knowledge that others are present and available to respond, even if the individual cannot see or be seen by them, allows the shifting of some of the responsibility for helping to them" (Latané & Nida, 1981, p. 309). Zimbardo supplies examples of groups that actually take steps to ensure the diffusion of responsibility, as when murderers pass around their weapons from hand to hand so that responsibility for the crime is distributed through the entire group rather than concentrated in the one person who pulls the trigger or wields the knife.

Group membership.   For a number of reasons group membership is another key input variable in the deindividuation process. First, being part of a group both increases feelings of anonymity and makes diffusion of responsibility possible. As Le Bon argued so many years ago, the crowd is "anonymous, and in consequence irresponsible," so the "sentiment of responsibility which always controls individuals disappears entirely" (1895/1960, p. 30). Second, contagion becomes more likely in groups, since more people are present to facilitate communication and provide behavioral examples (Dunand, Berkowitz, & Leyens, 1984). Third, social facilitation can, in some instances, trigger general arousal and even excitement (see Chapter 9). Lastly, studies suggest that self-awareness, along with self-regulation, often decreases when individuals join groups (Mullen, 1986a).

The empirical evidence indicates that anonymity paired with group membership is more likely to lead to deindividuation than is anonymity alone. Ed Diener and his associates examined this hypothesis by taking advantage of a unique tradition: Halloween trick-or-treating (Diener, Fraser, Beaman, & Kelem, 1976). Their subjects were 1352 children from the Seattle area who went trick-or-treating at one of the 27 experimental homes scattered throughout the city. The trick-or-treaters were greeted by a young woman (who did not live in the house) who told them they could each have one candy bar. She then said "I have to go back to my work in another room" and left them standing in front of a low table with two bowls on it, one containing small candy bars and a second filled with pennies and nickels. An observer hidden behind a decorative panel recorded transgressions—the number of extra candy bars taken and the amount of money stolen.

Diener and his associates manipulated several independent variables in the study, but the two of critical interest in the current discussion were group membership and anonymity. First, since the children came to the house alone or in small groups, group membership varied naturally (exceedingly large groups were not included in the study; nor were groups that included an adult). Second, since the children were already disguised, nothing was done to children assigned to the anonymous condition. Those in the nonanonymous condition, however, were asked to give their names and addresses.

The percentages of children transgressing in the four conditions of the experiment are shown in Figure 14-5. As the chart indicates, each variable contributed somewhat to transgression, with more money and candy being taken by children in groups rather than alone and by anonymous rather than nonanonymous children. However, the effects of anonymity on solitary children were not very pronounced, whereas in the group conditions the impact of anonymity was enhanced. These findings, which have been supported in other investigations, suggest that the term *deindividuation* is used most appropriately in reference to people who perform atypical behavior while members of a group (Cannavale, Scarr, & Pepitone, 1970; Mathes & Guest, 1976; Mathes & Kahn, 1975).

Group size.   Zimbardo does not state how large a group must be before deindividuation can occur, but several studies have found that bigger is better when it comes to atypical actions (Erffmeyer, 1984; Mann, 1981; Mullen, 1986a). Mann's (1981) studies of baiting crowds, for example, found that large crowds (more than 300 members) baited more than small

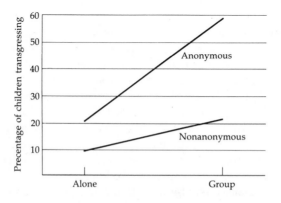

FIGURE 14-5. Percentage of children who transgressed by taking candy or money.
Source: Diener, Fraser, Beaman, & Kelem, 1976

crowds. Similarly, Brian Mullen (1986) presents evidence of the relationship between lynch-mob size and the savagery of the mob's actions. He examined the records of 60 lynchings in which the number of victims ranged from one to four and the size of the mob ranged from 4 to 15,000. He found that as the ratio of victims to mob size decreased, atrocities increased. Also, although Diener and his associates found that the size of ad hoc laboratory groups had no impact on behavior, they did find that group members felt less self-conscious in larger groups (Diener, Lusk, DeFour, & Flax, 1980).

Additional evidence comes from a recent study of persuasion during religious revivals (Newton & Mann, 1980). In most such meetings, when the speaker ends the lecture and sermon, he or she enjoins the listeners to make a public "decision" to accept the espoused teachings. For example, at the end of religious meetings conducted by the Billy Graham Evangelistic Association, the audience members are invited to become *inquirers* by coming forward and declaring their dedication to Christ. Although the crusaders consider this dedication to be a spiritual experience caused by divine prompting, from a group-dynamics perspective the actions can be viewed as crowd responses to a persuasive communication. Accordingly, if deindividuation is associated with larger groups, the proportion of listeners who become inquirers will be greater in large groups than in small groups. Supporting this contention, across 57 religious meetings a significant relationship between crowd size and the proportion of people who moved down to the stage to become inquirers was obtained ($r = .43$). Indeed, on Sunday the correlation rose to .78 and on weekdays the correlation was .84.

Arousal.   Zimbardo lists a number of other variables that stimulate deindividuated action, including altered temporal perspective, sensory overload, heightened involvement, lack of situational structure, and the use of drugs. Many of these factors, he suggests, function by arousing group members. He contends that arousal "increases the likelihood that gross, agitated behavior will be released, and that cues in the situation that might inhibit responding will not be noticed." Continuing, he proposes that "extreme arousal appears to be a necessary condition for achieving a true state of 'ecstasy'—literally, a stepping out of one's self" (1969, p. 257). Zimbardo even suggests that certain war rituals, such as war dances and group singing, enacted before battle are actually designed to arouse participants and enable them to be deindividuated when the fighting starts: "Among cannibals, like the Cenis or certain Maori and Nigerian tribes, the activity of ritual bonfire dance which precedes eating the flesh of another human being is always more prolonged and intense when the victim is to be eaten alive or uncooked" (1969, p. 257).

Although Zimbardo may be overstating his case in labeling arousal a necessary condition, certainly research has shown that reactions are intensified when group members are physiologically aroused. Arousal produced by anger or frustration has been repeatedly linked to increases in aggressive responses in humans, particularly when cues that are associated with aggression are present in the situation (Berkowitz, 1983; Ferguson & Rule, 1983). Evidence also indicates that emotionally neutral activities such as exercise and physical exertion can create a state of general physiological arousal that in certain situations is misinterpreted as excitement, anger, and hostility (Zillmann, 1983). Aroused individuals, too, are more likely to ignore inhibitory situational cues (Zillmann, Bryant, Cantor, & Day, 1975).

Experiencing Deindividuation

"I had the knife in my right hand and I was just swinging with the knife, and I remember hitting something four, five times repeatedly behind me. I didn't see what it was I was stabbing" [testimony of S. Atkins during the grand jury investigation of the Manson crimes (reported in Bugliosi, 1974, p. 239)].

"Everyone was pushing and I pulled out my knife. I saw this face—I never seen it before, so I stabbed it. He was laying on the ground lookin' up at us. Everyone was kicking, punching, stabbing. I kicked him on the jaw or someplace; then I kicked him in the stomach. That was the least I could do was kick 'im" [gang member's account of the stabbing of a polio victim in New York City (reported in Yablonsky, 1959, p. 113)].

"I began to have intervals of liberty—for waves of glory swept over me and when they came I praised God with a loud voice and in the spirit I clapped my hands and rejoiced [A.T. Boisen describing his conversion to a religious sect known as the Holy Rollers (1939, pp. 188–189)].

Each of these accounts suggests that individuals, when deindividuated, experience profound changes in emotions, memory, and self-regulation. These accounts, however, yield only a vague glimpse into the nature of the deindividuation experience, leaving unanswered the question "What transpires when an individual becomes deindividuated?"

Extending Zimbardo's initial theorizing, Diener proposes a *multicomponent theory* of deindividuation involving two discrete components: a loss of self-awareness and altered experiencing. First, as studies of **self-awareness** suggest, individuals can focus their attention outward, onto other group members or environmental objects, or inward, onto the self. When this focus is on the self, people become more self-aware and are more likely to attend to their emotional and cognitive states, carefully consider their behavioral options, and monitor their actions closely. When this focus is on features of the situation that are external to the person, people fail to monitor their actions and may therefore overlook any discrepancies between moral and social standards and their behavior (Carver & Scheier, 1981, 1983, 1984; Wicklund, 1980). Diener writes:

People who are deindividuated have lost self-awareness and their personal identity in the group situation. Because they are prevented by the situation from awareness of themselves as individuals and from attention to their own behavior, deindividuated persons do not have the capacity for self-regulation and the ability to plan for the future. Thus, prevented from self-attention and self-monitoring by the group situation, they become more reactive to immediate stimuli and emotions and are unresponsive to norms and the long-term consequences of behavior [1980, p. 210].

Consistent with Diener's theory, studies indicate that the reduction of self-awareness can lead to disinhibited action, including heightened susceptibility to incorrect interpretations of social situations (Scheier, Carver, & Gibbons, 1979), reductions in willingness to help others (Wegner & Schaefer, 1978), and increases in aggression (Carver, 1975) and stealing (Beaman, Klentz, Diener, & Svanum, 1979).

The second factor is *altered experiencing*. When individuals are deindividuated, they may undergo a host of cognitive and emotional changes, including disturbances in concentration and judgment, the feeling that time is moving slowly or rapidly, extreme emotions, a sense of unreality, and perceptual distortions. The individual may also experience intense pleasure. As Zimbardo notes, members of mobs, even when engaged in intensely violent and aggressive actions such as lynchings and rioting, often appear joyous, boisterous, and happy. Although the pleasure of deindividuation stems in part from the feeling of security that can be gained by immersion in a group, Zimbardo suggests that deindividuated behavior is evaluated as pleasurable at a more basic emotional level.

The duality of deindividuation has been confirmed in several studies (Diener, 1979; Mann, Newton, & Innes, 1982; Prentice-Dunn & Rogers, 1980, 1982; Prentice-Dunn & Spivey, 1986; Rogers & Prentice-Dunn, 1981). Diener (1979), for example, manipulated deindividuation by including a large number of confederates in each group he studied. The subjects thought that they were members of eight-person groups, but in actuality six of the group members were Diener's accomplices, trained to facilitate or inhibit the development of deindividuation across three conditions:

1. In the *self-aware condition* the confederates seemed restless and fidgety. The subjects wore name tags, and they worked on tasks designed to heighten self-awareness, such as providing personal responses to questions, sharing their opinions on topics, and disclosing personal information about themselves.

2. In the *non–self-aware condition* an attempt was made to shift the subjects' focus of attention outward by having them perform a series of mildly distracting tasks. In no case was their individuality emphasized, and though the problems were not difficult, they required a good deal of concentration and creativity.

3. In the *deindividuation condition* the experimenter and the confederates went to great lengths to try to foster a feeling of group cohesiveness, unanimity, and anonymity. The confederates always addressed their questions and comments to the group as a whole, and they even adopted a

TABLE 14-2. The nature of deindividuation.

Factor	Typical Characteristics
Loss of self-awareness	• Minimal self-consciousness • Lack of conscious planning as behavior becomes spontaneous • Lack of concern for what others think of you • Subjective feeling that time is passing quickly • Liking for the group and feelings of group unity • Uninhibited speech • Performing uninhibited tasks
Altered experiencing	• Unusual experiences such as hallucinations • Altered states of consciousness • Subjective loss of individual identity • Feelings of anonymity • Liking for the group and feelings of group unity

(Source: Diener, 1979)

group name when the experimenter suggested that this would be appropriate. During the study all eight group members wore coveralls, and the experimenter referred to them only by the group name. Lastly, the groups undertook a series of tasks and games designed to increase arousal, cohesiveness, and external focus, including group singing and dancing. For example, when listening to "loud Burundi drum music, the group clapped in unison, swayed in unison, and danced around the circle together. The lights in the room were dimmed" (Diener, 1979, p. 1163).

Immediately after their group experience the subjects were given the opportunity to perform uninhibited tasks (for example, playing in the mud, writing down the faults of their friends, sucking liquids from baby bottles, writing down all the obscenities they could think of) or more inhibited tasks (such as working on crossword puzzles, reading an essay on disarmament, answering moral dilemmas). While the subjects were working, their statements and actions were unobtrusively recorded by several of the confederates. Additionally, participants later completed a memory test and a questionnaire measure of feelings and thoughts.

Because Diener was seeking to understand the nature of the deindividuated state, he used a statistical procedure called factor analysis to search for clusters of highly intercorrelated variables in his observational and self-report data. Based on this analysis, he identified the two clusters or factors shown in Table 14-2. The first factor, self-awareness, encompasses a lack of self-consciousness, little planning of action, high group unity, and uninhibited action. The second dimension, altered experiencing, is also consistent with the theory in that it ties together a number of related processes such as "unusual" experiences, altered perceptions, and a loss of individual identity. When Diener compared the responses of subjects in the three conditions of his experiment, he discovered that (1) deindividuated subjects displayed greater losses of self-awareness than both the non–self-aware and the self-aware subjects and (2) deindividuated subjects reported more extreme altered experiencing than the self-aware subjects.

Subsequent research carried out by Steven Prentice-Dunn and Ronald W. Rogers (1980, 1982) extends these findings by suggesting that *both* components mediate the relationship between input factors and aggressive responses. They manipulated both self-awareness and the group members' accountability for their actions. Half of the subjects were led through a series of experiences that focused their attention on the situation, whereas the others were frequently reminded to pay attention to their personal feelings. Also, to manipulate accountability, some subjects were told that their actions would be carefully monitored, whereas others were led to believe that their actions weren't going to be linked to them personally. The subjects, who participated in four-man groups, were then given the opportunity to deliver ostensible electric shocks to a confederate (Prentice-Dunn & Rogers, 1982).

The results of the study supported the two-factor model of deindividuation on three counts. First, the subjects who were prompted to focus on the situation were lower in private self-awareness, and they tended to behave more aggressively. Second, analysis of the subjects' questionnaire responses revealed the two components emphasized by Diener: low self-awareness and altered experiencing. Third, using a statistical procedure known as path analysis, Prentice-Dunn and Rogers found that both of these components mediated the relationship between the variables they manipulated and subjects' aggressive response.

Deindividuated Behaviors

What kinds of actions are likely to be performed by deindividuated group members? Altruistic contributions to charity? Attempts to establish meaningful relationships with others? Goal-oriented achievement strivings? Usually not, for in Zimbardo's words, deindividuated behaviors often result in a "perversion of human potential," a regrettable replacement of reason and order with impulse and chaos (1969, 1975, 1977). According to Zimbardo (1975, p. 53), "conditions that reduce a person's sense of uniqueness, that minimize individuality are the wellsprings of antisocial behaviors, such as aggression, vandalism, stealing, cheating, rudeness, as well as a general loss of concern for others."

The studies discussed earlier certainly support Zimbardo's hypothesis, for deindividuated group members also tend to be hostile, uninhibited, aggressive, rude, obscene, thieving, and bizarre. Yet even Zimbardo notes that deindividuation can give rise to positive behaviors, including "intense feelings of happiness or sorrow, and open love for others" (1969, p. 251). In explanation, evidence now indicates that deindividuation tends to lead to extreme behaviors or polarized behaviors but that these actions are not necessarily negative ones. Rather, deindividuation sets the stage for the performance of either prosocial or antisocial behaviors, depending on the needs that are prominent for group members or the nature of the situation (Diener, 1980).

This extremism has been supported in several investigations. In one, women in college were told that they were to be members in four-person groups that would be administering shocks to a man taking part in a learning study (Johnson & Downing, 1979). Each time the man made an error, the subject could elect to administer either high, moderate, or slight increases in shock voltage ($+3$, $+2$, $+1$) or high, moderate, or slight decreases in shock voltage (-3, -2, -1). To manipulate anonymity, some subjects were told that their names and decisions regarding the voltage level would be known to other group members, whereas others were told that names and decisions could not be linked to any particular group member. To manipulate situational cues, subjects were given costumes to wear under the guise of masking individual characteristics. In the *prosocial-cues condition* nurses' gowns were used; the experimenter explained that "I was fortunate the recovery room let me borrow these nurses' gowns." In the *antisocial-cues conditions* the costumes resembled Ku Klux Klan outfits: "I'm not much of a seamstress; this thing came out looking kind of Ku Klux Klannish" (p. 1534).

The researchers hypothesized that the effects of anonymity would largely depend on the valence of the situational cues. They predicted that when prosocial cues were present, anonymity would lead to a reduction in the intensity of the punishment. If the situation contained antisocial cues, anonymity should promote increases in punishment. As Figure 14-6 shows, these hypotheses were supported. Taken in combination with other studies that have found significant effects of situational cues on

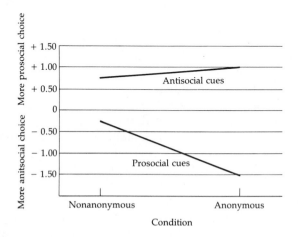

FIGURE 14-6. Mean shock selection in the four conditions of the "deindividuation and cues" experiment.

Source: Johnson & Downing, 1979

deindividuated group members, the findings suggest that deindividuation is neither "good" nor "bad" (Diener et al., 1975; N. R. Johnson, 1974; N. R. Johnson, Stemler, & Hunter, 1977; R. D. Johnson & Downing, 1979; Nadler, Goldberg, & Jaffe, 1982; Orive, 1984; Prentice-Dunn & Rogers, 1980; Reicher, 1982, 1984a, 1984b). (See Focus 14-4). As Diener summarizes:

> The deindividuated person in a certain situation might be more likely to donate a large amount of money to charity, might be more likely to risk his or her life to help another, and might be more likely to kiss friends—all behaviors that many consider laudatory. However, a deindividuated person might also be more likely to throw rocks at others, participate in a lynching, or set a building ablaze. Thus, less concerned with norms, personal punishment, or long-term consequences, the deindividuated person is quite reactive to emotions and situational cues that may lead to uninhibited behaviors that are judged to be prosocial, antisocial, or neutral by the individual's society [1980, p. 232].

• •
FOCUS 14-4: THE POSITIVE SIDE OF DEINDIVIDUATION

The study seemed simple enough. When a subject arrived, he or she was asked to fill out some questionnaires. After about 20 minutes the subject was led by an experimenter to another room, where just before entering the experimenter said:

> You will be left in the chamber for no more than an hour with some other people. There are no rules . . . as to what you should do together. At the end of the time period you will each be escorted from the room alone, and will subsequently depart from the experimental site alone. There will be no opportunity to meet the other participants [Gergen, Gergen, & Barton, 1973, p. 129].

Inside, the subject found a fairly small room (10 feet by 12 feet) that featured padded walls and floors. Occupying this comfortable space were approximately eight other people, some male and some female, all of whom were utter strangers to one another.

Would you be surprised to hear that some of the subjects in this experiment intimately embraced and kissed one another? that of the nearly 50 people who participated, 100% accidentally touched one another? that 89% purposefully touched one another? that 51% hugged one another? that 78% reported that they had felt sexually aroused? that over 50% changed their positions in the room every five minutes?

These statistics are a bit difficult to believe, but only because a crucial bit of information about the study has been omitted: the room was completely dark. When a well-lit room was used, none of these intimate actions occurred (see Figure 14-7). Only in the darkened chamber were individuals completely anonymous and, thus, able to engage in many be-

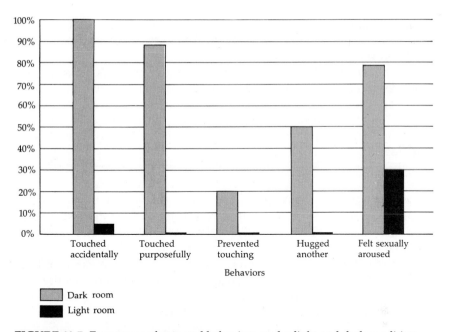

FIGURE 14-7. Frequency of assorted behaviors under light and dark conditions.
Source: Gergen, Gergen, & Barton, 1973

haviors that, under more usual circumstances, would have been considered counternormative and bizarre. In no case, however, did the anonymous (and possibly deindividuated) group members exhibit hostility, aggressiveness, or violence. Rather, nearly all became more intimately involved with one another in a positive fashion. In the words of one participant, a "group of us sat closely together, touching, feeling a sense of friendship and loss as a group member left. I left with a feeling that it had been fun and nice." Apparently the situation helped people express feelings that they would have otherwise kept hidden, but these feelings were those of affection rather than aggression (Gergen et al., 1973).

. . . .

Conclusions and Implications

In sum, research indicates that the three-step conception of deindividuation presented in Figure 14-4 is a viable approach to understanding disinhibited group behavior. Although large gaps in the empirical domain remain, the influence of certain situational variables (for example, anonymity, group members, and personal arousal), the nature of the deindividuated state, and the causal links between these components and behavioral outcomes have been tentatively confirmed. As investigators continue to expand their efforts in this area, we can hope that the puzzling behavioral and emotional misfirings of people in groups—riots, vandalism, gang violence, and panics—will become more predictable and thus more preventable.

Several interesting issues remain unresolved, however. One of these issues concerns the balance between individuation and deindividuation. Robert L. Dipboye (1977), in a review of deindividuation, calls attention to a paradox that permeates analyses of group membership and individuality. On the one hand, many theorists assume that deindividuation—and the freedom to act that it spawns—is a pleasurable, gratifying, and often-sought experience (Hoffer, 1951; Le Bon, 1895/1960; Zimbardo, 1969). Submersion in a group results in the attainment of power and an escape from societal inhibitions; hence, group members seek and try to maintain the experience of deindividuation. In contrast, humanistic theorists (for example, Fromm, 1965; Laing, 1960; Maslow, 1968) maintain that human beings can enjoy psychological well-being only when they are able to establish and maintain their own unique identities. In the words of R. D. Laing (1960, p. 44), "A firm sense of one's own autonomous identity is required in order that one may be related as one human being to another. Otherwise, any and every relationship threatens the individual with loss of identity." Thus, from this perspective deindividuation is unpleasant and identity-threatening; group members who feel "lost" in a group will try to reestablish their individual identities.

When deindividuation is considered an experience to be avoided rather than sought after, some of the output behaviors that had previously been interpreted as disinhibited, impulsive actions can be recast as identity-seeking behaviors. For example, although riots may stem from the loss of responsibility, anonymity, arousal, and group presence of deindividuation, rioters may also be attempting to reaffirm their individual identities. As one resident of the riot-torn community of Watts in Los Angeles explained, "I don't believe in burning, stealing, or killing, but I can see why the boys did what they did. They just wanted to be noticed, to let the world know the seriousness of their state of life" (Milgram & Toch, 1969, p. 576). Similarly, members of large groups, such as industrial workers, students in large classrooms, people working in bureaucratic organizations, and employees in companies with high turnover rates may perform atypical actions just to stand apart from the "crowd."

In one of the few studies that reports evidence of the need to seek individuation, Christina Maslach (1972) led the members of four-person groups to expect that one of their members was to be chosen to work on a particular task. During this screening interview two of the subjects were made to feel individuated; Maslach referred to them by name, made more personal comments to them, and maintained a significant amount of eye contact. The other two subjects were made to feel deindividuated, since she avoided close contact with them and addressed them impersonally. When these individuals were later given the opportunity to engage in a free-response group discussion and complete some questionnaires, the deindividuated subjects evidenced two different types of identity-seeking reactions. Some attempted to make themselves seem as different from the other group members as possible by giving more unusual answers to the questions, making longer comments, joining in the discussion more frequently, and attempting to capture the attention of the experimenter. In contrast, other subjects seemed to redefine their identities by revealing more intimate details of their personalities and beliefs through longer and more unusual self-descriptions.

In fairness to both of these perspectives, in some situations group members may prefer to become deindividuated, whereas at other times the need to be individuated may predominate (Diener, 1980; Ziller, 1964). Spectators at a college football game, celebrants at the Mardi Gras, shy listeners in a large audience, and soldiers standing for inspection may all feel quite comfortable when submerged in the group. Yet when these same persons seek rewards for their personal skills and contributions, wish to make lasting impressions on others, or hope to establish one-to-one relationships with other group members, they would no doubt prefer to stand out as individuals. Indeed, it is a reflection on the value of groups in human affairs that joining with others makes both of these goals possible; only by becoming members of groups can we both lose ourselves in the crowd while also securing an audience for our identity-defining self-presentations.

SUMMARY

Le Bon, the author of *The Crowd*, believed that when people joined large, relatively unstructured social groups, they sometimes engaged in spontaneous and atypical *collective behavior.* Subsequent studies of *crowds* support some of Le Bon's arguments, although the extremity of the action clearly depends, in large part, on the type of crowd being observed. In general members of *casual crowds, audiences (conventional crowds),* and *queues* conform to social norms, whereas members of *mobs* and crowds in *panic* display hostile and fearful actions, respectively. Also, individuals need not be concentrated in a single location to display atypical actions, for such *collective movements* as *fads, crazes, fashions,* rumors, *mass hysteria,* and *social movements* can influence widely dispersed individuals.

Several theories have been developed to account for collective behavior. Le Bon proposes that crowds seem to be governed by a collective mind, and that *contagion* causes crowd members to experience similar thoughts and emotions. *Convergence theory,* in contrast, proposes that the individuals who join groups often possess similar needs and personal characteristics. Freud, for example, argues that individuals, by joining crowds, are able to satisfy some basic needs for membership, hostility, and so on. Turner and Killian, however, argue that the similarity of behavior seen in crowds is caused by *emergent norms.* Their *emergent-norm theory* posits that crowds often develop unique standards for behavior and that these atypical norms exert a powerful influence on behavior.

Zimbardo's *deindividuation theory* draws on all three of these theories to explain the reduction of inner constraints that is sometimes seen in groups. This process, which is termed *deindividuation*, can be broken down into three components: (1) inputs, (2) internal changes, and (3) behavioral outcomes. Inputs, or causes of deindividuation, include feelings of anonymity, reduced responsibility (*diffusion of responsibility*), membership in large groups, and a heightened state of physiological arousal. The deindividuated state itself appears to involve two basic components: reduced *self-awareness* (minimal self-consciousness, lack of conscious planning, uninhibited speech, and performing uninhibited tasks) and altered experiencing (disturbances in concentration and judgment, the feeling that time is moving slowly or rapidly, extreme emotions, a sense of unreality, and perceptual distortions). Lastly, evidence indicates that this state of deindividuation sets the stage for more extreme, or more polarized, behaviors. Although Zimbardo emphasizes the negative consequences of deindividuation, violent actions do not always follow losses of identity and self-awareness. In fact, evidence indicates that, given certain prosocial cues, deindividuated group members may behave altruistically and that some of the atypical behaviors that had previously been interpreted as disinhibited, impulsive actions were actually attempts to reestablish a sense of individuality. Thus, deindividuation has both a positive and a negative side.

·15·

Groups and Change

The group's first hour-long meeting was, in a word, boring. Dr. R. and Dr. M., the group's coleaders, introduced themselves to the group and asked each member to do the same, but no one said much more than "I teach school for a living" or "I was born in New York, but my family moved to Palo Alto when I was six." Several of the members could barely bring themselves to speak to the group, and most stared at the floor rather than make eye contact with anyone. Even when the leaders asked members direct questions about their feelings or thoughts, they remained reticent. The hour passed by slowly.

The members of this group were very different from one another in many ways, but they did share one common quality: when interviewed by psychologists at the Stanford University clinic, they complained of severe problems developing and sustaining relationships with other people. All had a history of loneliness and interpersonal isolation, and some were so withdrawn that they were diagnosed as schizoid personalities. They had been placed together in a therapeutic group to help them solve their problems in social adjustment. The two therapists did not lead the discussion but preferred, instead, to let the members identify issues, raise questions, and offer their own solutions. As necessary, however, the therapists stepped in and subtly guided the group toward an analysis of the processes that were taking place in the group at that moment. When, for example, two members began criticizing each other, when a client tried to use powerful influence tactics, or when one of the members refused to get involved in a discussion of another member's inability to ask a woman out for a date, the therapists forced the group to examine and explain the members' interaction (Yalom, 1985).

Ever so slowly the members of the group began to change. Members who had been so socially anxious that they were tongue-tied when they tried to carry on a conversation with another person identified the causes of this anxiety and overcame it. People who had never been able to converse openly about their feelings practiced disclosing this kind of personal information. Group members learned how to understand and interpret other people's feelings and to respond to those feelings appropriately. Also, despite their many previous failures at maintaining any type of relationship, the members' bonds with one another became very strong. The therapists felt that the group seemed dull at times, but the clients themselves were very satisfied with their group, and they rarely missed a session. It took over two years of weekly sessions, but eventually the group members felt that their problems relating to other people had been corrected.

The idea that a group can be used as a change-promoting agent is not a new one. Throughout history personal change has often been achieved through social mechanisms rather than individualistic, asocial processes. As early as 1905 a Boston physician arranged for patients who were suffering from tuberculosis to meet in groups to ward off feelings of depression and to discuss ways to overcome their disease. Jacob L. Moreno (1932), who developed sociometry, also advocated acting out troubling relationships and feelings in a group process he called psychodrama. Sigmund Freud (1922) presented a cogent analysis of group processes that provided the foundation for conducting psychoanalysis in groups, and Kurt Lewin (1936) was an outspoken champion of group approaches to achieving social and personal change. Indeed, it was Lewin who stated the basic "law" of group therapy in its most simple form: "It is easier to change individuals formed into a group than to change any of them separately" (1951, p. 228).

This chapter asks some basic "what," "how," and "why" questions about groups and change. We begin with the question "What are some of the ways in which groups are used to achieve change in individual members?" Although often used to foster therapeutic change, groups can also be used in nonclinical settings to help well-adjusted individuals improve their social skills, to solve interpersonal problems in work settings, and to aid individuals who are trying to cope with a personal crisis or overcome an addiction. After reviewing these various uses of groups, we then turn to the question "How effective are groups in bringing about change?" The group led by Dr. R. and Dr. M. benefited the members tremendously, but do groups sometimes do more harm than good? After exploring this controversial topic, we close by asking *why:* why do people change when they are placed in groups? To answer this query the chapter explores some of the interpersonal processes that make groups effective agents of change.

THE GROUP AS AN AGENT OF CHANGE

People join groups to achieve a variety of goals. Some want to get rid of something: too much weight, too much grief over the passing of a loved one, irrational thoughts, or overwhelming feelings of worthlessness and despair. Others are seeking new skills and outlooks: insight into their own characteristics, a better sense of how others see them, or a new repertoire of behaviors they can use to improve their relationships with others. Some seek the strength they need to resist an addiction or obsession: the temptation to drink alcohol, use drugs, batter their spouse, or molest their children. And still others are seeking a brief respite from the stresses and strains of a too-impersonal world.

The variety of change-promoting groups reflects the variety of individuals' goals. Although the excesses of the 1960s and '70s have been tempered somewhat—communes, nude encounter groups, marathon encounter groups, and LSD-using sensitivity groups are rarities—these groups have been replaced by jogging and fitness clubs; consciousness-raising groups (such as gay-rights groups and women's groups); support groups for parents, children, grandparents, and ex-spouses; workshops and leadership seminars; marital- and family-counseling groups, religious retreats; self-help groups; and on and on. These groups, despite their many varieties, all help individuals achieve goals that they cannot reach on their own. Moreover, most of these group-level approaches to change fit one of the three basic categories shown in Table 15-1. **Group therapy,** which is usually conducted by a mental-health professional, is most often used to help people overcome troublesome psychological and social problems. **Interpersonal-learning groups,** in contrast, involve attempts to help relatively well-adjusted individuals extend their self-understanding and improve their relationships with others. Last, **self-help groups** are voluntarily formed groups of people who help one another cope with or overcome a common problem. These three varieties are considered below (Klein, 1983; Lakin, 1972; Lieberman, 1980; Rudestam, 1982).

TABLE 15-1. Some basic approaches to using groups as agents of personal and interpersonal change.

Type of Group	Basic Goal	Leader's Characteristics	Examples
Group therapy	Improve psychological functioning and adjustment of individual members	Mental-health professional: psychologist, psychiatrist, clinical social worker	Psychodynamic and Gestalt groups, interactional group therapy, behavior therapy
Interpersonal-learning group	Help members gain self-understanding and improve their interpersonal skills	Varied and unregulated; trained professional or untrained layperson	T-groups, encounter groups, skills-training seminars and workshops
Self-help group	Help members cope with or overcome specific problems or life crises	Typically, a volunteer layperson; many groups do not include a leadership role	Alcoholics Anonymous, Weight Watchers, support groups for parents of terminally ill children

Group Therapy

Like any other form of psychotherapy, the group led by Dr. R. and Dr. M. was designed to help patients overcome troublesome psychological and personal problems. But unlike individual therapies, group therapies involve treating individuals "in groups, with the group itself constituting an important element in the therapeutic process" (Slavson, 1950, p. 42). When they were initially proposed, skeptics questioned the wisdom of putting people who are suffering from psychological problems together in one group. How, they asked, could troubled individuals be expected to cope in a group when they had failed individually? And how could the therapist guide the therapeutic process in a group, given the subtle nuances that pervade one-to-one therapies? History, however, has proven the skeptics wrong, and at present a number of distinct group therapies have been developed (Kaplan & Sadock, 1983; Klein, 1983; Long, 1988). The sample we consider here includes psychoanalytic groups, Gestalt groups, and behavior-therapy groups.

Psychoanalytic groups. Freud's method of helping people cope with psychological problems is well known. Given his belief that most behavior reflects repressed motivations that people can only dimly perceive, he insisted that his patients talk about their memories, fantasies, dreams, and fears in the hope that they would gain insight into their unconscious mind. As necessary, Freud also offered *interpretations* of his patients' free associations that helped them identify the sources of their motivations and emotions, and he took advantage of *transference:* the tendency for patients to transfer the emotions they feel for their parents or siblings to the therapist. By capitalizing on transference, Freud succeeded in helping his patients work through unresolved family conflicts.

These methods, although used primarily with individual patients, form the basis of **psychoanalytic group therapy.** Freud himself, some suggest, practiced group psychoanalysis when he and his students met to discuss his theories and cases (Kanzer, 1983). In such groups the therapist is very much the leader, for he or she directs the group's discussion during the session, offers interpretations, and summarizes the group's efforts. Most psychoanalytic groups adhere to the *principle of shifting attention,* in that therapists shift their focus from one patient to the next during the course of a single group session. This shifting of attention means that group members change their roles during the session, sometimes acting as the patient seeking help, at other times the observer of others' problems, and on occasion the helper who gives counsel to a fellow group member. This rotation gives patients an opportunity to develop empathic listening skills, and it also gives them time to reflect on the information uncovered during the session. The group setting also offers more opportunities to work through problems that result from early family conflicts. Although individual therapy usually stimulates parental transference, during group psychoanalysis sibling transference also occurs. Members may find themselves reacting to one another inappropriately, but their actions, when examined more closely, may parallel the way they treated a brother or a sister when they were young (Day, 1981; Wolf, 1983).

Gestalt groups.   Frederick S. ("Fritz") Perls is generally recognized as the founder of Gestalt therapy. Perls drew his theoretical principles from Gestalt psychologists, who argue that perception requires the active integration of perceptual information. The word *Gestalt,* which means "whole" or "form," suggests that we perceive the world as unified, continuous, and organized. Like Freud, Perls assumed that we often repress many of our emotions and that family conflicts turn into "unfinished business" that continues to influence us even as adults. Perls, however, believed that we are capable of self-regulation and great emotional awareness, and he used therapy to help patients reach this potential (Perls, 1969; Perls, Hefferline, & Goodman, 1951).

In some cases **Gestalt group therapy** is one-to-one Gestalt therapy conducted in a group setting. Group members observe one another's "work," but they do not interact (Roth, 1983; Yalom, 1975). More frequently, however, interaction takes place among group members, with the therapist actively orchestrating the events. Rather than examining prior experiences or events that transpire outside the group, the focus is on immediate experiences in the group: the **here and now** rather than the *then and there.* Therapists often rely on a variety of *experiments,* or experiential exercises designed to stimulate emotional understanding (see Focus 15-1). When using the *hot seat,* one person in the group sits in the center of the room and publicly works through his or her emotional experiences. The *empty-chair* method involves imagining that another person or a part of oneself is sitting in an empty chair and then carrying on a dialogue with the person. These techniques are quite powerful, and as a result individuals often become very emotional during the session. Also, because of the difficulties inherent in trying to understand the emotional experiences of another person, Gestalt therapists resist offering interpretations to their patients.

• •
FOCUS 15-1. A GESTALT EXPERIMENT
──

Unlike many of the groups discussed in earlier chapters, therapeutic groups keep what transpires in the sessions confidential. This description by the therapist Robert L. Harman of a hypothetical group experiment, however, vividly captures the power of the Gestalt method (Harman, 1988, pp. 250–251):

> Rich, agitated, is tapping both feet, wringing his hands, and I ask him what is going on. He responds that he feels "so cooped up," and he goes on talking, with what seems to me to be forced humor, telling of all the "things he

has to do." Gradually his voice takes on a dull monotone. I consider saying to him that one way for him to coop himself up is to think of all the "things he has to do"; resisting this, I propose an experiment. Would he be willing, I ask, to give a voice to the part of him responsible for "cooping up" and let it speak to the rest of him? He agrees. His voice picks up energy as he says to this part of himself, "Look Buddy, I'm in control! Don't try to slide away from me; you know you wouldn't be able to get rid of me." I ask him to move to another seat and to give the other part a voice, the part that feels "cooped up." He moves, and in a whine, begs the other part to lighten up. As he continues to move from place to place, from voice to voice, in this enactment he asks the "cooping up" part what it is trying to do for him. He switches places and says, "To keep you from getting hurt." At this point he starts to sob. This is quite new behavior for Rich, who is a "big bear" of a man and has alternated between looking foreboding and making superficial jokes.

I check to see the impact he is having on others. Most appear to be paying close attention and Becky looks as if she wants to reach out to him or say something to him. She does not do so. I do not want to interfere or in any way cut off what Rich is getting into; I am thinking of what I could do to facilitate his becoming more involved with his experience so that he will be able to "finish" with it. His sobbing peaks and he begins to take a few deep breaths. I ask him what is going on. He starts sobbing again and says,

"I really hurt."

"Can you tell me how you hurt?"

"I am keeping in so much from the woman I live with," he replies.

• •

Behavior-therapy groups.   Behavior therapists utilize methods that differ substantially from those employed by psychoanalytic and Gestalt therapists. Rather than searching for the cause of the problematic behavior in unseen unconscious conflicts, behavior therapists focus on the problematic behavior itself. They also assume that problematic behaviors, like virtually all other behaviors, are acquired through experience, so they base their interventions on principles derived from learning theories. The goals of behavior therapy also tend to be specific and are defined in terms of desirable behaviors that will be encouraged (for example, expressing positive emotions with one's spouse) and undesirable behaviors that will be extinguished (for example, drinking alcohol).

Behavior-therapy groups use these principles with two or more individuals (Flowers, 1979; Hollander & Kazaoka, 1988; Rose, 1977, 1983). If, for example, Drs. M. and R. are behavior therapists, they will follow a series of standard procedures before, during, and after the group intervention. Prior to treatment they will measure their patients' social skills using behavioral rating methods. They will also review with each patient the purpose of the therapy and, in some cases, ask the patients to watch videotaped examples of group-therapy sessions. Such pretherapy reviews not only create change-enhancing expectancies but also help members identify the specific goals of the therapeutic intervention (Higginbotham,

West, & Forsyth, 1988). At this point the therapists may also ask the patients to sign a **behavioral contract** that describes in objective terms the goals the group members are trying to achieve.

During the therapy itself Drs. M. and R. rely on a number of proven therapeutic methods, including modeling, behavior rehearsal, and feedback. **Modeling** involves demonstrating particular behaviors while the group members observe (Bandura, 1977). The group leaders may engage in a one-minute conversation with each other, videotape the interaction, and then play it back to the group while identifying the nonverbal and verbal behaviors that made the conversation flow smoothly. During **behavior rehearsal** group members practice particular skills themselves, either with one another or through role-playing exercises. These practice sessions can be videotaped and played back to the group so the participants can see precisely what they are doing correctly and what aspects of their behavior need improvement. This **feedback** phase involves not only reassurance and praise from the leaders but also support from the other group members (Bellack & Hersen, 1979; Curran, 1977; Galassi & Galassi, 1979).

Interpersonal Learning Groups

Humanistic psychologists are united in their belief that the human race too frequently fails to reach its full potential. Although our relationships with others should be rich and satisfying, they are more often than not superficial and limiting. Also, although we are capable of profound self-understanding and acceptance, in many cases we do not understand ourselves very well. These limitations are not so severe that we seek treatment from a psychotherapist, but our lives would be richer if we could overcome them (Friedman, 1976).

Lewin was one of the first to suggest using small groups as "training laboratories" for teaching people interpersonal skills (see Focus 15-2). Lewin believed that in many cases groups and organizations fail because their members aren't trained in human relations. He therefore recommended using specialized **training groups, or T-groups,** to give group members experience in group dynamics. Other theorists expanded on this basic idea, and by 1965 the *human potential movement* was in high gear (Back, 1973; Gazda & Brooks, 1985; Lakin, 1972).

· ·
FOCUS 15-2: THE ORIGIN OF T-GROUPS

Group-dynamics folklore suggests that the first human-relations-training group, or T-group for short, was serendipitously initiated by Kurt Lewin in 1946. Lewin, as part of a series of problem-solving workshops, arranged for his graduate students to observe and later discuss the dynamics of work groups. These discussions were held in private until one evening a few of the work-group members asked if they could listen to the students' interpretations. Lewin reluctantly agreed to their request, and sure enough the participants confirmed Lewin's expectations by sometimes vehemently disagreeing with the observations and interpretations offered by Lewin's students. However, the animated discussion that followed proved to be highly educational, and Lewin realized that everyone in the group was benefiting enormously from the analysis of the group's processes and dynamics.

Lewin helped organize the National Training Laboratory (NTL) at Bethel, Maine, which later flourished under the leadership of Leland P. Bradford. This center further developed the concept of training groups in special workshops, or "laboratories," and during the last 40 years thousands of executives have participated in programs offered by NTL and other training centers. Although the long-term effectiveness of T-groups is still being debated, T-group training continues to play a key role in many organization-development interventions (Bednar & Kaul, 1979; Burke & Day, 1986; Kaplan, 1979).

• •

Training groups (T-groups).   How can people learn about group dynamics? Members could learn the facts about effective interpersonal relations by attending lectures or by reading a book about group dynamics, but Lewin argued that good group skills are most easily acquired by actually experiencing human relations. Hence, he developed a laboratory training program in which members were encouraged to actively confront and resolve interpersonal issues with the goal of better understanding of self and others. As one advocate of group training explained, "The training laboratory is a special environment in which they learn new things about themselves. . . . It is a kind of emotional re-education" (Marrow, 1964, p. 25).

One of the most noteworthy aspects of T-groups is their lack of structure. Although from time to time the conferees might meet in large groups to hear lectures or presentations, during the program most learning takes place in small groups. Even though the group includes a designated leader, often called a *facilitator* or *trainer,* this individual acts primarily as a catalyst for discussion rather than as director of the group. Indeed, during the first few days of a T-group's existence group members usually complain of the lack of structure and the situational ambiguity, blaming the trainer for their discomfort. This ambiguity is intentional, however, for it shifts responsibility for structuring, understanding, and controlling the group's activities to the participants themselves. As the group grapples with problems of organization, agenda, goals, and structure, the members reveal their preferred interaction styles to others. They also learn to disclose their feelings honestly, gain conflict-reduction skills, and find enjoyment from working in collaborative relationships.

Sensitivity-training groups and encounter groups.   The T-group was a precursor of group techniques designed to enhance spontaneity, increase personal awareness, and maximize members' sensitivity to others. As the purpose of the group experience shifted from training in group dynamics to increasing sensitivity, the name changed from T-group to **sensitivity-training group,** or **encounter group** (Johnson, 1988).

The humanistic therapist Carl Rogers was a leader in the development of encounter groups (1970). Rogers believed that most of us lose sight of our basic goodness because our needs for approval and love are rarely satisfied. We reject many aspects of ourselves, deny our failings, and hold our feelings in when interacting with other people. Rogers felt that the encounter group helps us restore our trust in our own feelings, our acceptance of our most personal qualities, and our openness when interacting with others. If Rogers had been leading the group of seven socially isolated individuals, he would have encouraged the members to "open up" to one another by displaying their inner emotions, thoughts, and worries. Recognizing that the group members probably felt insecure about their social competences, Rogers would have given each one unconditional positive regard and helped them express their feelings by repeating any statements they made. Rogers would also have used role playing and other exercises to encourage them to experience and express intense feelings of anger, caring, loneliness, and helplessness. Stripped of defensiveness and facades, Rogers believed, group members would encounter each other "authentically."

Structured learning groups.   Both T-group training and encounter groups are open-ended, *unstructured* approaches to interpersonal learning. Members of such groups follow no agenda, examine events that unfold spontaneously within the confines of the group itself, and give one another feedback about their interpersonal effectiveness when appropriate. **Structured learning groups,** in contrast, are planned interventions that focus on a specific interpersonal problem or skill. Integrating behavior therapy with experiential learning, the group leaders identify specific learning outcomes before the sessions. They then develop behaviorally focused exercises that will help members practice these targeted skills. In a session on nonverbal communication, group members may be assigned a partner and then be asked to communicate a series of feelings without using spoken language. During assertiveness training, group members might practice saying no to one another's requests. In a leadership training seminar, group members may be asked to role-play various leadership styles in a small group. To develop problem-solving skills, the members may be told to imagine that they are stranded in a desert and that they must rank several objects in terms of their importance to the group's survival. In a negotiation workshop participants may complete a questionnaire that measures their preferred approach to dealing with conflict. These exercises are similar in that they actively involve the group members in the learning process.

Examples of structured groups abound. At present, hundreds of local and national institutes offer seminars and workshops on a variety of topics, with such titles as How to Manage People Effectively, Stress-Management Seminar, Negotiate Your Way to Success, How Successful Women Manage, Time Management, and so on. Although the formats for these structured experiences differ substantially, most are based on the interpersonal learning cycle summarized in Figure 15-1. First, the group members perform an *experiential exercise* that requires self-assessment or active interaction within the group. Second, they *describe* their experiences within the group by discussing their personal feelings, thoughts, and reactions. This descriptive phase can involve open-ended discussion, or it, too, can be structured through the use of questioning, information-exchange procedures, or videotape recording. Third, the consultant helps the group members conceptualize their experiences by *processing* the exercise. Going beyond summary, the consultant guides the group's analysis of underlying group dynamics and offers a conceptual analysis that gives meaning to the event. Lastly, the interpersonal learning cycle is completed when the group members identify ways in which they can apply their newfound knowledge in their own work, family, and other interpersonal settings.

Self-Help Groups

Bill Wilson had tried to quit drinking for years, but no matter what he tried, he always returned to his addiction. But in 1935, after a fourth hospital stay for acute alcoholism, Wilson experienced a profound, almost mystical, experience that convinced him that he could overcome his

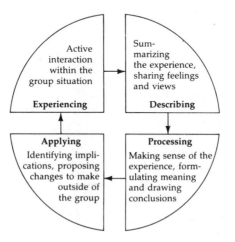

FIGURE 15-1. The experiencing/describing/processing/applying cycle of interpersonal learning.

drinking problem. Together with his friend, physician, and fellow alcoholic William D. Silkworth, Wilson developed a series of guidelines for maintaining abstinence. Wilson's program formed the basis of Alcoholics Anonymous, or AA, which grew to be an international organization with well over 1 million members. Despite AA's size, change is still achieved through local chapters of alcoholics who meet regularly to review their success in maintaining their sobriety. AA meetings emphasize testimonials, mutual self-help, and adherence to the "12 steps" of the AA doctrine. These steps include admitting one's powerlessness over alcohol; surrendering one's fate to a greater power; taking an inventory of personal strengths, weaknesses, and moral failings; and helping others fight their addiction (Flores, 1988).

Alcoholics Anonymous is an example of a *self-help group:* a voluntary group whose members combine their energies and effort in an attempt to cope with or overcome a common problem. Although antiaddiction groups like AA, Gamblers Anonymous, and Weight Watchers are among the best known self-help groups, the variety of such groups is enormous (see Table 15-2). Like AA many such groups form because the members' needs are not being met by existing educational, social, or health agencies. These groups usually gather in public settings, such as churches, community centers, or schools, and the meetings are conducted by laypeople rather than professional helpers. Although different groups use different methods, most make use of the following (Cole, 1983; Flores, 1988; Killilea, 1976; Robinson, 1980):

1. inspirational testimonials in which members share information and relate their experiences with the problem
2. mutual help that benefits both the person in need and the person giving the help

TABLE 15-2. Varieties of self-help groups.

Type of Group	Examples
Antiaddiction groups	AA, Gamblers Anonymous, Take Off Pounds Sensibly (TOPS), Weight Watchers
Family-support groups	In Touch (for parents of mentally handicapped children), Adult Children of Alcoholics, Al-Anon
Rehabilitation-support groups	CARE (Cancer Aftercare and Rehabilitation Society), Recovery, Inc. (for recovering psychotherapy patients), Reach to Recovery (for breast-cancer patients)
Social-rights groups	Campaign for Homosexual Equality, local chapters of the National Organization for Women, the Gay Activists' Alliance
General social-support groups	Association of the Childless and Childfree, Parents without Partners, Singles Anonymous

3. sharing similarities in the problems that members are experiencing
4. collective encouragement and praise for any improvements reported by group members and social support when individuals experience setbacks

THE EFFECTIVENESS CONTROVERSY

What would you do if you were bothered by some personal problem? Perhaps, like the men and women in the therapy group led by Drs. R. and M., you have trouble making friends. Or maybe you are having problems adjusting to a new job or wish that you could be more productive when you are at work. Perhaps you have finally resolved to stop smoking or drinking, you want to end a long-term romantic relationship that has been causing turmoil in your life, or you just can't seem to get over the depression that has enveloped you since your mother passed away last year. Whatever the problem, your personal resources may not be sufficient for you to achieve the changes you desire on your own. So, after reviewing your options, you decide to join a therapy group, an interpersonal-learning group, or a self-help group.

But would this group really help you achieve the changes you desire? Researchers and therapists have been debating this question for many years. Initial attempts to test the value of groups yielded favorable results, but in many cases the research methods were flawed. Richard L. Bednar and Theodore J. Kaul (1978), for example, examined hundreds of studies evaluating the effectiveness of group interventions, but they rejected over 85% as so methodologically flawed that they yielded no information whatsoever. In some cases researchers studied only one or two groups at a time, so they couldn't be certain if the changes they observed were produced by the group treatment or by some uncontrolled characteristic of the group or groups they were observing. Often, too, they measured change with self-report instruments administered to subjects before and after the intervention, so the subjects may have reported change because they realized that change was expected. Last, very few of the early studies included a no-treatment condition or other comparison group, so the relative benefits of treatment were difficult to quantify (Bednar & Kaul, 1978).

Despite these flaws, Bednar and Kaul (1978, 1979) conclude that the bulk of the properly conducted studies weigh in favor of group-level interventions, and they write that "group treatments have been more effective than no treatment, than placebo treatment, or than other accepted forms of psychological treatment" (1979, p. 314). They qualify this positive conclusion, however, in several ways. First, they note that the changes brought about by group experiences are often more perceptual than behavioral. Second, in some cases groups can do more harm than good for participants. Third, all groups are not created equal: some are more effective in promoting change than others. These issues are examined next.

Perceptions Versus Behaviors

Bednar and Kaul, after culling the studies of change in groups that were methodologically flawed, concluded that most studies had reported changes only on self-report data, rather than behavioral data. Reviews of experiential groups, for example, generally find stronger evidence of perceptual changes than of behavioral changes (Bates & Goodman, 1986; Berman & Zimpfer, 1980; Knapp & Shostrom, 1976). One review, for example, identified 26 controlled studies of personal-growth groups that (1) used both pretest and posttest measures, (2) met for at least ten hours, and (3) had a long-term follow-up (at least one month after termination). Summarizing these methodologically superior studies, the reviewers concluded that group treatments did result in enduring positive changes, particularly at the self-report level (Berman & Zimpfer, 1980). These and other findings suggest that groups are most useful in promoting changes in the "ability to manage feelings, directionality of motivation, attitudes towards the self, attitudes towards others, and interdependence" but that behavior changes are slight (Gibb, 1970, p. 2114; Shaw, 1981).

Evidence of Negative Effects

Of the seven men and women who began their therapy with Drs. R. and M., only five completed the experience successfully. One dropped out of the group to join the armed forces. Another, however, quit the group after only a few months. She complained that the experience was too stressful and that it was causing her more harm than good.

Bednar and Kaul note that groups can fail in two distinct ways: first, a participant may decide to leave the group before he or she has benefited in any way; such an individual is usually labeled a **premature termination,** or *dropout* (Holmes, 1983). A **casualty,** in contrast, is significantly harmed by the group experience. A casualty might, for example, commit suicide as a result of the group experience, require individual therapy to correct harm caused by the group, or report continued deteriorations in adjustment over the course of the group. The number of casualties reported in studies has ranged from none among 94 participants in a human-relations training lab followed up after five months (Smith, 1975, 1980) to a high of 8% of the participants in a study of 17 encounter groups (Lieberman, Yalom, & Miles, 1973). A relatively high casualty rate (18%) was obtained in one study of 50 married couples who participated in marathon encounter groups, but this rate was inflated by the problems the couples were experiencing before entering the group (Doherty, Lester, & Leigh, 1986). No evidence is available concerning the rate of casualties in self-help groups, but statistics maintained by the NTL indicate that 25 individuals who participated in the program prior to 1974 experienced a severe psychological reaction (Back, 1974). This number is less than 0.2% of the participants.

Bednar and Kaul (1978) note that most premature terminations result from failed expectations about the purposes of the group or an inadequate match between the group member's goals and the leader's methods. Casualties, in contrast, can most often be traced to a particularly negative event in the group. In one study, for example, an individual sought psychiatric treatment immediately after the group attacked her for being overweight:

> She stated that the group was an extremely destructive one for her. The group operated by everybody "ganging up on one another, thirteen to one, and bulldozing them until they were left on the ground panting." She was bitterly attacked by the group and finally dropped out after an attack on her in which she was labeled "a fat Italian mama with a big shiny nose." She was also told that she probably had "a hell of a time getting any man to look at her" [Lieberman, Yalom, & Miles, 1973, p. 189].

Given these potential problems, group therapists, trainers, facilitators, and members themselves are urged to use care when interacting in their groups. Casualities can be minimized by limiting conflict during sessions and making certain that the group atmosphere is supportive, nonevaluative, and nonthreatening (Mitchell & Mitchell, 1984; Scheuble, Dixon, Levy, & Kagan-Moore, 1987).

Factors That Influence Effectiveness

Studies of group treatments, although far from unanimous, are for the most part positive. Bednar and Kaul note, however, that researchers have succeeded in identifying certain group procedures that tend to be more effective than others. Several of the variables that are related to effectiveness, including pretraining, group development, leadership, and the type of group intervention used, are examined below.

Pretraining participants.   Bednar and his colleagues have repeatedly argued that pregroup training, by reducing members' anxieties about the group experience, facilitates change (Bednar & Battersby, 1976; Bednar & Kaul, 1978; Bednar & Lawlis, 1971; Bednar, Melnick, & Kaul, 1974). This training need not be elaborate to be effective. In one study, for example, group members were exposed to a film describing the basis for psychotherapy, group members' roles, and the activities to be undertaken during therapy. In clarifying what was expected of members, the film also emphasized a number a specific points, including expression of personal feelings, the value of emotional expression, the responsibilities of the group member, the difference between adaptive and maladaptive behavior, and the potential gains that could be reasonably expected. On measures of improvement, satisfaction with treatment, symptom discomfort, and motivation, clients who saw the film responded more positively than clients who saw an irrelevant film (Strupp & Bloxom, 1973). These and other studies suggest that attempts to clarify the processes used to achieve change in groups by providing either pregroup training or information during the therapy lead to more positive therapeutic outcomes. As Bednar and Kaul (1978) conclude, "Ambiguity and lack of clarity tend to be associated with increased anxiety and diminished productivity and learning in a variety of settings," (p. 793), whereas interventions designed to decrease ambiguity "have been associated with significant and constructive effects" (p. 794; see Hardin, Subich, & Holvey, 1988).

Group development.   Many theorists note that the success of the group depends to a large extent on its movement through stages of development. Although the stages receive various labels from various theorists, many accept the five emphasized by Bruce Tuckman (1965): forming, storming, norming, performing, and adjourning. As noted in Chapter 4, during the forming stage individual members are seeking to understand their relationship to the newly formed group and strive to establish clear intermember relations. During the storming stage group members often find themselves in conflict over status and group goals, and, in consequence, hostility, disruption, and uncertainty dominate group discussions. During the next phase, norming, the group strives to develop a group structure that increases cohesiveness and harmony. The performing stage is typified by a focus on group productivity and decision making. Lastly, when the group fulfills its goals, it reaches its final stage of development, adjourning. If a group does not move through these stages, its members will not be able to benefit from the experience (Bennis & Shepard, 1956; Lewis, 1984; Pedigo & Singer, 1982; Shambaugh, 1978).

Dennis Kivlighan and his colleagues illustrated the important impact of group development on therapeutic outcomes by matching interventions to the developmental "maturity" of the group. Group members were given structured help in expressing either anger or intimacy before either the fourth or ninth group session of their therapy. The information dealing with anger clarified the value of anger as a natural part of group participation and provided suggestions for communicating it. In contrast, the information dealing with intimacy clarified the value of intimacy in groups and provided suggestions for its appropriate expression toward others. As anticipated, when the interventions were matched to the most appropriate developmental stage—for example, group members received the information on anger during the storming phase (session four) or the information on intimacy during the norming phase (session nine)—the subjects displayed more comfort in dealing with intimacy, more appropriate expressions of intimacy and anger, fewer inappropriate expressions of intimacy, and more congruence between self-ratings and other ratings of interpersonal style (Kivlighan, McGovern, & Corazzini, 1984).

Leadership.   The question "How much should a leader/therapist participate in the group process?" has been called the "greatest single problem in group psychotherapy" (Gorlow, Hoch, & Telschow, 1952, p. 15). On the one hand, many clinicians advocate the leader-centered approaches typical of psychoanalytic, Gestalt, and behavioral groups. In such groups the leader is the central figure. He or she controls the course of the interaction, assigns various tasks to the group members, and occupies the center of the centralized communication network. In some instances the group members may not even communicate with one another but only with the group leader. In contrast, other therapists advocate a nondirective style of leadership in which all group members communicate with one another. These group-oriented approaches, which are typified by encounters or T-groups, encourage the analysis of the group's processes, with the therapist/leader sometimes facilitating the process but at other times providing no direction whatsoever.

Studies of groups indicate that both directive and nondirective leaders are effective agents of change. As noted in earlier chapters, provided the direct leader is accepted by the group, he or she should succeed in influencing the group members. In contrast, studies of minority influence also suggest that indirect-influence agents can be successful, provided they are consistent over time. Several studies do suggest, however, that group members prefer membership in groups led by supportive but nondirective leaders and that groups with two leaders produce more change than groups with only one leader (Higginbotham, West, & Forsyth, 1988). (See Focus 15-3.)

● ●

FOCUS 15-3: COLEADERSHIP IN CHANGE-PROMOTING GROUPS

Coleadership is a relatively recent development within change-oriented groups. The two leaders can lend support to each other and can also offer the group members their combined knowledge, insight, and experience. Also, male/female teams may be particularly beneficial, since they offer a fuller perspective on gender issues and serve as models of positive but nonromantic heterosexual relationships. The advantages of coleadership, however, are lost if the leaders are unequal in status or engage in power struggles during group sessions (Thune, Manderscheid, & Silbergeld, 1981).

Coleading heterosexual pairs, however, must be aware of group members' sexist biases concerning leadership. As in most groups, members often erroneously assume that men make better leaders than women, even though the available evidence indicates that men and women are equal in leadership skill (see Chapter 8). In one illustrative study of co-led groups, the male and female coleaders performed virtually identical behaviors. Yet the men were perceived as significantly more potent, active, instrumental, and insightful than the women. Moreover, the women were viewed as more emotional (Greene, Morrison, & Tischler, 1981). Other researchers, too, have found that gender is a more important determinant of status in therapy groups than either professional experience or professional affiliation (Thune et al., 1981). These findings suggest that coleaders must be careful to maintain a positive relationship with each other while also demonstrating to the group that they are equal in status and influence.

● ●

Type of group. As noted earlier in this chapter, groups conform to no single set of procedures: some groups are leader-centered (psychoanalytic or Gesalt groups), whereas others are group-focused (encounter groups and T-groups), and the group's activities can range from the highly structured (interpersonal learning groups) to the unstructured (encounter groups). Some groups members are responsible for running the meeting itself (self-help groups), whereas in other situations the facilitator runs the session (structured groups). Group practitioners also vary greatly in their orientations and techniques, for some focus on emotions with Gestalt exercises, others concentrate on the here and now of the group's interpersonal process, and others train members to perform certain behaviors through videotaped feedback, behavioral rehearsal, and systematic reinforcement.

Given this diversity in purposes and procedures, one might expect some types to emerge as more effective than others. Yet differences among treatments are relatively rare. Consider, for example, Morton Lieberman, Irvin Yalom, and Matthew Miles's classic investigation of encounter groups. They investigated the overall impact of a 12-week experiential group on members' adjustment (Yalom, 1985; Lieberman, Yalom, & Miles, 1973). They began by assigning 206 Stanford University students to 1 of 18 therapy groups representing ten theoretical orientations: Gestalt, transactional analysis, NTL T-groups, Synanon, Esalen, psychoanalysis, marathon, psychodrama, encounter tape, and encounter. Trained observers coded the groups' interactions, with particular attention to the leaders' style. Before, during, immediately after, and six months following the participation they administered a battery of items assessing group members' self-esteem, attitudes, self-satisfaction, values, satisfaction with friendships, and so on. Measures were also completed by the co-members, the leaders, and by group members' acquaintances.

Somewhat unexpectedly, the project discovered that no one theoretical approach had a monopoly on effectiveness. For example, two separate Gestalt groups with different leaders were included in the design, but the members of these two groups evidenced widely discrepant gains. One of the Gestalt groups ranked among the most successful in stimulating participant growth, but the other group yielded fewer benefits than all of the other groups.

A number of factors could account for this apparent equivalence of therapies (Stiles, Shapiro, & Elliott, 1986). First, the various group therapies may be differentially effective, but researchers' measures may not be sensitive enough to detect these variations. Second, a group's effectiveness may depend as much on who is in the group and who leads the group as on the methods used. The question isn't "Is Therapy X more effective than Therapy Y?" but "What type of group run by which therapist is effective for this individual with this type of problem?" (Paul, 1967). Third, although group interventions are based on widely divergent theoretical assumptions, these assumptions may not lead to differences in practice. A leader of a Gestalt group and the leader of a psychodynamic group, for example, may explain their goals and methods in very different theoretical terms, but they may nonetheless rely on identical methods when in their groups.

A (fourth) plausible explanation, however, remains. This explanation suggests that despite their heterogeneity in purposes and procedures, therapeutic groups have certain characteristics in common. In all types of groups the members have the opportunity to learn from others. They can rely on one another for support and guidance. They receive feedback from other group members that is self-sustaining and corrective, and they also gain an audience for their self-disclosures. Might these common aspects of groups and their dynamics account for the therapeutic effects of group interventions? These change-promoting factors are examined in the next section.

SOURCES OF CHANGE IN GROUPS

Bednar and Kaul (1978), while documenting the relatively greater impact of groups on perceptions rather than behavior and the value of certain techniques over others, also note that very little is known of the processes underlying group-induced change. They speculate that participation in a "developing social microcosm," "interpersonal feedback and consensual validation," and "reciprocal opportunities to be both helpers and helpees in group settings" (p. 781) are essential ingredients, but they admit that groups may derive their power to change people from a variety of other sources.

Several other theorists have described these sources as well, but Irvin Yalom's **curative-factors model** is by far the most comprehensive and well-researched (Yalom 1975, 1985). Yalom proposes that the factors listed in Table 15-3 operate to promote change in most groups. The list includes the installing of hope, universality, the imparting of information, altruism, the corrective recapitulation of the primary family group, the development of socializing techniques, imitative behavior, interpersonal learning, group cohesiveness, catharsis, and existential factors. Some of the factors on Yalom's list are mechanisms that are reponsible for facilitating change, whereas others describe the general group conditions that should be present within effective groups (Butler & Fuhriman, 1983a, 1983b; Markovitz & Smith, 1983; Maxmen, 1973, 1978; Rohrbaugh & Bartels, 1975; Rugel & Myer, 1984; Sherry & Hurley, 1976).

Yalom gleaned these factors from his clinical experience and empirical research. His list, however, is consistent with theoretical analyses of groups in general. Following a tradition established by sociologists such as William Graham Sumner and Charles Horton Cooley and the psychologist Lewin, social psychologists have long argued that groups are the shapers of individuals. Small groups are society's primary socializing

TABLE 15-3. The curative factors common to many change-promoting groups.

Factor	Meaning to the Member
Instilling of hope	If other members can change, so can I.
Universality	We all have problems.
Imparting of information	I learn alternative methods to solve my problems.
Altruism	I can help others in my group, and they can help me.
Corrective recapitulation of the family	My group is like reliving and understanding my family relationships.
Development of socializing techniques	I learn how to listen and relate to other people.
Imitative behavior	I see how other people cope with this problem.
Interpersonal learning	I learn how other people see me.
Group cohesiveness	My group members accept me.
Catharsis	I'm able to express emotions freely.
Existential factors	I feel responsible for my own life despite its circumstances.

(Source: Yalom, 1975, 1985)

agents, for they provide their members with a particular world view and then sustain that view through direct instruction, selective social reinforcement, and corrective social influence as necessary. Individuals, too, sustain their groups by defending them against other groups, by contributing their effort in group activities, and by changing the group when existing norms and forms of activity are antiquated or become maladaptive. These aspects of groups are examined in more detail below.

Universality and Hope

Yalom (1985) notes that the act of joining with people who share a particular problem is, in and of itself, reassuring, because it reduces anxiety that emanates from uncertainty: "Fear and anxiety that stem from uncertainty of the source, meaning, and seriousness of psychiatric symptoms may so compound the total dysphoria that effective exploration becomes vastly more difficult" (p. 12).

Studies of uncertainty and social comparison provide strong support for Yalom's speculations. Stanley Schachter's 1959 studies, for example, indicate that individuals seek out other people whenever they feel uncertain of the validity of their attitudes or beliefs. Confronted by an ambiguous and anxiety-provoking situation, the college women who served as subjects clearly preferred to wait with others, provided these others could provide them with information. Individuals may also find reassurance by comparing themselves with others in the group who are experiencing more severe problems or coping less effectively than themselves. This downward social-comparison process is likely to occur when we are uncertain of abilities and lack confidence in our beliefs, and hence it may serve a protective, adaptive function (Wills, 1981, in press). Studies of breast-cancer patients, for example, indicate that women who compare themselves with superior copers describe their own adjustment in more negative terms. Perhaps as a result of these negative implications, over 60% of the women engaged in downward social comparison by choosing a comparison patient who wasn't coping effectively (Wood, Taylor, & Lichtman, 1985).

Interpersonal Learning

Many theorists have underscored the value of groups as arenas for interpersonal learning (Lieberman, 1980; Yalom, 1975). By participating in a group, individuals gain information about themselves, their problems, and their social relationships with others. As Yalom (1985) notes, some of this information is conveyed through direct instruction, as clients trade advice and information and the therapist provides structure and direction. The group also provides members with the opportunity to gather reactions to their own interpersonal behavior. Interaction in groups is social behavior, and so it has implications for self-definition that go beyond the confines of the temporary group situation. Within the social microcosm of the small group, individuals "become aware of the significant aspects of their interpersonal behavior: their strengths, their limitations, their parataxic disortions, and their maladaptive behavior that elicits unwanted responses from others" (Yalom, 1975, p. 40). Through feedback from the group leader and other group members, as well as self-observations formulated within the group setting, individuals gain an increased understanding of their social selves, and this self-understanding provides the basis for changes in cognitions and actions. The value of interpersonal learning is also recognized by group members themselves, for when rating the most valuable aspect of the group experience, they tend to emphasize feedback and interpersonal processes: "the group's teaching me about the type of impression I make on others," "learning how I come across to others," and "other members honestly telling me what they think of me" (Yalom, 1975, p. 79). Of the 12 curative factors noted by Yalom (1985), 4 of them pertain to social learning: guidance (direct instruction), interpersonal learning via feedback, interpersonal learning by examining relationships with others, and identification with others within the group. (See Focus 15-4.)

· ·
FOCUS 15-4: THE JOHARI WINDOW OF SELF-UNDERSTANDING
_____

The need for self-understanding is a prominent motive in human beings. Individuals are continually scrutinizing and assessing the self, and in most cases we think that we understand fully our own personal strengths, weaknesses, values, and beliefs. Yet we do not have complete knowledge of our own attributes. A person with a fiery temper, for example, may insist that she is good-natured. Or a person who is easily manipulated by others may not recognize his lack of assertiveness. Groups promote self-understanding by exposing us to these unknown areas of our selves.

Joseph Luft (1984) illustrates this process with the model of the **Johari window** (see Figure 15-2). Many of our attributes are known to both ourselves and to other people; these are the qualities in the *open* quadrant. Attributes in the *blind* quadrant, in contrast, are known to other people, but we ourselves do not recognize them. All of our friends may know that we are boring, but we think of ourselves as the life of the party, or our spouse may think we are cold when we consider ourselves to be warm. In the *hidden* quadrant we find aspects of ourselves that we accept but that we keep hidden from other people, and in the *unknown* quadrant are qualities that are known neither to us nor to others. (Luft developed the model after long discussions with Harrington ["Harry"] Ingham, so he named it the Joe-Harry, or Johari, window.)

Luft believes that groups help us shrink the size of the blind, hidden, and unknown quadrants by expanding the size of the open quadrant. Although we are not particularly open to feedback about our own attributes, when several individuals provide us with the same feedback, we are more likely to internalize this information (Jacobs, 1974; Kivlighan, 1985). Also, when the feedback is given in the context of a long-term, reciprocal relation, it cannot be so easily dismissed as biased or subjective. Group leaders, too, often reward members for accepting rather than rejecting feedback, and the setting itself works to intensify self-awareness. In a supportive, accepting group, we can reveal hidden aspects of ourselves, and

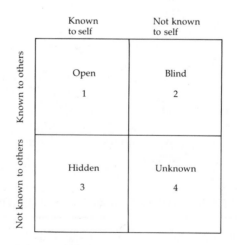

FIGURE 15-2. The Johari window.
Source: Luft, 1984

we therefore feel more open and honest in our relationships. Lastly, even qualities that are unknown to others and to ourselves can emerge and be recognized during group interactions. Thus, when we look at groups through Luft's Johari window, we can see that this interpersonal learning situation offers a means of increasing our self-awareness by decreasing our self-deception and self-denial.

• •

Cohesiveness and Altruism

According to Yalom (1985), though cohesion may not be a sufficient condition for effective groups, it could be a necessary condition; without cohesion, feedback would not be accepted, norms would never develop, and groups could not retain their members. In emphasizing the value of highly cohesive groups, Yalom and his colleagues join a long line of researchers who have reached similar conclusions. As early as 1951 Dorwin Cartwright suggested that if groups were used as change agents, the members should have a strong sense of group identity and belonging or otherwise the group would not exert sufficient influence over its members. Others, too, have noted that the "cotherapeutic influence of peers" in the therapy group requires group cohesion (Bach, 1954, p. 348; Frank, 1957; Goldstein, Heller, & Sechrest, 1966).

Yet in the face of this widespread agreement about the value of cohesiveness, some researchers have noted that cohesion may not always enhance group outcomes. On the positive side cohesiveness is associated with group stability, satisfaction, effective communication, positive intrapersonal consequences for members, and increased group influence. On the negative side, however, cohesion has also been linked to social pressures of such intensity that individual members are overwhelmed and prey to illusions, misperceptions, and faulty communication. Furthermore, given the right (or wrong) combination of circumstances, cohesiveness also decreases the quality of group performance, encourages hostility and interpersonal rejection, and promotes disabling overdependence in long-term members. If group members reject the therapist's attempts to establish change-producing norms, for example, cohesiveness will only intensify their resistance. Similarly, if the group accepts the fact that the expression and resolution of hostility and conflict are legitimate group goals, cohesiveness will generate even higher levels of conflict and growth. If the group members tend to avoid hostile exchanges, however, this tendency will be exacerbated when cohesiveness increases.

Cohesive groups, however, do offer individuals the opportunity to help others and to be helped by them. When we are members of such groups, we tend to be buffered from the everyday stresses of life, and our health often improves (Barrera, 1986). Studies of social support, for example, indicate that the emotional support, advice and guidance, tangible assistance, and positive feedback we receive from other people protect us from stress and its aftereffects. Evidence also supports the buffering hypothesis: during times of stress individuals who are part of a social network experience fewer psychological and physical problems than individuals who receive no social support (Cohen & Wills, 1985). Often, too, individuals' attempts to maintain personal change depend on the degree to which their interpersonal network provides them with reassurance and support (Baranowski, 1984).

Intimacy Needs

Groups also function by fulfilling our unsatisfied need for interpersonal intimacy (Shaver & Buhrmester, 1983). Although our need for intimacy is often satisfied by long-term dyadic pairings such as close friendships and love relationships, a highly cohesive therapeutic group, encounter group, or self-help group also meets these needs. As Yalom notes, the effective group allows members to give and receive help (altruism), provides them emotional support and positive feedback (cohesiveness), serves as an audience for self-disclosures and venting of emotions (catharsis), and offers answers to questions of value and meaning (existential factors). An intimate group takes the place of the original family group and provides the member with a sense of belonging, protection from harm, and acceptance (recapitulation of the family).

SUMMARY

What would you do if, after years of trying to change, you were still troubled by your inability to make friends or a health-endangering addiction to drugs? One solution involves using a group as a vehicle for achieving personal change. As Lewin argued 40 years ago, change is often more easily accomplished when we are part of group than when we are isolated, because groups are a natural arena for change-evoking and change-maintaining processes.

Most change-oriented groups focus either on therapeutic adjustment (*group therapy*), interpersonal and emotional growth (*interpersonal learning groups*), or overcoming addictions or other life stresses (*self-help groups*). Group therapy, which is usually conducted by a mental-health professional, focuses on relatively severe psychological and social problems:

1. In *psychoanalytic group therapy* the therapist helps members gain insight into their problems by offering interpretations and working through sibling and parental transference effects.
2. In *Gestalt group therapy* the therapist promotes emotional growth by focusing on the *here and now*, using experiments, and avoiding interpretations.
3. In *behavior-therapy groups* the therapist uses principles derived from learning theory to encourage specific behaviors while extinguishing others. This approach makes use of a number of behavioral methods, including *behavioral contracts, modeling, behavior rehearsal*, and *feedback*.

Interpersonal-learning groups, in contrast, involve attempts to help relatively well-adjusted individuals improve their self-understanding and relationships with others:

1. In *training groups,* or *T-groups,* members are encouraged to actively confront and resolve interpersonal issues through unstructured discussions.
2. In *sensitivity-training groups* or *encounter groups* individuals are urged to disclose personal aspects of themselves to others and to provide other members with positive feedback.
3. In *structured learning groups* members take part in planned exercises that focus on a specific interpersonal problem or skill. Most of these interventions involve a learning cycle that begins with an experiential event and then moves from description to process and to application.

The third type of change-promoting group, the self-help group, often forms spontaneously when people combine their energies and efforts in an attempt to cope with or overcome a common problem. These groups tend to use inspirational testimonials, mutual help, shared similarities, and collective encouragement.

Despite the popularity of groups for achieving change, researchers and therapists continue to debate their effectiveness. Bednar and Kaul, for example, note that the changes fostered by group experiences are often more perceptual than behavioral. Participation in groups can also lead to a number of negative consequences, although every *premature termination* from a group is not necessarily a psychological *casualty.* Bednar and Kaul also identify a number of factors that determine the effectiveness of group approaches, including pretraining, group development, leadership style, *coleadership* and the type of group intervention used. All in all, however, they note that most group approaches are superior to individualistic methods of achieving change.

What factors lie at the core of the group's power as an agent of change? Although many theorists have discussed this question, Yalom's *curative-factors model* argues that effective groups possess certain common characteristics. By providing opportunities to engage in social comparison and mutual support, they instill a sense of hope and convince members of the universality of their problems. Groups also facilitate interpersonal learning, including guidance (direct instruction), feedback, identification with others within the group, and increased self-knowledge (as illustrated by the *Johari window*). Groups, when cohesive, also provide members with the social support they need to overcome the negative effects of stress, and they even satisfy members' needs for interpersonal intimacy (including catharsis, existential factors, and recapitulation of the primary family).

· Glossary ·

Action research: Lewin's term for scientific inquiry that provides information about basic theoretical questions while yielding solutions to significant social problems.

Additive task: A task that can be completed by adding together individual group members' inputs.

Agentic state: The loss of autonomy individuals experience when they become the agent of a higher authority.

Anticonformity (or Counterconformity): The public expression of ideas, beliefs, judgments, or actions that conflict with the group's standards simply to disagree with the group.

Applied research: Scientific inquiry conducted to increase the investigator's understanding of a practical problem and identify possible solutions.

Archival analysis: A type of nonreactive measurement method that requires collecting and analyzing existing records and public archives.

Arousal/aggression hypothesis: A motivational explanation of aggressive behavior that argues aversive events lead to arousal, which in turn can prompt aggression.

Attraction relations: Patterns of liking and disliking in a group; the group's sociometric structure.

Attribution: An inference about the cause of a behavior or event; also, the cognitive processes underlying these inferences.

Attribution theory: A social-psychological explanation of how people make inferences about the causes of behaviors and events.

Audience: Individuals who deliberately gather in a particular area to observe some event or activity.

Authority relations: Patterns of relative status or power in a group; the "chain of command" or hierarchy of dominance.

$B = f(P, E)$: Lewin's interactionism formula that states behavior is a function of the person and the environment.

Balance: A satisfying equilibrium in a group's attraction patterns that exists when all relationships among members are positive or the number of negative relationships is even.

Balance theory: A theoretical framework advanced by Heider that assumes interpersonal relationships can be either balanced (integrated units with elements that fit together

485

without stress) or unbalanced (inconsistent units with elements that conflict with one another). Heider believed that unbalanced relationships create an unpleasant tension that must be relieved by changing some element of the system.

Bargaining theory: A theoretical framework that assumes coalition formation depends upon bargaining, negotiation, promises, threats, and concessions.

Basic research: A scientific investigation conducted to increase the investigator's understanding of theoretically significant hypotheses.

Basking in reflected glory (BIRGing): Seeking direct or indirect association with prestigious groups or individuals.

Behavior therapy group: The treatment of interpersonal and psychological problems through the application of behavioral principles in a group setting.

Behavioral assimilation: The eventual matching of the behaviors displayed by interacting group members.

Behavioral contract: An agreement accepted by participants in behavior therapy that sets forth the goals that the members of the group should achieve.

Behavioral rehearsal: A component of behavior therapy that gives group members the opportunity to practice particular skills with one another through role-play exercises.

Behavioral sink: A significant distortion of courting rituals, mating, nest building, territoriality, aggression, and rearing practices observed by Calhoun in his studies of overcrowded rats.

Brainstorming: A method for enhancing creativity in groups that calls for heightened expressiveness, inhibited evaluation, quantity rather than quality, and deliberate attempts to build on earlier ideas.

Case study: A research technique that involves examining, in as much detail as possible, the dynamics of a single group or individual.

Casual crowd: A group of otherwise unrelated individuals who, while going about their own personal business, end up in the same general vicinity and share a common focus.

Casualty: An individual who is significantly harmed by his or her experiences in a change-promoting group.

Charismatic leader: An individual who influences large numbers of people by relying primarily on referent power.

Choice Dilemmas Questionnaire (CDQ): An instrument developed by Wallach, Kogan, and Bem to measure riskiness in decisions.

Coleadership: Installing two equal-status leaders within a single group; a practice often used in therapeutic groups.

Coalition: A subgroup within a larger group.

Coercive power: The capacity to punish or threaten group members who do not comply with requests or demands.

Cognitive dissonance: An aversive psychological state that occurs when an individual simultaneously accepts two conflicting cognitions.

Cohesiveness: The strength of the relationships linking the members of a group to one another and to the group as a whole.

Collective behavior: Spontaneous and often atypical actions performed by individuals when they become part of a large group.

Collective induction: A process of cooperative problem solving in groups that involves pooling information, searching for and identifying explanations and generalizations, and testing these explanations and principles through discussion or through observation.

Collective movements: A mass phenomenon in which individuals who are physically dispersed are similarly influenced and act in novel and often atypical ways.

Collectivism: A cultural outlook that stresses the primacy of group needs, interests, and goals relative to individual needs, interests, and goals.

Communication network: Well-defined patterns of communication in a group that describe who speaks most frequently to whom (for example, wheel, circle, chain).

Communication relations: Patterns of information exchange in a group.

Comparison level (CL): In Thibaut and Kelley's social-exchange theory, the standard by which the individual evaluates the quality of any social relationship.

Comparison level for alternatives (CLalt): In Thibaut and Kelley's social-exchange theory, the standard by which the individual evaluates the quality of other groups that he or she may join.

Compensatory task: A task that can be completed by averaging together individual group members' inputs.

Competition: A performance situation structured in such a way that any one member of the group will succeed only if another member of the group fails.

Complementarity hypothesis: A prediction that maintains coercive, powerful influence tactics often lead to submissive, passive reactions in the target.

Complementarity-of-needs hypothesis: A prediction pertaining to attraction that states that people like others who possess characteristics complementing their own personal qualities.

Complexity bias: The tendency of individuals' conception of their own group to be complex and extremely differentiated relative to their conception of the out-group.

Compliance: Change that occurs when the targets of social influence publicly accept the influencer's position, but privately continue to maintain their original beliefs.

Compresence: The performance of actions when others are present.

Confirmatory biases: Perceptual, cognitive, and behavioral tendencies that serve to affirm erroneous assumptions about other people.

Conflict: Disagreement, discord, and friction that occur when the actions and/or beliefs of one individual or group of individuals are incompatible with those adopted by another individual or group of individuals.

Conflict spiral: An escalating pattern of conflict.

Conformity: A change in beliefs and/or behaviors brought about through social influence.

Conjunctive task: A task that requires input from all group members.

Contact hypothesis: The prediction that equal-status contact between the members of different groups will reduce intergroup conflict.

Contagion: The transmission of behaviors and emotions from one member of a collective to another.

Contingency model of leadership: Any model predicting that leadership depends on the interaction of personal characteristics of the leader and the nature of the group situation; usually used in reference to the leadership theory developed by Fiedler.

Conventional crowds: An aggregate of individuals, such as an audience, people in a shopping mall, or a queue, who deliberately gather in a particular area.

Convergence theory: An explanation of collective behavior that assumes that individuals with similar needs, values, or goals tend to converge to form a single group.

Conversion (or **Private acceptance**): Change that occurs when the targets of social influence personally accept the influencer's position.

Cooperation: A performance situation structured in such a way that the success of any one member of the group improves the chances of other members to succeed.

Coordination problems: Inefficiency that results from group members' inability to combine their resources in a maximally productive fashion.

Correlation coefficient: A statistic that measures the strength and direction of a relationship between two variables. Often symbolized by r, correlations can range from -1.0 to $+1.0$.

Correlational study: A research technique that involves systematically measuring all variables of interest and then examining the relationship among measures statistically.

Counterconformity (or **Anticonformity**): The public expression of ideas, beliefs, judgments, and actions that conflict with the group's standards simply to disagree with the group.

Covert observation: A measurement method that requires recording group members' actions from a concealed location without the subjects' knowledge.

Crazes: Irrational, costly, or widespread fads.

Crowd: An aggregate of individuals who share a common focus and are concentrated in a single location.

Crowding: A psychological reaction that occurs when individuals feel that the amount of space available to them is insufficient for their needs.

Curative factors in groups: Elements present in group settings that aid and promote personal growth and adjustment. Yalom's list of such factors includes the installation of hope, universality, imparting of information, altruism, the corrective recapitulation of the primary family group, development of socializing techniques, imitative behavior, interpersonal learning, group cohesiveness, catharsis, and existential factors.

Cyclical models: A class of theories describing group development that assumes groups pass through various phases over time but that these phases reoccur repeatedly across the lifespan of the group.

Deindividuation: An experiential state, caused by a number of input factors such as group membership and anonymity, that is characterized by the loss of self-awareness, altered experiencing, and atypical behavior.

Deindividuation theory: A process model proposed by Zimbardo that specifies the causes (inputs), mediating mechanisms (process), and consequences (outputs) of the reduction of individuality that sometimes occurs in groups.

Density: The number of individuals per unit of space.

Density-intensity hypothesis: An explanation of crowding predicting that high density makes unpleasant situations more unpleasant but pleasant situations more pleasant.

Dependent variable: The responses of the subject measured by the researcher; the effect variable in a cause-effect relationship.

Diffusion of responsibility: A reduction of personal responsibility that results from membership in a group.

Discretionary task: A relatively unstructured task that can be solved by using a variety of social-combination procedures.

Discussion stage: The decision-making stage characterized by the gathering of information about the situation and the identification/weighing of options.

Disjunctive task: An either/or or yes/no task that is completed only when the group members reach agreement on a single answer that will stand as the group's product.

Distraction/conflict theory: An explanation of social facilitation that assumes the distraction and attentional conflict produced by the presence of others facilitates productivity on simple tasks but inhibits performance on complex tasks.

Dominant responses: Well-learned or instinctive behaviors that the organism has practiced and is primed to perform.

Downward social comparison: The tendency to compare oneself to others who are performing less effectively.

Emergent norm: A standard for behavior that develops spontaneously within a group and often conflicts with more generally accepted social standards.

Emergent-norm theory: An explanation of collective behavior that suggests that aberrant behaviors in groups stem from unique norms that develop in the group situation.

Emotional loneliness: Feelings of isolation and depression that occur when individuals desire, but cannot achieve, a meaningful, intimate relationship with another person.

Encounter group: A form of sensitivity training that provides individuals with the opportunity to gain deep interpersonal intimacy with other group members.

Entitativity: The quality of being an entity; perceived groupness.

Entrapment: A form of escalation in which the parties expend more of their resources in the conflict than seems appropriate or justifiable by external standards.

Equality norm: A social standard that encourages allocating resources equally among all members.

Equilibrium model of personal space: An explanation of distancing behavior in interpersonal settings that argues that the amount of eye contact, the intimacy of the topic, and smiling influence the amount of personal space required by interactants.

Equity norm: A social standard that encourages allocating individuals' outcomes in proportion to their inputs.

Ethnocentrism: The belief that one's own group or country is superior to other groups and other countries.

Eureka task: A task with a solution that, once suggested, seems obviously correct.

Evaluation-apprehension: Concern over being appraised by observers; a possible mediator of social-facilitation effects.

Expectation-states theory: An explanation of status differentiation in groups that emphasizes the individual's standing on positively and negatively valued status characteristics.

Experimental study: A research design in which the investigator manipulates at least one variable, systematically measures at least one other variable, and maintains control over other influential variables.

Expert power: Influence that derives from group members' assumption that the powerholder possesses superior skills and abilities.

Extremity bias: The tendency for judgments about out-group members to be more extreme than judgments made about in-group members.

Fad: An abrupt but short-lived change in the opinions, behaviors, or life-styles of a large number of widely dispersed individuals.

Fashions: Fads that pertain to styles of dress or manners.

Feedback: The transfer of information from the process or output component of a system to the input component; in behavior therapy, the delivery of reassurance, praise, and corrective information to group members.

FIRO (Fundamental Interpersonal Relations Orientation): Schutz's theory of group formation that emphasizes compatibility among three basic needs: inclusion, control, and affection.

Fundamental attribution error: The tendency to overestimate the causal influence of dispositional factors while underemphasizing the causal influence of situational factors.

Genogram: A sociogram of a family.

Gestalt group therapy: An approach to group therapy in which clients are taught to understand the unity of their emotions and cognitions through a leader-guided analysis of their behavior in the group situation.

Graduated and Reciprocal Initiative in Tension Reduction (GRIT): A ten-step system for reducing intergroup conflict by increasing trust and cooperation.

Group: Two or more interdependent individuals who influence one another through social interaction.

Group attribution error: The tendency for perceivers to assume that a group's decision reflects the group members' personal beliefs.

Group development: Growth and change across the group's life span that begins when the group first forms and ends when it dissolves.

Group dynamics: The scientific study of groups; also a general term for group processes.

Groupmind (or collective consciousness): A unifying mental force linking group members together.

Group-polarization hypothesis: An explanation of risky and cautious shifts in judgments following group discussion that assumes judgments made after group discussion will be more extreme in the same direction as the average of individual judgments made prior to discussion.

Group socialization: A pattern of change in the relationship between an individual and a group that begins when an individual first considers joining the group and ends when he or she leaves it.

Group space: An area surrounding a group into which nonmembers cannot intrude without arousing discomfort.

Group structure: A stable pattern of relationships among the members of a group.

Group therapy: The treatment of psychological and social problems in a group context.

Groupthink: A strong concurrence-seeking tendency that interferes with effective group decision making.

Hawthorne effect: A change in behavior that occurs when individuals know they are being observed by researchers.

Here and now: A therapeutic technique that requires processing events that occur within the group rather than outside the group.

Identification: Kelman's term for conformity and attitude change that occurs when a person likes, respects, or seeks to imitate another person.

Idiosyncrasy credits: Psychological credits or bonuses earned when an individual makes a contribution to the group.

Illusory correlations: Assumed relationships between two variables that are not actually related to one another; also, overestimations of the strength of the relationship between unrelated characteristics possessed by the members of a particular group.

Implementation stage: The final stage of decision making during which the group's decision is implemented and its effectiveness appraised.

Implicit leadership theories: The group members' personal assumptions about the naturally occurring relationships among various traits and leadership effectiveness.

Independence: The public expression of ideas, beliefs, judgments, and so on that are consistent with one's own personal standards, irrespective of group pressure to conform.

Independent variable: The aspect of the situation manipulated by the researcher in an experimental study; the causal variable in a cause-effect relationship.

Individualism: A cultural outlook that stresses the primacy of individual needs, interests, and goals relative to group needs, interests, and goals.

Information saturation: The point at which the individual can no longer efficiently monitor, collate, or route incoming and outgoing messages.

Informational influence: Social influence that results from discovering new information about a situation by observing others' responses.

In-group/out-group bias: The tendency to view people who are members of one's own group more favorably than those who are not members.

Integrative negotiation (or Principled negotiation): A conflict-resolution strategy in which both parties work together to generate a mutually satisfying solution.

Interaction: The mutual influence of two or more components of a system.

Interaction Process Analysis: A structured coding system developed by Bales that can be used to classify group behavior into socioemotional or task-oriented categories.

Interactional model of leadership: A theory of leadership that assumes the leader's qualities, the nature of the situation, and the group members' qualities interact to determine leadership emergence and effectiveness.

Interactionism: A theoretical framework based on the assumption that individuals' personal qualities interact with aspects of the social situation to determine social behavior.

Intergroup conflict: Disputes between members of two or more groups.

Intergroup contact: A conflict-resolution strategy that requires equal-status contact between the members of different groups.

Internalization: Conformity or attitude change that occurs when an individual personally adopts another person's beliefs, attitudes, and so on.

Interpersonal influence: Social influence that results from direct and indirect social pressure, including persuasion, bargaining, threats, and promises.

Interpersonal learning group: A group intervention designed to help relatively well-adjusted individuals extend their self-understanding and improve their relationships with others.

Interpersonal style: An individual-differences variable that describes variations in group members' general behavioral orientations; many theoretical analyses of interpersonal style distinguish between cooperators and competitors.

Interpersonal zones: Situationally determined interpersonal distances; Hall describes four such zones (intimate, personal, social and public).

Interrole conflict: Incompatibility between two simultaneously enacted roles.

Intragroup conflict: Disputes among members of a single group.

Intrarole conflict: Incompatibility among the behaviors that make up a single role, often resulting from inconsistent expectations on the part of the role taker and the role sender.

Investigation phase: The initial period of group socialization characterized by reconnaissance on the part of the prospective group members and recruitment efforts on the part of the group.

Jigsaw technique: A team-learning technique that involves assigning topics to each group member, allowing students with the same topics to study together, and then requiring these students to teach their topics to the other members of their groups.

Johari window: A model of personal awareness that assumes one's personal attributes can be known or unknown to both oneself and to other people.

Jury: A group of individuals chosen from the community who weigh evidence presented in a court case before deciding guilt or liability.

Law of small numbers: The assumption that one can make generalizations about an entire group after observing a small number of individual members of that group.

Leader prototypes: An abstract set of qualities and characteristics expected in a leader.

Leadership: A reciprocal, transactional, and transformational process in which individuals are permitted to influence and motivate others to facilitate the attainment of group and individual goals.

Leadership Behavior Description Questionnaire (LBDQ): An instrument used for measuring two dimensions of leadership: interpersonal relationships (consideration) and task orientation (initiating structure).

Leadership emergence: The process by which an individual becomes the leader of a formerly leaderless group.

Leadership substitutes: Factors in the group situation that take the place of the leader.

Least Preferred Co-worker Scale (LPC Scale): A self-report method for assessing leadership style developed by Fiedler; those individuals who give relatively high ratings to their least preferred co-worker tend to adopt a relationship-oriented leadership style, whereas those who give low ratings to their least preferred co-worker tend to adopt a task-oriented style.

Legitimate power: Power that stems from an authority's legitimate right to require and demand compliance.

Maintenance: In Moreland and Levine's model of group socialization, a period of time during which group members negotiate their roles within the group.

Managerial Grid: A theory of management and leadership, proposed by Blake and Mouton, that assumes people vary in their concern for people and concern for results, and that individuals who are high on both dimensions (9,9) are the best leaders.

Mandate phenomenon: A tendency to overstep the bounds of authority when one feels he or she has the overwhelming support of the group.

Mass hysteria: The spontaneous outbreak of atypical thoughts, feelings, and/or actions in a group or aggregate, including psychogenic illness, common hallucinations, and bizarre actions.

Mere exposure: Increased liking for

stimuli that are merely presented repeatedly to individuals.

Mindlessness: A state of reduced cognitive activity in which individuals respond without considering the meaning of their behavior or its possible consequences.

Minimum-power theory: An explanation of coalitions that predicts that the coalition that is sufficient to win but includes partners with the most minimal pivotal power is the most likely one to form.

Minimum-resource theory: An explanation of coalitions that predicts that the coalition that is sufficient to win but involves partners with the most minimal resources is the most likely one to form.

Mirror-image thinking: The tendency for groups in conflict to adopt the same distorted misperceptions about one another.

Mixed-motive situations: Performance settings in which the interdependence among interactants involves both cooperative and competitive goal structures.

Mob: A hostile crowd of emotionally charged individuals.

Modeling: Learning new behaviors by observing and imitating another person; also, a method of treatment used in behavior therapy that involves demonstrating particular behaviors while the group members observe.

***n* Affiliation:** The need for affiliation; the dispositional tendency to seek out others.

***n* Power:** The need for power; the dispositional tendency to seek control over others.

Natural selection: The evolutionary favoring of species with qualities that promote their survival.

Negotiation: A reciprocal communication process that is used to identify a basis of agreement between two parties in conflict.

Nominal group technique (NGT): A group performance method that calls for combining individuals' inputs in a structured group setting.

Nonconformity: Refusing to change one's beliefs and/or behaviors despite social pressures.

Nondominant responses: Novel, complicated, or untried behaviors that the organism has never performed before or has performed only infrequently.

Nonreactive measures: Measurement methods that have little or no impact on the participants in the research.

Norm: An implicit social standard that describes what behaviors should or should not be performed in a social setting; guidelines for actions.

Norm of reciprocity: A social standard enjoining individuals to pay back in kind what they receive from others.

Normative influence: Social influence that results from personal and interpersonal pressures to conform to group norms.

Normative model of group effectiveness: A process model of productivity, proposed by Hackman, that assumes that situational inputs (organizational context, group design, and synergy) and group process (effort, knowledge, and task performance strategies) determine group effectiveness.

Normative model of leadership: A theory of leadership developed by Vroom that predicts the effectiveness of group-centered, consultative, and autocratic leaders across a number of group settings.

Observational measure: Any measurement method that involves watching and recording another individual's actions.

Organizational development (OD): A general label for a wide variety of organizational interventions designed to assess current level of development, clarify and prioritize goals, promote adequate planning, and create innovation in organizations.

Orientation stage: The first stage of decision making, characterized by the identification of the problem to be solved and planning of the process to be used in reaching the decision.

Other-total ratio (OTR): A formula, proposed by Mullen, that assumes self-awareness depends on the ratio of the number of other people in the group (T) to the number of people in the majority (O).

Out-group-homogeneity bias: The tendency for people to assume that the out-group is much more homogeneous than the in-group.

Overload: An excessive number of inputs that come so rapidly that the information cannot be processed effectively.

Panic: A feeling of fear and of being threatened; a group of people who are seeking escape en masse from a dangerous situation.

Parity norm (or **Equity norm**): A norm of resource allocation that suggests individuals' payoffs should be proportional to their inputs.

Participant observation: An observational method that involves making observations while taking part in the social process.

Participatory leadership: A form of leadership that allows group members to participate in the decision making process.

Personal space: The area individuals maintain around themselves into which others cannot intrude without arousing discomfort.

Persuasive-arguments theory: An explanation of polarization in groups that assumes that group members shift in the direction of the more valued pole because they can generate more arguments favoring the more valued pole.

Power: The capacity to influence others, even when these others try to resist this influence.

Premature termination: The withdrawal of a participant from a change-promoting group that occurs before the individual has benefited in any way.

Primary groups: Influential groups characterized by face-to-face interaction, interdependency, and strong group identification.

Primary tension: Feelings of discomfort and awkwardness that frequently occur in newly formed groups.

Primary territory: Well-controlled areas that are possessed on a long-term basis.

Principled negotiation (or Integrative negotiation): A conflict-resolution strategy in which both parties work together to generate a mutually satisfying solution.

Prisoner's dilemma game (PDG): A laboratory procedure in which players must make either cooperative or competitive choices in order to earn points or money; used in the study of cooperation, competition, and the development of mutual trust.

Private acceptance: Change that occurs when the targets of social influence personally accept the influencer's position.

Process consultation: Training group members to identify group processes (leadership, conflict) within the organization through didactic instruction, role playing, structured process analysis, and training in observational methods.

Process losses: Aspects of the group's dynamics that inhibit successful performance; these losses include coordination losses and social loafing.

Proximity/attraction effect: The tendency to like individuals who are located nearby.

Psychoanalytic group therapy: An approach to group therapy that uses Freud's methods of interpretation, transference, and shifting attention to help members gain insight into the causes of their psychological problems.

Public territory: An area that the occupants control only when physically present in the situation; no expectation of future use exists.

Quality circle: Small self-regulated groups of employees charged with identifying ways to improve product quality.

Queue: A waiting line.

Reactance: A complex emotional and cognitive reaction that occurs when individuals feel that their freedom to make choices has been threatened or eliminated.

Realistic-conflict theory: The view that conflict stems from competition between individuals and groups for scarce resources.

Reciprocity: Paying back in kind what you receive from others.

Reference group: A group that provides individuals with a reference point for defining their own personal attitudes and beliefs.

Referent power: Influence that is based on group members' identification with, attraction to, or respect for, the powerholder.

Relationship behaviors: Actions performed by group members or the group leader that improve interpersonal relations within the group; consideration, supportiveness, and socioemotionality.

Remembrance: In Moreland and Levine's model of group socialization, a period of time during which remaining group members reminisce about a former group member and the former group member appraises his or her experiences in the group.

Resocialization: In Moreland and Levine's model of group socialization, a period of time during which

group members who have failed to fulfill their role as full group members renegotiate their roles within the group.

Revolutionary coalition: A subgroup formed within the larger group that seeks to overthrow the current group leader.

Reward power: The ability to mediate the distribution of positive or negative reinforcers.

Ringelmann effect: The tendency for group members to become less productive as the size of their group increases.

Risky-shift phenomenon: The tendency for groups to make riskier decisions than individuals.

Robbers Cave Experiment: A study performed by the Sherifs and their colleagues in an attempt to better understand the causes and consequences of intergroup conflict.

Role: A behavior characteristic of persons in a context; the part played by a member of a group.

Role ambiguity: Unclear expectations about the behaviors to be performed by individuals who occupy particular positions within the group.

Role conflict: Intragroup and intraindividual conflict that results from incompatibility in role relations.

Role differentiation: The development of distinct roles in a group, such as leader, follower, isolate.

Role transition: The movement from one role to another that occurs during the group socialization process.

Secondary tension: Feelings of discord, friction, and discomfort that occur in groups that have passed through an earlier period of primary tension.

Secondary territories: Areas that are controlled on a regular basis, even though the individual has no exclusive claim to the space.

Self-attention theory: A social impact model proposed by Mullen that argues self-awareness increases as the number of people in the majority becomes larger and the individual's subgroup becomes smaller.

Self-awareness: The psychological state in which one's attention is focused on the self, personal standards, or inner experiences.

Self-evaluation maintenance model: A theory proposed by Tesser and Campbell that assumes individuals seek membership in groups provided (a) they feel superior to the other group members in areas that are central to their self-concept and (b) the other group members excel in areas that are not central to the individual's self-concept.

Self-fulfilling prophecy: A perceiver's inaccurate belief that can evoke new behaviors in the person being observed that confirm the perceiver's original inaccurate conception.

Self-help group: A group of people who voluntarily help one another cope with or overcome a problem they hold in common.

Self-perception theory: A theoretical model that assumes individuals come to know their own attitudes, emotions, and other internal states by inferring them from observations of their own overt behavior.

Self-report measures: Assessment devices, such as questionnaires, tests, or interviews, that ask respondents to describe their feelings, attitudes, or beliefs.

Sensitivity training: An unstructured group experience designed to enhance spontaneity, increase personal awareness, and maximize members' sensitivity to others.

Similarity/attraction effect: The tendency to like people with characteristics that are similar to our own.

Situational leadership theory: Hersey and Blanchard's theory of leadership that suggests that groups benefit

from leadership that meshes with the maturity level of the group.

Situational model of leadership: Any framework that assumes leadership emergence is determined by factors operating in the group situation and not personality characteristics of the group members.

Social categorization: The perceptual classification of people into various social groups.

Social combination rule: The procedure used by group members for combining individuals' inputs to yield a group product.

Social comparison: Evaluating the accuracy of personal beliefs and attitudes by comparing oneself to others.

Social-comparison theory: A theoretical framework that explains when and why individuals revise their beliefs by comparing themselves to others.

Social-decision scheme: The process by which individual inputs are combined to yield a group decision.

Social-exchange theory: An economic model of interpersonal relationships that argues individuals seek out relationships that offer them many rewards while exacting few costs.

Social facilitation: The enhancement of an individual's performance when that person works in the presence of other people.

Social identity theory: A theoretical framework that assumes individuals are motivated to maintain a positive public and private self-image and that one way to achieve the goal is to praise the in-group and derogate the out-group.

Social impact theory: An analysis of social influence processes that proposes the impact of any source of influence depends upon the strength, immediacy, and number of influencers involved.

Social influence: Actions undertaken to change the beliefs or behaviors of another person; also, any change that results from such interpersonal pressures.

Social loafing: The reduction of individual effort exerted when people work in groups compared to when they work alone.

Social loneliness: Feelings of isolation and depression that occur when individuals believe that their relationships with friends and acquaintances are too few or unsatisfying.

Social movement: A deliberate, organized attempt to achieve a change or resist a change in a social system.

Social support: Advice, guidance, assistance, positive feedback, and emotional support provided by other individuals.

Social trap: Situations that prompt individuals to act in their own immediate self-interest to the detriment of other group members' needs or their own long-term outcomes.

Socialization: The gradual acquisition of language, attitudes, and other socially approved values through reinforcement, observation, and other social learning processes; also, a period of group socialization during which the potential group member becomes assimilated to the group and the group accommodates the new group member.

Sociobiology: A biological approach to understanding social behavior that assumes recurring patterns of behavior in animals ultimately stem from evolutionary pressures that increase the likelihood of adaptive social actions while extinguishing nonadaptive practices.

Socioemotional role: A position in a group whose occupant is expected to perform supportive, interpersonally accommodative behaviors.

Sociofugal spaces: Seating arrangements that discourage or prevent interaction among group members.

Sociograms: Graphic representations of the patterns of attraction among groups' members created through sociometry.

Sociometric differentiation: The development of patterns of liking and disliking in a group.

Sociometric structure: Patterns of liking and disliking in a group; the group's attraction structure.

Sociometry: A measurement technique developed by Moreno that can be used to summarize graphically and mathematically patterns of interpersonal attraction in groups.

Sociopetal spaces: Seating arrangements that promote interaction among group members.

Staffing theory: An explanation of the consequences of overcrowded and understaffed behavior settings based on ecological psychology.

Status: Authority or prestige in the group.

Status differentiation: The gradual development of authority relations within groups.

Status generalization: The tendency for irrelevant, extragroup status characteristics to influence the status hierarchy in the group.

Status liability: The condition that prevails when deviancy is so extreme that high-status individuals' idiosyncrasy credits are no protection against sanction and they are held especially responsible for the negative consequences.

Steinzor effect: The tendency for members of a group to comment immediately after the person sitting opposite them.

Stereotypes: Cognitive generalizations about the qualities and characteristics of the members of a particular group or social category.

Stressor: An environmental event that threatens an individual's existence or sense of well-being.

Structure: Patterns of relationships among members of a group.

Structured learning groups: Planned interventions, such as workshops, seminars, or retreats, that focus on a specific interpersonal problem or skill.

Structured observational measure: A method of measurement that involves classifying (coding) the subject's actions under clearly defined categories; Bales's Interaction Process Analysis (IPA) and SYMLOG are examples of such coding systems.

Successive-stage theory: Any theory of group development that specifies the usual order of the phases through which the developing group typically progresses.

Superordinate goals: Goals that can only be attained if the members of two or more groups work together by pooling their efforts and resources.

Survey feedback: The assessment of the organization's current state of development through the use of interviews, surveys, focus groups, and structured and unstructured observation.

Synergy: A gain in energy and motivation that occurs in group situations.

Synomorphy: Barker's term describing the quality of the fit between the human occupants and the physical situation.

System of Multiple Level Observation of Groups (SYMLOG): A three-dimensional theory and observational system developed by Bales for the classification of group behavior.

Task behaviors: Actions performed by group members or the group leader that are relevant to the group's tasks.

Task demands: The combination processes dictated by the problem or group activity.

Task role: A position in a group whose occupant is expected to perform goal-oriented, task-focused behaviors.

Team building: Fostering cohesion, clarifying structure, and reducing conflict through the use of role analysis, interpersonal-skills training, communication training, retreats, and workshops.

Territories: Specific geographic areas that individuals or groups of individuals claim, mark, and defend against intrusion by others.

Threshold theory: Bormann's theory of conflict that argues that conflict serves a useful function in groups so long as it does not surpass the tolerance threshold for too long.

Training groups (T-groups): Helping individuals improve their interpersonal skills by arranging for them to work for a substantial period of time in an unstructured group setting.

Trait model of leadership: A framework that assumes that leaders possess certain personality characteristics distinguishing them from nonleaders.

Vigilant information processing: Recognizing and weighing all information relevant to the decision at hand; requires the avoidance of such discussion-limiting strategies as procrastination, bolstering, and satisficing.

Voir dire: The verbal or written questioning of prospective jurors by counsel.

· References ·

Adams, J. S. (1965). Inequity in social exchange. In L. Berkowitz (Ed.), *Advances in experimental social psychology* (Vol. 2, pp. 267–299). New York: Academic Press.

Aiello, J. R. (1987). Human spatial behavior. In D. Stokols & I. Altman (Eds.), *Handbook of environmental psychology* (Vol. 1, pp. 389–504). New York: Wiley.

Aiello, J. R., Baum, A., & Gormley, F. (1981). Social determinants of residential crowding stress. *Personality and Social Psychology Bulletin, 7*, 643–644.

Aiken, M., & Hage, J. (1968) Organizational interdependence and intraorganizational structure. *American Sociological Review, 33*, 912–930.

Ainsworth, M. D. S. (1979). Infant-mother attachment. *American Psychologist, 34*, 932–937.

Ainsworth, M. D. S., Blehar, M. C., Waters, E., & Wall, S. (1978). *Patterns of attachment: A psychological study of the strange situation.* Hillsdale, NJ: Erlbaum.

Akin, G., & Hopelain, D. (1986). Finding the culture of productivity. *Organizational Dynamics, 14*, 19–32.

Allen, H. (1978). Cults: The battle for the mind. In C. A. Krause, *Guyana massacre: The eyewitness account* (pp. 111–121). New York: Berkley.

Allen, V. L. (1965). Situational factors in conformity. In L. Berkowitz (Ed.), *Advances in experimental social psychology* (Vol. 2, pp. 133–175). New York: Academic Press.

Allen, V. L. (1975). Social support for nonconformity. In L. Berkowitz (Ed.), *Advances in experimental social psychology* (Vol. 8, pp. 2–43). New York: Academic Press.

Allen, V. L., & Wilder, D. A. (1980). Impact of group consensus and social support on stimulus meaning: Mediation of conformity by cognitive restructuring. *Journal of Personality and Social Psychology, 39*, 1116–1124.

Allison, S. T., & Messick, D. M. (1985a). Effects of experience on performance in a replenishable resource trap. *Journal of Personality and Social Psychology, 49*, 943–948.

Allison, S. T., & Messick, D. M. (1985b). The group attribution error. *Journal of Experimental Social Psychology, 21*, 563–579.

Allison, S. T., & Messick, D. M. (1987). From individual inputs to group outputs, and back again: Group processes and inferences about members. In C. Hendrick (Ed.), *Review of Personality and Social Psychology: Group Process* (Vol. 8, pp. 111–143). Newbury Park, CA: Sage.

Allport, F. H. (1920). The influence of the group upon association and thought. *Journal of Experimental Psychology, 3*, 159–182.

Allport, F. H. (1924). *Social psychology.* Boston: Houghton Mifflin.

Allport, F. H. (1961). The contemporary appraisal of an old problem. *Contemporary Psychology, 6*, 195–197.

Allport, F. H. (1962). A structuronomic conception of behavior: Individual and collective. I. Structural theory and the master problem of social psychology. *Journal of Abnormal and Social Psychology*, 64, 3–30.

Allport, G. W. (1954). *The nature of prejudice*. New York: Addison-Wesley.

Allport, G. W. (1985). The historical background of social psychology. In G. Lindzey & E. Aronson (Eds.), *Handbook of Social Psychology* (Vol. 1, 3rd ed., pp. 1–46). New York: Random House.

Allport, G. W., & Postman, L. J. (1947). *The psychology of rumor*. New York: Henry Holt.

Altman, I. (1973). An ecological approach to the functioning of socially isolated groups. In J. E. Rasmussen (Ed.), *Man in isolation and confinement* (pp. 241–269). Chicago: Aldine.

Altman, I. (1975). *The environment and social behavior*. Pacific Grove, CA: Brooks/Cole.

Altman, I. (1977). Research on environment and behavior: A personal statement of strategy. In D. Stokols (Ed.), *Perspectives on environment and behavior* (pp. 303–324). New York: Plenum.

Altman, I., & Chemers, M. M. (1980). *Culture and environment*. Pacific Grove, CA: Brooks/Cole.

Altman, I., & Haythorn, W. W. (1967). The ecology of isolated groups. *Behavioral Science*, 12, 169–182.

Altman, I., & Taylor, D. A. (1973). *Social penetration*. New York: Holt, Rinehart, & Winston.

Altman, I., Taylor, D. A., & Wheeler, L. (1971). Ecological aspects of group behavior in social isolation. *Journal of Applied Social Psychology*, 1, 76–100.

Amir, Y. (1969). Contact hypothesis in ethnic relations. *Psychological Bulletin*, 71, 319–342.

Amir, Y. (1976). The role of intergroup contact in change of prejudice and ethnic relations. In P. A. Katz (Ed.), *Towards the elimination of racism*. New York: Pergamon.

Anderson, C. A. (1989). Temperature and aggression: Ubiquitous effects of heat on occurrence of human violence. *Psychological Bulletin*, 106, 74–96.

Ansari, M. A., & Kapoor, A. (1987). Organizational context and upward influence

tactics. *Organizational Behavior and Human Decision Processes*, 40, 39–49.

Apfelbaum, E. (1974). On conflicts and bargaining. In L. Berkowitz (Ed.), *Advances in experimental social psychology* (Vol. 7, pp. 103–156). New York: Academic Press.

Apodoca v. Oregon, 406 U.S. 404 (1972).

Archibald, W. P. (1976). Psychology, sociology, and social psychology: Bad fences make bad neighbors. *British Journal of Sociology*, 27, 115–129.

Ardry, R. (1970). *The territorial imperative: A personal inquiry into the animal origins of property and nations*. New York: Atheneum.

Argyle, M. (1969). *Social interaction*. New York: Atherton.

Argyle, M., & Dean, J. (1965). Eye-contact, distance, and affiliation. *Sociometry*, 28, 289–304.

Arkin, R. M., & Burger, J. M. (1980). Effects of unit relation tendencies on interpersonal attraction. *Social Psychology Quarterly*, 43, 380–391.

Arnold, D. W., & Greenberg, C. I. (1980). Deviate rejection within differentially manned groups. *Social Psychology Quarterly*, 43, 419–424.

Aronson, E. (1980). *The social animal* (3rd ed.). San Francisco: Freeman.

Aronson, E., & Mills, J. (1959). The effect of severity of initiation on liking for a group. *Journal of Abnormal and Social Psychology*, 59, 177–181.

Aronson, E., Stephan, C., Sikes, J., Blaney, N., & Snapp, M. (1978). *The Jigsaw classroom*. Newbury Park, CA: Sage.

Asch, S. E. (1952). *Social psychology*. Englewood Cliffs, NJ: Prentice-Hall.

Asch, S. E. (1955). Opinions and social pressures. *Scientific American*, 193(5), 31–35.

Asch, S. E. (April, 1957). An experimental investigation of group influence. In *Symposium on preventive and social psychiatry*, Walter Reed Army Institute of Research. Washington, DC: U.S. Government Printing Office.

Aschenbrenner, K. M., & Schaefer, R. E. (1980). Minimal group situations: Comments on a mathematical model and on the research paradigm. *European Journal of Social Psychology*, 10, 389–398.

Ashour, A. S. (1973a). Further discussion of Fiedler's contingency model of leadership effectiveness. *Organizational Behavior and Human Performance, 9*, 369–376.

Ashour, A. S. (1973b). The contingency model of leadership effectiveness: An evaluation. *Organizational Behavior and Human Performance, 9*, 339–355.

Atthowe, J. M., Jr. (1961). Interpersonal decision making: The resolution of a dyadic conflict. *Journal of Abnormal and Social Psychology, 62*, 114–119.

Axelrod, R., & Hamilton, W. D. (1981). The evolution of cooperation. *Science, 211*, 1390–1396.

Bach, G. R. (1954). *Intensive group psychotherapy*. New York: Ronald Press.

Bacharach, S. B., & Aiken, M. (1979). The impact of alienation, meaninglessness, and meritocracy on supervisor and subordinate satisfaction. *Social Forces, 57*, 853–870.

Back, K. W. (1951). Influence through social communication. *Journal of Abnormal and Social Psychology, 46*, 9–23.

Back, K. W. (1973). *Beyond words: The story of sensitivity training and the encounter movement*. Baltimore: Penguin Books.

Back, K. W. (1974). Intervention techniques: Small groups. In M. Rosenzweig & L. Porter (Eds.), *Annual Review of Psychology*, 1974.

Backman, C. W. (1983). Toward an interdisciplinary social psychology. In L. Berkowitz (Ed.), *Advances in experimental social psychology* (Vol. 16, pp. 219–260). New York: Academic Press.

Backman, C. W. (August, 1986). *Interdisciplinary social psychology: Prospects and problems*. Paper presented at the meetings of the American Psychological Association: Washington, DC.

Baker, P. M. (1981). Social coalitions. *American Behavioral Scientist, 24*, 633–647.

Bales, R. F. (1950). *Interaction process analysis: A method for the study of small groups*. Reading, MA: Addison-Wesley.

Bales, R. F. (1955). How people interact in conferences. *Scientific American, 192*(3), 31–35.

Bales, R. F. (1958). Task roles and social roles in problem-solving groups. In E. E. Maccoby, T. M. Newcomb, & E. L. Hartley (Eds.), *Readings in social psychology*. New York: Holt, Rinehart, & Winston.

Bales, R. F. (1965). The equilibrium problem in small groups. In A. P. Hare, E. F. Borgatta, & R. F. Bales (Eds.), *Small groups: Studies in social interaction*. New York: Knopf.

Bales, R. F. (1970). *Personality and interpersonal behavior*. New York: Holt, Rinehart, & Winston.

Bales, R. F. (1980). *SYMLOG case study kit*. New York: Free Press.

Bales, R. F. (1985). The new field theory in social psychology. *International Journal of Small Group Research, 1*, 1–18.

Bales, R. F., & Cohen, S. P. with Williamson, S. A. (1979). *SYMLOG: A system for the multiple level observation of groups*. New York: Free Press.

Bales, R. F., & Strodtbeck, F. L. (1951). Phases in group problem solving. *Journal of Abnormal and Social Psychology, 46*, 485–495.

Bandura, A. (1986). *Social foundations of thought and action: A social cognitive theory*. Englewood Cliffs, NJ: Prentice-Hall.

Baranowski, T. (1984). Social support and health-related behavior change maintenance. *Society for the Advancement of Social Psychology Newsletter, 10*(1), 12–18.

Barash, D. P. (1982). *Sociobiology and behavior* (2nd ed.). New York: Elsevier.

Barker, R. G. (1968). *Ecological psychology*. Stanford, CA: Stanford University Press.

Barker, R. G. (1987). Prospecting in ecological psychology: Oskaloosa revisited. In D. Stokols & I. Altman (Eds.), *Handbook of environmental psychology* (Vol. 2, pp. 1413–1432). New York: Wiley.

Barker, R. G., & Associates. (1978). *Habitats, environments, and human behavior: Studies in ecological psychology and eco-behavioral sciences from the Midwest Psychological Field Station, 1947–1972*. San Francisco: Jossey-Bass.

Barnard, C. I. (1938). *The functions of the executive*. Cambridge, MA: Harvard University Press.

Baron, R. A. (1978). Aggression and heat: The "long hot summer" revisited. In A. Baum, J. E. Singer, & S. Valins (Eds.), *Advances in environmental psychology* (Vol. 1, pp. 57–84). Hillsdale, NJ: Erlbaum.

Baron, R. M., & Rodin, J. (1978). Personal control as a mediator of crowding. In A. Baum, J. E. Singer, & S. Valins (Eds.), *Advances in environmental psychology* (Vol. 1, pp. 145–190). Hillsdale, NJ: Erlbaum.

Baron, R. S. (1986). Distraction-conflict theory: Progress and problems. In L. Berkowitz (Ed.), *Advances in experimental social psychology* (Vol. 19, pp. 1–40). New York: Academic Press.

Baron, R. S., Moore, D. L., & Sanders, G. S. (1978). Distraction as a source of drive in social facilitation research. *Journal of Personality and Social Psychology, 36*, 816–824.

Barrera, M., Jr. (1986). Distinctions between social support concepts, measures, and models. *American Journal of Community Psychology, 14*, 413–422.

Barrow, J. C. (1977). The variables of leadership: A review and conceptual framework. *Academy of Management Review, 2*, 231–251.

Bartol, K. M., & Martin, D. C. (1986). Women and men in task groups. In R. D. Ashmore & F. K. DelBoca (Eds.), *The social psychology of female-male relations* (pp. 259–310). New York: Academic Press.

Barton, A. H., & Lazarfeld, P. H. (1969). Some functions of qualitative analysis in social research. In G. J. McCall & J. L. Simmons (Eds.), *Issues in participant observation* (pp. 163–196). Reading, MA: Addison-Wesley.

Bass, B. M. (1981). *Stogdill's handbook of leadership*. New York: Free Press.

Bass, B. M. (1985a). Good, better, best. *Organizational Dynamics, 13*, 26–40.

Bass, B. M. (1985b). *Leadership and performance beyond expectations*. New York: Free Press.

Bass, B. M., Avolio, B. J., & Goldheim, L. (1987). Biography and the assessment of transformational leadership at the world-class level. *Journal of Management, 13*, 7–19.

Bass, B. M., & Ryterband, E. C. (1979). *Organizational psychology* (2nd ed.). Boston: Allyn and Bacon.

Batchelor, J. P., & Goethals, G. R. (1972). Spatial arrangements in freely formed groups. *Sociometry, 35*, 270–279.

Bates, B., & Goodman, A. (1986). The effectiveness of encounter groups: Implications of research for counselling practice. *British Journal of Guidance and Counselling, 14*, 240–251.

Batson, C. D. (1975). Rational processing or rationalization?: The effect of disconfirming information on a stated religious belief. *Journal of Personality and Social Psychology, 32*, 176–184.

Battistich, V. A., & Thompson, E. G. (1980). Students' perceptions of the college milieu: A multidimensional scaling analysis. *Personality and Social Psychology Bulletin, 6*, 74–82.

Baum, A., Calesnick, L. E., Davis, G. E., & Gatchel, R. J. (1982). Individual differences in coping with crowding: Stimulus screening and social overload. *Journal of Personality and Social Psychology, 43*, 821–830.

Baum, A., & Davis, G. E. (1980). Reducing the stress of high-density living: An architectural intervention. *Journal of Personality and Social Psychology, 38*, 471–481.

Baum, A., Davis, G. E., & Valins, S. (1979). Generating behavioral data for the design process. In J. R. Aiello & A. Baum (Eds.), *Residential crowding and design* (pp. 175–196). New York: Plenum.

Baum, A., Harpin, R. E., & Valins, S. (1976). The role of group phenomena in the experience of crowding. In S. Saegert (Ed.), *Crowding in real environments*. Newbury Park, CA: Sage.

Baum, A., & Paulus, P. (1987). Crowding. In D. Stokols & I. Altman (Eds.), *Handbook of environmental psychology* (Vol. 1, pp. 533–570). New York: Wiley.

Baum, A., Singer, J., & Baum, C. (1982). Stress and the environment. *Journal of Social Issues, 37*(1), 4–35.

Baum, A., & Valins, S. (1977). *Architecture and social behavior: Psychological studies of social density*. Hillsdale, NJ: Erlbaum.

Baumeister, R. F. (1984). Choking under pressure: Self-consciousness and paradoxical effects of incentives on skillful performance. *Journal of Personality and Social Psychology, 46*, 610–620.

Baumeister, R. F. (1985). The championship choke. *Psychology Today, 19*(4), 48–52.

Baumeister, R. F., Hamilton, J. C., & Tice, D. M. (1985). Public versus private expectancy of success: Confidence booster or performance pressure? *Journal of Personality and Social Psychology, 48*, 1447–1457.

Baumeister, R. F., & Showers, C. J. (1986). A review of paradoxical performance effects: Choking under pressure in sports and mental tests. *European Journal of Social Psychology, 16*, 361–383.

Baumeister, R. F., & Steinhilber, A. (1984). Paradoxical effects of supportive audiences on performance under pressure:

The home field disadvantage in sports championships. *Journal of Personality and Social Psychology, 47*, 85–93.

Baumrind, D. (1964). Some thoughts on ethics of research: After reading Milgram's "Behavioral study of obedience." *American Psychologist, 19*, 421–423.

Bavelas, A. (1948). A mathematical model for group structures. *Applied Anthropology, 7*, 16–30.

Bavelas, A. (1950). Communication patterns in task oriented groups. *Journal of the Acoustical Society of America, 22*, 725–730.

Bavelas, A., & Barrett, D. (1951). An experimental approach to organization communication. *Personnel, 27*, 367–371.

Beach, B. H., Mitchell, T. R., & Beach, L. R. (1975). *Components of situational favorableness and probability of success.* Tech. Rep. 75-66. Seattle: University of Washington, Organizational Research Group.

Beaman, A. L., Klentz, B., Diener, E., & Svanum, S. (1979). Objective self-awareness and transgression in children: A field study. *Journal of Personality and Social Psychology, 37*, 1835–1846.

Bedell, J., & Sistrunk, F. (1973). Power, opportunity, costs, and sex in a mixed-motive game. *Journal of Personality and Social Psychology, 25*, 219–226.

Bednar, R. L., & Battersby, C. (1976). The effects of specific cognitive structure on early group development. *Journal of Applied Behavioral Sciences, 12*, 513–522.

Bednar, R. L., & Kaul, T. (1978). Experiential group research: Current perspectives. In S. Garfield and A. Bergin (Eds.), *Handbook of psychotherapy and behavior change.* New York: Wiley.

Bednar, R. L., & Kaul, T. (1979). Experiential group research: What never happened. *Journal of Applied Behavioral Science, 15*, 311–319.

Bednar, R. L., & Lawlis, F. (1971). Empirical research in group psychotherapy. In A. E. Bergin & S. L. Garfield (Eds.), *Handbook of psychotherapy and behavior change.* New York: Wiley.

Bednar, R. L., Melnick, J., & Kaul, T. (1974). Risk, responsibility and structure: A conceptual framework for initiating group counseling and psychotherapy. *Journal of Counseling Psychology, 21*, 31–37.

Belk, S. S., Snell, W. E., Jr., Garcia-Falconi, R., Hernandez-Sanchez, J. E., Hargrove, L., & Holtzman, W. H., Jr. (1988). Power strategy use in the intimate relationships of women and men from Mexico and the United States. *Personality and Social Psychology Bulletin, 14*, 439–447.

Bell, P. A. (1981). Physiological, comfort, performance, and social effects of heat stress. *Journal of Social Issues, 37*, 71–94.

Bellack, A., & Hersen, M. (1979). *Research and practice in social skills training.* New York: Plenum.

Bem, S. L. (1975). Sex role adaptability: One consequence of psychological androgyny. *Journal of Personality and Social Psychology, 31*, 634–643.

Bem, S. L. (1985). Androgyny and gender schema theory: A conceptual and empirical integration. *Nebraska symposium on motivation, 32*, 179–226.

Benne, K. D., & Sheats, P. (1948). Functional roles of group members. *Journal of Social Issues, 4*(2), 41–49.

Bennett, H. S. (1980). *On becoming a rock musician.* Amherst: University of Massachusetts Press.

Bennis, W. G. (1975). *Where have all the leaders gone?* Washington, DC: Federal Executive Institute.

Bennis, W. G., & Shepard, H. A. (1956). A theory of group development. *Human Relations, 9*, 415–437.

Berg, J. H., & Clark, M. S. (1986). Social exchange and the decision to pursue close friendship. In V. J. Derlega & B. Winstead (Eds.), *Friendship and social interaction.* New York: Springer-Verlag.

Berger, J., Cohen, B. P., & Zelditch, M., Jr. (1972). Status characteristics and social interaction. *American Sociological Review, 37*, 241–255.

Berger, J., Conner, T. L., & Fisek, M. H. (Eds.). (1974). *Expectation states theory: A theoretical research program.* Cambridge, MA: Winthrop.

Berger, J., Fisek, M. H., Norman, R. Z., & Zelditch, M., Jr. (1977). *Status characteristics and social interaction.* New York: Elsevier.

Berger, J., Webster, M., Jr., Ridgeway, C., & Rosenholtz, S. J. (1986). Status cues, expectations, and behavior. In E. J. Lawler (Ed.), *Advances in group processes* (Vol. 3, pp. 1–22). Greenwich, CT: JAI Press.

Berger, R. E. (1981). *Heart rate, arousal, and the "mere presence" hypothesis of social facilitation.* Unpublished doctoral dissertation, Virginia Commonwealth University, Richmond, VA.

Berger, S. M., Carli, L. C., Garcia, R., & Brady, J. J., Jr. (1982). Audience effects in anticipatory learning: A comparison of drive and practice-inhibition analyses. *Journal of Personality and Social Psychology, 42,* 478–486.

Berger, S. M., Hampton, K. L., Carli, L. L., Grandmaison, P. S., Sadow, J. S., Donath, C. H., & Herschlag, L. R. (1981). Audience-induced inhibition of overt practice during learning. *Journal of Personality and Social Psychology, 40,* 479–491.

Berkowitz, L. (1962). *Aggression: A social psychological analysis.* New York: McGraw-Hill.

Berkowitz, L. (1971). Reporting an experiment: A case study in leveling, sharpening, and assimilation. *Journal of Experimental Social Psychology, 7,* 237–243.

Berkowitz, L. (1978). Whatever happened to the frustration-aggression hypothesis? *American Behavioral Scientist, 32,* 691–708.

Berkowitz, L. (1983). The experience of anger as a parallel process in the display of impulsive, "angry" aggression. In R. G. Geen & E. I. Donnerstein (Eds.), *Aggression: Theoretical and empirical reviews* (Vol. 1). New York: Academic Press.

Berkowitz, L. (1989). Frustration-aggression hypothesis: Examination and reformulation. *Psychological Bulletin, 106,* 59–73.

Berkowitz, L., & Geen, J. A. (1962). The stimulus qualities of the scapegoat. *Journal of Abnormal and Social Psychology, 64,* 293–301.

Berkowitz, L., & Howard, R. C. (1959). Reactions to opinion deviates as affected by affiliation need (n) and group member interdependence. *Sociometry, 22,* 81–91.

Berman, J. J., & Zimpfer, D. G. (1980). Growth groups: Do the outcomes really last? *Review of Educational Research, 50,* 505–524.

Berscheid, E. (1985). Interpersonal attraction. In G. Lindzey & E. Aronson (Eds.), *Handbook of social psychology* (3rd ed., Vol. 2, pp. 413–484). New York: Random House.

Bertram, B. C. R. (1978). Living in groups: Predators and prey. In P. P. G. Bateson &

R. A. Hinde (Eds.), *Behavioral ecology: An evolutional approach.* London: Blackwell.

Biddle, B. J. (1979). *Role theory: Expectations, identities, and behavior.* New York: Academic Press.

Billig, M. G. (1976). *Social psychology and group relations.* New York: Academic Press.

Billig, M. G., & Tajfel, H. (1973). Social categorization and similarity in intergroup behavior. *European Journal of Social Psychology, 3,* 27–52.

Binning, J. F., Zaba, J. F., & Whattam, J. C. (1986). Explaining the biasing effects of performance cues in terms of cognitive categorizations. *Academy of Management Journal, 29,* 521–535.

Bion, W. R. (1961). *Experiences in groups.* New York: Basic Books.

Black, T. E., & Higbee, K. L. (1973). Effects of power, threat, and sex on exploitation. *Journal of Personality and Social Psychology, 27,* 382–388.

Blake, R. R., & Mouton, J. S. (1964). *The managerial grid.* Houston, TX: Gulf.

Blake, R. R., & Mouton, J. S. (1978). *The new managerial grid.* Houston, TX: Gulf.

Blake, R. R., & Mouton, J. S. (1980). *The versatile manager: A Grid profile.* Homewood, IL: Dow Jones-Irwin.

Blake, R. R., & Mouton, J. S. (1982). How to choose a leadership style. *Training and Development Journal, 36,* 39–46.

Blake, R. R., & Mouton, J. S. (1984). *Solving costly organizational conflicts: Achieving intergroup trust, cooperation, and teamwork.* San Franscisco: Jossey-Bass.

Blake, R. R., & Mouton, J. S. (1985). Presidential (Grid) styles. *Training and Development Journal, 39,* 30–34.

Blake, R. R., & Mouton, J. S. (1986). From theory to practice in interface problem solving. In S. Worchel & W. G. Austin (Eds.), *Psychology of intergroup relations* (2nd ed., pp. 67–87). Chicago: Nelson-Hall.

Blake, R. R., Shepard, H. A., & Mouton, J. S. (1964). *Managing intergroup conflict in industry.* Houston, TX: Gulf.

Blanchard, F. A., Adelman, L., & Cook, S. W. (1975). Effect of group success and failure upon interpersonal attraction in cooperating interracial groups. *Journal of Personality and Social Psychology, 31,* 1020–1030.

Blanchard, F. A., & Cook, S. W. (1976). Effects of helping a less competent member of a cooperating interracial group on the development of interpersonal attraction. *Journal of Personality and Social Psychology, 34,* 1245–1255.

Blanchard, F. A., Weigel, R. H., & Cook, S. W. (1975). The effect of relative competence of group members upon interpersonal attraction in cooperating interracial groups. *Journal of Personality and Social Psychology, 32,* 519–530.

Blanchard, K., & Johnson, S. (1981). *The one minute manager.* New York: Berkley Books.

Blascovich, J., Ginsburg, G. P., & Howe, R. C. (1975). Blackjack and the risky shift, II: Monetary stakes. *Journal of Experimental Social Psychology, 11,* 224–232.

Blascovich, J., Ginsburg, G. P., & Howe, R. C. (1976). Blackjack, choice shifts in the field. *Sociometry, 39,* 274–276.

Blascovich, J., Ginsburg, G. P., & Veach, T. L. (1975). A pluralistic explanation of choice shifts on the risk dimension. *Journal of Personality and Social Psychology, 31,* 422–429.

Blascovich, J., Nash, R. F., & Ginsburg, G. P. (1978). Heart rate and competitive decision making. *Personality and Social Psychology Bulletin, 4,* 115–118.

Blau, P. M. (1954). Cooperation and competition in a bureaucracy. *American Journal of Sociology, 59,* 530–535.

Blau, P. M. (1964). *Exchange and power in social life.* New York: Wiley.

Bleda, P. R., & Sandman, P. H. (1977). In smoke's way: Socioemotional reactions to another's smoking. *Journal of Applied Psychology, 62,* 452–458.

Blumer, H. (1946). Collective behavior. In A. M. Lee (Ed.), *New outline of the principles of sociology.* New York: Barnes and Noble.

Blumer, H. (1951). Collective behavior. In A. M. Lee (Ed.), *Principles of sociology.* New York: Barnes and Noble.

Blumer, H. (1957). Collective behavior. In J. B. Gittler (Ed.), *Review of sociology: Analysis of a decade.* New York: Wiley.

Bobo, L. (1983). Whites' opposition to busing: Symbolic racism or realistic group conflict? *Journal of Personality and Social Psychology, 45,* 1196–1210.

Bodenhausen, G. V., Gaelick, L., & Wyer, R. S., Jr. (1987). Affective and cognitive factors in intragroup and intergroup communication. In C. Hendrick (Ed.), *Review of Personality and Social Psychology: Group Process* (Vol. 9, pp. 137–166). Newbury Park, CA: Sage.

Bogardus, E. S. (1954). Group behavior and groupality. *Sociology and Social Research, 38,* 401–403.

Bohrnstedt, G. W., & Fisher, G. A. (1986). The effects of recalled childhood and adolescent relationships compared to current role performances on young adults' affective functioning. *Social Psychology Quarterly, 49,* 19–32.

Boire, J. A. (1980). Collective behavior in sport. *Review of Sport and Leisure, 5*(1), 2–45.

Boisen, A. T. (1939). Economic distress and religious experience. A study of the Holy Rollers. *Psychiatry, 2,* 185–194.

Bond, C. F. (1982). Social facilitation: A self-presentational view. *Journal of Personality and Social Psychology, 42,* 1042–1050.

Bond, C. F., & Titus, L. J. (1983). Social facilitation: A meta-analysis of 241 studies. *Psychological Bulletin, 94,* 265–292.

Bonner, H. (1959). *Group dynamics: Principles and applications.* New York: Ronald.

Bonney, M. E. (1947). Popular and unpopular children: A sociometric study. *Sociometry Monographs,* No. 9.

Bonney, W. C., Randall, D. A., & Cleveland, J. D. (1986). An analysis of client perceived curative factors in a therapy group of former incest victims. *Small Group Behavior, 17,* 303–321.

Booth, A. (1972). Sex and social participation. *American Sociological Review, 37,* 183–193.

Borah, L. A., Jr. (1963). The effects of threat in bargaining: Critical and experimental analysis. *Journal of Abnormal and Social Psychology, 66,* 37–44.

Borgatta, E. F., & Bales, R. F. (1953). Task and accumulation of experience as factors in the interaction of small groups. *Sociometry, 16,* 239–252.

Borgatta, E. F., Cottrell, L. S., Jr., & Mann, J. H. (1958). The spectrum of individual characteristics: An interdimensional analysis. *Psychological Reports, 4,* 279–319.

Borgatta, E. F., Cottrell, L. S., Jr., & Meyer, H. J. (1956). On the dimensions of group behavior. *Sociometry, 19,* 223–240.

Borgatta, E. F., Couch, A. S., & Bales, R. F. (1954). Some findings relevant to the great man theory of leadership. *American Sociological Review, 19*, 755–759.

Bormann, E. G. (1975). *Discussion and group methods: Theory and practices* (2nd ed.). New York: Harper & Row.

Bornstein, F., Crum, L., Wittenbraker, J., Harring, K., Insko, C. A., & Thibaut, J. (1983). On the measurement of social orientations in the Minimal Group Paradigm. *European Journal of Social Psychology, 13*, 321–350.

Bouchard, T. J. (1972a). A comparison of two group brainstorming procedures. *Journal of Applied Psychology, 56*, 418–421.

Bouchard, T. J. (1972b). Training, motivation, and personality as determinants of the effectiveness of brainstorming groups and individuals. *Journal of Applied Psychology, 56*, 324–331.

Bouchard, T. J., Barsaloux, J., & Drauden, G. (1974). Brainstorming procedure, group size, and sex as determinants of the problem-solving effectiveness of groups and individuals. *Journal of Applied Psychology, 59*, 135–138.

Bouchard, T. J., Drauden, G., & Barsaloux, J. (1974). A comparison of individual, subgroup, and total group methods of problem solving. *Journal of Applied Psychology, 59*, 226–227.

Bouchard, T. J., & Hare, M. (1970). Size, performance, and potential in brainstorming groups. *Journal of Applied Psychology, 54*, 51–55.

Bowers, D. G., & Seashore, S. E. (1966). Predicting organizational effectiveness with a four-factor theory of leadership. *Administrative Science Quarterly, 11*, 238–263.

Bowlby, J. (1980). *Attachment and loss* (Vol. 1). London: Hogarth.

Boyd, R., & Lorberbaum, J. P. (1987). No pure strategy is evolutionarily stable in the repeated Prisoner's Dilemma game. *Nature, 327*, 58–59.

Bradley, P. H. (1978). Power, status, and upward communication in small decision-making groups. *Communication Monographs, 45*, 33–43.

Braginsky, D. D. (1970). Machiavellianism and manipulative interpersonal behavior in children. *Journal of Experimental Social Psychology, 6*, 77–99.

Bramel, D., & Friend, R. (1981). Hawthorne, the myth of the docile worker, and class bias in psychology. *American Psychologist, 36*, 867–878.

Bray, R. M., Johnson, D., & Chilstrom, J. T., Jr. (1982). Social influence by group members with minority opinions: A comparison of Hollander & Moscovici. *Journal of Personality and Social Psychology, 43*, 78–88.

Bray, R. M., Kerr, N. L., & Atkin, R. S. (1978). Effects of group size, problem difficulty, and sex on group performance and member reactions. *Journal of Personality and Social Psychology, 36*, 1224–1240.

Brechner, K. C. (1977). An experimental analysis of social traps. *Journal of Experimental Social Psychology, 13*, 552–564.

Brehm, J. W. (1976). Responses to loss of freedom: A theory of psychological reactance. In J. W. Thibaut, J. T. Spence, & R. C. Carson (Eds.), *Contemporary topics in social psychology* (pp. 51–78). Morristown, NJ: General Learning Press.

Brehm, J. W., & Mann, M. (1975). Effect of importance of freedom and attraction to group members on influence produced by group pressure. *Journal of Personality and Social Psychology, 31*, 816–824.

Brehm, J. W., & Sensenig, J. (1966). Social influence as a function of attempted and implied usurpation of choice. *Journal of Personality and Social Psychology, 4*, 703–707.

Brehm, S. S., & Brehm, J. W. (1981). *Psychological reactance: A theory of freedom and control*. New York: Academic Press.

Breiger, R. L., & Ennis, J. G. (1979). Personae and social roles: The network structure of personality types in small groups. *Social Psychology Quarterly, 42*, 262–270.

Brenner, O. C., & Vinacke, W. E. (1979). Accommodative and exploitative behavior of males versus females versus managers versus nonmanagers as measured by the Test of Strategy. *Social Psychology Quarterly, 42*, 289–293.

Brewer, M. B. (1979). In-group bias in the minimal intergroup situation: A cognitive-motivational analysis. *Psychological Bulletin, 86*, 307–324.

Brewer, M. B. (1986). The role of ethnocentrism in intergroup conflict. In S. Worchel & W. G. Austin (Eds.), *Psychology of intergroup relations* (2nd ed., pp. 88–102). Chicago: Nelson-Hall.

Brewer, M. B., & Campbell, D. T. (1976). *Ethnocentrism and intergroup attitudes: East African evidence*. New York: Halsted Press.

Brewer, M. B., & Kramer, R. M. (1985). The psychology of intergroup attitudes and behavior. *Annual Review of Psychology, 36,* 219–243.

Brewer, M. B., & Kramer, R. M. (1986). Choice behavior in social dilemmas: Effects of social identity, group size, and decision framing. *Journal of Personality and Social Psychology, 50,* 543–549.

Brewer, M. B., & Miller, N. (1984). Beyond the contact hypothesis: theoretical perspectives on desegregation. In N. Miller & M. Brewer (Eds.), *Groups in contact: The psychology of desegregation* (pp. 281–302). New York: Academic Pess.

Brickman, P., Becker, L. J., & Castle, S. (1979). Making trust easier and harder through two forms of sequential interaction. *Journal of Personality and Social Psychology, 37,* 515–521.

Brickner, M. A., Harkins, S. G., & Ostrom, T. M. (1986). Effects of personal involvement: Thought-provoking implications for social loafing. *Journal of Personality and Social Psychology, 51,* 763–770.

Brief, A. P., Schuler, R. S., & Van Sell, M. (1981). *Managing job stress.* Boston: Little Brown.

Brockner, J., & Rubin, J. Z. (1985). *The social psychology of conflict escalation and entrapment.* New York: Springer-Verlag.

Brockner, J., Shaw, M. C., & Rubin, J. Z. (1979). Factors affecting withdrawal from an escalating conflict: Quitting before it's too late. *Journal of Experimental Social Psychology, 15,* 492–503.

Brockner, J., & Swap, W. C. (1976). Effects of repeated exposure and attitudinal similarity on self-disclosure and interpersonal attraction. *Journal of Personality and Social Psychology, 33,* 531–540.

Bronfenbrenner, U. (1961). The mirror image in Soviet-American relations: A social psychologist's report. *Journal of Social Issues, 17*(3), 45–56.

Brown, B. B. (1987). Territoriality. In D. Stokols & I. Altman (Eds.), *Handbook of environmental psychology* (Vol. 1, pp. 505–531). New York: Wiley.

Brown, B. B., & Lohr, M. J. (1987). Peer-group affiliation and adolescent self-esteem: An integration of ego-identity and symbolic-interaction theories. *Journal of Personality and Social Psychology, 52,* 47–55.

Brown, B. R. (1977). Face-saving and face-restoration in negotiation. In D. Druckman (Ed.), *Negotiations* (pp. 275–299). Newbury Park, CA: Sage.

Brown, R. (1988). *Group processes: Dynamics within and between groups.* New York: Blackwell.

Brown, R., Condor, S., Matthews, A., Wade, G., & Williams, J. A. (1986). Explaining intergroup differentiation in an industrial organization. *Journal of Occupational Psychology, 59,* 273–286.

Brown, R. W. (1954). Mass phenomena. In G. Lindzey (Ed.), *Handbook of social psychology* (Vol. 2, pp. 833–876). Cambridge, MA: Addison-Wesley.

Brown, R. (1965). *Social Psychology.* New York: Free Press.

Brown, S., & Beletsis, S. (1986). The development of family transference in groups for the adult children of alcoholics. *International Journal of Group Psychotherapy, 36,* 97–114.

Brown, V., & Geis, F. L. (1984). Turning lead into gold: Evaluations of men and women leaders and the alchemy of social consensus. *Journal of Personality and Social Psychology, 46,* 811–824.

Browning, L. (1978). A grounded organizational communication theory derived from qualitative data. *Communication Monographs, 45,* 93–109.

Buby, C. M., & Penner, L. A. (1974). Conformity as a function of response position. *Psychological Reports, 34,* 938.

Buckley, W. (1967). *Sociology and modern systems theory.* Englewood Cliffs, NJ: Prentice-Hall.

Budman, P. H. (1981). Significant treatment factors in short term group psychotherapy. *Group, 5,* 25–31.

Bugliosi, V. (1974). *Helter Skelter.* New York: Bantam.

Buller, P. F. (1986). The team building-task performance relation: Some conceptual and methodological refinements. *Group and Organization Studies, 11,* 147–168.

Buller, P. F. (1988). For successful strategic change: Blend OD practices with strategic management. *Organizational Dynamics, 16,* 52–55.

Burgoon, J. K. (1983). Nonverbal violations of expectations. In J. M. Wiemann & R. P. Harrison (Eds.), *Sage annual reviews of com-*

munication: Nonverbal interaction (Vol. 11). Newbury Park, CA: Sage.

Burke, M. J., & Day, R. R. (1986). A cumulative study of the effectiveness of managerial training. *Journal of Applied Psychology, 71,* 232–245.

Burke, P. J. (1967). The development of task and social-emotional role differentiation. *Sociometry, 30,* 379–392.

Burke, P. J. (1974). Participation and leadership in small groups. *American Sociological Review, 39,* 832–842.

Burke, R. J. (1970). Methods of resolving superior-subordinate conflict: The constructive use of subordinate differences and disagreements. *Organizational Behavior and Human Performance, 5,* 393–411.

Burns, J. M. (1978). *Leadership.* New York: Harper.

Burnstein, E., & Vinokur, A. (1973). Testing two classes of theories about group-induced shifts in individual choice. *Journal of Experimental Social Psychology, 9,* 123–137.

Burnstein, E., & Vinokur, A. (1975). What a person thinks upon learning he has chosen differently from others: Nice evidence for the persuasive-arguments explanation of choice shifts. *Journal of Experimental Social Psychology, 11,* 412–426.

Burnstein, E., & Vinokur, A. (1977). Persuasive arguments and social comparison as determinants of attitude polarization. *Journal of Experimental Social Psychology, 13,* 315–332.

Burwitz, L., & Newell, K. M. (1972). The effects of the mere presence of coactors on learning a motor skill. *Journal of Motor Behavior, 4,* 99–102.

Bushman, B. J. (1984). Perceived symbols of authority and their influence on compliance. *Journal of Applied Social Psychology, 14,* 501–508.

Bushman, B. J. (1988). The effects of apparel on compliance: A field experiment with a female authority figure. *Personality and Social Psychology Bulletin, 14,* 459–467.

Buss, A. H. (1961). *The psychology of aggression.* New York: Wiley.

Buss, D. M. (1981). Sex differences in the evaluation and performance of dominant acts. *Journal of Personality and Social Psychology, 40,* 147–154.

Buss, D. M., Gomes, M., Higgins, D. S., & Lauterbach, K. (1987). Tactics of manip-

ulation. *Journal of Personality and Social Psychology, 52,* 1219–1229.

Butler, T., & Fuhriman, A. (1983a). Curative factors in group therapy: A review of the recent literature. *Small Group Behavior, 14,* 131–142.

Butler, T., Fuhriman, A. (1983b). Level of functioning and length of time in treatment variables influencing patients' therapeutic experience in group psychotherapy. *International Journal of Group Psychotherapy, 33,* 489–505.

Buys, C. J. (1978). Humans would do better without groups. *Personality and Social Psychology Bulletin, 4,* 123–125.

Byrne, D. (1971). *The attraction paradigm.* New York: Academic Press.

Byrne, D., Ervin, C. R., & Lamberth, J. (1970). Continuity between the experimental study of attraction and real-life computer dating. *Journal of Personality and Social Psychology, 16,* 157–165.

Calhoun, J. B. (1962). Population density and social pathology. *Scientific American, 206,* 139–148.

Callaway, M. R., & Esser, J. K. (1984). Groupthink: Effects of cohesiveness and problem-solving procedures on group decision making. *Social Behavior and Personality, 12,* 157–164.

Callaway, M. R., Marriott, R. G., & Esser, J. K. (1985). Effects of dominance on group decision making: Toward a stress- reduction explanation of groupthink. *Journal of Personality and Social Psychology, 49,* 949–952.

Campbell, D. T. (1958a). Common fate, similarity, and other indices of the status of aggregates of persons as social entities. *Behavioral Science, 3,* 14–25.

Campbell, D. T. (1958b). Systematic error on the part of human links in communication systems. *Information and Control, 1,* 334–369.

Campbell, D. T. (1965). Ethnocentric and other altruistic motives. In D. Levine (Ed.), *Nebraska symposium on motivation* (Vol. 13). Lincoln: University of Nebraska Press.

Campbell, J. D., Tesser, A., & Fairey, P. J. (1986). Conformity and attention to the stimulus: Some temporal and contextual dynamics. *Journal of Personality and Social Psychology, 51,* 315–324.

Canary, D. J., Cody, M. J., & Marston, P. J. (1986). Goal types, compliance-gaining, and locus of control. *Journal of Language and Social Psychology, 5*, 249–269.

Canetti, E. (1962). *Crowds and power*. London: Gollancz.

Cannavale, F. J., Scarr, H. A., & Pepitone, A. (1970). Deindividuation in the small group: Further evidence. *Journal of Personality and Social Psychology, 16*, 141–147.

Cantril, H. (1940). *The invasion from Mars*. Princeton: Princeton University Press.

Caplow, T. (1956). A theory of coalitions in the triad. *American Sociological Review, 21*, 489–493.

Caplow, T. (1968). *Two against one*. Englewood Cliffs, NJ: Prentice-Hall.

Carew, D. K., Parisi-Carew, E., & Blanchard, K. H. (1986). Group development and situational leadership: A model for managing groups. *Training and Development Journal, 40*(6), 46–50.

Carlyle, T. (1841). *On heroes, hero-worship, and the heroic*. London: Fraser.

Carment, D. W. (1970). Rate of simple motor responding as a function of coaction, competition, and sex of the participants. *Psychonomic Science, 19*, 340–341.

Carneiro, R. L. (1970). A theory of the origin of the state. *Science, 169*, 239–249.

Carnevale, P. J. D. (1986a). Mediating disputes and decisions in organizations. In R. J. Lewicki, B. H. Sheppard, & M. H. Bazerman (Eds.), *Research on negotiation in organizations* (Vol. 1, pp. 251–269). Greenwich, CT: JAI Press.

Carnevale, P. J. D. (1986b). Strategic choice in mediation. *Negotiation Journal, 2*, 41–56.

Carnevale, P. J. D., Pruitt, D. G., & Seilheimer, S. (1981). Looking and competing: Accountability and visual access in integrative bargaining. *Journal of Personality and Social Psychology, 40*, 111–120.

Carpenter, C. R. (1958). Territoriality: A review of concepts and problems. In A. Roe & G. G. Simpson (Eds.), *Behavior and evolution*. New Haven: Yale University Press.

Carroll, J. W. (1987). Indefinite terminating points and the iterated Prisoner's Dilemma. *Theory and Decision, 22*, 247–256.

Carron, A. V. (1980). *Social psychology of sport*. Ithaca, NY: Mouvement Publications.

Carron, A. V., & Chelladurai, P. (1981). The dynamics of group cohesion in sport. *Journal of Sport Psychology, 3*, 123–139.

Carson, R. C. (1969). *Interaction concepts of personality*. Chicago: Aldine.

Carter, L. F. (1954). Recording and evaluating the performance of individuals as members of small groups. *Personnel Psychology, 7*, 477–484.

Carter, L. F., Haythorn, W., & Howell, M. (1950). A further investigation of the criteria of leadership. *Journal of Abnormal and Social Psychology, 45*, 350–358.

Cartwright, D. (1951). Achieving change in people: Some applications of group dynamics theory. *Human Relations, 4*, 381–392.

Cartwright, D. (1959). A field theoretical conception of power. In D. Cartwright (Ed.), *Studies in social power*. Ann Arbor, MI: Institute for Social Research.

Cartwright, D. (1968). The nature of group cohesiveness. In D. Cartwright & A. Zander (Eds.), *Group dynamics: Research and theory* (3rd ed., pp. 91–109). New York: Harper & Row.

Cartwright, D. (1978). Theory and practice. *Journal of Social Issues, 34*(4), 168–175.

Cartwright, D., & Harary, F. (1956). Structural balance: A generalization of Heider's theory. *Psychological Review, 63*, 277–293.

Cartwright, D., & Harary, F. (1970). Ambivalence and indifference in generalizations of structural balance. *Behavioral Science, 14*, 497–513.

Cartwright, D., & Zander, A. (1968). *Group dynamics: Research and theory* (3rd ed.). New York: Harper & Row.

Carver, C. S. (1975). Physical aggression as a function of objective self-awareness and attitudes toward punishment. *Journal of Experimental Social Psychology, 11*, 510–519.

Carver, C. S., & Scheier, M. F. (1981). *Attention and self-regulation: A control-theory approach to human behavior*. New York: Springer-Verlag.

Carver, C. S., & Scheier, M. F. (1983). Two sides of the self: One for you and one for me. In J. Suls & A. G. Greenwald (Eds.), *Psychological perspectives on the self* (Vol. 2). Hillsdale, NJ: Erlbaum.

Carver, C. S., & Scheier, M. F. (1984). Self-focused attention in test anxiety: A general theory applied to a specific phenomenon. In H. van der Ploeg, R. Schwarzer, & C. D. Spielberger (Eds.), *Advances in test anxiety research* (Vol. 3). Hillsdale, NJ: Erlbaum.

Castore, C. H., & Murnighan, J. K. (1978). Determinants of support for group decisions. *Organizational Behavior and Human Performance, 22*, 75–92.

Cattell, R. B. (1948). Concepts and methods in the measurement of group syntality. *Psychological Review, 55*, 48–63.

Cavalli, L. (1986). Charismatic domination, totalitarian dictatorship, and plebiscitary democracy in the twentieth century. In C. F. Graumann & S. Moscovici (Eds.), *Changing conceptions of leadership* (pp. 67–81). New York: Springer-Verlag.

Chapanis, A., Garner, W. R., & Morgan, C. T. (1949). *Applied experimental psychology: Human factors in engineering design.* New York: Wiley.

Chapman, A. J. (1973). Funniness of jokes, canned laughter, and recall performance. *Sociometry, 36*, 569–578.

Chemers, M. M. (1983). Leadership theory and research: A systems-process integration. In P. B. Paulus (Ed.), *Basic group processes* (pp. 9–39). New York: Springer-Verlag.

Chemers, M. M. (1987). Leadership processes: Intrapersonal, interpersonal, and societal influences. In C. Hendrick (Ed.), *Review of Personality and Social Psychology: Group Process* (Vol. 8, pp. 252–277). Newbury Park, CA: Sage.

Chemers, M. M., Hays, R. B., Rhodewalt, F., & Wysocki, J. (1985). A person-environment analysis of job stress: A contingency model explanation. *Journal of Personality and Social Psychology, 49*, 628–635.

Chemers, M. M., & Skrzypek, G. J. (1972). Experimental test of the contingency model of leadership effectiveness. *Journal of Personality and Social Psychology, 24*, 173–177.

Cheng, J. L. (1983). Organizational context and upward influence: An experimental study of the use of power tactics. *Group and Organization Studies, 8*, 337–355.

Cheyne, J. A., & Efran, M. G. (1972). The effect of spatial and interpersonal variables on the invasion of group controlled territories. *Sociometry, 35*, 477–487.

Childers, T. L., Dubinsky, A. J., & Gencturk, E. (1986). On the psychometric properties of a scale to measure leadership substitutes. *Psychological Reports, 59*, 1215–1226.

Cialdini, R. B., Borden, R., Thorne, A., Walker, M., Freeman, S., & Sloane, L. R. (1976). Basking in reflected glory: Three (football) field studies. *Journal of Personality and Social Psychology, 34*, 366–375.

Cialdini, R. B., & Richardson, K. D. (1980). Two indirect tactics of image management: Basking and blasting. *Journal of Personality and Social Psychology, 39*, 406–415.

Clark, G. (1969). What happens when the police strike? *New York Times Magazine*, November, 45.

Clark, K. B. (1971). The pathos of power. *American Psychologist, 26*, 1047–1057.

Clark, R. D., III. (1971). Group-induced shift toward risk: A critical appraisal. *Psychological Bulletin, 76*, 251–270.

Clark, R. D., III, & Sechrest, L. B. (1976). The mandate phenomenon. *Journal of Personality and Social Psychology, 34*, 1057–1061.

Clayton, D. A. (1978). Socially facilitated behavior. *The Quarterly Review of Biology, 53*, 373–392.

Clore, G. L., & Byrne, D. (1974). A reinforcement-affect model of attraction. In T. Huston (Ed.), *Foundations of interpersonal attraction.* New York: Academic Press.

Coalter, F. (1985). Crowd behaviour at football matches: A study in Scotland. *Leisure Studies, 4*, 111–117.

Coch, L., & French, J. R. P. (1948). Overcoming resistance to change. *Human Relations, 1*, 512–532.

Cohen, D. J., Whitmyre, J. W., & Funk, W. H. (1960). Effect of group cohesiveness and training upon group thinking. *Journal of Applied Psychology, 44*, 319–322.

Cohen, E. G. (1982). Expectation states and interracial interaction in school settings. *Annual Review of Sociology, 8*, 209–235.

Cohen, E. G., & Roper, S. (1972). Modification of interracial interaction disability: An application of status characteristics theory. *American Sociological Review, 37*, 643–655.

Cohen, J. L. (1979). Social facilitation: Increased evaluation apprehension through permanency of record. *Motivation and Emotion, 3*, 19–33.

Cohen, S. (1980). Aftereffects of stress on human performance and social behavior: A review of research and theory. *Psychological Bulletin, 88*, 82–108.

Cohen, S., & Weinstein, N. (1981). Non-auditory effects of noise on behavior and health. *Journal of Social Issues, 37*(1), 36–70.

Cohen, S., & Wills, T. A. (1985). Stress, social support, and the buffering hypothesis. *Psychological Bulletin, 98*, 310–357.

Coie, J. D., Dodge, K. A., & Coppotelli, H. (1982). Dimensions and types of social status: A cross-age perspective. *Developmental Psychology, 18*, 557–570.

Cole, D. W. (1987). Organization development and its implications for innovative management in the 1990s. *Organization Development Journal, 5*, 5–10.

Cole, S. A. (1983). Self-help groups. In H. I. Kaplan & B. J. Sadock (Eds.), *Comprehensive group psychotherapy* (2nd. ed., pp. 144–150). Baltimore: Williams & Wilkins.

Coleman, J. F., Blake, R. R., & Mouton, J. S. (1958). Task difficulty and conformity pressures. *Journal of Abnormal and Social Psychology, 57*, 120–122.

Colligan, M. J., & Murphy, L. R. (1982). A review of mass psychogenic illness in work settings. In M. J. Colligan, J. W. Pennebaker, & L. R. Murphy (Eds.), *Mass psychogenic illness: A social psychological analysis* (pp. 33–52). Hillsdale, NJ: Erlbaum.

Colligan, M. J., Pennebaker, J. W., & Murphy, L. R. (Eds.). (1982). *Mass psychogenic illness: A social psychological analysis.* Hillsdale, NJ: Erlbaum.

Comer, R., & Laird, J. D. (1975) Choosing to suffer as a consequence of expecting to suffer: Why do people do it? *Journal of Personality and Social Psychology, 32*, 92–101.

Condor, S., & Brown, R. (1988). Psychological processes in intergroup conflict. In W. Stroebe, A. W. Kruglanski, D. Bar-Tal, & M. Hewstone (Eds.), *The social psychology of intergroup conflict* (pp. 3–26). New York: Springer-Verlag.

Condry, J. (1977). Enemies of exploration: Self initiated versus other initiated learning. *Journal of Personality and Social Psychology, 35*, 459–477.

Cook, M. (1977). The social skill model and interpersonal attraction. In S. Duck (Ed.), *Theory and practice in interpersonal attraction.* New York: Academic Press.

Cook, S. W. (1978). Interpersonal and attitudinal outcomes in cooperating interracial groups. *Journal of Research and Development in Education, 12*, 97–113.

Cook, S. W. (1981). Ethical implications. In L. H. Kidder (Ed.), *Research methods in social relations* (4th ed.). New York: Holt, Rinehart, & Winston.

Cook, S. W. (1984). The 1954 social science statement and school desegregation: A reply to Gerard. *American Psychologist, 39*, 819–832.

Cook, S. W. (1985). Experimenting on social issues: The case of school desegregation. *American Psychology, 40*, 452–460.

Cook, T. D. (1985). Postpositivist critical multiplism. In R. L. Shotland & M. M. Marks (Eds.), *Social science and social policy.* Newbury Park, CA: Sage.

Cook, T. D., & Campbell, D. T. (1979). *Quasi-experimentation: Design and analysis issues for field settings.* Boston: Houghton-Mifflin.

Cooley, C. H. (1902). *Human nature and the social order.* New York: Scribner.

Cooley, C. H. (1909). *Social organization.* New York: Scribner.

Cooper, C. L. (1981). Social support at work and stress management. *Small Group Behavior, 12*, 285–297.

Cooper, G. E., White, M. D., & Lauber, J. K. (Eds.) (1979, June). *Resource management on the flight deck (NASA Report No. CP-2120).* Moffett Field, CA: NASA-Ames Research Center. NTIS No. N80-22283.

Cooper, H. M. (1979). Statistically combining independent studies: A metaanalysis of sex differences in conformity research. *Journal of Personality and Social Psychology, 37*, 131–146.

Cooper, J., & Fazio, R. H. (1986). The formation and persistence of attitudes that support intergroup conflict. In S. Worchel & W. G. Austin (Eds.), *Psychology of intergroup relations* (2nd ed., pp. 183–195). Chicago: Nelson-Hall.

Coser, L. A. (1956). *The functions of social conflict.* Glencoe, IL: Free Press.

Cotton, J., & Cook, M. (1982). Meta-analyses and effects of various systems: Some different conclusions from Johnson et al. *Psychological Bulletin, 92*, 176–183.

Cottrell, N. B. (1972). Social facilitation. In C. G. McClintock (Ed.), *Experimental social psychology* (pp. 185–236). New York: Holt, Rinehart, & Winston.

Cottrell, N. B., Wack, D. L., Sekerak, G. J., & Rittle, R. H. (1968). Social facilitation of dominant responses by the presence of an audience and the mere presence of others. *Journal of Personality and Social Psychology, 9,* 245–250.

Courtright, J. A. (1978). A laboratory investigation of groupthink. *Communication Monographs, 43,* 229–246.

Cowan, G., Drinkard, J., & MacGavin, L. (1984). The effects of target, age, and gender on use of power strategies. *Journal of Personality and Social Psychology, 47,* 1391–1398.

Cox, V. C., Paulus, P. B., & McCain, G. (1984). Prison crowding research: The relevance for prison housing standards and a general approach regarding crowding phenomena. *American Psychologist, 39,* 1148–1160.

Craddock, A. E. (1985). Centralized authority as a factor in small group and family problem solving. *Small Group Behavior, 16,* 59–73.

Crago, M., Yates, Beutler, L. E., & Arizmendi, T. G. (1985). Height-weight ratios among female athletes: Are collegiate athletics the precurors to an anorexic syndrome? *International Journal of Eating Disorders, 4,* 79–87.

Craig, J. M., & Sherif, C. W. (1986). The effectiveness of men and women in problem-solving groups as a function of group gender composition. *Sex Roles, 14,* 453–466.

Crandall, C. S. (1988). Social contagion of binge eating. *Journal of Personality and Social Psychology, 55,* 588–598.

Cribbin, J. J. (1972). *Effective managerial leadership.* New York: American Management Association.

Crocker, J., & McGraw, K. M. (1984). What's good for the goose is not good for the gander: Solo status as an obstacle to occupational achievement for males and females. *American Behavioral Scientist, 27,* 357–369.

Crocker, J., Thompson, L. L., McGraw, K. M., & Ingerman, C. (1987). Downward comparison, prejudice, and evaluations of others: Effects of self-esteem and threat. *Journal of Personality and Social Psychology, 52,* 907–916.

Crocker, O. L., Chiu, J. S. L., & Charney, C. (1984). *Quality circles.* Ontario, Canada: Methuen.

Cronshaw, S. F., & Lord, R. G. (1987). Effects of categorization, attribution, and encoding processes on leadership perceptions. *Journal of Applied Psychology, 72,* 97–106.

Crook, J. H. (1981). The evolutionary ethology of social processes in man. In H. Kellerman (Ed.), *Group cohesion.* New York: Grune & Stratton.

Crosbie, P. V. (1979). Effects of status inconsistency: Negative evidence from small groups. *Social Psychology Quarterly, 42,* 110–125.

Crow, W. J. (1963). A study of strategic doctrines using the Inter-Nation Simulation. *Journal of Conflict Resolution, 7,* 580–589.

Crutchfield, R. S. (1955). Conformity and character. *American Psychologist, 10,* 191–198.

Csoka, L. S., & Bons, P. M. (1978). Manipulating the situation to fit the leader's style—Two validation studies of Leader Match. *Journal of Applied Psychology, 63,* 295–300.

Cummings, L. L., Harnett, D. L., & Stevens, O. J. (1971). Risk, fate, conciliation and trust: An international study of attitudinal differences among executives. *Academy of Management Journal, 14,* 285–304.

Cunningham, J. D., Starr, P. A., & Kanouse, D. E. (1979). Self as actor, active observer, and passive observer: Implications for causal attributions. *Journal of Personality and Social Psychology, 37,* 1146–1152.

Curran, J. P. (1977). Skills training as an approach to the treatment of heterosexual-social anxiety: A review. *Psychological Bulletin, 84,* 140–157.

Curry, T. J., & Emerson, R. M. (1971). Balance theory: A theory of interpersonal attraction? *Sociometry, 33,* 216–238.

Cutrona, C. E. (1986). Objective determinants of perceived social support. *Journal of Personality and Social Psychology, 50,* 349–355.

Cyert, R. M., & March, J. G. (1963). *A behavioral theory of the firm.* Englewood Cliffs, NJ: Prentice-Hall.

Dahrendorf, R. (1958). Toward a theory of social conflict. *Journal of Conflict Resolution, 2,* 170–183.

Dahrendorf, R. (1959). *Class and class conflict in industrial society.* Palo Alto, CA: Stanford University Press.

Dale, R. (1952). *Planning and developing the company organization structure.* New York: American Management Association.

Dane, F. C., & Wrightsman, L. S. (1982). Effects of defendants' and victims' characteristics on jurors' verdicts. In N. L. Kerr & R. M. Bray (Eds.), *Psychology of the courtroom* (pp. 83–115). New York: Academic Press.

Darley, J. G., Gross, N., & Martin, W. E. (1951). Studies of group behavior: The stability, change, and interrelations of psychometric and sociometric variables. *Journal of Abnormal and Social Psychology, 46,* 565–576.

Darley, J. M., & Aronson, E. (1966). Self-evaluation vs. direct anxiety reduction as determinants of the fear-affiliation relationship. *Journal of Experimental Social Psychology,* Supplement 1, 66–79.

Darley, J. M., & Fazio, R. H. (1980). Expectancy confirmation processes arising in the social interaction sequence. *American Psychologist, 35,* 867–881.

Darley, J. M., & Gilbert, D. T. (1985). Social psychological aspects of environmental psychology. In G. Lindzey & E. Aronson (Eds.), *Handbook of Social Psychology* (Vol. 2, 3rd ed., pp. 949–991). New York: Random House.

Darley, J. M., & Gross, P. H. (1983). A hypothesis-confirming bias in labeling effects. *Journal of Personality and Social Psychology, 44,* 20–33.

Dashiell, J. F. (1930). An experimental analysis of some group effects. *Journal of Abnormal and Social Psychology, 25,* 190–199.

Davis, J. H. (1969). *Group performance.* Reading, MA: Addison-Wesley, 1969.

Davis, J. H. (1973). Group decision and social interaction: A theory of social decision schemes. *Psychological Review, 80,* 97–125.

Davis, J. H. (1982). Social interaction as a combinatorial process in group decision. In H. Brandstatter, J. H. Davis, & G. Stocker-Kreichgauer (Eds.), *Group decision making* (pp. 27–58). London: Academic Press.

Davis, J. H., Bray, R. M., & Holt, R. W. (1977). The empirical study of decision processes in juries: A critical review. In J. L. Tapp & F. J. Levine (Eds.), *Law, justice, and the individual in society.* New York: Holt, Rinehart, & Winston.

Davis, J. H., Kerr, N. L., Atkin, R. S., Holt, R., & Meek, D. (1975). The decision processes of 6- and 12-person juries assigned unanimous and 2/3 majority rules. *Journal of Personality and Social Psychology, 32,* 1–14.

Davis, J. H., Kerr, N. L., Stasser, G., Meek, D., & Holt, R. (1977). Victim consequences, sentence severity, and decision processes in mock juries. *Organizational Behavior and Human Performance, 18,* 346–365.

Davis, J. H., & Stasson, M. F. (1988). Small group performance: Past and present research trends. In E. J. Lawler & B. Markovsky (Eds.), *Advances in group processes* (Vol. 5, pp. 245–277). Greenwich, CT: JAI Press.

Davis, J. H., Stasson, M., Ono, K., & Zimmerman, S. (1988). Effects of straw polls on group decision making: Sequential voting pattern, timing, and local majorities. *Journal of Personality and Social Psychology, 55,* 918–926.

Davis, J. R. (1982). *Street gangs: Youth, biker, and prison groups.* Dubuque, IO: Kendall/Hunt.

Dawes, R. M. (1980). Social dilemmas. *Annual Review of Psychology, 31,* 169–193.

Dawes, R. M., & Smith, T. L. (1985). Attitude and opinion measurement. In G. Lindzey & E. Aronson (Eds.), *Handbook of Social Psychology* (Vol. 1, 3rd ed., pp. 509–566). New York: Random House.

Day, M. (1981). Psychoanalytic group therapy in clinic and private practice. *American Journal of Psychiatry, 138,* 64–69.

Dean, L. M., Willis, F. N., & Hewitt, J. (1975). Initial interaction distance among individuals equal and unequal in military rank. *Journal of Personality and Social Psychology, 32,* 294–299.

Deaux, K. (1976). *The behavior of women and men.* Pacific Grove, CA: Brooks/Cole.

Deci, E. L., & Ryan, R. M. (1985). *Intrinsic motivation and self-determination in human behavior.* New York: Plenum.

Dedrick, D. K. (1978). Deviance and sanctioning within small groups. *Social Psychology, 41,* 94–105.

Defoe, D. (1908). *The life and strange surprising adventures of Robinson Crusoe, of York, mariner, as related by himself.* Philadelphia: Altemus.

DeLamater, J. A. (1974). A definition of "group." *Small Group Behavior, 5,* 30–44.

Delbecq, A. L., & Van de Ven, A. H. (1971). A group process model for problem identification and program planning. *Journal of Applied Behavioral Science, 7,* 466–492.

Delbecq, A. L., Van de Ven, A. H., & Gustafson, D. H. (1975). *Group techniques for program planning.* Glenview, IL: Scott, Foresman.

Deming, W. E. (1975). On some statistical aids towards economic production. *Interfaces, 5,* 1–15.

Deutsch, M. (1949a). An experimental study of the effects of cooperation and competition upon group process. *Human Relations, 2,* 199–231.

Deutsch, M. (1949b). A theory of cooperation and competition. *Human Relations, 2,* 129–152.

Deutsch, M. (1958). Trust and suspicion. *Journal of Conflict Resolution, 2,* 265–279.

Deutsch, M. (1960). The effect of motivational orientation upon trust and suspicion. *Human Relations, 13,* 123–139.

Deutsch, M. (1968). Group behavior. In D. L. Sills (ed.), *International Encyclopedia of the Social Sciences* (Vol 6). New York: Macmillan.

Deutsch, M. (1969). Socially relevant science: Reflections on some studies of interpersonal conflict. *American Psychologist, 24,* 1076–1092.

Deutsch, M. (1973). *The resolution of conflict.* New Haven, CT: Yale University Press.

Deutsch, M. (1980). Fifty years of conflict. In L. Festinger (Ed.), *Retrospections on social psychology* (pp. 46–77). New York: Oxford University Press.

Deutsch, M. (1985). *Distributive justice: A social psychological perspective.* New Haven, CT: Yale University Press.

Deutsch, M., & Gerard, H. B. (1955). A study of normative and informational social influences upon individual judgment. *Journal of Abnormal and Social Psychology, 51,* 629–636.

Deutsch, M., & Krauss, R. M. (1960). The effect of threat upon interpersonal bargaining. *Journal of Abnormal and Social Psychology, 61,* 181–189.

Deutsch, M., & Krauss, R. M. (1962). Studies of interpersonal bargaining. *Journal of Conflict Resolution, 6,* 52–76.

Deutsch, M., & Lewicki, R. J. (1970). "Locking in" effects during a game of Chicken. *Journal of Conflict Resolution, 14,* 367–378.

Deutsch, M., & Solomon, L. (1959). Reactions to evaluations by others as influenced by self-evaluations. *Sociometry, 22,* 93–112.

DeVries, D. L., Edwards, K. J., & Fennessey, G. M. (1973). *Using Teams-Games-Tournaments (TGT) in the classroom.* Baltimore, MD: Center for Social Organization in Schools, Johns Hopkins University.

Dewey, J. (1910). *How we think.* New York: Heath.

Diehl, M., & Stroebe, W. (1987). Productivity loss in brainstorming groups: Toward the solution of a riddle. *Journal of Personality and Social Psychology, 53,* 497–509.

Diener, E. (1979). Deindividuation, self-awareness, and disinhibition. *Journal of Personality and Social Psychology, 37,* 1160–1171.

Diener, E. (1980). Deindividuation: The absence of self-awareness and self-regulation in group members. In P. B. Paulus (Ed.), *Psychology of group influence* (209–242). Hillsdale, NJ: Erlbaum.

Diener, E., Dineen, J., Endresen, K., Beaman, A. L., & Fraser, S. C. (1975). Effects of altered responsibility, cognitive set, and modeling on physical aggression and deindividuation. *Journal of Personality and Social Psychology, 31,* 328–337.

Diener, E., Fraser, S. C., Beaman, A. L., & Kelem, R. T. (1976). Effects of deindividuating variables on stealing by Halloween trick-or-treaters. *Journal of Personality and Social Psychology, 33,* 178–183.

Diener, E., Lusk, R., DeFour, D., & Flax, R. (1980). Deindividuation: Effects of group size, density, number of observers, and group member similarity on self-consciousness and disinhibited behavior. *Journal of Personality and Social Psychology, 39,* 449–459.

Dillard, J. P., & Fitzpatrick, M. A. (1985). Compliance-gaining in marital interaction. *Personality and Social Psychology Bulletin, 11*, 419–433.

Dion, K. K., & Stein, S. (1978). Physical attractiveness and interpersonal influence. *Journal of Experimental Social Psychology, 14*, 97–108.

Dion, K. L. (1973). Cohesiveness as a determinant of ingroup-outgroup bias. *Journal of Personality and Social Psychology, 28*, 163–171.

Dion, K. L. (1979). Intergroup conflict and intragroup cohesiveness. In W. G. Austin & S. Worchel (Eds.), *The social psychology of intergroup relations* (pp. 211–224). Pacific Grove, CA: Brooks/Cole.

Dion, K. L. (1985). Sex, gender, and groups: Selected issues. In V. O'Leary, R. K. Unger, & B. Strudler-Wallston (Eds.), *Women, gender, and social psychology* (pp. 293–347). Hillsdale, NJ: Erlbaum.

Dion, K. L., Baron, R. S., & Miller, N. (1970). Why do groups make riskier decisions than individuals? In L. Berkowitz (Ed.), *Advances in experimental social psychology* (Vol. 5, pp. 306–377). New York: Academic Press.

Dipboye, R. L. (1977). Alternative approaches to deindividuation. *Psychological Bulletin, 84*, 1057–1075.

Dittes, J. E., & Kelley, H. H. (1956). Effects of different conditions of acceptance upon conformity to group norms. *Journal of Abnormal and Social Psychology, 53*, 100–107.

Dobbins, G. H., & Platz, S. J. (1986). Sex differences in leadership: How real are they? *Academy of Management Review, 11*, 118–127.

Dobbins, G. H., Stuart, C., Pence, E. C., & Sgro, J. A. (1985). Cognitive mechanisms mediating the biasing effects of leader sex on ratings of leader behavior. *Sex Roles, 12*, 549–560.

Dodd, D. K. (1985). Robbers in the classroom: A deindividuation exercise. *Teaching of Psychology, 12*, 89–91.

Doherty, W. J., Lester, M. E., & Leigh, G. K. (1986). Marriage Encounter weekends: Couples who win and couples who lose. *Journal of Marital and Family Therapy, 12*, 49–61.

Doherty, W. J., & Walker, B. J. (1982). Marriage Encounter casualties: A preliminary investigation. *American Journal of Family Therapy, 10*, 15–25.

Doise, W. (1969). Intergroup relations and polarization of individual and collective judgments. *Journal of Personality and Social Psychology, 12*, 136–143.

Doise, W. (1986). *Levels of explanation in social psychology.* New York: Cambridge University Press.

Doms, M., & Van Avermaet, E. (1980). Majority influence, minority influence, and conversion behavior: A replication. *Journal of Experimental Social Psychology, 16*, 283–292.

Donnerstein, E., Donnerstein, M., Simon, S., & Ditrichs, R. (1972). Variables in interracial aggression: Anonymity, expected retaliation, and a riot. *Journal of Personality and Social Psychology, 22*, 236–245.

Donohue, W. A. (1978). An empirical framework for examining negotiation processes and outcomes. *Communication Monographs, 45*, 247–256.

Doob, L. (1952). *Social psychology.* New York: Holt.

Doreian, P. (1986). Measuring relative standing in small groups and bounded social networks. *Social Psychology Quarterly, 49*, 247–259.

Douglas, J. D. (1976). *Investigative social research.* Newbury Park, CA: Sage.

Drescher, S., Burlingame, G., & Fuhriman, A. (1985). Cohesion: An odyssey in empirical understanding. *Small Group Behavior, 16*, 3–30.

Drucker, P. F. (1981). Behind Japan's success. *Harvard Business Review, 59*, 83–90.

Druckman, D. (Ed.). (1977). *Negotiations.* Newbury Park, CA: Sage.

Druckman, D. (1987). New directions for a social psychology of conflict. In D. J. D. Sandole & I. Sandole-Staroste (Eds.), *Conflict management and problem solving: Interpersonal to international applications* (pp. 50–56). London: Frances Pinter.

Dunand, M., Berkowitz, L., & Leyens, J. P. (1984). Audience effects when viewing aggressive movies. *British Journal of Social Psychology, 21*, 69–76.

Duncan, B. L. (1976). Differential social perception and attribution of intergroup violence: Testing the lower limits of stereotyping of blacks. *Journal of Personality and Social Psychology, 34*, 590–598.

Dunnette, M. D., Campbell, J., & Jaastad, K. (1963). The effect of group participation on brainstorming effectiveness for two industrial samples. *Journal of Applied Psychology, 47*, 30–37.

Dunning, E. G., Maguire, J. A., Murphy, P. J., & Williams, J. M. (1982). The social roots of football hooligan violence. *Leisure Studies, 1*, 139–156.

Dunning, E. G., Murphy, P. J., & Williams, J. M. (1986). Spectator violence at football matches: Towards a sociological explanation. *British Journal of Sociology, 37*, 221–244.

Durand, D. E. (1977). Power as a function of office space and physiognomy: Two studies of influence. *Psychological Reports, 40*, 755–760.

Durkheim, E. (1897/1966). *Suicide.* New York: Free Press.

Durkheim, E. (1964). *The division of labor in society.* New York: Free Press.

Dutton, D. (1973). Attribution of cause for opinion change and liking for audience members. *Journal of Personality and Social Psychology, 26*, 208–216.

Duval, S., & Wicklund, R. A. (1972). *A theory of objective self-awareness.* New York: Academic Press.

Dyer, W. G. (1977). *Team building: Issues and alternatives.* Reading, MA: Addison-Wesley.

Eagly, A. H. (1974). Comprehensibility of persuasive arguments as a determinant of opinion change. *Journal of Personality and Social Psychology, 29*, 758–773.

Eagly, A. H. (1978). Sex differences in influenceability. *Psychological Bulletin, 85*, 86–116.

Eagly, A. H. (1983). Gender and social influence: A social psychological analysis. *American Psychologist, 38*, 971–983.

Eagly, A. H. (1987). *Sex differences in social behavior: A social-role interpretation.* Hillsdale, NJ: Erlbaum.

Eagly, A. H., & Carli, L. L. (1981). Sex of researchers and sex-typed communications as determinants of sex differences in influenceability: A meta-analysis of social influence studies. *Psychological Bulletin, 90*, 1–20.

Eagly, A. H., & Johnson, B. (in press). Gender and leadership style: A meta-analysis. *Psychological Bulletin.*

Eagly, A. H., & Warren, R. (1976). Intelligence, comprehension, and opinion change. *Journal of Personality, 44*, 226–242.

Eagly, A. H., Wood, W., & Fishbaugh, L. (1981). Sex differences in conformity: Surveillance by the group as a determinant of male nonconformity. *Journal of Personality and Social Psychology, 40*, 384–394.

Earle, W. B. (1986). The social context of social comparison: Reality versus reassurance? *Personality and Social Psychology Bulletin, 12*, 159–168.

Ebbesen, E., Kjos, G., & Konecni, V. (1976). Spatial ecology: Its effects on the choice of friends and enemies. *Journal of Experimental Social Psychology, 12*, 505–518.

Edman, I. (1919). *Human traits and their social significance.* New York: Houghton Mifflin.

Edney, J. (1975). Territoriality and control: A field experiment. *Journal of Personality and Social Psychology, 31*, 1108–1115.

Edney, J. J. (1976). Human territories: Comment on functional properties. *Environment and Behavior, 8*, 31–48.

Edney, J. J. (1980). The commons problem: Alternative perspectives. *American Psychologist, 35*, 131–150.

Edney, J. J., & Bell, P. A. (1984). Sharing scarce resources: Group-outcome orientation, external disaster, and stealing in a simulated commons. *Small Group Behavior, 15*, 87–108.

Edney, J. J., & Grundmann, M. J. (1979). Friendship, group size, and boundary size: Small group spaces. *Small Group Behavior, 10*, 124–135.

Edney, J. J., & Jordan-Edney, N. L. (1974). Territorial spacing on a beach. *Sociometry, 37*, 92–104.

Edney, J. J., & Uhlig, S. R. (1977). Individual and small group territories. *Small Group Behavior, 8*, 457–468.

Edwards, D. J. A. (1972). Approaching the unfamiliar: A study of human interaction distances. *Journal of Behavioral Sciences, 1*, 249–250.

Edwards, J. D. (1979). The home field advantage. In J. H. Goldstein (Ed.), *Sports, games, and play.* Hillsdale, NJ: Erlbaum.

Eisenberg, E. M., Monge, P. R., & Miller, K. I. (1983). Involvement in communication networks as a predictor of organizational commitment. *Human Communication Research, 10*, 179–201.

Emerson, R. M. (1954). Deviation and rejection: An experimental replication. *American Sociological Review, 19*, 688–693.

Emerson, R. M. (1962). Power-dependence relations. *American Sociological Review, 27,* 31–40.

Emerson, R. M. (1981). Social exchange theory. In M. Rosenberg & R. H. Turner (Eds.), *Social psychology: Sociological perspectives* (pp. 30–65). New York: Basic Books.

Endler, N. S., & Hartley, S. (1973). Relative competence, reinforcement, and conformity. *European Journal of Social Psychology, 3,* 63–72.

Erez, M., Rim, Y., & Keider, I. (1986). The two sides of the tactics of influence: Agent vs. target. *Journal of Occupational Psychology, 59,* 25–39.

Erffmeyer, E. S. (1984). Rule-violating behavior on the golf course. *Perceptual and Motor Skills, 59,* 591–596.

Esser, A. H. (1968). Dominance hierarchy and clinical course of psychiatrically hospitalized boys. *Child Development, 39,* 147–157.

Esser, A. H. (1973). Cottage Fourteen: Dominance and territoriality in a group of institutionalized boys. *Small Group Behavior, 4,* 131–146.

Esser, A. H., Chamberlain, A. S., Chapple, E. D., & Kline, N. S. (1965). Territoriality of patients on a research ward. In J. Wortis (Ed.), *Recent advances in biological psychiatry.* New York: Plenum.

Etzioni, A. (1967). The Kennedy experiment. *The Western Political Quarterly, 20,* 361–380.

Evans, G. W. (1979). Behavioral and physiological consequences of crowding in humans. *Journal of Applied Social Psychology, 9,* 27–46.

Evans, G. W., & Cohen, S. (1987). Environmental stress. In D. Stokols & I. Altman (Eds.), *Handbook of environmental psychology* (Vol. 1, pp. 571–610). New York: Wiley.

Evans, G. W., & Howard, R. B. (1973). Personal space. *Psychological Bulletin, 80,* 334–344.

Evans, N. J., & Jarvis, P. A. (1986). The group attitude scale: A measure of attraction to group. *Small Group Behavior, 17,* 203–216.

Falbo, T. (1977). The multidimensional scaling of power strategies. *Journal of Personality and Social Psychology, 35,* 537–548.

Falbo, T., & Peplau, L. A. (1980). Power strategies in intimate relationships. *Journal of Personality and Social Psychology, 38,* 618–628.

Fanon, F. (1963). *The wretched of the earth.* New York: Grove.

Farrell, M. P. (1982). Artists' circles and the development of artists. *Small Group Behavior, 13,* 451–474.

Fassheber, P., & Terjung, B. (1985). SYMLOG rating data and their relationship to performance and behavior beyond the group situation. *International Journal of Small Group Research, 1,* 97–108.

Fazio, R. H. (1979). Motives for social comparison: The construction-validation distinction. *Journal of Personality and Social Psychology, 37,* 1683–1698.

Felson, R. B. (1981). An interactionist approach to aggression. In J. T. Tedeschi (Ed.), *Impression management theory and social psychological research.* New York: Academic Press.

Felson, R. B., & Reed, M. D. (1986). Reference groups and self-appraisals of academic ability and performance. *Social Psychology Quarterly, 49,* 103–109.

Ferber, M., Huber, J., & Spitze, G. (1979). Preference for men as bosses and professionals. *Social Forces, 58,* 466–476.

Ferguson, T. J., & Rule, B. G. (1983). An attributional analysis of anger and aggression. In R. G. Geen & E. I. Donnerstein (Eds.), *Aggression: Theoretical and empirical reviews* (Vol. 1). New York: Academic Press.

Ferris, G. R., & Rowland, K. M. (1983). Social facilitation effects on behavioral and perceptual task performance measures: Implications for work behavior. *Group and Organization Studies, 8,* 421–438.

Festinger, L. (1950). Informal social communication. *Psychological Review, 57,* 271–282.

Festinger, L. (1953). An analysis of compliant behavior. In M. Sherif & M. O. Wilson (Eds.), *Group relations at the crossroads.* New York: Harper.

Festinger, L. (1954). A theory of social comparison processes. *Human Relations, 7,* 117–140.

Festinger, L. (1957). *A theory of cognitive dissonance.* Evanston, IL: Row, Peterson.

Festinger, L., Gerard, H. B., Hymovitch, B., Kelley, H. H., & Raven, B. (1952). The influence process in the presence of extreme deviates. *Human Relations, 5,* 327–346.

Festinger, L., Pepitone, A., & Newcomb, T. (1952). Some consequences of deindividuation in a group. *Journal of Abnormal and Social Psychology, 47,* 382–389.

Festinger, L., Riecken, H. W., & Schachter, S. (1956). *When prophecy fails.* Minneapolis: University of Minnesota Press.

Festinger, L., Schachter, S., & Back, K. (1950). *Social Pressures in informal groups.* New York: Harper.

Festinger, L., & Thibaut, J. (1951). Interpersonal communication in small groups. *Journal of Abnormal and Social Psychology, 46,* 92–99.

Fiedler, F. E. (1955). The influence of leader-keyman relations on combat crew effectiveness. *Journal of Abnormal and Social Psychology, 51,* 227–235.

Fiedler, F. E. (1964). A contingency model of leadership effectiveness. In L. Berkowitz (Ed.), *Advances in experimental social psychology* (Vol. 1, pp. 150–190). New York: Academic Press.

Fiedler, F. E. (1967). *A theory of leadership effectiveness.* New York: McGraw-Hill.

Fiedler, F. E. (1971a). *Leadership.* Morristown, NJ: General Learning Press.

Fiedler, F. E. (1971b). Note on the methodology of Graen, Orris, and Alvarez studies testing the Contingency Model. *Journal of Applied Psychology, 55,* 202–204.

Fiedler, F. E. (1972). Personality, motivational systems, and behavior of high and low LPC persons. *Human Relations, 25,* 391–412.

Fiedler, F. E. (1973). The contingency model—A reply to Ashour. *Organizational Behavior and Human Performance, 9,* 356–368.

Fiedler, F. E. (1978). The contingency model and the dynamics of the leadership process. In L. Berkowitz (Ed.), *Advances in experimental social psychology* (Vol. 12, pp. 59–112). New York: Academic Press.

Fiedler, F. E. (1981). Leadership effectiveness. *American Behavioral Scientist, 24,* 619–632.

Fiedler, F. E., & Chemers, M. M. (1974). *Leadership and effective management.* Glenview, IL: Scott, Foresman.

Fiedler, F. E., Chemers, M. M., & Mahar, L. (1976). *Improving leadership effectiveness: The Leader Match Concept.* New York: Wiley.

Field, R. H. G. (1979). A critique of the Vroom-Yetton contingency model of leadership behavior. *Academy of Management Review, 4,* 249–257.

Filley, A. C. (1976). *Interpersonal conflict resolution.* Glenview, IL: Scott, Foresman.

Fine, G. A., & Stoecker, R. (1985). Can the circle be unbroken? Small groups and social movements. In E. J. Lawler (Ed.), *Advances in group processes* (Vol. 2, pp. 1–28). Greenwich, CT: JAI Press.

Fisek, M. H., & Ofshe, R. (1970). The process of status evolution. *Sociometry, 33,* 327–346.

Fishbein, M. (1963). The perception of non-members: A test of Merton's reference group theory. *Sociometry, 26,* 271–286.

Fisher, B. A. (1980). *Small group decision making* (2nd ed.). New York: McGraw-Hill.

Fisher, C. D., & Gitelson, R. (1983). A meta-analysis of the correlates of role conflict and ambiguity. *Journal of Applied Psychology, 68,* 320–333.

Fisher, J. D., Bell, P. A., & Baum, A. (1984). *Environmental psychology* (2nd ed.). New York: Holt, Rinehart, & Winston.

Fisher, J. D., & Byrne, D. (1975). Too close for comfort: Sex differences in response to invasions of personal space. *Journal of Personality and Social Psychology, 32,* 15–21.

Fisher, R. (1964). Fractionating conflict. In R. Fisher (Ed.), *International conflict and behavioral science: The Craigville papers.* New York: Basic Books.

Fisher, R. (1983). Negotiating power. *American Behavioral Science, 27,* 149–166.

Fisher, R., & Ury, W. (1981). *Getting to yes: Negotiating agreement without giving in.* Boston: Houghton-Mifflin.

Fiske, S. T., & Taylor, S. E. (1984). *Social cognition.* Reading, MA: Addison-Wesley.

Flapan, D., & Fenchel, G. H. (1987). Terminations. *Group, 11,* 131–143.

Fleischer, R. A., & Chertkoff, J. M. (1986). Effects of dominance and sex on leader selection in dyadic work groups. *Journal of Personality and Social Psychology, 50,* 94–99.

Flores, P. J. (1982). Modifications of Yalom's interactional group therapy model as a mode of treatment for alcoholism. *Group, 6,* 3–16.

Flores, P. J. (1988). *Group psychotherapy with addicted populations.* New York: Haworth Press.

Flowers, J. (1979). Behavioral analysis of group therapy and a model for behavioral group therapy. In D. Upper & S. Ross (Eds.), *Behavioral group therapy, 1979: An annual review.* Champaign, IL: Research Press.

Flowers, M. L. (1977). A laboratory test of some implications of Janis' groupthink hypothesis. *Journal of Personality and Social Psychology, 35,* 888–896.

Foa, U. G. (1957). Relation of worker's expectation to satisfaction with supervisor. *Personnel Psychology, 10,* 161–168.

Foa, U. G., & Foa, E. B. (1971). Resource exchange: Toward a structural theory of interpersonal relations. In A. W. Siegman & B. Pope (Eds.), *Studies in dyadic communication.* New York: Pergamon Press.

Fodor, E. M. (1984). The power motive and reactivity to power stresses. *Journal of Personality and Social Psychology, 47,* 853–859.

Fodor, E. M. (1985). The power motive, group conflict, and physiological arousal. *Journal of Personality and Social Psychology, 49,* 1408–1415.

Folberg, J., & Taylor, A. (1984). *Mediation: A comprehesive guide to resolving conflicts without litigation.* San Francisco: Jossey-Bass.

Folk, G. E., Jr. (1974). *Textbook of environmental physiology.* Philadelphia: Lea & Febiger.

Folkes, V. S. (1985). Mindlessness or mindfulness: A partial replication and extension of Langer, Blank, & Chanowitz. *Journal of Personality and Social Psychology, 48,* 600–604.

Forsyth, D. R. (1976). Crucial experiments and social psychological inquiry. *Personality and Social Psychology Bulletin, 2,* 454–459.

Forsyth, D. R. (1981). A psychological perspective on ethical uncertainties in behavioral research. In A. J. Kimmel (Ed.), *New Directions for Methodology of Social and Behavioral Science: Ethics of Human Subject Research* (No. 10). San Francisco: Jossey-Bass.

Forsyth, D. R., Berger, R., & Mitchell, T. (1981). The effects of self-serving vs. other-serving claims of responsibility on attraction and attribution in groups. *Social Psychology Quarterly, 44,* 59–64.

Forsyth, D. R., Schlenker, B. R., Leary, M. R., & McCown, N. E. (1985). Self-presen-

tational determinants of sex differences in leadership behavior. *Small Group Behavior, 16,* 197–210.

Forsyth, D. R., & Strong, S. R. (1986). The scientific study of counseling and psychotherapy: A unificationist view. *American Psychologist, 41,* 113–119.

Foschi, M., Warriner, G. K., & Hart, S. D. (1985). Standards, expectations, and interpersonal influence. *Social Psychology Quarterly, 48,* 108–117.

Foss, R. D. (1981). Structural effects in simulated jury decision making. *Journal of Personality and Social Psychology, 40,* 1055–1062.

Foti, R. J., Fraser, S. L., & Lord, R. G. (1982). Effects of leadership labels and prototypes on perceptions of political leaders. *Journal of Applied Psychology, 67,* 326–333.

Foti, R. J., & Lord, R. G. (1987). Prototypes and scripts: The effects of alternative methods of processing information on rating accuracy. *Organizational Behavior and Human Decision Processes, 39,* 318–340.

Foushee, H. C. (1984). Dyads and triads at 35,000 feet: Factors affecting group process and aircrew performance. *American Psychologist, 39,* 885–893.

Foushee, H. C. (August, 1986). *Group performance in space: Lessons learned from aviation.* Paper presented at the Annual Meetings of the American Psychological Association, Washington, DC.

Foushee, H. C., & Helmreich, R. L. (1988). Group interaction and flightcrew performance. In E. L. Wiener & D. C. Nagel (Eds.), *Human factors in modern aviation.* New York: Academic Press.

Fox, J., & Moore, J. C., Jr. (1979). Status characteristics and expectation states: Fitting and testing a recent model. *Social Psychology Quarterly, 42,* 126–134.

Foy, E., & Harlow, A. F. (1928/1956). *Clowning through life.* New York: Dutton.

Frager, R. (1970). Conformity and anticonformity in Japan. *Journal of Personality and Social Psychology, 15,* 203–210.

Frank, F., & Anderson, L. R. (1971). Effects of task and group size upon group productivity and member satisfaction. *Sociometry, 34,* 135–149.

Frank, J. D. (1957). Some determinants, manifestations, and effects of cohesiveness in therapy groups. *International Journal of Group Psychotherapy, 7,* 53–63.

Franke, R. H. (1979). The Hawthorne experiments: Re-view. *American Sociological Review, 44*, 861–867.

Franke, R. H., & Kaul, J. D. (1978). The Hawthorne experiments: First statistical interpretation. *American Sociological Review, 43*, 623–643.

Fraser, N. M., & Hipel, K. W. (1984). *Conflict analysis: Models and resolutions.* New York: North-Holland.

Fraser, T. M. (1966). *The effects of confinement as a factor in manned space flight.* NASA Contractor Report, NASA CR-511. Washington, D.C.: NASA.

Freedman, J. L. (1975). *Crowding and behavior.* San Francisco: Freeman.

Freedman, J. L. (1979). Reconciling apparent differences between responses of humans and other animals to crowding. *Psychological Review, 86*, 80–85.

Freedman, J. L., Klevansky, S., & Ehrlich, P. R. (1971). The effect of crowding on human task performance. *Journal of Applied Social Psychology, 1*, 7–25.

Freedman, J. L., & Perlick, D. (1979). Crowding, contagion, and laughter. *Journal of Experimental Social Psychology, 15*, 295–303.

Freeman, L. C. (1977). A set of measures of centrality based on betweenness. *Sociometry, 40*, 35–41.

Freeze, L., & Cohen, B. P. (1973). Eliminating status generalization. *Sociometry, 36*, 177–193.

French, J. R. P., Jr. (1941). The disruption and cohesion of groups. *Journal of Abnormal and Social Psychology, 36*, 361–377.

French, J. R. P., Jr., Morrison, H., & Levinger, G. (1960). Coercive power and forces affecting conformity. *Journal of Abnormal and Social Psychology, 61*, 93–101.

French, J. R. P., Jr., & Raven, B. (1959). The bases of social power. In D. Cartwright (Ed.), *Studies in social power.* Ann Arbor, MI: Institute for Social Research.

French, W. L., & Bell, C. H., Jr. (1984). *Organization development: Behavioral science interventions for organization improvement.* Englewood Cliffs, NJ: Prentice-Hall.

Freud, S. (1922). *Group psychology and the analysis of the ego.* London: Hogarth.

Friedkin, N. E. (1983). Horizons of observability and limits of informal control in organizations. *Social Forces, 62*, 54–77.

Friedland, N. (1976). Social influence via threats. *Journal of Experimental Social Psychology, 12*, 552–563.

Friedman, L. (1981). How affiliation affects stress in fear and anxiety situations. *Journal of Personality and Social Psychology, 40*, 1102–1117.

Friedman, M. (1976). Aiming at the self: The paradox of encounter and the human potential movement. *Journal of Humanistic Psychology, 16*, 5–34.

Froman, L. A., Jr., & Cohen, M. D. (1969). Threats and bargaining efficiency. *Behavioral Science, 14*, 147–153.

Fromm, E. (1965). *Escape from freedom.* New York: Holt, Rinehart, & Winston.

Gabarro, J. J. (1987). The development of working relationships. In J. W. Lorsch (Ed.), *Handbook of organizational behavior* (pp. 172–189). Englewood Cliffs, NJ: Prentice-Hall.

Galassi, J. P., & Galassi, M. D. (1979). Modification of heterosocial skills deficits. In A. S. Bellack & M. Hersen (Eds.), *Research and practice in social skills training.* New York: Plenum.

Galle, O. R., Gove, W. R., & McPherson, J. M. (1972). Population density and pathology: What are the relationships for man? *Science, 176*, 23–30.

Gallo, P. S., Jr. (1966). Effects of increased incentives upon the use of threat in bargaining. *Journal of Personality and Social Psychology, 4*, 14–20.

Gamson, W. A. (1961a). An experimental test of a theory of coalition formation. *American Sociological Review, 26*, 565–573.

Gamson, W. A. (1961b). A theory of coalition formation. *American Sociological Review, 26*, 373–382.

Gamson, W. A. (1964). Experimental studies of coalition formation. In L. Berkowitz (Ed.), *Advances in experimental social psychology* (Vol. 1, pp. 82–110). New York: Academic Press.

Gamson, W. A. (1968). *Power and discontent.* Belmont, CA: Wadsworth.

Gannon, T. M. (1966). Emergence of the "defensive" group norm. *Federal Probation, 30*(4), 44–47.

Gardner, J. W. (1965). *The antileadership vaccine.* Annual Report of the Carnegie Corporation. New York: Carnegie Corporation.

Garfinkel, H. (1956). Conditions of successful degradation ceremonies. *American Journal of Sociology, 61,* 420–424.

Garner, D. M., & Garfinkel, P. E. (1980). Socio-cultural factors in the development of anorexia nervosa. *Psychological Medicine, 10,* 647–656.

Garner, K., & Deutsch, M. (1974). Cooperative behavior in dyads: Effects of dissimilar goal orientations and differing expectations about the partner. *Journal of Conflict Resolution, 18,* 634–645.

Gastorf, J. W., Suls, J., & Sanders, G. S. (1980). Type A coronary-prone behavior pattern and social facilitation. *Journal of Personality and Social Psychology, 38,* 773–780.

Gazda, G. M., & Brooks, D. K. (1985). The development of the social/life skills training movement. *Journal of Group Psychotherapy, Psychodrama and Sociometry, 38,* 1–10.

Geen, R. G. (1980). The effects of being observed on performance. In P. B. Paulus (Ed.), *Psychology of group influence* (pp. 61–97). Hillsdale, NJ: Erlbaum.

Geen, R. G. (1981). Evaluation apprehension and social facilitation: A reply to Sanders. *Journal of Experimental Social Psychology, 17,* 252–256.

Geen, R. G., & Bushman, B. J. (1987). Drive theory: Effects of socially engendered arousal. In B. Mullen & G. R. Goethals (Eds.), *Theories of group behavior* (pp. 89–109). New York: Springer-Verlag.

Geen, R. G., & Gange, J. J. (1977). Drive theory of social facilitation: Twelve years of theory and research. *Psychological Bulletin, 84,* 1267–1288.

Geffner, R., & Gross, M. M. (1984). Sex-role behavior and obedience to authority: A field study. *Sex Roles, 10,* 973–985.

Geis, F. L., Boston, M. B., & Hoffman, N. (1985). Sex of authority role models and achievement by men and women: Leadership performance and recognition. *Journal of Personality and Social Psychology, 49,* 636–653.

Gelman, E., with Rogers, M., Lubenow, G. C., Marbach, W. D., Friday, C., & Cook, W. J. (1985). Showdown in Silicon Valley. *Newsweek, 106,* September 30, 46–50.

Gemmill, G. (1986). The mythology of the leader role in small groups. *Small Group Behavior, 17,* 41–50.

Genevie, L. E. (Ed.). (1978). *Collective behavior and social movements.* Itasca, IL: Peacock.

Gerard, H. B. (1953). The effect of different dimensions of disagreement on the communication process in small groups. *Human Relations, 6,* 249–271.

Gerard, H. B. (1963). Emotional uncertainty and social comparison. *Journal of Abnormal and Social Psychology, 66,* 568–573.

Gerard, H. B. (1983). School desegregation: The social science role. *American Psychologist, 38,* 869–877.

Gerard, H. B., & Mathewson, G. C. (1966). The effect of severity of initiation on liking for a group: A replication. *Journal of Experimental Social Psychology, 2,* 278–287.

Gerard, H. B., & Orive, R. (1987). The dynamics of opinion formation. In L. Berkowitz (Ed.), *Advances in experimental social psychology* (Vol. 20, pp. 171–202). New York: Academic Press.

Gerard, H. B., Wilhelmy, R. A., & Conolley, E. S. (1968). Conformity and group size. *Journal of Personality and Social Psychology, 8,* 79–82.

Gergen, K. J., Gergen, M. M., & Barton, W. H. (1973). Deviance in the dark. *Psychology Today, 10,* 129–130.

Gewirtz, J. L. (1969). Mechanisms of social learning: Some rules of stimulation and behavior in early human development. In D. A. Goslin (Ed.), *Handbook of socialization theory and research* (pp. 57–212). Chicago: Rand McNally, 1969.

Gewirtz, J. L., & Baer, D. M. (1958a). Deprivation and satiation of social reinforcers as drive conditions. *Journal of Abnormal and Social Psychology, 57,* 165–172.

Gewirtz, J. L., & Baer, D. M. (1958b). The effect of brief social deprivation on behaviors for a social reinforcer. *Journal of Abnormal and Social Psychology, 56,* 49–56.

Gibb, C. A. (1969). Leadership. In G. Lindzey & E. Aronson (Eds.), *The handbook of social psychology* (Vol. 4, 2nd ed., pp. 205–282). Reading, MA: Addison-Wesley.

Gibb, J. R. (1970). Effects of human relations training. In A. E. Bergin & S. L. Garfield (Eds.), *Handbook of psychotherapy and behavior change.* New York: Wiley, 1971.

Giesen, M., & McClaren, H. A. (1976). Discussion, distance, and sex: Changes in impressions and attraction during small group interaction. *Sociometry, 39,* 60–70.

Gifford, R., & O'Connor, B. (1987). The interpersonal circumplex as a behavior map. *Journal of Personality and Social Psychology, 52*, 1019–1026.

Gilchrist, J. C. (1952). The formation of social groups under conditions of success and failure. *Journal of Abnormal and Social Psychology, 47*, 174–187.

Giles, H. (Ed.). (1977). *Language, ethnicity, and intergroup relations*. London: Academic Press.

Giles, H., & Johnson, P. (1981). The role of language in ethnic group relations. In J. C. Turner & H. Giles (Eds.), *Intergroup behavior* (pp. 199–272). Oxford: Basil Blackwell.

Giordano, P. C. (1983). Sanctioning the high-status deviant: An attributional analysis. *Social Psychology Quarterly, 46*, 329–342.

Gist, M. E., Locke, E. A., & Taylor, M. S. (1987). Organizational behavior: Group structure, process, and effectiveness. *Journal of Management, 13*, 237–257.

Gladstein, D. L. (1984). Groups in context: A model of task group effectiveness. *Administrative Science Quarterly, 29*, 499–517.

Glaser, B. G., & Strauss, A. L. (1967). *The discovery of grounded theory: Strategies for qualitative research*. Chicago: Aldine.

Glaser, B. G., & Strauss, A. L. (1971). *Status passage*. Chicago: Aldine.

Glaser, D. (1964). *The effectiveness of a prison and parole system*. Indianapolis: Bobbs-Merrill.

Glass, D. C., & Singer, J. E. (1972). *Urban stress*. New York: Academic Press.

Glass, D. C., Singer, J. E., & Pennebaker, J. W. (1977). Behavioral and physiological effects of uncontrollable environmental events. In D. Stokols (Ed.), *Perspectives on environment and behavior* (pp. 131–151). New York: Plenum.

Godfrey, D. K., Jones, E. E., & Lord, C. G. (1986). Self-promotion is not ingratiating. *Journal of Personality and Social Psychology, 50*, 106–115.

Goethals, G. R. (1986). Social comparison theory: Psychology from the lost and found. *Personality and Social Psychology Bulletin, 12*, 261–278.

Goethals, G. R., & Darley, J. M. (1977). Social comparison theory: An attributional approach. In J. M. Suls & R. L. Miller (Eds.), *Social comparison processes: Theoretical and empirical perspectives*. Washington, DC: Hemisphere.

Goethals, G. R., & Darley, J. M. (1987). Social comparison theory: Self-evaluation and group life. In B. Mullen & G. R. Goethals, (Eds.), *Theories of group behavior* (pp. 21–47). New York: Springer-Verlag.

Goethals, G. R., & Zanna, M. P. (1979). The role of social comparison in choice shifts. *Journal of Personality and Social Psychology, 37*, 1469–1476.

Goetsch, G. G., & McFarland, D. D. (1980). Models of the distribution of acts in small discussion groups. *Social Psychology Quarterly, 43*, 173–183.

Gold, M., & Yanof, D. S. (1985). Mothers, daughters, and girlfriends. *Journal of Personality and Social Psychology, 49*, 654–659.

Goldberg, C. (1974). Sex roles, task competence, and conformity. *Journal of Psychology, 86*, 157–164.

Goldberg, C. (1975). Conformity to majority type as a function of task and acceptance of sex-related stereotypes. *Journal of Psychology, 89*, 25–37.

Goldberg, L. (1968). Ghetto riots and others: The faces of civil disorder in 1967. *Journal of Peace Research, 2*, 116–132.

Goldman, M., & Fraas, L. A. (1965). The effects of leader selection on group performance. *Sociometry, 28*, 82–88.

Goldman, M., Stockbauer, J. W., & McAuliffe, T. G. (1977). Intergroup and intragroup competition and cooperation. *Journal of Experimental Social Psychology, 13*, 81–88.

Goldstein, A. P., Heller, K., & Sechrest, L. B. (1966). *Psychotherapy and the psychology of behavior change*. New York: Wiley.

Goodacre, D. M. (1953). Group characteristics of good and poor performing combat units. *Sociometry, 16*, 168–178.

Goodman, P. S., Ravlin, E., & Schminke, M. (1987). Understanding groups in organizations. *Research in Organizational Behavior, 9*, 121–173.

Goodstadt, B. E., & Hjelle, L. A. (1973). Power to the powerless: Locus of control and use of power. *Journal of Personality and Social Psychology, 27*, 190–196.

Gordon, B. (1965). Influence, social comparison, and affiliation. *Dissertation Abstracts, 26*(4), 2366.

Gordon, W. (1961). *Synectics: The development of creative capacity.* New York: Harper & Row.

Gorlow, L., Hoch, E. L., & Telschow, E. F. (1952). *Non-directive group psychotherapy.* New York: Teacher's College Studies in Education, Columbia University Press.

Gove, W. R., Hughes, M., & Galle, O. R. (1983). *Overcrowding in the household: An analysis of determinants and effects.* New York: Academic Press.

Graeff, C. L. (1983). The situational leadership theory: A critical view. *Academy of Management Review, 8,* 285–291.

Graen, G. (1976). Role-making processes within complex organizations. In M. D. Dunnette (Ed.), *Handbook of industrial organizational psychology.* Chicago: Rand McNally.

Graen, G. B., Alvares, K. M., Orris, J. B., & Martella, J. A. (1970). The contingency model of leadership effectiveness: Antecedent and evidential results. *Psychological Bulletin, 74,* 285–296.

Graen, G. B., Orris, J. B., & Alvares, K. M. (1971). Contingency model of leadership effectiveness: Some experimental results. *Journal of Applied Psychology, 55,* 196–201.

Green, S. G., & Nebeker, D. M. (1977). The effects of situational factors and leadership style on leader behavior. *Organizational Behavior and Human Performance, 19,* 368–377.

Greenberg, C. I., & Firestone, I. J. (1977). Compensatory responses to crowding: Effects of personal space intrusion and privacy reduction. *Journal of Personality and Social Psychology, 35,* 637–644.

Greene, C. N. (1989). Cohesion and productivity in work groups. *Small Group Behavior, 20,* 70–86.

Greene, L. R., Morrison, T. L., & Tischler, N. G. (1981). Gender and authority: Effects on perceptions of small group coleaders. *Small Group Behavior, 12,* 401–413.

Greenstein, T. N. (1981). Scope conditions and critical tests: Comment on Lee and Ofshe. *Social Psychology Quarterly, 44,* 381–383.

Greenstein, T. N., & Knottnerus, J. D. (1980). The effects of differential evaluations on status generalization. *Social Psychology Quarterly, 43,* 147–154.

Greer, D. L. (1983). Spectator booing and the home advantage: A study of social influence in the basketball arena. *Social Psychology Quarterly, 46,* 252–261.

Griffitt, W. (1970). Environmental effects on interpersonal affective behavior: Ambient effective temperature and attraction. *Journal of Personality and Social Psychology, 15,* 240–244.

Griffitt, W., & Veitch, R. (1971). Hot and crowded: Influence of population density and temperature on interpersonal affective behavior. *Journal of Personality and Social Psychology, 17,* 92–98.

Griffitt, W., & Veitch, R. (1974). Preacquaintance attitude similarity and attraction revisited: Ten days in a fall-out shelter. *Sociometry, 37,* 163–173.

Grimes, A. J. (1978). Authority, power, influence and social control: A theoretical synthesis. *Academy of Management Review, 3,* 724–737.

Groff, B. D., Baron, R. S., & Moore, D. L. (1983). Distraction, attentional conflict, and drivelike behavior. *Journal of Experimental Social Psychology, 19,* 359–380.

Grofman, B., & Owen, G. (1982). A game theoretic approach to measuring degree of centrality in social networks. *Social Networks, 4,* 213–224.

Gross, E., & Stone, G. P. (1964). Embarrassment and the analysis of role requirements. *American Journal of Sociology, 70,* 1–15.

Grush, J. E. (1979). A summary review of mediating explanations of exposure phenomena. *Personality and Social Psychology Bulletin, 5,* 154–159.

Guerin, B. (1983). Social facilitation and social monitoring: A test of three models. *British Journal of Social Psychology, 22,* 203–214.

Guerin, B. (1986). Mere presence effects in humans: A review. *Journal of Experimental Social Psychology, 22,* 38–77.

Guerin, B., & Innes, J. M. (1983). Social facilitation and social monitoring: A new look at Zajonc's mere presence hypothesis. *British Journal of Social Psychology, 21,* 7–18.

Guerin, P. J. & Pendagast, E. G. (1976). Evaluation of family system and genogram. In P. J. Guerin (Ed.), *Family therapy: Theory and practice* (pp. 450–464). New York: Gardner.

Gunderson, E. K. E. (1973). Individual behavior in confined or isolated groups. In

J. E. Rasmussen (Ed.), *Man in isolation and confinement* (pp. 145–164). Chicago: Aldine.

Gurr, T. R. (1970). *Why men rebel.* Princeton, NJ: Princeton University Press.

Gustafson, D. H., Shukla, R. M., Delbecq, A. L., & Walster, G. W. (1973). A comparative study of differences in subjective likelihood estimates made by individuals, interacting groups, Delphi groups, and nominal groups. *Organizational Behavior and Human Performance, 9,* 280–291.

Guthman, E. (1971). *We band of brothers.* New York: Harper & Row.

Guzzo, R. A. (1986). Group decision making and group effectiveness in organizations. In P. S. Goodman (Ed.), *Designing effective work groups* (pp. 34–71). San Francisco: Jossey-Bass.

Haas, D. F., & Deseran, F. A. (1981). Trust and symbolic exchange. *Social Psychology Quarterly, 44,* 3–13.

Haber, G. M. (1980). Territorial invasion in the classroom: Invadee response. *Environment and Behavior, 12,* 17–31.

Haber, G. M. (1982). Spatial relations between dominants and marginals. *Social Psychology Quarterly, 45,* 219–228.

Hackman, J. R. (1983). *A normative model of work team effectiveness.* Technical Report No. 2, Research Program on Group Effectiveness, Yale School of Organization and Management, New Haven, CT.

Hackman, J. R. (1987). The design of work teams. In J. W. Lorsch (Ed.), *Handbook of organizational behavior* (pp. 315–342). Englewood Cliffs, NJ: Prentice Hall.

Hackman, J. R., Brousseau, K. R., & Weiss, J. A. (1976). The interaction of task design and group performance strategies in determining group effectiveness. *Organizational Behavior and Human Performance, 16,* 350–365.

Hackman, J. R., & Morris, C. G. (1975). Group tasks, group interaction process, and group performance effectiveness: A review and proposed integration. In L. Berkowitz (Ed.), *Advances in experimental social psychology* (Vol. 8, pp. 47–99). New York: Academic Press.

Hackman, J. R., & Oldham, G. R. (1980). *Work redesign.* Reading, MA: Addison-Wesley.

Hackman, J. R., & Walton, R. E. (1986). Leading groups in organizations. In P. S. Goodman (Ed.), *Designing effective work groups* (pp. 72–119). San Francisco: Jossey-Bass.

Hall, E. T. (1966). *The hidden dimension.* New York: Doubleday.

Hallinan, M. T. (1981). Recent advances in sociometry. In S. R. Asher & J. M. Gottman (Eds.), *The development of children's friendships* (pp. 91–115). Cambridge, England: Cambridge University Press.

Halpin, A. W., & Winer, B. J. (1952). *The leadership behavior of the airplane commander.* Columbus: Ohio State University Research Foundation.

Hamblin, R. L. (1958). Leadership and crises. *Sociometry, 21,* 322–335.

Hamilton, D. L. (1979). A cognitive-attributional analysis of stereotyping. In L. Berkowitz (Ed.), *Advances in experimental social psychology* (Vol. 12, pp. 53–84). New York: Academic Press.

Hamilton, D. L., & Rose, T. L. (1980). Illusory correlation and the maintenance of stereotypic beliefs. *Journal of Personality and Social Psychology, 39,* 832–845.

Hamilton, R. W. (1972). Weekend retreat. In R. H. Turner & L. M. Killian (Eds.), *Collective behavior* (2nd ed.). Englewood Cliffs, NJ: Prentice-Hall.

Hamilton, V. L. (1986). Chains of command: Responsibility attribution in hierarchies. *Journal of Applied Social Psychology, 16,* 118–138.

Hanks, M., & Eckland, B. K. (1978). Adult voluntary associations and adolescent socialization. *Sociological Quarterly, 19,* 481–490.

Hans, V. P., & Vidmar, N. (1982). Jury selection. In N. L. Kerr & R. M. Bray (Eds.), *Psychology of the courtroom* (pp. 39–82). New York: Academic Press.

Hansell, S. (1984). Cooperative groups, weak ties, and the integration of peer friendships. *Social Psychology Quarterly, 47,* 316–328.

Hansen, W. B., & Altman, I. (1976). Decorating personal places: A descriptive analysis. *Environment and Behavior, 8,* 491–504.

Hanson, P. S., & Lubin, B. (1986). Team building as group development. *Organization Development Journal, 4,* 27–35.

Hardin, G. (1968). The tragedy of the commons. *Science, 162,* 1243–1248.

Hardin, S. I., Subich, L. M., & Holvey, J. M. (1988). Expectancies for counseling in relation to premature termination. *Journal of Counseling Psychology, 35,* 37–40.

Hardy, C., & Latané, B. (1986). Social loafing on a cheering task. *Social Science, 71*(2–3), 165–172.

Hare, A. P. (1967). Small group development in the relay assembly testroom. *Sociological Inquiry, 37,* 169–182.

Hare, A. P. (1976). *Handbook of small group research* (2nd ed.). New York: Free Press.

Hare, A. P. (1982). *Creativity in small groups.* Newbury Park, CA: Sage.

Hare, A. P. (1985). The significance of SYM-LOG in the study of group dynamics. *International Journal of Small Group Research, 1,* 38–50.

Hare, A. P., & Bales, R. F. (1963). Seating position and small group interaction. *Sociometry, 26,* 480–486.

Hare, A. P., Borgatta, E. F., & Bales, R. F. (1955). *Small groups: Studies in social interaction.* New York: Knopf.

Hare, A. P., & Naveh, D. (1986). Conformity and creativity: Camp David, 1978. *Small Group Behavior, 17,* 243–268.

Harkins, S. G. (1987). Social loafing and social facilitation. *Journal of Experimental Social Psychology, 23,* 1–18.

Harkins, S. G., & Jackson, J. M. (1985). The role of evaluation in eliminating social loafing. *Personality and Social Psychology Bulletin, 11,* 457–465.

Harkins, S. G., Latané, B., & Williams, K. (1980). Social loafing: Allocating effort or taking it easy. *Journal of Experimental Social Psychology, 16,* 457–465.

Harkins, S. G., & Petty, R. E. (1982). Effects of task difficulty and task uniqueness on social loafing. *Journal of Personality and Social Psychology, 43,* 1214–1229.

Harkins, S. G., & Szymanski, K. (1987). Social loafing and social facilitation: New wine in old bottles. In C. Hendrick (Ed.), *Review of Personality and Social Psychology: Group Process and Intergroup Relations* (Vol. 9, pp. 167–188). Newbury Park, CA: Sage.

Harlow, H. F., & Harlow, M. K. (1966). Learning to love. *American Scientist, 54,* 244–272.

Harman, R. L. (1988). Gestalt group therapy. In S. Long (Ed.), *Six group therapies* (pp. 217–256). New York: Plenum.

Harnett, D. L., Cummings, L. L., & Hamner, W. C. (1973). Personality, bargaining style, and payoff in bilateral monopoly bargaining among European managers. *Sociometry, 36,* 325–245.

Harper, N. L., & Askling, L. R. (1980). Group communication and quality of task solution in a media production organization. *Communication Monographs, 47,* 77–100.

Harrison, A. A. (1977). Mere exposure. In L. Berkowitz (Ed.), *Advances in experimental social psychology* (Vol. 10). New York: Academic Press.

Harrison, A. A., & Connors, M. M. (1984). Groups in exotic environments. In L. Berkowitz (Ed.), *Advances in experimental social psychology* (Vol. 18, pp. 50–87). New York: Academic Press.

Harvey, P. H., & Greene, P. J. (1981). Group composition: An evolutionary perspective. In H. Kellerman (Ed.), *Group cohesion.* New York: Grune & Stratton.

Hastie, R. (1986). Review essay: Experimental evidence on group accuracy. In G. Owen & B. Grofman (Eds.), *Information pooling and group decision making* (pp. 129–157). Westport, CT: JAI.

Hastie, R., Penrod, S. D., & Pennington, N. (1984). *Inside the jury.* Cambridge, MA: Harvard University Press.

Hastorf, A. H., & Cantril, H. They saw a game. (1954). *Journal of Abnormal and Social Psychology, 49,* 129–134.

Hayduk, L. A. (1978). Personal space: An evaluative and orienting overview. *Psychological Bulletin, 85,* 117–134.

Hayduk, L. (1983). Personal space: Where we now stand. *Psychological Bulletin, 94,* 293–335.

Hays, R. B. (1985). A longitudinal study of friendship development. *Journal of Personality and Social Psychology, 48,* 909–924.

Hays, R. B., & Oxley, D. (1986). Social network development functioning during a life transition. *Journal of Personality and Social Psychology, 50,* 304–313.

Haythorn, W. W. (1973). The miniworld of isolation: Laboratory studies. In J. E. Rasmussen (Ed.), *Man in isolation and confinement* (pp. 219–239). Chicago: Aldine.

Hearne, G. (1957). Leadership and the spatial factor in small groups. *Journal of Abnormal and Social Psychology, 54,* 269–272.

Heffron, M. H. (1972). The naval ship as an urban design problem. *Naval Engineers Journal, 12,* 49–64.

Heider, F. (1958). *The psychology of interpersonal relations.* New York: Wiley.

Heinicke, C. M., & Bales, R. F. (1953). Developmental trends in the structure of small groups. *Sociometry, 16,* 7–38.

Heller, J. F., Groff, B. D., & Solomon, S. H. (1977). Toward an understanding of crowding: The role of physical interaction. *Journal of Personality and Social Psychology, 35,* 183–190.

Helmreich, R. L. (1974). Evaluation of environments: Behavioral observations in an undersea habitat. In J. Lang, C. Burnette, W. Moleski, & D. Vachon (Eds.), *Designing for human behavior.* Stroudsburg, PA: Dowden, Hutchinson, & Ross.

Helmreich, R. L., & Collins, B. E. (1967). Situational determinants of affiliative preference under stress. *Journal of Personality and Social Psychology, 6,* 79–85.

Hembroff, L. A. (1982). Resolving status inconsistency: An expectation states theory and test. *Social Forces, 61,* 183–205.

Hembroff, L. A., & Myers, D. E. (1984). Status characteristics: Degrees of task relevance and decision process. *Social Psychology Quarterly, 47,* 337–346.

Hemphill, J. K. (1950). Relations between the size of the group and the behavior of "superior" leaders. *Journal of Social Psychology, 32,* 11–22.

Hemphill, J. K. (1961). Why people attempt to lead. In L. Petrullo & B. M. Bass (Eds.), *Leadership and interpersonal behavior.* New York: Holt, Rinehart, & Winston.

Henchy, T., & Glass, D. C. (1968). Evaluation apprehension and the social facilitation of dominant and subordinate responses. *Journal of Personality and Social Psychology, 10,* 446–454.

Hensley, T. R., & Griffin, G. W. (1986). Victims of groupthink: The Kent State University Board of Trustees and the 1977 gymnasium controversy. *Journal of Conflict Resolution, 30,* 497–531.

Hensley, V., & Duval, S. (1976). Some perceptual determinants of perceived similarity, liking, and correctness. *Journal of Personality and Social Psychology, 34,* 159–168.

Herbert, T. T., & Estes, R. W. (1977). Improving executive decisions by formalizing dissent: The corporate devil's advocate. *Academy of Management Review, 2,* 662–667.

Herek, G., Janis, I. L., & Huth, P. (1987). Decisionmaking during international crises: Is quality of process related to outcome? *Journal of Conflict Resolution, 31,* 203–226.

Hermann, M. G., & Kogan, N. (1977). Effects of negotiators' personalities on negotiating behavior. In D. Druckman (Ed.), *Negotiations.* Newbury Park, CA: Sage.

Hersey, P. (1985). A letter to the author of "Don't be misled by LEAD." *Journal of Applied Behavioral Sciences, 21,* 152–153.

Hersey, P., & Blanchard, K. H. (1976). Leader effectiveness and adaptability description (LEAD). In J. W. Pfeiffer & J. E. Jones (Eds.), *The 1976 annual handbook for group facilitators* (Vol. 5). La Jolla, CA: University Associates.

Hersey, P., & Blanchard, K. H. (1977). *Management of organizational behavior: Utilizing human resources* (3rd ed.). Englewood Cliffs, NJ: Prentice-Hall.

Hersey, P., & Blanchard, K. H. (1982). *Management of organizational behavior* (4th ed). Englewood Cliffs, NJ: Prentice-Hall.

Heshka, S., & Nelson, Y. (1972). Interpersonal speaking distance as a function of age, sex, and relationship. *Sociometry, 25,* 491–498.

Hewstone, M. (1988). Attributional bases of intergroup conflict. In W. Stroebe, A. W. Kruglanski, D. Bar-Tal, & M. Hewstone (Eds.), *The social psychology of intergroup conflict* (pp. 47–71). New York: Springer-Verlag.

Hewstone, M., & Brown, R. J. (1986). Contact is not enough: An intergroup perspective on the "contact hypothesis." In M. Hewstone & R. J. Brown (Eds.), *Contact and conflcit in intergroup encounters.* Oxford: Blackwell.

Higginbotham, H. N., West, S. G., & Forsyth, D. R. (1988). *Psychotherapy and behavior change: Social, cultural, and methodological perspectives.* New York: Pergamon.

Hill, C. T., & Stull, D. E. (1981). Sex differences in effects of social and value similarity in same-sex friendship. *Journal of Personality and Social Psychology, 41,* 488–502.

Hill, T. E., & Schmitt, N. (1977). Individual differences in leadership decision making. *Organizational Behavior and Human Performance, 19*, 353–367.

Hill, W. F. (1977). Hill Interaction Matrix (HIM): The conceptual framework, derived rating scales, and an updated bibliography. *Small Group Behavior, 8*, 251–268.

Hill, W. F., & Gruner, L. (1973). A study of development in open and closed groups. *Small Group Behavior, 4*, 355–381.

Hiltrop, J. M., & Rubin, J. Z. (1982). Effect of intervention mode and conflict of interest on dispute resolution. *Journal of Personality and Social Psychology, 42*, 665–672.

Hinkle, S., & Schopler, J. (1986). Bias in the evaluation of in-group and out-group performance. In S. Worchel & W. G. Austin (Eds.), *Psychology of intergroup relations* (2nd ed., pp. 196–212). Chicago: Nelson-Hall.

Hirokawa, R. Y. (1980). A comparative analysis of communication patterns within effective and ineffective decision-making groups. *Communication Monographs, 47*, 312–321.

Hirokawa, R. Y. (1984). Does consensus really result in higher quality group decisions? In G. M. Phillips & J. T. Wood (Eds.), *Emergent issues in human decision making* (pp. 40–49). Carbondale, IL: Southern Illinois University Press.

Hirokawa, R. Y., Gouran, D. S., & Martz, A. E. (1988). Understanding the sources of faulty group decision making: A lesson from the Challenger disaster. *Small Group Behavior, 19*, 411–433.

Hoffer, E. (1951). *The true believer*. New York: Harper & Row.

Hoffman, L. R. (1982). Improving the problem-solving process in managerial groups. In R. A. Guzzo (Ed.), *Improving group decision making in organizations* (pp. 95–126). New York: Academic Press.

Hoffman, L. R., & Maier, N. R. F. (1961). Sex differences, sex composition, and group problem solving. *Journal of Abnormal and Social Psychology, 63*, 453–456.

Hofstede, G. (1983). Dimensions of national cultures in fifty countries and three regions. In J. B. Deregowaki, S. Dziurawiec, & R. C. Annis (Eds.), *Expiscations in cross-cultural psychology* (pp. 335–355). Lisse, the Netherlands: Swets and Zeitlinger B. V.

Hollander, E. P. (1958). Conformity, status, and idiosyncrasy credit. *Psychological Review, 65*, 117–127.

Hollander, E. P. (1960). Competence and conformity in the acceptance of influence. *Journal of Abnormal and Social Psychology, 61*, 365–369.

Hollander, E. P. (1961). Some effects of perceived status on responses to innovative behavior. *Journal of Abnormal and Social Psychology, 63*, 247–250.

Hollander, E. P. (1964). *Leaders, groups, and influence*. New York: Oxford University Press.

Hollander, E. P. (1965). Validity of peer nominations in predicting a distant performance criterion. *Journal of Applied Psychology, 49*, 434–438.

Hollander, E. P. (1971). *Principles and methods of social psychology* (2nd ed.). New York: Oxford University Press.

Hollander, E. P. (1975). Independence, conformity, and civil liberties: Some implications from social psychological research. *Journal of Social Issues, 31(2)*, 55–67.

Hollander, E. P. (1978). *Leadership dynamics: A practical guide to effective relationships*. New York: Free Press.

Hollander, E. P. (1981). *Principles and methods of social psychology*. New York: Oxford University Press.

Hollander, E. P. (1983). Women and leadership. In H. H. Blumberg, A. P. Hare, V. Kent, & M. Davies (Eds.), *Small groups and social interaction* (Vol. 1, pp. 423–429). New York: Wiley.

Hollander, E. P. (1985). Leadership and power. In G. Lindzey & E. Aronson (Eds.), *Handbook of social psychology* (Vol 2, 3rd ed., pp. 485–537). New York: Random House.

Hollander, E. P., & Julian, J. W. (1969). Contemporary trends in the analysis of leadership processes. *Psychological Bulletin, 71*, 387–397.

Hollander, M., & Kazaoka, K. (1988). Behavior therapy groups. In S. Long (Ed.), *Six group therapies* (pp. 257–326). New York: Plenum.

Hollingworth, H. L. (1935). *The psychology of the audience*. New York: American Books.

Holmes, J. G., & Miller, D. T. (1976). Interpersonal conflict. In J. W. Thibaut, J. T. Spence, & R. C. Carson (Eds.), *Contemporary topics in social psychology*. Morristown, NJ: General Learning Press.

Holmes, P. (1983). "Dropping out" from an adolescent therapeutic group: A study of factors in the patients and their parents which may influence this process. *Journal of Adolescence, 6,* 333–346.

Holsti, O. R., & North, R. (1965). The history of human conflict. In E. B. McNeil (Ed.), *The nature of human conflict.* Englewood Cliffs, NJ: Prentice-Hall.

Homans, G. C. (1950). *The human group.* New York: Harcourt, Brace, & World.

Homans, G. C. (1967). *The nature of social science.* New York: Harcourt, Brace, & World.

Homans, G. C. (1974). *Social behavior: Its elementary forms.* San Diego: Harcourt Brace Jovanovich.

Horai, J. (1977). Attributional conflict. *Journal of Social Issues, 33*(1), 88–100.

Horwitz, M., & Rabbie, J. M. (1982). Individuality and membership in the intergroup system. In H. Tajfel (Ed.), *Social identity and intergroup relations* (pp. 241–274). New York: Cambridge University Press.

Hottes, J. H., & Kahn, A. (1974). Sex differences in a mixed-motive conflict situation. *Journal of Personality, 42,* 260–275.

House, J. S. (1977). The three faces of social psychology. *Sociometry, 40,* 161–177.

House, R. J. (1971). A path goal theory of leader effectiveness. *Administrative Science Quarterly, 16,* 321–338.

House, R. J., Schuler, R. S., & Levanoni, E. (1983). Role conflict and ambiguous scales: Realities or artifacts. *Journal of Applied Psychology, 68,* 334–337.

Howard, J. A., Blumstein, P., & Schwartz, P. (1986). Sex, power, and influence tactics in intimate relationships. *Journal of Personality and Social Psychology, 51,* 102–109.

Howard, J. W., & Rothbart, M. (1980). Social categorization and memory for in-group and out-group behavior. *Journal of Personality and Social Psychology, 38,* 301–310.

Howells, L. T., & Becker, S. W. (1962). Seating arrangement and leadership emergence. *Journal of Abnormal and Social Psychology, 64,* 148–150.

Hudgins, M. K., & Preston, J. C. (1981). Psychodramatic expansion of the Johari Window. *Journal of Group Psychotherapy, Psychodrama and Sociometry, 34,* 93–99.

Huesmann, L. R., & Levinger, G. (1976). Incremental exchange theory: A formal model for progression in dyadic social interaction. In L. Berkowitz (Ed.), *Advances in experimental social psychology* (Vol. 9, pp. 192–229). New York: Academic Press.

Humphreys, P., & Berger, J. (1981). Theoretical consequences of the status characteristics formulation. *American Journal of Sociology, 86,* 953–983.

Hunt, E. B., & Rowe, R. R. (1960). Group and individual economic decision making in risk conditions. In D. W. Taylor (Ed.), *Experiments on decision making and other studies.* Arlington, VA: Armed Services Technical Information Agency.

Huston, T. L., & Burgess, R. L. (1979). Social energy in developing relationships: An overview. In R. L. Burgess & T. L. Huston (Eds.), *Social exchange in developing relationships.* New York: Academic Press.

Hyman, H. (1942). The psychology of status. *Archives of Psychology, 38* (Whole No. 269).

Hyman, H. M., & Tarrant, C. M. (1975). Aspects of American trial jury history. In R. J. Simon (Ed.), *The jury system in America.* Newbury Park, CA: Sage.

Iacocca, J. L. (1984). *Iacocca: An autobiography.* New York: Bantam.

Ickes, W. (1983). Influences of past relationships on subsequent ones. In P. B. Paulus (Ed.), *Basic group processes* (pp. 315–337). New York: Springer-Verlag.

Ickes, W., & Turner, M. (1983). On the social advantages of having an older, opposite-sex sibling: Birth order influence in mixed-sex dyads. *Journal of Personality and Social Psychology, 45,* 210–222.

Ilgen, D. R., & Fujji, D. S. (1976). An investigation of the validity of leader behavior descriptions obtained from subordinates. *Journal of Applied Psychology, 61,* 642–651.

Indik, B. P. (1965). Organization size and member participation: Some empirical tests of alternate explanations. *Human Relations, 15,* 339–350.

Ingham, A. G., Levinger, G., Graves, J., & Peckham, V. (1974). The Ringelmann effect: Studies of group size and group performance. *Journal of Personality and Social Psychology, 10,* 371–384.

Insko, C. A., Gilmore, R., Drenan, S., Lipsitz, A., Moehle, D., & Thibaut, J. (1983). Trade versus expropriation in open groups: A comparison of two types of social power. *Journal of Personality and Social Psychology, 44*, 977–999.

Insko, C. A., Pinkley, R. L., Hoyle, R. H., Dalton, B., et al. (1987). Individual versus group discontinuity: The role of intergroup contact. *Journal of Experimental Social Psychology, 23*, 250–267.

Insko, C. A., & Schopler, J. (1972). *Experimental social psychology*. New York: Academic Press.

Insko, C. A., Smith, R. A., Alicke, M. D., Wade, J., & Taylor, S. (1985). Conformity and group size: The concern with being right and the concern with being liked. *Personality and Social Psychology Bulletin, 11*, 41–50.

Insko, C. A., Thibaut, J. W., Moehle, D., Wilson, M., Diamond, W. D., Gilmore, R., Solomon, M. R., & Lipsitz, A. (1980). Social evolution and the emergence of leadership. *Journal of Personality and Social Psychology, 39*, 431–448.

Insko, C. A., & Wilson, M. (1977). Interpersonal attraction as a function of social interaction. *Journal of Personality and Social Psychology, 35*, 903–911.

Instone, D., Major, B., & Bunker, B. B. (1983). Gender, self confidence, and social influence strategies: An organizational simulation. *Journal of Personality and Social Psychology, 44*, 322–333.

Isenberg, D. J. (1986). Group polarization: A critical review and meta-analysis. *Journal of Personality and Social Psychology, 50*, 1141–1151.

Isenberg, D. J., & Ennis, J. G. (1981). Perceiving group members: A comparison of derived and imposed dimensions. *Journal of Personality and Social Psychology, 41*, 293–305.

Iverson, M. A. (1964). Personality impressions of punitive stimulus persons of differential status. *Journal of Abnormal and Social Psychology, 68*, 617–626.

Ivie, R. L. (1980). Images of savagery in American justifications for war. *Communication Monographs, 47*, 279–294.

Izraeli, D. N., Izraeli, D., & Eden, D. (1985). Giving credit where credit is due: A case of no sex bias in attribution. *Journal of Applied Social Psychology, 15*, 516–530.

Jablin, F. M. (1979). Superior-subordinate communication: The state of the art. *Psychological Bulletin, 86*, 1201–1222.

Jackson, J. M. (1986). In defense of social impact theory: Comment on Mullen. *Journal of Personality and Social Psychology, 50*, 511–513.

Jackson, J. M. (1987). Social impact theory: A social forces model of influence. In B. Mullen & G. R. Goethals (Eds.), *Theories of group behavior* (pp. 112–124). New York: Springer-Verlag.

Jackson, J. M., & Harkins, S. G. (1985). Equity in effort: An explanation of the social loafing effect. *Journal of Personality and Social Psychology, 49*, 1199–1206.

Jackson, J. M., & Latané, B. (1981). All alone in front of all those people: Stage fright as a function of number and type of co-performances and audience. *Journal of Personality and Social Psychology, 40*, 73–85.

Jackson, J. M., & Williams, K. D. (In press). *A review and theoretical analysis of social loafing.*

Jacobs, A. (1974). The use of feedback in groups. In A. Jacobs & W. W. Spradlin (Eds.), *Group as an agent of change* (pp. 408–448). New York: Behavioral Publications.

Jacobs, R. C., & Campbell, D. T. (1961). The perpetuation of an arbitrary tradition through several generations of a laboratory microculture. *Journal of Abnormal and Social Psychology, 62*, 649–658.

Jacobson, M. B., & Effertz, J. (1974). Sex roles and leadership perceptions of the leaders and the led. *Organizational Behavior and Human Performance, 12*, 383–396.

Jago, A. G. (1978). Configural cue utilization in implicit models of leader behavior. *Organizational Behavior and Human Performance, 22*, 474–496.

James, J. (1951). A preliminary study of the size determinant in social group interactions. *American Sociological Review, 16*, 474–477.

James, J. (1953). The distribution of free-forming small group size. *American Sociological Review, 18*, 569–570.

James, R. (1959). Status and competency of jurors. *American Journal of Sociology, 64*, 563–570.

Janis, I. L. (1963). Group identification under conditions of external danger. *British Journal of Medical Psychology, 36*, 227–238.

Janis, I. L. (1972). *Victims of groupthink*. Boston: Houghton-Mifflin, 1972.

Janis, I. L. (1982). *Victims of groupthink* (2nd ed.). Boston: Houghton-Mifflin.

Janis, I. L. (1983). Groupthink. In H. H. Blumberg, A. P. Hare, V. Kent, & M. F. Davis (Eds.), *Small groups and social interaction* (Vol. 2, pp. 39–46). New York: Wiley.

Janis, I. L. (1985). International crisis management in the nuclear age. *Applied Social Psychology Annual, 6,* 63–86.

Janis, I. L. (1989). *Crucial decisions: Leadership in policymaking and crisis management.* New York: Free Press.

Janis, I. L., & Mann, L. (1977). *Decision making: A psychological analysis of conflict, choice, and commitment.* New York: Free Press.

Javornisky, G. (1979). Task context and sex differences in conformity. *Journal of Social Psychology, 108,* 213–220.

Johnson, C. (1974). Planning for termination of the group. In P. Glasser, R. Sarri, & R. Vinter (Eds.), *Individual change through small groups* (pp. 258–265). New York: Free Press.

Johnson, D. W. (1980). Group processes: Influences of student-student interaction on school outcomes. In J. H. McMillan (Ed.), *The social psychology of school learning.* New York: Academic Press.

Johnson, D. W., Johnson, R. T., & Maruyama, G. (1984). Goal interdependence and interpersonal attraction in heterogeneous classrooms: A metanalysis. In N. Miller & M. Brewer (Eds.), *Groups in contact: The psychology of desegregation* (pp. 187–212). New York: Academic Press.

Johnson, D. W., Johnson, R. T., & Smith, K. A. (1986). Academic conflict among students: controversy and learning. In R. S. Feldman (Ed.), *The social psychology of education* (pp. 199–231). New York: Cambridge University Press.

Johnson, D. W., Maruyama, G., Johnson, R., Nelson, D., & Skon, L. (1981). Effects of cooperative, competitive, and individualistic goal structures on achievement: A meta-analysis. *Psychological Bulletin, 89,* 47–62.

Johnson, F. (1988). Encounter group therapy. In S. Long (Ed.), *Six group therapies* (pp. 115–158). New York: Plenum.

Johnson, M. P., & Ewens, W. (1971). Power relations and affective style as determinants of confidence in impression formation in a game situation. *Journal of Experimental Social Psychology, 7,* 98–110.

Johnson, N. R. (1974). Collective behavior as group-induced shift. *Sociological Inquiry, 44,* 105–110.

Johnson, N. R. (1987). Panic at "The Who concert stampede": An empirical assessment. *Social Problems, 34,* 362–373.

Johnson, N. R., Stemler, J. G., & Hunter, D. (1977). Crowd behavior as "risky shift": A laboratory experiment. *Sociometry, 40,* 183–187.

Johnson, R. D., & Downing, L. L. (1979). Deindividuation and valence of cues: Effects on prosocial and antisocial behavior. *Journal of Personality and Social Psychology, 37,* 1532–1538.

Jones, A. P., & James, L. R. (1979). Psychological climate: Dimensions and relationships of individual and aggregated work environment perceptions. *Organizational Behavior and Human Performance, 23,* 201–250.

Jones, E. E. (1985). Major developments in social psychology during the past five decades. In G. Lindzey & E. Aronson (Eds.), *Handbook of Social Psychology* (Vol. 1, 3rd ed., pp. 47–108). New York: Random House.

Jones, G. V. (1983). Identifying basic categories. *Psychological Bulletin, 1–94,* 423–428.

Jones, S. C. (1973). Self- and interpersonal evaluations: Esteem theories versus consistency theories. *Psychological Bulletin, 79,* 185–199.

Judd, C. M., & Park, B. (1988). Out-group homogeneity: Judgments of variability at the individual and group levels. *Journal of Personality and Social Psychology, 54,* 778–788.

Kahn, A., Hottes, J., & Davis, W. L. (1971). Cooperation and optimal responding in the Prisoner's Dilemma Game: Effects of sex and physical attractiveness. *Journal of Personality and Social Psychology, 17,* 267–279.

Kahn, A., & Ryen, A. H. (1972). Factors influencing the bias towards one's own group. *International Journal of Group Tensions, 2,* 33–50.

Kahn, R. L., Wolfe, D. M., Quinn, R. P., Snoek, J. D., & Rosenthal, R. A. (1964). *Organizational stress: Studies in role conflict and ambiguity.* New York: Wiley.

Kalven, H., Jr., & Zeisel, H. (1966). *The American jury*. Boston: Little, Brown.

Kandel, D. B. (1978). Similarity in real-life adolescent friendship pairs. *Journal of Personality and Social Psychology, 36,* 306–312.

Kanzer, M. (1983). Freud: The first psychoanalytic group leader. In H. I. Kaplan & B. J. Sadock (Eds.), *Comprehensive group psychotherapy* (2nd ed., pp. 8–14). Baltimore: Williams & Wilkins.

Kaplan, H. I., & Sadock, B. J. (Eds.). (1983). *Comprehensive group psychotherapy* (2nd ed.). Baltimore: Williams & Wilkins.

Kaplan, K. J., Firestone, I. J., Klein, K. W., & Sodikoff, C. (1983). Distancing in dyads: A comparison of four models. *Social Psychology Quarterly, 46,* 108–115.

Kaplan, M. F. (1982). Cognitive processes in the individual juror. In N. L. Kerr & R. M. Bray (Eds.), *Psychology of the courtroom* (pp. 197–220). New York: Academic Press.

Kaplan, M. F., & Miller, C. E. (1983). Group discussion and judgment. In P. B. Paulus (Ed.), *Basic group processes* (pp. 65–94). New York: Springer-Verlag.

Kaplan, M. F., & Miller, C. E. (1987). Group decision making and normative versus informational influence: Effects of type of issue and assigned decision rule. *Journal of Personality and Social Psychology, 53,* 306–313.

Kaplan, R. E. (1979). The conspicuous absence of evidence that process consultation enhances task performance. *Journal of Applied Behavioral Science, 15,* 346–360.

Kaplan, R. E. (1982). The dynamics of injury in encounter groups: Power, splitting, and the mismanagement of resistance. *International Journal of Group Psychotherapy, 32,* 163–187.

Kaplowitz, S. A. (1978). Towards a systematic theory of power attribution. *Social Psychology, 41,* 131–148.

Karabenick, S. A. (1983). Sex-relevance of content and influenceability: Sistrunk and McDavid revisited. *Personality and Social Psychology Bulletin, 9,* 243–252.

Katz, D., & Braly, K. W. (1933). Racial stereotypes of 100 college students. *Journal of Abnormal and Social Psychology, 28,* 280–290.

Katz, D., & Kahn, R. L. (1978). *The social psychology of organizations* (2nd ed.). New York: Wiley.

Katz, G. M. (1982). Previous conformity, status, and the rejection of the deviant. *Small Group Behavior, 13,* 403–422.

Katz, I. (1970). Experimental studies in Negro-white relationships. In L. Berkowitz (Ed.), *Advances in experimental social psychology* (Vol. 5, 71–117). New York: Academic Press.

Katz, R., & Tushman, M. (1979). Communication patterns, project performance, and task characteristics: An empirical evaluation and integration in an R & D setting. *Organization Behavior and Group Performance, 23,* 139–162.

Keller, R. T., & Holland, W. E. (1983). Communicators and innovators in research and development organizations. *Academy of Management Journal, 26,* 742–749.

Kelley, H. H. (1952). Two functions of reference groups. In G. E. Swanson, T. M. Newcomb, & E. L. Hartley (Eds.), *Readings in social psychology* (2nd ed.). New York: Holt.

Kelley, H. H. (1968). Interpersonal accommodation. *American Psychologist, 23,* 399–410.

Kelley, H. H. (1979). *Personal relationships: Their structures and processes*. Hillsdale, NJ: Erlbaum.

Kelley, H. H. (1983). Love and commitment. In H. H. Kelley, E. Berscheid, A. Christensen, J. H. Harvey, T. L. Huston, G. Levinger, E. McClintock, L. A. Peplau, & D. R. Peterson, *Close relationships*. New York: Freeman.

Kelley, H. H., Berscheid, E., Christensen, A., Harvey, J. H., Huston, T. L., Levinger, G., McClintock, E., Peplau, L. A., & Peterson, D. R. (1983). *Close relationships*. New York: Freeman.

Kelley, H. H., & Shapiro, M. M. (1954). An experiment on conformity to group norms where conformity is detrimental to group achievement. *American Sociological Review, 19,* 557–567.

Kelley, H. H., & Stahelski, A. J. (1970a). Errors in perceptions of intentions in a mixed-motive game. *Journal of Experimental Social Psychology, 6,* 379–400.

Kelley, H. H., & Stahelski, A. J. (1970b). Social interaction basis of cooperators' and competitors' beliefs about others. *Journal of Personality and Social Psychology, 16,* 66–91.

Kelley, H. H., & Stahelski, A. J. (1970c). The inference of intentions from moves in the Prisoner's Dilemma Game. *Journal of Experimental Social Psychology, 6,* 401–419.

Kelley, H. H., & Thibaut, J. W. (1978). *Interpersonal relations: A theory of interdependence.* New York: Wiley.

Kelman, H. C. (1958). Compliance, identification, and internalization: Three processes of attitude change. *Journal of Conflict Resolution, 2,* 51–60.

Kelman, H. C. (1961). Processes of opinion change. *Public Opinion Quarterly, 25,* 57–78.

Kemery, E. R., Bedeian, A. G., Mossholder, K. W., & Touliatos, J. (1985). Outcomes of role stress: A multisample constructive replication. *Academy of Management Review, 28,* 363–375.

Kennedy, R. F. (1969). *Thirteen days.* New York: Norton.

Kenny, D. A., & Zaccaro, S. J. (1983). An estimate of variance due to traits in leadership. *Journal of Applied Psychology, 68,* 678–685.

Kerckhoff, A. C., & Back, K. W. (1968). *The June Bug: A study of hysterical contagion.* New York: Appleton-Century-Crofts.

Kerckhoff, A. C., Back, K. W., & Miller, N. (1965). Sociometric patterns in hysterical contagion. *Sociometry, 28,* 2–15.

Kerckhoff, A. C., & Davis, K. E. (1962). Value consensus and need complementarity in mate selection. *American Sociological Review, 27,* 295–303.

Kerr, N. L. (1982). Social transition schemes: Model, method, and applications. In H. Brandstatter, J. H. Davis, & G. Stocker-Kreichgauer (Eds.), *Group decision making* (pp. 59–79). London: Academic Press.

Kerr, N. L. (1983). Motivation losses in small groups: A social dilemma analysis. *Journal of Personality and Social Psychology, 45,* 819–828.

Kerr, N. L., Atkin, R. S., Stasser, G., Meek, D., Holt, R. W., & Davis, J. H. (1976). Guilt beyond a reasonable doubt: Effect of concept definition and assigned decision rule on the judgments of mock jurors. *Journal of Personality and Social Psychology, 34,* 282–294.

Kerr, N. L., & Bruun, S. E. (1981). Ringelmann revisited: Alternative explanations for the social loafing effect. *Personality and Social Psychology Bulletin, 7,* 224–231.

Kerr, N. L., & Bruun, S. E. (1983). Dispensability of member effort and group motivation losses: Free-rider effects. *Journal of Personality and Social Psychology, 44,* 78–94.

Kerr, N. L., & Huang, J. Y. (1986). Jury verdicts: How much difference does one juror make? *Personality and Social Psychology Bulletin, 12,* 325–343.

Kerr, N. L., & MacCoun, R. J. (1985). The effects of jury size and polling method on the process and product of jury deliberation. *Journal of Personality and Social Psychology, 48,* 349–363.

Kerr, N. L., & Sullaway, M. (1983). Group sex composition and member motivation. *Sex Roles, 9,* 403–417.

Kerr, S., & Jermier, J. M. (1978). Substitutes for leadership: Their meaning and measurement. *Organizational Behavior and Human Performance, 22,* 375–403.

Kerr, S., Schriesheim, C. A., Murphy, C. J., & Stogdill, R. M. (1974). Toward a contingency theory of leadership based upon the consideration and initiating structure literature. *Organizational Behavior and Human Performance, 12,* 62–82.

Kidder, L. H. (1981). *Research methods in social relations* (4th ed.). New York: Holt, Rinehart, & Winston.

Kiesler, C. A., & Kiesler, S. B. (1976). *Conformity* (2nd ed.). Reading, MA: Addison-Wesley.

Kiesler, C. A., & Pallak, M. S. (1975). Minority influence: The effect of majority reactionaries and defectors, and minority and majority compromisers, upon majority opinion and attraction. *European Journal of Social Psychology, 5,* 237–256.

Kiesler, D. J. (1983). The 1982 interpersonal circle: A taxonomy for complementarity in human transactions. *Psychological Review, 90,* 185–214.

Kiesler, S., Siegel, J., & McGuire, T. W. (1984). Social psychological aspects of computer-mediated communication. *American Psychologist, 39,* 1123–1134.

Kilham, W., & Mann, L. (1974). Level of destructive obedience as a function of transmitter and executant roles in the Milgram obedience paradigm. *Journal of Personality and Social Psychology, 29,* 696–702.

Killian, L. M. (1984). Organization, rationality, and spontaneity in the civil rights movement. *American Sociological Review, 49*, 770–783.

Killilea, M. (1976). Mutual help organizations: Interpretations in the literature. In G. Caplan & M. Killilea (Eds.), *Support systems and mutual help: multidisciplinary explorations.* New York: Grune & Stratton.

Kinder, D. R., & Sears, D. O. (1981). Prejudice and politics: Symbolic racism versus racial threats to the good life. *Journal of Personality and Social Psychology, 40*, 414–431.

King, G. A., & Sorrentino, R. M. (1983). Psychological dimensions of goal-oriented interpersonal situations. *Journal of Personality and Social Psychology, 44*, 140–162.

Kipnis, D. (1972). Does power corrupt? *Journal of Personality and Social Psychology, 24*, 33–41.

Kipnis, D. (1974). *The powerholders.* Chicago: University of Chicago Press.

Kipnis, D. (1984). The use of power in organizations and in interpersonal settings. In S. Oskamp (Ed.), *Applied social psychology annual* (Vol. 5, pp. 179–210). Newbury Park, CA: Sage.

Kipnis, D., Castell, P. J., Gergen, M., & Mauch, D. (1976). Metamorphic effects of power. *Journal of Applied Psychology, 61*, 127–135.

Kipnis, D., & Consentino, J. (1969). Use of leadership powers in industry. *Journal of Applied Psychology, 53*, 460–466.

Kipnis, D., Schmidt, S. M., Swaffin-Smith, C., & Wilkinson, I. (1984). Patterns of managerial influence: Shotgun managers, tacticians, and bystanders. *Organizational Dynamics, 12(3)*, 58–67.

Kirchler, E., & Davis, J. H. (1986). The influence of member status differences and task type on group consensus and member position change. *Journal of Personality and Social Psychology, 51*, 83–91.

Kivlighan, D. M., Jr. (1985). Feedback in group psychotherapy: Review and implications. *Small Group Behavior, 16*, 373–386.

Kivlighan, D. M., Jr., McGovern, T.V., & Corazzini, J. G. (1984). Effects of content and timing of structuring interventions on group therapy process and outcome. *Journal of Counseling Psychology, 31*, 363–370.

Klein, R. H. (1983). Group treatment approaches. In M. Hersen, A. E. Kazdin, & A. S. Bellack (Eds.), *The clinical psychology handbook* (pp. 593–610). New York: Pergamon.

Knapp, R. P., & Shostrom, E. L. (1976). POI outcomes in studies of growth groups: A selected review. *Group and Organization Studies, 1*, 187–202.

Knight, H. C. (1921). *A comparison of the reliability of group and individual judgment.* Unpublished master's thesis, Columbia University.

Knowles, E. S. (1973). Boundaries around group interaction: The effect of group size and member status on boundary permeability. *Journal of Personality and Social Psychology, 26*, 327–331.

Knowles, E. S. (1980). An affiliative conflict theory of personal and group spatial behavior. In P. B. Paulus (Ed.), *Psychology of group influence* (pp. 133–188). Hillsdale, NJ: Erlbaum.

Knowles, E. S., & Bassett, R. L. (1976). Groups and crowds as social entities: The effects of activity, size, and member similarity on nonmembers. *Journal of Personality and Social Psychology, 34*, 837–845.

Knowles, E. S., Kreuser, B., Haas, S., Hyde, M., & Schuchart, G. E. (1976). Group size and the extension of social space boundaries. *Journal of Personality and Social Psychology, 1976, 33*, 647–654.

Koberg, C. S. (1985). Sex and situational influences on the use of power: A follow-up study. *Sex Roles, 13*, 625–639.

Kochan, T. A., Schmidt, S. M., & DeCotiis, T. A. (1975). Superior-subordinate relations: Leadership and headship. *Human Relations, 28*, 279–294.

Kogan, N., & Wallach, M. A. (1964). *Risk taking: A study of cognition and personality.* New York: Holt, Rinehart, & Winston.

Kohler, W. (1947). *Gestalt psychology.* New York: Liveright.

Komorita, S. S., & Chertkoff, J. M. (1973). A bargaining theory of coalition formation. *Psychological Review, 80*, 149–162.

Komorita, S. S., & Ellis, A. L. (1988). Level of aspiration in coalition bargaining. *Journal of Personality and Social Psychology, 54*, 421–431.

Komorita, S. S., Hamilton, T. P., & Kravitz, D. A. (1984). Effects of alternatives in coalition bargaining. *Journal of Experimental Social Psychology, 20*, 116–136.

Komorita, S. S., & Kravitz, D. A. (1983). Coalition formation: A social psychological approach. In P. B. Paulus (Ed.), *Basic group processes* (pp. 179–202). New York: Springer-Verlag.

Komorita, S. S., & Meek, D. D. (1978). Generality and validity of some theories of coalition formation. *Journal of Personality and Social Psychology, 36*, 392–404.

Komorita, S. S., & Miller, C. E. (1986). Bargaining strength as a function of coalition alternatives. *Journal of Personality and Social Psychology, 51*, 325–332.

Komorita, S. S., & Moore, D. (1976). Theories and processes of coalition formation. *Journal of Personality and Social Psychology, 33*, 371–381.

Komorita, S. S., & Nagao, D. (1983). The functions of resources in coalition bargaining. *Journal of Personality and Social Psychology, 44*, 95–106.

Korda, M. (1975). *Power! How to get it, how to use it.* New York: Ballantine.

Korman, A. K. (1974). Contingency approaches to leadership: An overview. In J. G. Hunt & L. L. Larson (Eds.), *Contingency approaches to leadership*. Carbondale, IL: Southern Illinois University Press.

Kounin, J. S. (1970). *Discipline and group management in classrooms.* New York: Holt, Rinehart, & Winston.

Kounin, J. S., & Gump, P. V. (1958). The ripple effect in discipline. *Elementary School Journal, 59*, 158–162.

Krackhardt, D., & Porter, L. W. (1986). The snowball effect: Turnover embedded in communication networks. *Journal of Applied Psychology, 71*, 50–55.

Krause, C. A. (1978). *Guyana massacre: The eyewitness account.* New York: The Washington Post.

Krauss, R. M., & Deutsch, M. (1966). Communication in interpersonal bargaining. *Journal of Personality and Social Psychology, 4*, 572–577.

Kravitz, D. A. (1981). Effects of resources and alternatives on coalition formation. *Journal of Personality and Social Psychology, 41*, 87–98.

Kravitz, D. A. (1987). Size of smallest coalition as a source of power in coalition bargaining. *European Journal of Social Psychology, 17*, 1–21.

Kravitz, D. A., & Iwaniszek, J. (1984). Number of coalitions and resources as sources of power in coalition bargaining. *Journal of Personality and Social Psychology, 47*, 534–548.

Kravitz, D. A., & Martin, B. (1986). Ringelmann rediscovered: The original article. *Journal of Personality and Social Psychology, 50*, 936–941.

Krebs, D., & Adinolfi, A. A. (1975). Physical attractiveness, social relations, and personality style. *Journal of Personality and Social Psychology, 31*, 245–253.

Kriesberg, L. (1973). *The sociology of social conflicts.* Englewood Cliffs, NJ: Prentice-Hall.

Kushell, E., & Newton, R. (1986). Gender, leadership style, and subordinate satisfaction: An experiment. *Sex Roles, 14*, 203–209.

Kushnir, T. (1984). Social psychological factors associated with the dissolution of dyadic business partnerships. *Journal of Social Psychology, 122*, 181–188.

Kuypers, B. C., Davies, D., & Glaser, K. H. (1986). Developmental arrestations in self-analytic groups. *Small Group Behavior, 17*, 269–302.

Kuypers, B. C., Davies, D., & Hazewinkel, A. (1986). Developmental patterns in self-analytic groups. *Human Relations, 39*, 793–815.

La Gaipa, J. J. (1977). Interpersonal attraction and social exchange. In S. Duck (Ed.), *Theory and practice in interpersonal attraction.* New York: Academic Press.

Lacoursiere, R. B. (1980). *The life cycle of groups.* New York: Human Sciences Press.

LaFrance, M. (1985). Postural mirroring and intergroup relations. *Personality and Social Psychology Bulletin, 11*, 207–217.

Laing, R. D. (1960). *The divided self.* London: Tavistock.

Lakin, M. (1972). *Experiential groups: The uses of interpersonal encounter, psychotherapy groups, and sensitivity training.* Morristown, NJ: General Learning Press.

Lal Goel, M. (1980). Conventional political participation. In D. H. Smith, J. Macaulay and Associates (Eds.), *Participation in social and political activities: A comprehensive analysis of political involvement, expressive leisure time, and helping behavior* (pp. 108–132). San Francisco: Jossey-Bass.

Lamm, H., & Myers, D. G. (1978). Group-induced polarization of attitudes and behavior. In L. Berkowitz (Ed.), *Advances in*

Experimental Social Psychology (Vol. 11, 145–195). New York: Academic Press.

Lamm, H., & Trommsdorff, G. (1973). Group versus individual performance on tasks requiring ideational proficiency (Brainstorming): A review. *European Journal of Social Psychology, 3,* 361–388.

Landsberger, H. A. (1958). *Hawthorne revisited.* Ithaca, NY: Cornell University.

Langer, E. J., Blank, A., & Chanowitz, B. (1978). The mindlessness of ostensibly thoughtful action. *Journal of Personality and Social Psychology, 36,* 635–642.

Langer, E. J., Chanowitz, B., & Blank, A. (1985). Mindlessness-mindfulness in perspective: A reply to Valerie Folkes. *Journal of Personality and Social Psychology, 48,* 605–607.

Langer, E. J., & Newman, H. M. (1979). The role of mindlessness in a typical social psychology experiment. *Personality and Social Psychology Bulletin, 5,* 295–298.

Lanzetta, J. T., & Roby, T. B. (1960). The relationship between certain group process variables and group problem-solving efficiency. *Journal of Social Psychology, 52,* 135–148.

LaPiere, R. (1938). *Collective behavior.* New York: McGraw-Hill.

Larson, L. L., Hunt, J. G., & Osborn, R. N. (1976). The great Hi-Hi leader behavior myth: A lesson from Occam's Razor. *Academy of Management Journal, 19,* 628.

Latané, B. (1981). The psychology of social impact. *American Psychologist, 36,* 343–356.

Latané, B. (1986). Responsibility and effort in organizations. In P. S. Goodman (Ed.), *Designing effective work groups* (pp. 277–304). San Francisco: Jossey-Bass.

Latané, B., & Bidwell, L. D. (1977). Sex and affiliation in college cafeterias. *Personality and Social Psychology Bulletin, 3,* 571–574.

Latané, B., & Darley, J. M. (1970). *The unresponsive bystanders: Why doesn't he help.* New York: Appleton-Century-Crofts.

Latané, B., & Nida, S. (1981). Ten years of research on group size and helping. *Psychological Bulletin, 39,* 308–324.

Latané, B., Williams, K., & Harkins, S. (1979). Many hands make light the work: The causes and consequences of social loafing. *Journal of Personality and Social Psychology, 37,* 822–832.

Latané, B., & Wolf, S. (1981). The social impact of majorities and minorities. *Psychological Review, 88,* 438–453.

LaTour, S. (1978). Determinants of participant and observer satisfaction with adversary and inquisitorial modes of adjudication. *Journal of Personality and Social Psychology, 36,* 1531–1545.

LaTour, S., Houlden, P., Walker, L., & Thibaut, J. (1976). Some determinants of preference for modes of conflict resolution. *Journal of Conflict Resolution, 20,* 319–356.

Lauderdale, P. (1976). Deviance and moral boundaries. *American Sociological Review, 41,* 660–676.

Lauderdale, P., Smith-Cunnien, P., Parker, J., & Inverarity, J. (1984). External threat and the definition of deviance. *Journal of Personality and Social Psychology, 46,* 1058–1068.

Laughlin, P. R. (1980). Social combination processes of cooperative problem solving groups on verbal intellective tasks. In M. Fishbein (Ed.), *Progress in social psychology.* Hillsdale, NJ: Erlbaum.

Laughlin, P. R. (1988). Collective induction: Group performance, social combination processes, and mutual majority and minority influence. *Journal of Personality and Social Psychology, 54,* 254–267.

Laughlin, P. R., & Adamopoulos, J. (1980). Social combination processes and individual learning for six-person cooperative groups on an intellective task. *Journal of Personality and Social Psychology, 38,* 941–947.

Laughlin, P. R., & Futoran, G. C. (1985). Collective induction: Social combination and sequential transition. *Journal of Personality and Social Psychology, 48,* 608–613.

Laughlin, P. R., & McGlynn, R. P. (1967). Cooperative versus competitive concept attainment as a function of sex and stimulus display. *Journal of Personality and Social Psychology, 7,* 398–402.

Laughlin, P. R., & McGlynn, R. P. (1986). Collective induction: Mutual group and individual influence by the exchange of hypotheses and evidence. *Journal of Experimental Social Psychology, 22,* 567–589.

Laughlin, P. R., & Shippy, T. A. (1983). Collective induction. *Journal of Personality and Social Psychology, 45,* 94–100.

Lawler, E. J. (1975). An experimental study of factors affecting the mobilization of revolutionary coalitions. *Sociometry, 38,* 163–179.

Lawler, E. J. (1986). Bilateral deterrence and conflict spiral: A theoretical analysis. In E. J. Lawler (Ed.), *Advances in group processes* (Vol. 3, pp. 107–130). Greenwich, CT: JAI Press.

Lawler, E. J., Ford, R. S., & Blegen, M. A. (1988). Coercive capability in conflict: A test of bilateral deterrence versus conflict spiral theory. *Social Psychology Quarterly, 51,* 93–107.

Lawler, E. J., & Thompson, M. E. (1978). Impact of a leader's responsibility for inequity on subordinate revolts. *Social Psychology Quarterly, 41,* 264–268.

Lawler, E. J., & Thompson, M. E. (1979). Subordinate response to a leader's cooptation strategy as a function of type of coalition power. *Representative Research in Social Psychology, 9,* 69–80.

Leana, C. R. (1985). A partial test of Janis' groupthink model: Effects of group cohesiveness and leader behavior on defective decision making. *Journal of Management, 11,* 5–17.

Leary, M. R. (1983). *Understanding social anxiety.* Newbury Park, CA: Sage.

Leary, M. R., & Forsyth, D. R. (1987). Attributions of responsibility for collective endeavors. In C. Hendrick (Ed.), *Review of Personality and Social Psychology: Group Process* (Vol. 8, pp. 167–188). Newbury Park, CA: Sage.

Leary, M. R., Jenkins, T. B., & Wheeler, D. S. (1986). Aspects of identity and behavioral preferences: Studies of occupational and recreational choice. *Social Psychology Quarterly, 49,* 11–18.

Leary, M. R., Robertson, R. B., Barnes, B. D., & Miller, R. S. (1986). Self-presentations of small group leaders: Effects of role requirements and leadership orientation. *Journal of Personality and Social Psychology, 51,* 742–748.

Leary, M. R., Rogers, P. A., Canfield, R. W., & Coe, C. (1986). Boredom in interpersonal encounters: Antecedents and social implications. *Journal of Personality and Social Psychology, 51,* 968–975.

Leavitt, H. J. (1951). Some effects of certain communication patterns on group perfor-

mance. *Journal of Abnormal and Social Psychology, 46,* 38–50.

Le Bon, G. (1895/1960). *The crowd* (translation of *Psychologie des foules*). New York: The Viking Press.

Leffler, A., Gillespie, D. L., & Conaty, J. C. (1982). The effects of status differentiation on nonverbal behavior. *Social Psychology Quarterly, 45,* 153–161.

Lemyre, L., & Smith, P. M. (1985). Intergroup discrimination and self-esteem in the minimal group paradigm. *Journal of Personality and Social Psychology, 49,* 660–670.

Leonard, W. M., II. (1980). *A sociological perspective on sport.* Minneapolis: Burgess.

Lepsius, M. R. (1986). Charismatic leadership: Max Weber's model and its applicability to the rule of Hitler. In C. F. Graumann & S. Moscovici (Eds.), *Changing conceptions of leadership* (pp. 53–66). New York: Springer-Verlag.

Lerner, M. J. (1974). Social psychology of justice and interpersonal attraction. In T. Huston (Ed.), *Perspectives on interpersonal attraction.* New York: Academic Press.

Lerner, M. J., & Miller, D. T. (1978). Just world research and the attribution process: Looking back and ahead. *Psychological Bulletin, 85,* 1030–1051.

Leszcz, M., Yalom, I. D., & Norden, M. (1985). The value of inpatient group psychotherapy: Patients' perceptions. *International Journal of Group Psychotherapy, 35,* 411–433.

Leung, K., & Lind, E. A. (1986). Procedural justice and culture: Effects of culture, gender, and investigator status on procedural preferences. *Journal of Personality and Social Psychology, 50,* 1134–1140.

Levine, J. M. (1980). Reaction to opinion deviance in small groups. In P. B. Paulus (Ed.), *Psychology of group influence.* Hillsdale, NJ: Erlbaum.

Levine, J. M. (1983). Social comparison and education. In J. M. Levine & M. C. Wang (Eds.), *Teacher and student perception: Implications for learning* (pp. 29–56). Hillsdale, NJ: Erlbaum.

Levine, J. M., & Ranelli, C. J. (1978). Majority reaction to shifting and stable attitudinal deviates. *European Journal of Social Psychology, 8,* 55–70.

Levine, J. M., & Ruback, R. B. (1980). Reaction to opinion deviance: Impact of a fence-straddler's rationale on majority evaluation. *Social Psychology Quarterly, 43,* 73–81.

Levine, J. M., & Russo, E. M. (1987). Majority and minority influence. In C. Hendrick (Ed.), *Review of personality and social psychology: Group process* (Vol. 8, pp. 13–54). Newbury Park, CA: Sage.

Levine, J. M., Saxe, L., & Harris, H. J. (1976). Reaction to attitudinal deviance: Impact of deviate's direction and distance of movement. *Sociometry, 39,* 97–107.

Levine, J. M., Sroka, K. R., & Snyder, H. N. (1977). Group support and reaction to stable and shifting agreement/disagreement. *Sociometry, 40,* 214–224.

LeVine, R. A., & Campbell, D. T. (1972). *Ethnocentrism: Theories of conflict, ethnic attitudes, and group behavior.* New York: Wiley.

Levinger, G., Senn, D. J., & Jorgensen, B. W. (1970). Progress toward permanence in courtship: A test of the Kerckhoff-Davis hypothesis. *Sociometry, 33,* 427–433.

Lewin, K. (1936). *Principles of topological psychology.* New York: McGraw-Hill.

Lewin, K. (1943). Forces behind food habits and methods of change. *Bulletin of the National Research Council, 108,* 35–65.

Lewin, K. (1948). *Resolving social conflicts: Selected papers on group dynamics.* New York: Harper.

Lewin, K. (1951). *Field theory in social science.* New York: Harper.

Lewin, K., Lippitt, R., & White, R. (1939). Patterns of aggressive behavior in experimentally created "social climates." *Journal of Social Psychology, 10,* 271–299.

Lewis, C. M. (1984). The impact of tasks of group development on the psychotherapeutic treatment of depression in groups. *International Journal of Mental Health, 13,* 105–118.

Lewis, H. S. (1974). *Leaders and followers: Some anthropological perspectives.* Reading, Mass.: Addison-Wesley.

Lewis, S. A., Langan, C. J., & Hollander, E. P. (1972). Expectation of future interaction and the choice of less desirable alternatives in conformity. *Sociometry, 35,* 404–447.

Ley, D., & Cybriwsky, R. (1974a). The spatial ecology of stripped cars. *Environment and Behavior, 6,* 53–68.

Ley, D., & Cybriwsky, R. (1974b). Urban graffiti as territorial markers. *Annals of the Association of American Geographers, 64,* 491–505.

Lieberman, M. A. (1976). Change induction in small groups. *Annual Review of Psychology, 27,* 217–250.

Lieberman, M. A. (1980). Group methods. In F. H. Kanfer & A. P. Goldstein (Eds.), *Helping people change.* New York: Pergamon.

Lieberman, M. A., Yalom, I., & Miles, M. (1973). *Encounter groups: First facts.* New York: Basic Books.

Likert, R. (1961). *New patterns of management.* New York: McGraw-Hill.

Likert, R. (1967). *The human organization.* New York: McGraw-Hill.

Lind, E. A., Kurtz, S., Musante, L., Walker, L., & Thibaut, J. W. (1980). Procedure and outcome effects on reactions to adjudicated resolution of conflicts of interest. *Journal of Personality and Social Psychology, 39,* 643–656.

Lindblom, C. E. (1965). *The intelligence of democracy.* New York: Free Press.

Lindskold, S. (1978). Trust development, the GRIT proposal, and the effects of conciliatory acts on conflict and cooperation. *Psychological Bulletin, 85,* 772–793.

Lindskold, S. (1979). Conciliation with simultaneous or sequential interaction. *Journal of Conflict Resolution, 23,* 704–714.

Lindskold, S. (1986). GRIT: Reducing distrust through carefully introduced conciliation. In S. Worchel & W. G. Austin (Eds.), *Psychology of intergroup relations* (2nd ed., pp. 305–322). Chicago: Nelson-Hall.

Lindskold, S., Albert, K. P., Baer, R., & Moore, W. C. (1976). Territorial boundaries of interacting groups and passive audiences. *Sociometry, 39,* 71–76.

Lindskold, S., & Arnoff, J. R. (1980). Conciliatory strategies and relative power. *Journal of Experimental Social Psychology, 16,* 187–198.

Lindskold, S., & Collins, M. G. (1978). Inducing cooperation by groups and individuals. *Journal of Conflict Resolution, 22,* 679–690.

Lindskold, S., Finch, M. L. (1982). Anonymity and the resolution of conflicting pressures from the experimenter and from peers. *Journal of Psychology, 112,* 79–86.

Lindskold, S., Han, G., & Betz, B. (1986). Essential elements of communication in GRIT strategy. *Personality and Social Psychology Bulletin, 12,* 179–186.

Lindzey, G., & Borgatta, E. F. (1954). Sociometric measurement. In G. Lindzey (Ed.), *Handbook of social psychology.* Cambridge, MA: Addison-Wesley.

Linville, P. W. (1982). The complexity-extremity effect and age-based stereotyping. *Journal of Personality and Social Psychology, 42,* 193–211.

Linville, P. W., & Jones, E. E. (1980). Polarized appraisals of out-group members. *Journal of Personality and Social Psychology, 38,* 689–703.

Lippitt, R. (1947). Kurt Lewin, 1890–1947: Adventures in the exploration of interdependence. *Sociometry, 10,* 87–97.

Lippmann, W. (1922). *Public opinion.* New York: Harcourt & Brace.

Litman-Adizes, T., Fontaine, G., & Raven, B. (1978). Consequences of social power and causal attribution for compliance as seen by powerholder and target. *Personality and Social Psychology Bulletin, 4,* 260–264.

Littlepage, G. E., Cowart, L., & Kerr, B. (1989). Relationships between group environment scales and group performance and cohesion. *Small Group Behavior, 20,* 50–61.

Littlepage, G. E., West, W. B., Beard, D., Robeson, L., & Bryant, J. (1988, April). *Effects of group size and task characteristics on group performance: A test of Steiner's model.* Paper presented at the Eleventh Biennial Psychology Conference, United States Air Force Academy, Colorado Springs, Colorado.

Llewelyn, S. P., & Haslett, A. V. (1986). Factors perceived as helpful by the members of self help groups: An exploratory study. *British Journal of Guidance and Counselling, 14,* 252–262.

Lockheed, M. E., & Hall, K. (1976). Conceptualizing sex as a status characteristic: Applications to leadership training strategies. *Journal of Social Issues, 32,* 111–124.

Lockheed, M. E., Harris, A. M., & Nemceff, W. P. (1983). Sex and social influence: Does sex function as a status characteristic in mixed-sex groups of children? *Journal of Educational Psychology, 75,* 877–888.

Lombardo, M. M., & McCall, M. W., Jr. (1984). The intolerable boss. *Psychology Today, 18*(1), 45–54.

Long, S. (Ed.). (1988). *Six group therapies.* New York: Plenum.

Longley, J., & Pruitt, D. G. (1980). Groupthink: A critique of Janis's theory. In L. Wheeler (Ed.), *Review of personality and social psychology* (Vol. 1). Newbury Park, CA: Sage.

Lord, R. G. (1977). Functional leadership behavior: Measurement and relation to social power and leadership perceptions. *Administrative Science Quarterly, 22,* 114–133.

Lord, R. G. (1985). An information processing approach to social perceptions, leadership, and behavioral measurement in organizations. In L. L. Cummings and B. M. Staw (Eds.), *Research in organizational behavior* (Vol. 7, pp. 87–128). Greenwich, CT: JAI Press.

Lord, R. G., & Alliger, G. M. (1985). A comparison of four information processing models of leadership and social perception. *Human Relations, 38,* 47–65.

Lord, R. G., Binning, J. F., Rush, M. C., & Thomas, J. C. (1978). The effect of performance cues and leader behavior on questionnaire ratings of leadership behavior. *Organizational Behavior and Human Performance, 21,* 27–39.

Lord, R. G., De Vader, C. L., & Alliger, G. M. (1986). A meta-analysis of the relation between personality traits and leadership perceptions: An application of validity generalization procedures. *Journal of Applied Psychology, 71,* 402–410.

Lord, R. G., Foti, R. J., & De Vader, C. L. (1984). A test of leadership categorization theory: Internal structure, information processing, and leadership perceptions. *Organization Behavior and Human Performance, 34,* 343–378.

Lorge, I., Fox, D., Davitz, J., & Brenner, M. (1958). A survey of studies contrasting quality of group performance and individual performance, 1920–1957. *Psychological Bulletin, 55,* 337–372.

Lorge, I., & Solomon, H. (1955). Two models of group behavior in the solution of Eureka-type problems. *Psychometrika, 20,* 139–148.

Lott, A. J., & Lott, B. E. (1965). Group cohesiveness as interpersonal attraction: A review of relationships with antecedent and consequent variables. *Psychological Bulletin, 64,* 259–309.

Lott, A. J., Lott, B. E., Reed, T., & Crow, T. (1970). Personality-trait descriptions of differentially liked persons. *Journal of Personality and Social Psychology, 16,* 284–290.

Lubenow, G. C., & Rogers, M. (1985, September 30). Jobs talks about his rise and fall. *Newsweek, 106,* 51–57.

Luce, R. D., & Raiffa, H. (1957). *Games and decisions.* New York: Wiley.

Lueder, D. C. (1985a). Don't be misled by LEAD. *Journal of Applied Behavioral Science, 21,* 143–151.

Lueder, D. C. (1985b). A rejoinder to Dr. Hersey. *Journal of Applied Behavioral Science, 21,* 154.

Luft, J. (1984). *Groups process: An introduction to group dynamics* (3rd. ed.). Palo Alto, CA: Mayfield.

Luthans, F., Welsh, D. H., & Taylor, L. A. (1988). A descriptive model of managerial effectiveness. *Group and Organizational Studies, 13,* 148–162.

Lyman, S. M., & Scott, M. B. (1967). Territoriality: A neglected sociological dimension. *Social Problems, 15,* 236–249.

Maass, A., & Clark, R. D., III. (1984). Hidden impact of minorities: Fifteen years of minority influence research. *Psychological Bulletin, 95,* 428–450.

Maass, A., West, S. G., & Cialdini, R. B. (1987). Minority influence and conversion. In C. Hendrick (Ed.), *Review of Personality and social psychology: Group process* (Vol. 8, pp. 55–79). Newbury Park, CA: Sage.

MacCracken, M. J., & Stadulis, R. E. (1985). Social facilitation of young children's dynamic balance performance. *Journal of Sport Psychology, 7,* 150–165.

Mack, R. W., & Snyder, R. C. (1957). The analysis of social conflict—Toward an overview and synthesis. *Journal of Conflict Resolution, 1,* 212–248.

McAdam, D., McCarthy, J. D., & Zald, M. N. (1988). Social movements. In N. J. Smelser (Ed.), *The handbook of sociology* (pp. 695–737). Newbury Park, CA: Sage.

McAdams, D. P., & Constantian, C. A. (1983). Intimacy and affiliation motives in daily living: An experience sampling analysis. *Journal of Personality and Social Psychology, 45,* 851–861.

McAdams, D. P., Healy, S., & Krause, S. (1984). Social motives and patterns of friendship. *Journal of Personality and Social Psychology, 47,* 828–383.

McArthur, L. Z. & Friedman, S. (1980). Illusory correlation in impression formation: Variations in the shared distinctiveness effect as a function of the distinctive person's age, race, and sex. *Journal of Personality and Social Psychology, 39,* 615–624.

McBride, G. (1964). A general theory of social organization of behavior. *University of Queensland Papers, 1,* 75–110.

McBurney, D. H., Levine, J. M., & Cavanaugh, P. H. (1977). Psychophysical and social ratings of human body odor. *Personality and Social Psychology Bulletin, 3,* 135–138.

McCallum, D. M., Harring, K., Gilmore, R., Drenan, S., Chase, J. P., Insko, C. A., & Thibaut, J. (1985). Competition and cooperation between groups and between individuals. *Journal of Experimental Social Psychology, 21,* 301–320.

McCallum, R., Rusbult, C. E., Hong, G. K., Walden, T., & Schopler, J. (1979). Effects of resource availability and importance of behavior on the experience of crowding. *Journal of Personality and Social Psychology, 37,* 1304–1313.

McCauley, C. C., Stitt, L., & Segal, M. (1980). Stereotyping: From prejudice to prediction. *Psychological Bulletin, 87,* 195–208.

McClelland, D. C. (1975). *Power: The inner experience.* New York: Irvington.

McClelland, D. C. (1985). How motives, skills, and values determine what people do. *American Psychologist, 40,* 812–825.

McClintock, C. G., Stech, F. J., & Keil, L. J. (1983). The influence of communication on bargaining. In P. B. Paulus (Ed.), *Basic group processes* (pp. 205–233). New York: Springer-Verlag.

McCranie, E. W., & Kimberly, J. C. (1973). Rank inconsistency, conflicting expectations, and injustice. *Sociometry, 36,* 152–176.

McDougall, W. (1908). *An introduction to social psychology.* London: Methuen.

McGill, M. E. (1977). *Organization development for operating managers.* New York: AMACOM.

McGillicuddy, N. B., Pruitt, D. G., & Syna, H. (1984). Perceptions of firmness and strength in negotiation. *Personality and Social Psychology Bulletin, 10,* 402–409.

McGlynn, R. (1982). A comment on the meta-analysis of goal structures. *Psychological Bulletin, 92,* 184–185.

McGrath, J. E. (1978). Small group research. *American Behavioral Scientist, 21,* 651–674.

McGrath, J. E. (1984). *Groups: Interaction and performance.* Englewood Cliffs, NJ: Prentice-Hall.

McGraw, K. M., & Bloomfield, J. (1987). Social influence on group moral decisions: The interactive effects of moral reasoning and sex role orientation. *Journal of Personality and Social Psychology, 53,* 1080–1087.

McGregor, D. (1960). *The human side of enterprise.* New York: McGraw-Hill.

McGuire, T. W., Kiesler, S., & Siegel, J. (1987). Group and computer-mediated discussion effects in risk decision making. *Journal of Personality and Social Psychology, 52,* 917–930.

MacKenzie, K. R. (1987). Therapeutic factors in group psychotherapy: A contemporary view. *Group, 11,* 26–34.

MacKenzie, K. R., & Livesley, W. J. (1984). Developmental stages: An integrating theory of group psychotherapy. *Canadian Journal of Psychiatry, 29,* 247–251.

Mackie, D. M., & Goethals, G. R. (1987). Individual and group goals. *Review of Personality and Social Psychology, 8,* 144–166.

McMahon, J. T. (1972). The contingency model: Logic and method revised. *Personnel Psychology, 25,* 697–710.

McMahon, N., & Links, P. S. (1984). Cotherapy: The need for positive pairing. *Canadian Journal of Psychiatry, 29,* 385–389.

MacNeil, M. K., & Sherif, M. (1976). Norm change over subject generations as a function of arbitrariness of prescribed norm. *Journal of Personality and Social Psychology, 34,* 762–773.

McPhail, C., & Wohlstein, R. R. (1983). Individual and collective behaviors within gatherings, demonstrations, and riots. *Annual Review of Sociology, 9,* 579–600.

Magaro, P. A., & Ashbrook, R. M. (1985). The personality of societal groups. *Journal of Personality and Social Psychology, 48,* 1479–1489.

Maier, N. R. F. (1950). The quality of group decisions as influenced by the discussion leader. *Human Relations, 3,* 155–174.

Maier, N. R. F., & Solem, A. R. (1952). The contribution of a discussion leader to the quality of group thinking: The effective use of minority opinions. *Human Relations, 5,* 277–288.

Maki, J. E., Thorngate, W. B., & McClintock, C. G. (1979). Prediction and perception of social motives. *Journal of Personality and Social Psychology, 37,* 203–220.

Manis, M., Cornell, S. D., & Moore, J. C. (1974). Transmission of attitude-relevant information through a communication chain. *Journal of Personality and Social Psychology, 30,* 81–94.

Mann, F. C. (1965). Toward an understanding of the leadership role in formal organizations. In R. Dubin, G. C. Homans, F. C. Mann, & D. C. Miller (Eds.), *Leadership and productivity.* San Francisco: Chandler.

Mann, F. C., & Likert, R. (1952). The need for research on the communication of research results. *Human Organization, 11*(4), 14–19.

Mann, L. (1969). Queue culture. The waiting line as a social system. *American Journal of Sociology, 75,* 340–354.

Mann, L. (1970). The psychology of waiting lines. *American Scientist, 58,* 390–398.

Mann, L. (1979). Sports crowds viewed from the perspective of collective behavior. In J. H. Goldstein (Ed.), *Sports, games, and play: Social and psychological viewpoints.* Hillsdale, NJ: Erlbaum.

Mann, L. (1980). Cross-cultural studies of small groups. In H. C. Triandis & R. W. Brislin (Eds.), *Handbook of Cross-Cultural Psychology: Social Psychology* (Vol. 5). Boston: Allyn & Bacon.

Mann, L. (1981). The baiting crowd in episodes of threatened suicide. *Journal of Personality and Social Psychology, 41,* 703–709.

Mann, L., Newton, J. W., & Innes, J. M. (1982). A test between deindividuation and emergent norm theories of crowd aggression. *Journal of Personality and Social Psychology, 42,* 260–272.

Mann, R. D. (1959). A review of the relationships between personality and performance in small groups. *Psychological Bulletin, 56,* 241–270.

Manz, C. C., & Sims, H. P. (1982). The potential for "groupthink" in autonomous work groups. *Human Relations, 35,* 773–784.

March, J. G., & Simon, H. A. (1958). *Organization.* New York: Wiley.

Markovitz, R. J., & Smith, J. E. (1983). Patients' perceptions of curative factors in short term group psychotherapy. *International Journal of Group Psychotherapy, 33,* 21–39.

Markovsky, B., Smith, L. F. & Berger, J. (1984). Do status interventions persist? *American Sociological Review, 49,* 373–382.

Markus, H. (1978). The effect of mere presence on social facilitation: An unobtrusive test. *Journal of Experimental Social Psychology, 14,* 389–397.

Markus, H. (1981). The drive for integration: Some comments. *Journal of Experimental Social Psychology, 17,* 257–261.

Markus, H., & Zajonc, R. B. (1985). The cognitive perspective in social psychology. In G. Lindzey & E. Aronson (Eds.), *Handbook of Social Psychology* (Vol. 1, 3rd ed., pp. 137–230). New York: Random House.

Marquart, D. I. (1955). Group problem solving. *Journal of Social Psychology, 41,* 103–113.

Marrow, A. J. (1964). *Behind the executive mask.* New York: American Management Association.

Marrow, A. J. (1969). *The practical theorist: The life and work of Kurt Lewin.* New York: Basic Books.

Marrow, A. J., Bowers, D. G., & Seashore, S. E. (1967). *Management by participation.* New York: Harper & Row.

Martens, R., & Landers, D. M. (1972). Evaluation potential as a determinant of coaction effects. *Journal of Experimental Social Psychology, 8,* 347–359.

Martens, R., Landers, D. M., & Loy, J. (1972). *Sports cohesiveness questionnaire.* American Association of Health, Physical Education, and Recreation.

Martin, E. D. (1920). *The behavior of crowds.* New York: Harper.

Martin, J., Lobb, B., Chapman, G. C., & Spillane, R. (1976). Obedience under conditions demanding self-immolation. *Human Relations, 29,* 345–356.

Martin, M. W., & Sell, J. (1985). The effect of equating status characteristics on the generalization process. *Social Psychology Quarterly, 48,* 178–182.

Marwell, G., & Schmitt, D. R. (1967). Dimensions of compliance-gaining behavior: An empirical analysis. *Sociometry, 30,* 350–364.

Marx, K., & Engels, F. (1947). *The German ideology.* New York: International Publishers.

Maslach, C. (1972). Social and personal bases of individuation. *Proceedings of the 80th Annual Convention of the American Psychological Association, 7,* 213–214.

Maslach, C., Santee, R. T., & Wade, C. (1987). Individuation, gender role, and dissent: Personality mediators of situational forces. *Journal of Personality and Social Psychology, 53,* 1088–1093.

Maslow, A. H. (1968). *Toward a psychology of being.* New York: Van Nostrand Reinhold.

Mathes, E. W., & Guest, T. A. (1976). Anonymity and group antisocial behavior. *Journal of Social Psychology, 100,* 257–262.

Mathes, E. W., & Kahn, A. (1975). Diffusion of responsibility and extreme behavior. *Journal of Personality and Social Psychology, 5,* 881–886.

Maxmen, J. (1973). Group therapy as viewed by hospitalized patients. *Archives of General Psychiatry, 28,* 404–408.

Maxmen, J. (1978). An educative model for in-patient group therapy. *International Journal of Group Psychotherapy, 28,* 321–338.

Mayadas, N., & Glasser, P. (1985). Termination: A neglected aspect of social group work. In M. Sundel, P. Glasser, R. Sarri, & R. Vinter (Eds.), *Individual change through small groups* (2nd ed., pp. 251–261). New York: Free Press.

Mayer, T. (1975). *Mathematical models of group structure.* New York: Bobbs-Merrill.

Mayo, E. (1933). *The human problems of an industrial civilization.* Cambridge, MA: Harvard University Press.

Mayo, E. (1945). *The social problems of an industrial civilization.* Cambridge, MA: Harvard University Press.

Mazur, A. (1973). Cross-species comparison of status in established small groups. *American Sociological Review, 38,* 513–529.

Mazur, A. (1983). Hormones, aggression, and dominance in humans. In B. Svare (Ed.), *Hormones and aggressive behavior*. New York: Plenum.

Mazur, A., Rosa, E., Faupel, M., Heller, J., Leen, R., & Thurman, B. (1980). Physiological aspects of communication via mutual gaze. *American Journal of Sociology, 86*, 50–74.

Meadow, A., Parnes, S. J., & Reese, H. (1959). Influence of brainstorming instructions and problem sequence on a creative problem solving test. *Journal of Applied Psychology, 43*, 413–416.

Medalia, N. Z., & Larsen, O. N. (1958). Diffusion and belief in a collective delusion: The Seattle windshield pitting epidemic. *American Sociological Review, 23*, 180–186.

Meerloo, J. A. (1950). *Patterns of panic*. New York: International Universities Press.

Megargee, E. I. (1969). Influence of sex roles on the manifestation of leadership. *Journal of Applied Psychology, 53*, 377–382.

Mehrabian, A. (1972). *Nonverbal communication*. Chicago: Aldine-Atherton.

Mehrabian, A. (1980). *Basic dimensions of a general psychological theory*. Cambridge, MA: Oelgeschlanger, Gunn, and Hain.

Mehrabian, A., & Diamond, S. G. (1971). Effects of furniture arrangement, props, and personality on social interaction. *Journal of Personality and Social Psychology, 20*, 18–30.

Meindl, J. R., & Lerner, M. J. (1984). Exacerbation of extreme responses to an outgroup. *Journal of Personality and Social Psychology, 47*, 71–84.

Melton, J. G. (1986). *Encyclopedic handbook of cults in America*. New York: Garland.

Merei, F. (1958). Group leadership and institutionalization. In E. E. Maccoby, T. M. Newcomb, & E. L. Hartley (Eds.), *Readings in social psychology* (3rd ed.). New York: Holt, Rinehart, & Winston.

Merton, R. K. (1957). *Social theory and social structure*. New York: Free Press.

Messé, L. A., Stollak, G. E., Larson, R. W., & Michaels, G. Y. (1979). Interpersonal consequences of person perception in two social contexts. *Journal of Personality and Social Psychology, 37*, 369–379.

Messick D. M., & Brewer, M. B. (1983). Solving social dilemmas: A review. In L. Wheeler & P. Shaver (Eds.), *Review of Personality and Social Psychology* (Vol. 4, pp. 11–44). Newbury Park, CA: Sage.

Meumann, E., (1904) Haus- und Schularbeit: Experimente an Kindern der Volkschule. *Die Deutsche Schule, 8*, 278–303, 337–359, 416–431.

Meuwese, W., & Fiedler, F. E. (1965). *Leadership and group creativity under varying conditions of stress*. Urbana, IL: University of Illinois, Group Effectiveness Research Laboratory.

Meyer, J. P., & Pepper, S. (1977). Need compatibility and marital adjustment in young married couples. *Journal of Personality and Social Psychology, 35*, 331–342.

Michels, R. (1915/1959). *Political parties: A sociological study of the oligarchical tendencies of modern democracy*. New York: Dover.

Michener, H. A., & Burt, M. R. (1975a). Components of "authority" as determinants of compliance. *Journal of Personality and Social Psychology, 31*, 606–614.

Michener, H. A., & Burt, M. R. (1975b). Use of social influence under varying conditions of legitimacy. *Journal of Personality and Social Psychology, 32*, 398–407.

Michener, H. A., & Lawler, E. J. (1975). The endorsement of formal leaders: An integrative model. *Journal of Personality and Social Psychology, 31*, 216–223.

Middlemist, R. D., Knowles, E. S., & Matter, C. F. (1976). Personal space invasions in the lavatory: Suggestive evidence for arousal. *Journal of Personality and Social Psychology, 33*, 541–546.

Milburn, T. W. (1977). The nature of threat. *Journal of Social Issues, 33*(1), 126–139.

Miles, R. H. (1976). A comparison of the relative impacts of role perceptions of ambiguity and conflict by role. *Academy of Management Journal, 19*, 25–35.

Milgram, S. (1963). Behavioral study of obedience. *Journal of Abnormal and Social Psychology, 67*, 371–378.

Milgram, S. (1964). Issues in the study of obedience: A reply to Baumrind. *American Psychologist, 19*, 848–852.

Milgram, S. (1965). Liberating effects of group pressure. *Journal of Personality and Social Psychology, 1*, 127–134.

Milgram, S. (1970). The experience of living in cities. *Science, 167*, 1461–1468.

Milgram, S. (1974). *Obedience to authority*. New York: Harper & Row.

Milgram, S. (1977, October). Subject reaction: The neglected factor in the ethics of experimentation. *Hastings Center Report*, 19–23.

Milgram, S., Bickman, L., & Berkowitz, L. (1969). Note on the drawing power of crowds of different size. *Journal of Personality and Social Psychology, 13,* 79–82.

Milgram, S., Liberty, H. J., Toledo, R., & Wackenhut, J. (1986). Response to intrusion into waiting lines. *Journal of Personality and Social Psychology, 51,* 683–689.

Milgram, S., & Toch, H. (1969). Collective behavior: Crowds and social movements. In G. Lindzey & E. Aronson (Eds.), *The handbook of social psychology* (Vol. 4, 2nd ed.). Reading, MA: Addison-Wesley.

Miller, A. G. (1982). Historical and contemporary perspectives on stereotyping. In A. G. Miller (Ed.), *In the eye of the beholder: Contemporary issues in stereotyping*. New York: Praeger.

Miller, A. G. (1986). *The obedience experiments*. New York: Praeger.

Miller, C. E. (1980a). A test of four theories of coalition formation: Effects of payoffs and resources. *Journal of Personality and Social Psychology, 38,* 153–164.

Miller, C. E. (1980b). Coalition formation in characteristic function games: Competitive tests of three theories. *Journal of Experimental Social Psychology, 16,* 61–76.

Miller, C. E. (1980c). Effects of payoffs on coalition formation: A test of three theories. *Social Psychology Quarterly, 43,* 154–164.

Miller, C. E., & Crandall, R. (1980). Experimental research on the social psychology of bargaining and coalition formation. In P. B. Paulus (Ed.), *Psychology of group influence* (pp. 333–374). Hillsdale, NJ: Erlbaum.

Miller, C. E., Jackson, P., Mueller, J., & Schersching, C. (1987). Some social psychological effects of group decision rules. *Journal of Personality and Social Psychology, 52,* 325–332.

Miller, C. E., & Komorita, S. S. (1986a). Changes in outcomes in coalition bargaining. *Journal of Personality and Social Psychology, 51,* 720–729.

Miller, C. E., & Komorita, S. S. (1986b). Coalition formation in organizations: What laboratory studies do and do not tell us. In R. J. Lewicki, B. H. Sheppard, & M. H.

Bazerman (Eds.), *Research on negotiation in organizations* (Vol. 1, pp. 117–137). Greenwich, CT: JAI.

Miller, C. E., & Wong, J. (1986). Coalition behavior: Effects of earned versus unearned resources. *Organizational Behavior and Human Decision Processes, 38,* 257–277.

Miller, D. L. (1985). *Introduction to collective behavior*. Belmont, CA: Wadsworth.

Miller, D. T., & Holmes, J. G. (1975). The role of situational restrictiveness on self-fulfilling prophecies: A theoretical and empirical extension of Kelley and Stahelski's triangle hypothesis. *Journal of Personality and Social Psychology, 31,* 661–673.

Miller, D. T., & Norman, S. A. (1975). Actor-observer differences in perceptions of effective control. *Journal of Personality and Social Psychology, 31,* 503–515.

Miller, F. D. (1983). Group processes in successful community groups. In H. H. Blumberg, A. P. Hare, V. Kent, & M. F. Davies (Eds.), *Small groups and social interaction* (Vol. 2, pp. 329–335). New York: Wiley.

Miller, N., & Brewer, M. B. (1986a). Categorization effects on ingroup and outgroup perception. In J. Dovidio & S. Gaertner (Eds.), *Prejudice, discrimination, and racism: Theory and research* (pp. 209–230). New York: Academic Press.

Miller, N., & Brewer, M. B. (1986b). Social categorization theory and team learning procedures. In R. S. Feldman (Ed.), *The social psychology of education* (pp. 172–198). New York: Cambridge University Press.

Miller, N., & Davidson-Podgorny, G. (1987). Theoretical models of intergroup relations and the use of cooperative teams as an intervention for desegregated settings. In C. Hendrick (Ed.), *Review of Personality and Social Psychology: Group Process* (Vol. 9, pp. 41–67). Newbury Park, CA: Sage.

Mills, T. M. (1962). A sleeper variable in small groups research: The experimenter. *Pacific Sociological Review, 5,* 21–28.

Miner, J. B. (1975). The uncertain future of the leadership concept: An overview. In J. G. Hunt & L. Larson (Eds.), *Leadership frontiers*. Kent, OH: Kent State University Press.

Mintzberg, H. (1975). The manager's job: Folklore and fact. *Harvard Business Review, 53,* 49–61.

Mintzberg, H. (1979). *The structuring of organizations*. Englewood Cliffs, NJ: Prentice-Hall.

Mintzberg, H. (1980). *The nature of managerial work* (2nd ed.). Englewood Cliffs, NJ: Prentice-Hall.

Misumi, J. (1985). *The behavioral science of leadership*. Ann Arbor: University of Michigan Press.

Mitchell, R. C., & Mitchell, R. R. (1984). Constructive management of conflict in groups. *Journal for Specialists in Group Work, 9*, 137–144.

Mitroff, I. I., & Kilmann, R. H. (1978). *Methodological approaches to social science*. San Francisco: Jossey-Bass.

Miyamoto, M. (1985) Effects of audience status upon free recall performance. *Japanese Journal of Psychology, 56*, 171–174.

Mobley, W. H., Griffeth, R. W., Hand, H. H., & Meglino, B. M. (1979). Review and conceptual analysis of employee turnover process. *Psychological Bulletin, 86*, 493–522.

Moede, W. (1927). Die Richtlinien der Leistungs-Psychologie. *Industrielle Psychotechnik, 4*, 193–207.

Mohr, P. B. (1986). Demeanor, status cue or performance? *Social Psychology Quarterly, 49*, 228–236.

Molm, L. D. (1986). Gender, power, and legitimation: A test of three theories. *American Journal of Sociology, 91*, 1156–1186.

Molm, L. D. (1987). Extending power-dependence theory: Power processes and negative outcomes. In E. J. Lawler & B. Markovsky (Eds.), *Advances in group processes* (Vol. 4, pp. 171–198). Greenwich, CT: JAI.

Molm, L. D. (1988). The structure and use of power: A comparison of reward and punishment power. *Social Psychology Quarterly, 51*, 108–122.

Monge, P. R., Edwards, J. A., & Kirste, K. K. (1983). Determinants of communication network involvement: Connectedness and integration. *Group and Organization Studies, 8*, 83–111.

Moore, L. E. (1973). *The jury*. Cincinnati: W. H. Anderson.

Moorhead, G. (1982). Groupthink: Hypothesis in need of testing. *Group and Organization Studies, 7*, 429–444.

Moorhead, G., & Montanari, J. R. (1986). An empirical investigation of the groupthink phenomenon. *Human Relations, 39*, 399–410.

Moos, R. H., & Humphrey, B. (1974). *Group environment scale, Form R*. Palo Alto, CA: Consulting Psychologists Press.

Moos, R. H., Insel, P. M., & Humphrey, B. (1974). *Preliminary manual for family environment scale, work environment scale, and group environment scale*. Palo Alto, CA: Consulting Psychologists Press.

Morasch, B., Groner, N., & Keating, J. (1979). Type of activity and failure as mediators of perceived crowding. *Personality and Social Psychology Bulletin, 5*, 223–226.

Moreland, R. L. (1985). Social categorization and the assimilation of "new" group members. *Journal of Personality and Social Psychology, 48*, 1173–1190.

Moreland, R. L. (1987). The formation of small groups. *Review of Personality and Social Psychology, 8*, 80–110.

Moreland, R. L., & Levine, J. M. (1982). Socialization in small groups: Temporal changes in individual-group relations. In L. Berkowitz (Ed.), *Advances in experimental social psychology* (Vol. 15, 137–192). New York: Academic Press.

Moreland, R. L., & Levine, J. M. (1984). Role transitions in small groups. In V. L. Allen & E. van de Vliert (Eds.), *Role transitions: Explorations and explanations* (pp. 181–195). New York: Plenum.

Moreland, R. L., & Levine, J. M. (1988). Group dynamics over time: Development and socialization in small groups. In J. E. McGrath (Ed.), *The social psychology of time: New perspectives* (pp. 151–181). Newbury Park, CA: Sage.

Morelock, T. C. (1980). Sex differences in susceptibility to social influence. *Sex Roles, 6*, 537–548.

Moreno, J. L. (1932). *Who shall survive?* Washington, DC: Nervous and Mental Disease Publishing Co.

Moreno, J. L. (1953). *Who shall survive?* (rev. ed.). Beacon, New York: Beacon House.

Moreno, J. L. (Ed.). (1960). *The sociometry reader*. Glencoe, New York: Free Press.

Moreno, Z. T. (1973). Origins of the group psychotherapy movement. *Handbook of International Sociometry, 7*, 5–13.

Morris, W. N., & Miller, R. S. (1975a). Impressions of dissenters and conformers: An attributional analysis. *Sociometry, 38*, 327–339.

Morris, W. N., & Miller, R. S. (1975b). The effects of consensus-breaking and consensus-preempting partners on reduction of conformity. *Journal of Experimental Social Psychology, 11*, 215–223.

Morris, W. N., Worchel, S., Bois, J. L., Pearson, J. A., Rountree, C. A., Samaha, G. M., Wachtler, J., & Wright, S. L. (1976). Collective coping with stress: Group reactions to fear, anxiety, and ambiguity. *Journal of Personality and Social Psychology, 33*, 674–679.

Moscovici, S., (1976). *Social influence and social change.* London: Academic Press.

Moscovici, S. (1980). Toward a theory of conversion behavior. In L. Berkowitz (Ed.), *Advances in experimental social psychology* (Vol. 13, pp. 209–239). New York: Academic Press.

Moscovici, S. (1985). Social influence and conformity. In G. Lindzey & E. Aronson (Eds.), *Handbook of social psychology* (Vol. 2, 3rd ed., pp. 347–412). New York: Random House.

Moscovici, S., & Faucheux, C. (1972). Social influence, conformity bias, and the study of active minorities. In L. Berkowitz (Ed.), *Advances in experimental social psychology* (Vol. 6, 150–202). New York: Academic Press.

Moscovici, S., & Lage, E. (1976). Studies in social influence. III. Majority versus minority influence in a group. *European Journal of Social Psychology, 6*, 149–174.

Moscovici, S. & Nemeth, C. J. (1974). Minority influence. In C. J. Nemeth (Ed.), *Social psychology: Classic and contemporary integrations* (pp. 217–249). Chicago: Rand McNally.

Moscovici, S., & Personnaz, B. (1980). Studies in social influence. V. Minority influence and conversion behavior in a perceptual task. *Journal of Experimental Social Psychology, 16*, 270–282.

Moscovici, S., & Zavalloni, M. (1969). The group as a polarizer of attitudes. *Journal of Personality and Social Psychology, 12*, 125–135.

Moxley, R. L., & Moxley, N. F. (1974). Determining point centrality in uncontrived social networks. *Sociometry, 37*, 122–130.

Mudd, S. A. (1968). Group sanction severity as a function of degree of behavior deviation and relevance of norm. *Journal of Personality and Social Psychology, 8*, 258–260.

Mudrack, P. E. (1989). Defining group cohesiveness: A legacy of confusion? *Small Group Behavior, 20*, 37–49.

Mulder, M., & Stemerding, A. (1963). Threat, attraction to group, and need for strong leadership. *Human Relations, 16*, 317–334.

Mulder, M., Van Kijk, R., Soutenkijk, S., Stelwagen, T., & Verhagen, J. (1964). Non-instrumental liking tendencies toward powerful group members. *Acta Psychologica, 22*, 367–386.

Mullen, B. (1983). Operationalizing the effect of the group on the individual: A self-attention perspective. *Journal of Experimental Social Psychology, 19*, 295–322.

Mullen, B. (1985). Strength and immediacy of sources: A meta-analytic evaluation of the forgotten elements of social impact theory. *Journal of Personality and Social Psychology, 48*, 1458–1466.

Mullen, B. (1986a). Atrocity as a function of lynch mob composition: A self-attention perspective. *Personality and Social Psychology Bulletin, 12*, 187–197.

Mullen, B. (1986b). Effects of strength and immediacy in group contexts: Reply to Jackson. *Journal of Personality and Social Psychology, 50*, 514–516.

Mullen, B. (1986c). Stuttering, audience size, and the other-total ratio: A self-attention perspective. *Journal of Applied Social Psychology, 16*, 139–149.

Mullen, B. (1987a). Introduction: The study of group behavior. In B. Mullen & G. R. Goethals, (Eds.), *Theories of group behavior* (pp. 1–19). New York: Springer-Verlag.

Mullen, B. (1987b). Self-attention theory: The effects of group composition on the individual. In B. Mullen & G. R. Goethals (Eds.), *Theories of group behavior* (pp. 125–146). New York: Springer-Verlag.

Mullen, B., & Baumeister, R. F. (1987). Group effects on self-attention and performance: social loafing, social facilitation, and social impairment. In C. Hendrick (Ed.), *Review of Personality and Social Psychology: Group Process and Intergroup Relations* (Vol. 9, pp. 189–206). Newbury Park, CA: Sage.

Mullen, B., & Johnson, C. (1989). *Productivity loss in brainstorming groups: A meta-analytic integration and a different solution to the riddle*. Unpublished manuscript, Syracuse University, New York.

Mumpower, J. L., & Cook, S. W. (1978). The development of interpersonal attraction in cooperating interracial groups: The effects of success-failure, race and competence of groupmates, and helping a less competent groupmate. *International Journal of Group Tensions, 8*, 18–50.

Murata, K. (1982). Attribution processes in a mixed-motive interaction: The role of active observer's behavior. *Behaviormetrika, 12*, 47–61.

Murnighan, J. K. (1978). Models of coalition formation: Game theoretic, social psychological, and political perspectives. *Psychological Bulletin, 85*, 1130–1153.

Murnighan, J. K. (1985). Coalitions in decision-making groups: Organizational analogs. *Organizational Behavior and Human Decision Processes, 35*, 1–26.

Murnighan, J. K. (1986). Organizational coalitions: Structural contingencies and the formation process. In R. J. Lewicki, B. H. Sheppard, & M. H. Bazerman (Eds.), *Research on negotiation in organizations* (Vol. 1, pp. 155–174). Greenwich, CT: JAI Press.

Murnighan, J. K., Komorita, S. S., & Szwajkowski, E. (1977). Theories of coalition formation and the effects of reference groups. *Journal of Experimental Social Psychology, 13*, 166–181.

Murphy-Berman, V., & Berman, J. (1978). Importance of choice and sex invasions of personal space. *Personality and Social Psychology Bulletin, 4*, 424–428.

Myers, A. E. (1962). Team competition, success, and the adjustment of group members. *Journal of Abnormal and Social Psychology, 65*, 325–332.

Myers, D. G. (1978). The polarizing effects of social comparison. *Journal of Experimental Social Psychology, 14*, 554–563.

Myers, D. G. (1982). Polarizing effects of social interaction. In H. Brandstätter, J. H. Davis, & G. Stocker-Kreichgauer (Eds.), *Group decision making*. New York: Academic Press.

Myers, D. G., & Lamm, H. (1975). The polarizing effect of group discussion. *American Scientist, 63*, 297–303.

Myers, D. G., & Lamm, H. (1976). The group polarization phenomenon. *Psychological Bulletin, 83*, 602–627.

Nachmias, D. (1974). Coalition politics in Israel. *Comparative Political Studies, 7*, 316–333.

Nadler, A., Goldberg, M., Jaffe, Y. (1982). Effect of self-differentiation and anonymity in group on deindividuation. *Journal of Personality and Social Psychology, 42*, 1127–1136.

Nail, P. R. (1986). Toward an integration of some models and theories of social response. *Psychological Bulletin, 100*, 190–206.

Nail, P. R., & Cole, S. G. (1985). A critical comparison of bargaining theory and the weighted probability model of coalition behaviour. *British Journal of Social Psychology, 24*, 259–266.

Nathan, B. R., Hass, M. A. & Nathan, M. L. (August, 1987). *Meta-analysis of Fiedler's leadership theory: A figure if worth a thousand words*. Paper presented at the Annual Meetings of American Psychological Association, New York City.

National Transportation Safety Board. (1979, June). *Aircraft accident report (NTSB Report No. AAR-79-7)*. Washington, DC.

Nemeth, C. J. (1973). A critical analysis of research utilizing the Prisoner's Dilemma paradigm for the study of bargaining. In L. Berkowitz (Ed.), *Advances in experimental social psychology* (Vol. 6, 203–234). New York: Academic Press.

Nemeth, C. J. (1980). Jury trials: Psychology and the law. In L. Berkowitz (Ed.), *Advances in experimental social psychology* (Vol. 14, pp. 309–367). New York: Academic Press.

Nemeth, C. J. (1986). Differential contributions of majority and minority influence. *Psychological Review, 93*, 23–32.

Nemeth, C. J. (1987). Influence processes, problem solving, and creativity. In M. P. Zanna, J. M. Olson, & C. P. Herman (Eds.), *Social influences: The Ontario Symposium* (Vol. 5, pp. 237–246). Hillsdale, NJ: Erlbaum.

Nemeth, C. J., Endicott, J., & Wachtler, J. (1976). From the '50s to the '70s: Women in jury deliberations. *Sociometry, 39*, 293–304.

Nemeth, C. J., & Kwan, J. L. (1985). Originality of word associations as a function of majority vs. minority influence. *Social Psychology Quarterly, 48*, 277–282.

Nemeth, C. J., & Kwan, J. L. (1987). Minority influence, divergent thinking, and detection of correct solutions. *Journal of Applied Social Psychology, 17*, 788–799.

Nemeth, C. J., & Wachtler, J. (1974). Creating the perceptions of consistency and confidence: A necessary condition for minority influence. *Sociometry, 37*, 529–540.

Nemeth, C. J., & Wachtler, J. (1983). Creative problem solving as a result of majority vs. minority influence. *European Journal of Social Psychology, 13*, 45–55.

Newcomb, A. F., & Bukowski, W. M. (1983). Social impact and social preference as determinants of children's peer group status. *Developmental Psychology, 19*, 856–867.

Newcomb, T. M. (1943). *Personality and social change*. New York: Dryden.

Newcomb, T. M. (1956). The prediction of interpersonal attraction. *American Psychologist, 11*, 575–586.

Newcomb, T. M. (1960). Varieties of interpersonal attraction. In D. Cartwright and A. Zander (Eds.), *Group dynamics: Research and theory* (2nd ed., pp. 104–119). Evanston, IL: Row, Peterson.

Newcomb, T. M. (1961). *The acquaintance process*. New York: Holt, Rinehart & Winston.

Newcomb, T. M. (1963). Stabilities underlying changes in interpersonal attraction. *Journal of Abnormal and Social Psychology, 66*, 376–386.

Newcomb, T. M. (1978). Individual and group. *American Behavioral Scientist, 5*, 631–650.

Newcomb, T. M. (1979). Reciprocity of interpersonal attraction: A nonconfirmation of a plausible hypothesis. *Social Psychology Quarterly, 42*, 299–306.

Newcomb, T. M. (1981). Heiderian balance as a group phenomenon. *Journal of Personality and Social Psychology, 40*, 862–867.

Newcomb, T. M., Koenig, K., Flacks, R., & Warwick, D. (1967). *Persistence and change: Bennington College and its students after 25 years*. New York: Wiley.

Newman, O. (1972). *Defensible space*. New York: Macmillan.

Newman, P. R., & Newman, B. M. (1976). Early adolescence and its conflict: Group identity vs. alienation. *Adolescence, 11*, 261–274.

Newton, J. W., & Mann, L. (1980). Crowd size as a factor in the persuasion process: A study of religious crusade meetings. *Journal of Personality and Social Psychology, 39*, 874–883.

Nicholls, J. R. (1985). A new approach to situational leadership. *Leadership and Organization Development Journal, 6*(4), 2–7.

Nicholson, N., Cole, S. G., & Rocklin, T. (1986). Coalition formation in parliamentary situations as a function of simulated ideology, resources, and electoral systems. *Political Psychology, 7*, 103–116.

Nicholson, P. J., & Goh, S. C. (1983). The relationship of organization structure and interpersonal attitudes to role conflict and ambiguity in different work environments. *Academy of Management Journal, 26*, 148–155.

Nordholm, L. A. (1975). Effects of group size and stimulus ambiguity on conformity. *Journal of Social Psychology, 97*, 123–130.

Norman, P. (1981). *Shout!* New York: Simon & Schuster.

North, R. C., Brody, R. A., & Holsti, O. R. (1964). Some empirical data on the conflict spiral. *Peace Research Society International Papers, 1*, 1–14.

Northway, M. L. (1967). *A primer of sociometry* (2nd ed.). Toronto: University of Toronto Press.

Norvell, N., & Forsyth, D. R. (1984). The impact of inhibiting or facilitating causal factors on group members' reactions after success and failure. *Social Psychology Quarterly, 47*, 293–297.

Nosanchuk, T. A., & Erickson, B. H. (1985). How high is up? Calibrating social comparison in the real world. *Journal of Personality and Social Psychology, 48*, 624–623.

Nosanchuk, T. A., & Lightstone, J. (1974). Canned laughter and public and private conformity. *Journal of Personality and Social Psychology, 29*, 153–156.

Nye, J. L. (1988). *The effects of performance cues on perceptions of male and female leaders*. Unpublished dissertation, Virginia Commonwealth University, Richmond, VA.

Nye, J. L., & Forsyth, D. R. (August, 1987). *Cognitive mediators of biases in leadership appraisals*. Paper presented at the Annual

Meetings of American Psychological Association, New York City.

Nyquist, L. V., & Spence, J. T. (1986). Effects of dispositional dominance and sex role expectations on leadership behaviors. *Journal of Personality and Social Psychology, 50,* 87–93.

Nystrom, P. C. (1978). Managers and the Hi-Hi leader myth. *Academy of Management Journal, 21,* 325–331.

Oakes, P. J., & Turner, J. C. (1980). Social categorization and intergroup behavior: Does minimal intergroup discrimination make social identity more positive? *European Journal of Social Psychology, 10,* 295–302.

Offermann, L. R., & Schrier, P. E. (1985). Social influence strategies: The impact of sex, role, and attitudes toward power. *Personality and Social Psychology Bulletin, 11,* 286–300.

Ofshe, R., & Lee, M. T. (1981). Reply to Greenstein. *Social Psychology Quarterly, 44,* 383–385.

Okiishi, R. W. (1987). The genogram as a tool in career counseling. *Journal of Counseling and Development, 66,* 139–143.

Orcutt, J. D. (1973). Societal reaction and the response to deviation in small groups. *Social Forces, 52,* 261–267.

O'Reilly, C. A. (1978). The intentional distortion of information in organizational communication: A laboratory and field investigation. *Human Relations, 31,* 173–193.

Orive, R. (1984). Group similarity, public self-awareness, and opinion extremity: A social projection explanation of deindividuation effects. *Journal of Personality and Social Psychology, 47,* 727–737.

Orive, R. (1988a). Group consensus, action immediacy, and opinion confidence. *Personality and Social Psychology Bulletin, 14,* 573–577.

Orive, R. (1988b). Social projection and social comparison of opinions. *Journal of Personality and Social Psychology, 54,* 943–964.

Orkin, M. (1987). Balanced strategies for Prisoner's Dilemma. *Journal of Conflict Resolution, 31,* 186–191.

Orne, M. T., & Holland, C. H. (1968). On the ecological validity of laboratory deceptions. *International Journal of Psychiatry, 6,* 282–293.

Orpen, C. (1986). Improving organizations through team development. *Management and Labor Studies, 11,* 1–12.

Orvis, B. B., Kelley, H. H., & Butler, D. (1976). Attributional conflict in young couples. In J. H. Harvey, W. J. Ickes, & R. E. Kidd (Eds.), *New directions in attribution research* (Vol. 1). Hillsdale, NJ: Erlbaum.

Osborn, A. F. (1957). *Applied imagination.* New York: Scribner.

Osgood, C. E. (1979). GRIT for MBFR: A proposal for unfreezing force-level postures in Europe. *Peace Research Reviews, 8*(2), 77–92.

Oskamp, S., & Hartry, A. (1968). A factor-analytic study of the double standard in attitudes toward U.S. and Russian actions. *Behavioral Science, 13,* 178–188.

Padawer-Singer, A. M., Singer, A. N., Singer, R. L. J. (1977). An experimental study of twelve vs. six member juries under unanimous vs. nonunanimous decisions. In B. D. Sales (Ed.), *Psychology in the legal process.* New York: Spectrum.

Page, R. A., & Moss, M. K. (1976). Environmental influences on aggression: The effects of darkness and proximity of victim. *Journal of Applied Social Psychology, 6,* 126–133.

Palmer, G. J. (1962). Task ability and effective leadership. *Psychological Reports, 10,* 863–866.

Pandey, J., & Singh, P. (1987). Effects of machiavellianism, other-enhancement, and power-position on affect, power feeling, and evaluation of the ingratiator. *Journal of Psychology, 121,* 287–300.

Paolillo, J. G. P. (1987). Role profiles for managers in different functional areas. *Group and Organization Studies, 12,* 109–118.

Park, B., & Rothbart, M. (1982). Perception of out-group homogeneity and levels of social categorization: Memory for the subordinate attributes of in-group and out-group members. *Journal of Personality and Social Psychology, 42,* 1051–1068.

Parkinson, C. N. (1957). *Parkinson's law and other studies in administration.* Boston: Houghton Mifflin.

Parkum, K. H., & Parkum, V. C. (1980). Citizen participation in community planning and decision making. In D. H. Smith, J. Macaulay and Associates (Eds.), *Partici-*

pation in social and political activities: A comprehensive analysis of political involvement, expressive leisure time, and helping behavior (pp. 153–167). San Francisco: Jossey-Bass.

Parsons, H. M. (1976). Work environments. In I. Altman & J. Wohlwill (Eds.), *Human behavior and environment* (Vol. 1). New York: Plenum.

Parsons, T. (1962). On the concept of influence. *Public Opinion Quarterly, 27*, 37–63.

Parsons, T., Bales, R. F., & Shils, E. (1953). *Working papers in the theory of action.* New York: Free Press.

Patten, S. C. (1977). Milgram's shocking experiments. *Philosophy, 52*, 425–440.

Patterson, M. L. (1973). Compensation in nonverbal immediacy behaviors: A review. *Sociometry, 36*, 237–252.

Patterson, M. L. (1975). Personal space—Time to burst the bubble? *Man-Environment Systems, 5*, 67.

Patterson, M. L. (1976). An arousal model of interpersonal intimacy. *Psychological Review, 83*, 235–245.

Patterson, M. L. (1982). A sequential function model of verbal exchange. *Psychological review, 89*, 231–249.

Patterson, M. L., Kelley, C. E., Kondracki, B. A., & Wulf, L. J. (1979). Effects of seating arrangement on small group behavior. *Social Psychology Quarterly, 42*, 180–185.

Patterson, M. L., Roth, C. P., & Schenk, C. (1979). Seating arrangement, activity, and sex differences in small group crowding. *Personality and Social Psychology Bulletin, 5*, 100–103.

Patterson, M. L., & Sechrest, L. B. (1970). Interpersonal distance and impression formation. *Journal of Personality, 38*, 161–166.

Paul, G. L. (1967). Strategy of outcome research in psychotherapy. *Journal of Consulting Psychology, 31*, 109–118.

Paulus, P. B., Annis, A. B., Seta, J. J., Schkade, J. K., & Matthews, R. W. (1976). Density does affect task performance. *Journal of Personality and Social Psychology, 34*, 248–353.

Pavelshak, M. A., Moreland, R. L., & Levine, J. M. (1986). Effects of prior group memberships on subsequent reconnaissance activities. *Journal of Personality and Social Psychology, 50*, 56–66.

Pearce, J. A., & Ravlin, E. C. (1987). The design and activation of self-regulating work groups. *Human Relations, 40*, 751–782.

Pearce, J. L., Stevenson, W. B., & Porter, L. W. (1986). Coalitions in the organizational context. In R. J. Lewicki, B. H. Sheppard, & M. H. Bazerman (Eds.), *Research on negotiation in organizations* (Vol. 1, pp. 97–115). Greenwich, CT: JAI Press.

Pedigo, J. M., & Singer, B. (1982). Group process development: A psychoanalytic view. *Small Group Behavior, 13*, 496–517.

Pennebaker, J. W. (1982). Social and perceptual factors affecting symptom reporting and mass psychogenic illness. In M. J. Colligan, J. W. Pennebaker, & L. R. Murphy (Eds.), *Mass psychogenic illness: A social psychological analysis* (pp. 139–153). Hillsdale, NJ: Erlbaum.

Penrod, S., & Hastie, R. (1979). Models of jury decision making: A critical review. *Psychological Bulletin, 86*, 462–492.

Penrod, S., & Hastie, R. (1980). A computer simulation of jury decision making. *Psychological Review, 87*, 133–159.

Pepitone, A. (1981). Lessons from the history of social psychology. *American Psychologist, 36*, 972–985.

Pepitone, A., & Reichling, G. (1955). Group cohesiveness and the expression of hostility. *Human Relations, 8*, 327–337.

Pepitone, A., & Wilpinski, C. (1960). Some consequences of experimental rejection. *Journal of Abnormal and Social Psychology, 60*, 359–364.

Perlman, D., & Fehr, B. (1987). The development of intimate relationships. In D. Perlman & S. Duck (Eds.), *Intimate relationships: Development, dynamics, and deterioration* (pp. 13–42). Newbury Park, CA: Sage.

Perls, F. (1969). *Gestalt therapy verbatim.* Lafayette, CA: Real People Press.

Perls, F., Hefferline, R., & Goodman, P. (1951). *Gestalt therapy: Excitement and growth in the human personality.* New York: Julian Press.

Pessin, J. (1933). The comparative effects of social and mechanical stimulation on memorizing. *American Journal of Psychology, 45*, 263–270.

Peteroy, E. T. (1983). Cohesiveness development in an ongoing therapy group: An exploratory study. *Small Group Behavior, 14,* 269–272.

Peters, L. H., Hartke, D. D., & Pohlmann, J. T. (1985). Fiedler's contingency theory of leadership: An application of the meta-analytical procedures of Schmidt and Hunter. *Psychological Bulletin, 97,* 274–285.

Petty, R. E., & Cacioppo, J. T. (1986). The elaboration likelihood model of persuasion. In L. Berkowitz (Ed.), *Advances in experimental social psychology* (Vol. 19, pp. 124–205). New York: Academic Press.

Pfeffer, J. (1977). The ambiguity of leadership. *Academy of Management Review, 2,* 104–112.

Philipsen, G., Mulac, A., & Dietrich, D. (1979). The effects of social interaction on group idea generation. *Communication Monographs, 46,* 119–125.

Phillips, J. S., & Lord, R. G. (1986). Notes on the practical and theoretical consequences of implicit leadership theories for the future of leadership measurement. *Journal of Management, 12,* 31–41.

Phoon, W. H. (1982). Outbreaks of mass hysteria at workplaces in Singapore: Some patterns and modes of presentation. In M. J. Colligan, J. W. Pennebaker, & L. R. Murphy (Eds.), *Mass psychogenic illness: A social psychological analysis* (pp. 21–31). Hillsdale, NJ: Erlbaum.

Pigors, P. *Leadership or domination.* Boston: Houghton Mifflin, 1935.

Pilisuk, M., Brandes, B., & van den Hove, D. (1976). Deceptive sounds: Illicit communication in the laboratory. *Behavioral Science, 21,* 515–523.

Pinney, E. L. (1978). The beginnings of group psychotherapy: John Henry Pratt, M.D. and the Reverend Dr. Elwood Worcester. *International Journal of Group Psychotherapy, 28,* 109–114.

Pinney, E. L. (1979). Paul Schilder and group psychotherapy: The development of psychoanalytic group psychotherapy. *Psychiatric Quarterly, 50,* 133–143.

Pittard-Payne, B. (1980). Nonassociational religious participation. In D. H. Smith, J. Macaulay and Associates (Eds.), *Participation in social and political activities: A comprehensive analysis of political involvement, expressive leisure time, and helping behavior* (pp. 214–243). San Francisco: Jossey-Bass.

Platt, J. (1973). Social traps. *American Psychologist, 28,* 641–651.

Podsakoff, P. M., & Schriesheim, C. A. (1985). Field studies of French and Raven's bases of power: Critique, reanalysis, and suggestions for future research. *Psychological Bulletin, 97,* 387–411.

Polley, R. B. (1984). Subjectivity in issue polarization. *Journal of Applied Social Psychology, 14,* 426–440.

Polley, R. B. (1986). Rethinking the third dimension. *International Journal of Small Group Research, 2,* 134–140.

Polley, R. B. (1987). The dimensions of social interaction: A method for improved rating scales. *Social Psychology Quarterly, 50,* 72–82.

Polley, R. B. (1989). On the dimensionality of interpersonal behavior: A reply to Lustig. *Small Group Behavior, 20,* 270–278.

Pollis, N. P., Montgomery, R. L., & Smith, T. G. (1975). Autokinetic paradigms: A reply to Alexander, Zucker, and Brody. *Sociometry, 38,* 358–373.

Porter, N., Geis, F. L., Cooper, E., & Newman, E. (1985). Androgyny and leadership in mixed-sex groups. *Journal of Personality and Social Psychology, 49,* 808–823.

Prentice-Dunn, S., & Rogers, R. W. (1980). Effects of deindividuating situation cues and aggressive models on subjective deindividuation and aggression. *Journal of Personality and Social Psychology, 39,* 104–113.

Prentice-Dunn, S., & Rogers, R. W. (1982). Effects of public and private self-awareness on deindividuation and aggression. *Journal of Personality and Social Psychology, 43,* 503–513.

Prentice-Dunn, S., & Rogers, R. W. (1983). Deindividuation and aggression. In R. G. Geen & E. I. Donnerstein (Eds.), *Aggression: Theoretical and empirical reviews* (Vol. 1). New York: Academic Press.

Prentice-Dunn, S., & Spivey, R. W. (1986). Extreme deindividuation in the laboratory: Its magnitude and subjective components. *Personality and Social Psychology Bulletin, 12,* 206–215.

Prince, G. (1970). *The practice of creativity.* New York: Harper & Row.

Prince, G. (1975). The mind spring theory. *Journal of Creative Behavior, 9*(3), 159–181.

Pritchard, R. D., Roth, P. L., Jones, S. D., Galgay, P., Watson, M. D. (1988). Designing a goal-setting system to enhance performance: A practical guide. *Organizational Dynamics, 17,* 69–78.

Pruitt, D. G. (1971a). Choice shifts in group discussion: An introductory review. *Journal of Personality and Social Psychology, 20,* 339–360.

Pruitt, D. G. (1971b). Conclusions: Toward an understanding of choice shifts in group discussion. *Journal of Personality and Social Psychology, 20,* 495–510.

Pruitt, D. G. (1981). *Negotiation behavior.* New York: Academic Press.

Pruitt, D. G. (1983). Strategic choice in negotiation. *American Behavioral Science, 27,* 167–194.

Pruitt, D. G. (1987). Creative approaches to negotiation. In D. J. D. Sandole & I. Sandole-Staroste (Eds.), *Conflict management and problem solving: Interpersonal to international applications* (pp. 62–76). London: Frances Pinter.

Pruitt, D. G., & Rubin, J. Z. (1986). Social conflict: *Escalation, stalemate, and settlement.* New York: Random House.

Pugh, M. D., & Wahrman, R. (1983). Neutralizing sexism in mixed-sex groups: Do women have to be better than men? *American Journal of Sociology, 88,* 746–762.

Quadagno, J. S. (1979). Paradigms on evolutionary theory: The sociobiological model of natural selection. *American Sociological Review, 44,* 100–109.

Quattrone, G. A. (1986). On the perception of a group's variability. In S. Worchel & W. G. Austin (Eds.), *Psychology of intergroup relations* (2nd ed., pp. 25–48). Chicago: Nelson-Hall.

Quattrone, G. A., & Jones, E. E. (1980). The perception of variability within in-groups and out-groups: Implications for the law of small numbers. *Journal of Personality and Social Psychology, 38,*141–152.

Quinn, R. E., & McGrath, M. R. (1982). Moving beyond the single solution perspective. *Journal of Applied Behavioral Science, 18,* 463–472.

Rabbie, J. M., Benoist, F., Oosterbaan, H., & Visser, L. (1974). Differential power and effects of expected competitive and cooperative intergroup interaction upon intra- and outgroup attitudes. *Journal of Personality and Social Psychology, 30,* 46–56.

Rabbie, J. M., & Horwitz, M. (1969). Arousal of ingroup-outgroup bias by a chance win or loss. *Journal of Personality and Social Psychology, 13,* 269–277.

Rabbie, J. M., Visser, L., & van Oostrum, J. (1982). Conflict behavior of individuals, dyads, and triads in mixed-motive games. In H. Brandstatter, J. H. Davis, & G. Stocker-Kreichgauer (Eds.), *Group decision making.* London: Academic Press.

Radloff, R., & Helmreich, R. (1968). *Groups under stress: Psychological research in SEALAB II.* New York: Irvington.

Ragone, G. (1981). Fashion, "craze," and collective behavior. *Communications, 7,* 249–268.

Raiffa, H. (1983). Mediation of conflicts. *American Behavioral Science, 27,* 195–210.

Rapoport, A. (1985). Editorial comment on articles by Diekmann and Molander. *Journal of Conflict Resolution, 29,* 619–622.

Rapoport, A., & Bornstein, G. (1987). Intergroup competition for the provision of binary public goods. *Psychological Review, 94,* 291–299.

Rasinski, K. A., Tyler, T. R., & Fridkin, K. (1985). Exploring the function of legitimacy: Mediating effects of personal and institutional legitimacy on leadership endorsement and system support. *Journal of Personality and Social Psychology, 49,* 386–394.

Raven, B. H. (1965). Social influence and power. In I. D. Steiner & M. Fishbein (Eds.), *Current studies in social psychology* (pp. 371–382). New York: Holt, Rinehart, & Winston.

Raven, B. H., & Kruglanski, A. W. (1970). Conflict and power. In P. Swingle (Ed.), *The structure of conflict.* New York: Academic Press.

Raven, B. H., & Rubin, J. Z. (1976). *Social psychology: People in groups.* New York: Wiley.

Rawlins, W. K. (1984). Consensus in decision-making groups: A conceptual history. In G. M. Phillips & J. T. Wood (Eds.), *Emergent issues in human decision making* (pp. 19–39). Carbondale, IL: Southern Illinois University Press.

Read, P. P. (1974). *Alive.* New York: Avon.

Reckman, R. F., & Goethals, G. R. (1973). Deviancy and group orientation as determinants of group composition preferences. *Sociometry, 36,* 419–423.

Reddin, W. J. (1970). *Managerial effectiveness*. New York: McGraw-Hill.

Regan, D. T., & Totten, J. (1975). Empathy and attribution: Turning observers into actors. *Journal of Personality and Social Psychology, 32*, 850–856.

Regan, J. W. (1976). Liking for evaluators: Consistency and self-esteem theories. *Journal of Experimental Social Psychology, 12*, 159–169.

Reicher, S. (1982). The determination of collective behavior. In H. Tajfel (Ed.), *Social identity and intergroup relations* (pp. 41–83). New York: Cambridge University Press.

Reicher, S. (1984a). Social influence in the crowd: Attitudinal and behavioural effects of de-individuation in conditions of high and low group salience. *British Journal of Social Psychology, 23*, 341–350.

Reicher, S. (1984b). The St. Pauls riot: An explanation of the limits of crowd action in terms of a social identity model. *European Journal of Social Psychology, 14*, 1–21.

Reis, H. T., Earing, B., Kent, A., & Nezlek, J. (1976). The tyranny of numbers: Does group size affect petition signing? *Journal of Applied Social Psychology, 6*, 228–234.

Reynolds, P. D. (1979). *Ethical dilemmas and social science research*. San Francisco: Jossey-Bass.

Rice, O. K. (1978). *The Hatfields and the McCoys*. Lexington, KY: University Press of Kentucky.

Rice, R. W. (1978a). Construct validity of the Least Preferred Co-worker (LPC) score. *Psychological Bulletin, 85*, 1199–1237.

Rice, R. W. (1978b). Psychometric properties of the Esteem for Least Preferred Co-worker (LPC) Scale. *Academy of Management Review, 3*, 106–118.

Rice, R. W. (1979). Reliability and validity of the LPC scale: A reply. *Academy of Management Review, 4*, 291–294.

Rice, R. W., Instone, D., & Adams, J. (1984). Leader sex, leader success, and leadership process: Two field studies. *Journal of Applied Psychology, 69*, 12–31.

Rickards, T. (1974). *Problem solving through creative analysis*. London: Halsted Press.

Ridgeway, C. L. (1978). Conformity, group-oriented motivation, and status attainment in small groups. *Social Psychology, 41*, 175–188.

Ridgeway, C. L. (1982). Status in groups: The importance of motivation. *American Sociological Review, 47*, 76–88.

Ridgeway, C. L. (1984). Dominance, performance, and status in groups: A theoretical analysis. In E. J. Lawler (Ed.), *Advances in group processes* (Vol. 1, pp. 59–93). Greenwich, CT: JAI Press.

Ridgeway, C. L., Berger, J., & Smith, L. F. (1985.) Nonverbal cues and status: An expectation states approach. *American Journal of Sociology, 90*, 955–978.

Riess, M. (1982). Seating preferences as impression management: A literature review and theoretical integration. *Communication, 11*, 85–113.

Riess, M., & Rosenfeld, P. (1980). Seating preferences as nonverbal communication: A self-presentational analysis. *Journal of Applied Communications Research, 8*, 22–30.

Ringelmann, M. (1913). Research on animate sources of power: The work of man. *Annales de l'Institut National Agronomique*, 2e serie—tome XII, 1–40.

Ringer, R. J. (1973). *Winning through intimidation*. Greenwich, CT: Fawcett.

Riordan, C. (1983). Sex as a general status characteristic. *Social Psychology Quarterly, 46*, 261–267.

Riordan, C., & Riggiero, J. (1980). Producing equal-status interracial interaction: A replication. *Social Psychology Quarterly, 43*, 131–136.

Robert, H. M. (1915/1971). *Robert's rules of order* (Revised ed.). New York: Morrow.

Robinson, D. (1980). Self-help health groups. In P. B. Smith (Ed.), *Small groups and personal change* (pp. 176–193). New York: Methuen.

Rodin, J. (1976). Crowding, perceived choice, and response to controllable and uncontrollable outcomes. *Journal of Experimental Social Psychology, 12*, 564–578.

Rodin, J., & Baum, A. (1978). Crowding and helplessness: Potential consequences of density and loss of control. In A. Baum & Y. Epstein (Eds.), *Human responses to crowding*. Hillsdale, NJ: Erlbaum.

Rodin, J., Solomon, S. K., & Metcalf, J. (1978). Role of control in mediating perceptions of density. *Journal of Personality and Social Psychology, 36*, 988–999.

Roethlisberger, F. J., & Dickson, W. J. (1939). *Management and the worker*. Cambridge, MA: Harvard University Press.

Rofé, Y. (1984). Stress and affiliation: A utility theory. *Psychological Review, 91*, 235–250.

Rogers, C. (1970). *Encounter groups*. New York: Harper & Row.

Rogers, R. W., & Prentice-Dunn, S. (1981). Deindividuation and anger-mediated interracial aggression: Unmasking regressive racism. *Journal of Personality and Social Psychology, 41*, 63–73.

Rohrbaugh, M., & Bartels, B. D. (1975). Participants' perceptions of curative factors in therapy and growth groups. *Small Group Behavior, 6*, 430–456.

Rook, K. S. (1984). The negative side of social interaction: Impact on psychological well-being. *Journal of Personality and Social Psychology, 46*, 1097–1108.

Roos, P. D. (1968). Jurisdiction: An ecological concept. *Human Relations, 21*, 75–84.

Rose, S. D. (1977). *Group therapy: A behavioral approach*. Englewood Cliffs, NJ: Prentice-Hall.

Rose, S. D. (1983). Behavior therapy in groups. In H. I. Kaplan & B. J. Sadock (Eds.), *Comprehensive group psychotherapy* (2nd. ed., pp. 101–108). Baltimore: Williams & Wilkins.

Rosen, B., & Jerdee, T. H. (1973). The influence of sex-role stereotypes on evaluations of male and female supervisory behavior. *Journal of Applied Psychology, 57*, 44–48.

Rosen, B., & Jerdee, T. H. (1978). Perceived sex differences in managerially relevant characteristics. *Sex Roles, 4*, 837–843.

Rosenberg, S. W., & Wolfsfeld, G. (1977). International conflict and the problem of attribution. *Journal of Conflict Resolution, 21*, 75–103.

Rosenthal, R., & Jacobson, L. (1968). *Pygmalion in the classroom*. New York: Holt, Rinehart, & Winston.

Rosnow, R. L. (1980). Psychology of rumor reconsidered. *Psychological Bulletin, 87*, 578–591.

Rosnow, R. L., & Kimmel, A. J. (1979). Lives of a rumor. *Psychology Today, 13*(6), 88–92.

Rosnow, R. L., Yost, J. H., & Esposito, J. L. (1986). Belief in rumor and likelihood of rumor transmission. *Language and Communication, 6*, 189–194.

Ross, L. (1977). The intuitive psychologist and his shortcomings: Distortions in the attribution process. In L. Berkowitz (Ed.), *Advances in experimental social psychology* (Vol. 10). New York: Academic Press.

Ross, L., Bierbrauer, G., & Hoffman, S. (1976). The role of attribution processes in conformity and dissent: Revisiting the Asch situation. *American Psychologist, 31*, 148–157.

Rossi, P. H., & Berk, R. A. (1985). Varieties of normative consensus. *American Sociological Review, 50*, 333–347.

Roth, B. E. (1983). Gestalt and other types of group psychotherapy. In H. I. Kaplan & B. J. Sadock (Eds.), *Comprehensive group psychotherapy* (2nd. ed., pp. 210–214). Baltimore: Williams & Wilkins.

Rothbart, M., Evans, M., & Fulero, S. (1979). Recall for confirming events: Memory processes and the maintenance of social stereotypes. *Journal of Experimental Social Psychology, 15*, 343–355.

Rothbart, M., Fulero, S., Jensen, C., Howard, J., & Birrell, P. (1978). From individual to group impressions: Availability heuristics in stereotype formation. *Journal of Experimental Social Psychology, 14*, 237–255.

Ruback, R. B., Dabbs, J. M., Jr., & Hopper, C. H. (1984). The process of brainstorming: An analysis with individual and group vocal parameters. *Journal of Personality and Social Psychology, 47*, 558–567.

Rubenstein, C. M., & Shaver, P. (1980). Loneliness in two northeastern cities. In J. Hartog & R. Audy (Eds.), *The anatomy of loneliness*. New York: International Universities Press.

Rubin, J. Z. (1980). Experimental research on third-party intervention in conflict: Toward some generalizations. *Psychological Bulletin, 87*, 379–391.

Rubin, J. Z. (1983). Negotiation. *American Behavioral Science, 27*, 135–147.

Rubin, J. Z. (1986). Third parties within organizations: A responsive commentary. In R. J. Lewicki, B. H. Sheppard, & M. H. Bazerman (Eds.), *Research on negotiation in organizations* (Vol. 1, pp. 271–283). Greenwich, CT: JAI Press.

Rubin, J. Z., & Brown, B. R. (1975). *The social psychology of bargaining and negotiation*. New York: Academic Press.

Rudestam, K. E. (1982). *Experiential groups in theory and practice*. Pacific Grove, CA: Brooks/Cole.

Rugel, R. P., & Meyer, D. J. (1984). The Tavistock group: Empirical findings and implications for group therapy. *Small Group Behavior, 15*, 361–374.

Rusbult, C. E. (1983). A longitudinal test of the investment model: The development (and deterioration) of satisfaction and commitment in heterosexual involvements. *Journal of Personality and Social Psychology, 45*, 101–117.

Rusbult, C. E., Zembrodt, I. M., & Gunn, L. K. (1982). Exit, voice, loyalty, and neglect: Responses to dissatisfaction in romantic involvements. *Journal of Personality and Social Psychology, 43*, 1230–1242.

Rush, M. C., Thomas, J. C., & Lord, R. G. (1977). Implicit leadership theory: A potential threat to the internal validity of the leader behavior questionnaires. *Organizational Behavior and Human Performance, 20*, 93–110.

Russell, B. (1938). *Power*. London: George Allen & Unwyn.

Russell, D., Peplau, L. A., & Cutrona, C. E. (1980). The revised UCLA Loneliness Scale: Concurrent and discriminant validity evidence. *Journal of Personality and Social Psychology, 39*, 472–480.

Ryen, A. H., & Kahn, A. (1975). The effects of intergroup orientation on group attitudes and proxemic behavior: A test of two models. *Journal of Personality and Social Psychology, 31*, 302–310.

Sabini, J., & Silver, M. (1983). Dispositional vs. situational interpretations of Milgram's obedience experiments: "The fundamental attribution error." *Journal for the Theory of Social Behavior, 13*, 147–154.

Sackhoff, J., & Weinstein, L. (1988). The effects of potential self-inflicted harm on obedience to an authority figure. *Bulletin of the Psychonomic Society, 26*, 347–348.

Saegart, S. (1978). High-density environments: Their personal and social consequences. In A. Baum & Y. M. Epstein (Eds.), *Human response to crowding*. Hillsdale, NJ: Erlbaum.

Saegert, S., Swap, W., & Zajonc, R. B. (1973). Exposure, context, and interpersonal attraction. *Journal of Personality and Social Psychology, 25*, 234–242.

Safer, M. A. (1980). Attributing evil to the subject, not the situation. *Personality and Social Psychology Bulletin, 6*, 205–209.

Sagar, H. A., & Schofield, J. W. (1980). Racial and behavioral cues in black and white children's perceptions of ambiguously aggressive acts. *Journal of Personality and Social Psychology, 39*, 590–598.

Saks, M. J. (1977). *Jury verdicts*. Lexington, MA: D. C. Heath.

Saks, M. J., & Hastie, R. (1978). *Social psychology in court*. New York: Van Nostrand Reinhold.

Sampson, E. E. (1971). *Social psychology and contemporary society*. New York: Wiley.

Sampson, E. E., & Brandon, A. C. (1964). The effects of role and opinion-deviation on small group behavior. *Sociometry, 27*, 261–281.

Sampson, R. V. (1965). *Equality and power*. London: Heinemann.

Samuelson, R. J. (1985, October 7). Steve Jobs and Apple pie. *Newsweek, 106*, 59.

Sanders, G. S. (1981a). Driven by distraction: An integrative review of social facilitation theory and research. *Journal of Experimental Social Psychology, 17*, 227–251.

Sanders, G. S. (1981b). Toward a comprehensive account of social facilitation: Distraction/conflict does not mean theoretical conflict. *Journal of Experimental Social Psychology, 17*, 262–265.

Sanders, G. S. (1984). Self-presentation and drive in social facilitation. *Journal of Experimental Social Psychology, 20*, 312–322.

Sanders, G. S., & Baron, R. S. (1975). The motivating effects of distraction on task performance. *Journal of Personality and Social Psychology, 32*, 956–963.

Sanders, G. S., & Baron, R. S. (1977). Is social comparison irrelevant for producing choice shifts? *Journal of Experimental Social Psychology, 13*, 303–314.

Sanders, G. S., Baron, R. S., & Moore, D. L. (1978). Distraction and social comparison as mediators of social facilitation effects. *Journal of Experimental Social Psychology, 14*, 291–303.

Santee, R. T., & Jackson, S. E. (1982). Sex differences in evaluative implications of conformity and dissent. *Social Psychology Quarterly, 45*, 121–125.

Santee, R. T., & Maslach, C. (1982). To agree or not to agree: Personal dissent amid social pressure to conform. *Journal of Personality and Social Psychology, 42,* 690–700.

Sarason, B. R., Shearin, E. N., Pierce, G. R., & Sarason, I. G. (1987). Interrelations of social support measures: Theoretical and practical implications. *Journal of Personality and Social Psychology, 52,* 813–832.

Sarri, R. C., & Galinsky, M. J. (1985). In M. Sundel, P. Glasser, R. Sarri, & R. Vinter (Eds.), *Individual change through small groups* (2nd ed., pp. 70–86). New York: Free Press.

Sasfy, J., & Okun, M. (1974). Form of evaluation and audience expertness as joint determinants of audience effects. *Journal of Experimental Social Psychology, 10,* 461–467.

Schachter, S. (1951). Deviation, rejection, and communication. *Journal of Abnormal and Social Psychology, 46,* 190–207.

Schachter, S. (1959). *The psychology of affiliation.* Palo Alto, CA: Stanford University Press.

Schachter, S., Ellertson, N., McBride, D., & Gregory, D. (1951). An experimental study of cohesiveness and productivity. *Human Relations, 4,* 229–238.

Schauer, A. H., Seymour, W. R., & Geen, R. G. (1985). Effects of observation and evaluation on anxiety in beginning counselors: A social facilitation analysis. *Journal of Counseling and Development, 63,* 279–285.

Scheier, M. F., Carver, C. S., & Gibbons, F. X. (1979). Self-directed attention, awareness of bodily states, and suggestibility. *Journal of Personality and Social Psychology, 37,* 1576–1588.

Schein, E. H. (1971). *Process consultation: Its role in organization development.* Reading, MA: Addison-Wesley.

Schein, V. E. (1985). Organizational realities: The politics of change. *Training and Development Journal, 39,* 37–41.

Schellenberg, J. A. (1978). *Masters of social psychology.* New York: Oxford.

Scheuble, K. J., Dixon, K. N., Levy, A. B., & Kagan-Moore, L. (1987). Premature termination: A risk in eating disorder groups. *Group, 11,* 85–93.

Schindler, W. (1976). The development of group psychotherapy. *Praxis der Psychotherapie, 21,* 59–67.

Schlenker, B. R. (1975). Liking for a group following an initiation: Impression management or dissonance reduction? *Sociometry, 38,* 99–118.

Schlenker, B. R., & Bonoma, T. V. (1978). Fun and games: The validity of games for the study of conflict. *Journal of Conflict Resolution, 22,* 7–37.

Schlenker, B. R., & Forsyth, D. R. (1977). On the ethics of psychological research. *Journal of Experimental Social Psychology, 13,* 369–396.

Schlenker, B. R., & Goldman, H. J. (1978). Cooperators and competitors in conflict: A test of the "triangle model." *Journal of Conflict Resolution, 22,* 393–410.

Schlenker, B. R., Nacci, P., Helm, B., & Tedeschi, J. T. (1976). Reactions to coercive and reward power: The effects of switching influence modes on target compliance. *Sociometry, 39,* 316–323.

Schlesinger, A. M., Jr. (1965). *A thousand days.* Boston: Houghton Mifflin.

Schmidt, D. E., & Keating, J. P. (1979). Human crowding and personal control: An integration of the research. *Psychological Bulletin, 86,* 680–700.

Schmidt, N., & Sermat, V. (1983). Measuring loneliness in different relationships. *Journal of Personality and Social Psychology, 44,* 1038–1047.

Schmitt, B. H., Gilovich, T., Goore, N., & Joseph, L. (1986). Mere presence and social facilitation: One more time. *Journal of Experimental Social Psychology, 22,* 242–248.

Schmitt, D. R. (1981). Performance under cooperation or competition. *American Behavioral Scientist, 24,* 649–679.

Schneier, C. E. (1978). The contingency model of leadership: An extension to emergent leadership and leader's sex. *Organizational Behavior and Human Performance, 21,* 220–239.

Schofield, J. W. (1978). School desegregation and intergroup relations. In D. Bar-Tal & L. Saxe (Eds.), *The social psychology of education.* Washington, DC: Halstead.

Schofield, J. W., & Sagar, H. A. (1977). Peer interaction patterns in an integrated middle school. *Sociometry, 40,* 130–138.

Schofield, J. W., & Whitely, B. E., Jr. (1983). Peer nomination vs. rating scale measurement of children's peer preferences. *Social Psychology Quarterly, 46,* 242–251.

Schopler, J., & Layton, B. D. (1972a). *Attributions of interpersonal influence and power*. Morristown, NJ: General Learning Press.

Schopler, J., & Layton, B. D. (1972b). Determinants of the self-attribution of having influenced another person. *Journal of Personality and Social Psychology, 22*, 326–332.

Schriesheim, C. A., Bannister, B. D., & Money, W. H. (1979). Psychometric properties of the LPC Scale: An extension of Rice's review. *Academy of Management Review, 4*, 287–290.

Schriesheim, C. A., & Kerr, S. (1977). Theories and measures of leadership: A critical appraisal of current and future directions. In J. G. Hunt and L. L. Larson (Eds.), *Leadership: The cutting edge*. Carbondale, IL: Southern Illinois University Press.

Schroeder, D. A., Irwin, M. E., & Sibicky, M. E. (June, 1988). *Social dilemmas: A unifying framework*. Paper presented at the Eleventh International Conference on Groups, Networks, and Organizations, Nags Head, NC.

Schutz, W. C. (1958). *FIRO: A three-dimensional theory of interpersonal behavior*. New York: Rinehart.

Schutz, W. (1967/1973). *Joy: Expanding human awareness*. New York: Ballantine books.

Schutz, W. (1983). A theory of small groups. In H. H. Blumberg, A. P. Hare, V. Kent, & M. F. Davies (Eds.), *Small groups and social interaction* (Vol. 2, pp. 479–486). New York: Wiley.

Schwartz, H., & Jacobs, J. (1979). *Qualitative sociology: A method to the madness*. New York: Free Press.

Schwartz, M. S., & Schwartz, C. G. (1955). Problems in participant observation. *American Journal of Sociology, 60*, 343–354.

Scott, J. P. (1981). Biological and psychological bases of social attachment. In H. Kellerman (Ed.), *Group cohesion*. New York: Grune & Stratton.

Scott, J. W. (1942). Mating behavior of the sage grouse. *Auk, 59*, 477–498.

Scott, W. A., & Scott, R. (1981). Intercorrelations among structural properties of primary groups. *Journal of Personality and Social Psychology, 41*, 279–292.

Sculley, J. (with J. A. Byrne). (1987). *Odyssey: Pepsi to Apple . . . A journey of adventure, ideas, and the future*. New York: Harper & Row.

Sears D. O., & Kinder, D. R. (1985). Whites' opposition to busing: On conceptualizing and operationalizing group conflict. *Journal of Personality and Social Psychology, 48*, 1141–1147.

Seashore, S. E. (1954). *Group cohesiveness in the industrial work group*. Ann Arbor, MI: Institute for Social Research.

Seashore, S. E., & Bowers, D. G. (1970). The durability of organizational change. *American Psychologist, 25*, 227–233.

Seeger, J. A. (1983). No innate phases in group problem solving. *Academy of Management Review, 8*, 683–689.

Segal, M. W. (1979). Varieties of interpersonal attraction and their interrelationships in natural groups. *Social Psychology Quarterly, 42*, 253–261.

Semmel, A. K. (1976). *Group dynamics and the foreign policy process: The choice-shift phenomenon*. Paper presented at the Annual Meetings of the Southern Political Science Association.

Sermat, V. (1964). Cooperative behavior in a mixed-motive game. *Journal of Social Psychology, 62*, 217–239.

Service, E. R. (1975). Origins of the state and civilization. New York: Norton.

Shambaugh, P. W. (1978). The development of the small group. *Human Relations, 31*, 283–295.

Shapiro, D. E., Heil, J., & Hager, F. (1983). Validation of the JoHari Window Test as a measure of self disclosure. *Journal of Social Psychology, 120*, 289–290.

Shapley, L. S. (1953). A value for *n*-person games. In H. W. Kuhn & A. W. Tucker (Eds.), *Contributions to the theory of games* (Vol. 2). Princeton, NJ: Princeton University Press.

Shaver, P., & Buhrmester, D. (1983). Loneliness, sex-role orientation, and group life: A social needs perspective. In P. B. Paulus (Ed.), *Basic group processes* (pp. 259–288). New York: Springer-Verlag.

Shaw, J. I., & Condelli, L. (1986). Effects of compliance outcome and basis of power on the powerholder-target relationship. *Personality and Social Psychology Bulletin, 12*, 236–246.

Shaw, M. (Marjorie) E. (1932). A comparison of individuals and small groups in the rational solution of complex problems. *American Journal of Psychology, 44*, 491–504.

Shaw, M. E. (1963). *Scaling group tasks: A method for dimensional analysis.* Technical Report No. 1, ONR contract NR 170-266, Nonr-580(11).

Shaw, M. E. (1964). Communication networks. In L. Berkowitz (Ed.), *Advances in experimental social psychology* (Vol. 1, pp. 111–147). New York: Academic Press.

Shaw, M. E. (1976). *Group dynamics: The psychology of small group behavior* (2nd ed.). McGraw-Hill.

Shaw, M. E. (1978). Communication networks fourteen years later. In L. Berkowitz (Ed.), *Group processes.* Academic Press.

Shaw, M. E. (1981). *Group dynamics: The psychology of small group behavior* (3rd ed.). McGraw-Hill.

Shaw, M. E., & Breed, G. R. (1970). Effects of attribution of responsibility for negative events on behavior in small groups. *Sociometry, 33,* 382–393.

Shaw, M. E., & Costanzo, P. R. (1982). *Theories of social psychology* (2nd. ed.). New York: McGraw-Hill.

Shaw, M. E., & Harkey, B. (1976). Some effects of congruency of member characteristics and group structure upon group behavior. *Journal of Personality and Social Psychology, 34,* 412–418.

Shaw, M. E., & Shaw, L. M. (1962). Some effects of sociometric grouping upon learning in a second grade classroom. *Journal of Social Psychology, 57,* 453–458.

Shears, L. M. (1967). Patterns of coalition formation in two games played by male tetrads. *Behavioral Science, 12,* 130–137.

Shepher, J., & Tiger, L. (1983). Kibbutz and parental investment. In H. H. Blumberg, A. P. Hare, V. Kent, & M. F. Davies (Eds.), *Small groups and social interaction* (Vol. 2, pp. 279–292). New York: Wiley.

Sheridan, C. L., & King, R. G., Jr. (1972). Obedience to authority with an authentic victim. *Proceedings of the 80th Annual Convention of the American Psychological Association, 7,* 165–166.

Sherif, C. W. (1976). *Orientation in social psychology.* New York: Harper & Row.

Sherif, M. (1936). *The psychology of social norms.* New York: Harper & Row.

Sherif, M. (1966). *In common predicament: Social psychology of intergroup conflict and cooperation.* Boston: Houghton Mifflin.

Sherif, M., Harvey, O. J., White, B. J., Hood, W. R., & Sherif, C. W. (1961). *Intergroup conflict and cooperation. The Robbers Cave Experiment.* Norman, OK: Institute of Group Relations.

Sherif, M., & Sherif, C. W. (1953). *Groups in harmony and tension.* New York: Harper & Row.

Sherif, M., & Sherif, C. W. (1956). *An outline of social psychology* (rev. ed.). New York: Harper & Row.

Sherif, M., & Sherif, C. W. (1964). *Reference groups.* New York: Harper & Row.

Sherif, M., White, B. J., & Harvey, O. J. (1955). Status in experimentally produced groups. *American Journal of Sociology, 60,* 370–379.

Sherman, S. J. (1983). Expectation-based and automatic behavior: A comment on Lee and Ofshe, and Berger and Zelditch. *Social Psychology Quarterly, 46,* 66-70.

Sherrod, D. R., & Cohen, S. (1979). Density, personal control, and design. In J. R. Aiello & A. Baum (Eds.), *Residential crowding and design* (pp. 217–227). New York: Plenum.

Sherry, P., & Hurley, J. R. (1976). Curative factors in psychotherapeutic and growth groups. *Journal of Clinical Psychology, 32,* 835–837.

Shiflett, S. (1979). Toward a general model of small group productivity. *Psychological Bulletin, 86,* 67–79.

Shiflett, S. C. (1973). The contingency model of leadership effectiveness: Some implications of its statistical and methodological properties. *Behavioral Science, 18,* 429–440.

Shrauger, J. S. (1975). Responses to evaluation as a function of initial self-perceptions. *Psychological Bulletin, 82,* 581–596.

Shure, G. H., & Meeker, J. R. (1967). A personality/attitude scale for use in experimental bargaining studies. *Journal of Psychology, 65,* 233–252.

Shure, G. H., Rogers, M. S., Larsen, I. M., & Tassone, J. (1962). Group planning and task effectiveness. *Sociometry, 25,* 263–282.

Sigall, H. (1970). Effects of competence and consensual validation on a communicator's liking for the audience. *Journal of Personality and Social Psychology, 16,* 251–258.

Sigelman, C. K., & Sigelman, L. (1976). Authority and conformity: Violation of a traffic regulation. *Journal of Social Psychology, 100,* 35–43.

Silver, M., & Geller, D. (1978). On the irrelevance of evil: The organization and individual actions. *Journal of Social Issues, 34*(4), 125–135.

Simmel, G. (1902). The number of members as determining the sociological form of the group. *American Journal of Sociology, 8*, 1–46, 158–196.

Simmel, G. (1950). *The sociology of Georg Simmel.* New York: Free Press.

Simmel, G. (1955). *Conflict.* New York: Free Press.

Simon, B., & Brown, R. (1987). Perceived intragroup homogeneity in minority majority contexts. *Journal of Personality and Social Psychology, 53*, 703–711.

Simon, H. A. (1976). *Administrative behavior: A study of decision-making processes in adminstrative organizations* (3rd. ed.). New York: Free Press.

Simon, R. J. (1980). *The jury: Its role in American society.* Lexington, MA: D. C. Heath.

Simonton, D. K. (1980). Land battles, generals, and armies: Individual and social determinants of victory and casualties. *Journal of Personality and Social Psychology, 38*, 110–119.

Simonton, D. K. (1985). Intelligence and personal influence in groups: Four nonlinear models. *Psychological Review, 92*, 532–547.

Simonton, D. K. (1987). *Why presidents succeed.* New Haven, CT: Yale University Press.

Singer, J. E., Baum, C. S., Baum, A., & Thew, B. D. (1982). Mass psychogenic illness: The case for social comparison. In M. J. Colligan, J. W. Pennebaker, & L. R. Murphy (Eds.), *Mass psychogenic illness: A social psychological analysis* (pp. 155–169). Hillsdale, NJ: Erlbaum.

Singer, J. E., Brush, C. A., & Lublin, S. C. (1965). Some aspects of deindividuation: Identification and conformity. *Journal of Experimental Social Psychology, 1*, 356–378.

Sistrunk, F., & McDavid, J. W. (1971). Sex variable in conforming behavior. *Journal of Personality and Social Psychology, 17*, 200–207.

Skrypnek, B. J., & Snyder, M. (1982). On the self-perpetuating nature of stereotypes about women and men. *Journal of Experimental Social Psychology, 18*, 277–291.

Slater, P. E. (1955). Role differentiation in small groups. *American Sociological Review, 20*, 300–310.

Slavin, R. E. (1983). When does cooperative learning increase student achievement? *Psychological Bulletin, 94*, 429–445.

Slavin, R. E. (1986). Cooperative learning: Engineering social psychology in the classroom. In R. S. Feldman (Ed.), *The social psychology of education* (pp. 153–171). New York: Cambridge University Press.

Slavson, S. R. (1950). Group psychotherapy. *Scientific American, 183*(6), 42–45.

Sloan, L. R. (1979). The function and impact of sports for fans: A review of theory and contemporary research. In J. H. Goldstein (Ed.), *Sports, games, and play: Social and psychological viewpoints.* Hillsdale, NJ: Erlbaum.

Smelser, N. J. (1962). *Theory of collective behavior.* New York: Free Press.

Smith, D. H. (1980). Participation in outdoor recreation and sports. In D. H. Smith, J. Macaulay and Associates (Eds.), *Participation in social and political activities: A comprehensive analysis of political involvement, expressive leisure time, and helping behavior* (pp. 177–201). San Francisco: Jossey-Bass.

Smith, K. K., & White, G. L. (1983). Some alternatives to traditional social psychology of groups. *Personality and Social Psychology Bulletin, 9*, 65–73.

Smith, M. B. (1972). Is experimental social psychology advancing? *Journal of Experimental Social Psychology, 8*, 86–96.

Smith, P. B. (1975). Controlled studies of the outcome of sensitivity training. *Psychological Bulletin, 82*, 597–622.

Smith, P. B. (1980). The outcome of sensitivity training and encounter. In P. B. Smith (Ed.), *Small groups and personal change* (pp. 25–55). New York: Methuen.

Smith, W. P., & Anderson, A. J. (1975). Threats, communication, and bargaining. *Journal of Personality and Social Psychology, 32*, 76–82.

Smoke, W. H., & Zajonc, R. B. (1962). On the reliability of group judgments and decisions. In J. H. Criswell, H. Solomon, & P. Suppes (Eds.), *Mathematical methods in small group processes.* Stanford, CA: Stanford University Press.

Snodgrass, S. E., & Rosenthal, R. (1984). Females in charge: Effects of sex of subordinate and romantic attachment status upon self-ratings of dominance. *Journal of Personality, 52,* 355–371.

Snyder, C. R., Lassegard, M., & Ford, C. E. (1986). Distancing after group success and failure: Basking in reflected glory and cutting off reflected failure. *Journal of Personality and Social Psychology, 51,* 382–388.

Snyder, M., & Swann, W. B., Jr. (1978). Behavioral confirmation in social interaction: From social perception to social reality. *Journal of Experimental Social Psychology, 14,* 148–162.

Snyder, M., Tanke, E. D., & Berscheid, E. (1977). Social perception and interpersonal behavior: On the self-fulfilling nature of social stereotypes. *Journal of Personality and Social Psychology, 35,* 656–666.

Solomon, L. (1960). The influence of some types of power relationships and game strategies upon the development of interpersonal trust. *Journal of Abnormal and Social Psychology, 61,* 223–230.

Sommer, R. (1959). Studies in personal space. *Sociometry, 22,* 247–260.

Sommer, R. (1967). Small group ecology. *Psychological Bulletin, 67,* 145–152.

Sommer, R. (1969). *Personal space.* Englewood Cliffs, NJ: Prentice-Hall.

Sommer, R. (1972). *Design awareness.* San Francisco: Rinehart.

Sorensen, T. C. (1966). *Kennedy.* New York: Bantam.

Sorokin, P. A., & Lundin, W. A. (1959). *Power and morality: Who shall guard the guardians?* Boston, MA: Sargent.

Sorrels, J. P., & Kelley, J. (1984). Conformity by omission. *Personality and Social Psychology Bulletin, 10,* 302–305.

Sorrentino, R. M., & Boutillier, R. G. (1975). The effect of quantity and quality of verbal interaction on ratings of leadership ability. *Journal of Experimental Social Psychology, 11,* 403–411.

Sorrentino, R. M., & Field, N. (1986). Emergent leadership over time: The functional value of positive motivation. *Journal of Personality and Social Psychology, 50,* 1091–1099.

Sorrentino, R. M., King, G., & Leo, G. (1980). The influence of the minority on perception: A note on a possible alternative explanation. *Journal of Experimental Social Psychology, 16,* 293–301.

Spitzer, C. E., & Davis, J. H. (1978). Mutual social influence in dynamic groups. *Social Psychology, 41,* 24–33.

Squire, S. (1983). *The slender balance.* New York: Pinnacle.

Stang, D. J. (1976). Group size effects on conformity. *Journal of Social Psychology, 98,* 175–181.

Stanton & Poors. (1967). *Register of corporations, directors, and executives.* New York: Stanton & Poors.

Stasser, G., Kerr, N. L., & Bray, R. M. (1982). The social psychology of jury deliberations: Structure, process, and product. In N. L. Kerr & R. M. Bray (Eds.), *Psychology of the courtroom* (pp. 221–256). New York: Academic Press.

Stasser, G., Kerr, N. L., & Davis, J. H. (1980). Influence processes in decision-making groups: A modeling approach. In P. B. Paulus (Ed.), *Psychology of group influence.* Hillsdale, NJ: Erlbaum.

Stasser, G., Kerr, N. L., & Davis, J. H. (in press). Influence processes and consensus models in decision-making groups. In P. B. Paulus (Ed.), *Psychology of group influence* (2nd ed.). Hillsdale, NJ: Erlbaum.

Stasser, G., & Titus, W. (1985). Pooling of unshared information in group decision making: Biased information sampling during discussion. *Journal of Personality and Social Psychology, 48,* 1467–1478.

Stasser, G., & Titus, W. (1987). Effects of information load and percentage of shared information on the dissemination of unshared information during group discussion. *Journal of Personality and Social Psychology, 53,* 81–93.

Staub, E. (1985). The psychology of perpetrators and bystanders. *Political Psychology, 6,* 61–85.

Staw, B. M., & Ross, J. (1987). Behavior in escalation situations: Antecedents, prototypes, and solutions. *Research in Organizational Behavior, 9,* 39–78.

Stech, F. J., & McClintock, C. G. (1981). Effects of communicating timing on duopoly bargaining outcomes. *Journal of Personality and Social Psychology, 40,* 664–674.

Stein, R. T. (1982). High-status group members as exemplars: A summary of field research on the relationship of status to congruence conformity. *Small Group Behavior, 13,* 3–21.

Stein, R. T., & Heller, T. (1979). An empirical analysis of the correlations between leadership status and participation rates reported in the literature. *Journal of Personality and Social Psychology, 37*, 1993–2002.

Stein, R. T., & Heller, T. (1983). The relationship of participation rates to leadership status: A meta-analysis. In H. H. Blumberg, A. P. Hare, V. Kent, & M. Davies (Eds.), *Small groups and social interaction* (Vol. 1, pp. 401–406.). New York: Wiley.

Steiner, I. D. (1972). *Group process and productivity*. New York: Academic Press.

Steiner, I. D. (1974). Whatever happened to the group in social psychology? *Journal of Experimental Social Psychology, 10*, 94–108.

Steiner, I. D. (1976). Task-performing groups. In J. W. Thibaut, J. T. Spence, & R. C. Carson (Eds.), *Contemporary topics in social psychology* (pp. 393–422). Morristown, NJ: General Learning Press.

Steiner, I. D. (1983). What ever happened to the touted revival of the group? In H. Blumberg, A. Hare, V. Kent, & M. Davies (Eds.), *Small groups and social interaction* (Vol. 2, pp. 539–547). New York: Wiley.

Steiner, I. D. (1986). Paradigms and groups. In L. Berkowitz (Ed.), *Advances in experimental social psychology* (Vol. 19, pp. 251–289). New York: Academic Press.

Steinhauer, P. D. (1987). The family as small group: The process model of family function. In T. Jacob (Ed.), *Family interaction and psychopathology: Theories, methods, and findings* (pp. 67–115). New York: Plenum.

Steinzor, B. (1950). The spatial factor in face to face discussion groups. *Journal of Abnormal and Social Psychology, 45*, 552–555.

Stephan, C. W., & Stephan, W. G. (1985). *Two social psychologies: An integrative approach*. Belmont, CA: Wadsworth.

Stephan, C. W., & Stephan, W. G. (1986, August). *Social psychology at the crossroads*. Paper presented at the meetings of the American Psychological Association: Washington, DC.

Stephan, W. G. (1985). Intergroup relations. In G. Lindzey & E. Aronson (Eds.), *Handbook of Social Psychology* (Vol. 2, 3rd ed., pp. 599–658). New York: Random House.

Stephan, W. G. (1987). The contact hypothesis in intergroup relations. In C. Hendrick (Ed.), *Review of Personality and Social Psychology: Group Process* (Vol. 9, pp. 13–40). Newbury Park, CA: Sage.

Sternberg, R. J., & Soriano, L. J. (1984). Styles of conflict resolution. *Journal of Personality and Social Psychology, 47*, 115–126.

Stevenson, W. B., Pearce, J. L., & Porter, L. W. (1985). The concept of "coalition" in organization theory and research. *Academy of Management Review, 10*, 256–268.

Stiles, W. B. (1978). Verbal response modes and dimensions of interpersonal roles: A method of discourse analysis. *Journal of Personality and Social Psychology, 36*, 693–703.

Stiles, W. B. (1980). Comparison of dimensions derived from rating versus coding of dialogue. *Journal of Personality and Social Psychology, 38*, 359–374.

Stiles, W. B. (1981). Classification of intersubjective elocution. *Language in Society, 10*, 227–249.

Stiles, W. B., Orth, J. E., Scherwitz, L., Hennrikus, D., & Vallbona, C. (1984). Role behaviors in routine medical interviews with hypertensive patients: A repertoire of verbal exchanges. *Social Psychology Quarterly, 47*, 244–254.

Stiles, W. B., Putnam, S. M., & Jacob, M. C. (1982). Verbal exchange structure of initial medical interviews. *Health Psychology, 1*, 315–336.

Stiles, W. B., Shapiro, D. A., & Elliott, R. (1986). "Are all psychotherapies equivalent?" *American Psychologist, 41*, 165–180.

Stiles, W. B., Tupler, L. A., & Carpenter, J. C. (1982). Participants' perceptions of self-analytic group sessions. *Small Group Behavior, 13*, 237–254.

Stiles, W. B., Waszak, C. S., & Barton, L. R. (1979). Professorial presumptuousness in verbal interactions with university students. *Journal of Experimental Social Psychology, 15*, 158–169.

Stockard, J., van de Kragt, A. J. C., & Dodge, P. J. (1988). Gender roles and behavior in social dilemmas: Are there sex differences in cooperation and in its justification? *Social Psychology Quarterly, 51*, 154–163.

Stogdill, R. M. (1948). Personal factors associated with leadership. *Journal of Psychology, 23*, 35–71.

Stogdill, R. M. (1959). *Individual behavior and group achievement*. New York: Oxford.

Stogdill, R. M. (1974). *Handbook of leadership*. New York: Free Press.

Stokes, G. (1980). *The Beatles*. New York: Rolling Stone Press.

Stokes, J. P. (1983). Components of group cohesion: Intermember attraction, instrumental value, and risk taking. *Small Group Behavior, 14,* 163–173.

Stokes, J. P. (1985). The relation of social network and individual difference variables to loneliness. *Journal of Personality and Social Psychology, 48,* 981–990.

Stokes, J. P., & Wilson, D. G. (1984). The inventory of socially supportive behaviors: Dimensionality, prediction, and gender differences. *American Journal of Community Psychology, 12,* 53–69.

Stokols, D. (1972). On the distinction between density and crowding: Some implications for future research. *Psychological Review, 79,* 275–278.

Stokols, D. (1978). In defense of the crowding construct. In A. Baum, J. E. Singer, & S. Valins (Eds.), *Advances in environmental psychology* (Vol. 1, pp. 111–130). Hillsdale, NJ: Erlbaum.

Stokols, D., & Altman, I. (Eds.) (1987). *Handbook of environmental psychology* (Vol. 1 & Vol. 2). New York: Wiley.

Stoner, J. A. F. (1961). *A comparison of individual and group decisions involving risk*. Unpublished master's thesis, Massachusetts Institute of Technology.

Stones, C. R. (1982). A community of Jesus people in South Africa. *Small Group Behavior, 13,* 264–272.

Stoop, J. R. (1932). Is the judgment of the group better than that of the average member of the group? *Journal of Experimental Psychology, 15,* 550–562.

Storms, M. D., & Thomas, G. C. (1977). Reactions to physical closeness. *Journal of Personality and Social Psychology, 35,* 319–328.

Stratham, A. (1987). The gender model revisited: Differences in the management styles of men and women. *Sex Roles, 16,* 409–429.

Strauss, A. L. (1944). The literature on panic. *Journal of Abnormal and Social Psychology, 39,* 317–328.

Streufert, S., & Streufert, S. C. (1986). The development of internation conflict. In S. Worchel & W. G. Austin (Eds.), *Psychol-ogy of intergroup relations* (2nd ed., pp. 134–152). Chicago: Nelson-Hall.

Stricker, L. J., Messick, S., & Jackson, D. N. (1970). Conformity, anticonformity, and independence: Their dimensionality and generality. *Journal of Personality and Social Psychology, 16,* 494–507.

Strickland, L. H. (1958). Surveillance and trust. *Journal of Personality, 26,* 206–215.

Strickland, L. H., Barefoot, J. C., & Hockenstein, P. (1976). Monitoring behavior in the surveillance and trust paradigm. *Representative Research in Social Psychology, 7,* 51–57.

Strodtbeck, F. L., & Hook, L. H. (1961). The social dimensions of a twelve-man jury table. *Sociometry, 24,* 397–415.

Strodtbeck, F. L., James, R. M., & Hawkins, C. (1957). Social status in jury deliberations. *American Sociological Review, 22,* 713–719.

Strodtbeck, F. L., & Lipinski, R. M. (1985). Becoming first among equals: Moral considerations in jury foreman selection. *Journal of Personality and Social Psychology, 49,* 927–936.

Strodtbeck, F. L., & Mann, R. D. (1956). Sex role differentiation in jury deliberations. *Sociometry, 19,* 3–11.

Stroebe, W., Lenkert, A., & Jonas, K. (1988). Familiarity may breed contempt: The impact of student exchange on national stereotypes and attitudes. In W. Stroebe, A. W. Kruglanski, D. Bar-Tal, & M. Hewstone (Eds.), *The social psychology of intergroup conflict* (pp. 167–187). New York: Springer-Verlag.

Strong, S. R., Hills, H. I., Kilmartin, C. T., DeVries, H., Lanier, K., Nelson, B. N., Strickland, D., & Meyer, C. W., III. (1988). The dynamic relations among interpersonal behaviors: A test of complementarity and anticomplementarity. *Journal of Personality and Social Psychology, 54,* 798–810.

Strube, M. J., & Garcia, J. E. (1981). A meta-analytic investigation of Fiedler's contingency model of leadership effectiveness. *Psychological Bulletin, 90,* 307–321.

Strube, M. J., & Garcia, J. E. (1983). On the proper interpretation of empirical findings: Strube and Garcia (1981) revisited. *Psychological Bulletin, 93,* 600–603.

Strupp, H. H., & Bloxum, A. L. (1973). Preparing lower-class patients for group psychotherapy: Development and evaluation of a role-induction film. *Journal of Consulting and Clinical Psychology, 41,* 373–384.

Stryker, S. (1977). Developments in "Two social psychologies": Toward an appreciation of mutual relevance. *Sociometry, 40,* 145–160.

Stryker, S. (August, 1986). *Consequences of the gap between the "Two social psychologies."* Paper presented at the meetings of the American Psychological Association: Washington, DC.

Stryker, S., & Statham, A. (1985). Symbolic interaction and role theory. In G. Lindzey & E. Aronson (Eds.), *Handbook of social psychology* (3rd ed., Vol. 1, pp. 311–378). New York: Random House.

Stults, D. M., & Messe, L. A. (1985). Behavioral consistency: The impact of public versus private statements of intentions. *Journal of Social Psychology, 125,* 277–278.

Stumpf, S. A., Freedman, R. D., & Zand, D. E. (1979). Judgmental decisions: A study of interactions among group members, group functioning, and the decision situation. *Academy of Management Journal, 22,* 765–782.

Suedfeld, P. (1987). Extreme and unusual environments. In D. Stokols & I. Altman (Eds.), *Handbook of environmental psychology* (Vol. 1, pp. 863–887). New York: Wiley.

Suenaga, T., Andow, K., Ohshima, T. (1981). Social facilitation: History, current studies, and future perspectives. *Japanese Psychological Review, 24,* 423–457.

Suls, J. M., & Miller, R. L. (Eds.). (1977). *Social comparison processes.* Washington, DC: Hemisphere.

Sumner, W. G. (1906). *Folkways.* New York: Ginn.

Sundstrom, E. (1975). An experimental study of crowding: Effects of room size, intrusion, and goal-blocking on nonverbal behavior, self-disclosure, and self-reported stress. *Journal of Personality and Social Psychology, 32,* 645–654.

Sundstrom, E. (1987). Work environments: Offices and factories. In D. Stokols & I. Altman (Eds.), *Handbook of environmental psychology* (Vol. 1, pp. 733–782). New York: Wiley.

Sundstrom, E., & Altman, I. (1974). Field study of dominance and territorial behav-

ior. *Journal of Personality and Social Psychology, 30,* 115–125.

Swap, W. C., & Rubin, J. Z. (1983). Measurement of interpersonal orientation. *Journal of Personality and Social Psychology, 44,* 208–219.

Swingle, P. G., & Santi, A. (1972). Communication in non-zero sum games. *Journal of Personality and Social Psychology, 23,* 54–63.

Szymanski, K., & Harkins, S. G. (1987). Social loafing and self-evaluation with a social standard. *Journal of Personality and Social Psychology, 53,* 891–897.

Tajfel, H. (1978a). Interindividual behavior and intergroup behavior. In H. Tajfel (Ed.), *Differentiation between social groups* (pp. 27–60). New York: Academic Press.

Tajfel, H. (1978b). Social categorization, social identity, and social comparison. In H. Tajfel (Ed.), *Differentiation between social groups* (pp. 61–76). New York: Academic Press.

Tajfel, H. (1978c). The achievement of group differentiation. In H. Tajfel (Ed.), *Differentiation between social groups* (pp. 77–98). New York: Academic Press.

Tajfel, H. (1981). *Human groups and social categories.* New York: Cambridge University Press.

Tajfel, H. (1982). The social psychology of intergroup relations. *Annual Review of Psychology, 33,* 1–39.

Tajfel, H., Sheikh, A. A., & Gardner, R. C. (1964). Content of stereotypes and the inference of similarity between members of stereotyped groups. *Acta Psychologica, 22,* 191–201.

Tajfel, H., & Turner, J. C. (1986). The social identity theory of intergroup behavior. In S. Worchel & W. G. Austin (Eds.), *Psychology of intergroup relations* (2nd ed., pp. 7–24). Chicago: Nelson-Hall.

Tallman, I. (1970). The family as a small problem-solving group. *Journal of Marriage and the Family, 32,* 94–104.

Tanford, S., & Penrod, S. (1983). Computer modeling of influence in the jury: the role of the consistent juror. *Social Psychology Quarterly, 46,* 200–212.

Tanford, S., & Penrod, S. (1984). Social influence model: A formal integration of research on majority and minority influence processes. *Psychological Bulletin, 95,* 189–225.

Tarde, G. (1903). *The laws of imitation.* New York: Holt.

Taylor, D. A., & Moriarty, B. F. (1987). Ingroup bias as a function of competition and race. *Journal of Conflict Resolution, 1,* 192–199.

Taylor, D. M., & Moghaddam, F. M. (1987). *Theories of intergroup relations.* New York: Praeger.

Taylor, D. W., Berry, P. C., & Block, C. H. (1958). Does group participation when using brainstorming facilitate or inhibit creative thinking? *Administrative Science Quarterly, 3,* 23–47.

Taylor, F. W. (1923). *The principles of scientific management.* New York: Harper.

Taylor, H. F. (1970). *Balance in small groups.* New York: Van Nostrand Reinhold.

Taylor, S. E. (1983). Adjustment to threatening events: A theory of cognitive adaptation. *American Psychologist, 38,* 1161–1173.

Tedeschi, J. T., Gaes, G. G., & Rivera, A. N. (1977). Aggression and the use of coercive power. *Journal of Social Issues, 33*(1), 101–125.

Tedeschi, J. T., Schlenker, B. R., & Bonoma, T. V. (1973). *Conflict, power, and games.* Chicago: Aldine.

Tedeschi, J. T., Smith, R. B., III, & Brown, R. C. (1974). A reinterpretation of research on aggression. *Psychological Bulletin, 81,* 540–563.

Teger, A. (1980). *Too much invested to quit.* New York: Pergamon.

Terborg, J. R., Castore, C., & DeNinno, J. A. (1976). A longitudinal field investigation of the impact of group composition on group performance and cohesion. *Journal of Personality and Social Psychology, 34,* 782–790.

Terhune, K. W. (1970). The effects of personality in cooperation and conflict. In P. Swingle (Ed.), *The structure of conflict.* New York: Academic Press.

Tesser, A., & Campbell, J. (1983). Self-definition and self-evaluation maintenance. In J. Suls & A. G. Greenwald (Eds.), *Psychological perspectives on the self* (Vol. 2). Hillsdale, NJ: Erlbaum.

Tesser, A., Campbell, J., & Smith, M. (1984). Friendship choice and performance: Self-evaluation maintenance in children. *Journal of Personality and Social Psychology, 46,* 561–574.

Tesser, A., & Rosen, S. (1975). The reluctance to transmit bad news. In L. Berkowitz (Ed.), *Advances in experimental social psychology* (Vol. 8, pp. 194–232). New York: Academic Press.

Tetlock, P. E. (1979). Identifying victims of groupthink from public statements of decision makers. *Journal of Personality and Social Psychology, 37,* 1314–1324.

Thibaut, J. W. (1950). An experimental study of the cohesiveness of underprivileged groups. *Human Relations, 3,* 251–278.

Thibaut, J. W., & Coules, J. (1952). The role of communication in the reduction of interpersonal hostility. *Journal of Abnormal and Social Psychology, 47,* 770–777.

Thibaut, J. W., & Kelley, H. H. (1959). *The social psychology of groups.* New York: Wiley.

Thomas, E. J., & Fink, C. F. (1961). Models of group problem solving. *Journal of Abnormal and Social Psychology, 63,* 53–63.

Thompson, S. C. (in press). Intervening to enhance perceptions of control. In C. R. Snyder & D. R. Forsyth (Eds.), *Handbook of social and clinical psychology: The health perspective.* New York: Pergamon.

Thrasher, F. M. (1927). *The gang.* Chicago: University of Chicago Press.

Thune, E. S., Manderscheid, R. W., & Silbergeld, S. (1981). Sex, status, and cotherapy. *Small Group Behavior, 12,* 415–442.

Tiger, L. (1969). *Men in groups.* New York: Random House.

Tiger, L., & Fox, R. (1971). *The imperial animal.* New York: Random House.

Tiger, L., & Shepher, J. (1975). *Women in the kibbutz.* New York: Harcourt Brace Jovanovich.

Tjosvold, D. (1986). *Working together to get things done.* Lexington, MA: Lexington Books.

Tolstoy, L. (1952).*War and peace.* Chicago: Encyclopaedia Britannica.

Towler, G. (1986). From zero to one hundred: Coaction in a natural setting. *Perceptual and Motor Skills, 62,* 377–378.

Travis, L. E. (1925). The effect of a small audience upon eye-hand coordination. *Journal of Abnormal and Social Psychology, 20,* 142–146.

Travis, L. E. (1928). The influence of the group upon the stutterer's speed in free association. *Journal of Abnormal and Social Psychology, 23*, 45–51.

Triandis, H. C. (1978). Some universals of social behavior. *Personality and Social Psychology Bulletin, 4*, 1–16.

Triandis, H. C. (1986). Commentary. In S. Worchel & W. G. Austin (Eds.), *Psychology of intergroup relations* (2nd ed., pp. 366–378). Chicago: Nelson-Hall.

Triplett, N. (1898). The dynamogenic factors in pacemaking and competition. *American Journal of Psychology, 9*, 507–533.

Trujillo, N. (1986). Toward a taxonomy of small group interaction-coding systems. *Small Group Behavior, 17*, 371–394.

Tsui, A. S. (1984). A role-set analysis of managerial reputation. *Organizational Behavior and Human Performance, 34*, 64–96.

Tsui, A. S., & Gutek, B. A. (1984). A role set analysis of gender differences in performance, affective relationships, and career success of industrial middle managers. *Academy of Management Journal,* 619–635.

Tucker, R. C. (1977). Personality and political leaders. *Political Science Quarterly, 92*, 383–393.

Tuckman, B. W. (1965). Developmental sequences in small groups. *Psychological Bulletin, 63*, 384–399.

Tuckman, B. W., & Jensen, M. A. C. (1977). Stages of small group development revisited. *Group and Organizational Studies, 2*, 419–427.

Tuddenham, R. D. (1959). Correlates of yielding to a distorted group norm. *Journal of Personality, 27*, 272–284.

Turner, J. C. (1981). The experimental social psychology of intergroup behavior. In J. C. Turner & H. Giles (Eds.), *Intergroup behavior* (pp. 144–167). Oxford: Blackwell.

Turner, J. C. (1982). Towards a cognitive redefinition of the social group. In H. Tajfel (Ed.), *Social identity and intergroup relations* (pp. 15–40). New York: Cambridge University Press.

Turner, J. C. (1983). Some comments on "The measurement of social orientations in the minimal group paradigm." *European Journal of Social Psychology, 13*, 351–367.

Turner, J. C. (1985). Social categorization and the self-concept: A social-cognitive theory of group behavior. In E. J. Lawler (Ed.), *Advances in group processes* (Vol. 2, pp. 77–122). Greenwich, CT: JAI Press.

Turner, J. C. (1987). *Rediscovering the social group: A self-categorization theory.* New York: Blackwell.

Turner, J. C., Sachdev, I., & Hogg, M. A. (1983). Social categorization, interpersonal attraction, and group formation. *British Journal of Social Psychology, 22*, 227–239.

Turner, R. H. (1964). Collective behavior. In R. E. L. Faris (Ed.), *Handbook of modern sociology.* Chicago: Rand McNally.

Turner, R. H., & Killian, L. M. (1972). *Collective behavior* (2nd ed.). Englewood Cliffs, NJ: Prentice-Hall.

Turner, R. H., & Killian, L. M. (1987). *Collective behavior* (3rd ed.). Englewood Cliffs, NJ: Prentice-Hall.

Turner, R. H., & Surace, S. J. (1956). Zootsuiters and Mexicans: Symbols in crowd behavior. *The American Journal of Sociology, 62*, 14–20.

Tuthill, D., & Forsyth, D. R. (1982). Sex differences in opinion conformity and dissent. *Journal of Social Psychology, 116*, 205–210.

Tutzauer, F. (1985). Toward a theory of disintegration in communication networks. *Social Networks, 7*, 263–285.

Tuzlak, A., & Moore, J. C., Jr. (1984). Status, demeanor, and influence: An empirical reassessment. *Social Psychology Quarterly, 47*, 178–183.

Tyerman, A., & Spencer, C. (1983). A critical test of the Sherifs' Robber's Cave Experiments: Intergroup competition and cooperation between groups of well-acquainted individuals. *Small Group Behavior, 14*, 515–531.

Tyler, T. R., & Sears, D. O. (1977). Coming to like obnoxious people when we must live with them. *Journal of Personality and Social Psychology, 35*, 200–211.

Ulschak, F. L., Nathanson, L., & Gillan, P. G. (1981). *Small group problem solving.* Reading, MA: Addison-Wesley.

Uris, A. (1978). *Executive dissent: How to say no and win.* New York: AMACOM.

Urruti, G., & Miller, C. E. (1984). Test of the bargaining and equal excess theories of coalition formation: Effects of experience, information about payoffs, and monetary stakes. *Journal of Personality and Social Psychology, 46*, 825–836.

Uttal, B. (1985, August 5). Behind the fall of Steve Jobs. *Fortune,* 20–24.

Van de Ven, A. H. (1974). *Group decision-making effectiveness*. Kent, OH: Kent State University Center for Business and Economic Research Press.

Van de Ven, A. H., & Delbecq, A. L. (1971). Nominal versus interacting group process for committee decisionmaking effectiveness. *Academy of Management Journal, 14*, 203–212.

Van Egeren, L. F. (1979). Cardiovascular changes during social competition in a mixed-motive game. *Journal of Personality and Social Psychology, 37*, 858–864.

Van Sell, M., Brief, A. P., & Schuler, R. S. (1981). Role conflict and role ambiguity: Integration of the literature and directions for future research. *Human Relations, 34*, 43–71.

Varela, J. A. (1971). *Psychological solutions to social problems*. New York: Academic Press.

Varney, G. H. (1977). *Organization development for managers*. Reading, MA: Addison-Wesley.

Vecchio, R. P. (1977). An empirical examination of the validity of Fiedler's model of leadership effectiveness. *Organizational Behavior and Human Performance, 19*, 180–206.

Vecchio, R. P. (1983). Assessing the validity of Fiedler's contingency model of leadership: A closer look at Strube and Garcia. *Psychological Bulletin, 93*, 600–603.

Vecchio, R. P. (1987). Situational leadership theory: An examination of a prescriptive theory. *Journal of Applied Psychology, 72*, 444–451.

Verba, S. (1961). *Small groups and political behavior: A study of leadership*. Princeton, NJ: Princeton University Press.

Villaseñor, V. (1977). *Jury: The people vs. Juan Corona*. Boston: Little, Brown.

Vinacke, W. E. (1971). Negotiations and decisions in a politics game. In B. Lieberman (Ed.), *Social choice*. New York: Gordon & Breach.

Vinokur, A. (1971). A review and theoretical analysis of the effects of group processes upon individual and group decisions involving risk. *Psychological Bulletin, 76*, 231–250.

Vinokur, A., & Burnstein, E. (1974). The effects of partially shared persuasive arguments on group-induced shifts: A group-problem-solving approach. *Journal of Personality and Social Psychology, 29*, 305–315.

Vinokur, A., & Burnstein, E. (1978). Depolarization of attitudes in groups. *Journal of Personality and Social Psychology, 36*, 872–885.

Vinokur, A., Burnstein, E., Sechrest, L., & Wortman, P. M. (1985). Group decision making by experts: Field study of panels evaluating medical technologies. *Journal of Personality and Social Psychology, 49*, 70–84.

Vinsel, A., Brown, B. B., Altman, I., & Foss, C. (1980). Privacy regulation, territorial displays, and effectiveness of individual functioning. *Journal of Personality and Social Psychology, 39*, 1104–1115.

Vollrath, D. A., & Davis, J. H. (1980). Jury size and decision rule. In R. J. Simon (Ed.), *The jury: Its role in American society*. Lexington, MA: Heath.

Vroom, V. H. (1973). A new look at managerial decision making. *Organizational Dynamics, 1*, 66–80.

Vroom, V. H. (1974). Decision making and the leadership process. *Journal of Contemporary Business, 3*, 47–64.

Vroom, V. H. (1976). Leadership. In M. D. Dunnette (Ed.), *Handbook of industrial and organizational psychology*. Chicago: Rand McNally.

Vroom, V. H., & Jago, A. G. (1978). On the validity of the Vroom/Yetton model. *Journal of Applied Psychology, 63*, 151–162.

Vroom, V. H., & Mann, F. C. (1960). Leader authoritarianism and employee attitudes. *Personnel Psychology, 13*, 125–140.

Vroom, V. H., & Yetton, P. W. (1973). *Leadership and decision making*. Pittsburgh, PA: University of Pittsburgh Press.

Wahrman, R., & Pugh, M. D. (1972). Competence and conformity: Another look at Hollander's study. *Sociometry, 35*, 376–386.

Wahrman, R., & Pugh, M. D. (1974). Sex, nonconformity, and influence. *Sociometry, 37*, 137–147.

Walden, T. A., & Forsyth, D. R. (1981). Close encounters of the stressful kind: Affective, physiological, and behavioral reactions to the experience of crowding. *Journal of Nonverbal Behavior, 6*, 46–64.

Walker, C. J., & Berkerle, C. A. (1987). The effect of state anxiety on rumor transmission. *Journal of Social Behavior and Personality, 2,* 353–360.

Wallach, M. A., Kogan, N., & Bem, D. J. (1962). Group influence on individual risk taking. *Journal of Abnormal and Social Psychology, 65,* 75–86.

Wanous, J. P., Reichers, A. E., & Malik, S. D. (1984). Organizational socialization and group development: Toward an integrative perspective. *Academy of Management Review, 9,* 670–683.

Warriner, C. H. (1956). Groups are real: A reaffirmation. *American Sociological Review, 21,* 549–554.

Watson, R. I., Jr. (1973). Investigation into deindividuation using a cross-cultural survey technique. *Journal of Personality and Social Psychology, 25,* 342–345.

Webb, E. J., Campbell, D. T., Schwartz, R. D., Sechrest, L., Grove, J. B. (1981). *Nonreactive measures in the social sciences.* Boston: Houghton Mifflin.

Weber, M. (1921/1946). The sociology of charismatic authority. In H. H. Gert, & C. W. Mills (Trans. & Eds.), *From Max Weber: Essay in sociology* (pp. 245–252). New York: Oxford University Press.

Weber, M. (1947). *The theory of social and economic organization.* New York: Oxford.

Webster, M., Jr., & Driskell, J. E., Jr. (1978). Status generalization: A review and some new data. *American Sociological Review, 43,* 220–236.

Webster, M., Jr., & Driskell, J. E., Jr. (1983). Processes of status generalization. In H. H. Blumberg, A. P. Hare, V. Kent, & M. F. Davies (Eds.), *Small groups and social interaction* (Vol. 1, pp. 57–67). New York: Wiley.

Webster, N. (1976). *Webster's new twentieth century dictionary of the English language.* New York: Collins World.

Wegner, D. M., & Schaefer, D. (1978). The concentration of responsibility: An objective self-awareness analysis of group size effects in helping situations. *Journal of Personality and Social Psychology, 36,* 147–155.

Weick, K. E. (1985). Systematic observational methods. In G. Lindzey & E. Aronson (Eds.), *Handbook of Social Psychology* (Vol. 1, 3rd ed., pp. 567–634). New York: Random House.

Weigel, R. H., & Cook, S. W. (1975). Participation in decision-making: A determinant of interpersonal attraction in cooperating interracial groups. *International Journal of Group Tension, 5,* 179–195.

Weiler, D. J., & Castle, J. E. (November, 1972). *The need for an open systems approach to naval ship habitability design.* Paper presented at the meetings of the Society of Naval Architects and Marine Engineers, New York.

Weiss, R. F., & Miller, F. G. (1971). The drive theory of social facilitation. *Psychological Review, 78,* 44–57.

Weiss, R. S. (1973). *Loneliness: The experience of emotional and social isolation.* Cambridge, MA: MIT Press.

Wentworth, D. K., & Anderson, L. R. (1984). Emergent leadership as a function of sex and task type. *Sex Roles, 11,* 513–524.

Wertheimer, M. (1938). The general theoretical situation. In W. D. Ellis (Ed.), *A source book of Gestalt psychology.* New York: Harcourt, Brace, & World.

West, S. G., Gunn, S. P., & Chernicky, P. (1975). Ubiquitous Watergate: An attributional analysis. *Journal of Personality and Social Psychology, 23,* 55–65.

Weston, S. B., & English, H. B. (1926). The influence of the group on psychological test scores. *American Journal of Psychology, 37,* 600–601.

Wetherby, T. (1977). *Conversations.* Millbrae, CA: Les Femmes.

Weybrew, B. B. (1963). Psychological problems of prolonged marine submergence. In J. N. Burns, R. Chambers, & E. Hendler (Eds.), *Unusual environments and human behavior.* New York: Macmillan.

Wheeler, D. D., & Janis, I. L. (1980). *A practical guide for making decisions.* New York: Free Press.

Wheeler, L. (1966). Toward a theory of behavioral contagion. *Psychological Review, 73,* 179–192.

Wheeler, L., Reis, H. T., & Bond, M. H. (1989). Collectivism-individualism in everyday social life: The middle kingdom and the melting pot. *Journal of Personality and Social Psychology, 57,* 79–86.

Wheeler, L., Reis, H. T., & Nezlek, J. (1983). Loneliness, social interaction, and sex roles. *Journal of Personality and Social Psychology, 45,* 943–953.

Wheeless, L. R., Barraclough, R., & Stewart, R. (1983). Compliance-gaining and power in persuasion. In R. N. Bostrom (Ed.),

Communication yearbook (Vol. 7, pp. 105–145). Newbury Park, CA: Sage.

Wheeless, L. R., Wheeless, V. E., & Dickson-Markman, F. (1982). A research note: The relations among social and task perceptions in small groups. *Small Group Behavior, 13*, 373–384.

White, M. J. (1977). Counternormative behavior as influenced by deindividuating conditions and reference group salience. *Journal of Social Psychology, 103*, 73–90.

White, R. K. (1965). Images in the context of international conflict. In H. Kelman (Ed.), *International behavior*. New York: Holt, Rinehart, & Winston.

White, R. K. (1966). Misperception and the Vietnam war. *Journal of Social Issues, 22*(3), 1–156.

White, R. K. (1969). Three not-so-obvious contributions of psychology to peace. *Journal of Social Issues, 25*(4), 23–29.

White, R. K. (1970). *Nobody wanted war: Misperception in Vietnam and other wars* (rev. ed.). New York: Doubleday/Anchor.

White, R. K. (1977). Misperception in the Arab-Israeli conflict. *Journal of Social Issues, 33*(1), 190–221.

White, R. K., & Lippitt, R. (1960). *Autocracy and democracy*. New York: Harper & Row.

White, R. K., & Lippitt, R. (1968). Leader behavior and member reaction in three "social climates." In D. Cartwright and A. Zander (Eds.), *Group dynamics: Research and theory* (3rd ed., pp. 318–335). New York: Harper & Row.

Whitehead, T. N. (1938). *The industrial worker*. Cambridge, MA: Harvard University Press.

"The Who." The what, but why? (1979, December 5). *Richmond News Leader*, p. A-19.

Whyte, W. F. (1943). *Street corner society*. Chicago: University of Chicago Press.

Wicker, A. W. (1979). *An introduction to ecological psychology*. Pacific Grove, CA: Brooks/Cole.

Wicker, A. W. (1987). Behavior settings reconsidered: Temporal stages, resources, internal dynamics, context. In D. Stokols & I. Altman (Eds.), *Handbook of environmental psychology* (Vol. 1, pp. 613–653). New York: Wiley.

Wicker, A. W., Kirmeyer, S. L., Hanson, L., & Alexander, D. (1976). Effects of manning levels on subjective experiences, performance, and verbal interaction in groups. *Organizational Behavior and Human Performance, 17*, 251–274.

Wicklund, R. A. (1980). Group contact and self-focused attention. In P. B. Paulus (Ed.), *Psychology of group influence* (p. 189–208). Hillsdale, NJ: Erlbaum.

Wiesenthal, D. L., Endler, N. S., Coward, T. R., & Edwards, J. (1976). Reversibility of relative competence as a determinant of conformity across different perceptual tasks. *Representative Research in Social Psychology, 7*, 35–43.

Wiggins, J. A., Dill, F., & Schwartz, R. D. (1965). On "status-liability." *Sociometry, 28*, 197–209.

Wilder, D. A. (1977). Perception of groups, size of opposition, and social influence. *Journal of Experimental Social Psychology, 13*, 253–268.

Wilder, D. A. (1978a). Perceiving persons as a group: Effects of attributions of causality and beliefs. *Social Psychology, 41*, 13–23.

Wilder, D. A. (1978b). Reduction of intergroup discrimination through individuation of the out-group. *Journal of Personality and Social Psychology, 36*, 1361–1374.

Wilder, D. A. (1986a). Cognitive factors affecting the success of intergroup contact. In S. Worchel & W. G. Austin (Eds.), *Psychology of intergroup relations* (2nd ed., pp. 49–66). Chicago: Nelson-Hall.

Wilder, D. A. (1986b). Social categorization: Implications for creation and reduction of intergroup bias. In L. Berkowitz (Ed.), *Advances in experimental social psychology* (Vol. 19, pp. 293–355). New York: Academic Press.

Wilder, D. A., & Thompson, J. E. (1980). Intergroup contact with independent manipulations of in-group and out-group interaction. *Journal of Personality and Social Psychology, 38*, 589–603.

Wilkinson, I., & Kipnis, D. (1978). Interfirm use of power. *Journal of Applied Psychology, 63*, 315–320.

Williams *v.* Florida, 399 U.S. 78 (1970).

Williams, K. B., Harkins, S., & Latané, B. (1981). Identifiability as a deterrent to social loafing: Two cheering experiments. *Journal of Personality and Social Psychology, 40*, 303–311.

Williams, K. B., & Williams, K. D. (1983). Social inhibition and asking for help: The effects of number, strength, and immediacy of potential help givers. *Journal of Personality and Social Psychology, 44,* 67–77.

Willis, F. N. (1966). Initial speaking distance as a function of the speakers' relationship. *Psychonomic Science, 5,* 221–222.

Willis, R. H. (1963). Two dimensions of conformity-nonconformity. *Sociometry, 26,* 499–512.

Wills, T. A. (1981). Downward comparison principles in social psychology. *Psychological Bulletin, 90,* 245–271.

Wills, T. A. (in press). Social comparison processes in coping and health. In C. R. Snyder & D. R. Forsyth (Eds.), *Handbook of Social and Clinical Psychology: The Health Perspective.* New York: Pergamon.

Wilson, E. O. (1975). *Sociobiology: The new synthesis.* Cambridge, MA: Belknap Press.

Wilson, S. R. (1970). Some factors influencing instrumental and expressive ratings in task-oriented groups. *Pacific Sociological Review, 13,* 127–131.

Wilson, W., & Miller, N. (1961). Shifts in evaluations of participants following intergroup competition. *Journal of Abnormal and Social Psychology, 63,* 428–431.

Winslow, C. N. (1944). Sympathetic pennies: A radio case study. *Journal of Abnormal and Social Psychology, 39,* 174–179.

Winstead, B. (1986). Sex differences in same sex friendships. In V. J. Derlega & B. Winstead (Eds.), *Friendship and social interaction.* New York: Springer-Verlag.

Winter, D. G. (1973). *The power motive.* New York: Free Press.

Wiseman, R. L., & Schenck-Hamlin, W. (1981). A multidimensional scaling validation of an inductively derived set of compliance-gaining strategies. *Communication Monographs, 48,* 251–270.

Wish, M., Deutsch, M., & Kaplan, S. J. (1976). Perceived dimensions of interpersonal relations. *Journal of Personality and Social Psychology, 33,* 409–420.

Wolf, A. (1983). Psychoanalysis in groups. In H. I. Kaplan & B. J. Sadock (Eds.), *Comprehensive group psychotherapy* (2nd. ed., pp. 113–131). Baltimore: Williams & Wilkins.

Wolf, S. (1985). Manifest and latent influence of majorities and minorities. *Journal of Personality and Social Psychology, 48,* 899–908.

Wolf, S. (1987). Majority and minority influence: A social impact analysis. In M. P.

Zanna, J. M. Olson, & C. P. Herman (Eds.), *Social influences: The Ontario Symposuim* (Vol. 5, pp. 207–235). Hillsdale, NJ: Erlbaum.

Wolpe, J., & Lazarus, A. A. (1966). *Behavior therapy techniques.* Oxford: Pergamon Press.

Wood, J. T. (1984). Alternative methods of group decision making: A comparative examination of consensus, negotiation, and voting. In G. M. Phillips & J. T. Wood (Eds.), *Emergent issues in human decision making* (pp. 3–18). Carbondale, IL: Southern'Illinois University Press.

Wood, J. V., Taylor, S. E., Lichtman, R. R. (1985). Social comparison in adjustment to breast cancer. *Journal of Personality and Social Psychology, 49,* 1169–1183.

Wood, W. (1987). A meta-analytic review of sex differences in group performance. *Psychological Bulletin, 102,* 53–71.

Wood, W., & Karten, S. J. (1986). Sex differences in interaction style as a product of perceived sex differences in competence. *Journal of Personality and Social Psychology, 50,* 341–347.

Wood, W., Polek, D., & Aiken, C. (1985). Sex differences in group task performance. *Journal of Personality and Social Psychology, 48,* 63–71.

Worchel, S. (1978). The experience of crowding: An attributional analysis. In A. Baum & Y. M. Epstein (Eds.), *Human response to crowding.* Hillsdale, NJ: Erlbaum.

Worchel, S. (1986). The role of cooperation in reducing intergroup conflict. In S. Worchel & W. G. Austin (Eds.), *Psychology of intergroup relations* (2nd ed., pp. 288–304). Chicago: Nelson-Hall.

Worchel, S., Andreoli, V. A., & Folger, R. (1977). Intergroup cooperation and intergroup attraction: The effect of previous interaction and outcome of combined effort. *Journal of Experimental Social Psychology, 13,* 131–140.

Worchel, S. & Austin, W. G. (Eds.). (1986). *Psychology of intergroup relations.* Chicago: Nelson-Hall.

Worchel, S., Axsom, D., Ferris, F., Samaha, C., & Schweitzer, S. (1978). Factors determining the effect of intergroup cooperation on intergroup attraction. *Journal of Conflict Resolution, 22,* 429–439.

Worchel, S., & Brehm, J. W. (1971). Direct and implied social restoration of freedom.

Journal of Personality and Social Psychology, 18, 294–304.

Worchel, S., Lind, E., & Kaufman, K. (1975). Evaluations of group products as a function of expectations of group longevity, outcome of competition, and publicity of evaluations. *Journal of Personality and Social Psychology, 31*, 1089–1097.

Worchel, S., & Norvell, N. (1980). Effect of perceived environmental conditions during cooperation on intergroup attraction. *Journal of Personality and Social Psychology, 38*, 764–772.

Worchel, S., & Teddlie, C. (1976). The experience of crowding: A two-factor theory. *Journal of Personality and Social Psychology, 34*, 30–40.

Worchel, S., & Yohai, S. (1979). The role of attribution in the experience of crowding. *Journal of Experimental Social Psychology, 15*, 91–104.

Word, C. O., Zanna, M. P., & Cooper, J. (1974). The nonverbal mediation of self-fulfilling prophecies in interracial interaction. *Journal of Experimental Social Psychology, 10*, 109–120.

Worringham, C. J., & Messick, D. M. (1983). Social facilitation of running: An unobtrusive study. *Journal of Social Psychology, 121*, 23–29.

Worth, L.T., Allison, S. T., & Messick, D. M. (1987). Impact of a group decision on perception of one's own and others' attitudes. *Journal of Personality and Social Psychology, 53*, 673–682.

Wright, C. L., & Hyman, H. (1958). Voluntary association memberships in American adults: Evidence from national sample surveys. *American Sociological Review, 23*, 284–294.

Wright, J. C., Giammarino, M., & Parad, H. W. (1986). Social status in small groups: Individual-group similarity and the social "misfit." *Journal of Personality and Social Psychology, 50*, 523–536.

Wright, P. H., & Crawford, A. C. (1971). Agreement and friendship: A close look and some second thoughts. *Representative Research in Social Psychology, 2*, 52–69.

Wright, T. L., Ingraham, L. J., & Blackmer, D. R. (1984). Simultaneous study of individual differences and relationship effects in attraction. *Journal of Personality and Social Psychology, 47*, 1059–1062.

Wrightsman, L. S. (1977). *Social psychology* (2nd ed.). Belmont, CA: Wadsworth.

Wrightsman, L. S. (1978). The American trial jury on trial: Empirical evidence and procedural modifications. *Journal of Social Issues, 34*(4), 137–164.

Wrightsman, L. S. (1987). *Psychology and the legal system*. Pacific Grove, CA: Brooks/Cole.

Wrightsman, L. S., O'Connor, J., & Baker, N. J. (Eds.). (1972). *Cooperation and competition: Readings on mixed-motive games*. Belmont, CA: Wadsworth.

Wrong, D. H. (1979). *Power*. New York: Harper.

Yablonsky, L. (1959). The delinquent gang as a near group. *Social Problems, 7*, 108–117.

Yablonsky, L. (1962). *The violent gang*. New York: Macmillan.

Yalom, I. D. (1975). *The theory and practice of group psychotherapy* (2nd ed.). New York: Basic Books.

Yalom, I. D. (1982). The "terrestrial" meanings of life. *International Forum for Logotherapy, 5*, 92–102.

Yalom, I. D. (1985). *The theory and practice of group psychotherapy* (3rd ed.). New York: Basic Books.

Youngs, G. A., Jr. (1986). Patterns of threat and punishment reciprocity in a conflict setting. *Journal of Personality and Social Psychology, 51*, 541–546.

Yukl, G. A. (1981). *Leadership in organizations*. Englewood Cliffs, NJ: Prentice-Hall.

Zaccaro, S. J. (1984). Social loafing: The role of task attractiveness. *Personality and Social Psychology Bulletin, 10*, 99–106.

Zajonc, R. B. (1965). Social facilitation. *Science, 149*, 269–274.

Zajonc, R. B. (1968). Attitudinal effect of mere exposure. *Journal of Personality and Social Psychology*, Monograph Supplement, *9*, (2, part 2), 2–27.

Zajonc, R. B. (1980). Compresence. In P. B. Paulus (Ed.), *Psychology of group influence* (pp. 35–60). Hillsdale, NJ: Erlbaum.

Zajonc, R. B., Heingartner, A., & Herman, E. M. (1969). Social enhancement and impairment of performance in the cockroach. *Journal of Personality and Social Psychology, 13*, 83–92.

Zald, M. N., & McCarthy, J. D. (Eds.). (1987). *Social movements in an organizational society*. New Brunswick, NJ: Transaction Books.

Zamarripa, P. O., & Krueger, D. L. (1983). Implicit contracts regulating small group leadership. *Small Group Behavior, 14*, 187–210.

Zander, A. (1968). Group aspirations. In D. Cartwright & A. Zander (Eds.), *Group dynamics: Research and theory* (3rd ed., pp. 418–429). New York: Harper & Row.

Zander, A. (1971). *Motives and goals in groups*. New York: Academic Press.

Zander, A. (1977). *Groups at work*. San Francisco: Jossey-Bass.

Zander, A. (1979). The psychology of group processes. *Annual Review of Psychology, 30*, 417–451.

Zander, A. (1982). *Making groups effective*. San Francisco: Jossey-Bass.

Zander, A. (1983). The value of belonging to a group in Japan. *Small Group Behavior, 14*, 3–14.

Zander, A. (1985). *The purposes of groups and organizations*. San Francisco: Jossey-Bass.

Zander, A., & Cohen, A. R. (1955). Attributed social power and group acceptance: A classroom experimental demonstration. *Journal of Abnormal and Social Psychology, 51*, 490–492.

Zander, A., Cohen, A. R., & Stotland, E. (1959). Power and relations among the professions. In D. Cartwright (Ed.), *Studies in social power*. Ann Arbor, MI: Institute for Social Research.

Zander, A., Stotland, E., & Wolfe, D. (1960). Unity of group, identification with group, and self-esteem of members. *Journal of Personality, 28*, 463–478.

Zanna, M. P., & Pack, S. J. (1975). On the self-fulfilling nature of apparent sex differences in behavior. *Journal of Experimental Social Psychology, 11*, 583–591.

Zeisel, H., & Diamond, S. S. (1976). The jury selection in the Mitchell-Stans conspiracy trial. *American Bar Foundation Research Journal, 1*, 151–174.

Ziller, R. C. (1964). Individuation and socialization: A theory of assimilation in large organizations. *Human Relations, 17*, 341–360.

Zillmann, D. (1983). Arousal and aggression. In R. G. Geen & E. I. Donnerstein (Eds.), *Aggression: Theoretical and empirical reviews* (Vol. 1). New York: Academic Press.

Zillmann, D., Bryant, J., Cantor, J. R., & Day, K. D. (1975). Irrelevance of mitigating circumstances in retaliatory behavior at high levels of excitation. *Journal of Research in Personality, 9*, 282–293.

Zillmann, D., & Cantor, J. R. (1976). Effect of timing of information about mitigating circumstances on emotional responses to provocation and retaliatory behavior. *Journal of Experimental Social Psychology, 12*, 38–55.

Zillmann, D., Sapolsky, B. S., & Bryant, J. (1979). The enjoyment of watching sport contests. In J. H. Goldstein (Ed.), *Sports, games and play: Social and psychological viewpoints*. Hillsdale, NJ: Erlbaum.

Zimbardo, P. G. (1969). The human choice: Individuation, reason, and order versus deindividuation, impulse, and chaos. In W. J. Arnold & D. Levine (Eds.), *Nebraska Symposium on Motivation*, Lincoln: University of Nebraska Press.

Zimbardo, P. G. (1975). Transforming experimental research into advocacy for social change. In M. Deutsch & H. A. Hornstein (Eds.), *Applying social psychology* (pp. 33–66). Hillsdale, NJ: Erlbaum.

Zimbardo, P. G. (1977). *Psychology and life*. Glenview, IL: Scott, Foresman.

Zimpfer, D. G. (1986). Planning for groups based on their developmental phases. *Journal for Specialists in Group Work, 11*, 180–187.

Zurcher, L. A., Jr. (1969). Stages of development in poverty program neighborhood action committees. *Journal of Applied Behavioral Science, 15*, 223–258.

· Name Index ·

· Subject Index ·

· Credits ·

These pages constitute an extension of the copyright page.

CHAPTER 2: 28, Quotation reprinted from *Street Corner Society,* by W. F. Whyte, by permission of the University of Chicago Press. Copyright © 1943 by the University of Chicago Press. **8,** Figure 2-1 adapted from "They Saw a Game," by A. H. Hastorf and H. Cantril, *Journal of Abnormal and Social Psychology,* 1954, *49.* Copyright 1954 by the American Psychological Association. **31,** Table 2-1 from *Personality and Interpersonal Behavior* by Robert Freed Bales. Copyright © 1970 by Holt, Rinehart, and Winston, Inc. Reprinted by permission of Holt, Rinehart and Winston, CBS College Publishing. **40 and 42,** Figure 2-4 and quotation from *Personality and Social Change,* by T. M. Newcomb. Copyright © 1943 by Dryden Press. **CHAPTER 3: 56,** Table 3-2 from *FIRO: A Three-Dimensional Theory of Interpersonal Behavior* by W. C. Schutz. Copyright 1958 by Holt, Rinehart & Winston, Inc. **60,** Table 3-4 adapted from Zander, A., *The Purposes of Groups and Organizations.* San Francisco: Jossey-Bass Inc., 1985, pp. 24–25. Used with permission. **68,** Table 3-5 from "Boredom in Interpersonal Encounters: Antecedents and Social Implications," by M. R. Leary, P. A. Rogers, R. W. Canfield, and C. Coe, *Journal of Personality and Social Psychology,* 1986, *51,* 968–975. Copyright 1986 by the American Psychological Association. Reprinted by permission. **70,** Figure 3-1 from "Friendship Choice and Performance: Self-evaluation Maintenance in Children," by A. Tesser, J. Campbell, and M. Smith. In J. Suls and A. G. Greenwald (Eds.), *Psychological Perspectives on the Self* (Vol. 2). Copyright 1983 by Lawrence Erlbaum Associates, Inc. Reprinted with permission. **70,** Figure 3-2 from "Physical Attractiveness, Social Relations, and Personality Style," by D. Krebs and A. A. Adinolfi, *Journal of Personality and Social Psychology,* 1975, *31,* 245–253. Copyright 1975 by the American Psychological Association. Reprinted by permission. **CHAPTER 4: 80 and 81,** Figures 4-1 and 4-2 adapted from *Discussion and Group Methods,* 2nd Edition by Ernest G. Bormann. Copyright © 1969, 1975 by Ernest G. Bormann. Reprinted by permission of Harper & Row Publishers, Inc. (Also adapted from *Small Group Decision-Making,* 2nd Edition by B. A. Fisher. Copyright © 1980 by McGraw-Hill, Inc. Reprinted by permission. **94,** Figure 4-4 data from "The Effect of Severity of Initiation on Liking for a Group," by E. Aronson and J. Mills, *Journal of Abnormal and Social Psychology,* 1959, *59,* 177–181. Copyright 1959 by the American Psychological Association. **96,** Figure 4-5 adapted from "Socialization in Small Groups: Temporal Changes in Individual-Group Relations," by R. L. Moreland and M. J. Levine, *Advances in Experimental Social Psychology,* Vol. 15. Copyright © 1982 by Academic Press. Reprinted by permission. **103,** Figure 4-6 from *Human Organization* by R. Likert. Copyright © 1961 by McGraw-Hill, Inc. Reprinted by permission. **CHAPTER 5: 113,** Table 5-1 adapted from "Functional Roles of Group Members," by K.D. Benne and P. Sheats, *Journal of Social Issues,* 1948, *4*(2), 41–49. Copyright 1948 by the Society for the Psychology of Social Issues. Reprinted by permission. **117,** Table 5-2 adapted from "A Meta-Analysis of the Correlates of Role Conflict and Ambiguity," by C. D. Fisher and R. Gitelson, *Journal of Applied Psychology,* 1983, *68,* 320–333. Copyright 1983 by the American Psychological Association. Adapted by permission. **123,** Table 5-3 adapted from "Verbal Response Modes and Dimensions of Interpersonal Roles: A Method of Discourse Analysis," by W. B. Stiles, *Journal of Personality and Social Psychology,* 1978, *36,* 693–703. Copyright 1978 by the American Psychological Association. Adapted by permission. **128,** Table 5-4 from "Social Status in Small Groups: Individual-Group Similarity and the Social 'Misfit'," by J. C. Wright, M. Giammarino, and H. W. Parad, *Journal of Personality and Social Psychology,* 1986, *50,* 523–536. Copyright 1978 by the American Psychological Association. Reprinted by permission. **131,** Figure 5-3 from "Communication Networks," by M. E. Shaw. In L. Berkowitz (Ed.), *Advances in Experimental Social Psychology,* (Vol. 1). Copyright © 1964 by Academic Press. Reprinted by permission. **135,** Figure 5-4 reprinted with permission of The Free Press, a Division of Macmillan, Inc. from *SYMLOG: A System for the Multiple Level Observation of Groups,* by Robert F. Bales, Stephen P. Cohen with Stephen A. Williamson. Copyright © 1979 by The Free Press. **CHAPTER 6: 143,** Table 6-1 and quotations adapted from *Jury: The People vs. Juan Corona* by V. Villaseñor. Copyright 1977 by Little, Brown, Inc. **144,** Figure 6-1 adapted from "An Experimental Investigation of Group Influence," by S. E. Asch. In *Symposium on Preventive and Social Psychiatry,* April 15–17, Walter Reed Army Institute of Research. Washington, DC: Government Printing Office. **145,** Figure 6-2 from "Opinions and Social Pressures," by S. E. Asch, *Scientific American,* 1955, *193*(5). Reprinted by permission. **147,** Figure 6-3 from *Social Psychology.* by L. S.

Wrightsman, Brooks/Cole Publishing Company, 1977. **149,** Figure 6-4 adapted from "The Psychology of Social Impact," by B. Latané, *American Psychologist,* 1981, *36,* 343–356. And from "Social Influence Model: A Formal Integration of Research on Majority and Minority Influence Processes," by S. Tanford and S. Penrod, *Psychological Bulletin,* 1984, *95,* 189–225. And from "Strength and Immediacy of Sources: A Meta-Analytic Evaluation of the Forgotten Elements of Social Impact Theory," by B. Mullen, *Journal of Personality and Social Psychology,* 1985, *48.* 1458–1466. Copyrights 1981, 1984, and 1985 by the American Psychological Association. **153,** Table 6-3 from "A Computer Simulation of Jury Decision-Making," by S. Penrod and R. Hastie, *Psychological Bulletin,* 1980, *87,* 133–159. Copyright 1980 by the American Psychological Association. **158,** Figure 6-5 from "Sex Variable in Conforming Behavior," by F. Sistrunk and J. W. McDavid, *Journal of Personality and Social Psychology,* 1971, *17,* 200–207. Copyright 1971 by the American Psychological Association. Reprinted by permission. **162,** Figure 6-6 data from *The Psychology of Social Norms,* by Muzafer Sherif. Copyright © 1936 by Harper & Row, Publishers, Inc; renewed by Muzafer Sherif. Adapted by permission of the publisher. **168,** Table 6-5 from "Deviance, Rejection, and Communication," by S. Schachter, *Journal of Abnormal and Social Psychology,* 1951, *46,* 190–207. Copyright 1951 by the American Psychological Association. **169,** Figure 6-7 data from "Reaction to Attitudinal Deviance: Impact of Deviate's Direction and Distance of Movement," by J. M. Levine, L. Saxe, and H. J. Harris, *Sociometry,* 1976, *39,* 97–107. Copyright 1976 by the American Sociological Association. Reprinted by permission. **CHAPTER 7: 192,** Figure 7-1 based on data from "Effects of Compliance Outcome and Basis of Power on the Powerholder-Target Relationship," by J. I. Shaw and L. Condelli, *Personality and Social Psychology Bulletin,* 1986, *12,* 236–246, Sage Publication, Inc. **196,** Table 7-3 from Gary A. Yukl, Leadership in Organizations, © 1981, pp. 44–58. Adapted by permission of Prentice Hall, Inc., Englewood Cliffs, New Jersey. **202,** Focus 7-3 quotations and Figure 7-2 from *Obedience to Authority: An Experimental View,* by Stanley Milgram. Copyright © 1974 by Stanley Milgram. Reprinted by permission of Harper & Row, Publishers, Inc. **207,** Figure 7-3 data from "Ubiquitous Watergate: An Attributional Analysis," by S. G. West, S. P. Gunn, and P. Chernicky, *Journal of Personality and Social Psychology,* 1975, *23,* 55–56. Copyright 1975 by the American Psychological Association. Reprinted by permission. **CHAPTER 8: 218–219,** Focus 8-2 from "The Manager's Job: Folklore and Fact," by H. Mintzberg, *Harvard Business Review,* 1975, *53,* 49–61. **p. 221,** Table 8-2 from "Substitutes for Leadership: Their Meaning and Measurement," by S. Kerr and J. M. Jermier. In *Organizational Behavior and Human Performance,* 1978, *22,* 375–403. Copyright © 1978 by Academic Press. Reprinted by permission. **p. 228,** Focus 8-3 from *Small Group Decision-Making,* 2nd Edition, by B. A. Fisher, 1980, McGraw-Hill, Inc. **230 and 233,** Quotations and Figure 8-1 from "The Contingency Model and the Dynamics of the Leadership Process," by F. E. Fiedler. In L. Berkowitz (Ed.), *Advances in Experimental Social Psychology* (Vol. 12). Copyright © 1978 by Academic Press. Reprinted by permission. **238,** Figure 8-2 from "Management Facades," by R. R. Blake and J. S. Mouton, *Advanced Management Journal,* July 1966, *31.* Reprinted by permission. **239,** Figure 8-3 from "Leader Effectiveness and Adaptability Description (LEAD)," by P. Hersey and K. H. Blanchard. In J. W. Pfeiffer and J. E. Jones (Eds.), *The 1976 Annual Handbook for Group Facilitators,* 1976, Vol. 5. **241,** Figure 8-4 from Figure 1 in *Autocracy and Democracy,* by R. K. White and R. Lippitt. Copyright © 1960 by Ralph K. White and Ronald Lippitt. Reprinted by permission of Harper & Row Publishers, Inc. **243,** Figure 8-5 reprinted from *Leadership and Decision-Making,* by Victor H. Vroom and Philip W. Yetton, by permission of the University of Pittsburgh Press. © 1973 by University of Pittsburgh Press. **CHAPTER 9: 252,** Figure 9-1 from "The Dynamogenic Factors in Pacemaking and Competition," by N. Triplett, *American Journal of Psychology,* 1897, *9,* 507–533. **255,** Table 9-1 data from "Social Enhancement and Impairment of Performance in the Cockroach," by R. B. Zajonc, A. Heingartner, and E. M. Herman, *Journal of Personality and Social Psychology,* 1969, *13,* 83–92. Copyright 1969 by the American Psychological Association. **262,** Table 9-2 adapted from *Group Processes and Productivity,* by I. D. Steiner. Copyright © 1972 by Academic Press. **270,** Figure 9-2 data from "Research on Animate Sources of Power: The Work of Man," by M. Ringelmann, *Annales de l'Institut National Agronomique,* 2e séries—tome XXI, 1–24. **271,** Figure 9-2 from "Many Hands Make Light the Work: The Causes and Consequences of Social Loafing," by B. Latané, K. Williams, and S. Harkins, *Journal of Personality and Social Psychology,* 1979, *37,* 822–832. Copyright 1979 by the American Psychological Association. Reprinted by permission. **279,** Figure 9-4 from *A Normative Model of Work Team Effectiveness,* by J. R. Hackman. Technical Report No. 2, Research Program on Group Effectiveness, Yale School of Organization and Management (1983). Used with permission. **CHAPTER 10: 303,** Figure 10-4 data from "A Laboratory Investigation of Groupthink," by J. A. Courtright, *Communication Monographs,* 1978, *45,* 229. Reprinted by permission of the Speech Communication Association. **310,** Focus 10-4 and Table 10-1 adapted from "Group Influence on Individual Risk Taking," by M. A. Wallach, N. Kogan, and D. J. Bem, *Journal of Abnormal and Social Psychology,* 1962, *65,* 75–86. Copyright 1962 by the American Psychological Association. **CHAPTER 11: 319,** Figure 11-1 from *Groups Under Stress: Psychological Research in Sealab II,* by R. Rad-